Game Programming Tricks of the Trade

PREMIER PRESS

GAME DEVELOPMENT

GAME
PROGRAMMING
TRICKS OF THE
TRADE

Lorenzo D. Phillips Jr., Editor

André LaMothe, Series Editor

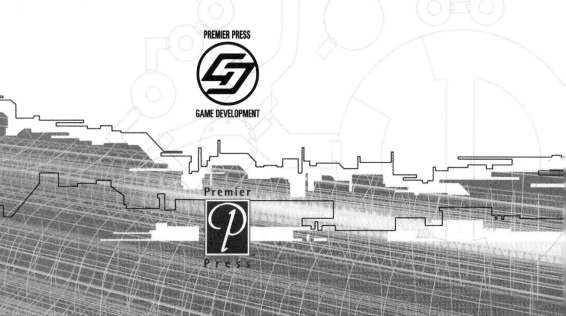

PREMIER PRESS

GAME DEVELOPMENT

Premier

p

Press

Premier

Press

Premier Press, Inc. is a registered trademark of Premier Press, Inc.

The Premier Press logo and related trade dress are trademarks of Premier Press, Inc. and may not be used without written permission. All other trademarks are the property of their respective owners.

Publisher: Stacy L. Hiquet

Marketing Manager: Heather Hurley

Managing Editor: Sandy Doell

Acquisitions Editor: Emi Smith

Project Editor: Argosy Publishing

Editorial Assistants: Margaret Bauer and Elizabeth Barrett

Marketing Coordinator: Kelly Poffenbarger

Technical Reviewer: André LaMothe

Interior Layout: Argosy Publishing

Cover Design: Mike Tanamachi

CD-ROM Producer: Carson McGuire

All trademarks are the property of their respective owners.

Important: Premier Press cannot provide software support. Please contact the appropriate software manufacturer's technical support line or Web site for assistance.

Premier Press and the author have attempted throughout this book to distinguish proprietary trademarks from descriptive terms by following the capitalization style used by the manufacturer.

Information contained in this book has been obtained by Premier Press from sources believed to be reliable. However, because of the possibility of human or mechanical error by our sources, Premier Press, or others, the Publisher does not guarantee the accuracy, adequacy, or completeness of any information and is not responsible for any errors or omissions or the results obtained from use of such information. Readers should be particularly aware of the fact that the Internet is an ever-changing entity. Some facts may have changed since this book went to press.

ISBN: 1-931841-69-1

Library of Congress Catalog Card Number: 2001099848

Printed in the United States of America

02 03 04 05 BA 10 9 8 7 6 5 4 3 2 1

Premier Press, a division of Course Technology

2645 Erie Avenue, Suite 41

Cincinnati, Ohio 45208

I dedicate this book to Sayun, Lorenzo IV, Tylen, and to the rest of my other family and friends.

—Lorenzo D. Phillips, Jr.

Foreword

I started programming games over 25 years ago, and although I have been on both sides of the business, that is, the development side and the business side, I can say wholeheartedly, I much prefer making games to selling them! The game business is like magic to me. Although, I am practically as old as Yoda compared to many of the new young game programmers, all these years have clarified in my mind that I simply love making and playing games. Video games are the most impressive artistic accomplishments of our generation. They are the fusion of science, art, sound, music, and prose. And the cool thing has been watching them grow from nothing to photo-real simulations that have you blinking your eyes saying, "that looks real!"

I remember the very first game that I played—Pong. Shortly after, I played Space War in an arcade in Oak Ridge Mall, San Jose, CA. I was amazed by these games. I couldn't believe my eyes; it was like magic, but better, since it was *real*. It was real, and I could learn how to do it. So I decided that I would spend my life learning how to do it, and I have pretty much done that.

In my travels, I have met the most interesting people you can imagine, from Bill Gates to Steve Wozniak. I had lunch with the guy who invented Defender, and sat in a dark room and talked about DOOM with John Carmack. I can say without a doubt there's nothing in the world I would rather do. And now with the turn of the century behind us, it's up to you, the next generation of game developers, to take games to the places that we all dream about.

I admit I would much rather make games than write books, but writing books is much more constructive and more meaningful to me, personally, than writing games. However, I am eager to start creating games as I did in the '80s and early '90s. But, for now, I still have a few tricks up my sleeve, and this book is one of them.

When I first came up with the idea for a compilation book, the first comment to me was "the *Game Programming Gems* series is doing well, and in fact, you are one of the co-authors!" True, but this book is completely different. Personally, I have never gotten that much out of books that have small 1- to 5-page articles. I believe that a compilation book needs to have coherent and complete chapters wherein explain a topic to a point that the reader really learns how to do it. So, my goal was to have a

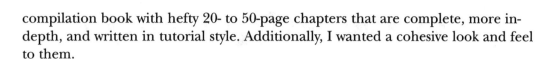

compilation book with hefty 20- to 50-page chapters that are complete, more in-depth, and written in tutorial style. Additionally, I wanted a cohesive look and feel to them.

With all that said, this book hits the mark. It's the first in our series of compilation books, but I think that it more than delivers its weight in Pentiums. There are some really interesting subjects covered in this book from advanced mathematics to scripting, as well as topics like OpenGL, 2D, Skyboxes, Optimizations techniques, Assembly Language, and so on. Each topic is a complete treatise on the subject, not just introductions or little blurbs that leave you wondering.

Of course, the authors are to thank for the content, but Lorenzo Phillips, the managing editor of the book, is to thank for making this idea a reality. If you're reading this book and have worked on any kind of engineering job in your life, you will appreciate the incredible complexity of getting people to do their jobs on time. Now, try getting 15 to 20 people to all do their jobs on time and do it with consistency—that's a miracle. Lorenzo is really the person who I feel should get the most "props"—without his determination and hard work, this book would just be another idea and would never have come to fruition.

Lastly, as someone with experience in the trenches, and now that I have your attention, I would like to leave you with some real advice about making games—or making anything for that matter. This stuff is hard—really hard. If you are serious about it, then, as I have said many times, forget about having fun, forget about vacations, forget about that cute blonde next door—it's not going to happen (especially the cute blonde). You simply don't have time for anything, but work, work, and work. Talk is cheap; don't waste your time on web boards describing your newest game, engine, technology, whatever—spend your time making it!

Remember, the few short moments of free time we have fade away all too quickly, and reality sets in. All those things you wanted to do, thought you would do, never get done. So while you have the chance, do everything you can and finish it. Whatever it is. . .

André LaMothe

"Surrounded by 14 computers in his laboratory and one of them is getting impatient!"

Acknowledgments

Wow, my first book project is finally complete! There are so many people to thank that I hope I don't forget anyone, but please know that if I forgot you, it was not intentional.

First and foremost, I have to thank my mother, Novella Phillips, for her guidance, love, and support and for keeping me out of harm's way all these years. I love you, Mom. I'd like to thank my wife, Sayun Phillips, for her love, her support, and for growing with me over the years. I thank you for making sure that I ate during those long stretches of no sleep and for the times when we just chilled out and played Tetris against each other. I love you, babe. I'd like to thank my sister, Sharnell Phillips, for being the greatest big sister a little brother could ever ask for. I must thank the little people in my life (that is, the kids), starting with Lorenzo IV and Tylen, my two sons, for their unconditional love, Jordan and Shane for the endless hours of game play on the PCs and consoles, and Tessa for all of the laughter she provides on a daily basis. To round out the family acknowledgements, I'd like to thank Joe and Kurt (my brothers-in-law), Su (my sister-in-law), and Myong (my mother-in-law), for being the best in-laws a man could hope for when two families are joined by marriage.

I have to thank my man André LaMothe for getting me involved in the game industry in the way I have always envisioned, for introducing me to book writing, for picking me to grow businesses with, and for simply being a great friend. I'd like to thank Emi Smith and Morgan Halstead for putting up with me and my authors and for being such nice people to work with. Emi, you have also grown into a good friend, and I know I still owe you a glass of wine –SMILE-. I have to thank all of the authors because without them this book would not have been possible. Thanks to all of you for your hard work and dedication to make the project a reality. I hope the project has been enjoyable for each of you, and I would love to work with you all on future book projects.

Finally, I would like to thank all of the gamers around the world for sharing my love and passion for creating and playing games.

—Lorenzo D. Phillips Jr.

About the Authors

Lorenzo D. Phillips Jr. is a gamer at heart and is involved in game development in every aspect. He spends hours upon hours developing and writing games. He is the Founder and President of RenWare, Inc. and is the Chief Development Officer of Xtreme Games, LLC and Nurve Networks, LLC. He has 10+ years of experience in the Information Technology community. He has performed a wide range of duties that include software development, analysis and design, networking, database, quality assurance, and most recently configuration management. He is formally educated and holds an associate's degree in Computer Science, a bachelor's degree in Business and Information Systems, and a master's degree in Computers and Information Systems.

Kevin Hawkins is co-author of *OpenGL Game Programming* and a software engineer at Raydon Corporation in Daytona Beach, FL. He is working on his master's degree in Software Engineering at Embry-Riddle University, where he obtained his bachelor's degree in Computer Science and played on the intercollegiate baseball team. Kevin is also the co-founder and CEO of **www.gamedev.net**, the leading online community for game developers. When he's not toying with the computer, he can be found playing guitar, reading, bodyboarding, and playing baseball. He was drafted by the Cleveland Indians in the 35th round of the 2002 Major League Baseball Amateur Draft.

Ernest Pazera is a self-taught programmer, starting at age 13 with a TRS-80 including a tape deck. A month later, he was already writing video games. Before long Mr. Pazera couldn't imagine himself doing anything but game programming. Mr. Pazera is one of the developers who helped create one of the most popular and respected game development sites on the Web: **www.gamedev.net**. He is the moderator of an isometric/hexagonal forum on the site and has extensive experience with game development.

Wendy Jones is currently a game programmer with Humongous Entertainment in Seattle. She is currently focusing her professional attention on next-generation console projects, and her personal attention on her three children. In the past, she has done everything from tech support to web development to interface design in her eight short years in the computer industry.

Trent Polack is a high school senior who has been programming in various languages since he was nine years old. Other than programming, he is interested in sports, reading, and just enjoying life! He is also the cofounder of **www.CodersHQ.com**, a site with a wealth of game programming tutorials and demos.

Born and raised in Seattle Washington, **Ben Humphrey** knew he wanted to be a game programmer since childhood. He has been programming since he was very young. Right out of high school he applied and was accepted to DigiPen Institute of Technology, which at the time was only accepting around 100 people. After leaving DigiPen, he was picked up by Infogames Interactive where he is currently working. During that time, Ben also had the opportunity to teach C++ for a year at Bellevue Community College. Aside from his day job as a game programmer, he is also the co-web host of **www.GameTutorials.com**, which has hundreds of tutorials that teach game programming from the ground up, all the way to advanced 3-D concepts.

Heather Holland is a software engineer for Navsys in Colorado Springs. In her free time, she works on small shareware games, moderates a forum at **www.gamedev.net**, and plays her MMORPG of the month way too much.

Jeff Wilkinson is a game programmer at Terminal Reality, Inc. He received his degree from DigiPen Institute of Technology.

Dave Astle is a game programmer at Avalanche Software in Salt Lake City. He is also one of the owners and operators of **www.gamedev.net**, where he has been actively involved in the game development community for over three years. He coauthored *OpenGL Game Programming* and has contributed to several other game development books.

Alex Varanese, alex@xenonstudios.com.

Mason McCuskey is the leader of Spin Studios (**www.spin-studios.com**), an independent game studio currently hard at work on a brand new game. Mason has been programming games since the days of the Apple II. He has also written a book (*Special Effects Game Programming*), along with a bunch of articles on the glorious craft of coding and designing games. He likes programming games more than wrestling Siberian grizzlies.

André LaMothe has been involved with gaming for more than 25 years and is still the best-selling game programming author in the world (he wants someone to take over soon!). He holds degrees in Mathematics, Computer Science, and Electrical Engineering. Additionally, he is founder and CEO of Xtreme Games LLC, Nurve

Networks LLC, and eGameZone Netwoks LLC. He is also the creator of the "not-for-profit" Xtreme Games Developers conference **www.xgdc.com**, which is a game developer conference that everyone can enjoy because of its affordable price.

Richard Benson is a software engineer at Electronic Arts Los Angeles. He can be reached at **rbenson@earthlink.net**.

Chris Hobbs is a senior software engineer for Flying Blind Technologies. The company is focused on developing software for the blind and visually impaired. He has also worked with storage technology, game development, and educational software over the course of his 5 years as a professional programmer. In his spare time, Chris is currently working on a product that merges his experience from the educational software and game development industries. He is married and expecting his first child in July of 2002.

Contents at a Glance

Section 4: Appendices

Contents

Section 3: Advanced Game Programming Tricks

Trick 13: High-Speed Image Loading Using Multiple Threads

Trick 14: Space Partitioning with Octrees

Trick 15: Serialization Using XML Property Bags

Section 4: Appendices

LETTER FROM THE SERIES EDITOR

This book has been a long time in the making. My original motivation for wanting a game programming tricks compilation book was that although there are other compilation books on the market they simply try and cover too many topics. The results are a collection of 50-60 authors that only have a few pages each to cover topics that simply take much more time to do justice to. Therefore, my goal with this book was to create more of a collection of complete tutorials of game programming tricks that had enough page count each to really make a dent in the subject area. Additionally, I wanted to create a template of sorts, so that as you're reading each trick or tutorial you see a familiar structure rather than a smorgasbord of layouts.

Game Programming Tricks of the Trade fills a gap between the game programming bibles that are 1000+ pages of the same thing, and the other compilation books that use the shotgun approach. I think that by the time you complete this book you will have a strong theoretical and practical grasp of every single subject covered. And let me tell you some of the demos are pretty cool! Make sure to check out the quadtree and scripting engine demos for sure.

This book covers a lot of interesting ground, moreover there are actual complete code listings, and working demos! You aren't going to see comments like, "this is how you would do it, I leave it to you…" Rather, you are going to see how to do it, and then it will be done! Furthermore, the authors really made an effort to make the book as cool as possible, no stuffy talk, no trying to impress or confuse the readers, but just plain brain to brain coverage of some of the most interesting facets of game programming that are discussed in many game programming books, but never really covered in a complete manner.

In conclusion, this book is a must for any level of game programmer, I guarantee you will get something out of even if you're starting out or you just finished HALO II! You can't know everything!

Additionally, we would love to hear your feedback on Game Programming Tricks of the Trade and what topics you would like to see covered in the future, so feel free to email me personally at gds_suggestions@hotmail.com with any ideas for material you would like covered in the next volume. These books are for you, so you might as well have a say in it!

Sincerely,

André LaMothe

Series Editor

Introduction

by Lorenzo D. Phillips Jr.,
www.renwareinc.com,
lorenzo.phillips@renwareinc.com

Welcome to *Game Programming Tricks of the Trade*! This book is a compilation of "tricks" that you can use when you are making games. Each trick provides you with a unique tip that you can add to your games. You can even use a combination of tricks if you like. The tricks that are taught in this book are a combination of OpenGL and DirectX. This will ensure that we have something for all of you game programmers out there.

I should point out that this book is not intended to be a complete resource for game programming, OpenGL, or DirectX. Rather, it is a collection of techniques that will serve as a guide for you.

This book is organized into three parts:

1. Part I, Game Programming Development Tricks, provides you with some needed foundation to make you an effective game programmer. Topics include cross-platform game programming, application frameworks, and so on. There is even a chapter included that discusses configuration management. Configuration management is becoming more and more popular in the industry and it is important to know what it is and how it will help you with your game programming projects. If you plan to deal with larger companies, you should definitely look into the configuration management movement.

2. Part II, General Game Programming Tricks, is a compilation or techniques mainly for beginners at heart. The topics covered are those that you will not be able to do without for larger scale game projects. After all, if you do not understand 2D then how do you expect to learn and understand 3D?

3. Part III, Advanced Game Programming Tricks, is filled with tricks that will help you create games that are optimized. It will also help you create intelligent life forms that will make your game players quake in their boots once the enemy is hot on their trail. There is also a complete tutorial on how to develop a game using Assembly Language. Now you tell me, what other book

covers Assembly Language game programming? And in case you happen to know of one, you tell me if what you found will result with a completed game at the end of the reading.

In addition to the techniques taught throughout this book, the CD-ROM has a collection of source code, demos, and games. So, without any further delay, let's jump right into the first trick and get started on your journey to enhancing your game programming skills.

In short, there is enough information in here to be useful to anyone interested in game programming. I know there are complaints from the advanced community about books not having enough advanced information. Well, I ask those of you in that crowd to stick with this series, because if this one does not have what you are looking for, you can believe one of the future books will! In fact, one is already in the planning stages.

Either way, I hope you enjoy the book as the authors and I put a lot of effort into this project because we believe in sharing game programming information so that the level of quality in the games continues to get better!

NOTE

Due to some of the formatting constraints of the book, you may see some of the source code fall onto the next line and indent three spaces. We have all tried our very best to ensure that the code is still in a format that will not cause errors in the compilers. However, if you type or enter the code from the book in via the keyboard, please be sure to place the code on a single line so the compiler will recognize it correctly or in most cases you can refer to the CD-ROM and copy and paste the code you need.

SECTION I

GAME PROGRAMMING DEVELOPMENT TRICKS

Welcome to Game Programming Tricks of the Trade! As you may have guessed, this is the first of three sections. This section is made up of five chapters all of which cover some aspect of game programming development tricks. You will learn how to create platform independent source code. You will also learn to create a flexible user interface and an application framework. Since the game industry has started taking a more serious look at software configuration management, there is even an introductory chapter on this topic. Part I is meant to help you with good game programming practices that will save you a lot of time and a lot of heartache.

So without any further delay, let's jump right in and get started on your journey to becoming a better game programmer!

TRICK I

Software Configuration Management in the Game Industry

Lorenzo D. Phillips Jr.,
www.renwareinc.com,
lorenzo.phillips@renwareinc.com

Introduction

Here we are about to discuss one of the most hated topics in software development—Software Configuration Management (SCM). Maybe it's not that much of a hated topic, but it is truly a discipline that no one seems to have time to implement properly. SCM is often viewed as additional overhead that will cause the project to slip its schedule, or it's simply just seen as a pain in the butt. This is the farthest thing from the truth. If done properly, SCM is one of the major factors in successfully delivering your product on time and under budget. But, as with most things, if it is not implemented appropriately it can be disastrous!

This chapter will introduce the game world to the SCM discipline. Well, maybe not introduce it, but rather make an effort to discuss what SCM really is at a high level. This chapter, however, will not make an attempt to cover SCM in too much depth because this topic could easily generate a book of several hundred pages. This chapter will cover what SCM is, a typical Software Development Life Cycle (SDLC), the pitfalls of SDLC, and the importance of the SCM role on every project. So, without further hesitation, let's jump right in and figure out what true SCM is all about.

What Is Software Configuration Management (SCM)?

Simply stated, SCM is the process of bringing control to a software development effort.

We can always expect some level of confusion any time a number of individuals get together. The larger the group is, the greater the chance of confusion or miscommunication. The software development world is producing some of the most complex applications and systems ever seen. Because of this fact, SCM is needed more than ever. SCM is the art of identifying, tracking, and controlling the changes to the software or system being built. It is becoming more and more common that software releases are being produced in a faster timeframe. This means there is little room for error and that defects are being reported more quickly. With this type of acceleration, it is important that a clear line of communication is established so that everyone on the project knows exactly where the project is and what is going on at all times.

But where did SCM come from? How long has it been around? What functions do SCM serve? And, why is it so important? I will attempt to answer these questions in the following subsections.

A Brief History on SCM

It is understood by many that SCM got its start in the U.S. defense industry. Back in those days, software applications were small and their level of sophistication was fairly simple (or at least as simple as it could be for that time period). But, as with most everything in life, things began to change and grow in new directions. The software applications became more complex and the project teams began to grow in size. It became virtually impossible to use the existing processes and procedures with the existing staff because design changes and the overall production of the product was too much for a single person or small group of people to control.

As time passed, computers became a hot item and the applications that automated many tasks on the computer became more and more visible. Of course, this was great for the software industry, but with this growth came public demand. The demands for new software features opened the door for other software firms to enter the software development industry with new and improved products that constantly took advantage of the latest technologies. As a result, the project team dynamics changed. There were more people with diverse backgrounds that needed to communicate well with others in order to understand the vision of the project. You no longer had a small team of experts, but a large team of entry-level employees mixed in with those expert employees. As with any communication, the larger the group, the less effective communication can become. Just like the old grapevine example. You can start a rumor and if the group is small that rumor stands a good chance of staying intact. In addition, if the rumor started to change, the group communicating was small enough to correct any misunderstandings. However, in larger groups the rumor would not be in its original form by the time it reached every single person. Since the group is much larger, not everyone speaks to everyone, so there would be no corrective action taken to keep the rumor in its original format.

The growing demands of the public forced the software developers to automate more and more tasks, which translates to new or improved functionality. The changing dynamic of the project team itself results in poor communication. Now, let's throw in new technological paradigms, like Internet-based software, and the faster release cycles that society demands and we have a potential mess on our hands. The result of all this is software that has too many bugs in it or that does not function as requested. So, how do we manage all of this? We control this chaos through the proper use and application of SCM.

SCM Concepts and Functions

Many people in the world think they really understand what SCM is and what purpose it serves. Of course, a very high percentage of people are totally wrong. I have been in numerous organizations, both large and small, implementing SCM. Following, I have listed some of the statements or thoughts I have come across from those that claim to know all about SCM.

- SCM can be done by a developer or the development team lead.
- SCM gets in the way of productive work.
- I don't need SCM because I know exactly what is to be developed.
- Our software never has bugs in it when we release it.
- All we need is version control because that is what SCM is all about.

If you know anything about SCM, then you are probably laughing at the previous statements because you have heard these comments before or because they are simply that ridiculous.

First of all, I have to point out that SCM is a discipline! Just like software development is a discipline and testing is a discipline. Unless you have been trained or have experience in this discipline, you are not qualified to create, manage, or enforce it. As a discipline, SCM has a set of rules that applies to the project based on the SCM analysis work that has been performed. That's right! There is an analysis phase in the SCM discipline. How do you expect to create, manage, and enforce the rules if you do not have a solid understanding of why those rules need to exist?

Second, SCM is more than simple version control of the project artifacts. There is a piece of the puzzle called Change Control, which makes the previously mentioned third bullet point sound absurd. Does the development team fully expect to understand every detail of the application in the beginning? Do they not expect the original requirements of the application to change at all?

Finally, SCM does not get in the way of productive work. In fact, SCM enhances the ability of the project to work productively and gives management an easy way to track the project's progress and perform an audit any time it feels the need to do so. With SCM, the project manager does not have to hunt down the information or spend long periods of time putting something together for those unplanned meetings. Many of the SCM tools available today handle things like reporting with ease, but I will talk more about that later on in the chapter. So, let's talk about some of the basic concepts of SCM, just so we are on the same page for the rest of the chapter.

We have already established that SCM is a discipline, but what is the basic function of the SCM organization? SCM identifies the configuration items and then documents their physical and functional characteristics. The configuration items can be things like documentation, source code modules, third-party software, data, and so on. All of these items make up the software product. At that point, SCM documents their physical characteristics, such as size, function, and libraries, as well as functional characteristics, such as what each artifact's purpose (or function) is and their features. This is not a complete list, of course, but I think you will get the point.

Once the functional and physical characteristics have been documented, it is time to baseline the artifacts and control any changes to them. Any changes to these artifacts must go through the established change control process that the Change Control Board (CCB) oversees for the duration of the project. Control is often mistaken as prevention. The goal of SCM is not to prevent work from being done, but rather to control the work or changes made to project artifacts. A typical process would be that anyone that desires to change an artifact or a collection of artifacts must submit a Change Request (CR) to the CCB for review. This review is essential to controlling the changes made on the project because it prevents scope creep and minimizes the impact to the schedule and budget.

The CCB will approve, postpone, or reject the CR. If the CR is approved, then it will be assigned a project resource to be implemented for the next build and, eventually, tested to ensure it was implemented properly and did not break any existing functionality. If it is postponed, then it simply goes into a holding queue and will be reviewed again at a later time. If the CR is rejected, then it goes into another queue with a justification as to why it was rejected. This cycle would go on for the duration of the project. Again, this is a simple example of a process and, as with most processes, is not meant to work for every project. It was merely an example to provide you with some idea of what a process could entail. However, it demonstrates that there is a change control process that is documented and enforced for every project. Each CR is documented and tracked throughout its life cycle. This is an effective communication method and it ensures that:

1. Each person on the project is aware of proposed changes, the state of each such request, and which build the requests are associated with, and

2. That the information is readily available to all project members at any time.

Lastly, SCM is the point of verification for the product. This means that the SCM organization is responsible for ensuring that each release is consistent with the requirements and the design it is being developed from. In short, SCM ensures that what was developed matches exactly with what was specified at the beginning of the project by the customer. And believe me, there is nothing more embarrassing than doing a demo or presentation to your customer and having them tell you that the system you are showing them is not the one they specified. Not to mention the millions of dollars they paid you for the project or that you did not find out until the very end that you wasted your time and effort developing the wrong system.

Is SCM Important?

SCM plays a major role in the successful delivery of the product or system. SCM creates, controls, and enforces the rules necessary to be successful. Changes are tracked and SCM performs audits at major (and sometimes minor) milestones to ensure that the application is evolving according to the plan and design that has been established. Believe it or not, SCM saves money! With the proper implementation of SCM, the proper tracking, reviewing, and auditing take place. If these activities were not in place, then the cost of communication breakdown, delivery of the wrong systems, and so on, would be great. It is common knowledge that the longer it takes to catch or identify any problems, the more it will cost. For example, if a problem with the requirements is identified in the requirements gathering phase, then the level of effort to correct the problem is small because you are still in that phase and thus, an update to the requirement is made to fix the issue. If the problem is not discovered until after development has begun, then the problem is much larger because now it needs to be fixed in three different places at a minimum. It has to be fixed in the source code (and any associated documentation), the design, and the requirement itself. A manager of mine always says, "Why don't we have time to do it right, but we always have time to do it over?" This is in response to requirement requests, design, or code reviews. The response he always received was that there was not enough time or that the schedule would not allow for it. I say that those projects have bad project managers and are already in serious jeopardy. The concern is how to explain to upper-management why the project plan is longer than projected. However, I would rather explain to upper-management that the project plan is longer because we want to do it right, rather than have to explain why my project is several million dollars over the projected budget!

In short, just know that SCM—in its simplest form—will save you time and money if it is implemented properly. And without it, you will continue the trends you are familiar with currently—working long hours and weekends, missed deadlines, scope creep, delivery of an incorrect system, projects that are way over budget and schedule, and other unexplainable events that no one ever seems to know what happened.

The Software Development Life Cycle (SDLC)

The Software Development Life Cycle (SDLC) has been around for many, many years! It is a well-defined process that has many success stories—but true success comes only when SDLC is implemented properly. SDLC is similar to SCM in that it is made up of a set of rules in order to accomplish a goal, which, in this case, is to deliver a product. The next two sections will talk about the various models and typical phases of SDLC.

Software Development Models

Over the years, SDLC has evolved to meet the needs of the industry and take advantage of new and evolving technology. New and improved technology has forced the industry to constantly review and evaluate the effectiveness of the existing models to ensure they provide what is needed to be successful. Every software product has a lifetime that starts in response to a need and evolves until it becomes obsolete. Models implement certain phases for the life of the software and they also dictate the order the phases are to be executed. The standard phases are discussed in more detail in the next subsection, so for now, let's focus on the different types of models.

The Waterfall Model

The waterfall model is a linear approach to software development. The phases that one would implement in this model are done in a sequential fashion. The next one cannot officially start until the current phase is completed.

The waterfall model was accepted because of its ease-of-use and it was visually easy to follow (especially for management- or business-type people).

Most humans function in some orderly fashion to the degree that they perform one task and then another, but they only begin the next task after the current task is complete. This model also allowed management to plan to visibly determine where each phase began and ended. This model also uses the concept of "freezing" artifacts. For example, after the requirements phase is complete, you would "freeze" the requirements so they would not change. The same is true for the design. After the design phase is complete, the design would be "frozen" so that it would not change. This is a good concept and it gave the project members the confidence that they were actually achieving their goals.

It became apparent, however, that this model could only be used for certain types of software development. The software development process can be quite complex and the waterfall model cannot be used to represent the complexities very easily. Furthermore, this type of model did lend itself very well to risk management. By this, I mean that problems were often found in the later phases when it was more expensive to correct them. This is not to say that this is a bad model, but to simply point out that it has its purpose and its limitations. These things should be reviewed carefully for each project to determine if the model can be implemented to the degree that it enhances the success of the project, not hinder that success.

The Spiral Model

The spiral model differs from the waterfall method in that its beginning and end are not really visible. Instead, this model gives the project members the feeling of a never-ending project because there was constant refinement and enhancement to the software. One of the key concepts of this model is the assessment of risk at established intervals. The thought here is that because risks were identified, a corrective action could be taken to counteract those risks. Another key concept is the review before proceeding to the next cycle in the spiral. This also allowed project management to assess the "lessons learned," so that corrective action could be taken in the next cycle to improve anything that did not work in the last cycle. This model is also good for modular development and is viewed as a transformation of an application into a production system, but again, the downfall is that project members did not really view an end to a project that implemented this model.

The Iterative Model

This is the model I use most often at my company. However, I promise to remain objective in my description of this model. The Iterative Model's key concept is that every phase is implemented in each iteration. Better yet, this model lends itself to incremental development of a system. I find that this works well for my game development projects because I can develop a set of requirements based on a piece of the design, and test it until that functionality is working according to the specs. I can then repeat this process until I have the finished product of a market-ready game. For example, in iteration 1, I can construct the entire game world and make sure everything looks as expected. In iteration 2, I can create the player and other creatures to make the world come alive. This process would continue until the entire game is developed.

This model takes the best of the waterfall and spiral models and allows for risk identification and corrective action to be taken during and prior to the next iteration. However, it also offers clear and well-defined beginnings and endings to each iteration, as well as the project as a whole. What more can you ask of a model?

The Other Models

No discussion would be complete without at least mentioning some of the other models being used in the industry. Who am I to break tradition?

The Prototype Model is an approach that gives the developer and end user a graphical method of communication. Based on initial conversations, the development team will construct a prototype and present that to the end user. The end user can then evaluate the prototype and make the necessary requests for changes. The prototype will evolve from this process until it is finished and represents the needs of the end user.

The Operation Model is based on algorithms rather than implementation. To successfully implement this model, it is extremely important that the specifications be accurately captured because the specifications have to be executable once they are complete. If you have not heard of this model, then you probably do not spend too much time using CASE tools. This model thrives on its ability to develop systems for different environments. The downside is accurately capturing the specifications so that the resulting system is the desired system.

The Component Assembly Model is known for its ability to reduce software development time. This is because this model takes advantage of existing components, more commonly known as reusability. The resulting system is made of components either from in-house libraries, third-party libraries, or existing systems.

Software Development Phases

Now that we have talked about the various software development models, it is time to discuss the phases that each model uses. I have to point out that this section uses the typical phases on a project. This section is not meant to state that all projects use each of these phases. Some projects might combine some of these phases or may not use some of the phases being discussed. Again, this is meant to give you a little bit of background so that you can understand what the weaknesses are and why SCM is needed. So, without any further delays, let's jump in and talk about the phases of the models.

The Project Startup Phase

The project startup aspect is often overlooked as a phase or is not counted as a phase. I feel that this is an important phase because it is where the review of the project takes place and it officially marks your effort as a funded project. During this phase, the project contracts are constructed and reviewed, the project members are recruited, and a project plan is constructed. Other activities are the formalization of project standards and templates for documentation. The purpose for counting this as a phase is because this is where SCM should come into the project picture. SCM has to be involved from this point forward if the project wants to have a high-level of confidence of the SCM implementation. It is so sad that this is not an accepted fact because rarely is SCM in the picture at this point of the project. The perception of many people is that SCM gets involved right before the development of the software begins. But think about it; SCM has to begin in this phase because key decisions are being made here. Decisions regarding the direction of the project, the standards that will be enforced, and the templates that will go under version control all appear in this phase. There are already artifacts that need to be identified (i.e., configuration identification) and tracked. And because those artifacts need to be identified and tracked, they need an environment setup so that they can be tracked. This is also where the SCM plan comes into play. The SCM plan is constructed by the SCM group to capture some of the initial information that will become vital to the success of the project. So as you can see, if SCM is not involved in this phase, then the group is already behind. Another point to be made here is that key project members begin to meet and make decisions for the project. These individuals may not know it yet, but they will evolve into the Configuration/Change Control Board (CCB).

The Requirements Phase

This is the phase where the work that will be done is defined—meaning the business analysts will meet with the end users. The interaction between the end users and the business analysts will evolve in one of two ways. If the resulting application is created from scratch, then the interaction is that of requirements gathering. If there is an existing system that requires enhancements or new features, then the interaction begins with understanding the existing system and then capturing the requirements of the new and improved system. Some industry veterans classify this interaction as capturing the functional specification. Another aspect of this interaction is to capture the non-functional requirements. Non-functional requirements can be the capturing of information, for example, the frequency of system and data backups, the backup and restore process, the up time of the system, the availability of those systems and the network, the requirements for planned downtime or outages, hardware specs, and so on.

Once these requirements have been defined and documented in the Requirements Definition Document (RDD), they are reviewed and, upon approval, baselined into the SCM repository. This process is known as the creation of the functional baseline.

The Analysis Phase

Now that the requirements of the system have been defined and documented in the RDD, it is time to create and evaluate the potential solutions that meet those requirements. This information is captured in the Systems Analysis Document (SAD). If the proposed solutions use any commercial off-the-shelf (COTS) products, then the analysts must also create a usability plan. The information stored in the usability plan simply compares a variety of packages that might be a potential fit for the proposed solutions. Some of the criteria used to determine the effectiveness of COTS products in a solution are cost effectiveness, the flexibility/scalability of the product, the amount of customization that the product allows, and so on.

Another key activity in this phase is the review of the SCM plan, the RDD, and the project plan. Dates may need to be shifted and the project budget may need to be adjusted based on the solution that is chosen. Of course, some of these items may have already been approved, signed off, and baselined in the SCM repository, so any changes made to them would need to be approved. This responsibility would fall on the trusty shoulders of those key individuals I talked about in the Project Startup Phase earlier. At this point, they still may not be calling themselves the CCB, but the group and its responsibilities are evolving in that direction.

The High-Level Design Phase

In this phase, an effort is made to begin to model the proposed system. The result of this effort is the system architecture diagram. Sometimes a prototype is generated to graphically demonstrate to the end user what the proposed system will look like at the end, but this is not always the case. The main element of this phase is the system architecture diagram, which addresses questions like whether or not the system will be modeled as a client/server, mainframe, or distributed system architecture. It also answers questions regarding what technology will be used, how the network will be set up, and how data will be transferred throughout the system. Another task that is commonly handled in this phase is the construction and normalization of the database.

The output of this phase is the high-level design document. Now, some people might say that activities such as the creation of the system test plan and system test cases are generated here, while some others may argue that the system test activities occur immediately following the finalization of the requirements. Again, this is not meant to be a means to an end and things can (and usually do) differ from project-to-project. However, it is essential to have the high-level design when this phase ends. Of course, any existing documentation can be reviewed at this point and changes to those documents can be made if approved through the established change control process. But at a bare minimum, the high-level design document must be reviewed, approved, and added to the baseline.

The Low-Level Design Phase

This phase picks up right where the last phase left off. The low-level phase is a phase that is typically combined with the high-level design phase, but I like to separate the two because they each serve a different purpose. The main purpose of the high-level design phase is to model the system. The focus of this phase is to create the specifications for each program or module in the system. The program logic is captured, the inputs, outputs, and system messages are determined, and the program specification document is prepared. The unit test plan is also prepared at this point.

Of course, the output of this phase is the low-level design document. The review of the other documentation is performed and any changes required to those artifacts are subject to approval through the change control process.

The end of this phase brings about another important event. The allocated baseline is created. This baseline basically represents the logical evolution from the functional baseline and the link between the design process and the development process.

The Development/Construction Phase

This is the phase that everyone knows and sometimes tries to skip directly to, bypassing the previous phases. The SCM team should have evolved the SCM environment to the point that it is ready for the workload that accompanies this phase. All of the SCM client software should be installed at this point and all of the processes should be in full swing. Those key people I mentioned a couple of times before are now known as the CCB (if they aren't already). And the system or software application is developed. All of the various project groups are involved at this point. This is the phase that has the most communication between all of the project members. It is very important to enforce the predefined processes and project standards to ensure the project stays on track.

The output of this phase is the unit tested components that make up the system at key points in time. The amount of artifacts under SCM control also increases quite a bit. Such artifacts can include all source code, test results, documentation that is associated with each release, and so on.

The Testing Phase

The activities of this phase basically surround the testing of the system or software application. The test plans that were generated based on the requirements are used to test that the system is doing what is required. I listed this phase as the testing phase because this is another one of the phases that can be combined or broken out into smaller pieces. This phase is commonly known as the system test of integration test phase. However, activities such as regression testing are not uncommon here. This phase can also be broken into alpha and beta testing phases. The alpha and beta testing phases are common in the game industry and are heavily relied upon.

The cycle between the development and testing phases is repeated until:

1. there are no bugs in the release, or
2. the product is 100% completed.

In either case, there is also a testing process known as User Acceptance Testing (UAT). This is when the product is released to the customer for testing to ensure that the product does what the customer expects and wants it to do. I don't think UAT is all that common in the game industry unless someone pays for the ground-up development effort, but it is a big part of the testing phase nonetheless.

Once the system or product has been successfully tested and the necessary audits (functional and physical) have been performed to ensure that this release of the product meets the established specification, a product baseline is created. A product baseline simply captures a version of the product in a point in time. The product baseline would include the associated documentation like user manuals, release notes, and so on.

The Maintenance Phase

Now I know we all want to believe that we write perfect code and deliver systems that function absolutely according to the customer's requirements and without any bugs in them, but the reality is that software developments are huge undertakings. The chances of 100 percent customer satisfaction are about as good as Halle Berry seeing me and falling madly in love with me. Basically, it is not going to happen. There will always be bugs that will need to be fixed. There will always be requests for enhancements from the customer. And there will always be new features that can be added (especially to take advantage of new technology).

This is also where the SCM group can measure its level of success. If things were done properly, then the documentation that shows how to use the system will be readily available. The documentation that needs to go to the help desk folks will be provided to that team to assist them in troubleshooting the system. In short, whatever is needed in this phase should be accessible and very little time should be spent searching for the documents, product components, or bug fixes. And finally, if there is ever a need to reproduce the product or a particular version of the product, then all of that should be a snap.

Software Development Phases Summary

Okay, Okay, I know that was long and drawn out, but how can you understand the value of SCM if you do not understand the SDLC? Forgive me, but I must point out one more time that the models, phases, and the definitions in this section are generic in nature. Some phases can be combined and some can be broken out. The activities listed for each phase are not a complete list and some activities can occur in different phases. This section was merely to give you some insight into the SDLC so that you would understand what I am going to discuss in the next two sections—the pitfalls of SDLC and the importance of SCM based on those pitfalls.

SDLC Pitfalls

On projects with more than one person, anything can happen and typically does. There are times when the wrong SDLC model is selected and implemented and that can cause problems. However, the issues I discuss in this section deal more with problems that can occur even if you select the appropriate model and define the proper phases for your project. Read on and discover the issues that plague every project sooner or later.

Communication Breakdown

I feel that communication is the very foundation of any successful project. Why? Because no matter what model you choose, phases you define, or tools you select, it does not matter if the communication is bad. You can have the best process in the world, but if it is not properly communicated and understood, then it will fail the project because people are not using it as it was intended.

Numerous studies have been done on effective communication (both verbal and body language) and one thing everyone agrees on is that effective communication is a very complex system. If you have two people, you drastically increase the communication process because there are now two speakers and two listeners. This opens the door for something that is not commonly seen when there is a single person—interpretation. Anything that you say or do is subject to interpretation when two or more people are involved in the communication process. Now add in a project with 30 members performing large scale development.

Other things that tend to add to the communication breakdown are the different backgrounds of the project members. The different races, genders, skill levels, educational backgrounds, and so on, all play an important role in the communication breakdown. The result, of course, is total chaos.

Artifact Update Conflicts

This problem can be minor when the project team is made up of a few people. However, it grows out of control quickly as more and more resources are added to the project. If two project members have copies of a single file and they both update it, how do those changes get tracked? If that file is stored in a shared location and is copied back by each person when he or she is done, then one of the set of changes will be overwritten. Furthermore, these types of conflicts can result in bad builds of the software of a bad delivery of the product documentation. A lot of time will be wasted troubleshooting these types of issues. The number of resources that would have to be involved to figure it out would be costly both from a time and money standpoint.

The Importance of SCM

In a previous section, I touched briefly on the importance of SCM. Or rather I answered the question, "Is SCM important?" You may ask yourself why there is another section that basically addresses the same thing. Well, the importance of

SCM needs to be understood and the fallacies need to be put to rest. I want to ensure that you walk away with a different outlook on SCM. I want you to think about SCM a little more and compare what is in this chapter to some of your personal experiences. Plus, at this point, you should have a better understanding of SDLC and the problems that pop up on all projects at some point in time.

The most common question asked of me when I perform SCM consulting is, "What can you do for me?" SCM can dramatically increase the success of your current project when implemented correctly. It also gives you an easy way to track the progress of your project, as well as provides a mechanism for you to track the evolution of the product. SCM is not an overhead to the project as many people tend to claim and it is not so large that it impacts the project's productivity.

The following is a list of reasons why SCM is vital to the success of any project regardless of size and complexity. SCM provides:

- A mechanism to control the chaos experienced on most projects.
- A method of reducing wasted manhours.
- A way of controlling the complexity and demands placed on the project and its product.
- An increased method of deploying quality software products by reducing the number of bugs in the system.
- Faster problem identification and problem resolution.
- A level of comfort that the system that is being built is the system that was defined in the requirements and system architecture diagram.
- Traceability of all project artifacts and changes to those artifacts.
- And, contrary to popular belief, SCM even helps to lower the cost of developing the system or product.

The list could go on and on, but I think you get the point. The benefits of implementing SCM on your projects by far outweigh the negatives. By being organized and knowing where things are on your project, you save time and money. There is no other argument required! Organization has been, and always will be, more efficient and cost effective than chaos. Okay, except for those rare and extreme cases that one may find on *The X-Files*. But you get my meaning. It is time to stop arguing and just do it like the Nike commercials always tell us.

Conclusion: The Future of SCM

SCM is here to stay and there will always be a need for it as long as software development exists. SCM is still maturing and evolving as new technology emerges and consumers continue to demand more and more features out of the software. So are the SCM tools that support the discipline. But let me digress from traditional SCM and its future and talk a little bit about SCM in the game industry. Since I am an avid gamer, I follow the trends of SCM in the game industry. I see a lot of conversation taking place on bulletin boards and in chat rooms about this topic now. I have seen game-related books go from a paragraph to a couple of pages to a full section within a chapter regarding SCM. These are exciting times for us SCM people that have a true passion for game development.

This chapter just touched on some of the basic concepts of SCM and made an effort to point out the benefits of implementing an SCM strategy on your project. SCM is much more than using SourceSafe for version control of your source code! It is a full-blown discipline that deserves its respect. No one can prove that SCM is costly, inefficient, and a major overhead. Those that believe that either do not know what they are talking about or did not understand the SCM discipline well enough to implement it properly in their projects or organizations. I really hope that the game industry continues its current path to SCM implementations. On the surface, I think it is long overdue. Personally, I just get tired of reading about games that I get excited for and can't wait until they hit the market, only to read a couple of magazine issues later that the project was canned or delayed for an additional six months. I am certain that a high percentage of the reasons why these games never make it to the market or experience significant delays is the lack of SCM control to ensure that things stay on track and that the delivery dates do not slip.

It is really that simple of a solution. Well, nothing is really simple, but you get my meaning. Take the time up front to implement an SCM solution that will satisfy your project needs and be sure to see it through to the end. Most game titles have million dollar budgets and will take over a year to develop into a market-ready product. It absolutely kills us hard-core game players and game programmers when we have to wait longer before we can play a game we know we would enjoy, if it even makes it to the market at all.

TRICK 2

Using the UML in Game Development

Kevin Hawkins, GameDev.net,
kevin@gamedev.net

Introduction

As other sectors of the software industry begin to recognize the importance of software engineering best practices, the games industry is lagging behind. Those who try to rationalize the industry's lack of progress say that games involve too much creativity and that it is impossible to control such an ad-hoc and chaotic process. The reality is that these arguments are the exact reason why some of software engineering's best practices need to be incorporated into game-development processes.

The Unified Modeling Language (UML) is one such best practice that has taken the rest of the software industry by storm. It is now the standard object-oriented modeling language, after going through a standardization process with the *Object Management Group* (OMG). Starting as a unification of the methods of Grady Booch, Jim Rumbaugh, and Ivar Jacobson, the UML has expanded to become a well-defined and invaluable tool to the object-oriented software-development world.

Booch, Rumbaugh, and Jacobson have also developed a unified process called the *Rational Unified Process* (RUP), which makes extensive use of the UML. You don't have to use the RUP to use the UML because the UML is entirely independent of any software-development process, but you are welcome to take a look to see if the RUP is of any use in your organization.

In the meantime, you'll be presented with a lightweight process in this chapter that will help put the UML in the context of game development. This is not meant to be a primer on UML; rather, it's a look at how you can use the UML as an effective analysis and design tool in your game-development process.

What Will Be Covered?

This chapter will first provide an overview of the Unified Modeling Language, including use cases, interaction diagrams, class diagrams, activity diagrams, and statechart diagrams. There is an assumption that you have had some sort of exposure to UML at some point in the past or that you at least have more extensive UML materials readily available for you to reference. Complete coverage of the UML is impossible in a single chapter such as this, but you should at least get a decent understanding of what is going on through the overview.

After the overview, you will begin to see the real meat of the chapter as the UML is applied to a game-development process. You'll see what diagrams to use, when to use them, and how they're beneficial for modeling the design of your game.

The Unified Modeling Language

Although there is an abundance of notations and methods for object-oriented analysis and design of software, the Unified Modeling Language has emerged as the standard notation for describing object-oriented models. The UML allows you to model just about any type of application, including games, running on any type of operating system and in any programming language. Of course, its natural use is for object-oriented languages and environments such as Java, C++, and C#, but it can be used for modeling *non-Object-Oriented* (non-OO) applications as well, albeit in a restricted sense.

The latest version of UML at the time of this writing, UML 1.4, supports eight types of diagrams divided into three categories: static structure diagrams, dynamic behavior diagrams, and model management diagrams.

- *Basic UML diagrams* include the use of case diagram and static class diagram.
- *Dynamic behavior diagrams* include the interaction diagram, activity diagram, collaboration diagram, and statechart diagram.
- *Implementation diagrams* include component diagrams and deployment diagrams.

Most software-development methodologies do not use all of the UML diagrams when developing a software product, and chances are you will not want to use all of the diagrams in your game-development process either. Although the UML is much too broad to be covered in the space given here (the UML specification itself is over 550 pages!), let's take a brief look at a few of the more common diagrams and specifications in more detail.

Use Cases

A *use case* defines the behavior of a system by specifying a sequence of actions and interactions between actors and the software system. An *actor* represents a stimulus to the software system. It can be an external user or event, or the software itself can create it internally. Some examples of use cases in a first-person-shooter game might be "Player Shoots Gun," "Enemy Gets Shot," and "Player Opens Door." These are very simple examples, but hopefully you see where this is going.

The use cases for a software system are shown in a *use case diagram*. In the use case diagram, actors are depicted as stick figures, and a use case is drawn as an ellipse. Figure 2.1 shows a sample use case diagram.

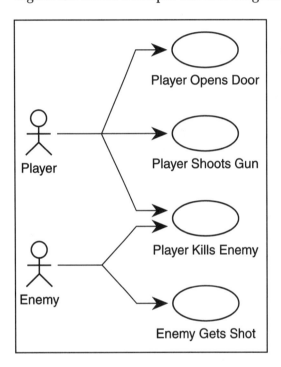

Figure 2.1

A sample use case diagram

The diagram might look wonderful, but it really doesn't have any meaning other than to provide a clear definition of the actors and the use cases they interact with. In reality, a use case is not complete without a corresponding *use case scenario*. The use case scenario describes the steps required for the completion of a use case. There is no standard format for use case scenarios, but they generally include the following items:

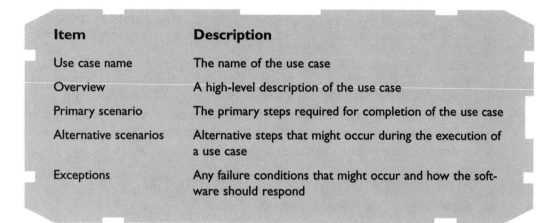

Item	Description
Use case name	The name of the use case
Overview	A high-level description of the use case
Primary scenario	The primary steps required for completion of the use case
Alternative scenarios	Alternative steps that might occur during the execution of a use case
Exceptions	Any failure conditions that might occur and how the software should respond

Although the UML does not have a specific naming convention for use cases, it typically is a good idea to create a specific format. For example, the "Player Shoots Gun" use case follows the format of *Actor Action Subject.* In this particular format, the actor is the actor that gets value from the use case, the action is the primary action that the actor is performing, and the subject is the primary subject on which the use case is performing. This format is what you'll be using in the rest of this chapter, but you can choose any format that works best for you.

The entire purpose of the use case is to capture requirements. Although the majority of your use cases should be generated during the initial phases of a project, you will discover more as you proceed through development. Every use case is a potential requirement, so you need to keep an eye out for them. Remember that you can't plan to deal with a requirement until you have captured it.

One question you may already be asking is, "How many use cases should I have?" The reality is that there have been projects of the same size and style that have had anywhere from 10 to more than 100 use cases. The answer is (as with most other things in software engineering) to use what works best for you.

There is a bit more to use cases than what has been covered here, so if you feel the need to explore use cases further, make sure you check out some of the references at the end of this chapter.

Class Diagrams

The *class diagram* is probably the one diagram people think of when they think of the UML. As a static view of the system, it describes the types of objects in the software system and the relationships among them, including the attributes and operations of a class and the constraints applied to the relationships between classes. Class diagrams are typically used to present two different perspectives of your software system:

- **Conceptual.** In this perspective, you are drawing a diagram that represents the concepts in the domain you are working with. While the concepts will naturally lead to implementation classes, there is not normally a direct mapping. The conceptual model should be drawn without regard to the programming language that might implement it.

- **Implementation.** The implementation, or design, perspective is a diagram with the real classes and full implementation of the software system. It is the most commonly used perspective.

> **NOTE**
>
> According to Martin Fowler (see *UML Distilled* [Addison-Wesley Pub. Co., 1999]), there is one more perspective of importance to class diagrams: the *specification perspective*. In this perspective, you define the interfaces of the software, not the implementation. If this doesn't make sense immediately, keep in mind that the key to object-oriented programming is to program to a class's interface and not its implementation. This concept is not easily seen because of the influence of object-oriented languages. If you would like to see some good discussion on the topic, look in the first chapter of *Design Patterns: Elements of Reusable Object-Oriented Software* (Addison-Wesley, 1995).

Perspective is not part of the standard UML, but it's a proven technique for creating a solid design of your software. The conceptual perspective is normally used during the object-oriented analysis phase of the development process, whereas the implementation perspective is used during the design and implementation phases.

Class diagrams typically use three types of relationships:

- **Aggregation.** This relationship focuses on one class being "made up of" a set of other classes. An example would be a Car class containing four Tire classes.

- **Inheritance.** This relationship focuses on similarities and differences between classes. It exists between a superclass and its subclasses. An example would be a BMW class and a Ford class inheriting from a Car class.

- **Association.** In this context, an association is any non-aggregation/inheritance relationship in which there is multiplicity and navigability between classes. For example, a Person class "drives 0..* (zero or more)" Car classes.

Figure 2.2 shows a sample class diagram with all of these relationships.

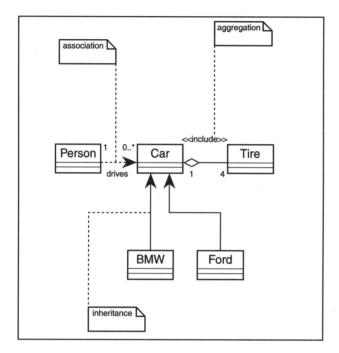

Figure 2.2

A class diagram with aggregation, inheritance, and association relationships

Another addition to the class diagram, particularly in more recent years, is the idea of constraints and assertions. An *assertion* is a boolean statement that should always evaluate to true; when it evaluates to false, you have a defect. In recent times, the OMG has been working to produce a formal language to define constraints called the *Object Constraint Language* (OCL). The OCL is making class diagrams more complete and well defined, but it's a rather lengthy topic and not suitable for this chapter. Check out the OMG Web site (see the URL at the end of this chapter) for more information on the OCL.

One of the dangers of class diagrams is that you can actually get too detailed and too specific in implementation details too early, such that it becomes difficult to make changes and update the models. To help prevent this, make sure you focus on the conceptual perspective first in an object-oriented analysis phase. Then, as you are further able to determine the operation and design of the system, you can move to the implementation perspective with more detail.

Interaction Diagrams

Interaction diagrams model the dynamic behavior of a group of objects involved in a single use case. They show which classes and methods are required and the order in which they are executed to satisfy the use case. There are two types of interaction diagrams: sequence diagrams and collaboration diagrams. These diagrams are very similar to each other in that they accomplish the same thing, but they do have some minor differences. In this chapter, we are only going to discuss sequence diagrams, but it is worth investigating collaboration diagrams elsewhere.

Figure 2.3 shows a sample sequence diagram. In this diagram, we are modeling the "Player Shoots Gun" use case mentioned earlier in the chapter.

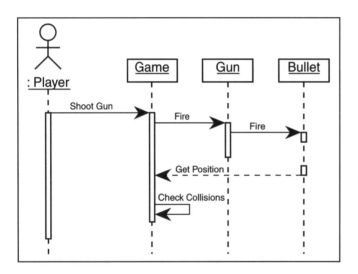

Figure 2.3

The sequence diagram for the "Player Shoots Gun" use case

As you can see, objects are shown as boxes at the top of a dashed vertical line called the object's *lifeline.* The lifeline represents the object's life during the sequence interaction. A box on the lifeline is called an *activation box* and indicates that the object is active.

Arrows between lifelines represent the messages sent between objects, and the ordering sequence of the messages is read from top to bottom of the diagram page. Conditions may also be specified for arrows between objects. An object may call itself with a *self-call arrow,* which is shown by sending the message arrow back to the same lifeline. There is also a dashed *return arrow,* which is used to indicate a return from a previously called message. You typically only use the return arrow when it

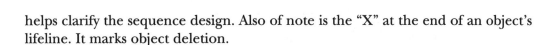

helps clarify the sequence design. Also of note is the "X" at the end of an object's lifeline. It marks object deletion.

You can also use sequence diagrams for concurrent processes, which some people may find particularly useful in game development. Figure 2.4 shows an example of a sequence diagram of concurrent processes and activations.

In Figure 2.4, you can see that asynchronous messages between objects are indicated by a half-arrowhead. These asynchronous messages can create a new thread, create a new object, or communicate with a thread already running.

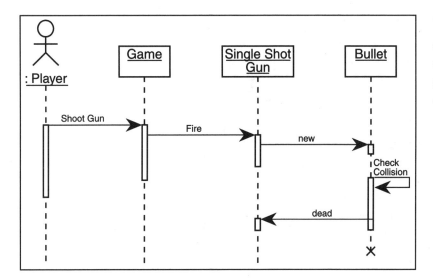

Figure 2.4

A sequence diagram of concurrent processes and activations

As you can see, interaction diagrams are a great way to look at the behavior of objects in a use case. They're very simple to create and easy to understand without looking into much detail, but they do have the drawback of not being able to provide a precise definition of the behavior of a use case.

Activity Diagrams

Activity diagrams focus on the sequencing of activities, or processes, in a use case or several use cases. They are similar to a flowchart, but they differ in that they support parallel activities and synchronization, whereas a flowchart depicts sequential execution. Typically, activity diagrams are used to provide a graphical view of a use case scenario, and they are particularly useful when you want to show how several use case behaviors interact. Figure 2.5 shows an activity diagram of the "Player Shoots Gun" use case.

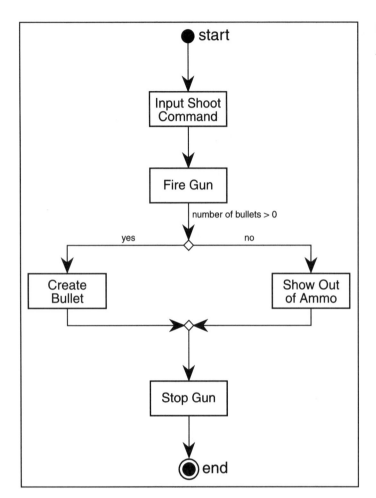

Figure 2.5

An activity diagram

Conditional behavior in activity diagrams is shown by *branches* and *merges*. Branches are similar to if-then-else statements in which, if a condition is true, execution flows in one direction; otherwise, it flows in another direction. Merges mark the end of a conditional branch.

Parallel behavior in activity diagrams is shown by *forks* and *joins*. When a fork is shown, all of the fork's outputs execute at the same time (in parallel). A join marks the end of a fork.

If you are going to use multiple use cases in an activity diagram, you can do so through the use of *swimlanes*. Each use case has its own swimlane, and any activities involved with a specific use case go in that use case's swimlane. You have to be careful, though, because things can get very confusing with complex diagrams.

As previously mentioned, activity diagrams are best used when analyzing use cases. They help provide a graphical overview of the use case and possibly use case interactions, which is much more understandable than the text in use case scenarios.

Activity diagrams will not be used in this chapter, but feel free to explore your options with them in your own development.

Statechart Diagrams

A *statechart diagram* is used to describe the behavior of an object and all its possible states. The statechart diagram essentially defines a finite state machine, where events control the transitions from one state to another. In object-oriented methods, statecharts typically are used to describe the behavior of a single class as opposed to the entire system. Figure 2.6 shows a sample statechart diagram.

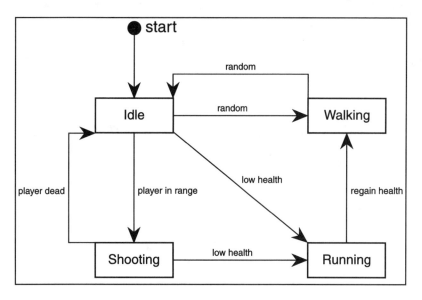

Figure 2.6

A statechart diagram for an enemy in a game

If you decide to use statechart diagrams, keep in mind that you don't need to draw them for every class in the software system. You should only use statechart diagrams for those classes that have some sort of state machine style of behavior, where drawing the statechart diagram will help you gain better understanding of what's happening. Also, in relation to game development, statechart diagrams are particularly useful for artificial intelligence system development.

Packages

The UML *package* (also called a *category*) is used to decompose a large software system into smaller ones. Inside each package is a set of related classes that make it up, but you can also have subpackages inside a package if your system needs to be decomposed in such a way. You can think of the software system itself as a single, high-level package, with everything else in the system contained in it. For instance, in a game, you might have a sound system package, a graphics package, a networking package, a main system package, and an input package, but all of these packages combine to form the entire game system.

You can also show the interactions and relationships between packages through dependencies, just like you do for class diagrams. If any dependency exists between any classes in any two packages, there's a dependency between the packages. There is not a standard diagram for showing packages, so you typically use a high-level class diagram that shows only the packages and their dependencies. Some people call these diagrams *package diagrams*; others call them *category diagrams*. Through the remainder of this chapter, they will be referred to as package diagrams. Figure 2.7 shows a sample package diagram.

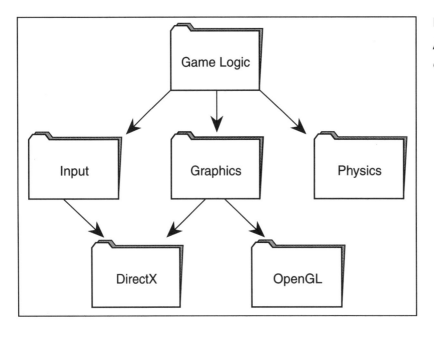

Figure 2.7

A sample package diagram

Packages and package diagrams can be as detailed and complex as you desire, so feel free to explore the topic further than what is covered here. They are particularly useful for minimizing dependencies across your software system while also providing a high-level view of your system architecture. Some developers even use packages instead of classes for primary unit testing. As with most of the elements in the UML, use what works best for you and your organization.

This concludes a brief overview of some of the UML's more common diagrams and techniques. Now it's time for the fun part of seeing how you can apply the UML in a game-development process.

Integrating the UML and Game Development

To keep things simple, a Pong game is going to be used to show how you can apply the UML to design your game software. The complete design is not going to be shown, but key ideas and diagrams will be so that you can get an idea of how the process works. The assumption is that you know what Pong is, but if you don't, read up on your video game history and learn about a tennis-like game with two paddles and a ball.

With Pong fresh on your mind, let's begin!

Build the Requirements Traceability Matrix

As with any software product, you need to know what you're going to build before you start to build it. This information, called the requirements, should be in a design document or some other specification (that is, a requirements specification) that becomes the cornerstone for the rest of the product's development. Granted, requirements evolve throughout a product's development (especially with games), so you're not going to be able to define all of them at first. As the project development continues, however, you need to keep track of changes to the requirements and make sure you are designing and developing your product according to the specified requirements. One particular tool that helps with this is the *Requirements Traceability Matrix* (RTM).

The RTM provides an easy way for you to trace through your analysis and design to ensure that you are building the software, or game, to the requirements. A simple

RTM might have columns for the requirement, the build number in which the requirement is to be implemented, and the use case, package, and class that will handle the requirement. Figure 2.8 shows a sample RTM form.

Requirements Traceability Matrix

Project_____

Req. #	Problem Statement	Build #	Use Case Name	Package	Class
1					
2					
3					
4					
5					
6					
7					
8					
9					
10					
11					
12					
13					
14					
15					
16					
17					
18					
19					
20					
21					
22					
23					
24					
25					
26					

Figure 2.8

A sample Requirements Traceability Matrix form

Let's apply the RTM to our Pong example. All you need to do is put the requirements in the RTM, as partially shown in Figure 2.9.

Requirements Traceability Matrix

Project Pong

Req. #	Problem Statement	Build #	Use Case Name	Package
1	1.1 The Pong game shall be a two player only game.	1		
2	1.2 Each player is represented by a paddle.	1		
3	1.3 The first player is located on the left side of the screen, and the right player is located on the right side of the screen.	1		

Figure 2.9

The Pong requirements applied to the RTM

Easy enough, right? Now you need to prioritize the requirements by build number. A *build* is a set of functionality to be built by a specific date. Since Pong is relatively small in size and effort, the majority of functionality can be developed completely in Build 1. In Build 2, the input and audio functionality is completed along with the win/lose conditions to complete the game. Naturally, more complex games would have more requirements resulting in more builds, but as with many software-

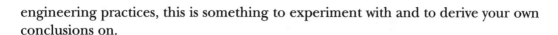
engineering practices, this is something to experiment with and to derive your own conclusions on.

Now that requirements have been defined and build numbers determined, we have a foundation from which to begin the analysis and design phases of the development process.

Identify Use Cases

In this phase, the requirements specified in the RTM are used to identify use cases. A use case diagram is then created to provide a visual representation of the actor–use case interactions. Use case scenarios are then created for each use case to describe the processes and activities involved in fulfilling a use case. There does not have to be a use case for every requirement, but make sure you specify enough use cases to have a thorough understanding of what you are trying to do.

When creating use cases, the first thing you need to do is identify the actors. Some developers stick with the rather inflexible notion that an actor is strictly external to the software. You may already be seeing the problem with this definition when applying it to games—the player would be the only actor.

A better, or at least more flexible, way to define an actor is anything that requests some sort of functionality. In a game, this might be the player, an enemy, or an item. In the Pong example, the actors can be the players and the ball. The definition of an actor is entirely up to you, but make sure the definition you choose gives you enough flexibility to properly determine the actors in your software.

Once the actors have been determined, you can begin to extract the use cases from the requirements. In the Pong example, Requirement 1.5 from the RTM deals with when the ball passes a player and the corresponding win/lose conditions. From this requirement, the following use cases can be derived:

- Player Wins Game
- Player Loses Game
- Ball Passes Player

To keep things organized, it is desirable to number the use cases as well. To do so, just prepend "UC#", where # is the number of the use case. For instance, in the Pong example, the first defined use case is "UC1_Player Wins Game."

You'll add each of these use cases to the RTM with the requirement it satisfies. Figure 2.10 shows how the Pong RTM will look after adding the use cases to the RTM.

	Req. #	Problem Statement	Build #	Use Case Name
1	1.1	The Pong game shall be a two player only game.	1	
2	1.2	Each player is represented by a paddle.	1	
3	1.3	The first player is located on the left side of the screen, and the right player is located on the right side of the screen.	1	
4	1.4	The Pong ball moves at constant speed around the game arena until it bounces off each paddle and the top and bottom walls (located at the top and bottom of the screen, respectively) at an angle equal to the angle of incidence.	1	UC7_Ball Hits Wall UC5_Player Touches Ball
5	1.5	If the ball moves past the vertical line that a paddle lies on, then the player represented by that paddle is declared the loser while the opposite player is declared the winner.	2	UC1_Player Wins Game UC2_Player Loses Game UC6_Ball Passes Player

Figure 2.10

The Pong RTM after adding use cases

Now we can create a use case diagram illustrating the interactions between the actors and the use cases. In the Pong example, we can also show a generalization from the Player actor to the Left Player and Right Player actors. Figure 2.11 shows the Pong use case diagram.

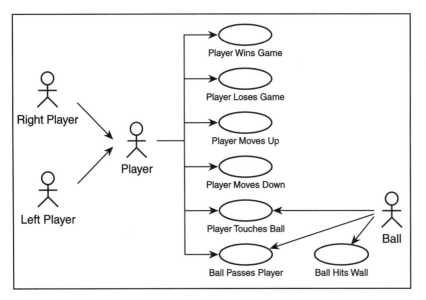

Figure 2.11

The Pong use case diagram

Each use case needs a use case scenario that specifies the steps required for completion of a use case. Scenarios were covered earlier in this chapter, so instead of discussing how to go about creating a scenario, look at Figure 2.12 as an example. It shows the use case scenario "UC1_Player Wins Game" from the Pong example.

Use Case Name: Player Wins Game

Overview:
This use case enables a player to win a game of Pong.

Primary Scenario:

Action	System Reaction
1. The first player paddle hits the ball.	1. The ball moves in the proper direction as a direct reaction of the ball hitting the paddle.
2. The ball moves past the paddle of the second player.	2. A win event occurs where the first player is declared the winner.
	3. Gameplay is stopped and "Player 1 is the winner!" is displayed on the screen.

Alternative Scenarios: none

Exceptions: none

Figure 2.12

Use case scenario for the "UC1_Player Wins Game" use case

As another example (including how to invoke another use case), Figure 2.13 shows the "UC6_Ball Passes Player" use case scenario.

Use Case Name: Ball Passes Player

Overview:
This use case enables the game ball to pass a player paddle.

Primary Scenario:

Action	System Reaction
1. Ball moves in its current direction.	1. Ball position is updated.
2. Ball reaches vertical location of player paddle.	2. If the player paddle position is located at the current ball position, then call Use Case 5; otherwise, ball position is updated.
3. Ball moves past player paddle.	3. Use Case 1 and Use Case 2 are invoked.

Alternative Scenarios: none

Exceptions:

Figure 2.13

Use case scenario for the "UC6_Ball Passes Player" use case

At this point you may be wondering, "Why do I need to include use cases in game development? I really don't see much value in them for helping me develop my game." Honestly, you may not need them, but you might find parts of them useful in determining a game's story line, how the player moves around, and especially actor interactions within the game world, among other things. Use cases are considered to be part of the *analysis* phase of development, and that is exactly what you are doing here: You are analyzing your game and determining how you want your game to look, act, and feel. Although you cannot predetermine all of these characteristics at this point in development, using use cases in your development process will help you get a better feel for what it is you are trying to create in your game.

Establish the Packages

In this phase, you develop a package list, allocate the packages to use cases in the RTM, and create the system package diagram. As previously mentioned, a package is essentially a collection of cohesive units. It can be a collection of classes, a subsystem, or even a collection of other packages.

The first thing you need to do is determine some candidate package names by looking at the actors and subjects in the use cases and using them as the candidate package names. Look for similarities in functionality, inheritance hierarchies ("Is this package a kind of another package?"), and aggregation hierarchies ("Is this package made up of another package?"). The roots of inheritance and aggregation hierarchies tend to be the names of packages. You may also find similarities in functionality that do not fit anywhere else, in which case you might want to create your own package named after the similarity.

The following is a list of the package names from the Pong example:

- Input
- Graphics
- Audio
- DirectX
- OpenGL
- Game Logic

The problem with using such a simple example as Pong becomes evident when trying to create package names—there just isn't very much to such a simple game! Hopefully, you will see the benefits of using packages beyond such a simple example.

In any case, the next step is to allocate these packages to use cases. Why do you do this? You need to allocate responsibility for use case development to the appropriate packages. This is a fairly easy step because all you do is go back to the use case(s) from which you got the package name. Figure 2.14 shows the updated Pong RTM.

4	1.4	The Pong ball moves at constant speed around the game arena until it bounces off each paddle and the top and bottom walls (located at the top and bottom of the screen, respectively) at an angle equal to the angle of incidence.	1	UC7_Ball Hits Wall UC5_Player Touches Ball	Game Logic
5	1.5	If the ball moves past the vertical line that a paddle lies on, then the player represented by that paddle is declared the loser while the opposite player is declared the winner.	2	UC1_Player Wins Game UC2_Player Loses Game UC6_Ball Passes Player	Game Logic
6	1.6	Each paddle may only move up and down, or vertically, and may not move horizontally.	1	UC3_Player Moves Up UC4_Player Moves Down	Game Logic
7	1.7	The Pong game shall use the keyboard up and down arrows for the second player and the keys 'A' and 'Z' for the first player.	1	UC3_Player Moves Up UC4_Player Moves Down	Game Logic Input
8	1.8	DirectX will be used for input and audio, while an option will be available to choose between DirectX and OpenGL for graphics rendering.	2		Input Sound and Music Graphics

Figure 2.14

The partial Pong RTM after allocating packages to use cases

Now that you have the packages defined, you need to specify how they relate through a *system package diagram* (SPD). This diagram is very much like a class diagram in how it shows dependencies and relationships between packages. Figure 2.15 shows the system package diagram for the Pong example.

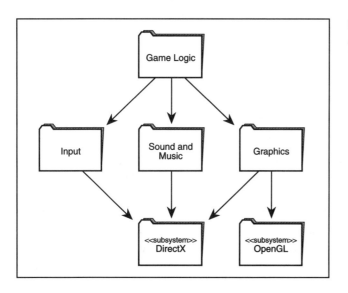

Figure 2.15

The system package diagram for Pong

Create Initial Class Diagrams

The next phase involves creating initial class diagrams for each package defined in the previous phase. You should also keep in mind that these initial diagrams should stay focused on the problem domain only, meaning you don't need to include language-specific features, design patterns, or other detailed design specifications. Probably the best way to show this is through an example, so take a look at Figure 2.16, which shows the initial class diagram for the Game Logic package.

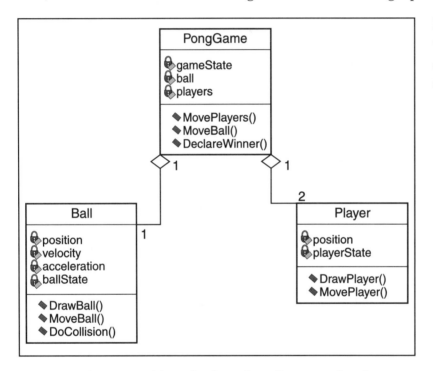

Figure 2.16

The package class diagram for the Game Logic package

You can, of course, add methods and attributes to the classes you created for the class diagram. You can also specify the access rights for the methods and attributes if you know what they should be at this point in the process.

The next part of this phase could be considered optional, depending on your software organization and development process. After creating the class diagrams, you create the class specifications for each class. In the class specification, you specify a description of the class, the list of class attributes and methods with descriptions, and any other items that may pertain to a particular project. As with any other document, the primary purpose of the class specifications is to provide a communication tool for development teams. If you are a solo developer, you might not need

the class specifications unless you just want a well-documented design. Again, as with most software engineering practices, use what works best for you.

Develop State Transition Diagrams

State transition diagrams (STDs) typically are used to define the states of entities in the game world, but they can also be used to represent the internal behavior of a class. An example of an entity for which you may want to create an STD would be the Ball actor in the Pong example. The Ball can be in one of four states: no contact, paddle contact, wall contact, and behind paddle. Figure 2.17 shows the Ball STD from the Pong example.

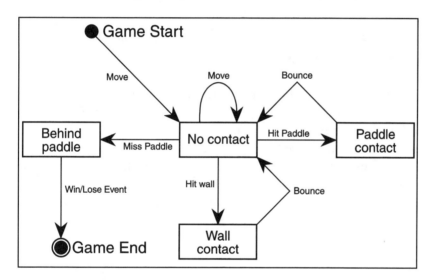

Figure 2.17

The Ball state transition diagram

An example of using an STD to represent the internal behavior of a class can be seen through the CPongGame class. This particular class represents the core of the game and controls everything from the gameplay to the menus. One of the attributes for the CPongGame class is an attribute called gameState. This particular attribute is called a *state attribute* because it has a set of values that represents the life cycle of the CPongGame class. These state values are main menu, play game, options menu, and scores screen. Figure 2.18 shows the CPongGame class STD.

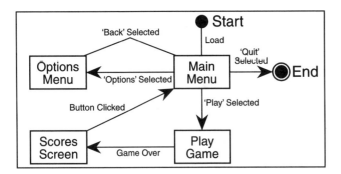

Figure 2.18

The CPongGame *class* gameState *STD*

Produce Package Interaction Diagrams

Package interaction diagrams (PIDs) provide a high-level view of the dynamic behavior between packages and their messages from the point of view of use cases. In use cases, an actor generates an event to the system, typically requesting some operation in response. The request event is what initiates the PID between the actor and the game system (that is, packages). For example, the PID for the "UC1_Player Wins Game" use case has the Player actor sending a "Move Paddle" message to the Game Logic package, along with the Ball actor sending a "Move Ball" message. The Game Logic package then sends a "Check Collision" message to itself to see if the ball collides with a paddle or wall or goes behind a paddle, before it sends itself a "Declare Winner" message to declare a winner of the game. All of this is shown in the PID for this use case in Figure 2.19.

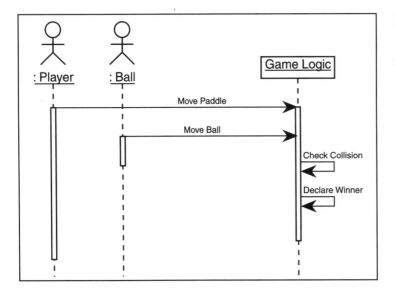

Figure 2.19

The "UC1_Player Wins Game" PID

Another good example of a PID from the Pong example is the PID for the "UC4_Player Moves Down" use case. In this PID, the Player actor sends a "Move Down" message to the Input package, which then sends a "Move Paddle Down" message to the Game Logic package. The Game Logic package splits execution at this point by sending a "Draw Paddle" message to the Graphics package and a "Paddle Move Sound" message to the Sound and Music package. Figure 2.20 shows the UC4 PID.

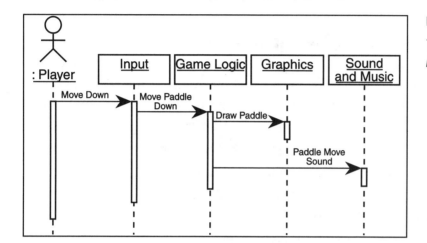

Figure 2.20

The "UC4_Player Moves Down" PID

Package interaction diagrams are an important part of understanding a game's behavior because they help isolate and illustrate operations that an actor requests from the game's packages.

The Transition from Analysis to Design

At this point in the process, you've reached a critical—yet oftentimes blurry—time in which you transition from problem and *domain object-oriented analysis* (OOA) to actual software *object-oriented design* (OOD) and implementation. You go from viewing the design as a set of logical entities to viewing it as more of a concrete and physical implementation of your game.

Because of the nature of this development process with UML, there is a fine line between analysis and design. For instance, you're mapping logical entities from OOA to implementation entities in OOD without any real changes in the design, simply a refinement. This means that the Ball class you created in OOA will map to the Ball class in OOD, but you might make some changes with respect to language implementation, use of design patterns, and of course going into more detail for the design specification itself.

As you may already be able to see, refinement becomes key at this point. Once you reach the OOD phase, you don't create many new diagrams unless you realize that you missed something in the OOA phase, and even then you would want to perform some sort of analysis before refining an implementation design.

But that's enough talk for now. Let's move on and take a look at how you go about refining and transitioning from OOA to OOD through the Pong example.

Update Class Diagrams

The first thing you should do when transitioning to OOD is take a look at the static view of your game system design through the class diagrams. Again, you are not introducing any new diagrams or specifications in this phase; you are refining your previous diagrams and specifications by adding more detail.

Some possible refinements of the class diagrams and specifications are as follows:

- Addition of parameterized classes, collection classes, and abstract classes
- Specification of access rights for attributes and methods
- Introduction and refinement of existing design patterns
- Identification of new association relationships

Figures 2.21 and 2.22 show the differences between the class diagram for the Game Logic package in the OOA phase and the OOD phase, respectively.

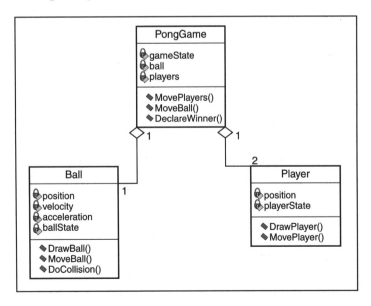

Figure 2.21

The Game Logic *OOA PCD*

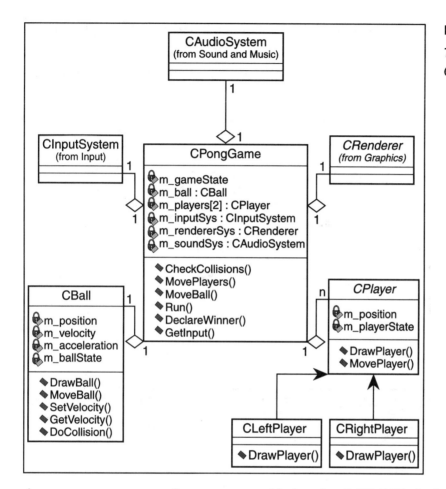

Figure 2.22

The Game Logic *OOD PCD*

As you can see, some refinement was added to the OOD PCD, including some dependencies to the graphics, audio, and input subsystems. Types for attributes were also specified, and although they are not shown in this particular example, you can also specify parameters and return types for methods as well.

Update Interaction Diagrams

Once the static view of the design is completed through the class diagrams, it's time to move on to the dynamic design of the game system with interaction diagrams. In this phase, you refine the package interaction diagrams created during OOA to include classes. The resulting product is called a *class interaction diagram* (CID).

In the CID, you illustrate the collaborative behavior of the classes you've discovered by specifying the messages that are passed between these classes. Through this refinement, you are trying to provide the level of detail necessary for implementation of the design.

Figures 2.23 and 2.24 show the PID and CID of the "UC4_Player Moves Down" use case, respectively.

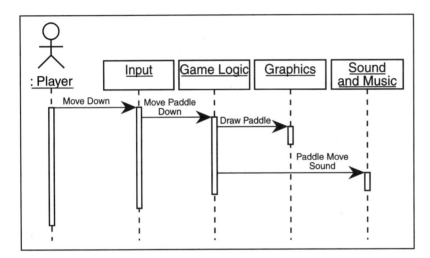

Figure 2.23

The "UC4_Player Moves Down" PID

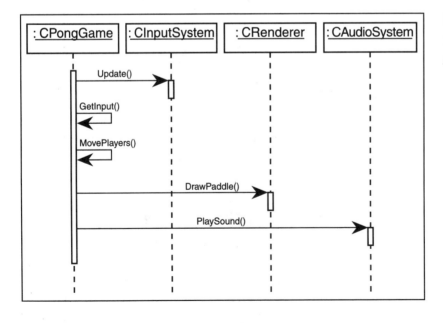

Figure 2.24

The "UC4_Player Moves Down" CID

Refinement and Iteration

The OOD phases of updating class diagrams and interaction diagrams are really one big loop of refinement and iteration. You aren't going to create a design you are happy with your first time through the phases, and chances are you aren't going to do it the second time through either. The idea is to refine and iterate through these phases until you find a design that fits your criteria for providing a baseline to move on to the implementation phases.

There is such a thing as overdesign, but at the same time, you can also underdesign. You and your team must decide when a design is complete, but don't shortchange yourself with an inadequate design. Ideally, you want to be able to minimize the number of changes you'll make to your documented design once you go into the implementation phases. Backtracking and making changes to previously developed material costs time, and everyone knows that time is money!

The Move to Implementation

Once you feel that your design is sufficient, it's time to head into the "fun" part of development—coding. There are many different ways in which you can transition your design to code, and it seems that every development team does this differently, so do what works for you. Some suggest that you should create the class interfaces and a skeleton of the class implementation that you fill in as development progresses; others suggest that you develop entire classes at once before moving onto the next class. Again, do what works for you. Remember, however, that if you change anything in your design while coding, you need to go back to your design on paper and make changes accordingly. You'll thank yourself for keeping everything well documented.

Summary and Review

Well, that completes your brief look at how you can use the UML in your game-development process. This is only one view of how to use UML, though. There are plenty of other processes and methodologies created for object-oriented analysis and design. How about a quick review?

You start off your analysis by defining use cases and creating use case scenarios that specify the steps required to fulfill the use case. Then you establish the packages and the system package diagram that defines the high-level architecture design of the game system.

Next you create class diagrams inside each package and state diagrams for state attributes inside the classes. Then you produce the package interaction diagrams from use cases that illustrate the behavior and collaboration across packages.

At this point, you begin the transition from object-oriented analysis to object-oriented design, where you begin an iterative process of updating the class diagrams for the static view of your design and the interaction diagrams for the dynamic view. You continue this cycle until you reach a point that is deemed sufficient, and then you move onto the implementation, or coding, phase.

Once at the coding phase, you are on your own for how you want to map the design to code. There are many different published methods for accomplishing this task, so choose the methods you like.

One thing that is not discussed in this chapter is testing. This is primarily because testing varies from project to project and from team to team. Typically, though, you'll want to generate unit tests for each package (and possibly for each class), but this really depends on your team and project. Naturally, you cannot test general gameplay issues, but the technical aspects of the game software can be tested very well.

Where to Go from Here

If this chapter has sparked some interest for using UML in game development, there are several resources you can check out for more general UML information, techniques, and discussions. Not much has been published in terms of UML's application specifically to game development, but hopefully, with this chapter and some of your own brainstorming, you'll be able to find something that works for you and your team.

Books

Booch, Grady, Jacobson, Ivar, Rumbaugh, J., *The Unified Modeling Language User Guide*. Boston: Addison-Wesley, 1998.

Texel, P., and Charles Williams, *Use Cases Combined with Booch/OMT/UML*. Upper Saddle River: Prentice Hall, 1997.

Web Sites

Object Management Group: **www.omg.org**

Rational Software: **www.rational.com**

Software Engineering Institute: **www.sei.cmu.edu**

Brad Appleton's Software Engineering: **www.enteract.com/~bradapp/**

Software Development Magazine: **www.sdmagazine.com**

GameDev.net Software Engineering: **www.gamedev.net/reference/**

UML Tools

Rational Rose by Rational Software: **www.rational.com**

ArgoUML, a free Java-based cognitive CASE tool: **www.argouml.com**

Dia, a diagram tool with UML support: **www.lysator.liu.se/~alla/dia/dia.html**

Conclusion

The Unified Modeling Language is a very broad topic and is difficult to discuss extensively in such a short chapter, but hopefully you've gained, if anything, a better understanding of how you can use the UML as a communication and design tool in your game-development process. Some people may not feel the need to use UML and be this elaborate in their process, and that's fine, but if you've found yourself redesigning, reworking, recoding, and re-other things, maybe you should give UML a chance. The rest of the software industry is giving new ideas a chance, so why shouldn't the game industry?

TRICK 3

Building an Application Framework

Ernest S. Pazera,
ernestpazera@msn.com

Introduction

Just as an object lesson, go start up your compiler and write, from scratch, a minimal Win32 application. Nothing fancy, just a WinMain and a window procedure. No, really. Go ahead and do it. I'll wait.

Are you back? Okay, now count the lines. For myself, I was able to do it with 39 lines of code. No blank lines, no comments, with one statement per line, and with braces each getting its own line. I'm certain that if I had wanted to get clever with it, I probably could have gotten it down to 30 lines or so, but that's not really the point here.

I just wrote 39 lines of code, and it gives me a window that does nothing (well, to be honest, my window can be moved around, it has a Close button, and so on), so to be more accurate, I wrote 39 lines that gave me a window that doesn't do anything *special*. In fact, these 39 lines are almost identical to the code I usually write when I'm making a WIN32 application.

For the sake of discussion, here are the 39 lines I wrote:

```
#include <windows.h>
const char* WINDOWTITLE="Example Window Title";
const char* WINDOWCLASSNAME="Example Window Class Name";
WNDCLASS g_WndCls;
HWND g_hWnd=NULL;
LRESULT CALLBACK TheWindowProc(HWND hWnd,UINT uMsg,WPARAM wParam,LPARAM lParam)
{
        switch(uMsg)
         {
        case WM_DESTROY:
                        PostQuitMessage(0);
                        return(0);
        default:
                        return(DefWindowProc(hWnd,uMsg,wParam,lParam));
         }
}
int WINAPI WinMain(HINSTANCE hInstance,HINSTANCE hPrevInstance,LPSTR lpCmdLine,
    int nShowCmd)
{
        memset(&g_WndCls,0,sizeof(WNDCLASS));
```

```
                g_WndCls.hbrBackground=(HBRUSH)GetStockObject(BLACK_BRUSH);

g_WndCls.hCursor=(HCURSOR)LoadCursor(NULL,MAKEINTRESOURCE(IDC_ARROW));
                g_WndCls.hInstance=hInstance;
                g_WndCls.lpfnWndProc=TheWindowProc;
                g_WndCls.lpszClassName=WINDOWCLASSNAME;
                g_WndCls.style=CS_DBLCLKS|CS_HREDRAW|CS_VREDRAW|CS_OWNDC;
                RegisterClass(&g_WndCls);

g_hWnd=CreateWindowEx(0,WINDOWCLASSNAME,WINDOWTITLE,WS_VISIBLE|WS_BORDER|WS_CAPTION|W
    S_SYSMENU,CW_USEDEFAULT,CW_USEDEFAULT,CW_USEDEFAULT,CW_USEDEFAULT,NULL,NULL,hInstan
    ce,NULL);
                MSG msg;
                for(;;)
                {
                                if(PeekMessage(&msg,NULL,0,0,PM_REMOVE))
                                {
                                                if(msg.message==WM_QUIT) break;
                                                TranslateMessage(&msg);
                                                DispatchMessage(&msg);
                                }
                }
                return(msg.wParam);
}
```

Undoubtedly, at some point you also got sick of writing this same exact code over and over again. Maybe you have a file with all the basic code in it and just cut and paste it when you create a new application. Or, like me, maybe you wrote an application framework. And so, we are brought to the topic of discussion: building application frameworks.

> **NOTE**
> You can find the preceding application on the accompanying CD-ROM if you really want to take the time to look at it. It is entitled appframe1.

Why Use an Application Framework?

Three words: *Rapid Application Development* (RAD). I don't care what kind of applications you are writing, whether they're business applications, games, level editors, or whatever. Ideally, you'd like to spend less time actually making them. If you start from scratch each time you make an application, you are spending more time than you need to on each application.

Instead, invest some time building a solid and flexible framework that you can use to quickly build other applications. If you spend 100 hours developing a robust, extensible framework that you can use to cut your development time for other projects in half, after a while, the time spent on the framework will pay for itself.

Let me give you a quick example. Whenever I write a book, the very first sample program I write will typically take me an hour (sometimes less). This is usually just a simple application that gets a window up and running, again doing nothing special. Thereafter, I copy the source code from that example and use it to build other examples. After the first example, it typically only takes me about 15 minutes (tops) to make something new based on what has gone before.

This is why engines and other frameworks already exist. If you are building a business application for Windows, you'd be a fool not to make use of the power of *Microsoft Foundation Classes* (MFC). If you are writing a high-end, bleeding-edge game, you'd be a fool not to use one of the commercially available engines that are out there.

Why Roll Your Own?

Okay, by now it should be pretty obvious that you should use an application framework. What may be a little less obvious is why you would want to make your own and not use one that is already available, like MFC or some game engine.

I am speaking from a focus of writing games and, more importantly, writing smallish games that are likely to be distributed as shareware or as a part of a game bundle on the racks of better computer stores everywhere.

In this situation, MFC is ill suited. It is a bloated framework that can do just about everything under the sun. However, most of its functionality will go unused in your games, so the extra bloat is just wasted space. A commercial engine isn't a great idea either because there's a high cost to make use of the engine, and you are a hungry developer just trying to make a buck or two.

Even if you aren't the small-time developer to whom I am writing, rolling your own application framework is a good idea because of what you will learn by doing so. Every other framework/engine is built on much the same principles, and by going ahead and doing it yourself, you will have a much easier time learning a different framework because you have already gone through how something similar works internally. If it takes you less time to get used to a new framework or engine, you've again saved time and added value to yourself as a developer.

Identify Your Needs

I'm going to take you through writing the core classes of an application framework. Since this is a book in which I only get a few pages to show you something, we won't be making a cutting-edge 3-D engine today.

What we will do, however, is get the pesky code that haunts every single Windows-based application . . . namely `WinMain` and the window procedure.

Programming is, as it has always been, a problem-solving endeavor. You start with a problem that you need to solve and then program the solution to that problem. So, the very first step in designing an application framework (or, indeed, any program) is to identify the problem we need to solve. This will keep us on task and productive and will keep us from wandering away from the mission.

So, what is the problem that we need to solve? Well, we want to give ourselves the core classes of an application framework that will allow us the freedom to never have to write another `WinMain` or `WindowProc` again.

Okay, that's something, but it's still sort of vague. Now we need to define what services `WinMain` and `WindowProc` provide us so that we can plan out how we will meet these needs ourselves.

The `WinMain` function does a number of things for us. Typically, it sets up a window class, creates a window, and then pumps messages. The `WindowProc` function handles messages received by various windows owned by that application.

From an object-oriented point of view, the `WinMain` function and the `WindowProc` function each embody two separate objects. However, they do communicate with one another. Also, each function is embodied with a particular Windows object. `WinMain` is the embodiment of an `HINSTANCE`, and `WindowProc` is the embodiment of an `HWND`.

`WinMain` also has an "ownership/parent" role toward the `HWND`, so this relationship extends to `WindowProc`.

And so, to get us started, we shall come up with two classes. One is called `CApplication`, and it takes the same responsibility that a `WinMain` function does (as well as embodying an `HINSTANCE`). The other is called `CEventHandler`, and it takes on the purposes of a `WindowProc` function and embodies an `HWND`.

The *CApplication* Design

We have stated already that CApplication has the duty of doing everything that a WinMain typically does. We can further state that only one CApplication will exist in a program, thus making it a singleton. It would be absurd to have more than one CApplication object at a time. Perhaps we would think differently if we were doing multithreaded programming, but that sort of thing is beyond the scope of this small chapter.

So, then, what tasks do we rely on WinMain to do? The WinMain function shown earlier in this chapter goes through the following steps:

1. Set up and register a window class.

2. Create a window.

3. Pump messages and wait for a quit message.

4. Terminate.

Of course, the application we are looking at is the simplest case. In reality, a WinMain function does a little bit more than this. It also sets up any application-level resources (setting up a window class and creating a window count as setting up application resources), and when no messages are waiting in the message queue, it will do something else for a little while during the idle state. Finally, it will free any resources that the program may be using before termination. Therefore, we revise what a CApplication must do:

1. Initialize application resources (register a window class, create a window, and so on).

2. Check for a message.

3. If a quit message has occurred, go to step 6.

4. If a nonquit message has occurred, send it to the appropriate message handler and then return to step 2.

5. If no message has occurred, do idle application activities and then return to step 2.

6. Clean up any resources in use by this application.

7. Terminate.

Now we can translate these steps into the beginnings of a class definition for CApplication. We'll return to it later, as we are not quite finished yet, but it does give us a start.

```
class CApplication
{
private:
                //CApplication is a singleton, and the sole instance will have its
    pointer
                //stored in a static member
                static CApplication* s_pTheApplication;
                //store the HINSTANCE
                static HINSTANCE s_hInstance;
public:
                //constructor
                CApplication();
                //destructor
                virtual ~CApplication();
                //retrieve the HINSTANCE
                static HINSTANCE GetHINSTANCE();
                //initialize application resources
                virtual bool OnInit();
                //idling behavior
                virtual void OnIdle();
                //pre-termination activities(clean up resources)
                virtual void OnTerminate();
                //run the application through a static member
                static int Execute(HINSTANCE hInstance,HINSTANCE hPrevInstance,
    LPSTR lpCmdLine,int nShowCmd);
                //retrieve the static application pointer
                static CApplication* GetApplication();
};
```

Based on this class definition, you might have a few questions as to why I made a particular member static or virtual. I'll do my best to answer them.

CApplication itself is not meant to be instantiated. Instead, whatever application you write will be an instance of a child class of CApplication. For example, you might create a child class called CMyApplication. After you have done so, you instantiate your application in the global scope as follows:

```
CMyApplication TheApp;
```

During the construction of the application, the static member s_pTheApplication will be set to point to your application. Later, when CApplication::Execute() is called, it will run your application. This is why the initialization, idling, and cleanup functions are all virtual. They are meant to be overridden.

The *CEventHandler* Design

And now for CEventHandler, which encapsulates the functionality of a WindowProc and embodies an HWND. Therefore, a CEventHandler has to do everything that a WindowProc can do as well as anything that an HWND can do. This is indeed a tall order, and we won't completely fill it here. Instead, we will make CEventHandler do the most common tasks associated with a WindowProc and an HWND, and we'll leave a way to extend this behavior later in child classes of CEventHandler.

The key to CEventHandler is that a single instance is bound tightly to a particular HWND and vice versa. On the CEventHandler side of things, this can easily be done by having a class member that stores the applicable HWND. On the HWND side, we have to store a pointer to the instance of the CEventHandler as the extra data with SetWindowLong, which we will look at a little later on.

Since we don't really want to duplicate the many functions that work with HWNDs as part of the CEventHandler class (although there's nothing to stop you from doing this if you really want to), we will simply leave a way to access the HWND through the CEventHandler instance, and then we'll leave it up to the user of the CEventHandler class to make use of the functions dealing with HWNDs.

And so, a good start on the design for CEventHandler might look like the following:

```
class CEventHandler
{
private:
            //registered window class
            static ATOM s_WndCls;
            //associated window handle
            HWND m_hWnd;
public:
            //constructor
            CEventHandler();
            //destructor
            ~CEventHandler();
            //conversion operator
            operator HWND();
```

```
            //retrieve HWND
            HWND GetHWND();
            //set HWND
            void SetHWND(HWND hWnd);
            //event handling function
            virtual bool HandleEvent(UINT uMsg,WPARAM wParam,LPARAM lParam);
            //event filtering
            virtual bool OnEvent(UINT uMsg,WPARAM wParam,LPARAM lParam);
            //event handlers: mouse
            virtual bool OnMouseMove(int iX,int iY,bool bShift, bool bControl,
    bool bLeft, bool bRight, bool bMiddle);
            virtual bool OnLButtonDown(int iX,int iY,bool bShift, bool bControl,
    bool bLeft, bool bRight, bool bMiddle);
            virtual bool OnLButtonUp(int iX,int iY,bool bShift, bool bControl,
    bool bLeft, bool bRight, bool bMiddle);
            virtual bool OnRButtonDown(int iX,int iY,bool bShift, bool bControl,
    bool bLeft, bool bRight, bool bMiddle);
            virtual bool OnRButtonUp(int iX,int iY,bool bShift, bool bControl,
    bool bLeft, bool bRight, bool bMiddle);
            //event handlers: keyboard
            virtual bool OnKeyDown(int iVirtKey);
            virtual bool OnKeyUp(int iVirtKey);
            virtual bool OnChar(TCHAR tchCode);
            //event handlers: window creation and destruction
            virtual bool OnCreate();
            virtual bool OnDestroy();
            //repaint
            virtual bool OnPaint(HDC hdc,const PAINTSTRUCT* pPaintStruct);
            //static member function for creating window class
            static void CreateWindowClass();
            //static member function for window procedure
            static LRESULT CALLBACK WindowProc(HWND hWnd,UINT uMsg,WPARAM
    wParam,LPARAM lParam);
};
```

Now we've got something to start with anyway. Certainly, we will want to have more event handlers in the finished class than the ones we currently have, but what we've got is fine to begin with.

Notice that all of the event-handling functions begin with the letters "On" and are virtual. (They are meant to be overridden.) Furthermore, they each return a bool.

If the event is processed properly, we need to have these functions return `true`. If unhandled, the event handlers can return `false`.

Unfortunately, because of the way Windows works, we will need to create our event handler *before* we create our window in order to properly bind the two of them together.

We could always get around this by using a factory method in derived classes of `CEventHandler`.

The *CMessageHandler* Design

Unfortunately, one part of the design is left out of the classes as we have designed them thus far. `CEventHandler` instances, like windows, can have a parent/child relationship. A `CEventHandler` can have a `CApplication` as its parent as well. Currently, there is no nice way to represent this in our code. Certainly, we could hack together something that would work most of the time, but that isn't very elegant. So, let's take a look at this new problem and see what we can come up with to solve it. We need the following features:

- A `CEventHandler` must be able to be a child of either a `CApplication` or another `CEventHandler`.

- A `CApplication` is at the root of the parent/child relationship tree. It will never have a parent but may have many children.

- A child must have some manner of notifying its parent when something is happening that the parent should know about.

To me, this sounds an awful lot like a need for another class that will be the parent class of both `CApplication` and `CEventHandler`. Since we only need to send messages down the tree (that is, toward the root), we only need to store a particular object's parent.

Here's what I've come up with for a `CMessageHandler` class:

```
class CMessageHandler
{
private:
            //the parent of this message handler
            CMessageHandler* m_pmhParent;
public:
            //constructor
            CMessageHandler(CMessageHandler* pmhParent);
```

```
            //destructor
            virtual ~CMessageHandler();
            //set/get parent
            void SetMessageParent(CMessageHandler* pmhParent);
            CMessageHandler* GetMessageParent();
            //handles messages, or passes them down the tree
            bool HandleMessage(int MessageID,int argc,void* argv[]);
            //triggered when a message occurs
            virtual bool OnMessage(int MessageID, int argc, void* argv[])=0;
};
```

Notice that `CMessageHandler::OnMessage` has the `=0` after it, making this class a pure virtual class. It cannot be instantiated, which is good, because it does nothing on its own. Now, once we set `CApplication` and `CEventHandler` to use `CMessageHandler` as its base class, we will also not implement their `OnMessage` functions, making them pure virtual classes as well. They aren't particularly useful on their own either.

For now, let's take a quick look at how `CApplication` and `CEventHandler` were changed by the addition of the `CMessageHandler` class as the parent class. First, here's `CApplication` (which really didn't change all that much):

```
class CApplication:  public CMessageHandler
{
private:
            //CApplication is a singleton, and the sole instance will have its
    pointer
            //stored in a static member
            static CApplication* s_pTheApplication;
            //store the HINSTANCE
            static HINSTANCE s_hInstance;
public:
            //constructor
            CApplication();
            //destructor
            virtual ~CApplication();
            //retrieve the HINSTANCE
            static HINSTANCE GetHINSTANCE();
            //initialize application resources
            virtual bool OnInit()=0;
            //idling behavior
            virtual void OnIdle()=0;
            //pre-termination activities(clean up resources)
```

```
                virtual void OnTerminate()=0;
                //run the application through a static member
                static int Execute(HINSTANCE hInstance,HINSTANCE hPrevInstance,LPSTR
     lpCmdLine,int nShowCmd);
                //retrieve the static application pointer
                static CApplication* GetApplication();
     };
```

For the most part, CApplication's definition remains unchanged. The first line is
modified to represent CMessageHandler's role as a parent class. The other changes
concern the modification of OnInit, OnIdle, and OnTerminate. I made them into pure
virtual functions. Since OnMessage from CMessageHandler already makes this class a
pure virtual class, requiring that the user implement these three functions doesn't
really hurt anything.

As for CEventHandler, here's what it looks like now:

```
class CEventHandler: public CMessageHandler
{
private:
                //registered window class
                static ATOM s_WndCls;
                //associated window handle
                HWND m_hWnd;
public:
                //constructor
                CEventHandler(CMessageHandler* pmhParent);
                //destructor
                ~CEventHandler();
                //conversion operator
                operator HWND();
                //retrieve HWND
                HWND GetHWND();
                //set HWND
                void SetHWND(HWND hWnd);
                //event handling function
                virtual bool HandleEvent(UINT uMsg,WPARAM wParam,LPARAM lParam);
                //event filtering
                virtual bool OnEvent(UINT uMsg,WPARAM wParam,LPARAM lParam);
                //event handlers: mouse
                virtual bool OnMouseMove(int iX,int iY,bool bShift, bool bControl,
     bool bLeft, bool bRight, bool bMiddle);
```

```
                virtual bool OnLButtonDown(int iX,int iY,bool bShift, bool bControl,
        bool bLeft, bool bRight, bool bMiddle);
                virtual bool OnLButtonUp(int iX,int iY,bool bShift, bool bControl,
        bool bLeft, bool bRight, bool bMiddle);
                virtual bool OnRButtonDown(int iX,int iY,bool bShift, bool bControl,
        bool bLeft, bool bRight, bool bMiddle);
                virtual bool OnRButtonUp(int iX,int iY,bool bShift, bool bControl,
        bool bLeft, bool bRight, bool bMiddle);
                //event handlers: keyboard
                virtual bool OnKeyDown(int iVirtKey);
                virtual bool OnKeyUp(int iVirtKey);
                virtual bool OnChar(TCHAR tchCode);
                //event handlers: window creation and destruction
                virtual bool OnCreate();
                virtual bool OnDestroy();
                //repaint
                virtual bool OnPaint(HDC hdc,const PAINTSTRUCT* pPaintStruct);
                //static member function for creating window class
                static void CreateWindowClass();
                //static member function for window procedure
                static LRESULT CALLBACK WindowProc(HWND hWnd,UINT uMsg,WPARAM
        wParam,LPARAM lParam);
};
```

In CEventHandler, not only did the first line of the declaration change but also the constructor. Now, because of polymorphism, you can pass a pointer to a CApplication (or any derived class) or to a CEventHandler (or any derived class) as the parent to the CEventHandler's constructor, and it will set that object as the new object's parent.

Implementation of a Simple Application Framework

There is certainly more we could design for this application framework, but this is meant to be a quick example to give you ideas, not an exhaustive treatise on application frameworks. Therefore, we'll call the three core classes "good enough" and implement them.

Implementation of *CMessageHandler*

We'll start with the base class, CMessageHandler. This is a rather elementary class. It essentially only stores a single CMessageHandler pointer as a parent. Table 3.1 shows the more simplistic member function implementations:

Table 3.1 *CMessageHandler* Member Functions

Function	Implementation
CMessageHandler(pmhParent)	{SetMessageParemt(pmhParent);}
~CMessageHandler()	{}
SetMessageParent(pmhParent)	{m_pmhParent=pmhParent;}
GetMessageParent()	{return(m_pmhParent);}

As you can see, Table 3.1 only shows you some rather standard getter and setter functions, and those are no big deal. The only function I had to be careful with was HandleMessage.

```
//handles messages, or passes them down the tree
bool CMessageHandler::HandleMessage(int MessageID,int argc,void* argv[])
{
          //attempt to handle message
          if(OnMessage(MessageID,argc,argv))
          {
                    //message has been handled, return true
                    return(true);
          }
          else
          {
                    //message has not been handled
                    //look for a parent to pass the message to...
                    if(GetMessageParent())
                    {
                              //found a parent
                              //let parent handle message
                              return(GetMessageParent()-
>HandleMessage(MessageID,argc,argv));
```

```
                                        }
                                        else
                                        {
                                                //did not find a parent
                                                //failed to handle message, return
        false

                                                return(false);

                                        }
                        }
        }
```

When a message handler (or any derived class) receives a message, we have to do a number of different things to get that message handled. First, we must try to handle the message ourselves. If we fail to handle the message on our own, we must try to pass it along to the parent message handler, if one exists. If no parent exists, the message remains unhandled. If a parent does exist, we pass it along to the parent.

The parameters for HandleMessage are structured so that there is a unique ID for the message (MessageID) and then a variable number of void* parameters. There is no way of knowing how many parameters we might need in the future, so we don't want to shoot ourselves in the foot.

Implementation of *CApplication*

CApplication, like CMessageHandler, is a simply implemented class. All of the data for this class is static. The only reason why not every member function of CApplication is static is because, to customize what an application does, we need to make use of virtual functions and polymorphism.

Of the CApplication member functions, OnInit, OnIdle, and OnTerminate are virtual, so we defer implementation until a derived class.

The static member functions, GetHINSTANCE and GetApplication, return our static members. They are simple enough that I shouldn't have to actually show them here in print.

That leaves us with the constructor, the destructor, and the static member function Execute. The destructor does absolutely nothing, so we can ignore it.

First, here's the constructor:

```
//constructor
CApplication::CApplication():
        CMessageHandler(NULL)//initialize message handler parent class
```

```
{
            //check for an instance of CApplication already existing
            if(s_pTheApplication)
            {
                        //instance of CApplication already exists, so termi-
   nate
                        exit(1);
            }

            //set application pointer
            s_pTheApplication=this;
}
```

Since a CApplication-derived object is meant to be declared in the global scope and furthermore is meant to be a singleton, the constructor for CApplication is concerned with two things. First, it makes certain that the static application pointer has not already been written to. (This static member starts with a value of NULL.) If an application has already been created, it causes the program to exit abruptly. Ideally, you should make some sort of alert system to make this easier to debug.

Second, if nothing has set the application pointer yet, the current application being initialized becomes the new value. This pointer is used later by Execute to make everything happen.

```
//run the application through a static member
int CApplication::Execute(HINSTANCE hInstance,HINSTANCE hPrevInstance,
   LPSTR lpCmdLine,int nShowCmd)
{
            //set instance handle
            s_hInstance=GetModuleHandle(NULL);
            //check for application instance
            if(!GetApplication())
            {
                        //no application instance, exit
                        return(0);
            }
            //attempt to initialize application
            if(GetApplication()->OnInit())
            {
                        //application initialized
                        //quit flag
                        bool bQuit=false;
```

```
//message structure
MSG msg;
//until quit flag is set
 while(!bQuit)
{
                //check for a message
                if(PeekMessage(&msg,NULL,0,0,PM_REMOVE))
                {
                                //a message has occurred
                                //check for a quit
                                if(msg.message==WM_QUIT)
                                {
                                                //quit message
                                                bQuit=true;
                                }
                                else
                                {
                                                //non quit
message
                                                //translate
and dispatch
TranslateMessage(&msg);

DispatchMessage(&msg);
                                }
                }
                else
                {
                                //application is idling
                                GetApplication()->OnIdle();
                }
}

                //terminate application
                GetApplication()->OnTerminate();
                //return
                 return(msg.wParam);
        }
          else
        {
```

```
                    //application did not initialize
                    return(0);
            }
}
```

`CApplication::Execute` looks very much like what a standard `WinMain` function looks like, minus window class creation and window creation. This function uses the static member function `GetApplication` to get a hold on whatever instance of a `CApplication`-derived class is the running application. `Execute` is also responsible for setting the static `HINSTANCE` member. Other than that, this function initializes the application, goes through a message pump (letting the application idle whenever no message is in the queue), and finally terminates once a quit message has been processed.

Our actual `WinMain` function (yes, despite our hard work, there still must be a `WinMain`) also is part of the `CApplication` implementation. Quite simply, here it is:

```
//winmain function
int WINAPI WinMain(HINSTANCE hInstance,HINSTANCE hPrevInstance,LPSTR lpCmdLine,
    int nShowCmd)
{
            //execute the application
    return(CApplication::Execute(hInstance,hPrevInstance,lpCmdLine,nShowCmd));
}
```

And behold! The mystically magical one-line `WinMain`! Everything is handled inside of `CApplication::Execute` anyway.

Implementing *CEventHandler*

NOTE

Just an FYI here: In case you were curious, this is exactly the same mechanism that **MFC** uses to get rid of `WinMain`. **Our** `CApplication` **class is the equivalent of** `CWinApp`.

`CEventHandler` is by far the most complicated class of the three, but even so, it is not particularly difficult to implement. Most of the functions (specifically those whose names begin with "On") are simply stubs and do nothing but return a value. Other functions include the `HWND` getter and setter, which are no-brainers. The functions that we really need to examine are `HandleEvent`, `CreateWindowClass`, `WindowProc`, and `Create`.

We'll start with `CreateWindowClass`. This is a static member function that sets up the window class to be used for all windows created for use with `CEventHandler` derived objects.

```
//static member function for creating window class
void CEventHandler::CreateWindowClass()
{
                //check for the atom
                if(!s_WndCls)
                {
                                //set up window class
                                WNDCLASSEX wcx;
                                wcx.cbClsExtra=0;
                                wcx.cbSize=sizeof(WNDCLASSEX);
                                wcx.cbWndExtra=0;
                                wcx.hbrBackground=NULL;
                                wcx.hCursor=NULL;
                                wcx.hIcon=NULL;
                                wcx.hIconSm=NULL;
                                wcx.hInstance=GetModuleHandle(NULL);
                                wcx.lpfnWndProc=CEventHandler::WindowProc;
                                wcx.lpszClassName="LAVALAMPSARECOOL";
                                wcx.lpszMenuName=NULL;
                                wcx.style=CS_DBLCLKS|CS_HREDRAW|CS_VREDRAW|CS_OWNDC;

                                //register the class
                                s_WndCls=RegisterClassEx(&wcx);
                }
}
```

This function checks to see whether the static window class member (s_WndCls) is
NULL (the initial value). If it is, it will create a rather generic window class. Please
don't laugh at the name I picked for it. After *CreateWindowClass* is called one time,
the window class is registered already and so the function henceforth does nothing
at all. This is a handy feature considering that each time CEventHandler::Create is
called, this function gets called, as you can see here:

```
//create a window and associate it with a pre-existing CEventHandler
HWND CEventHandler::Create(CEventHandler* pehHandler,DWORD dwExStyle,LPCTSTR
   lpWindowName,DWORD dwStyle,int x,int y,int nWidth,int nHeight,HWND
   hWndParent,HMENU hMenu)
{
                //create the window class
                CreateWindowClass();
```

```
                //create and return the window
    return(CreateWindowEx(dwExStyle,(LPCTSTR)s_WndCls,lpWindowName,dwStyle,x,y,nWidth,
    nHeight,hWndParent,hMenu,GetModuleHandle(NULL),pehHandler));
}
```

This function is the only function you should use to create CEventHandler-associated windows. It has most of the parameters of CreateWindowEx, with the exception of the class name and the HINSTANCE. An additional parameter is a pointer to a CEventHandler with which to associate the window.

To see how an HWND and a CEventHandler are associated with one another, we need to take a look at CEventHandler::WindowProc.

```
//static member function for window procedure
LRESULT CALLBACK CEventHandler::WindowProc(HWND hWnd,UINT uMsg,WPARAM wParam,
    LPARAM lParam)
{
                //check for WM_NCCREATE
                if(uMsg==WM_NCCREATE)
                {
                                //attach window to event handler and vice versa
                                //grab creation data
                                LPCREATESTRUCT lpcs=(LPCREATESTRUCT)lParam;
                                //grab event handler pointer
                                CEventHandler* peh=(CEventHandler*)lpcs->lpCreateParams;
                                //associate event handler with window
                                peh->SetHWND(hWnd);
                                //associate window with event handler
                                SetWindowLong(hWnd,GWL_USERDATA,(LONG)peh);
                }
                //look up event handler
                CEventHandler* peh=(CEventHandler*)GetWindowLong(hWnd,GWL_USERDATA);
                //check for a NULL event handler
                if(!peh)
                {
                                //use default window procedure
                                return(DefWindowProc(hWnd,uMsg,wParam,lParam));
                }
                //check for event filter
                if(peh->OnEvent(uMsg,wParam,lParam))
```

```
            {
                        //event filtered
                        return(0);
            }
            else
            {
                        //event not filtered
                        //attempt to handle event
                        if(peh->HandleEvent(uMsg,wParam,lParam))
                        {
                                    //event handled
                                    return(0);
                        }
                        else
                        {
                                    //event not handled
                                    //default processing

    return(DefWindowProc(hWnd,uMsg,wParam,lParam));
                        }
            }
}
```

There are really two parts to this function. One is when WM_NCCREATE occurs. (This message is sent to the window procedure during the call to CreateWindowEx.) This is where the CEventHandler and HWND become tied to one another. The CEventHandler has its HWND set to the window in question, and the HWND gets a pointer to the CEventHandler placed into its user data with a call to SetWindowLong.

If any other message besides WM_NCCREATE occurs, the function pulls out the CEventHandler pointer, checks that it is non-null (it can happen), and then tries to have the CEventHandler object handle the message. First, it sends it to the OnEvent filter; failing that, it goes to the HandleEvent function. If the event is still not handled, it defaults to DefWindowProc.

Finally, an event is dispatched to the appropriate handler by CEventHandler::HandleEvent.

```
//event handling function
bool CEventHandler::HandleEvent(UINT uMsg,WPARAM wParam,LPARAM lParam)
{
            //what message was received?
```

```
switch(uMsg)
{
case WM_MOUSEMOVE://mouse movement
                {
                                //grab x and y
                                int x=LOWORD(lParam);
                                int y=HIWORD(lParam);
                                //grab button states
                                bool bLeft=((wParam&MK_LBUTTON)>0);
                                bool bRight=((wParam&MK_RBUTTON)>0);
                                bool bMiddle=((wParam&MK_MBUTTON)>0);
                                //grab shift state
                                bool bShift=((wParam&MK_SHIFT)>0);
                                bool bCtrl=((wParam&MK_CONTROL)>0);
                                //send to event handling function
return(OnMouseMove(x,y,bShift,bCtrl,bLeft,bRight,bMiddle));
                        }break;
            case WM_LBUTTONDOWN://left mouse button press
                        {
                                //grab x and y
                                int x=LOWORD(lParam);
                                int y=HIWORD(lParam);
                                //grab button states
                                bool bLeft=((wParam&MK_LBUTTON)>0);
                                bool bRight=((wParam&MK_RBUTTON)>0);
                                bool bMiddle=((wParam&MK_MBUTTON)>0);
                                //grab shift state
                                bool bShift=((wParam&MK_SHIFT)>0);
                                bool bCtrl=((wParam&MK_CONTROL)>0);
                                //send to event handling function
return(OnLButtonDown(x,y,bShift,bCtrl,bLeft,bRight,bMiddle));
                        }break;
            case WM_LBUTTONUP://left mouse button release
                        {
                                //grab x and y
                                int x=LOWORD(lParam);
                                int y=HIWORD(lParam);
                                //grab button states
                                bool bLeft=((wParam&MK_LBUTTON)>0);
                                bool bRight=((wParam&MK_RBUTTON)>0);
                                bool bMiddle=((wParam&MK_MBUTTON)>0);
```

```
                                    //grab shift state
                                    bool bShift=((wParam&MK_SHIFT)>0);
                                    bool bCtrl=((wParam&MK_CONTROL)>0);
                                    //send to event handling function
        return(OnLButtonUp(x,y,bShift,bCtrl,bLeft,bRight,bMiddle));
                        }break;
            case WM_RBUTTONDOWN://right mouse button press
                        {
                                    //grab x and y
                                    int x=LOWORD(lParam);
                                    int y=HIWORD(lParam);
                                    //grab button states
                                    bool bLeft=((wParam&MK_LBUTTON)>0);
                                    bool bRight=((wParam&MK_RBUTTON)>0);
                                    bool bMiddle=((wParam&MK_MBUTTON)>0);
                                    //grab shift state
                                    bool bShift=((wParam&MK_SHIFT)>0);
                                    bool bCtrl=((wParam&MK_CONTROL)>0);
                                    //send to event handling function
        return(OnRButtonDown(x,y,bShift,bCtrl,bLeft,bRight,bMiddle));
                        }break;
            case WM_RBUTTONUP://right mouse button release
                        {
                                    //grab x and y
                                    int x=LOWORD(lParam);
                                    int y=HIWORD(lParam);
                                    //grab button states
                                    bool bLeft=((wParam&MK_LBUTTON)>0);
                                    bool bRight=((wParam&MK_RBUTTON)>0);
                                    bool bMiddle=((wParam&MK_MBUTTON)>0);
                                    //grab shift state
                                    bool bShift=((wParam&MK_SHIFT)>0);
                                    bool bCtrl=((wParam&MK_CONTROL)>0);
                                    //send to event handling function
        return(OnRButtonUp(x,y,bShift,bCtrl,bLeft,bRight,bMiddle));
                        }break;
            case WM_KEYDOWN://key press
                        {
                                    //send to event handler
                                    return(OnKeyDown(wParam));
                        }break;
```

```
case WM_KEYUP://key release
        {
                        //send to event handler
                        return(OnKeyUp(wParam));
        }break;
case WM_CHAR://character generated
        {
                        //send to event handler
                        return(OnChar(wParam));
        }break;
case WM_CREATE://window created
        {
                        return(OnCreate());
        }break;
case WM_DESTROY://window destroyed
        {
                        return(OnDestroy());
        }break;
case WM_PAINT://repaint
        {
                        //begin painting
                        PAINTSTRUCT ps;
                        HDC hdc=BeginPaint(GetHWND(),&ps);

                        //call handler
                        OnPaint(hdc,&ps);

                        //end painting
                        EndPaint(GetHWND(),&ps);
                        return(true);
        }break;
default://any other message
        {
                        //not handled
                        return(false);
        }break;
    }
}
```

This function operates just like a WindowProc without actually being one. It is missing the HWND parameter, but that is easily retrieved with a call to GetHWND, as shown in the

WM_PAINT handler. This function not only checks to see what event occurred, it also removes the applicable data from wParam and lParam before sending it off to the individual event-handling function. At the CEventHandler level, all of the event-handling functions, like OnMouseMove and OnKeyDown, just return false so that default processing can occur. The exception to this rule is OnPaint, which returns true even though it doesn't matter what it returns. All WM_PAINT messages are minimally handled.

In a derived class, you could add new events to handle and simply call CEventHandler::HandleEvent in the default block of the switch statement. See? It's extensible.

A Sample Program

The following sample program can be found on the accompanying CD-ROM. It is entitled appframe2.

As they currently exist, CMessageHandler, CApplication, and CEventHandler are useless because they are all pure virtual classes and cannot be instantiated. To make use of them, we need to derive some classes that implement the pure virtual functions. At a bare minimum, we need a derived class of CApplication and a derived class of CEvent-Handler. For this test case, I have created CTestApplication and CTestEventHandler.

The Design of *CTestApplication*

In our sample program, we simply want to create a window. Just so that this window responds to some sort of input, when the Esc key is pressed, we want the window to close and the application to terminate.

The only things we need to add to *CTestApplication* are a constructor and destructor (neither of which have to do anything in particular) and functions that implement OnMessage, OnInit, OnIdle, and OnTerminate. So, the definition for CTestApplication should look something like this:

```
class CTestApplication : public CApplication
{
private:
        //main event handler
        CTestEventHandler* m_pehMain;
public:
        //constructor
        CTestApplication();
```

```
            //destructor
            virtual ~CTestApplication();
            //implement pure virtual functions(message handler)
            bool OnMessage(int MessageID,int argc,void* argv[]);
            //implement pure virtual functions(application)
            bool OnInit();
            void OnIdle();
            void OnTerminate();
};
```

Our window will be controlled through a CTestEventHandler object, and even though we haven't yet designed that class, we know we will eventually need to store a pointer to it. Since we aren't making use of the message-handling functionality inherent in CMessagehandler, we know that the OnMessage function will basically do nothing except return a value. Similarly, since there is no idling activity for this application, OnIdle will wind up simply a stub function. So, really, only OnInit and OnTerminate need to have anything in them.

The Design of *CTestEventHandler*

Now this is some cool stuff. With CTestEventHandler, we only have to have a few member functions overridden. We first need a constructor, which will create the window and associate the window with the object being created. We also have to implement the OnMessage function from CMessageHandler, even though it will do nothing.

Other than that, we need only concern ourselves with the events we will be processing, namely OnKeyDown (to check for an Esc keypress) and OnDestroy (to post a quit message).

```
class CTestEventHandler : public CEventHandler
{
public:
            //constructor
            CTestEventHandler(CMessageHandler* pmhParent);
            //destructor
            virtual ~CTestEventHandler();
            //implement message handling function
            bool OnMessage(int MessageID,int argc,void* argv[]);
            //override key press handler
            bool OnKeyDown(int iVirtKey);
            //override destroy window handler
            bool OnDestroy();
```

};

This definition is a whole lot shorter than CEventHandler. Most of our events can undergo default processing, which is already handled by the CEventHandler implementation of the events. (This is why the individual event handlers are not pure virtual functions.) We only need to override the handlers that we actually need to deal with.

The Implementation of *CTestApplication*

The implementation for CTestApplication is so short that I can put the entire code here:

```
#include "TestApplication.h"
//constructor
CTestApplication::CTestApplication()
{
}
//destructor
CTestApplication::~CTestApplication()
{
}
//implement pure virtual functions(message handler)
bool CTestApplication::OnMessage(int MessageID,int argc,void* argv[])
{
            //simply return false
            return(false);
}
//implement pure virtual functions(application)
bool CTestApplication::OnInit()
{
            //create new event handler
            m_pehMain= new CTestEventHandler(this);
            //return true
            return(true);
}
void CTestApplication::OnIdle()
{
            //do nothing
}
```

```
void CTestApplication::OnTerminate()
{
                //destroy event handler
                delete m_pehMain;
}
//global application
CTestApplication TheApp;
```

There are only three items to which you should pay particular attention. First, during `CTestApplication::OnInit`, a `CTestEventHandler` is created and then the function returns `true`, allowing `CApplication::Execute` to continue with the application. Second, `CTestApplication::OnTerminate` destroys the `CTestEventHandler` (since it was dynamically created in `OnInit`). Third, after the implementation of `CTestApplication`, a single variable of type `CTestApplication` is created called `TheApp`. The actual name of this variable is unimportant, but this declaration causes the entire framework to do its job.

The Implementation of *CTestEventHandler*

The implementation of `CTestEventHandler` is only a few lines longer than the implementation of `CTestApplication`.

```
#include "TestEventHandler.h"
//constructor
CTestEventHandler::CTestEventHandler(CMessageHandler* pmhParent):
                CEventHandler(pmhParent)//initialize parent class
{
                //create a window
                CEventHandler::Create(this,0,"Test
  Application",WS_VISIBLE|WS_CAPTION|WS_SYSMENU|WS_BORDER,0,0,320,240,NULL,NULL);
}
//destructor
CTestEventHandler::~CTestEventHandler()
{
}
//implement message handling function
bool CTestEventHandler::OnMessage(int MessageID,int argc,void* argv[])
{
                //by default, return false
                return(false);
```

```
        }
//override key press handler
bool CTestEventHandler::OnKeyDown(int iVirtKey)
{
            //check for escape key
            if(iVirtKey==VK_ESCAPE)
            {
                        //destroy the window
                        DestroyWindow(GetHWND());
                        //handled
                        return(true);
            }
            //not handled
            return(false);
}
//override destroy window handler
bool CTestEventHandler::OnDestroy()
{
            //post a quit message
            PostQuitMessage(0);
            //handled
            return(true);
}
```

Essentially, the destructor and OnMessage functions can be ignored because they do nothing in particular. Notable functions include the constructor (which creates a window to associate with the event-handler object) and the handlers for OnKeyDown and OnDestroy. In the case of OnKeyDown, it simply checks for an escape key. If it detects one, it destroys the window (which causes OnDestroy to be called). Finally, OnDestroy posts a quit message to the event queue, which allows CApplication::Execute to get out of the event loop and terminate.

How Do We Benefit?

Now, if you are like me, you would have gone into the sample program, counted the lines in CTestApplication.h/cpp and CTestEventHandler.h/cpp, and seen that there are way more than double the lines of code compared to the beginning of the chapter. You would have scoffed and told me where to go for suggesting that by doubling the number of lines you are somehow working less.

But I never promised there would be fewer lines of code. I simply stated that you could get work done much faster if the core code that existed in all applications did not have to be rewritten each time.

The code for `CMessageHandler`, `CEventHandler`, and `CApplication` will never, ever need to be modified. You can derive classes from them all day long, and they'll serve you well. In addition, they have organized the core of your application rather well. Event handlers no longer require that you go into a gigantic switch, monkey around with a case here and there, and manipulate the `wParam` and `lParam` values to get the information you need. Certainly, the implementation of `CEventHandler` that I showed here could stand to have many more of the window message constants handled, but it's a decent start, and you could put in handlers for those other messages. Most importantly, you only have to implement that case one time and then use it ever after.

Right now, if I were to give you an assignment to take these core classes and build a small doodling application that draws white on a black background when the left mouse button is pressed, you could quickly throw it together with a derived class of `CApplication` and `CEventHandler`. You'd simply have to override `OnPaint`, `OnMouseMove`, and perhaps `OnLButtonDown` and `OnLButtonUp`.

Summary

Although this chapter gives you a decent application framework (albeit a very simple one), it is not intended to tell you how you should organize your code, nor is this framework necessarily the best framework to use in all cases. What you should get out of this chapter is ideas on how to build your own framework. Likely, many of the ideas you've seen here are ones you will want to follow. The framework I presented here is a simplified version of the framework I use in my "real" code. There is much, much more you can do with it to make it a nice, robust framework—usable for just about anything you need.

TRICK 4

User Interface Hierarchies

Ernest S. Pazera,
ernestpazera@msn.com

Introduction

A couple of years back, I was working on a value title (its name is not important). I started the day before the due date (never a good sign), and one of the items I was tasked with was to maintain the custom *user interface* (UI) system.

To give a small amount of background on exactly how it had to work, this game ran under Windows and used DirectX. (The graphics were run through DirectDraw.) The input was all gained through DirectInput. All of the drawing was done through the game's graphics "engine." The controls—including window frames, buttons, text, and so on—were all resources loaded into the game, and a simple function call would add whatever graphic was needed to the queue, which would be updated each frame.

As I was looking through the code for the UI system, my heart began to sink. This game had originally been written in C and then moved into C++ by taking groups of functions and putting a class around them. Each user interface element (window, button, text box, check box, horizontal scroll bar) was hard-coded as far as how it worked, and each window simply had an array (an array!) of 10 of each of the UI controls.

To make things worse, all of the input from a UI window and its controls was handled through a single function. That's right, a single function for *all* the different types of windows that could be called up in the game.

Now, I have been an object-oriented programmer for some time, and looking at the state of this user interface system just made me feel how wrongly designed it was. Obviously, not a whole lot of thought was put into it by the programmer who had worked on it before me. (That programmer had been fired, which was why I now had the task of working with it.)

To me, it seemed as though a UI system is a natural thing to which to apply object-oriented techniques. There is a master UI control (representing the entire screen), and each window would be a child of that master control. Buttons, text boxes, check boxes, and other widgets would be child controls of the windows, ad nauseam.

Essentially, this required that I rewrite the entire UI system (while at the same time not breaking the code, which worked even though it was kludgey). I learned a lot in the process. Most notably, I learned what *not* to do when making a UI system. In this chapter I hope to pass on the lessons I learned while working on that project so that you can avoid the same pains.

The Role of UI

Many game developers seem to think that a user interface is a trivial piece of the game and that as long as they can cobble together something really quick to do the job, they are done. This has caused the downfall of many games (especially in the value market). A klunky interface has caused many players to simply stop playing because they had to wrestle with the game to do what they wanted to get done.

Let's think about this logically for a moment. A computer game or console game is a piece of interactive entertainment. The key word here is "interactive." If we just wanted entertainment, we'd go out and rent a DVD, right?

To be interactive, a game has to respond to the player, the player then responds to the game, and so on. Without this interactivity, it's not a game.

Now, how can the game respond to the player? The player must, naturally, have some manner of communicating with the game. This takes the form of some sort of input device: a keyboard, a mouse, a gamepad, or any number of other input devices.

Another aspect of this is giving feedback to the player and letting him know that he has accomplished something or that he has failed to do something. Both positive and negative reinforcement will help the player gain better control over what he is doing in the game.

An example of this sort of feedback is just moving the mouse around. As the player moves the mouse, the cursor moves proportionally to how far the mouse has moved. Since we all use computers so much these days, it's easy to forget just how important that type of feedback is. We communicate with the computer by moving the mouse, and the computer responds by moving the cursor. Communication goes two ways.

Furthermore, there is other feedback that should be present. If the primary controlling device for the game is the mouse, then when the mouse is over something with which the player can interact, there should be some sort of feedback to show him that. Perhaps the text on a button changes its color or a red outline appears around an object in the game, indicating that if the player clicks on that object something will happen.

So, a user interface is not just buttons and windows and little icons. It is the communication pipeline between the player and the game, and vice versa. It should be obvious to anyone that making a UI system is anything but trivial. Instead, it is perhaps the most important aspect of your game. Sure, those Bézier surfaces are neat, your particle effects are spectacular, and the rendering of your 3-D world is breathtaking. But if you trivialized your UI system, you might as well just quit and go into film school.

UI Design Considerations

A good user interface system, despite all I have said so far, is not all that hard to design and implement. No, I am not contradicting myself here. A UI system is still a nontrivial piece of work, but like all other programming tasks, it is a problem-solving endeavor. If you just put a little effort into solving the problem and think about things in an organized manner rather than just throwing something together, you'll do just fine.

In the remainder of this chapter, we will be concentrating on performing the "normal" tasks of a UI—namely, things like windows, buttons, text boxes, and the like. Collectively, I refer to these things as "UI widgets" and, more often than not, simply "widgets."

I am making a separation here between interacting with these widgets and interacting with the game itself. When a window pops up on the screen and the user interacts with it instead of what is going on in the game itself, the UI preempts input from the game. That means that if user input is going to the UI system, it should *not* be filtering into the game afterward. With some widgets (like a full-screen status window), this might require that you pause what is going on in the game while the user fidgets with the UI. Other times this is not the case, and gameplay progresses even as the user plays with the UI (like in a real-time strategy game, when you are giving commands to a unit by pressing buttons off to the side of the screen).

The Widget Tree

Such a UI system is also hierarchical in nature. One widget will contain any number of other widgets, like a window that contains buttons to press. An individual button widget may not contain any other widgets at all. Also, there must be a single master widget that acts as the root of the tree from which all other widgets grow. The master widget (or, if you prefer, the "widget king"), doesn't really do anything on its own. It simply keeps the UI system together. Consider Figure 4.1.

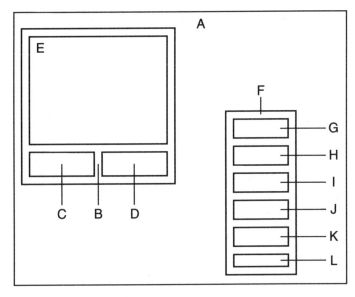

Figure 4.1

A sample UI layout

In Figure 4.1, A represents the entire screen, or the master widget. B and F represent "window" widgets. C, D, and G through L represent "button" widgets, and E represents a "label" widget containing textual information or perhaps a picture of something.

Just from looking at it, it is reasonably obvious that B and F are both "contained" by A; that C, D, and E are "contained" by B; and that G through L are "contained" by F. The relationship is shown in tree form in Figure 4.2.

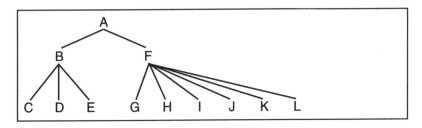

Figure 4.2

A tree view of the UI hierarchy

This sort of relationship is best represented as a parent/child relationship. A would then be the parent of B and F, and so on. In a hierarchy like this, it is paramount that any particular widget in the tree must be able to communicate with both its parent as well as its children, so there will need to be some mechanism in place to keep track of both of these things, and here is why.

The UI tree is used for two tasks. One task is to display whatever graphics are associated with the various widgets currently in existence. The other task is to trap user input to any of the widgets in the tree.

Z Ordering

Now we get into the concept of Z order. Certain widgets will be "closer" to the user than other widgets. Widget A, the master widget, is the farthest back and remains so at all times. All of its children are "in front" of it, just as all of their children are "in front" of them. Most of the time, this is not a problem. However, if two children of the same widget overlap on the screen, the one that is drawn last will appear to be "in front" of the one that was drawn first.

Why is this important? Because if the user interacts with a widget, he expects that the widget "closest" to him is the one with which he is interacting, even if two widgets overlap. Therefore, you have to be careful in how you handle input and how you handle displaying the widgets.

When updating the UI system on the display, you start at the root (the master widget) and follow this procedure:

1. Redraw the widget's background onto its own bitmap.
2. Redraw all child widgets in order from the first created to the last created.
3. Display the widget on its parent's bitmap.

It is important here that each widget get its own drawing area. Certainly, this can be done in other ways, but this is the way I have chosen for this chapter. I'm not saying that it is the one true way. You might instead just want child widgets to draw directly to the screen. The order remains the same.

When sending input to the UI system, the process is reversed, as follows:

1. Check all child widgets in order from the last created to the first created to see if input has been intercepted.
2. Check this widget for input interception.

To simplify these concepts, you will want to draw your widgets from back (farthest from user) to front (nearest to user) but check for input from front to back.

Notification

Another common task for a widget is to notify its parent that some event has occurred. You might have a window widget that contains two button widgets, one that says OK and one that says Cancel. The button widgets only have information pertaining to what they need to do. They know what text to display, and they typically will have an ID number of some sort. (For the sake of discussion, the OK button has an ID of 1, and the Cancel button has an ID of 2.) The buttons don't have a clue about what happens when they are clicked; they only know how to recognize when this occurs. When one of them is clicked, it notifies its parent, indicating what its button ID is. It is then up to the window to make sense of that information and pass down a new message to its own parent, indicating which button was pressed. This sort of thing typically filters down to the master widget, which communicates to the application that a particular command has been given through the UI system, and the application responds to that command.

Appearance

Now we get to what a particular widget might look like. Of course, each type of widget will look different from another type of widget. After all, a text box looks different than a button, which looks different than a check box, and so on. Basically what we are looking for here is how the appearance of a widget is similar to all other widgets. We get down to this basic level of sameness and put that into our design.

A widget, while theoretically it can have any shape and size, is probably most easily implemented as consisting of a rectangular area. Computers that make use of raster displays are well suited to rectangles rather than shapes like ovals or polygons. Plus, if we really feel a need to do so, we can still use a bounding rectangle and only draw to portions of the image that are the actual shape of the image, so we can have ovals and polygons if we really want.

The rectangular areas have a couple of aspects. First, a widget will have a position. This position will be in relation to its parent. Since it is convenient to do so, the position will record the upper-left corner of the rectangle. The other aspect is size, which we will store as the width and height of the widget.

Focus

Human beings and computers, although they can perform many tasks, can only perform one task at a time. When you are running applications on your computer, such as a spreadsheet, a word processor, a game, and a calculator, certainly all of these things are running on the computer at the same time, but you are only going to use one of them at a time and switch between them. You are "focused" on a single task, even though you are switching back and forth between tasks.

A similar concept applies to a user interface and the widgets that make it up. If there are two window widgets, you will only interact with one of them at a time. If you are typing information into a text box, only that text box should receive keyboard input, and all other widgets that might take keyboard input should be circumvented. This is the concept of input focus and/or input capture.

When you move the mouse over a button and press the left mouse button, the button will be the only widget to receive mouse input until you have released the left mouse button. If you release the left button while still inside of the widget, whatever action was to take place after clicking the button should occur. If you move the mouse outside of the widget, the action is canceled.

Most of the time, the idea of focus can be handled by the Z order of widgets. The widget at the top of the tree will receive input before other controls. Under certain circumstances, however, you need to override this behavior by having a particular widget "capture" input from one of the input devices, like for a text box or for a button when you press the left mouse button.

Widget Members

Now that we have really taken a look at the needs of a UI hierarchy, we can start to solidify it into a class definition. I like to start with what kind of data is abstracted (that is, members) and then work out what kinds of operations (that is, member functions) are required for everything to work properly.

From the previous discussion, we can determine that, at a bare minimum, the following pieces of information are needed if we want to take care of all of the design considerations:

1. A pointer to the widget's parent

2. An ordered container for all of the widget's children

3. A bitmap buffer/drawing context onto which the widget will be drawn and from which the widget can be drawn onto other widgets or the screen

4. The position and size of the widget

5. Static pointers to the widgets that currently have keyboard or mouse focus

Further, we must have a way, within this set of data, to determine the difference between the master widget and all other widgets. For our purposes, we can simply say that the master widget has a NULL parent, but we shall also provide a static pointer to the master widget.

So, if we were calling our class CWidget, this is one way to represent each of the data items:

```
class CWidget
{
            CWidget* m_pParentWidget;  //pointer to parent widget
            std::list<CWidget*> m_lstChildWidgets;  //list of child widgets
            HDC m_hDC;  //drawing context handle
            HBITMAP m_hbmWidget; //bitmap data for the widget's appearance
            HBITMAP m_hbmOld; //required for storing the old bitmap from a memory
  DC
            RECT m_rcBounds; //size and position of the widget
            static CWidget* s_pKeyboardFocus; //keyboard focus widget
            static CWidget* s_pMouseFocus; //mouse focus widget
            static CWidget* s_pMasterWidget; //main widget
            static std::list<CWidget*> s_lstDeleteList; //list of widgets to
  delete
            static std::list<CWidget*> s_lstMoveList; //list of widgets to move in
  the z order
            static CWidget* s_pMouseHover; //pointer to the widget over which the
  mouse is hovering
            static HWND s_hWnd; //window with which the master widget communicates
};
```

There are a few static members—namely s_lstDeleteList, s_lstMoveList, s_pMouseHover, and s_hWnd—that I did not discuss as a part of the design considera- tion. These are necessary because of the way the hierarchy is structured. During input processing and during displaying, we have to recursively loop through lists of children. If we have a need to move a widget to the top of a list or if we delete an item while in the midst of moving through these lists, we can start to have problems like a widget skipping its turn or getting two turns in the recursive loop. To combat this, whenever a widget is to be destroyed, instead of simply destroying it right then and there, we move it to the delete list (s_lstDeleteList) and process the delete list only after we have looped through all of the widgets in the tree. Similarly, when we want to move a widget to the top of its parent's Z order, we simply place it on the list and then process all of the moves once we have gone through all of the widgets in the tree. This makes things much less messy codewise.

The s_pMouseHover member is meant to represent the widget over which the mouse is currently hovering. Often, if hovering over a button, we would like to change the color of the button or the text on the button to give feedback to the user that click- ing here will do something.

Finally, s_hWnd is a window handle. Since the main widget will be interacting with a window, it cannot permanently have a Handle of a Device Context (HDC) to work with. Instead, it must borrow one before doing any drawing and must return it when done drawing. If you were implementing a UI system in DirectX, this would be replaced by a pointer to the back buffer.

One thing you might wonder about is my choice of the STL list template as the container for child widgets and for the delete list and move list. This was not the only possible container to use, of course. The other option was to use an STL vector. Both of these containers are resizable, and with an unknown number of children, this is necessary. I found vector to be a poor choice for two reasons. First, the strength of vector, which is that it provides fast random access into the container, goes unused. When going through a child list, we will simply be starting at one end and processing through to the other end, so random access is of no importance. Second, the slowness of insertion into a vector is not a good thing. We will only be adding children to the end of the list, so vector makes a poor choice.

There is, of course, a slight problem with using the STL list template. When a widget is removed from the child list, it will have to be iteratively searched for. Of course, this would also be true in the case of vector, and the lookup would take just as much time, so in conclusion, using list instead of vector is still not a bad choice.

Widget Member Functions

As you have probably been able to tell, I'm big into being object-oriented. As a result, I'm also a believer in encapsulation, so I tend not to have any data members that can be directly accessed by the user of a class. So, naturally, I would implement CWidget's member functions with a number of getter and setter functions. Your style might differ, so for your own UI system, you can implement it anyway you like. I'm not one to tell anybody that my way is the one true way. Suffice it to say, however, that I am going to make all of the data members private.

Static Member Accessors

This class has seven static members, and since they all need to be private, they need accessors. Some of the static members are read-only (or rather, read-mostly), so those setters will have to be private or protected rather than public. The getters, however, will almost universally be public.

And so, here is the scheme I have come up with for static member accessors. The data members are not listed here so that we can focus on only the member functions we are discussing.

```
class CWidget
{
private:
        static void SetHWND(HWND hWnd);//sets s_hWnd
        static void SetMasterWidget(CWidget* pWidget);//sets s_pMasterWidget
protected:
        static HWND GetHWND();//retrieves s_hWnd
        static void SetKeyboardFocus(CWidget* pWidget);//sets s_pKeyboardFocus
        static void SetMouseFocus(CWidget* pWidget);//sets s_pMouseFocus
        static void SetMouseHover(CWidget* pWidget);//sets s_pMouseHover
        static std::list<CWidget*>& GetDeleteList();//retrieve s_lstDeleteList
        static std::list<CWidget*>& GetMoveList();//retrieves s_lstMoveList
public:
        static CWidget* GetMasterWidget();//retrieves s_pMasterWidget
        static CWidget* GetKeyboardFocus();//retrieves s_pKeyboardFocus
        static CWidget* GetMouseFocus();//retrieves s_pMouseFocus
        static CWidget* GetMouseHover();//retrieves s_pMouseHover
};
```

For those of you keeping score, Table 4.1 shows each static member and whether the getter and setter are public, protected, or private. In a moment, I will describe my reasoning for each of these decisions.

Table 4.1 Static Member Accessor Accessibility

Member	Getter	Setter
s_pKeyboardFocus	Public	Protected
s_pMouseFocus	Public	Protected
s_pMasterWidget	Public	Private
s_lstDeleteList	Protected	N/A
s_lstMoveList	Protected	N/A
s_pMouseHover	Public	Protected
s_hWnd	Protected	Private

Two of the setters, the ones for s_pMasterWidget and for s_hWnd, are private and therefore will only be accessible by the member functions of CWidget itself. The reason for this is simply because there will never be a need for anything but CWidget to set these values. Eventually, we will have a constructor for creating the master widget, and this constructor will take care of the master widget pointer as well as the main window handle.

The rest of the setters have protected access. There simply is no need for the user of the class to directly manipulate these values. It should be all handled within the class and derived classes directly. The delete list and move list simply don't have setters. A setter is unnecessary in those cases.

For the getters, the delete list, the move list, and s_hWnd are protected. CWidget and its derived classes may have a need to look at these members, but looking at them outside of the class is not useful and can be dangerous.

The rest of the getters are public and can be examined at any time.

Indirect Static Member Accessors

Several of the static members of CWidget are simply pointers to various CWidgets. These include s_pKeyboardFocus, s_pMouseFocus, s_pMouseHover, and s_pMasterWidget. With the current few member functions we have come up with thus far, for a widget to determine whether it is the one that has mouse focus, you would have to use the following code:

```
if(GetMouseFocus()==this)
{
            //this widget has mouse focus
}
```

There is similar code to check and see whether the widget is the master control, has keyboard focus, or is the widget over which the mouse is hovering. I dislike code like the preceding example. Ideally, we should have some additional nonstatic member functions to check for these things, as follows:

```
class CWidget
{
public:
            bool HasMouseFocus();//checks if this widget has mouse focus
            bool HasKeyboardFocus();//checks if this widget has keyboard focus
            bool HasMouseHover();//check to see if this widget is the mouse hover
    widget
```

```
            bool IsMaster();//checks to see if this is the master widget
};
```

In my opinion, calling these member functions is a great deal more readable than doing an if with a ==this following it. These are indirect static member accessors.

Another set of indirect static member accessors is the manner in which we place a widget onto the delete list or the move list. In normal code, with the current accessors we have, it would look something like this:

```
//first, ensure that this widget isn't already on the list
GetDeleteList().remove(this);
//add this widget to the delete list
GetDeleteList().push_back(this);
```

Again, this code is a little unwieldy. For one thing, it is a two-step process and should only be a one-step thing. So, let's add a couple of member functions to automate this for us.

```
class CWidget
{
public:
            void Close();//add this widget to the delete list
            void BringToTop();//add this widget to the move list
};
```

Again, it is much more readable to simply tell a widget to close itself than to add it to a list directly (and a similar idea for moving the widget).

Nonstatic Member Accessors

There are six nonstatic members of CWidget: m_pParentWidget, m_lstChildWidgets, m_hDC, m_hbmWidget, m_hbmOld, and m_rcBounds. Only a few of these members require direct public access. Of these members, m_pParentWidget and m_hDC need public getter functions. The m_rcBounds member requires indirect public getters (to retrieve position and size information but not the RECT itself) as well as public accessors to manipulate position. (I prefer to keep controls a fixed size.) The rest of the members should only have protected access. Derived classes may need to look at them, but the user of the class should not need to. So, for nonstatic member accessors, this is what I've come up with:

```
class CWidget
{
protected:
            HDC& DC();//return reference to m_hDC
```

```
                HBITMAP& Bitmap();//return reference to m_hbmWidget
                HBITMAP& OldBitmap();//return reference to m_hbmOld
                RECT& Bounds();//return reference to m_rcBounds
                std::list<CWidget*>& ChildList();//return reference to child list
public:

                void SetParent(CWidget* pWidget);//set new parent widget
                CWidget* GetParent();//retrieve parent widget
                bool HasParent();//returns true if parent is non-null
                void AddChild(CWidget* pWidget);//add a child to the list
                bool RemoveChild(CWidget* pWidget);//remove a child from the list
                bool HasChild(CWidget* pWidget);//check for a child's existence
                bool HasChildren();//check to see if this widget has any children
                int GetX();//return x position (relative to parent)
                int GetY();//return y position (relative to parent)
                void SetX(int iX);//set x position(relative to parent)
                void SetY(int iY);//set y position(relative to parent)
                int GetWidth();//return the width of the widget
                int GetHeight();//return the height of the widget
                int GetLeft();//retrieve the left coordinate(global coordinates)
                int GetRight();//retrieve the right coordinate(global coordinates)
                int GetTop();//retrieve the top coordinate(global coordinates)
                int GetBottom();//retrieve the bottom coordinate(global coordinates)
                HDC GetDC();//return the m_hDC
};
```

We are starting to rack up quite a number of member functions for CWidget! So far, these have only been accessor functions, not functions that make CWidget do its job yet. I told you that this task is nontrivial!

Constructors and Destructors

As far as construction and destruction are concerned, we will need two separate constructors: one for constructing a master widget and one for constructing a non-master widget. A master widget has no parent and is associated with a window handle. A nonmaster widget has a parent and also requires a position and size. The destructor is just like any other destructor. Therefore:

```
class CWidget
{
public:
                CWidget(HWND hWnd);//master widget constructor
                CWidget(CWidget* pWidgetParent,int iX, int iY, int iWidth, int
```

```
iHeight);//nonmaster widget constructor
          virtual ~CWidget();//destructor
          static void Destroy();//destroy the master widget
};
```

The destructor of CWidget is responsible for cleaning up not only the widget in question but also all child widgets, so completely cleaning up the UI hierarchy is simply a matter of destroying the master widget. The static member function Destroy will allow us to do that without having a pointer to the master widget.

Displaying Widgets

One of the primary tasks of our UI hierarchy is to get the widgets to properly display. Each widget will know how to redraw and display itself. At the same time, though, the user of the UI hierarchy should be able to update the entire widget tree with a single call, and this call should not require having a pointer to the master widget.

Prior to the hierarchy displaying itself, any widgets on the delete list and move list should be taken care of. This might sound like a complicated process, but it can be simply implemented with only three functions.

```
class CWidget
{
public:
          void Display();//displays the widget and all child widgets
          virtual void OnRedraw();//redraws the widget
          static void Update();//updates all widgets
};
```

In derived classes of CWidget, only OnRedraw needs to be overridden. The Display function loops through all children and redraws them. When making use of CWidget, you need only call CWidget::Update(), and the entire hierarchy will be redrawn. The call to Update will also get rid of any widgets currently on the delete list and will move any widgets currently on the move list.

Receiving Input

As far as input processing is concerned, there are only eight types of events that we are really concerned with: key presses, key releases, character generation, mouse moves, left-mouse-button presses, left-mouse-button releases, right-mouse-button presses, and right-mouse-button releases. If we really wanted to, we could add left and right double-clicks, middle-mouse-button-events, and mouse wheel events, but we'll keep it simple for the moment.

Since our Windows application gets its events through `WndProc`, we will need to use the UI hierarchy as an event filter of sorts. If the UI system processes the event, we need not process it further. Also, we need only send the event data to the master control (although this will be a static function, so we won't need to have the master widget's pointer to do this), and it will send the event data up the hierarchy and attempt to handle it.

```
class CWidget
{
public:
                bool HandleEvent(UINT uMsg,WPARAM wParam,LPARAM lParam);
                virtual bool OnKeyDown(int iVirtKey);//handle a key press
                virtual bool OnKeyUp(int iVirtKey);//handle a key
                virtual bool OnChar(TCHAR tchCode);//handle character generation
                virtual bool OnMouseMove(int iX,int iY,bool bLeft, bool
    bRight);//mouse movement
                virtual bool OnLButtonDown(int iX,int iY,bool bLeft,bool
    bRight);//left button press
                virtual bool OnRButtonDown(int iX,int iY,bool bLeft,bool
    bRight);//right button press
                virtual bool OnLButtonUp(int iX,int iY,bool bLeft,bool bRight);//left
    button release
                virtual bool OnRButtonUp(int iX,int iY,bool bLeft,bool
    bRight);//right button release
                static bool FilterEvent(UINT uMsg,WPARAM wParam,LPARAM lParam);//send
    event to master control
};
```

Tying `CWidget`'s event filter will now be an easy task. With the data from a window message, you simply send it to `CWidget::FilterEvent`, and if this function returns `true`, you do no further processing. If it returns `false`, the application or game should process it.

Notification

Finally, we have to put in member functions for the task of notification. For this, I'm going to cheat a little bit and borrow some code from another part of this book (Trick 3, "Building an Application Framework"). I am going to borrow all three of the core classes presented there (it'll make life easier . . . trust me) but especially `CMessageHandler`, from which we will make `CWidget` a derived class.

So, for a brief rehash, here is `CMessageHandler`:

```
class CMessageHandler
{
private:
            //the parent of this message handler
            CMessageHandler* m_pmhParent;
public:
            //constructor
            CMessageHandler(CMessageHandler* pmhParent);
            //destructor
            virtual ~CMessageHandler();
            //set/get parent
            void SetMessageParent(CMessageHandler* pmhParent);
            CMessageHandler* GetMessageParent();
            //handles messages, or passes them down the tree
            bool HandleMessage(int MessageID,int argc,void* argv[]);
            //triggered when a message occurs
            virtual bool OnMessage(int MessageID, int argc, void* argv[])=0;
};
```

This class already has provisions for sending messages down a hierarchy. It also already has a parent/child type of structure but not one as rich as the one `CWidget` uses. Another reason we want to use `CMessageHandler` as a base class for `CWidget` is so we can set up the application and/or event handler to be the recipient of messages from the UI system.

Because of this, we do need to change one of `CWidget`'s constructors. Since we are using the application framework and we need to supply all widgets (even the master widget) with a message parent, we should change this:

```
CWidget::CWidget(HWND hWnd);//master widget constructor
```

to this:

```
CWidget::CWidget(CEventHandler* pehParent);//master widget constructor
```

We can grab the `HWND` from the event handler, so we don't actually need the window handle supplied to the widget. Also, the event handler will be the message parent of the master widget, so proper notification can take place. Neat. Figure 4.3 shows how the basic object hierarchy will work.

At the top of Figure 4.3 is the application, the root of the object tree. It is the parent of the event handler, which represents our main window. The event handler, in turn, is the parent of the master widget, which is the ultimate parent of all other widgets. The important thing here is that there is a line of communication possible between a child control six steps down the line and the application itself.

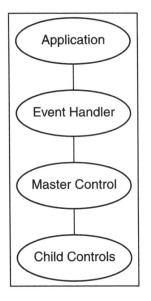

Figure 4.3

The object hierarchy using the application framework

Class Definition

Now, before we move on to actual implementation, let's take one final look at the class definition of CWidget. So far, we have only looked at bits and pieces, and it would be nice to finally see it all put together.

```
class CWidget: public CMessageHandler
{
private:
            CWidget* m_pParentWidget;  //pointer to parent widget
            std::list<CWidget*> m_lstChildWidgets;  //list of child widgets
            HDC m_hDC;  //drawing context handle
            HBITMAP m_hbmWidget; //bitmap data for the widget's appearance
            HBITMAP m_hbmOld; //required for storing the old bitmap from a memory
    DC
            RECT m_rcBounds; //size and position of the widget
            static CWidget* s_pKeyboardFocus; //keyboard focus widget
            static CWidget* s_pMouseFocus; //mouse focus widget
            static CWidget* s_pMasterWidget; //main widget
            static std::list<CWidget*> s_lstDeleteList; //list of widgets to
```

```
            delete
                static std::list<CWidget*> s_lstMoveList; //list of widgets to move in
        the z order
                static CWidget* s_pMouseHover; //pointer to the widget over which the
        mouse is hovering
                static HWND s_hWnd; //window with which the master widget communicates
                static void SetHWND(HWND hWnd);//sets s_hWnd
                static void SetMasterWidget(CWidget* pWidget);//sets s_pMasterWidget
        protected:
                HDC& DC();//return reference to m_hDC
                HBITMAP& Bitmap();//return reference to m_hbmWidget
                HBITMAP& OldBitmap();//return reference to m_hbmOld
                RECT& Bounds();//return reference to m_rcBounds
                std::list<CWidget*>& ChildList();//return reference to child list
                static HWND GetHWND();//retrieves s_hWnd
                static void SetKeyboardFocus(CWidget* pWidget);//sets s_pKeyboardFocus
                static void SetMouseFocus(CWidget* pWidget);//sets s_pMouseFocus
                static void SetMouseHover(CWidget* pWidget);//sets s_pMouseHover
                static std::list<CWidget*>& GetDeleteList();//retrieve s_lstDeleteList
                static std::list<CWidget*>& GetMoveList();//retrieves s_lstMoveList
        public:
                CWidget(CEventHandler* pehParent);//master widget constructor
                CWidget(CWidget* pWidgetParent,int iX, int iY, int iWidth, int
        iHeight);//nonmaster widget constructor
                virtual ~CWidget();//destructor
                bool HasMouseFocus();//checks if this widget has mouse focus
                bool HasKeyboardFocus();//checks if this widget has keyboard focus
                bool HasMouseHover();//check to see if this widget is the mouse hover
        widget
                bool IsMaster();//checks to see if this is the master widget
                void SetParent(CWidget* pWidget);//set new parent widget
                CWidget* GetParent();//retrieve parent widget
                bool HasParent();//returns true if parent is non-null
                void AddChild(CWidget* pWidget);//add a child to the list
                bool RemoveChild(CWidget* pWidget);//remove a child from the list
                bool HasChild(CWidget* pWidget);//check for a child's existence
                bool HasChildren();//check to see if this widget has any children
                int GetX();//return x position (relative to parent)
                int GetY();//return y position (relative to parent)
                void SetX(int iX);//set x position(relative to parent)
                void SetY(int iY);//set y position(relative to parent)
```

```
        int GetWidth();//return the width of the widget
        int GetHeight();//return the height of the widget
        int GetLeft();//retrieve the left coordinate(global coordinates)
        int GetRight();//retrieve the right coordinate(global coordinates)
        int GetTop();//retrieve the top coordinate(global coordinates)
        int GetBottom();//retrieve the bottom coordinate(global coordinates)
        HDC GetDC();//return the m_hDC
        void Display();//displays the widget and all child widgets
        virtual void OnRedraw();//redraws the widget
        void Close();//add this widget to the delete list
        void BringToTop();//add this widget to the move list
        bool HandleEvent(UINT uMsg,WPARAM wParam,LPARAM lParam);
        virtual bool OnKeyDown(int iVirtKey);//handle a key press
        virtual bool OnKeyUp(int iVirtKey);//handle a key
        virtual bool OnChar(TCHAR tchCode);//handle character generation
        virtual bool OnMouseMove(int iX,int iY,bool bLeft, bool
bRight);//mouse movement
        virtual bool OnLButtonDown(int iX,int iY,bool bLeft,bool bRight);//left
button press
        virtual bool OnRButtonDown(int iX,int iY,bool bLeft,bool
bRight);//right button press
        virtual bool OnLButtonUp(int iX,int iY,bool bLeft,bool bRight);//left
button release
        virtual bool OnRButtonUp(int iX,int iY,bool bLeft,bool bRight);//right
button release
        virtual bool OnMessage(int MessageID, int argc, void* argv[]);
        static bool FilterEvent(UINT uMsg,WPARAM wParam,LPARAM lParam);//send
event to master control
        static void Update();//updates all widgets
        static CWidget* GetMasterWidget();//retrieves s_pMasterWidget
        static CWidget* GetKeyboardFocus();//retrieves s_pKeyboardFocus
        static CWidget* GetMouseFocus();//retrieves s_pMouseFocus
        static CWidget* GetMouseHover();//retrieves s_pMouseHover
        static void Destroy();//destroy the master widget
};
```

Yes, this class is absolutely huge, but do not dismay. The vast majority of the member functions in CWidget are getters and setters or do other tasks that are so simple that they typically only take up one or two lines of code.

CWidget Implementation

Now that we've given proper thought to how CWidget should behave, it is finally time to implement. The code you are about to look at took about four hours of work (and an approximately equal amount of time testing and monkeying around with it).

Getters, Setters, and Other Simple Member Functions

Most of the functions, as I stated earlier, are simply implemented. Tables 4.2 through 4.4 show them all categorized. In Table 4.2, you can see all of the static member accessors, direct and indirect.

Table 4.2 Static Member Accessors (Direct and Indirect)

Function	Implementation
CWidget::SetHWND	{s_hWnd=hWnd;}
CWidget::GetHWND	{return(s_hWnd);}
CWidget::SetMasterWidget	{s_pMasterWidget=pWidget;}
CWidget::GetMasterWidget	{return(s_pMasterWidget);}
CWidget::IsMaster	{return(this==GetMasterWidget());}
CWidget::SetKeyboardFocus	{s_pKeyboardFocus=pWidget;}
CWidget::GetKeyboardFocus	{return(s_pKeyboardFocus);}
CWidget::HasKeyboardFocus	{return(this==GetKeyboardFocus());}
CWidget::SetMouseFocus	{s_pMouseFocus=pWidget;}
CWidget::GetMouseFocus	{return(s_pMouseFocus);}
CWidget::HasMouseFocus	{return(this==GetMouseFocus());}
CWidget::SetMouseHover	{s_pMouseHover=pWidget;}
CWidget::GetMouseHover	{return(s_pMouseHover);}
CWidget::HasMouseHover	{return(this==GetMouseHover());}
CWidget::GetDeleteList	{return(s_lstDeleteList);}
CWidget::Close	{GetDeleteList().remove(this); GetDeleteList().push_back(this);}

continues

Table 4.2 Static Member Accessors (Direct and Indirect) (continued)

Function	Implementation
CWidget::GetMoveList	{return(s_lstMoveList);}
CWidget::BringToTop	{GetMoveList().remove(this); GetMoveList().push_back(this);}

In Table 4.3 (by far the largest group of functions), you can see the nonstatic member accessors. Many of these are indirect, like the member functions dealing with position and size information.

Table 4.3 Nonstatic Member Accessors (Direct and Indirect)

Function	Implementation
CWidget::DC	{return(m_hDC);}
CWidget::Bitmap	{return(m_hbmWidget);}
CWidget::OldBitmap	{return(m_hbmOld);}
CWidget::Bounds	{return(m_rcBounds);}
CWidget::ChildList	{return(m_lstChildWidgets);}
CWidget::GetParent	{return(m_pParentWidget);}
CWidget::HasParent	{return(GetParent()!=NULL);}
CWidget::AddChild	{ChildList().remove(pWidget); ChildList().push_back(pWidget);}
CWidget::RemoveChild	{if(HasChild(pWidget)) {ChildList().remove(pWidget); return(true);}return(false);}
CWidget::HasChild	{std::list<CWidget*>::iterator iter=std::find(ChildList().begin(),ChildList().e nd(),pWidget);return(iter!=ChildList().end());}
CWidget::HasChildren()	{return(!ChildList().empty());}
CWidget::GetX	{return(Bounds().left);}
CWidget::GetY	{return(Bounds().top);}

Table 4.3 Nonstatic Member Accessors (Direct and Indirect)

Function	Implementation
CWidget::SetY	{OffsetRect(&Bounds(),0,iY-Bounds().top);}
CWidget::GetWidth	{return(Bounds().right-Bounds().left);}
CWidget::GetHeight	{return(Bounds().bottom-Bounds().top);}
CWidget::GetLeft	{if(HasParent()){return(GetX()+GetParent()->GetLeft());}else{return(0);}}
CWidget::GetRight	{return(GetLeft()+GetWidth());}
CWidget::GetTop	{if(HasParent()){return(GetY()+GetParent()->GetTop());}else{return(0);}}
CWidget::GetBottom	{return(GetTop()+GetHeight());}
CWidget::GetDC	{return(m_hDC);}
CWidget::SetX	{OffsetRect(&Bounds(),iX-Bounds().left,0);}

Next we have the functions in Table 4.4, which show the simple implementation for event- and message-handling functions. In all of these cases, the functions are just stubs. They only return a default value.

Table 4.4 Event Handlers/Message Handlers

Function	Implementation
CWidget::OnKeyDown	{return(false);}
CWidget::OnKeyUp	{return(false);}
CWidget::OnChar	{return(false);}
CWidget::OnMouseMove	{return(!IsMaster());}
CWidget::OnLButtonDown	{return(!IsMaster());}
CWidget::OnRButtonDown	{return(!IsMaster());}
CWidget::OnLButtonUp	{return(!IsMaster());}
CWidget::OnRButtonUp	{return(!IsMaster());}
CWidget::OnMessage	{return(false);}

Finally, Table 4.5 has the rest of the simply implemented functions. These are all static and typically will be the only members used outside of the class itself (other than constructors and destructors). Each of these functions in some way accesses the master widget.

Table 4.5 Other Static Member Functions

Function	Implementation
CWidget::FilterEvent	{if(GetMasterWidget()){return(GetMasterWidget()- >HandleEvent(uMsg,wParam,lParam));}return(false);}
CWidget::Update	{if(GetMasterWidget()){GetMasterWidget()->Display();}}
CWidget::Destroy	{if(GetMasterWidget()){delete GetMasterWidget();}}

Other Member Functions

We are left with six member functions: the two constructors, the destructor, CWidget::Display, CWidget::OnRedraw, and CWidget::HandleEvent. These functions do most of the work needed for widgets to exist.

Master Widget Constructor

The master widget has to be constructed like any other widget. However, it does get a special constructor. If you later want to change some of the behavior of the master widget, you can derive a new class and use the master widget constructor in the initializer list. In this way, you can have totally different class hierarchies for the master widget and nonmaster widgets.

```
CWidget::CWidget(CEventHandler* pehParent)://master widget constructor
CMessageHandler(pehParent),
m_pParentWidget(NULL),
m_lstChildWidgets(),
m_hDC(0),
m_hbmWidget(0),
m_hbmOld(0),
m_rcBounds()
{
            SetHWND(*pehParent);
            SetMasterWidget(this);
            GetClientRect(GetHWND(),&Bounds());
```

```
            HDC hdcScreen=::GetDC(NULL);
            DC()=CreateCompatibleDC(hdcScreen);
            Bitmap()=CreateCompatibleBitmap(hdcScreen,Bounds().right,Bounds().bot-
    tom);
            OldBitmap()=(HBITMAP)SelectObject(DC(),Bitmap());
            ReleaseDC(NULL,hdcScreen);
}
```

During testing, I decided to go with a double-buffered approach to updating my widgets, and so the master constructor, while it sets the static HWND to which it will do its updates, also creates a bitmap and HDC onto which it does drawing. If you were writing a game, you would access this HDC to do your screen updates, and you would then tell the master widget to update itself (but this would require overriding the default behavior in OnRedraw, as we will see a little later).

The size of the master control becomes the size of the client area of the window (which is as it should be).

Nonmaster Widget Constructor

Nonmaster widgets are created with fewer lines (since there is no need to grab a window handle):

```
CWidget::CWidget(CWidget* pWidgetParent,int iX, int iY, int iWidth, int
    iHeight)://nonmaster widget constructor
CMessageHandler(pWidgetParent),
m_pParentWidget(NULL),
m_lstChildWidgets(),
m_hDC(0),
m_hbmWidget(0),
m_hbmOld(0),
m_rcBounds()
{
            SetRect(&Bounds(),iX,iY,iX+iWidth,iY+iHeight);
            HDC hdcScreen=::GetDC(NULL);
            DC()=CreateCompatibleDC(hdcScreen);
            Bitmap()=CreateCompatibleBitmap(hdcScreen,iWidth,iHeight);
            OldBitmap()=(HBITMAP)SelectObject(DC(),Bitmap());
            ReleaseDC(NULL,hdcScreen);
            SetParent(pWidgetParent);
}
```

Like the master widget, a nonmaster widget creates a bitmap and an HDC. Since it isn't associated with a window, however, the size has to be set in the call to the constructor itself.

Destructor

Most of CWidget's destructor is concerned with cleaning up its resources. The destructor is also tasked with causing the destruction of all of the widget's child widgets.

```
CWidget::~CWidget()//destructor
{
            while(HasChildren())
            {
                        std::list<CWidget*>::iterator iter=ChildList().begin();
                        CWidget* pWidget=*iter;
                        delete pWidget;
            }
            SelectObject(DC(),OldBitmap());
            DeleteDC(DC());
            DeleteObject(Bitmap());
            SetParent(NULL);
            if(HasMouseFocus()) SetMouseFocus(NULL);
            if(HasKeyboardFocus()) SetKeyboardFocus(NULL);
            if(HasMouseHover()) SetMouseHover(NULL);
            if(IsMaster()) SetMasterWidget(NULL);
}
```

Finally, right at the end of the destructor, there are a series of checks to make sure that the mouse focus, keyboard focus, mouse hover, and master control always point to valid data, and if they don't, they are set to NULL. It would be disastrous if the mouse focus widget was destroyed and the pointer was not set to NULL.

Default *OnRedraw*

The default behavior of OnRedraw is simply to fill the widget's DC with black.

```
void CWidget::OnRedraw()//redraws the widget
{
            RECT rcFill;
            SetRect(&rcFill,0,0,GetWidth(),GetHeight());
            FillRect(DC(),&rcFill,(HBRUSH)GetStockObject(BLACK_BRUSH));
}
```

This function is simple enough, and I'll speak no more of it.

CWidget::Display

The Display function is the second longest function implementation in CWidget (the longest being HandleEvent, which is up next). The reason for this is that there is special processing depending on whether or not the control is the master.

When CWidget::Display is called on the master widget, it will go through and take care of the move list and delete list in that order. It moves all widgets currently in the move list to the top of their respective Z orders, and then it goes through all of the items on the delete list and destroys them. The reason it takes care of the move list first is so that if a widget is on both lists, it won't be destroyed before it is moved.

```
void CWidget::Display()//displays the widget and all child widgets
{
        if(IsMaster())
        {
                CWidget* pWidget;
                while(!GetMoveList().empty())
                {
                        pWidget=*GetMoveList().begin();
                        GetMoveList().remove(pWidget);
                        pWidget->SetParent(pWidget->GetParent());
                }
                while(!GetDeleteList().empty())
                {
                        pWidget=*GetDeleteList().begin();
                        GetDeleteList().remove(pWidget);
                        delete pWidget;
                }
        }
        OnRedraw();
        std::list<CWidget*>::iterator iter;
        CWidget* pChild;
        for(iter=ChildList().begin();iter!=ChildList().end();iter++)
        {
                pChild=*iter;
                pChild->Display();
        }
        if(IsMaster())
```

```
        {
                HDC hdcDst=::GetDC(GetHWND());
                BitBlt(hdcDst,0,0,GetWidth(),GetHeight(),DC(),0,0,SRCCOPY);
                ReleaseDC(GetHWND(),hdcDst);
        }
    else
        {
                BitBlt(GetParent()-
    >GetDC(),GetX(),GetY(),GetWidth(),GetHeight(),DC(),0,0,SRCCOPY);
        }
}
```

Master widget or not, the next step is to redraw the widget by calling OnRedraw. After that, a widget will draw any child widgets that happen to exist (in order from lowest to highest Z order). Finally, the widget updates its parent. In the case of the master control, this means writing its bitmap onto the window. In any other case, this simply means a write of its own bitmap onto its parent's bitmap with BitBlt.

CWidget::HandleEvent

Welcome to the nightmare that is CWidget::HandleEvent, the most evil function in the whole darn thing. CWidget has 54 member functions, and all but six of them are one- or two-liners that took perhaps a whole minute each to write. That takes all of about 45 minutes, maybe an hour if you add in time to write comments. CWidget, as I said, took about four hours to implement, however. If 90 percent of the class took only an hour, where did the other three hours go?

I'll tell you: About an hour was spent on the constructors, destructors, and Display and OnRedraw functions. The other two hours were spent on HandleEvent. Properly routing events is nontrivial. Here is the result of my two hours. (See you in a few pages!)

```
bool CWidget::HandleEvent(UINT uMsg,WPARAM wParam,LPARAM lParam)
{
        if(IsMaster())
        {
                switch(uMsg)
                {
                case WM_MOUSEMOVE:
                case WM_LBUTTONDOWN:
                case WM_LBUTTONUP:
                case WM_RBUTTONDOWN:
                case WM_RBUTTONUP:
```

```
                                        {
                                if(GetMouseFocus())
                                {
                                    SetMouseHover(GetMouseFocus());
                                        switch(uMsg)
                                        {
                                    case WM_MOUSEMOVE:
                                        {
return(GetMouseFocus()->OnMouseMove(LOWORD(lParam)-GetMouseFocus()-
    >GetLeft(),HIWORD(lParam)-GetMouseFocus()-
    >GetTop(),(wParam&MK_LBUTTON)>0,(wParam&MK_RBUTTON)>0));
}break;
                                                    case WM_LBUTTON-
    DOWN:
                                                        {
return(GetMouseFocus()->OnLButtonDown(LOWORD(lParam)-GetMouseFocus()-
    >GetLeft(),HIWORD(lParam)-GetMouseFocus()-
    >GetTop(),(wParam&MK_LBUTTON)>0,(wParam&MK_RBUTTON)>0));
                                                    }break;
                                        case WM_RBUTTONDOWN:
                                                        {
return(GetMouseFocus()->OnRButtonDown(LOWORD(lParam)-GetMouseFocus()-
    >GetLeft(),HIWORD(lParam)-GetMouseFocus()-
    >GetTop(),(wParam&MK_LBUTTON)>0,(wParam&MK_RBUTTON)>0));
                                                    }break;
                                        case WM_LBUTTONUP:
                                                        {
return(GetMouseFocus()->OnLButtonUp(LOWORD(lParam)-GetMouseFocus()-
    >GetLeft(),HIWORD(lParam)-GetMouseFocus()-
    >GetTop(),(wParam&MK_LBUTTON)>0,(wParam&MK_RBUTTON)>0));
                                                    }break;
                                        case WM_RBUTTONUP:
                                                        {
return(GetMouseFocus()->OnRButtonUp(LOWORD(lParam)-GetMouseFocus()-
    >GetLeft(),HIWORD(lParam)-GetMouseFocus()-
    >GetTop(),(wParam&MK_LBUTTON)>0,(wParam&MK_RBUTTON)>0));
                                                    }break;
                                                    }
                                            }
                                    }break;
                    case WM_KEYDOWN:
```

```
                            case WM_KEYUP:
                            case WM_CHAR:
                                         {
                                                        if(GetKeyboardFocus())
                                                        {

  switch(uMsg)

                                                                {
                                                        case WM_KEYDOWN:
                                                                {

return(GetKeyboardFocus()->OnKeyDown(wParam));
}break;

                                                        case WM_KEYUP:
                                                                {

return(GetKeyboardFocus()->OnKeyUp(wParam));

                                                                }break;
                                                        case WM_CHAR:
                                                                {

return(GetKeyboardFocus()->OnChar(wParam));

                                                                }break;
                                                                }
                                                        }
                                         }break;
                            default:
                                         {
                                                        return(false);
                                         }break;
                    }
                    SetMouseHover(NULL);
            }
            std::list<CWidget*>::reverse_iterator iter;
            for(iter=ChildList().rbegin();iter!=ChildList().rend();iter++)
            {
                    CWidget* pChild=(*iter);
                    if(pChild->HandleEvent(uMsg,wParam,lParam))
                    {
                            return(true);
                    }
            }
            if(IsMaster()) return(false);
            switch(uMsg)
```

```
                                    {
                            case WM_MOUSEMOVE:
                                            {
                                                            POINT ptHit;
                                                            ptHit.x=LOWORD(lParam);
                                                            ptHit.y=HIWORD(lParam);
                                                            RECT rcHit;

            SetRect(&rcHit,GetLeft(),GetTop(),GetRight(),GetBottom());
                                                            if(PtInRect(&rcHit,ptHit))
                                                            {
                                                                            if(!GetMouseHover())
            SetMouseHover(this);
return(OnMouseMove(LOWORD(lParam)-GetLeft(),HIWORD(lParam)-GetTop(),
    (wParam&MK_LBUTTON)>0,(wParam&MK_RBUTTON)>0));
                                                            }
                                    }break;
                            case WM_LBUTTONDOWN:
                                            {
                                                            POINT ptHit;
                                                            ptHit.x=LOWORD(lParam);
                                                            ptHit.y=HIWORD(lParam);
                                                            RECT rcHit;
SetRect(&rcHit,GetLeft(),GetTop(),GetRight(),GetBottom());
                                                            if(PtInRect(&rcHit,ptHit))
                                                            {
                                                                    if(!GetMouseHover())
            SetMouseHover(this);
return(OnLButtonDown(LOWORD(lParam)-GetLeft(),HIWORD(lParam)-
    GetTop(),(wParam&MK_LBUTTON)>0,(wParam&MK_RBUTTON)>0));
                                                            }
                                    }break;
                            case WM_LBUTTONUP:
                                            {
                                                            POINT ptHit;
                                                            ptHit.x=LOWORD(lParam);
                                                            ptHit.y=HIWORD(lParam);
                                                            RECT rcHit;
SetRect(&rcHit,GetLeft(),GetTop(),GetRight(),GetBottom());
                                                            if(PtInRect(&rcHit,ptHit))
                                                            {
```

```
                                                    if(!GetMouseHover())
        SetMouseHover(this);
    return(OnLButtonUp(LOWORD(lParam)-GetLeft(),HIWORD(lParam)-GetTop(),
        (wParam&MK_LBUTTON)>0,(wParam&MK_RBUTTON)>0)));
                                                    }
                        }break;
            //right button press
            case WM_RBUTTONDOWN:
                    {
                                                POINT ptHit;
                                                ptHit.x=LOWORD(lParam);
                                                ptHit.y=HIWORD(lParam);
                                                RECT rcHit;
    SetRect(&rcHit,GetLeft(),GetTop(),GetRight(),GetBottom());
                                                if(PtInRect(&rcHit,ptHit))
                                                {
                                                        if(!GetMouseHover())
    SetMouseHover(this);

    return(OnRButtonDown(LOWORD(lParam)-GetLeft(),HIWORD(lParam)-
    GetTop(),(wParam&MK_LBUTTON)>0,(wParam&MK_RBUTTON)>0)));
                                                }
                        }break;
            case WM_RBUTTONUP:
                    {
                                                POINT ptHit;
                                                ptHit.x=LOWORD(lParam);
                                                ptHit.y=HIWORD(lParam);
                                                RECT rcHit;
    SetRect(&rcHit,GetLeft(),GetTop(),GetRight(),GetBottom());
                                                if(PtInRect(&rcHit,ptHit))
                                                {
                                                        if(!GetMouseHover())
    SetMouseHover(this);
    return(OnRButtonUp(LOWORD(lParam)-GetLeft(),HIWORD(lParam)-GetTop(),
        (wParam&MK_LBUTTON)>0,(wParam&MK_RBUTTON)>0)));
                                                }
                        }break;
            case WM_KEYDOWN:
                    {
                                                return(OnKeyDown(wParam));
```

```
                    }break;
        case WM_KEYUP:
                    {
                                    return(OnKeyUp(wParam));
                    }break;
        case WM_CHAR:
                    {
                                    return(OnChar(wParam));
                    }break;
        }
        return(false);
}
```

You made it through the code! Yes, it's much like a trackless desert in there, and the listing doesn't even include any of the comments I have in the real code. Essentially, there are three parts to CWidget::HandleEvent: focus trapping, child trapping, and dispatching.

During focus trapping (which only occurs for the master widget), if a mouse event has occurred and there is a mouse focus widget, the input goes directly to the mouse focus widget without going through normal channels. Similarly, if a keyboard event has occurred and there is a keyboard focus widget, the input goes directly there.

During child trapping (which happens in either master or nonmaster widgets), we loop through all of the child widgets (in *reverse* Z order) and have the children attempt to handle the input.

If HandleEvent makes it all the way to the dispatch portion, the message in question is examined and sent to the proper event-handling function, and the return value there is handed down to the caller.

Now, all of this is handled iteratively and recursively by a single call to the master widget's HandleEvent function. This is what happens when CWidget::FilterEvent is called.

And Now for the Payoff

All of this hard work, and now what? Well, I'm about to show you. Go ahead and grab CApplication, CMessageHandler, and CEventHandler from the CD under Trick 3 on "Building an Application Framework." Add CWidget and let's put together a small demo.

On the accompanying CD-ROM, you can find this example under UIControls1. There you will find the full implementation of CWidget as described in the text in this chapter. In addition to that and the core classes of the application framework, there are three other classes: CTestApplication, CTestEventHandler, and CTestWidget. The CTestApplication class is identical to the one found in Trick 3, so I'll discuss it no more. CTestEventHandler and CTestWidget are specially designed and implemented to demonstrate the capabilities of CWidget (or, more importantly, the flexibility of CWidget's extensible design).

CTestEventHandler

The CTestEventHandler class is designed and implemented to interface with a CWidget master control.

```
class CTestEventHandler : public CEventHandler
{
private:
            CWidget* m_pMasterWidget;
public:
            CTestEventHandler(CMessageHandler* pmhParent);
            virtual ~CTestEventHandler();
            bool OnMessage(int MessageID,int argc,void* argv[]);
            bool OnDestroy();
            bool OnPaint(HDC hdc,const PAINTSTRUCT* pPaintStruct);
            bool OnEvent(UINT uMsg,WPARAM wParam,LPARAM lParam);
            CWidget* GetMasterWidget();
};
```

The OnMessage and OnDestroy functions are much as you would expect them to be. OnMessage simply returns false, and this function only exists so that CTestEventHandler can be instantiated. OnDestroy posts a quit message so that the application can terminate.

The GetMasterWidget function is simply an accessor to the member function m_pMasterWidget. This is not strictly necessary because you could simply use the GetMasterWidget static member function of CWidget to accomplish the same thing. I provided it here simply as a convenience.

So, we are left with the constructor (during which the master widget is created as well as a few other widgets), the destructor (during which the entire widget tree is destroyed), the OnPaint handler (during which the widget tree is displayed and updated), and finally the OnEvent handler (which allows the widget tree to filter out events it may need).

Said another way, I only needed to place four minor ties into another class for that class to interface with the CWidget UI hierarchy: one for creation, one for destruction, one for updating, and one for event handling. Now that system is pretty easy to interface with if I do say so myself. You can take a look at the implementation of CTestEventHandler on the accompanying CD-ROM.

CTestWidget

Now we've come to CTestWidget, and the luster of the UI hierarchy will shine before you. Here is the CTestWidget class definition:

```
class CTestWidget : public CWidget
{
private:
            HBRUSH m_hbrBackground;
            HBRUSH m_hbrOld;
            HPEN m_hpenOutline;
            HPEN m_hpenOld;
            HPEN m_hpenHilite;
public:
            CTestWidget(CWidget* pWidgetParent,int iX, int iY, int iWidth, int
   iHeight);
            virtual ~CTestWidget();
            void OnRedraw();
            bool OnLButtonDown(int iX,int iY,bool bLeft,bool bRight);
            bool OnLButtonUp(int iX,int iY,bool bLeft,bool bRight);
};
```

Behold the compactness of CTestWidget! Of 54 member functions, I only need to override five, and the only reason this class is so large is because of the numerous GDI objects needed for background and foreground colors.

CTestWidget is a simple, humble widget (it's only a *test* widget), so don't expect it to do much. It does, however, manage to do something: When the mouse pointer is hovering over it, it will be highlighted with yellow, and if you click on it, it captures mouse input. While the left mouse button is down, all input goes to it. If you release the left button while the mouse is inside of the widget, the widget will put itself on the delete list, later to be destroyed during the next widget tree update.

All of that from five little functions? You bet, and the implementations aren't that complex either, as you can see here:

```cpp
CTestWidget::CTestWidget(CWidget* pWidgetParent,int iX, int iY, int iWidth, int
    iHeight):
CWidget(pWidgetParent,iX,iY,iWidth,iHeight),
m_hbrBackground(NULL),
m_hbrOld(NULL),
m_hpenOutline(NULL),
m_hpenOld(NULL),
m_hpenHilite(NULL)
{
            m_hbrBackground=CreateSolidBrush(RGB(128,128,128));
            m_hpenOutline=CreatePen(PS_SOLID,0,RGB(192,192,192));
            m_hpenHilite=CreatePen(PS_SOLID,0,RGB(255,255,0));
            m_hbrOld=(HBRUSH)SelectObject(DC(),m_hbrBackground);
            m_hpenOld=(HPEN)SelectObject(DC(),m_hpenOutline);
}
CTestWidget::~CTestWidget()
{
            SelectObject(DC(),m_hbrOld);
            SelectObject(DC(),m_hpenOld);
            DeleteObject(m_hbrBackground);
            DeleteObject(m_hpenOutline);
            DeleteObject(m_hpenHilite);
}
void CTestWidget::OnRedraw()
{
            if(HasMouseHover())
            {
                        SelectObject(DC(),m_hpenHilite);
            }
            else
            {
                        SelectObject(DC(),m_hpenOutline);
            }
            RECT rcFill;
            CopyRect(&rcFill,&Bounds());
            OffsetRect(&rcFill,-rcFill.left,-rcFill.top);
            Rectangle(DC(),rcFill.left,rcFill.top,rcFill.right,rcFill.bottom);
}
bool CTestWidget::OnLButtonDown(int iX,int iY,bool bLeft,bool bRight)
{
            SetMouseFocus(this);
```

```
                    return(true);
}
bool CTestWidget::OnLButtonUp(int iX,int iY,bool bLeft,bool bRight)
{
            if(HasMouseFocus())
            {
                        SetMouseFocus(NULL);
                        if(iX>=0&&iY>=0&&iX<GetWidth()&&iY<GetHeight())
                                    //close the window
                                    Close();
            }
            return(true);
}
```

As you casually glance through the implementation, count how many of the lines of code are there simply to deal with the ugliness of GDI rendering. (Here's a clue: It's almost all of the lines in CTestWidget's implementation.) Only a small handful of CWidget member function calls sprinkle the big pile of GDI. If you were using a different rendering API, the implementation would be even shorter.

Summary

By now, the benefit of a well-designed UI hierarchy should be obvious. We never have to touch the implementation of CWidget again. It will be there for all time. But what CWidget allows us to do is derive child classes for which we can customize the behavior. Typically, this only means overriding OnRedraw and a few of the event-handling functions. The identity of a control is based solely on what it looks like and how it responds to input.

Another aspect of the UI hierarchy shown in this chapter was the idea of notification. The needed code is already in place, but there has been no example of how to make use of it. (I only have so many pages that I'm allowed to consume and only so much time in which to write them.)

Right now, using CWidget, you would not have a hard time writing a class that emulates the behavior of a button. You'd simply change OnRedraw and a few of the event-handling functions and then add a few notifications. The same goes for just about any type of control. None of them is terribly difficult to implement once you've got a core UI system in place. The rest is all customization.

TRICK 5

WRITING CROSS-PLATFORM CODE

WENDY JONES,
HUMONGOUS ENTERTAINMENT,
WWW.HUMONGOUS.COM

Introduction

You've been given the task of writing the next 3-D first-person shooter. The only problem is that your publisher wants you to write it for both the PC and the Playstation 2. Well, you could always write the version for the PC and worry about the pain of porting it to the Playstation 2 later, or you could develop your title for both platforms at the same time.

Cross-platform development isn't new to the world of software, but it's becoming more common in the game industry. No longer are developers and publishers content with releasing their latest game on a single platform. They want a wider audience, and they obtain it by porting their title across multiple systems. With the power of today's PCs and the popularity of console systems, games are reaching a record number of people, and publishers are perfectly happy to cash in on that market. Writing cross-platform code makes your game portable and more easily converted to whatever system is required.

Why Develop Cross-Platform Code?

So, why would we want to write cross-platform code? Why would we want to spend the extra time and effort up front, just to allow our game to run on different machines?

First and foremost, the possible market for your game title is greatly expanded. If you choose to create a game for only the Nintendo GameCube, you're restricting the possible audience and sales to only gamers owning that system. Porting your game to PCs or other consoles on the market enables your game to reach its full potential in the marketplace and hopefully its financial goals as well.

The second reason is less development time and lower cost when planning on releasing different versions of your game. Sure, we can write our game to run on the PC and write platform-specific to handle manipulating and rendering our graphics, but what happens when it comes time to port it to the Xbox? All the platform-specific code has to be ripped out and replaced with the same platform-specific code for the new system. We'd spend countless hours of development time just searching for all the pieces of code that reference the PC system. Then comes the task of actually replacing these sections; of course, we're assuming that the two systems work the same way. For example, writing a game for Microsoft Windows requires that our main game loop listen for messages coming from the operating system to keep the multitasking working correctly. Writing a game for a console system, however, skips the Windows messaging and focuses squarely on running your game loop. If we took this into account during the initial development cycle, we wouldn't have to spend this time replacing entire sections of code. A second drawback with porting after the fact is loss of momentum in the marketplace. Everyone may be hyping your PC product, but while they're waiting for the Xbox version, their interest is slowly fading. By the time the port is complete, there may no longer be an interest in your game.

Third, writing cross-platform code creates more portable source code base. While developing for one platform, the compiler may not catch errors in your code, or it may behave differently on separate systems. Sometimes due to the amount of memory or resources available on a particular system, overwriting a section of RAM without initializing it first can crash the system, whereas another system might allow the operation to complete successfully. Testing and debugging code on multiple systems helps us catch our own logic errors more readily. For instance, the debuggers used under Windows commonly are more mature and useful than the ones available for console systems. In this case, even if a Windows version isn't ever going to be seeing a release outside of your company, maintaining a PC version can help out in the debugging and testing process.

The final reason for cross-platform code is quality. If your development team is going to create only the first version of a game and then allow the port to other systems to be handled by a third-party, your game quality is going to suffer. By creating your code to be run on different systems from the start, the ports are kept in-house, and the quality of your game can me maintained.

Planning for a Cross-Platform Product

When you're designing your game with the goal of running it on multiple platforms, there are a few things to keep in mind before making the decision to start the development process. Remember that not all popular platforms are created equally, so you need to do your research first.

Console systems are great for titles such as fighting games, but will your PC role-playing game really translate well? For example, if you are planning to create a massive, multiplayer, role-playing game for the PC and also want the same title for the Nintendo GameCube, is the system really suited to the task? Here are a few questions you might want to ask yourself:

- Is the system powerful enough?
- Can the graphics and gameplay really be faithfully reproduced on the target platform?
- Will going from a mouse-and-keyboard input system on the PC hinder the users' ability to enjoy your game when they're restricted to a gamepad?
- If the game involves online play, will PC and console gamers be able to play online together?

Problems Between Platforms

Even after deciding for which platforms we're going to develop, there are still a few more things we need to look at. Each system is usually based on different hardware architectures. For example, a standard PC is normally based on an Intel processor that follows the 80×86 instruction set, whereas console systems can have a radically different architecture, as in the Sony Playstation 2. It is based on a proprietary processor with a unique instruction set. The instruction set isn't the only thing you have to worry about when comparing the processors in a system. The way the processor stores its data is also important. There are two ways in which current processors store their information; these ways are represented by the terms *big-endian* and *little-endian*.

Big-endian architectures consider the leftmost bytes (the lower address bytes) to be the most significant. In little-endian architectures, the rightmost (or higher) address bytes are considered most significant.

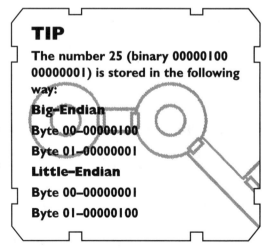

TIP

The number 25 (binary 00000100 00000001) is stored in the following way:

Big-Endian

Byte 00–00000100

Byte 01–00000001

Little-Endian

Byte 00–00000001

Byte 01–00000100

In game programming, this problem can arise when loading in data files for a particular platform. If a binary data file was created on the PC (little-endian architecture) and then loaded on a system using the Motorola 68000 processor (big-endian architecture) without accounting for the differences, the data we would be reading in would be mixed up. In this case, your code would have to support byte swapping for the data file loader. The following code demonstrates how to swap the bytes for an unsigned long (which, in this example, is 4 bytes). This is not a very fast piece of code, but it should demonstrate the concept clearly.

```
unsigned long byteSwap(unsigned long value)
{
  unsigned long newValue = 0;
  char* pcurValue = (char *)&value;
  char* pnewValue = (char *)&newValue;

  pnewValue[0] = pcurValue;[3]
  pnewValue[1] = pcurValue;[2]
  pnewValue[2] = pcurValue;[1]
  pnewValue[3] = pcurValue[0];

  return newValue;
}
```

I'll explain how this bit of code works. The byteSwap function is passed an unsigned long 4-byte value. Within the function, two new variables are declared as character pointers. pcurValue is initialized to the value passed to the byteSwap function, while pnewValue is initialized to zero. Since these two variables are character pointers, we can access each byte within them by using normal array notation. The first slot in pnewValue is set to the last slot of pcurValue. The next slot of pnewValue, slot 1, is then set to the second-from-the-last slot of pcurValue, and so on, until all the bytes have been dealt with. The function then returns newValue, which is holding the byte swapped value.

The hardware architecture of the targets' platforms isn't the only worry when dealing with cross-platform code. The differences in compilers for each platform can also cause problems. When dealing with standard C++ code under Microsoft Visual Studio, it's common to include #pragma statements, which are directives telling the compiler how to handle certain errors or how to compile a bit of code. For example, the following line of code tells the compiler to link in the opengl32.lib file during the link process.

```
#pragma comment (lib, "opengl32.lib");
```

This eliminates the need to add the LIB file to the link section of the project. While this is well and good when using MSVC, trying to compile this code under another compiler may fail because other compilers may not support the `#pragma` directive. When attempting to write portable code, it's best to leave these instructions within the makefile.

The easiest way to eliminate problems with your code across different compilers is to restrict yourself to the ANSI C/C++ standard. Microsoft Visual Studio has the following suggestions when trying to restrict your code to the ANSI standard when coding under Windows:

- Do not use the MFC library. Call the Win32 APIs directly.
- Disable Microsoft extensions.
- Use the iostream library from the ANSI Standard C++ library.
- Use the Standard Template Library (STL)

Programming for Multiple Platforms

Now that we've seen some of the differences between platforms and some of the pitfalls we have to watch out for, what can we do to make sure our code is portable? Most of the ways to keep your code portable are very simple to implement. By taking advantage of some of the built-in features of C and C++, we can keep a clean and cross-platform code base.

The *#if defined* Directive

One of the simplest ways to keep your code portable is to use the `#if defined` directive to create a conditional block of code. The `#if defined` directive checks to see if a specific constant has been defined and then compiles the code within the block. For instance, if compiling an application for Windows, you must deal with calling `WinMain` as the entry point to your application. Under a console system or DOS, only calling `main()` is required. So, how do we use `#if defined` to solve this problem? Look at the following example:

```
// Checking to see if we are running under Windows
#if defined(WINDOWS)
#include <windows.h>
#endif
```

```
#if defined (WINDOWS)
// we're under windows so use WinMain
int APIENTRY WinMain(HINSTANCE hInstance, HINSTANCE hPrevInstance,
LPSTR lpCmdLine, int nCmdShow)
#else
// we're not under Windows, so use the standard call to main()
int main()
#endif
{
    return 0;
}
```

This piece of code uses #if defined to check whether the constant WINDOWS has been defined. If it has been defined, #if is flagged as true, and the code following #if is compiled (as shown in the declaration of main()). If the constant WINDOWS has not been defined, the code following the #else is compiled.

The *typedef* Keyword

Typedef is used to basically create your own data types. During cross-platform development, you may find that an integer on one platform is 4 bytes, while on another platform it's only 2 bytes. If you use the default int data type, you may find yourself not having enough room to fit your data. Instead, you can create your own data types that will alleviate this problem. For example, on a platform that supports 4-byte integers, you would define your own type like this:

```
typdef  int Myint;
```

On the platform where to get the same 4-byte precision you must use an unsigned long, you would define your type like this:

```
typedef unsigned long Myint;
```

Most systems you come across will normally support the same size data types, but occasionally you'll come across a system that is completely different and causes elusive bugs. These types of bugs are difficult to track down.

Here's a sample header file called types.h that shows some common uses for creating your own data types.

```
/****************************************************
* types.h
****************************************************/
```

```
#ifndef TYPES_H
#define TYPES_H

// here we define the types
typdef unsigned char Mybool;
typedef int Myint;
typedef signed char Mychar;


#endif
/*****************************************************/
```

Always Use *sizeof()*

As previously explained, data types can be different sizes across platforms. If there is any spot in your code where you assume a certain number of bytes for a data type, go back and replace it with a call to sizeof(). Sizeof() returns the correct number of bytes for a data type based on the platform on which it's running. For instance, to display the size of an integer, we would use the following code:

```
printf("Number of bytes for an integer is %d\n", sizeof(int));
```

What Is an Abstraction Layer?

Abstraction layers are one of the more complicated—and yet powerful—ideas you can use to keep your game project portable. During the development process, you'll come across certain subsystems that will have to be platform-specific. Whether you're developing for consoles or just keeping to the PC, at some point you're going to have to call a piece of the hardware layer. This is where abstraction layers come into play.

An abstraction layer is basically just a small API that you create that sits between your game code and the hardware API layer. This allows you to keep any platform-specific calls separate from your actual game code (see Figure 5.1).

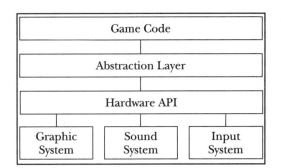

Figure 5.1

An abstraction layer is used to keep the game code from making platform-specific calls

Why Use an Abstraction Layer?

Using an abstraction layer within your code brings you benefits other than just portability. New hardware can be supported more easily. By keeping all the hardware-specific code separate, it's a simple matter of defining a new layer and adding the support within it. The game code needs no changes and doesn't need to know that the underlying hardware has been changed.

It's also a simple matter to change between multiple implementations within a layer. For instance, writing two versions of your graphic layer—one supporting Direct3D and the other supporting OpenGL—would give you the option of switching between the two during runtime. Users could be given the option of choosing which rendering engine to use for their system.

For What Systems Would We Want to Create an Abstraction Layer?

When planning your code design, a couple of systems that immediately come to mind would be useful to split out as an abstraction layer.

- **Video subsystem.** This includes any initialization of the video hardware and the drawing of anything to the screen. For instance, if you're creating a title on the PC, creating an abstraction layer above both OpenGL and DirectX would allow your game to run using either API.

- **Audio subsystem.** Not every platform plays music or sound effects the same way, but it's useful to be able to only use a standard call from your game code. An abstraction layer for audio would include functions such as `playsound()`, `stopstound()`, and `playbackgroundMusic()` just to start. With this layer in place, no matter what sound system the hardware supports, your main game code still makes the same call.

- **Input subsystem.** Another obvious subsystem is input. PCs have keyboards, mice, and gamepads available, but most console systems only have the gamepad. Keeping standard functions within your main loop for checking button presses keeps your code from getting confused with handling all the different ways in which the input can originate. For example, creating a layer to handle input from both the PC keyboard and a gamepad keeps your game code from having to deal with either specifically. Your game code would only have to worry about checking for the direction in which the player wants to go. For example, if the layer handled reading from a gamepad, it would only have to return the values for left, right, up, or down. The game code wouldn't care how the values were obtained.

Designing an Abstraction Layer

At this point, you should have the general idea of what an abstraction layer is and what it's used for. Now we'll go through the process of designing a simple layer. I chose the graphic layer because it's one of the more common and useful systems. The first thing we do is create an abstract parent class from which we derive the layers. The following is the prototype for the class:

```
/**********************************************************************
 * GraphicSystem.h
 **********************************************************************/
#if !defined(GRAPHICSYSTEM_H)
#define GRAPHICSYSTEM_H
class GraphicSystem
{
public:
            virtual void render() = 0;
            virtual void closeGraphicSystem() = 0;
            virtual bool initGraphicSystem(HWND hWnd) = 0;

            void setScreenResolution(int width, int height);
            GraphicSystem();
            virtual ~GraphicSystem();
private:
            static int screenHeight;
            static int screenWidth;
            HWND m_hWnd;
};
#endif
```

The GraphicSystem class has three private variables defined: screenHeight and
screenWidth (which are used to hold the resolution of the video mode) and m_hWnd
(which holds the handle to the main application window).

There are also three pure virtual functions defined that must be overridden in any
class that inherits from GraphicSystem.

The first is initGraphicSystem, which will be used to handle the creation of the render area of the application window. We pass in the hWnd (main application handle)
because systems like OpenGL and DirectX use this during their initialization
procedures.

The next function is closeGraphicSystem. This function handles the cleanup and
releasing of any memory we've used during our application.

The final function is render. Render is called once per frame and handles the actual
updating of the screen.

The code associated with this class is very minimal because its main use is just to be
overridden and to provide the framework for any child classes. The implementation of the GraphicSystem class is as follows:

```
/*********************************************************************
* GraphicSystem.cpp
* Parent abstraction layer class
*********************************************************************/
#include "GraphicSystem.h"

// constructor
GraphicSystem::GraphicSystem()
{
}
// destructor
GraphicSystem::~GraphicSystem()
{
}
// initializes the graphic system
// returns true if the system is initialized properly
// this class is meant to be overridden in a child class
bool GraphicSystem::initGraphicSystem(HWND hWnd)
{
            m_hWnd = hWnd;
            return true;
}
```

```
// closes down the graphic system and releases any memory that we used
// this class is meant to be overridden in a child class
void GraphicSystem::closeGraphicSystem()
{
}


// sets the two private variables screenWidth and screenHeight
// these two variables represent the resolution of the
// application window
void GraphicSystem::setScreenResolution(int width, int height)
{
                screenWidth = width;
                screenHeight = height;
}
// render is called once per frame. This is where the actual
// graphics will be drawn
// this class is meant to be overridden in a child class
void GraphicSystem::render()
{
}
```

The purpose of the code in the GraphicSystem.cpp file is just to provide default implementations of the class functionality. One function is provided that doesn't get overridden by inheriting from this class: setScreenResolution. This function takes two parameters (both integers), representing the width and height of the application window.

Deriving from the Abstraction Layer

The next step is to actually create an implementation based on the parent class GraphicSystem. Since this code is meant to run on the PC, the first system we will support will be OpenGL.

OpenGL, along with Direct3D, has become the de facto standard for 3-D on the PC. OpenGL eliminates the need for applications to deal with most 3-D and graphic code themselves. By providing a standard API, applications can be written to OpenGL without worrying about what hardware it's running on. OpenGL has been available for the PC for a couple of years and has really helped push the graphic accelerator market.

Since we chose OpenGL for the first layer, we need to create a prototype for a child class inheriting from GraphicSystem. The following is the code representing the openGLSystem.h file.

```
/*********************************************************************
* openGLSystem.h
*********************************************************************/
#if !defined(OPENGLSYSTEM_H)
#define OPENGLSYSTEM_H
#include "GraphicSystem.h"
class openGLSystem : public GraphicSystem
{
public:
            virtual ~openGLSystem();
            openGLSystem();

bool initGraphicSystem(HWND hWnd);
            void closeGraphicSystem();
            void render();

private:
// handle device context
            HDC         hDC;

// handle rendering context
            HGLRC   hRC;
};
#endif
```

As you can see from the class definition, we are inheriting from the GraphicSystem class.

```
Class openGLSystem: public Graphic System
```

The new class is also making sure to define the pure virtual functions required by the parent class. The code implementation of these functions will be placed in the openGLSystem.cpp file.

```
bool initGraphicSystem(HWND hWnd);
            void closeGraphicSystem();
            void render();
```

You'll also notice two new private variables that are not part of the parent class.

```
HDC      hDC;
HGLRC    hRC;
```

These two variables hold a handle to the device context and a handle to the rendering context for the application window.

```
/********************************************************************
* openGLSystem.cpp
********************************************************************/
#include "openGLSystem.h"

/* OpenGL specific includes */
#include <gl\gl.h>
#include <gl\glu.h>

/* constructor and destructor */
openGLSystem::openGLSystem()
{
}
openGLSystem::~openGLSystem()
{
}
/********************************************************************
* initGraphicSystem
* init the OpenGL graphic system
********************************************************************/
bool openGLSystem::initGraphicSystem(HWND hWnd)
{
// holds the chosen pixel format
        GLuint PixelFormat;

        GraphicSystem::initGraphicSystem(hWnd);
        Static PIXELFORMATDESCRIPTOR pfd = {
                sizeof(PIXELFORMATDESCRIPTOR),
                1,                      // Version Number
                PFD_DRAW_TO_WINDOW |    // Format Must Support Window
                PFD_SUPPORT_OPENGL |    // Format Must Support OpenGL
                PFD_DOUBLEBUFFER,       // Double Buffering
                PFD_TYPE_RGBA           // Request An RGBA Format
                16,                     // Select Our Color Depth
                0, 0, 0, 0, 0, 0,       // Color Bits Ignored
                0,                      // No Alpha Buffer
```

```
                              0,                    // Shift Bit Ignored
                              0,                    // No Accumulation Buffer
                              0, 0, 0, 0,           // Accumulation Bits Ignored
                              16,                   // 16Bit Z-Buffer
                              0,                    // No Stencil Buffer
                              0,                    // No Auxiliary Buffer
                              PFD_MAIN_PLANE,       // Main Drawing Layer
                              0,                    // Reserved
                              0, 0, 0               // Layer Masks Ignored
        };

// check for the device context
if (!( hDC = GetDC( hWnd )))        {
            closeGraphicSystem();
            return false;
}


// Did Windows Find A Matching Pixel Format?
if (!(PixelFormat = ChoosePixelFormat( hDC, &pfd )))          {
            closeGraphicSystem();
            return false;
}


// Can we set the pixel Format?
if(!SetPixelFormat( hDC, PixelFormat, &pfd )) {
            closeGraphicSystem();
            return false;
}


// can we get the rendering context?
if (!( hRC = wglCreateContext( hDC ))) {
            closeGraphicSystem();
            return false;
}


// attempt to activate the rendering context
if(!wglMakeCurrent( hDC, hRC )) {
            closeGraphicSystem();
            return false;
}
// we successfully have OpenGL initialized
```

```
            return true;
    }


/***********************************************************************
* render
* performs all the OpenGL rendering to the screen
***********************************************************************/
void openGLSystem::render()
{
            // clear the buffers
            glClear(GL_COLOR_BUFFER_BIT | GL_DEPTH_BUFFER_BIT);

            // Ensure we're working with the model matrix.
            glMatrixMode(GL_MODELVIEW);

            // load in the identity matrix
            glLoadIdentity();

            // swap the double buffers
            SwapBuffers(hDC);
    }

/***********************************************************************
* closeGraphicSystem
* close the OpenGL graphic system and performs cleanup
***********************************************************************/
void openGLSystem::closeGraphicSystem()
{
            // check for the rendering context
            // if it exists, let's release it
            if ( hRC ) {
                        // make this the current context
                        wglMakeCurrent( NULL, NULL );

                        // delete the rendering context
                        wglDeleteContext( hRC );

                        // Set to NULL
                        hRC = NULL;
            }
```

```
        // try to release the device context
        if (hDC && !ReleaseDC( m_hWnd, hDC )) {
                hDC = NULL;
        }
}
```

Explaining the Derived Layer

This section is just a very simple implementation of a derived layer. We're only supporting the bare minimum of functionality that you would want, but it's enough to explain the abstraction layer concept. Explaining in detail the OpenGL code in the preceding section isn't within the scope of this chapter. Now let's see how this layer works.

We start first by overriding the initGraphicSystem function. This function is created to take care of initializing OpenGL and preparing the application window for drawing.

Next we implemented the render function. This is where the main drawing for this layer takes place. The game itself will be given the task of sorting all the visible polygons into a format that the OpenGL layer will render.

Finally, we implemented the closeGraphicSystem function. Within this function, the device contexts we created are released back to the system. This is just our basic cleanup function.

Using the Derived Layer

Now it's time to put the layer we created to some use. We're going to create some code that allows switching between the OpenGL layer that we created in the last section and another layer supporting Direct3D.

The following code shows how to instantiate the gfxSystem object and call the functions defined within it.

```
#include <windows.h>
#include "GraphicSystem.h"

// defined if we want to use OpenGL rendering
#define USE_OPENGL 1

int APIENTRY WinMain(HINSTANCE hInstance, HINSTANCE hPrevInstance,
                                LPSTR lpCmdLine, int nCmdShow)
```

```
                {
                    // Windows Message Structure
                    MSG                         msg;

#ifdef USE_OPENGL
                    // use the OpenGL system
                    openGLSystem *gfxSystem = new openGLSystem();
#else
                    // use the Direct3D system
                    directXSystem *gfxSystem = new direct3DSystem();
#endif

                    // initialize the graphic system we chose
                    gfxSystem->initGraphicSystem( hWnd );
                    // loop control variable
                    bool done = false;

                    // main loop
                    while( !done )
                    {
                            // are there any windows messages waiting?
                            if (PeekMessage( &msg, NULL, 0, 0, PM_REMOVE ))
                            {
                                    // if so, check what they are
                                    if (msg.message == WM_QUIT) {
                                                done = true;
                                    }
                                    else {
                                                    TranslateMessage(
    &msg );
                                                    DispatchMessage(
    &msg );
                                    }
                            }
                            // otherwise, let's just do the rendering loop
                            else
                                    {
                                    // render to the window
                                    gfxSystem->render();
                                    }
                    }
```

```
            // shutdown the graphic system
            gfxSystem->closeGraphicSystem();

        // check for the existence of the gfxSystem
        // delete the pointer
        if ( gfxSystem )
        delete gfxSystem;

        return (msg.wParam);
```

The key to this code is actually the two lines nestled between #ifdef and #endif just within WinMain.

```
#ifdef USE_OPENGL
            // use the OpenGL system
            openGLSystem *gfxSystem = new openGLSystem();
#else
            // use the Direct3D system
            directXSystem *gfxSystem = new direct3DSystem();
#endif
```

The compiler checks to see if a constant USE_OPENGL has been defined. If so, the code creates an object based on OpenGL rendering. If the constant has not been defined, the code defaults to creating the object with the Direct3D system. A pointer gfxSystem is created that refers to the rendering system. The rest of the code at this point doesn't have to worry about what system is being used. All the proceeding calls refer directly to the pointer we created.

In Conclusion

The techniques we've described so far are just the tip of the iceberg when doing cross-platform development. Doing a search on the Web will give you a much greater understanding of the usefulness of keeping your code portable. With the growing popularity of Linux as a computing platform and the decreasing lifetime of console systems, the need for portable code going forward is only going to grow.

SECTION 2

General Game Programming Tricks

If you are reading this, then you have successfully made your way through Part I. At this point, you should have a clear understanding of some basic fundamentals that you can use for the rest of this book. Heck, you should be able to use what you have learned thus far for any of your game programming projects!

Part II will begin introducing some concepts that you will find useful for your game programming endeavors. You will cover topics such as OpenGL game programming, sound and music, 2D Sprite creation, and so on. There is even a special trick that instructs you on how to create text-based adventure games for you die-hard Zork fans out there. I hope it is a nice addition to the book and that it helps the beginners get their feet wet by programming a simple game to show off to their friends.

Are curious juices flowing yet? Well, let's satisfy that craving by moving right along into Part II.

TRICK 6

Tips from the Outdoorsman's Journal

Trent Pollack

Introduction: Life in the Great Outdoors

Ahhhh, everyone loves the outdoors . . . Well, maybe not everyone. Maybe the people with allergies loathe it, and maybe the people with really sensitive eyes don't like it either. So, let me rephrase that: Everyone loves a good outdoor image! That will be the goal for this chapter: to take your knowledge of creating an outdoor world from nil to being able to create a fully interactive and dynamic outdoor world.

What You Will Learn

In this chapter, you'll learn all about creating an outdoor world. I'm just going to give you a general overview. My goal for this chapter is to ease you into a wide variety of subjects and then give you links for how to make your implementation of that subject cooler and more complex. I'll start with an explanation about terrain, with an emphasis on height map manipulation, and then I'll tell you how to render that height map using brute force terrain. Brute force is definitely not the best choice for a terrain algorithm, but I want to keep things simple. I will then talk about texturing that terrain (using a multipass algorithm that I came up with). Then I'll introduce you to a very cool yet simple terrain lighting algorithm called "Slope Lighting."

Next on the ultrafun list is adding some environmental effects to your outdoor world. I will discuss the advantages of using fog, and then I'll give you another way to make a cool outdoor environment even cooler: skyboxes!

Height Maps 101

Imagine you have a grid of vertices that extends along the X-axis and the Z-axis. In case your mind is seriously lacking in the imagination department, I was nice enough to make an image of what your mind *should* have conjured up (see Figure 6.1).

Now that's a pretty boring image! How exactly are we going to go about making it more, well, terrain-ish? The answer is by using a *height map*. A height map, at least in our case, is a series of `unsigned char` values (perfect for grayscale images) we will be creating at runtime, or in a paint program, that defines the height values for a boring grid of vertices. Now, for a quick example, check out the height map in Figure 6.2. Once we load it and apply it to our terrain, the grid in Figure 6.1 will transform into the beautiful (well, sorta) terrain you see in Figure 6.3.

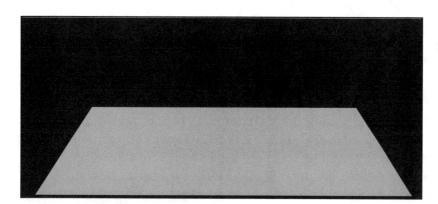

Figure 6.1

A grid of vertices with nondefined height values

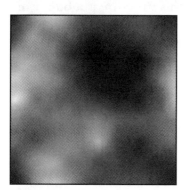

Figure 6.2

The 128×128 height map used to create Figure 6.3

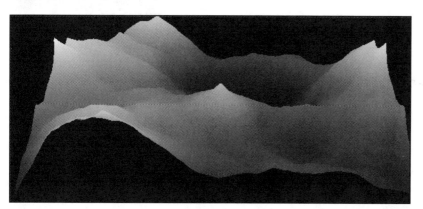

Figure 6.3

A brute force terrain image created using the height map in Figure 6.2

Granted, it looks pretty boring without any cool textures or lighting, but hey, we need to start somewhere. As I was previously explaining, height maps give us the power to shape a boring grid of vertices into a magnificent landscape. The question is, what exactly are they? Normally, a height map is a grayscale image in which each pixel represents a different height value. Dark colors represent a low height, and lighter colors represent a higher elevation. Look again at Figures 6.2 and 6.3. Notice how the 3-D terrain (in Figure 6.3) corresponds exactly to the height map (in Figure 6.2), with everything from the peaks to the ditches and even the colors? That's what we want our height maps to do: give us the power to mold a grid of vertices to create the terrain we want.

Now, in our case, the file format for our height maps is going to be the RAW format. (Though most of the demos create height maps dynamically, I included the option to save/load height maps using the RAW format.) I chose this format simply because it is incredibly simple to use, and since the RAW format only contains *pure* data, it is easy to load in and to use. Because we are using a grayscale RAW image, that just makes everything so much easier! Before we load a grayscale RAW image, we have a couple of things to do. First we need to create a simple data structure that can represent a height map. What we need for this structure is a buffer of unsigned char variables (we need to be able to allocate the memory dynamically) and a variable to keep track of the height map's size. Simple enough, eh? Well, here it is:

```
struct SHEIGHT_DATA
{
    unsigned char* m_pucData; //the height data
    int m_iSize;              //the height size (must be a power of 2)
};
```

Making the Base Terrain Class

Now, before we go any further, we need to create a base class from which we can derive a specific terrain implementation. (For this chapter, it's a brute force implementation, but I'm hoping you'll take a look at "Going Further: Deeper into the Wilderness" a bit later in this chapter and will implement your own more complicated algorithm.) We do not want the user to actually create an instance of this class; we just want this class to be a common parent for a variety of terrain implementations.

So far, all we need in our base class is three variables: an instance of SHEIGHT_DATA, a height scaling variable (which will let us dynamically scale the heights of our terrain), and a size variable (which should be exactly the same as the size member of SHEIGHT_DATA, or something is seriously screwed up). As far as functions go, we need some height map manipulation functions and the functions needed for the fractal terrain generation algorithms we talked about earlier. Here is what I came up with:

> **NOTE**
>
> The CTERRAIN class is what we C++ junkies like to refer to as an *abstract class*. An abstract class is a class that functions as a common interface for all of its children.[1] Think of it this way: A mother has red hair but a boring personality, and although her children all have red hair, each has a distinct personality that is incredibly entertaining. The same applies to an abstract class. Although it is boring by itself, its traits carry on to its children, and those children can define more "exciting" behavior for themselves.

```cpp
class CTERRAIN
{
    protected:
        SHEIGHT_DATA m_heightData;        //the height data

        float m_fHeightScale;             //scaling variable

    public:
        int m_iSize;     //must be a power of two



    bool LoadHeightMap( char* szFilename, int iSize );
    bool SaveHeightMap( char* szFilename );
    bool UnloadHeightMap( void );

    //-----------------------------------
    // Name:        CTERRAIN::SetHeightScale - public
    // Description:  Set the height scaling variable
    // Arguments:    -fScale: how much to scale the terrain
    // Return Value: None
    //-----------------------------------
    inline void SetHeightScale( float fScale )
```

```
{    m_fHeightScale= fScale;    }


//------------------------------------
// Name:         CTERRAIN::SetHeightAtPoint - public
// Description:   Set the true height value at the given point
// Arguments:    -ucHeight: the new height value for the point
//               -iX, iZ: which height value to retrieve
// Return Value: None
//------------------------------------
inline void SetHeightAtPoint( unsigned char ucHeight, int iX, int iZ)
{    m_heightData.m_ucpData[( iZ*m_iSize )+iX]= ucHeight;    }


//------------------------------------
// Name:         CTERRAIN::GetTrueHeightAtPoint - public
// Description:   A function to set the height scaling variable
// Arguments:    -iX, iZ: which height value to retrieve
// Return Value:  An float value: the true height at
//                the given point
//------------------------------------
inline unsigned char GetTrueHeightAtPoint( int iX, int iZ )
{    return ( m_heightData.m_ucpData[( iZ*m_iSize )+iX] );    }


//------------------------------------
// Name:         CTERRAIN::GetScaledHeightAtPoint - public
// Description:   Retrieve the scaled height at a given point
// Arguments:    -iX, iZ: which height value to retrieve
// Return Value:  A float value: the scaled height at the given
//                point.
//------------------------------------
inline float GetScaledHeightAtPoint( int iX, int iZ )
   {    return ( ( float )( m_heightData.m_ucpData[( iZ*m_iSize )+iX]
)*m_fHeightScale );    }

CTERRAIN( void )
{    }
~CTERRAIN( void )
{    }
};
```

Not too shabby, huh? Well, that's our "parent" terrain class. Every other implementation we develop will be derived from this class. I put quite a few height map manipulation functions in the class just to make things easier for both the users and us. I included two height retrieval functions for a reason: Although we, as the developers, will use the true function most often, the user will be using the scaled function most often (to perform collision detection). We will use the set height function when we get to deformation later in the book. With that said, let's discuss the height map loading/unloading functions.

Loading and Unloading a Height Map

I've been talking about both of these routines for a while now, and I think it's about time that we finally dive straight into them. These routines are very simple, so don't make them any harder than they should be. All we are doing is some simple C-style file I/O.

The best place to begin is with the loading routine because you can't unload something without it being loaded. So, let's get to it! All we need are two arguments for the function: the file name and the size of the map. Inside the function, we want to make a FILE instance (so we can load the requested height map), and then we want to check to make sure the class's height map instance is not already loaded with information. If it is, we'll call the unloading routine and continue about our business. Here is the code for what we just discussed:

> **NOTE**
>
> I tend to stick with C-style I/O because it is so much easier to read than C++-style I/O. It's as simple as that, so if you are really a true C++ junkie and absolutely loathe the "C way of doing things," feel free to change the routines to true C++! On the other hand, I really like C++-style memory operations, so if you're a true C-junkie, change those!

```
bool CTERRAIN::LoadHeightMap( char* szFilename, int iSize )
{
    FILE* pFile;

    //check to see if the data has been set
    if( m_heightData.m_pucData )
        UnloadHeightMap( );
```

Okay, next we need to just open the file, and then allocate memory in our height map instance's data buffer (`m_heightData.m_pucData`), and check to make sure that the memory was allocated correctly, and that something didn't go horribly wrong (which is always possible, I mean, sometimes I just turn my computer on, and the next minute it decides to format itself, go figure).

```
//allocate the memory for our height data
m_heightData.m_pucData= new unsigned char [iSize*iSize];

//check to see if memory was successfully allocated
if( m_heightData.m_pucData==NULL )
{
    //something is seriously wrong here
    printf( "Could not allocate memory for%s\n", szFilename );
    return false;
}
```

And for the next-to-last step in our loading process, and definitely the most important, we are going to load in the actual data, and place it in our height map instance's data buffer. And finally, we are going to close the file, set some of the class's instances, and print a success message!

```
//read the heightmap into context
fread( m_heightData.m_pucData, 1, iSize*iSize, pFile );

//Close the file
fclose( pFile );

//set the size data
m_heightData.m_iSize= iSize;
m_iSize                     = m_heightData.m_iSize;

//yahoo! The heightmap has been successfully loaded
printf( "Loaded %s\n", szFilename );
return true;
}
```

That's it for the loading routine. Now we'll move on to the unloading routine before I lose your attention! The unloading procedures are *very* simple. All we have to do

NOTE

The height map saving routine is almost the exact same thing as the loading routine. Basically, all that needs to be done is replace `fread` with `fwrite`. Yup, that's all there is to it!

is check to see if the memory has actually been allocated. If it has, delete it. That's all there is to it!

```
bool CTERRAIN::UnloadHeightMap( void )
{
    //check to see if the data has been set
    if( m_heightData.m_pucData )
    {
        //delete the data
        delete[] m_heightData.m_pucData;

        //reset the map dimensions also
        m_heightData.m_iSize= 0;
    }

    //the height map has been unloaded
    printf( "Successfully unloaded the height map\n" );
    return true;
}
```

I said a while back that we were going to be creating most of our height maps dynamically. How do we do that? I'm glad you asked. (Even if you didn't, I'm still going to explain it!) What we are going to do is use one of two fractal terrain generation algorithms (both from the first volume of *Game Programming Gems*): fault formation[2] or midpoint displacement[3]. Because the two chapters in *Gems* explain the concepts infinitely better than I could ever hope of doing, I'm going to refer you to those chapters. But that doesn't mean that I didn't include code. Check out the following functions:

```
void CTERRAIN::NormalizeTerrain( float* fpHeightData );
void CTERRAIN::FilterHeightBand( float* fpBand, int iStride, int iCount, float
   fFilter );
void CTERRAIN::FilterHeightField( float* fpHeightData, float fFilter );

bool CTERRAIN::MakeTerrainFault( int iSize, int iIterations, int iMinDelta, int
   iMaxDelta, int iIterationsPerFilter, float fFilter );
bool CTERRAIN::MakeTerrainPlasma( int iSize, float fRoughness );
```

In Figure 6.4, I created some quick examples of height maps using the midpoint displacement (MakeTerrainPlasma) creation function, with varying roughness as specified.

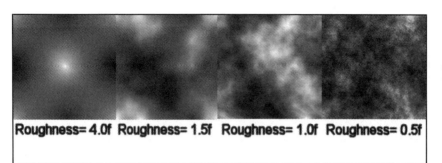

Figure 6.4

Height maps generated using the midpoint displacement algorithm, with varying levels of roughness

Roughness= 4.0f Roughness= 1.5f Roughness= 1.0f Roughness= 0.5f

The Brute Force of Things

Rendering terrain using brute force is incredibly simple and provides the best amount of detail possible. Unfortunately, it is the slowest of all the algorithms presented in this book. Basically, if you have a height map of 64×64 pixels, the terrain, when rendered using brute force, will consist of 64×64 vertices in a regular repeating pattern (see Figure 6.5).

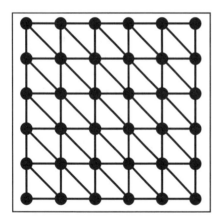

Figure 6.5

A 6×6 patch of brute force terrain vertices

In case you didn't immediately recognize it, we will be rendering each row of vertices as a trianglular strip, simply because it is the most logical way to render the vertices. I mean, you wouldn't exactly want to render them as individual triangles or as a triangle fan, would you?

For this chapter's first demo, I'm keeping things as simple as possible. So, for "lighting," we are just going to keep things, well, as simple as possible. The color for the vertex will be based on its height, so all vertices will be shades of gray. That's

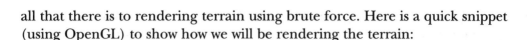

all that there is to rendering terrain using brute force. Here is a quick snippet (using OpenGL) to show how we will be rendering the terrain:

```cpp
void CBRUTE_FORCE::Render( void )
{
    unsigned char ucColor;
    int iZ;
    int iX;

    //loop through the Z-axis of the terrain
    for( iZ=0; iZ<m_iSize-1; iZ++ )
    {
        //begin a new triangle strip
        glBegin( GL_TRIANGLE_STRIP );

        //loop through the X-axis of the terrain
        //this is where the triangle strip is constructed
        for( iX=0; iX<m_iSize-1; iX++ )
        {
            //use height-based coloring (high-points are
            //light, low points are dark)
            ucColor= GetTrueHeightAtPoint( iX, iZ );

            //set the color with OpenGL, and render the point
            glColor3ub( ucColor, ucColor, ucColor );
            glVertex3f( iX, GetScaledHeightAtPoint( iX, iZ ), iZ );

            //use height-based coloring (high-points are
            //light, low points are dark)
            ucColor= GetTrueHeightAtPoint( iX, iZ+1 );

            //set the color with OpenGL, and render the point
            glColor3ub( ucColor, ucColor, ucColor );
            glVertex3f( iX, GetScaledHeightAtPoint( iX, iZ+1 ), iZ+1 );
        }

        //end the triangle strip
        glEnd( );
    }
}
```

Yup, that's all that there is to it. Now, do yourself a favor and check out OutdoorDemo_1 on the accompanying CD located in the folder associated with this chapter (i.e., Chapter 06). It's a nice demo with a ton of cool stuff to do, and there is even a nice little height map "mini map" up in the corner. Here are the controls and a screenshot of the demo (see Figure 6.6):

Key	Function
q or Escape	Quit the program
w/s	Move forward/backward
d/s	Strafe right/left
h	Save the current height map in the demo's directory
n	Switch to wireframe mode
m	Switch to "fill" mode
f	Form a new height map using fault formation
p	Form a new height map using midpoint displacement
=/-	Increase/decrease mouse sensitivity
]/[	Increase/decrease movement speed

Now, have some fun with that demo and meet me back here for some texture fun when you're done.

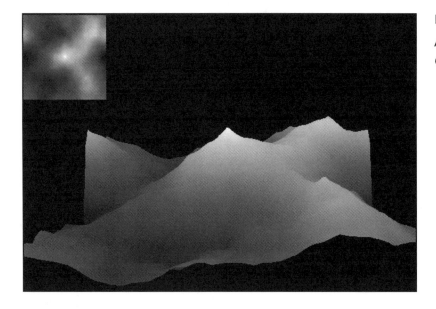

Figure 6.6

A screenshot from OutdoorDemo_1

Getting Dirty with Textures!

Sure, our terrain is great and all, but it still is seriously lacking in two areas: lighting, for one, and even more obviously, it lacks good textures! I mean, when was the last time you walked through a grayscale mountain?! So, we obviously have some work to do. I'm going to keep things very simple but also very cool. And although the approach I'm going to be presenting is probably not the best, it is very simple to implement. So, let's get started.

I'm going to be doing all of the texturing in this demo using some very simple methods. All we are going to be doing is stretching one texture (two a bit later) across the entire patch of terrain, which is easier than it sounds. Remember that texture coordinates are in a range of zero to one, so basically, all we have to do is take the current vertex we are rendering and divide it by the maximum length of the terrain. If we are rendering vertex (64, 32) in a 128×128 patch of terrain, that would provide us with the texture coordinate (64/128, 32/128) or (0.50, 0.25). So, all we are going to do (right now at least) is stretch a base grass texture (see Figure 6.7) across a patch of terrain, as in Figure 6.8.

Figure 6.7

The grass base texture for the textured terrain

Now for the fun part. The previous texture method was pretty trivial, but I can't make it *that* easy for you, can I? Notice the screenshot in Figure 6.8. Sure, it's pretty and all, but it looks a little . . . mountainous, doesn't it? Though when was the last

Figure 6.8

The texture in Figure 6.7 applied to a patch of terrain

time you saw a mountain completely covered in *grass*?! So, what we are going to do is have a little bit of fun with multipass rendering. We are going to be making two different texture passes: one for the base grass texture and one to apply a mountain texture based on height. To do this, we'll be increasing the alpha value of the vertex to be rendered as its height increases. Therefore, a vertex with a height value of 255 will be completely opaque, while a vertex with a height value of 32 will be barely noticeable.

Here's the exact same explanation, except this time I'll give it a bit more detail. As I said, we are going to be making two separate rendering passes. To do this, we are going to split the render function into three different sections: the base texture pass, the "mountain" pass, and finally a nontexture pass, just in case no textures are passed in the function's argument list. (Yes, I think this requires a code run-through.)

```
//----------------------------------
// Name:         CBRUTE_FORCE::Render - public
// Description:  Render the terrain height field
// Arguments:    -texTile1: the base texture to be used in the first pass
//               -texTile2: the additional texture
// Return Value:     None
//----------------------------------
void CBRUTE_FORCE::Render( IMAGE texTile1, IMAGE texTile2 )
{
```

```
float fTexLeft;
float fTexBottom;
float fTexTop;
float fColor;
int   z;
int   x;
```

The three `tex` variables are used for holding our texture coordinate generation for the current vertices being rendered. The other variables serve the same function as they did in the preceding section. Now let's go over the first section of the new rendering function. First we want to check to see if a base texture was even provided (both of the function arguments default to zero) because why would we want to waste a texture pass on something that's not getting textured? It's lunacy, I tell you! We then will bind the texture and render everything.

```
//make the first rendering pass
if( texTile1 )
{
    //bind the first texture (base texture)
    glBindTexture( GL_TEXTURE_2D, texTile1 );

    //loop through the Z-axis of the terrain
    for( z=0; z<m_iSize-1; z++ )
    {
        //begin a new triangle strip
        glBegin( GL_TRIANGLE_STRIP );

            //loop through the X-axis of the terrain
            //this is where the triangle strip is constructed
            for( x=0; x<m_iSize-1; x++ )
            {
                //calculate the texture coordinates
                fTexLeft  = ( float )x/m_iSize;
                fTexBottom= ( float )z/m_iSize;
                fTexTop   = ( float )( z+1 )/m_iSize;

                //use height-based coloring (high-points are
                //light, low points are dark)
                fColor= GetTrueHeightAtPoint( x, z )/255.0f;

                //set the color with OpenGL, and render the point
```

```
            glColor4f( fColor, fColor, fColor, 1.0f );
            glTexCoord2f( fTexLeft, fTexBottom );
            glVertex3f( x, GetScaledHeightAtPoint( x, z ), z );

            //use height-based coloring (high-points are
            //light, low points are dark)
            fColor= GetTrueHeightAtPoint( x, z+1 )/255.0f;

            //set the color with OpenGL, and render the point
            glColor4f( fColor, fColor, fColor, 1.0f );
            glTexCoord2f( fTexLeft, fTexTop );
            glVertex3f( x, GetScaledHeightAtPoint( x, z+1 ), z+1 );
        }


    //end the triangle strip
    glEnd( );
    }
}
```

Now, if that looks completely new to you, you obviously haven't been paying attention to what I've been writing, which hurts my feelings. But before I go cry and wallow in self-pity, I'm going to explain what is *different* from the old rendering routine. What should be most obvious are the three lines where we calculate the texture coordinates, but you already know how to do that because I did such an excellent job of explaining the calculations earlier—or didn't you listen to that either? The only other change present here is the two calls to glTexCoord2f, and those are pretty self-explanatory. So, now that we covered that, we need to move on to the second section of the rendering routine.

```
//make the second rendering pass
if( texTile2 )
{
    //bind the second texture (for higher areas on the terrain)
    glBindTexture( GL_TEXTURE_2D, texTile2 );

    //loop through the Z-axis of the terrain
    for( z=0; z<m_iSize-1; z++ )
    {
        //begin a new triangle strip
        glBegin( GL_TRIANGLE_STRIP );
```

```
//loop through the X-axis of the terrain
//this is where the triangle strip is constructed
for( x=0; x<m_iSize-1; x++ )
{
    //calculate the texture coordinates
    fTexLeft  = ( float )x/m_iSize;
    fTexBottom= ( float )z/m_iSize;
    fTexTop   = ( float )( z+1 )/m_iSize;

    //use height-based coloring (high-points are
    //light, low points are dark)
    fColor= GetTrueHeightAtPoint( x, z )/255.0f;

    //set the color with OpenGL, and render the point
    glColor4f( fColor, fColor, fColor, fColor );
    glTexCoord2f( fTexLeft, fTexBottom );
    glVertex3f( x, GetScaledHeightAtPoint( x, z ), z );

    //use height-based coloring (high-points are
    //light, low points are dark)
    fColor= GetTrueHeightAtPoint( x, z+1 )/255.0f;

    //set the color with OpenGL, and render the point
    glColor4f( fColor, fColor, fColor, fColor );
    glTexCoord2f( fTexLeft, fTexTop );
    glVertex3f( x, GetScaledHeightAtPoint( x, z+1 ), z+1 );
}

    //end the triangle strip
    glEnd( );
    }
}
```

The only difference here from the last section, in case you didn't notice, is in the alpha value that we pass for glColor4f, which defines the visibility of the second texture we are adding to the image. Remember that the higher the height value, the more opaque the second texture is. So, if we had a low value of 27, for example, it would be textured like a nice grassy field, but if we had a higher value of 227, it would be textured like a rugged mountaintop. Figure 6.9 shows the additional texture, and Figure 6.10 shows the multitextured version of Figure 6.8.

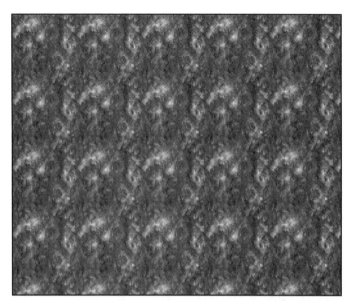

Figure 6.9

The additional texture for the terrain, just a rock texture that is repeated over and over

Figure 6.10

The multitextured version of Figure 6.8

That's all the information I'm going to give you about texturing in this chapter. If my nice little texturing technique was too simple or too slow for you, check out some of the excellent references in the section "Going Further: Deeper into the Wilderness" later in this chapter. In fact, I implore that you go check them out right now because making multiple passes for terrain isn't just a very fast technique; it's great for quick-and-dirty projects in which you need some good-looking results.

Adding Light to Your Life

Adding lighting to an outdoor world can make a *huge* difference in the overall mood and environment projected from your rendered scene. The lighting for the last couple of demos was, well, seriously flawed. It is probably the most unrealistic model possible. We just cannot have that, so I think it's about time for us to get to work on making a new lighting system for our outdoor world. For this task, we are going to use a *very* cool method called "Slope Lighting."[4]

To slope light terrain, all we are going to do is retrieve the height from the vertex next to the current vertex (which direction to go will be dictated by the light's direction) and then subtract it by the current vertex's height. The only kicker of the whole algorithm is that the light's direction must be in increments of 45 degrees. For instance, the direction of the light in the demo (OutdoorDemo_3) is (1, 1), but we could move it 90 degrees and give it a direction of (–1, 1), as seen in Figure 6.11.

Figure 6.11

Left image: Slope-lighted terrain with a light direction of (1, 1)

Right image: Slope-lighted terrain with a light direction of (–1, 1)

Now, does that look good, or does that look *good*? Yeah, that's what I thought! Anyway, let's do a code run-through and re-explain some of the concepts we just touched on in more detail. First of all, our slope-lighting system does all of its calculations per frame, so we might as well give the user as much power in customizing the lighting system as we can. To do this, we add a few variables to the ol' CTERRAIN class:

```
CVECTOR m_vecLightColor;     //the color of the light
float m_fLightSoftness;      //the light softness
float m_fMinBrightness;      //minimum shading value
float m_fMaxBrightness;      //maximum shading value
```

```
int    m_iDirectionX;       //X-direction of the light
int    m_iDirectionZ;       //Z-direction of the light
bool   m_bDoSlopeLighting;  //is slope lighting enabled/disabled?
```

These are all the variables we need. We also need to create a pair of functions to enable/disable slope lighting and one to customize the lighting system, but those are all very self-explanatory. What I want to concentrate on is the function that will be calculating the shading value for a pair of (X, Z) values.

```
//------------------------------------
// Name:           CTERRAIN::CalculateSlopeLighting - public
// Description:    Calculates the shading value using the Slope
//                 algorithm (Charlie Van Noland)
// Arguments:      -x, z: the vertex to calculate lighting for
// Return Value:   A floating point value: the shading level for a
//                 vertex
//------------------------------------
float CTERRAIN::CalculateSlopeLighting( int x, int z )
{
    float fShade;

    //if slope lighting is not enabled, then just return a very
    //bright color value (white)
    if( !m_bDoSlopeLighting )
        return 1;

    //ensure that we won't be stepping over array boundaries by
    //doing this
    if( z>=m_iDirectionZ && x>=m_iDirectionX )
    {
        //calculate the shading value using the "slope
        //lighting" algorithm
        fShade= 1-( GetTrueHeightAtPoint( x-m_iDirectionX,
                                          z-m_iDirectionZ ) -
                GetTrueHeightAtPoint( x, z ) )/m_fLightSoftness;
    }

    //if we are, then just return a very bright color value (white)
    else
        fShade= 1;
```

```
    //clamp the shading value to the min/max brightness boundaries
    if( fShade<m_fMinBrightness )
        fShade= m_fMinBrightness;
    if( fShade>m_fMaxBrightness )
        fShade= m_fMaxBrightness;

    //return the final shading value
    return fShade;
}
```

The most important part of this nice little snippet is the middle, where we calculate fShade. That is basically the whole slope lighting algorithm in one simple segment. Given the light direction, all we have to do is calculate the difference between the height of the vertex passed as an argument from the vertex before it (in the direction of the light). Here's a slight analogy: In a tightly packed city, there are some *huge* skyscrapers, and your little flower shop resides right next to one. Let's say the sun is directly behind the building from your point of view. Wouldn't things around you be a lot darker than if you were directly in front of the huge skyscraper (where you could receive the sun's rays in full)? Well, that's exactly what is going on here. In case you're more of a visual learner, check out Figure 6.12.

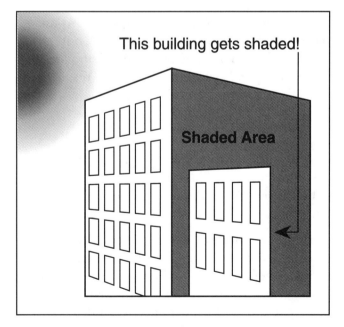

Figure 6.12

The slope lighting algorithm, using the building analogy

Now, for a better display of how a patch of terrain would get shaded, check out Figure 6.13. I didn't bother texturing the terrain at all, so you can see the full effect of how a blank patch of terrain would be shaded. Cool, huh?

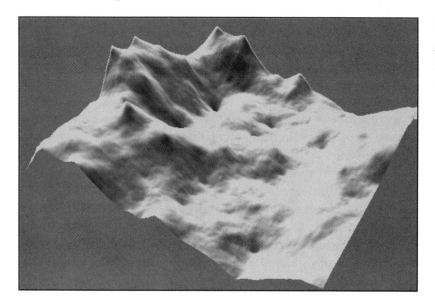

Figure 6.13

A nontextured but slope-lit patch of terrain

That's all that there is to slope lighting. I told you it was an easy algorithm to use, and yet it still provides great-looking results. It's all so exciting! Go check out OutdoorDemo_3 to see slope lighting in action. The controls for the demo are the exact same as they have been for the last couple. Next on the list is fog. Yes, fog!

Lost in the Fog

I'm not going into complicated fog issues here. I just want to discuss some of the benefits of fog and give you a simple demo to check out. I didn't use any compli-cated techniques to render the fog. I just used the API's hardware-accelerated fog features—nothing too great, but hey, it works!

Adding fog greatly increases the realism of an outdoor system. (Of course, you'd want to implement a better system than the one described here to be even more realistic. See the section "Going Further: Deeper into the Wilderness" later in this chapter.) Depending on how dense you make the fog, it can greatly change the mood of the entire scene. It also helps give the viewer a better sense of depth in the 3-D scene. Finally, fog helps hide the far clipping plane; once an object becomes completely absorbed in the fog, you might as well just clip it! So, you see, fog has other benefits in addition to its aesthetic value, so it's very worth your while to spend a bit of time making your fog system very high quality. Check out OutdoorDemo_4 for a simple implementation, just so you can see the benefits of fog that were previously listed (see Figure 6.14).

Figure 6.14

A patch of terrain covered in fog

Fun with Skyboxes

A skybox is just that, a box with a series of textures that together form a complete sky image. Remember when you were a little kid and your teacher made you cut out a series of little boxes that connected to form a cube? Well, that's basically what you're going to be doing here, except that little cube is a bit more complicated. It looks a little like Figure 6.15.

Now what we have to do is "cut" those images out and "glue" them together to make a nice-looking area surrounding our terrain. This isn't nearly as hard as it sounds. How many people, for their first 3-D project, made a simple cube? I'm hoping that most of you started out with something similar. The concept barely changes here except the position is a bit different, and you're adding textures to that simple cube.

To render the skybox, we just need six textures for the sides of the skybox, the center of the skybox (this should be the position of the camera), the minimum vertex of the skybox, and the maximum vertex of the skybox. Yup, that's all that we need! Check out Figure 6.16 for a visual list of the requirements.

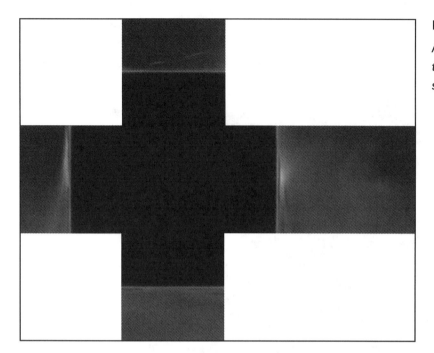

Figure 6.15

A series of textures that make up a skybox

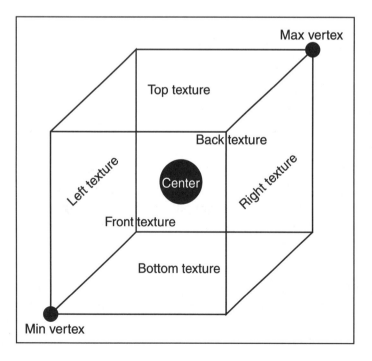

Figure 6.16

Visual requirements needed to render a skybox

We want the skybox to move along with the camera (we don't want the user to walk into a mountain that looks like it should still be an eternity away!), so we'll update the center of the skybox with the camera's position every frame. Also, skyboxes have one *huge* advantage that I have not discussed up to this point. If we disable depth testing and render the skybox directly after updating the view matrix (using our camera's utility function), we can eliminate the need to clear the color buffer (though we still need to clear the depth buffer). This provides a very large speed increase and makes a skybox both pretty and economical for our cause.

To render the skybox, you will want to "push" the current view matrix onto the stack and then translate to the skybox's center. You then would proceed to render the box using the min/max vertices, remembering to provide texture coordinates for each vertex (it's sort of important!). Alas, there's no code run-through this time because the code is very simple to understand and is rather repetitive to read. So, go ahead and check out OutdoorDemo_5 in Figure 6.17. Note how I changed the color of the slope lighting system to go along with the skybox textures. Now we are done with our fun outdoor world walkthrough . . . *dramatic music plays as lightning flares in the background and an evil maniacal laughter is heard*

Figure 6.17

Terrain rendered with a skybox used to provide the backdrop

Going Further: Deeper into the Wilderness

Brute force is definitely not the way to go for terrain rendering. Sure, it looks good and all, but it really is not practical in the slightest. Here are some great links that will give you information on more complicated, continuous-level-of-detail (CLOD) algorithms that are all very, very nice:

www.gamasutra.com/features/20000228/ulrich_01.htm

www.llnl.gov/graphics/ROAM/

http://gamasutra.com/features/20000403/turner_01.htm

www.flipcode.com/tutorials/tut_geomipmaps.shtml

For all of the demos in this chapter, I used a dynamic height map, so it was hard to predefine a texture map for it. I left out some stuff about how to generate good-looking texture maps ahead of time, so here are some good resources for doing that:

www.flipcode.com/tutorials/tut_terrtex.shtml

www.flipcode.com/tutorials/tut_proctext.shtml

My texture "tile" technique was okay, but it was far from fast and did not take advantage of hardware multitexturing at all. Jeff Lander, however, implemented a good-looking texture "tile" technique. A graphics card with at least three texture units is needed for good performance, but it's an interesting read nevertheless.

www.delphi3d.net/articles/printarticle.php?article=terraintex.htm

Finding a good terrain-lighting tutorial is definitely *not* an easy task. Fortunately, *Game Developer Magazine* is a very, very, very great resource. If you haven't subscribed to it yet, do yourself a favor and go get it. Check out the July 2001 issue, which contains an article called "Photorealistic Terrain Lighting in Real Time" by Naty Hoffman and Kenny Mitchell. The article describes two very good terrain-lighting algorithms and is definitely worth a look.

Since my fog explanation and demo weren't the greatest, here is a recent article about rendering volumetric fog:

www.gamasutra.com/features/20011003/boyd_pfv.htm

I know how much of a pain it is to generate skybox textures. In case *you* don't know how much of a pain it is, let me tell you: It's a pain! Some nice guys had the idea of making a tool whose sole purpose is to make the creation process easier. This tool is called "Skypaint," and you can check it out at the following site:

www.wasabisoft.com/

Conclusion: Back to the Indoors?

This chapter was a short whirlwind of topics related to outdoor world programming. There's so much more to cover, though, that it's impossible to fit it all into one short chapter. With that said, I'm hoping you have enjoyed this chapter thoroughly and are interested in a few of the variety of applicable topics. I'm also hoping you will continue your research into the world of outdoor world programming by using the links in the preceding section. Go off into the vast wilderness and continue your research!

Bibliography

[1]Gamma, E., et al. *Design Patterns: Elements of Reusable Object-Oriented Software.* Boston: Addison-Wesley, 1994.

[2]Shankel, Jason. "Fractal Terrain Generation—Fault Formation." *Game Programming Gems.* Rockland: Charles River Media, 2000.

[3]Shankel, Jason (2000). "Fractal Terrain Generation—Midpoint Displacement." *Game Programming Gems.* Rockland: Charles River Media, 2000.

[4]Van Noland, Charlie. "'Slope Lighting' Terrain." **www.gamedev.net/reference/articles/article1436.asp**, 2002.

TRICK 7

In the Midst of 3-D, There's Still Text

BEN HUMPHREY, GAMETUTORIALS,
www.GameTutorials.com

Introduction

In the age of advanced computer graphics and realism, many people forget the time (or weren't born yet) when games were just ASCII characters printed on the screen. With the creativity of a good writer, you were immersed in the fantastic world of text. There was no need for intense graphics cards that could pull off real-time masterpieces, and the only roadblock for a game designer was his own imagination. When someone thinks of text adventure games, what comes to mind is usually Zork, Spell Bound, or MUDDs (*multiuser Dungeons and Dragons*), to name a few. These are usually the first types of games that a game programmer attempts because they are so easy to create with one person and yet are incredibly fun, offering endless possibilities for creative game play.

For those of you who were born after 1985 or were lost with Amelia Earhart in the Bermuda Triangle, you might not know what constitutes a "text adventure." Let me explain. A *text adventure* is a game played by reading the text on the screen and typing commands into a DOS/UNIX-like prompt. There usually are no graphics in these games, unless they're created with ASCII characters. To maneuver around the world, you type directions such as north, south, up, down, east, west, left, or right. Think of it as reading a book, but you are the captain of the hero, as in a "Choose Your Own Adventure" book. Each room or area you are in generally is described to you in a few sentences. For example:

"The hallway off to your right is guarded by a bunch of rocks that appear impassible. A sobbing woman is kneeling down with her seemingly lifeless daughter. The earthquake continues to rumble. You'd better get out of here fast!

Directions [north right south]"

After reading the room's description, you then have the option of performing some task in that room, such as attacking an enemy, taking an object, dropping an object, looking at an object, or perhaps talking to a character that resides in the room. If you decide not to interact with anything or if there is nothing to do in that room, there is usually a list of valid directions in which you can go. After you manually type in the direction and hit Return, you either advance to a new room or area, or the game displays a message as to why you can't go that way.

Though many text adventures might not use any form of graphics other than the pixels of which the font is comprised, some add color to different parts of the text to make it more interesting to the eye. MUDDs are a perfect example of this technique to spice up what the viewer is seeing. As color became more popular, so did colored pictures of ASCII graphics. Surprisingly enough, one can make a pretty detailed representation of an image by using some color and the characters on the keyboard. There are many programs that actually take in an image and convert it to text. It's uncanny when you load it into your word processor and change the font to a small size—it looks almost identical to the picture! Unfortunately, we won't be delving into ASCII graphics in any of the following versions of our text adventure.

In the following sections, I will show you how to create a modular text adventure, which in the end will allow you to create a whole new game just by changing a text file. If you're a C/C++ programmer who is interested in making a text adventure but don't know where to begin, this is for you! It doesn't matter if you lack strong programming skills or just need a simple design to get you going—everything will be discussed here.

What Will Be Learned/Covered

Instead of throwing the source code of a finished, basic text adventure at you all at once, I will divide the final outcome into three different versions. Each of these versions will be a separate project on the accompanying CD-ROM to follow along with. Keep in mind that we will not cover every major aspect of a text adventure, but the base I provide should be enough to get you going toward creating the rest. Sometimes beginners just need a push in the right direction, and that's what I'm going to provide.

The first version will focus on getting the world up and running and being able to walk around with collision detection. After sparking your interest with that simple step, we will move on to the second version, which will add the capability to look at objects in the room that the character is currently in. This allows the user to find out more information about the room through interaction without being forced to read it all in a long paragraph. The final version will demonstrate adding enemies to your world. We will also add the basic fighting code. This should give you a base to do the rest of the text adventure yourself. By seeing how everything is set up, you will be able to pick up where I leave off. Near the end, I will discuss where to go from here and will provide some ideas for how to implement those ideas.

I am quite happy about the modularity of this design and how you can create a whole new game just by changing the data in the text file. That's not to say that the idea is anything compared with professional games—I would imagine most games that are developed allow this option within their level editors—but I am excited to share this simple idea with others who don't have much experience with programming and who need a boost to get their first game up and running. You can then apply these simple concepts to more advanced games that you make in the future.

Another large benefit to creating the game with one text file is that once you create your first game, you need only distribute the executable once and then the text file for each new game you make. This is also a cool thing to do with a little brother or sister who can't program but who wants to make his or her own games. All you need to do is just teach them how to set up the text file. You'll be surprised by how little code is used to create such a cool result.

To follow this chapter, you will need to be somewhat comfortable with the basics of programming. Some of these basics include functions, references, while loops, structures, and especially file input. The source code discussed will be in C++ created with Microsoft's Visual Studio. For more examples and to gain a better understanding of these concepts, you can check out a large collection of C++ tutorials at **www.GameTutorials.com** if you happen to find yourself lost while reading. Let's jump right in.

How Our Adventure Game Works

In this section, we will go over the design plan for how the game will work. The code in this chapter isn't as important as the theory behind it because everyone has his own way of programming an idea. With this in mind, before the code is introduced, I will go over each of the three stepping-stone versions that we will create. If you want to follow along with each version of the text adventure explanations and source code separately (and not confuse yourself with the other two versions before you fully understand the theory and implementation of the first), I suggest you read the overall description behind the first version, skip down to the implementation, and then come back and do the same for the second and third. Just to clarify for those of you who might be fairly new to programming terminology, when I say implementation, I am referring to the actual C++ code.

First Things First—Let's Get Ta Steppin'

Before you can create any type of adventure game, you need a world to move around in. This important part of the game is what we'll be covering first. Just so we are on the same page of understanding what is being mentioned, the areas in our world will be called *rooms*.

Describing a Room

A room will consist of a place where the main character is able to go, and it will initially have a room name and room description. In each room, there will also be a list of directions in which the player can and can't go, though he won't always know this information by the room description. For instance, some room descriptions might explicitly say something about a certain direction—perhaps that it is blocked off or that something exists off in that direction—whereas other descriptions may omit any details regarding directions.

A good text adventure usually will try to be as descriptive as possible so that players can immerse themselves in the world. A great description also helps the gamer become familiar with each room so that he knows where he is going and where he has been. It's a lot easier sometimes when playing a 2-D adventure game to orient yourself in the world, due to all the different colors and recognizable landmarks.

The rooms will be read from a text file simply titled World.txt. The file will be set up so that we can add unlimited rooms to our game without ever having to touch a bit of code. At the end of this first version, we will be able to move around the rooms with collision detection and view the room descriptions.

Our First Room Block

The basic premise of our game text file is to create room blocks that tell us everything there is to know about that room. Let's look at a sample room block:

```
<Middle>
You step into a house where you are nearly
blinded by the light shining through the window.
You have been searching for your friend who was captured.
The trail has led you to this mansion.
There is a door in every direction.*
<north> Top
<east>  Right
```

```
<south> Bottom
<west>  Left
```

The top header is the room's name, "Middle." We put the brackets (< >) around it to make it more obvious that it's a new room. The next paragraph is the room's description. I hope you are looking at these descriptions and thinking that you could write something 10 times better in your sleep. Notice at the end of the description that there is an asterisk (*). This tells us that the room description is done. You will see why this is important when we get to the code.

The next four lines in the block are the room names that are located in each associated direction. For example:

```
<north> Top
```

The <north> indicates the direction, and Top is the name of the room in that direction.

What if there isn't a room in a certain direction? In that situation, a None goes in place of the room name, as follows:

```
<north> None
```

This means that no room is in the north direction, and we can't go that way. This is how our simple collision detection works. Looking back at our original room block, if the user types "north", the game will already have the room name that is north of the current room stored in our room structure (which I will introduce later). The game will then look in the level file (World.txt) for a room header entitled <Top> and then will read its room data. As you can imagine, you can link rooms to other rooms without touching any extra code.

Another special keyword is End. If a room is titled "End," we know that the character has reached the end of the game. After the room is loaded, we check the room name for this reserved keyword. If the room bares this name, we display a quit message and exit from the program after the user hits a key. This is a simple solution, but most likely you will eventually want to give the user some options before quitting the game, like possibly loading a new game or starting once again from the beginning.

If there is an "End," there must be a beginning right? Well, yes, as a matter of fact there is. At the top of the game text file, there is this:

```
<start> Middle
```

The <start> section tells us that the room given after it will be the room in which the player ends up when the game begins. For instance, the room after the section is Middle. That will be the room block that is loaded first and displayed to the screen. Instead of creating a <start> section, you could just put the starting room as the first room block, but eventually, if you put in the option to save games, the starting room won't always be the beginning room (just some foresight you might want to think about).

Moving the Character from Room to Room

It's great that we understand a bit about the room block, but how does the movement really work? This is most likely one of the biggest stumbling blocks for beginners who are creating a text adventure. Should we load in the whole text file? No, that is definitely not needed. Since we are only displaying one room to the screen, there is no need to load more than one room at a time. This means that we will be loading from the file every time the character advances to a new room.

If you wanted to get really advanced, you could cache the rooms you have already visited or only the rooms that are visited more than once, but it isn't necessary. The only problem I foresee is if your game file is so huge that it takes three seconds to read from it between each room. In this case, you would just split up the levels into different files. Probably only a few more lines of code would be added to remedy this. You could then put a <File> section in the room block that would tell you which file to load from for the next room(s).

Getting back to the actual movement, how do you move the character to the next room once the action "north" is specified? Well, since we load all the data for the room we are currently in, we have the room name that is to the north of the current room. All we need to do is search for that room header in the game file. For instance, if the <north> section that was read in for the current room looked like this:

<north> Hallway2

We'd know that the room header is going to look like this:

<Hallway2>

We just have to add on the < and > characters to each end of the room name and then search for that string in the file. Once we find it, we know that the next line should hold the rest of the block information for that room. That's how it works. Simple enough, huh? This way, we only have to have one structure in code that holds the current room information read in. There's no need for a huge array that stores a bunch of rooms and their information, a simple concept for a beginning game programmer.

Mapping Out Your Game

As with any good game that is created, you are going to want to design it first. I suggest that you create a visual map on paper that has the rooms and their links to every other room. This will save you a lot of time when creating the world text file because you won't have to try to visualize the whole map and where rooms should go—it's right in front of you already done. Take a look at Figure 7.1.

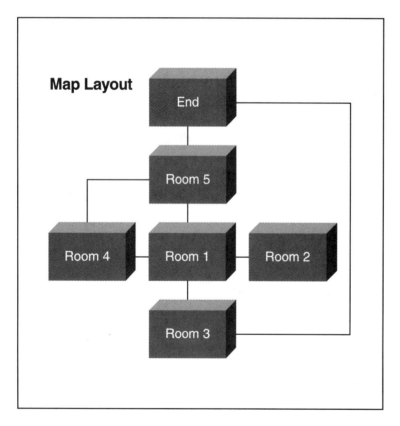

Figure 7.1

Map layout

Instead of creating your game levels on-the-fly, it's better to map them out first to get a visual idea of level design. Figure 7.1 is an example of one such map. We represent the rooms with 3-D boxes with the name of each room imprinted on its front. Of course, for your game, you will want to be more descriptive than just giving room numbers. You don't want such ambiguous names because it won't be clear what part of the world you are in. Names such as Desert1, Desert2, Oasis, Cottage5, Castle Entrance, and so on, will help you fully grasp what your world will be like before you create the text file.

Notice the lines that link from one room to another. This shows in which directions you can go from that room as well as which room(s) each direction leads to. Microsoft PowerPoint is a great tool for creating such maps. It has a wide variety of 2-D/3-D shapes and connectors that are easy to use and read.

The commands available in the first version are as follows:

```
look north south east west help quit.
```

You can imagine what they do, but let's list them here just in case:

- look   Displays the room description again
- north, south, east, and west   Moves the player in that direction
- help   Displays a list of all of the commands available
- quit   Umm . . . I forgot what this one does . . .

"Whatchu Lookin' At?"

This phrase does pose a good question regarding our text adventure. To extract more information from our rooms, we are going to need to be able to ask the game questions about certain things we see. Realistically, if we enter into a room or area, our eyes most likely peer around to learn more about our surroundings, possibly focusing on something or someone that might catch our eye or pique our interest. By allowing the player to investigate further into what he sees, the game becomes that much more real and enjoyable to play. This option is what we introduce in the next version of our text adventure.

Adding A *<look>* Section to Our Room Block

To allow the user to more closely examine things in a room, we need to add a new section to our room block entitled <look>. Adding onto our previous room block, take a look at the following new additions (which are italicized):

```
<Middle>
You step into a house where you are nearly
blinded by the light shining through the [window].
You have been searching for your friend who was captured.
```

```
The trail has led you to this mansion.
There is a door in every direction.*
<north> Top
<east>  Right
<south> Bottom
<west>  Left
<look>  1 window
```

```
<Middle|window>
The light pierces your eyes, causing you to wince in pain each time you look
    directly at the window.*
```

Let's dissect the new additions. First notice the new section in the room block:

```
<look>  1 window
```

The 1 tells us that there is only one thing to look at in the room. If there was a 0, that would mean there are no keywords to read in. The remaining information in that section is the word that the player is able to view. The "view" keyword will be a new command to add to our previous commands. When the user types "view", a prompt is given to have him type in the word he wishes to look at. If the word is valid, the description of that thing will be displayed on the screen; otherwise, an error message is displayed that indicates there is nothing to look at by that name. Keep in mind that we know which words can be viewed or not because we will read in all of the keywords when we read in the room information for the first time.

Adding a View Block

So, where does the description of the thing that was viewed come from? Let's look at the new header block that was added:

```
<Middle|window>
The light pierces your eyes, causing you to wince in pain each time you look
    directly at the window.*
```

We will call this the *view block*. Like the room block, the view block has a header and a description. However, it does not have any subsections attached to it. At the end of this chapter, I will give some suggestions for things you might want to add to it, but for now, we just want a description.

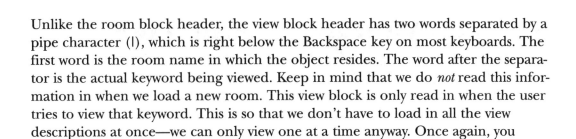

Unlike the room block header, the view block header has two words separated by a pipe character (|), which is right below the Backspace key on most keyboards. The first word is the room name in which the object resides. The word after the separator is the actual keyword being viewed. Keep in mind that we do *not* read this information in when we load a new room. This view block is only read in when the user tries to view that keyword. This is so that we don't have to load in all the view descriptions at once—we can only view one at a time anyway. Once again, you would probably want to change this if the game file was large enough to justify doing so.

If the player tries to view something, we store the keyword he typed in and then start concatenating some information. In pseudo code, we want to have something like this:

```
strViewHeader = "<" + strCurrentRoom + "|" + strKeyword + ">";
```

The result of this string gives us the view block header that we can then search for in the file. After finding that line, the next line is the description to be displayed, which can then be read in. It also must have an asterisk (*) at the end of the description, just like the room description. This is because we are using the function `getline()`, which allows us to read in a string from the file until a certain character is reached. It can be any character you decide, but I chose the asterisk. Keep in mind that this view block can be anywhere in the game file, but it's good to put it in the same area as the room to which it refers.

Looking at the room description of our newly updated room block, you'll notice that there are brackets around the `window` keyword.

```
...blinded by the light shining through the [window].
```

This has no significance other than letting the player know which words can be further investigated. Some people might not want to play a game in which they have to guess almost every word on the screen to see if it has any extra information. You might want to do both, however. Some words can be secret, and some can be obvious.

How Can We Have a Frag Count Without Any Monsters?

Who says that only first-person shooters can have frag counts? Okay, okay, so we won't implement a frag counter in our text adventure, but we will introduce monsters into the final mix. After all, as my grandma always says, "If I ain't killing something, I ain't happy." Keep in mind that when I use the term "monster," I am referring to the threat to our character in our game. In your game, you might call it a person or another entity.

Adding a Monster to Our Room Block

Very similar to the ⟨look⟩ section we added in the previous version, we want to add an ⟨enemy⟩ section that holds the enemy (if any) in the current room. Examine a sample room block with the following new section:

```
<Attic>
Entering into the upper loft of the house, a cool air runs through
your body as if a warning.  Something is definitely wrong here.
Your heartbeat seems to be imitating one of a squirrels'.
There is nowhere to go but back down.*
<north> None
<east>  None
<south> Bedroom
<west>  None
<look>  0
<enemy> goblin

<Attic|goblin>
<Health> 135
<Damage> 17
<Attack> The goblin claws your face off.*
```

In this example, there is nothing to look at, denoted by the 0 in the ⟨look⟩ section. There is, however, an enemy to fight. The ⟨enemy⟩ section works somewhat similarly to the ⟨look⟩ section. The only difference is that we only allow one enemy per room. I'll let you add the code to allow more than one. It should work exactly like the view keywords. Just put a number in front of the first enemy's name to specify how many there are.

Since we only have one monster per room, we can read in the monster's information immediately upon reading in the room. In our text adventure, the monster
will attack right when the player enters the room. In a good game, you want the
enemies to have different characteristics, but I chose to not complicate the code by
adding things you can do yourself. I provide the shell and base; you provide the
cool stuff.

Adding a Monster Block

Closely related to the view block, we want to create an *enemy block* that will store all
the information about the monster. Observe the following block:

```
<Attic|goblin>
<Health> 135
<Damage> 17
<Attack> The goblin claws your face off.*
```

The first line in this block is the header that stores the room that the monster is in,
along with the name of the monster.

```
<Attic|goblin>
```

Looking back on what we learned in the previous version, you can just concatenate
the appropriate information to form the header string to be searched for within
the game file. Once the header is found, the next three lines can be read in.

The remaining three lines are pretty self-explanatory. The first line holds the monster's health, the next line holds the damage that the monster takes off the player
each time they strike, and the remaining line is the attack message printed out to
the screen every time. This information is read in and stored in the monster structure we will create. Of course, in your game, you should add a bunch more quali-
ties that the monster should have, but once again, we will stick to a base to which
you can later add on.

Adding the Player Information

In the previous section, we mentioned that the monster had a damage attribute
that took off health from the player. For us to take off health, there first has to *be* a
player. In this final version of the text adventure (at least for our purposes), we will
add the player information to the top of the game file.

```
<Name>   Troy
<health> 275
```

```
<weapon> dagger
<damage> 21
<Start>  Middle
```

This information will be read in when we start the game. The player's name, health, weapon, and weapon damage will be loaded. Notice that the starting room is directly underneath the player data. For our purposes, the player won't be able to choose his name or information, but it will be the same every time. These stats and information will all be loaded into the player structure, which we will create in this version. I will talk more about incorporating saved games and such near the end of the chapter.

A new keyword will be added to our command list regarding the character's information. We will be able to type "status" and have all the player information displayed. That way, we at least know our current health so that we don't unwittingly go into battle with two hit points (hp).

"Hey, Take That Sword Out of My Stomach or I'm Tellin' Mom!"

So far, there has been mention of battles in our game, but how are they going to work? I'll tell you one thing: The battle scenes in our game are going to make the movie *Braveheart* seem like a nursery rhyme. Okay, maybe not, but don't worry. You can add on to them later. As a matter of fact, the monotony of our battles is going to be so great that it will force you to make them better for fear of getting beat up by your gaming audience.

The battle between the player and the monster begins immediately upon entering the room, assuming there is an enemy in the room. Surprisingly, the monster will attack first. Health from the player is taken according to the monster's damage stat. Then it's the player's turn to inflict damage. Depending on his damage stat, the monster loses some health after each blow. As this is going on, messages are being flashed to the screen about who lost what and the current health of each. This continues to go on until someone is dead. Fun, huh? I know, I know, but it should give you the desire to fix it.

In fact, there are no missed attacks, no random damages taken, and no stirring battle music—just pure brute force. You can imagine the emotions that will be evoked as your eyes glaze over each new status update after every successive attack. I recommend having some food and water nearby in case you become so engrossed in the game that you can't break yourself away from the computer to open the fridge.

Examining the Code

Now that we have introduced our design for the game, let's transfer it from thought to action. This section will go through all three versions of our text adventure's code and will shed some light on its meaning. Once again, after you finish each version, I would suggest that you go back and reread the next version's theory in the previous section. This will give you a fresh view of what's going on before diving into the code. I will, however, try to repeat as much as seems fit to help you better follow along.

Version 1—Mobility and Collision Detection

Get your shoes on because we'll be running around in no time (and yes, I give you permission to use this line on a blind date). Since there is only one source file for the first two versions, just assume we are discussing Main.cpp unless otherwise stated. In the final stepping stone, we will separate the game code into its own source and header file.

Creating the Room Structure and Defines

The following code is probably the most important since it will initialize GAME_FILE to the file that contains the data for the game world.

```
// This is a #define for our game file.
#define GAME_FILE "World.txt"
```

The level data will be read from a text file called World.txt. You can change this to whatever name you want, most likely the name of your game. It is a good idea to change the extension to .lev or something similar so that it's not so obvious that it's a text file. It's important to make sure that this file is in the same directory as the executable when running it outside your visual compiler, if you have one. I personally use Visual Studio C++.

```
// Defines to make our return values from GetInput() more clear
#define STILL_PLAYING     1
#define QUIT                              0
```

GetInput() is a function that handles our input from the user. It will return QUIT if we typed "quit"; otherwise, it returns STILL_PLAYING to let our main loop know to keep going. It's a good idea to always use #defines or constants, not numbers. That is what separates good, clean, readable code from bad code.

```
// This is our room structure, which holds the current room information
struct tRoom
{
    string strCurrentRoom;      // The current room we are in
    string strRoomDescription;  // The current room description
    string strRoomNorth;        // The room name that is to the north
    string strRoomEast;         // The room name that is to the east
    string strRoomSouth;        // The room name that is to the south
    string strRoomWest;         // The room name that is to the west
};
```

We need to know what the current room's name is, the current room's description, and what room names are off in each direction. We do not read in the whole level at the beginning, just the current room's information. When moving in a direction, we just search the game file (World.txt) for the room name that is in the direction we went. Then we read its information and start all over again in the loop. Notice that we put a t in front of Room to show that it's a structure. It's a good idea to get in the habit of doing this. If this were a class, we would call it CRoom. That is what many professionals try to use as a coding standard, but each project lead varies. It is not as important to follow the conventions I mention as to choose a convention and stick with it.

An str is also put in front of our variable names that are of type "string." Some people use sz (an old C standard). Next let's take a look at the main() function so that you see what is going on.

Defining Our *main()*

Now let's take a look at our main() function. This function is the workhorse of the entire program, so it is important to understand it.

```
// This is our main function that runs the program
int main()
{
```

The file pointer and room structure instances are created in main() and then passed down through our functions to eliminate global variables. We will be using the C++ ifstream class to read from our game file.

```
    // Create our file stream that will be open and read the file
```

```
ifstream fin;

// Create our room structure.  This will hold all of our room data.
tRoom room;
```

Once we have our important variables created, we then open the game file and check whether it was found and could be opened. Once the file is open, the output file stream should be pointing to the beginning of the file.

```
// Open the World.txt file
fin.open(GAME_FILE);

// Check if the file was found, if not, quit the program
if(fin.fail())
{
    // Display an error message and return -1 (Quit the program)
    cout << "Unable to find World.txt" << endl;
    return -1;
}
```

If we get here, we know that we found our game file, so let's read in the starting room. The starting room should be at the very top of the game file, as follows:

```
<Start> Middle
```

The `<Start>` word is just to make the game file more readable. We don't care about that when we are reading in the starting room; we just want the `Middle` part, which is the name of the first room block that should be read in. Since we don't want the `<Start>` string, we can't use `getline()`; otherwise, it would read in the whole line, and we would have to parse it ourselves. To get around this, we read in one word at a time. When we read in the first word, it will be `<Start>`. Then the next word can be read in, which will store the name of the room in which the character will start. The `room.strCurrentRoom` variable of our `tRoom` structure will store the starting room. Notice in the following code that we use it twice. The first time we read in the `<Start>` word, which is then stored in `room.strCurrentRoom`. Then we write over that with `Middle`. It's the same thing as if we did `cin >> num >> num`. If we typed in 10, hit return, typed in 12, and then hit return, `num` would equal 12 because it overwrote the 10.

```
// Store the starting room in our strCurrentRoom variable
fin >> room.strCurrentRoom >> room.strCurrentRoom;
```

After the starting room is determined, we want to find that room block in the text file to read its information. The information consists of the room description and the room names in each direction. Our next step is to display the room description to the screen.

```
// Pass the file stream and room data in to read the room data
GetRoomInfo(fin, room);

// Once the room data is read, display the current room description
DisplayRoom(room);
```

The following is our main game loop. It consists of an infinite `while` loop, with our `GetInput()` function returning a QUIT or a STILL_PLAYING value. If the return value == QUIT, we break from the main loop. So far, our game loop is just taking input from the user. There are no intros, cut scenes, level changes, and so on. This is the most basic game loop.

```
// Start our main game loop
    while(1)
    {
            // Get the input from the user and check game status
            if(GetInput(fin, room) == QUIT)
                break;       // Quit the main loop
        }
```

If we get here, the game is over and the player must have quit. The cleanup always comes last. When you are done using the file pointer, you need to close the file. I put a little delay before the program quits, allowing the user to see what happened.

```
// Close the file
fin.close();

// Delay the program for 3 seconds before quitting.
Sleep(3000);

// Return from main (Quit the program)
return 0;
}
```

Seeing the main game loop hopefully helps you better understand the use of the next functions we will be going over. How about we start with the easiest one, `DisplayRoom()`?

```
// This function shows the room description of our current room
void DisplayRoom(tRoom &room)
{
    // Use cout to display the room description of the current room
    cout << room.strRoomDescription << endl << endl;
}
```

DisplayRoom() will get called every time we enter "look" or enter into another room. Since we have all of our data stored in the room structure, we pass it in and query its strRoomDescription variable. This variable, among others, is set in our GetRoomInfo() function, which we will go over next.

Reading in the Room Block's Data

Now we begin to see how the room information gets read in from the file and stored in our room structure.

```
// This reads the current room information into our room structure
void GetRoomInfo(ifstream &fin, tRoom &room)
{
    // Create some temporary strings for reading in data from world.txt
    string strLine = "";
    string strTemp = "";
```

This function will be called when we start the game and then every time we move to another room. We only store the current room's data, so we need to load the next room's information when we move to it. The following creates a string that will store the room name with the < and > brackets around it. We need to do this because, in the text file we are reading from, it has the room blocks with brackets around it. This makes it more readable as a header. So, by adding < and > to each side of room.strCurrentRoom, it would turn Middle into <Middle>.

```
    // Save the current room with an appropriate header
    string strRoom = "<" + room.strCurrentRoom + ">";
```

First we want to return the file pointer to the beginning of the file. This way, we get a clean start when searching the file for the designed room block.

```
    // Set the file stream to the beginning and reset EOF flag
    fin.seekg(NULL,ios::beg);
    fin.clear();
```

Next it's time to start looking for the current room and read in its data. Here is the plan:

Since we start at the beginning of the file each time, we want to read in each line of the file, starting at the beginning, and then check whether that line is equal to the room block we are looking for (such as ⟨Middle⟩). If it is, we want to read in the "Middle" room's description. We do this by using getline(), and we stop reading characters when we hit an asterisk (*) symbol, which should be placed at the end of every room description in the text file. This allows us to read in multiple lines of text for the room description, but we needed a character to tell us when to stop reading. We will store the room description paragraph in our room.strRoomDescription variable. After the room description is loaded, we want to read in the rooms that are north, south, east, and west from the room being read in. The room names are stored after the direction block, as in ⟨north⟩ Top.

This tells us that to the north there is a room called "Top." Of course, these aren't good names, but in a game, you can make them more descriptive like "Hallway," "Library," and so on. We want to store the room names in each of the associated variables, depending on the direction. That means, for instance, that the Top in ⟨north⟩ Top should be stored in strRoomNorth. Since we don't want the ⟨north⟩ string, we can't use getline(); otherwise, it would read in the whole line. To get around this, we read in one word at a time. When we read in the first word, it will be ⟨north⟩. Then we can finally read in the next word, which will store the name of the room. This is coded in the following with fin >> strTemp >> room.strRoomNorth;.

We use strTemp to read in the ⟨north⟩ string, and then we store the next word in strRoomNorth. We want to do this for every direction. Once we finish reading in the last direction (west), we return from the function because we no longer need to read from the file anymore. Finally, the current room's description (strRoomDescription) is displayed, and we are now in the new room.

```
// Read in every line until we find the desired room header
while(getline(fin, strLine, '\n'))
{
    // Check if we found the room header we are looking for
    if(strLine == strRoom)
    {
        // Read in the room description until we hit the '*'
        // symbol, telling us to stop.
        getline(fin, room.strRoomDescription, '*');

        // Read past the direction blocks (I.E. <north>) and store
        // the room name for that direction.
        fin >> strTemp >> room.strRoomNorth;
```

```
            fin >> strTemp >> room.strRoomEast;
            fin >> strTemp >> room.strRoomSouth;
            fin >> strTemp >> room.strRoomWest;

            // Stop reading from the file because we got everything we
            // wanted.  The room info was read in so let's return.
            return;
        }
    }
}
```

I think GetRoomInfo() is the hardest part of the code to conceptualize. Once you grasp this, everything else is linear and obvious.

Handling Game Input

Moving on, we know that our main game loop calls GetInput(), but let's dissect this function and figure out what is going on. Bascially, GetInput() displays a prompt, waits for input, and then grabs the input and sends it through an if/else statement to check what command is desired.

This is the main control function that is called every time in the game loop. It displays a prompt, asks for the user's input, and then handles the desired command. If we want to quit the game, we return QUIT; otherwise, we return STILL_PLAYING.

```
// This handles our game input
int GetInput(ifstream &fin, tRoom &room)
{
    // Create a variable to hold the user's input
    string strInput = "";
```

The next couple of lines print a prompt out to the screen and grab the input. The rest of the function is just a large if/else statement to handle the command typed in.

```
    // Display a simple prompt
    cout << endl << ": ";

    // Read in the user's input
    cin >> strInput;
```

Just by looking at the comments, you can figure out exactly what the giant if/else statement is doing. If we type "look", display the room description. If we type any direction, move us to that room if there is a room to move to. If we type "help", display the available commands. Obviously, if we type "quit", return QUIT and leave the program. Finally, if the user types in something that is not recognized, we want to tell him so. I chose to just use the famous "Huh???" remark.

```cpp
if(strInput == "look")          // Check if the user typed "look"
{
    // Display the current room's description
    DisplayRoom(room);
}
else if(strInput == "north") // Check if the user typed "north"
{
    // Move to the room that is to the north (if it's a valid move)
    Move(fin, room, room.strRoomNorth);
}
else if(strInput == "east") // Check if the user typed "east"
{
    // Move to the room that is to the east (if it's a valid move)
    Move(fin, room, room.strRoomEast);
}
else if(strInput == "south") // Check if the user typed "south"
{
    // Move to the room that is to the south (if it's a valid move)
    Move(fin, room, room.strRoomSouth);
}
else if(strInput == "west") // Check if the user typed "west"
{
    // Move to the room that is to the west (if it's a valid move)
    Move(fin, room, room.strRoomWest);
}
else if(strInput == "quit") // Check if the user typed "quit"
{
    // Display a quit message and return QUIT to end our game loop
    cout << "Did you give up already?" << endl;
    return QUIT;
}
// Check if the user typed "help" or "?"
else if(strInput == "help" || strInput == "?")
{
    // Display a list of commands
    cout << endl << "Commands: look north south help quit" << endl;
```

```
    }
    else        // Otherwise we didn't recognize the command typed in
    {
        // Display a message indicating that we don't
        // understand what the user wants
        cout << endl << "Huh???" << endl;
    }


    // Return the default value saying that we still are playing
    return STILL_PLAYING;
}
```

Moving from Room to Room

There is one more function we haven't covered yet, and that is Move(). This was created because the code needed to check if we can go in the desired direction was
the same. The parameters are the file stream, the room structure, and the room
name we are trying to find. If you look back to where it's called in GetInput(), you
will see that we pass in the strings that store the room name for each direction,
such as strRoomNorth. Remember that these variables hold the name of the room in
that direction, so that is what we want to pass in to GetInput() for strRoom.

```
// This checks if we can move in a certain direction
void Move(ifstream &fin, tRoom &room, string strRoom)
{
```

First we want to check if the room that was passed in to strRoom was a valid room.
Remember that if the room == "None", there was no room in that direction.

```
    // Check if the room is a valid room
    if(strRoom == "None")
    {
        // Display a message that we can't go in that way and stop
        cout << "You can't go that way!" << endl;
        return;
    }
```

If we get here, the room name must be valid, and we should move to that room.
Before reading in the new room from our game file, we want to set strCurrentRoom
to the new room. After reading in the new room's data, the room description can
be displayed.

```
    // Set the current room to the new room we are moving to
```

```
room.strCurrentRoom = strRoom;

// Load the new room's data and store it in our room structure
GetRoomInfo(fin, room);

// Display the current room
DisplayRoom(room);
```

Once the room is loaded and the room description is displayed, we want to see if this is the final room in our game. This is done by checking whether the just-loaded room name bares the name of "End." That's our special keyword that we reserved. If we are at the end, we want to display a quit message and exit() the game.

```
        // Check if we are at the end room
        if(strRoom == "End")
        {
                // Display a quit message
                cout << "Press any key to quit the game...\n";

                // Wait for the player to hit any key
                getch();

                // Exit the game by using the system function
                //exit() and pass in a return value of 0
                exit(0);

        }
}
```

This concludes the code for our first version of the text adventure. Soon everyone will be dying to play your new game! Let me provide a recap of how the game file is set up:

```
<Start> Middle                    // This is the room that we will start at
```

The next block is the room block. The name of the room is surrounded in <> brackets to show that it's a header. This makes it easy to spot. The next few lines hold the room description. After the room description, there is an asterisk (*) symbol to show that it's done. That way, we can do a getline() and get multiple lines of text. The next four lines hold the rooms that are in each direction.

If there is *not* a room in a particular direction, we use the word "None" instead of putting in a room name. If we try to go north and the <north> section has the room name "None," it will tell us that we can't go that way. That's it! We can add as many rooms as we want in this way without touching any code. This makes it so the code is not dependent on the names of the rooms. That is why we read in the start room. It's incredibly modular.

```
<Middle>
You step into a house where you are nearly
blinded by the light shining through the window.
You have been searching for your friend who was captured.
The trail has led you to this mansion.
There is a door in every direction.*
<north> Top
<east>  Right
<south> Bottom
<west>  Left
```

Demonstrating a Test Run

Let's go through a test run of how this will work. Let's say we are at the start of the game. We will read in the starting room as "Middle." Then we search through the entire file for a room header called `<Middle>`. (Remember that we add the <>'s to the room name when searching.) We read in the data for the room and then display the room description to the screen. It should look like this:

You step into a house where you are nearly

blinded by the light shining through the window.

You have been searching for your friend who was captured.

The trail has led you to this mansion.

There is a door in every direction.:

There is a prompt (:) that awaits our input. Let's say we type "north" and hit Return. Since we have the room name that is stored in the `strRoomNorth` variable of our room object, we make sure it isn't "None." We know that it's "Top," so now we need to reset the file pointer to start at the beginning of the file. We are searching for the line `<Top>`. We check the first line. No, that's that starting room. Then we check the next. No, that's an empty line. And then the next . . . No, that's the `<Middle>` room, and so on. Eventually, we get to the line that says `<Top>`. We then read in its data because we know that we found the right room. See the following:

```
<Top>
```

```
As you get closer to the second story of the mansion, the sounds of someone
struggling can be heard more distinctly.  There is no turning back now.
One door is to the south and one is to the north up a stairwell.*
<north> End
<east>  None
<south> Middle
<west>  None
```

Now we are in the "Top" room. We display the room description on the screen and once again wait at the prompt for user input. Our only options are to go south and north. As you can see, east and west have "None" as the room name, meaning we can't go that way. Notice that there is a room with the name "End." This will always be the last room in our game. That way, you can always have an ending room for the game to be over (for mazes and such). We could have made a block at the top of the game file like the `<start>:` . . . `<end>` Attic and checked whether the `strEndRoom == strCurrentRoom`, but I like checking for a room named "End" better.

This pretty much sums up the first version of our simple text adventure. Before going on, I suggest that you try and code this yourself. That way, you will more fully grasp the next sections. With this simple version, you can already create a maze that has a beginning and an ending. Give it a shot.

Version 2—Taking a Look Around

In this next version, we will show how to allow the player to view something in the current room/area. It could be a person, an object, or anything else you can think of that the gamer will want to examine. To accomplish this new feature, let's look at the changes to our code that are needed to make it happen.

The first thing that needs to be added is a `#define`, which is used to restrict the maximum amount of things to look at in a room. I chose three as an arbitrary number. You can increase this to whatever you want. This means we will only be able to look at three different things in a room. If we have more than three keywords in the game file, it will read in only three and will ignore the rest. Our new `#define` is then used to allocate an array to hold all the viewable keywords in the room. To get around this restriction, you could just dynamically allocate the array when reading in the room. I chose not to since it might confuse others who aren't familiar with such techniques yet. This stores the size of our `strLookArray`

```
#define MAX_LOOKS                    3
```

New Additions to Our Room Structure

Next, two new variables will need to be added to our tRoom structure.

```
struct tRoom
{
    string strCurrentRoom;
    string strRoomDescription;
    string strRoomNorth;
    string strRoomEast;
    string strRoomSouth
    string strRoomWest;
```

Here we create an array with the size of MAX_LOOKS (3). That means we can hold three keywords for each room (for example, "floor," "creature," and "darkness"). We then need a variable to store the description of that keyword, like we do for the room description. Once we choose a keyword to look at, we first make sure it's in the strLookArray[] and then search the game file for its description.

As a reminder, we don't read in all of the view descriptions when loading the room, just their keywords. The description is only loaded when the player chooses to view something. If that keyword is valid, the description is loaded from the file.

```
    // This holds the names of the things to look at in the room
    string strLookArray[MAX_LOOKS];

    // This holds the description of the thing we look at
    string strLookDescription;
};
```

Reading In Our New Section

Moving on to the next function, let's revisit GetRoomInfo(). With the new data added to our structure, there needs to be some code to read it in. Since the <look> section is what is going to be parsed, the code must go after the sections of the adjacent room names are read (being that the section is after these).

```
void GetRoomInfo(ifstream &fin, tRoom &room)
{
    ...

    while(getline(fin, strLine, '\n'))
    {
```

```
if(strLine == strRoom)
{
    ...
    fin >> strTemp >> room.strRoomWest;
```

Assuming that the <west> section is right before the <look> section in your text file, this is where we read in the keywords for the current room. Take a look at the first room's look block:

`<look>  1 window`

We obviously need to read past the <look> word as we did with all the others, but then we need to read in how many keywords there are in this room. That is what the 1 is for. Since there is only one keyword, window, we put a 1 right after the <look> word. If we had two keywords like window and mansion, we would put a 2 instead of a 1, as follows:

`<look> 2 window mansion`

In the following, we use the strTemp string to read past the <look> word, and then we use a local created integer count to read in the number of keywords. Before we read in the keywords, we want to initialize the strLookArray. That way, if one room only has one keyword, we won't be able to look at two of the three keywords in the last room. This would cause a weird problem. Once we have the number of keywords, we need to do a loop that reads them into the strLookArray a word at a time. Notice that we mod (%) the count by MAX_LOOKS. This is so that we don't read in more than three keywords. If we read in four, the program would crash because we went outside the array boundaries.

```
// Create some local variables to use for counters
int count = 0, i = 0;

// Read past the "<look>" word and store keyword count
fin >> strTemp >> count;

// Go through and initialize all the indices in the array.
// This could also be done with a simple call to memset().
for(i = 0; i < MAX_LOOKS; i++)
{
    // Initialize the current index to nothing
    room.strLookArray[i] = "";
}
```

After the `strLookArray` is initialized, loop through and read in the keywords until all have been read. Also, make sure we don't read in more than our `strLookArray` can hold by using the % operator.

```
        for(i = 0; i < count % MAX_LOOKS; i++)
        {
            // Store the keyword into the index of our strLookArray
            fin >> room.strLookArray[i];
        }

        return;
    }
}
}
```

Adding the *View* Command

The data from the room block should now be able to be read. The view descriptions are still missing, however. These are only loaded when the player tries to view something using the `view` command, which is to be added to this second version. Our input function, `GetInput()`, will need to have a new `else if()` statement to allow the new command.

```
int GetInput(ifstream &fin, tRoom &room)
{
    ...

    // Check if the user typed "view"
    else if(strInput == "view")
    {
```

If the player chooses `view`, we want to prompt him to type in the keyword he wants to look at. Next, we check whether that keyword is in our list of keywords for the room. If it is, the description is read in from the game file and is displayed; otherwise, an error message is given saying that there is nothing to look at with that name.

Though we haven't covered the `CheckLook()` function, this basically searches our `strLookArray` for the keyword that the player types in. This way, we don't search the file for a keyword that doesn't even exit. The function returns `true` if that word is in our array, `false` if it's not. There are two other functions we haven't looked at yet, `GetLookInfo()` and `DisplayLook()`. Obviously, `DisplayLook()` just prints out the

strLookDescription, whereas GetLookInfo() finds the view header in the game file and
reads in its description.

```
// Display a prompt and read in the player's keyword to look at
cout << "What do you want to look at? ";
cin >> strInput;

// Check if what we typed in was valid in the room
if(CheckLook(room, strInput))
{
    // Read in and display the description for the keyword
    GetLookInfo(fin, room, strInput);
    DisplayLook(room.strLookDescription);
}
else
{
    // Display an error message due to an invalid keyword
    cout << "I don't see anything like that..." << endl;
}
    }
}
```

Determining a Valid *View* Keyword

This next function, CheckLook(), is called after the player types in "view" and has
chosen the keyword he wants to look at. It then searches through the strLookArray
to make sure what is being viewed is in the current room. If it is, it returns true;
otherwise, it returns false.

Here is an example run-through: Let's say we read in the keywords for a room in a
log cabin. There happens to be two keywords: "fork" and "chair." Let's say the
player chooses to look at "bed." It will then go through the whole strLookArray, fail
to find "bed," and then return false, which will appropriately display a mistake message to the screen.

The room structure is passed in to CheckLook(), along with the keyword that the
player wanted to look at.

```
bool CheckLook(tRoom &room, string strLook)
{
    // Go though all the slots in our strLookArray and check if the
    // word we are trying to look at is in this room's keywords.
```

```
        for(int i = 0; i < MAX_LOOKS; i++)
        {
            // Return TRUE if the desired word is in the current index
            if(strLook == room.strLookArray[i])
                return true;
        }

        // If we get here, we know that the keyword isn't in the list
        return false;
}
```

Almost identical to `DisplayRoom()`, `DisplayLook()` prints the description of what the player just looked at to the screen. This only gets called if `CheckLook()` verifies that the viewed keyword was valid. A simple `cout` is all it takes.

```
void DisplayLook(string strLookDescription)
{
    // Print the look description out to the screen
    cout << endl << strLookDescription << endl;
}
```

Reading in the View Block

The final addition to this version of our text adventure is the `GetLookInfo()` function. This is literally a rip-off of `GetRoomInfo()`, except that we don't need to read in the room names in each direction. All that we get from this function is the look description, found directly underneath the view header. The view header is similar to the room header, except that it also stores the current room's name that the keyword found. For instance, if a keyword "tub" were in the room named "bathroom," the room header would look like this:

```
<bathroom|tub>
```

There is a pipe character between the two words for aesthetics; it doesn't mean anything other than as a separator. You can use any syntax you want to make it understandable.

Since this function is very similar to `GetRoomInfo()`, we do the same types of things. The algorithm to get the look description is this: Go through every line in the game file and check whether it's the view block header that contains our desired description. Once the right header is reached, the description can then be read.

```
void GetLookInfo(ifstream &fin, tRoom &room, string strLook)
```

```
{
    // Create a string to hold each line that we read in
    string strLine = "";

    // Set the file pointer at the beginning of the file

    fin.seekg(NULL,ios::beg);
    fin.clear();

    // Read in a line at a time until we find the desired header
    while(getline(fin, strLine, '\n'))
    {
```

Here we check every line to see if it's the desired view header we want. Remember that we need to add the brackets <> and 'l' between the room name and the keyword to create the full string, like it's stored in the text file.

```
        // Check if the current line is the desired header
        if(strLine == "<" + room.strCurrentRoom + "|" + strLook + ">")
        {
```

If we get here, we just read in the right header (<Room1|jacket>). Now let's read in the description. Just like the room description, we do a getline() that reads all the characters of the description until we hit an asterisk (*) character, which tells us we are at the end of the description.

```
            getline(fin, room.strLookDescription, '*');

            // Leave this function since we read the description.
            return;
        }
    }
}
```

That's it for version two. Though it might have seemed like a lot of code was added in this version, in retrospect, it was really very similar to the code we added in the previous version. The next addition to our text adventure gets a bit more complicated. Be sure you understand and are comfortable with the previous ones before moving on.

Version 3—Adding Player and Enemy Data

This stands as the final version for our text adventure. Note that this does not mean you are done, just that you can now get started (in a sense). Don't forget to check near the end of this chapter for some further enhancements that can be done to make it a more robust game.

Still adding on to the previous version, a couple of new functions and classes will be added to our code. The new additions will allow us to battle monsters and define an actual player. I have moved the classes and our room structure, along with all the #defines and #includes into a header file called Main.h. Our Main.cpp now includes Main.h to reference this data.

Adding More Defines and Monster/Player Classes

First let's go over the new #defines that have been added. These #defines are exactly like the STILL_PLAYING and QUIT defines, except we will be using them for the outcome of fighting the monsters. New #defines were created to be more descriptive than "true" and "false." After a battle is over, one of these constants will be returned from AttackPlayer().

```
#define PLAYER_STILL_ALIVE          1
#define PLAYER_IS_DEAD              0
```

This is our newly created player class. An instance of this class is created in Main.cpp, which holds the player's information. We created a bunch of data access functions to set and query the player's data. The functions should be very straightforward in what they do. Though there isn't much in the player class now, you most likely will want to add more functions for the player's inventory, party members, and so on.

```
class CPlayer {
public:
    void SetName(string strPlayerName) { m_strName = strPlayerName; }
    void SetHealth(int playerHealth) { m_health = playerHealth; }
    void SetWeapon(string strWeapon) { m_strWeapon = strPlayerWeapon; }
    void SetDamage(int playerDamage) { m_damage = playerDamage; }

    string GetName() const    { return m_strName; }
    string GetWeapon() const    { return m_strWeapon; }
```

```
    int GetDamage() const        { return m_damage; }
    int GetHealth() const        { return m_health; }

private:
    string m_strName;      // This stores the player's name
    int m_health;          // This stores the player's health
    string m_strWeapon;    // This stores the name of the player's weapon
    int m_damage;          // This stores the weapon's inflicted damage
};
```

This is our newly created monster class. An instance of this class is created in our tRoom structure. A bunch of data access functions were created to set and query the monster's data. The functions should be very straightforward in what they do. Though there isn't much in the monster class now, you will add more functions for the monster's AI, inventory, and so on.

```
class CMonster {
public:
    void SetName(string strMonsterName) { m_strName = strMonsterName; }
    void SetAttackMessage(string strMessage)
        { m_strAttackMessage = strMessage; }
    void SetHealth(int monsterHealth) { m_health = monsterHealth; }
    void SetDamage(int monsterDamage) { m_damage = monsterDamage; }

    string GetName() const { return m_strName;      }
    string GetAttackMessage() const        { return m_strAttackMessage; }
    int GetHealth() const { return m_health;              }
    int GetDamage() const { return m_damage;       }

private:
    string m_strName;            // This stores the monster's name
    string m_strAttackMessage;   // The monster's attack message
    int m_health;                // This stores the monster's health
    int m_damage;                // This stores the weapon's damage
};
```

Notice the "C" in front of both the CMonster and CPlayer class definitions. This is a popular convention to show that these are classes. Also, the "m_" prefix before each of the class member variables indicates that these variables are member variables. This way, when you are writing code inside of a member function definition, it's obvious which variables are part of the class and which are passed in or local. Once again, I would like to reiterate that this convention is encouraged, but if it makes you want to vomit or kill people, you can pick a convention and stick to it. It's good to keep in mind that conventions, like most reasonable rules, are made for the purpose of helping you, not hindering you.

One thing you will eventually want to add to these classes is a constructor and possibly a deconstructor. Though our classes are small and simple now, if you intend to go any further with this code, it will get quite complex. For starters, a basic constructor that initializes all the member variables would be appropriate.

Adding Our Final Additions to the Room Structure

Since we added some new classes to our game, there also needs to be some extra data added to our tRoom structure. The first variable is an instance of the CMonster class. Remember that our game design specifies that there is only one monster per room. You will want to make an array of CMonsters if you want more than one. The bMonsterInRoom boolean tells us whether there is a monster in the room to attack. This variable will be explained more later on in "Reading in the Monster Block" section. Ideally, you eventually want to turn the tRoom structure into a CRoom class that has all the room functions as member functions and also uses member variables.

```
struct tRoom
{
    ...
    string strLookDescription;

    CMonster monster;            // Our monster data for this room
    bool bMonsterInRoom;    // This tells us if a monster is in the room
};
```

A few improvements were added to our main() function. Now that there is a player structure, we need to fill in its data. This information is stored at the top of the game file. The GetPlayerInfo() function will be used to locate and read in this data, which will be covered later in "Reading in the Player Data." Like the instance of our tRoom structure, the instance of our CPlayer class is declared locally in our main() and then is passed down to each function where appropriate.

Finishing Up Our *main()*

The final notable enhancement to our main() function is the call to AttackPlayer(). In our main loop, this is called to see if the player perhaps died from a monster in battle. It returns either PLAYER_IS_ALIVE or PLAYER_IS_DEAD. You'll notice that it's called every frame, but what if there isn't a monster in the room? Well, there is a check at the top of the function to return PLAYER_IS_ALIVE if there isn't a monster around. Ideally, the check could be outside of the function so that it doesn't have to enter the function, but I chose to stick to a cleaner main(), especially since it's a small text adventure. As your main game loop gets larger, you will want to create another function that encapsulates it all to avoid a cluttered main().

If there is a monster in the room, either the player or it will fight to the death. The winner of the battle is determined by the return value of AttackPlayer(). If the player is dead, the while loop is broken and we quit the game.

```
int main()
{
    // Read in the game file and make sure we found it
    ...

    // Create an instance of our player class to hold our player's data
    CPlayer player;

    // Since the player data is at the very beginning, we can just read
    // it in immediately without any searching.
    GetPlayerInfo(fin, player);

    // Initialize the flag that tells us if there is a monster in the
    // room.  This should most likely be done in a constructor.
    room.bMonsterInRoom = false;

    // Read in the starting room name, read in that room block, then
    // display the first room's description to the screen like normal.
    ...

    // Start our main game loop
    while(1)
    {
        // Get the input from the user and check game status
        if(GetInput(fin, room, player) == QUIT)
            break;              // Quit the main loop
```

Once again, this function is called to handle the battle scenes. If there is a monster in the current room, this function will loop continuously until either the player or the monster is dead. If you die, the game is over; otherwise, you keep on truckin'.

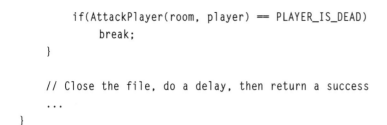

```
        if(AttackPlayer(room, player) == PLAYER_IS_DEAD)
            break;
    }

    // Close the file, do a delay, then return a success
    ...
}
```

Reading in the Monster Block

To have a monster in our game, it needs to have data. That data is read in from the game text file in the GetMonsterInfo() function. The parameters passed in are the file stream, the room, and name of the monster. One of the differences between getting the monster info and getting the look descriptions is that the monsters have three blocks of information. Let's look at a full monster block:

- <Right|goblin>   This is the header we search for.
- <Health> 125   This is the health of the monster.
- <Damage> 12   This is the damage that the monster inflicts on the player.
- <Attack> The goblin claws your face.*   This is the attack message.

If you know how to read in a room block, this works just the same. As with the look header, we check for the monster header in the exact same way. A sample header would be as follows:

<Forest2|goblin>

The room name is Forest2 and the monster's is goblin. In steps, it becomes the following:

```
"<" + room.strCurrentRoom + "|" + strMonsterName + ">" =
"<room.strCurrentRoom|strMonsterName>" =
"<Forest2|goblin>"
```

Take a look at the code that handles all this:

```
void GetMonsterInfo(ifstream &fin, tRoom &room, string strMonsterName)
{
    // Create a string to hold each line that we read in
    string strLine = "";

    // Reset the file stream to the beginning of the file
    fin.seekg(NULL,ios::beg);
    fin.clear();
```

It seems like a good idea to set the name of the new monster here because we obviously know there is a monster in the current room now, and we have it's name.

```
// Set the monster's name
room.monster.SetName(strMonsterName);

// Read in every line of the file until we reach the end
while(getline(fin, strLine, '\n'))
            {

    // Check if the current line read in is the monster header
    if(strLine=="<" + room.strCurrentRoom+"|"+strMonsterName + ">")
    {
        // Create an integer to store the health and damage
        int data = 0;

        // Read in the health of the monster
        fin >> strLine >> data;

        // Set the health of our monster
        room.monster.SetHealth(data);

        // Read in and assign the monster's damage
        fin >> strLine >> data;
        room.monster.SetDamage(data);

        // Read past the "<Attack>" word
        fin >> strLine;

        // Read the attack description until we hit a '*'
        getline(fin, strLine, '*');

        // Assign the attack message to our monster
        room.monster.SetAttackMessage(strLine);

        // Stop reading from the file and quit this function
        return;
    }
  }
}
```

Reading in the Player Data

To read in the player data, our `GetPlayerInfo()` function is used. Unlike the other `Get*Info()` functions, we don't need to search for the player data because we know that it's right at the beginning of the file. Just like every block of data in the game file, the player data is read in the same. You will want to read past the first word and then store what's after it.

```
void GetPlayerInfo(ifstream &fin, CPlayer &player)
{
    // Create some local variables to store data from the file
    string strWord;
    int data = 0;

    // Reset the file stream pointer to the beginning of the file
    fin.seekg(NULL,ios::beg);
    fin.clear();

    // Read in the player's name
    fin >> strWord >> strWord;

    // Set the player's name by its data access member function
    player.SetName(strWord);

    // Store the first word, then use the integer to store the health.
    fin >> strWord >> data;

    // To set the player's health, pass it into SetHealth()
    player.SetHealth(data);

    // Read in and store the player's weapon name
    fin >> strWord >> strWord;
    player.SetWeapon(strWord);

    // Read in and store the player's damage
    fin >> strWord >> data;
    player.SetDamage(data);
}
```

Handling the New *Status* Command

When the player types "status", DisplayPlayer() will be called to print out the player's details. Notice that the data access functions are being used instead of player.strName. This might seem silly now, but it is a safer way to program. A const is also put in front of the parameter CPlayer &player to ensure that we don't accidentally change anything. References are being used so that the player structure is not copied onto the stack; a pointer or "reference" to the memory address of the data is used instead.

```
void DisplayPlayer(const CPlayer &player)
{
    // Display our player's status to the screen
    cout << "Name: "   << player.GetName()   << endl;
    cout << "Health: " << player.GetHealth() << endl;
    cout << "Weapon: " << player.GetWeapon() << endl;
    cout << "Damage: " << player.GetDamage() << endl;
}
```

Speaking of the status command, let's add the code to our GetInput() function to allow this to happen in the game.

```
int GetInput(ifstream &fin, tRoom &room, CPlayer &player)
{
    // Display the prompt and read in the input
    ...

    ...
    // Check if the user typed "status"
    else if(strInput == "status")
    {
        // Display the player's current status
        DisplayPlayer(player);
    }
    ...
}
```

Reading in the New Section in Our Room Block

With a new <enemy> section added to our room block, more data will need to be read in each time the player enters a new room. This new section is read just like the room names in each direction:

```
<enemy> goblin
```

We will read past the first word and then read and store the next word, `goblin`. When there is not a monster in the room, `None` will substitute for the monster's name. Once it's determined whether there is a monster in the room, we need to read in its data immediately afterward because he is probably going to clobber us. The following is the code that needs to be added to our `GetRoomInfo()` function to read in the new section in our room block.

```
void GetRoomInfo(ifstream &fin, tRoom &room)
{
    // Go to the beginning of the file and set up local variables
    ...

    while(getline(fin, strLine, '\n'))
    {
        if(strLine == strRoom)
        {
            // Read in the standard room block information
            ...

            // Read in the monsters name, if any
            fin >> strTemp >> strTemp;

            // Check If there was no monster in the room
            if(strTemp == "None")
            {
                // Set our monster flag to false and return
                room.bMonsterInRoom = false;
                return;
            }

            // We must have a monster in the room
            room.bMonsterInRoom = true;
```

After we know that there is a monster in this room, we then need to search for the monster header and read in its info. The file stream, room structure, and header are passed in to our `GetMonsterInfo()` function.

```
            // Find the monster header and read in its info
            GetMonsterInfo(fin, room, strTemp);
        }
    }
}
```

Writing the Battle Code

This next function is probably the most complicated function in this program. To simplify the code so that no one gets lost, the battle sequence is *not* random and does *not* take off random damages. Though this would have been pretty easy to add, I chose to leave it out. It will give you something to do yourself that isn't too hard. Let's go over some pseudo code for the algorithm used for battle:

```
while(there is a monster in the room)
{
    The monster attacks first and subtracts its weapon damage from the player's
    health

    The player then attacks and subtracts his/her weapon damage from the monster's
    health

    Now we check:

            if(the player is dead)
                we return PLAYER_IS DEAD and the game is over

    else if(the monster is dead)
        display a victory message and set bMonsterInRoom to false
}
```

If the player and monster are still alive, it will continue to loop until at least one of them is dead. Pretty simple, huh? It doesn't get any easier than that. It would be fun to see what you guys come up with for your fighting sequences.

```
int AttackPlayer(tRoom &room, CPlayer &player)
{
    // Check if there is a monster in the room
    while(room.bMonsterInRoom)
    {
        // Before the monster attacks, display its attack message
        cout << room.monster.GetAttackMessage() << endl;
```

Subtract the monster's damage from our health because we just got hit. The result of player.GetHealth() - room.monster.GetDamage() will then be passed in to SetHealth(), which will change the player's health to a lower number.

```
        // Take health from the player, according to the monster stats
        player.SetHealth(player.GetHealth() -room.monster.GetDamage());
```

```cpp
        // Display our current health
        cout << "You now have " << player.GetHealth()
             << " health." << endl;

        // Display our attack message before we pound the enemy
        cout << "You attack the " << room.monster.GetName()
             << " with your "      << player.GetWeapon() << " for "
             << player.GetDamage() << " hit points!"    << endl;

        // Subtract our damage from the monster's health
        room.monster.SetHealth(room.monster.GetHealth() -
                               player.GetDamage() );

        // Display the monster's status
        cout << "It now has " << room.monster.GetHealth()
             << " health." << endl;

        // Our health is less than 0 (we died)...
        if(player.GetHealth() <= 0)
        {
          // Display a defeating message and quit the game
          cout << "You are dead!" << endl;
          return PLAYER_IS_DEAD;
        }
        // Else if the monster is dead...
        else if(room.monster.GetHealth() <= 0)
        {
            // Display our victory and set bMonsterInRoom to false
            cout << "You killed the "
                 << room.monster.GetName() << "!" << endl;

            room.bMonsterInRoom = false;
        }

        // Put in a delay between each round
        Sleep(1500);
    }

    // The monster didn't stand a chance, so return our ALIVE define
    return PLAYER_STILL_ALIVE;
}
```

That's it! You now have the knowledge to start on your own text adventure! Do you feel that funny feeling in your tummy? If so, you're pretty weird . . . It won't take you long to get bored of the game as we currently have it, so don't delay in building on it to create your own text adventure masterpiece.

Summary and Review

Though it seems as if I repeated myself many times throughout this chapter, let's go over everything we accomplished here. The point of this chapter was to show you how to set up a simple modular text adventure. Many times, we need to be shown how to do things in order to get our brain started; that is what was intended. Just remember, don't expect a sweet game from our final version. It should just be used as a base to start from. You will want to either work off of the code or just use some of the ideas to create your own from scratch.

This chapter broke up the task of creating a text adventure into three versions. The first version showed how to allow the player to walk around the world with collision detection. To store the world, a text file was used that had room blocks with all the pertinent information for that room. A room or area was where the player currently resided in the game. Each room had a section for north, south, east, and west that gave a room name that was off in that area. If there was no room in that direction, it was replaced with "None." This allowed us to know whether the character was able to move in that direction. Also in the first version, the player was able to type "help" to get a list of available commands.

The second version of our game added an option to view things in the room. A new section was added to the room block, giving the number of viewable things and their names. When the player tried to look at something, the name of the thing being looked at was first checked in our list; if found, the description of the viewed item was read from our game file and displayed to the screen. This required us to add the view command to the player's available options.

A text adventure isn't complete without some threat or resistance, and this is why our final version added the capability to fight monsters. Once again, a new section was added to our room block, storing the name of the monster in the room; otherwise, it would have "None." At the time the player entered the room, the monster's data was loaded and then initiated an attack. The battle continued until someone died. If the player died, the game would be over.

Let me now try to speak to some of your thoughts or questions:

What if I don't understand all of this stuff?

That's okay! You don't need to understand it all right now. As long as you can add to it, you should be fine. Once you start to build on it, many things will come together in your mind, and it will become clearer to you. If you don't understand most of it, I suggest starting with a simple game first. Try a simple number-guessing game and then work up from there.

Is this the only way to do this?

Absolutely not. The intent of this chapter was not so much to give you source code to use but to give you ideas as to how you might be able to build a text adventure yourself. As your game gets bigger, many more things will need to be added and moved around (or possibly redone, for that matter). Don't stress out about the code; just make sure you understand the basic concepts of how the game functions. There is a famous saying that if you ask six programmers how to code something, you are likely to get six different answers.

I can't imagine ever thinking of something like this on my own. Am I doomed to program-ming databases in a damp cellar?

I doubt it. (Well, unless maybe that's where your computer is.) Programming takes a colossal amount of devoted time. If you stick with it, you are bound to get better. Some people get better faster than others. I figure that, as long as you enjoy it enough to continue doing it, you usually can't go wrong. In my case, it took me a while to get the hang of it, but one day—after intense study and dedication—my brain just popped into the right place. From then on it only got better.

Can I call you if I need help on creating something for my game?

Probably not.

If not, can I call your mom?

I guess so . . . But she wouldn't be able to help you very much.

Well, where can I go for help then?

If you check out any of the popular sites like **www.GameDev.net**, **www.GameTutorials.com**, or **www.FlipCode.com**, they have great message boards being used by thousands of people who have gone through the same things you have and would love to help.

Where to Go from Here

Obviously, this game lacks much. Let's take a look at a list of things that could or should be added to make it more robust. The player should be able to ...

- Pick up and drop objects
- Save/load games
- Encrypt game files or save in binary
- Add party members
- Add NPCs (nonplayer characters: villagers, townsmen, and so on)
- Add music (FMOD or BASS libraries, which support most formats)
- Add a menu system that allows for mouse navigation
- Add intelligent monsters (shy, aggressive, random)
- Add roaming monsters that don't stay in the same room
- Add a Lose keyword like End for rooms that lose the game
- Add action IDs to the view and monster blocks
- Add trap doors that bring you to another room
- Add networking for multiplayer games such as MUDDs

These are just some ideas to get the juices flowing in that nerdy brain of yours. I would like to comment on some of these, starting with the save game options. This is one of the most popular options that people want to add to their game. To do this, I suggest first creating a file like <playername>.sav to holds the player's data. For instance, the basics would be:

```
<Name> Dartanion
<CurrentRoom> Temple
<Health>  255
<Weapon> Axe
<Damage> 45
<Inventory> 6 potion potion key3 pouch muffin muffin
```

This data would be at the top of the save file for the player. You wouldn't need to store the objects/weapon/armor information in the save file, just the name. When the player is loaded, it would then fill in that information by searching the original game file for that name. Next, whenever the player picks up an object or kills a monster, have it write some information about that room block:

```
<Corridor>
```

```
<enemy> none
<objects> 2 shield bow
```

If the player then picks up one of the objects or a monster walks into the room, it could say:

```
<Corridor>
<enemy> troll
<objects> 1 bow
```

This means that, before you write any new room block data to the player's save game file, be sure to first check whether it's already there.

Another important part of the game that I want to mention is the sound/music. You can go to **www.FMOD.org** and get an excellent library that allows you to play almost every popular sound format there is. You can find some tutorials on how to use this library at **www.GameTutorials.com**.

The last item I thought I should talk about is the action IDs. Let's say you want to have something special happen after you talk to someone or enter a room. For instance, if you talk to the Mage in the temple, you want a door to now open somewhere in the game. Possibly, you also might want to have it trigger someone else to tell you something new. This can be done with action numbers. You would want to add an `<action>` section to the NPC (nonplayer character) section and the room block section. It could look like this:

```
<action> 152
```

You could have an array like this in your game:

```
bool g_actionArray[MAX_ACTIONS];
```

When the player comes across an action number, that number is then used to index into the `g_actionArray[]` and sets the index to `true`. If you want to have something happen only if a certain action is set, you just need to query whether that needed action number in the global array is `true`. Perhaps then you would want to also add a `<neededAction>` section to the NPC block.

For cases that require a lot of special code, you would create a function as follows:

```
void HandleAction(int action);
```

All actions that are found could be passed in to this function to handle special things such as cut scenes. This should be enough to get your mind on the right page.

Conclusion

Hopefully the ideas discussed here were helpful enough to get your mind thinking in the right direction. I suggest that you try to re-create the game from scratch with your own code, just using the theory of how it works to guide you. If you intend to build on the base I provided, you might find yourself stuck because you didn't create the original code, and you might not understand it all.

In addition to my day job as a game programmer, I also am the co-Web host of **www.GameTutorials.com**. Our site has well over 200 tutorials that teach C or C++ from the ground up, all the way to advanced 3-D concepts. If you find that this game was too easy for you, there are enough tutorials on the site to get you where you want to go.

TRICK 8

Sound and Music: Introducing WAV and MIDI into Your Game

Heather "felisandria" Holland, GameDev.net, www.gamedev.net

Introduction

Sound and music are the polish that makes your game look professional and complete. Particle effects, sprites, and rendering might look spiffy, but the player won't be entirely immersed unless he can hear the rounds firing into the creepily moaning creature currently making a virtual attempt at eating his brain. In this chapter, we're going to look at some of the file formats used to store sound and music data, and we'll examine some relatively simple ways to turn that data into what you hear coming out of the speakers.

We are going to start off by discussing the WAV and MIDI file formats and how to glean from them the information you will need to turn those bytes into something playable. Once we are familiar with the data involved, we will look at a range of techniques from the very simple Win32 API and MCI versions to the more complex DirectSound and DirectMusic libraries. So, without further ado, let's dive directly into the data files and take a look at what we start out with . . . a RIFF file.

A Quick Overview of WAV

WAV is the most common sound file format for Windows. As with most standard Windows multimedia files, it generally uses a Resource Interchange File Format (RIFF). We're going to take a quick look at what a native Windows WAV file looks like. You probably won't need any of this information if you're doing very simple sound work, but if you decide you want to put all your sound files in one big data file to be clever, you will need to know the file format to do that properly.

All RIFF files start off with an 8-byte RIFF header, indicating that they are RIFF files and giving the file length. If you open a WAV file in Notepad or Visual Studio, you will see the letters "RIFF" followed by a 4-byte (DWORD) indication of how long the file is, minus the 8-byte header. The next 4 bytes give the type; for a WAV file, this will be "WAVE." Now that it has been established that this is, indeed, a RIFF file and the length and type of RIFF file have been established, the remainder of the file is broken into chunks. Each chunk begins with an 8-byte header that indicates the type of chunk (format, data, and so on) and the length of the chunk, not counting the chunk header. We're going to look specifically at format and data chunks because those are the important ones for our purposes.

The Format Chunk

In WAV files, there must always be a format chunk before the data chunk. The format chunk can be recognized by the "fmt " (note the space) in the first 4 bytes of the chunk header. The second 4 bytes are a DWORD indicating the length of this format chunk, not counting the 8-byte chunk header. The rest of the format chunk can be read as follows:

```
struct {
          WORD    wFormatTag;
          WORD    wChannels;
          DWORD   dwSamplesPerSec;
          DWORD   dwAvgBytesPerSec;
          WORD    wBlockAlign;
}
```

- `wFormatTag` This gives the WAV format category of the data chunk, indicating the compression type. If `wFormatTag` is 1, no compression is being used (normal Pulse Code Modulation). If compression is used, additional information will be appended to the format and in a fact chunk to allow for appropriate decompression. Too many types of compression are available to list them here. Most of the WAV files you use will not be compressed, especially if you produce them yourself.

- `wChannels` 1 for mono, 2 for stereo. Keep in mind that DirectSound is much better at handling mono waveforms.

- `dwSamplesPerSec` The sampling frequency of the waveform. Commonly used values are 11025, 22050, and 44100. Frequencies other than the three common ones are allowed but are not encouraged.

- `dwAvgBytesPerSec` The average bytes per second for transferal of the waveform.

- `wblockAlign` The size of a single sample frame, in bytes. This can be calculated using the following formula:

  ```
  wChannels • (wBitsPerSample % 8)
  ```

For a 16-bit mono waveform, the number would be 2 (4 bytes required per block); for stereo 16-bit waveforms, it would be 4.

The Data Chunk

The ID for a data chunk is "data," found in the first 4 bytes of the chunk header. The second 4 bytes, as always, are the chunk size not counting the 8 bytes of header. From there until the end of the chunk (which you can find by looking at the handy chunk size indicator), the rest is the actual waveform.

A Look at MIDI

MIDI files (.mid) are broken into chunks like WAV files. MIDI files contain a header chunk followed by track chunks. Each instrument, voice, staff, and so on, has its own track. Unlike WAV files, which involve sampling, MIDI first specifies the voice or instrument to be used on a track and then gives information such as note on, note off, pressure, and so on . . . much like a music box or player piano records notes.

The MIDI File Header

The MIDI file header starts with the 4 byte "MThd," which identifies this as a MIDI file, followed by 4 bytes giving the length of the header not counting the 8-byte header indicator. The header length will always be 6 bytes.

In the 6 bytes of the header, the first 2 bytes describe file format. File formats are as follows:

- **0—single track.** Only one track to worry about.
- **1—multiple tracks, synchronous.** Several tracks, all starting at the same time.
- **2—multiple tracks, asynchronous.** Several tracks, potentially starting at different times.

The second 2 bytes give the number of tracks. The third pair of bytes gives the number of ticks per quarter note.

Track Chunks

Track chunks start with "MTrk" and contain MIDI events (as previously described). Each MIDI event consists of 4 bits of command identifier (note on, note off, and so on) followed by 4 bits that indicate on which MIDI channel it should be executed. In addition to "normal" MIDI events, meta-events can be present. Meta-events contain information such as key changes, text (to allow a description to be physically inserted within the file), lyrics, track instrument names, cues, markers, tempo, and other information not directly related to track events. I could spend an entire chapter on everything a MIDI file can contain, but I won't . . . we need to play them!

Let's Play: Simply Win32

The simplest way to get sound and music in your games is merely to use the Win32 APIs. Granted, they have some glaring problems that we'll discuss later, but if all you really need is the occasional sound—and perhaps a little MIDI tune playing in the background—Win32 API sound will work.

"How simple is it?" you ask. Well, to play a WAV file, all you have to do is include winmmsystem.h and then use this function:

```
BOOL PlaySound(
      LPCSTR pszSound, // specifies the sound to play
      HMODULE hmod, // handle to the executable containing the resource
      DWORD fdwSound // control flags
);
```

The pszSound can be an alias to a system sound, a resource, or a WAV file, depending on the flag settings in fdwSound. The handle hmod is only required if you are using a resource; otherwise, it should be NULL. If you want to use a system alias, fdwSound should contain SND_ALIAS. If the sound is part of a resource contained in the executable, fdwSound should contain SND_RESOURCE. If you just want to use a WAV file, fdwSound should use the SND_FILENAME flag. If none of these flags is specified, PlaySound will use the pszSound first to search the WIN.INI for a matching alias, then to search for a matching resource, and then it will attempt to use it as a file name.

When trying to find your sound, PlaySound will search (in this order) the current directory, the Windows directory, the Windows system directory, the directories listed in the Path environment variable, and then the list of directories mapped in a network. If for some reason PlaySound is unable to find a sound that matches the pszSound, it will play the default system event sound. If you do not want PlaySound to play the default system event sound when it cannot find the specified pszSound, SND_NODEFAULT will instruct it to merely return silently.

fdwSound contains several other useful flags in addition to the ones used to specify the source of the sound. Two of the more important flags are SND_SYNC and SND_ASYNC. When SND_SYNC is used, PlaySound will wait until the sound is played entirely before it returns. SND_ASYNC returns immediately once the sound starts playing. In general, it is best to use SND_ASYNC because it will allow subsequent sounds to play immediately, preempting currently playing sounds. Using SND_SYNC will cause sounds to queue up and will likely make sounds that are the result of an event in your game appear to be very out of place. If you don't want currently playing sounds to yield to more recently triggered sound events but you do want your sounds to play asynchronously, using SND_NOSTOP will cause the newer sound events to return FALSE without playing anything.

Another interesting flag is SND_PURGE. Rather than playing a sound, SND_PURGE stops all sounds specified by pszSound. If pszSound is NULL, all sounds are stopped. If you want a sound to loop repeatedly, simply use the SND_LOOP flag.

Playing MIDI Using Win32

Win32 can play MIDI using the media control interface (MCI) contained in the Software Development Kit (SDK). Keep in mind that this is dependent on your sound card.

MCI is a generic interface for multimedia devices and is used to both record and play. We are going to look primarily at the commands necessary to play MIDI using MCI, but keep in mind that MCI is capable of quite a bit more than simply playing MIDI files. MCI fires notification messages when it encounters certain events, such as reaching the end of a MIDI file.

CAUTION

MIDI files sound different with different sound cards because the voices are generally stored on the card itself and the MCI commands use those voices. This is unlike DirectX, which emulates the Roland sound fonts.

The following is a function I wrote for a little peg game. It wasn't complex enough to use DirectX (the graphics were all GDI), and I wanted it to work on NT, so I used the MCI MIDI player.

```
void CGameBoard::PlayMusic()
{
  UINT deviceID;
  DWORD dwReturn;
  MCI_OPEN_PARMS openParms;
  MCI_PLAY_PARMS playParms;
  char buff[100];
```

```
openParms.lpstrDeviceType = "sequencer";
openParms.lpstrElementName = "pegmusic.mid";
if (dwReturn = mciSendCommand(NULL, MCI_OPEN,
            MCI_OPEN_TYPE|MCI_OPEN_ELEMENT|MCI_WAIT,
            (DWORD)(LPVOID)&openParms))
{
  mciGetErrorString(dwReturn, buff, sizeof(buff));
  MessageBox(buff, "ERROR", MB_OK|MB_ICONEXCLAMATION);
  return;
}
deviceID = openParms.wDeviceID;
playParms.dwCallback = (DWORD)m_hWnd;
if (dwReturn = mciSendCommand(deviceID, MCI_PLAY, MCI_NOTIFY,
                        (DWORD)(LPVOID)&playParms))
  return;
m_deviceID = deviceID;
m_playParms = playParms;
}
```

As you can see, it's relatively straightforward. The MCI commands open the MIDI device (your sound card) and use it to play the MIDI file (in my case, pegmusic.mid).

MCI_OPEN_PARMS is the structure that gives necessary information for the MCI_OPEN command to initialize the MIDI device. As you can see, the MIDI device is specified by setting the lpstrDeviceType to "sequencer." The MIDI file that we are initializing it to play is specified in lpstrElementName.

The generic MCI send command is as follows:

```
MCIERROR mciSendCommand(
      MCIDEVICEID IDDevice, // the device to send this to, NULL for MCI_OPEN
      UINT uMsg, // the message to send
      DWORD fdwCommand, // command flags
      DWORD dwParam // command parameters
);
```

With these specified, we send the command to initialize as follows:

```
mciSendCommand(
      NULL,  // IDDevice is always NULL for an MCI_OPEN command
      MCI_OPEN,  // we are initializing the specified device
      MCI_OPEN_TYPE|MCI_OPEN_ELEMENT|MCI_WAIT,  // command flags
```

```
        (DWORD)(LPVOID)&openParms // These are the parameters we specified above
);
```

The MCI_OPEN_TYPE flag specifies that the type name or constant can be found in the lpstrDeviceType member of the MCI_OPEN_PARMS structure. The flag MCI_OPEN_ALIAS could be used instead if lpstrAlias were being used to specify the device, or MCI_OPEN_TYPE_ID could be used if the device were specified in the lpstrDeviceType member. MCI_OPEN_ELEMENT states that there is a file name in the lpstrElementName. If the driver is to interpret the value in lpstrElementName as something internal to the driver, MCI_OPEN_ELEMENT_ID should be used instead, though with MIDI it is doubtful that you will do so. MCI_WAIT specifies that the open operation should finish before the function returns.

Now that we have initialized the device, we are ready to send the command to play. MCI commands are generic, so the command to play and the command to initialize look very similar. Because we want the music to loop, we are going to set up a notification message that will fire when the song ends. We are going to put our MCI notification handlers in the game window's message handlers, so we specify the handle to the window as the dwCallback of the MCI_PLAY_PARMS. We send the MCI command as follows:

```
mciSendCommand(
        deviceID,  // the device ID we initialized in MCI_OPEN
        MCI_PLAY,  // specify that this is a play command
        MCI_NOTIFY,  // instruct MCI to notify when the song finishes playing
        (DWORD)(LPVOID)&playParms  // the play parameters we gave
);
```

We did not specify MCI_WAIT this time because we want the game to work while the music plays. The song has started playing; it won't bother us until the notification that it's run out of MIDI to play. You will note that we stored the device ID and the play parameters for later use.

But, you say, what if I want to shut my music off?

Well, that's quite simple. All you need to do is tell MCI to shut that device off. You can specify which device to shut off in the first parameter if you want, but personally, this is the only thing I'm using MCI for, so I'm just going to shut MCI off wholesale:

```
mciSendCommand(MCI_ALL_DEVICE_ID, MCI_CLOSE, NULL, NULL);
```

This both stops and closes the initialized device. All you have to do to restart it is call your PlayMusic function to initialize the device and play the music again. Be sure to use this command to shut everything down when the user exits your game.

Let's look at the notification messages now so that we can restart the song when we are notified by MCI that it's run out of MIDI to play. I'm not going to tell you how to catch the notification message because, depending on whether you're using pure Win32 or MFC, it will change. I'm going to assume that you can handle any Windows messages that get fired at you. As you can see, you can catch several notification messages from MCI other than the "done" notification. I'm just going to handle restarting the music because the appropriate reaction to the examples I've given of a notification indicating failure or the playback being superseded is up to you.

```
LONG CGameBoard::OnMciNotify(UINT wFlags, LONG lDevId)
{
  MCI_PLAY_PARMS playParms;
  playParms.dwFrom = 0;
  switch(wFlags) {
    case MCI_NOTIFY_SUCCESSFUL:
      playParms.dwCallback = (DWORD)m_hWnd;
      mciSendCommand(lDevId, MCI_PLAY, MCI_NOTIFY|MCI_FROM,
                     (DWORD)(LPVOID)&playParms);
      break;
    case MCI_NOTIFY_FAILURE:
      // MCI has notified us of a failure.
      break;
    case MCI_NOTIFY_SUPERSEDED:
      // MCI has notified us that its play has been superseded.
      break;
  }
  return 0L;
}
```

The device has already been initialized and wasn't closed, so we don't have to perform the MCI_OPEN again. As you can see, the dwFrom value has been set to zero in the MCI_PLAY_PARMS. This ensures that the position in the MIDI file is set to the beginning so that we are ready to play it again. The device ID that is registering a successful completion message is given to us in the message, which is very handy. We make sure our MCI_PLAY_PARMS dwCallback value will still send notifications to this window, and then we send a command to start playing again. This time, to be sure that the song starts playing again in the right spot, we use the MCI_FROM flag to instruct MCI to use the dwFrom value in the play parameters.

Sound in DirectX

DirectSound uses DSound.lib when you include DSound.h. It can handle any number of recording formats, but it will help a great deal if you create or reformat all your sounds to have the same bits per sample and frequency. If you don't, DirectSound will have to convert all your samples to 22KHz 8-bit, which is both slow and likely to sound weird. DirectSound sounds best when using mono, so save some memory and storage space and use mono rather than stereo. DirectSound does have 3-D sound capability, but I won't be discussing the use of it here because it is very complicated and rarely used. The DirectX SDK documentation is a good reference if you are interested in attempting it.

As with most of DirectX, when using DirectSound, you will be talking to your sound card as an object. If you have more than one sound card, you can detect and enumerate them to get their globally unique identifiers (GUIDs) and pick which one you want to use as your sound device, but generally speaking, you will ignore the detection part and simply work with the default sound card for the system. Obviously, DirectSound will sound best on sound cards that have DirectSound drivers, but the DirectSound libraries can emulate the drivers. Granted, this will be a bit slower, but as long as your user has the DirectSound libraries, the sound card and the computer will still be able to make the noise you want.

As usual when using DirectX, to use DirectSound, you have to create the appropriate COM object and then get the interfaces you need. The objects and interfaces are as follows:

- IUnknown This is the usual base COM object.
- IDirectSound This is the main COM object, representing the sound card itself. If you want to represent more than one sound card, you will need an IDirectSound for each of them.
- IDirectSoundBuffer These represent the actual sounds and the mixing hardware. You will have one primary buffer and probably several secondary buffers. The primary buffer is the buffer that is playing and being mixed by either emulation or hardware (preferably hardware). Secondary buffers are sounds that are stored to be played using the primary buffer in the future, and they can be held either in the sound RAM on your sound card or in sys-

tem memory. You can make as many secondary buffers as you want until you run out of memory. When you want to play the sounds in the secondary buffers, you just feed them into the primary sound buffer.

- `IDirectSoundCapture` This interface is used to capture and record sounds. You probably won't need this unless you're doing something really special in your game that requires the player to actually talk through a microphone to the computer. I'm not going to cover this functionality because it's unlikely that you'll need it.

- `IDirectSoundNotify` This is another interface you probably won't use. It is set up to send notification messages to DirectSound in response to certain events, but in games, you will usually just want to ship the sound off to play and forget about it.

Now that we've looked at the objects and interfaces, let's get to the meat of it and look at the actual initialization and use of DirectSound.

Creating the DirectSound Object

I'm going to assume that most games will merely want to use the default sound card rather than checking the system to detect and enumerate multiple sound cards, setting up GUIDs for each of them, and deciding which one you want to use. So, let's look at `DirectSoundCreate`.

```
HRESULT DirectSoundCreate(
        LPGUID lpGuid, // guid of the sound card, use NULL to get the default device
        LPDIRECTSOUND •lpDS, // interface pointer to the object
        IUnknown FAR •pUnkOuter) // this will always be NULL
```

If we're using the default device, the call will look something like this:

```
LPDIRECTSOUND lpds;
  // DirectSound object pointer, you might want to store this to use later and
  eventually release when you shut down
if ( DirectSoundCreate(NULL, &lpds, NULL) != DS_OK )
{ // do your error handling }
```

Keep in mind that you are responsible for the `LPDIRECTSOUND` object you created, so when you are done using DirectSound entirely (probably around the time you shut your game down), be sure to use the following:

```
lpds->Release();
```

Cooperative Levels: Getting Along with Other Application Processes on Your System

Now that we have a DirectSound object, we need to decide whether or not we're going to make it play nice with other application processes on your system that might also want to use the sound card. There are four basic cooperation levels that range from having hardly any control over the primary buffer to having total control over the primary buffer. Microsoft generally suggests that you play nice and share with other applications, but you don't absolutely have to.

- DSSCL_NORMAL With this setting, DirectSound will create a default primary buffer set to 22KHz 8-bit stereo. DirectSound won't let you have permission to write to the primary buffer. Your game will be allowed to play sounds when it has focus but so will the other applications you might have running.

- DSSCL_PRIORITY This setting should be used if you want to be able to change the mixer settings of the primary buffer, change the primary buffer's data format, or do something complicated like in-memory compaction.

- DSSCL_EXCLUSIVE This setting gives you control over the primary buffer much like Priority mode, but your application must be in the foreground for any sound it makes to be heard.

- DSSCL_WRITEPRIMARY This gives you complete control over the primary buffer. It is the highest priority, and you probably won't use it unless you decide to write your own sound mixer. If you use this setting, you'd better know what you're doing because you can easily distort or even crash the sound for your application and whatever else you have running.

To set the cooperation level, call SetCooperativeLevel from the interface of your main DirectSound object. SetCooperativeLevel looks like this:

```
HRESULT SetCooperativeLevel(
        HWND hwnd, // handle of the window you're playing sounds for
        DWORD dwLevel ) // one of the above cooperative levels
```

If you want to set your game to the DDSCL_NORMAL cooperative level, it would look like this:

```
if ( lpds->SetCooperativeLevel( m_hWnd, DSSCL_NORMAL ) != DS_OK )
{ // do your error handling here }
```

Now we have our game all set up with a primary sound buffer initialized and a cooperative level set, and we're cleaning up after ourselves when we're done. It's time to use it to actually play something!

Working with Sound Buffers

Unless you set your cooperative level to DSSCL_WRITEPRIMARY, DirectSound will make you a primary sound buffer to use. As previously discussed, the default primary sound buffer is 22 KHz 8-bit stereo. If you want to use something other than this, you will need to set your cooperative level to at least DSSCL_PRIORITY and then set the data format you want for the primary buffer.

Secondary Sound Buffers

These buffers are the sounds you want to play, but they are not currently playing. Size doesn't matter as long as you have enough memory to hold them all in your sound RAM and system memory.

There are two basic types of secondary buffers: static and streaming. Generally speaking, you will be using static sound buffers because they are relatively small buffers that you will want to play again and again, such as the sound of a bullet being fired or a footstep. Streaming buffers are for the huge sound files you want to play, such as CD audio or a narrator voiceover of an intro movie. You wouldn't have enough room to store the entire sound file in a static buffer, so the data chunks are constantly read out of the file, streamed to the DirectSound buffer to play, and then released in a manner very similar to streaming audio you find on the Web. This keeps you from running out of memory when playing the truly huge sound files.

To make it easier to do static and streaming buffers, DirectSound uses circular buffering. Sounds are stored into circular buffers, and DirectSound keeps track of a play cursor and a write cursor. The *write cursor* is slightly ahead of the play cursor and is the point in the buffer in which new data is being read in from the file. The *play cursor* is the point at which the buffer is being played. This allows you to simultaneously read in and play your sounds. There will be a slight lapse between where it is reading and where it is playing, but you will never notice because you won't be looking directly at the memory. Most of the time, you won't care when using sound in games because you will probably store your sounds in a static buffer for a while before you find it necessary to play them.

Getting Ready to Use *CreateSoundBuffer()*

When you use `CreateSoundBuffer`, an `LPDIRECTSOUNDBUFFER` is created and initialized for your use. To make one, we must first fill a `DirectSoundBuffer` struct with the information DirectSound needs to properly create the buffer. The `LPDSBUFFERDESC` is as follows:

```
typedef struct
{
     DWORD dwSize; // size of this description buffer
     DWORD dwFlags; // creation control flags, as described below
     DWORD dwBufferBytes; // size of the actual sound buffer, in bytes
     DWORD dwReserved; // not currently used
     LPWAVEFORMATEX lpwfxFormat; // wave format, described below
} DSBUFFERDESC, *LPDSBUFFERDESC;
```

The creation control flags (`dwFlags`) that you can use to describe your buffer are as follows:

- `DSBCAPS_CTRLALL` This "all control" flag was removed from DirectX, but I mention it because some old code might contain it and be impossible to build as a result. I assume this was done because each control flag you add slows down the sound processing, so the DirectSound developers decided to make you specify each control flag.

- `DSBCAPS_CTRLDEFAULT` This default flag once specified `DSBCAPS_CTRLFREQUENCY_ DSBCAPS_CTRLPAN| DSBCAPS_CTRLVOLUME`, but like `DSBCAPS_CTRLALL`, it has been removed.

- `DSBCAPS_CTRLFREQUENCY` This gives the buffer frequency control capability.

- `DSBCAPS_CTRLPAN` This gives the buffer pan (left to right) control capability.

- `DSBCAPS_CTRLVOLUME` This gives the buffer volume control capability.

- `DSBCAPS_LOCDEFER` This allows the buffer to be assigned to a hardware or software resource when `AcquireResources` is called or at playtime.

- `DSBCAPS_LOCHARDWARE` This tells DirectX to use hardware mixing for this buffer.

- `DSBCAPS_LOCSOFTWARE` This tells DirectX to use software mixing for this buffer and place it in software memory.

- `DSBCAPS_PRIMARYBUFFER` This indicates that this buffer is the primary buffer. Unless you're sure you know what you're doing and are using `DSSCL_WRITEPRIMARY`, don't make one of these.

- `DSBCAPS_STATIC` This specifies that this is a static sound buffer.

The next structure we need to be concerned with to load our secondary buffer is the `WAVEFORMATEX` struct so that we can supply `CreateSoundBuffer()` with the proper `lpwfxFormat`. You will note that much of the information in the `WAVEFORMATEX` is contained in the RIFF file header as previously discussed, and that's where we will be getting it. The `WAVEFORMATEX` struct is as follows:

```
typedef struct
{
    WORD wFormatTag; // describes the wave file's format, you will usually use
  WAVE_FORMAT_PCM
    WORD nChannels; // number of audio channels involved, 1 for mono, 2 for stereo
    DWORD nSamplesPerSecond; // samples per second
    DWORD nAvgBytesPerSec; // average data rate in bytes per second
    WORD nBlockAlign; // (nAvgBytesPerSec/nSamplesPerSecond) • nChannels
    WORD wBitsPerSample; // bits per sample
    WORD cbSize; // don't need this, set it to 0
}WAVEFORMATEX;
```
]

Most of the information in this `WAVEFORMATEX` is information we will be getting directly from the file, so it's time to look at reading the file so we can populate it.

Reading WAV Files

Now that we know what we need for our sound buffer, let's take a look at extracting the information to set it up from a standard WAV file. Keep in mind the WAV RIFF discussion from earlier in this chapter. Using the information I gave you there, you could write your own parser, but why bother when Microsoft has been so kind as to write one for you? The multimedia I/O interface (MMIO) that will let you load WAV files can be used when you include mmsystem.h and link to winmm.lib.

As I showed you in the RIFF file, the format is based on chunks. We need to extract the header chunk and use the information there to set up our wave format parameters for the buffer. Then we need to get the data chunk for our actual sound buffer. MMIO is very handy for this because it is capable of parsing the wave format parameters for us.

MMIO Commands and Structures

A few basic MMIO structures are used to extract data from a file. The first one you will need to be familiar with is HMMIO, which is basically a handle to the file from which you intend to extract information. The file can be a standard file, an in-memory file, or part of a custom storage system.

The second important structure is MMIOINFO, which deals with the file itself. This specifies the type of file, the state of the file, and other information. You will not need to use this structure unless you are doing something special—such as making your own data files for all your sounds—that would require you to tell MMIO where to start reading for that particular chunk of RIFF information. Therefore, I will give a brief overview and suggest you look at the MSDN documentation if you need to do more. The MMIOINFO struct looks like this:

```
typedef struct {
    DWORD dwFlags; // flags specifying how the file was opened
    FOURCC fccIOProc; // four-character code defining the I/O procedure
    LPMMIOPROC pIOProc; // address of the file's I/O procedure
    UINT wErrorRet; // error value if mmioOpen fails
    HTASK hTask; // local I/O procedure handle
    LONG cchBuffer; // size of the file's I/O buffer in bytes
    HPSTR pchBuffer; // address of the file's I/O buffer
    HPSTR pchNext; // address of the next location to be read or written
    HPSTR pchEndWrite; // location 1 byte past the last location that can be
written
    LONG lBufOffset; // reserved
    LONG lDiskOffset; // current position in bytes from the beginning of the file
    DWORD adwInfo[4]; // state information of the I/O procedure
    DWORD dwReserved1; // reserved
    DWORD dwReserved2; // reserved
    HMMIO hmmio; // handle of the opened file
}  MMIOINFO;
```

The third important MMIO structure is MMCKINFO. This struct contains "chunk" information pertaining to the RIFF file you're working with. The MMCKINFO struct looks like this:

```
typedef struct {
    FOURCC ckid; // chunk identifier
    DWORD cksize; // size of the data in the chunk, not including the identifier or
chunk size
```

```
    FOURCC fccType; // format type as discussed in the RIFF file information
previously
    DWORD dwDataOffset; // offset of this chunk's data member from the beginning of
the file
    DWORD dwFlags; // either 0 or MMIO_DIRTY to indicate changes in chunk length
and the need to update
} MMCKINFO;
```

You probably noticed the FOURCC data type. As you read in the RIFF file synopsis, chunk headers, type indicators, and so on, are four letters long. FOURCC, or four-character code, is merely four characters' worth of space designed to hold those strings, such as "WAVE," "fmt " (note the space), "data," and others. To easily convert, we can use mmioFOURCC. If, for example, we wanted to convert "WAVE" to FOURCC, we would use the following:

```
FOURCC fccWAVE = mmioFOURCC('W','A','V','E');
```

Before we take a broader look at the actual parsing of it, let's look briefly at the MMIO commands we will be using to load things from the file. A few standard commands will let you move easily through the WAV file, parsing out the data you need and storing it for later use.

To begin parsing a file, we first need to open it. To do so, we use the following:

```
HMMIO mmioOpen(
    LPSTR szFilename, // file name or other indicator
    LPMMIOINFO, // unless you are doing something special, this should be NULL to
merely open the specified file
    DWORD dwOpenFlags, // flags for the open operation
};
```

There are several options for dwOpenFlags. The purpose for which the file is opened is specified by MMIO_READ, MMIO_WRITE, and MMIO_READWRITE. We will be opening the file to read the sound into a buffer, so we will use MMIO_READ. We will also use MMIO_ALLOCBUFF to specify that we want to use buffered I/O. The default buffer is 8k, which should be fine for our purposes. To open a sound file with the name specified by the CString fileName and to store the resulting MMIO handle, we would use the following:

```
hFile = mmioOpen(fileName.GetBuffer(0), NULL, MMIO_READ| MMIO_ALLOCBUF);
```

Once the file is open, several commands are used to move about the file and to extract the information from it. We will move around in the file using mmioDescend and mmioAscend and then extract the data using mmioRead. So, to get the information we need, we are going to use `mmioDescend`, `mmioRead`, and `mmioAscend` repeatedly until we have extracted everything we need to know.

To search for and descend into a RIFF chunk to get the information from it, we use `mmioDescend`, which looks like this:

```
MMRESULT mmioDescend(
        HMMIO hmmio, // MMIO file handle returned by mmioOpen
        LPMMCKINFO lpck, // information on the chunk we're looking for
        LPMMCKINFO lpckParent, // parent chunk in which to search for this chunk
        UINT wFlags // search flags
);
```

Appropriate values of `wFlags` include `MMIO_FINDCHUNK` to look for RIFF chunk identifiers, `MMIO_FINDLIST` to look for chunks with the LIST identifier, and `MMIO_FINDRIFF` to look for the RIFF identifier chunk. The first flag we will use is `MMIO_FINDRIFF` so that we can figure out where to start in the RIFF file we've opened. From there, we will use `MMIO_FINDCHUNK` to find chunks of the type we've specified in the `fccType` member of our `MMCKINFO` struct.

Now that we're in the chunk from which we want to extract information, we need to read the information, so we use `mmioRead`, which looks like this:

```
LONG mmioRead(
        HMMIO hmmio, // MMIO file handle returned by mmioOpen
        HPSTR pch, // address of the buffer to contain the data we read
        LONG cch // number of bytes to read from the file
);
```

The `pch` is simply an address, so we can read the file into any type of structure we want. Later on, we're going to read the file's information directly into a `WAVEFORMATEX` structure for the format and a buffer for the sound data.

Once we have the data we need from the chunk we're looking at, we need to ascend so that we can descend into another chunk. We use `mmioAscend` to do this, and it looks like the following:

```
MMRESULT mmioAscend(
                HMMIO hmmio, // MMIO file handle returned by mmioOpen
                LPMMCKINFO lpck, // this should match mmioDescend's lpck
                UINT wFlags // reserved, must be zero
);
```

Once we've done all the ascending and descending we need to do and have extracted all the data we need (or if we run into an error we can't recover from), it's time to close the file. We do this by using `mmioClose`, which looks like this:

```
MMRESULT mmioClose(
     HMMIO hmmio, // MMIO file handle returned by mmioOpen
     UINT wFlags // flags for close operation
);
```

For our purposes, `wFlags` will usually be 0. The other allowed value is `MMIO_FHOPEN`, which should be used if the file was opened using a non-MMIO file handle so that the standard file handle can remain open while only the MMIO file handle is closed.

Now that we've discussed the MMIO commands we will be using to extract data, it's time to look at an actual example of loading a WAV file using MMIO.

Using MMIO to Load a WAV

The following is an excerpt from a sound library I wrote. It takes a file name and uses it to load a `CSoundWAV`, which is a class I designed to represent an actual WAV file in a format that I can use with DirectSound.

```
CString       m_szFileName;  // name of the file to load
UINT          m_nResID;      // name of the resource to load
WAVEFORMATEX  *m_FormatEx;   // wave format info
void          *m_pByte;      // pointer to data, from disk = NULL

DWORD         m_dwLength;    // length of data
HMODULE       m_hModule;     // module to load resource from

BOOL          m_bResource;   // resource flag
BOOL          m_bValid;      // valid flag
```

As you can see, I store pertinent information such as the file name from which I loaded the buffer, the `WAVEFORMATEX` that will be read in the load from the file header, the data buffer that contains the actual sound, the data length, and a few other tidbits that might prove useful.

In parsing and loading the information contained in the WAV file, the following MMIO functions are used. The `CDSoundWAV`'s `Load` function is as follows. I have thoroughly commented it, and it's fairly self-explanatory. Using MMIO, we are finding and parsing the RIFF header information and storing it in our `WAVEFORMATEX`, as well as finding the actual sound data and storing it into a character array to be used later.

```cpp
BOOL CDSoundWAV::Load(CString fileName)
{
  m_szFileName = fileName;

  WAVEFORMATEX formatEx;

  DWORD bufSize1 = 0;
  DWORD bufSize2 = 0;

  // file handle
  HMMIO hFile;

  // chunks
  MMCKINFO primary;
  MMCKINFO secondary;
  // set up the primary chunk
  primary.ckid          = (FOURCC)0;
  primary.cksize        = 0;
  primary.fccType       = (FOURCC)0;
  primary.dwDataOffset  = 0;
  primary.dwFlags       = 0;
  // secondary needs the same stuff so copy it over
  secondary = primary;

  // buffers for storage
  UCHAR *tempBuffer = NULL;
  UCHAR *buffer1    = NULL;
  UCHAR *buffer2    = NULL;

  // open the file
  // check for validity
  if ((hFile = mmioOpen(fileName.GetBuffer(0), NULL, MMIO_READ|MMIO_ALLOCBUF)) ==
  NULL)
  {
    MessageBox(NULL, "Failed to open the .WAV file.", "Load Failed",
  MB_OK|MB_ICONEXCLAMATION);
    return FALSE;
  }
```

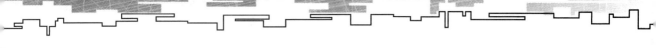

```
// find the WAV file notice
primary.fccType = mmioFOURCC('W','A','V','E');

// make sure it is a real WAV file
if (mmioDescend(hFile, &primary, NULL,MMIO_FINDRIFF))
{
  // doh! close it.
  mmioClose(hFile,0);
  MessageBox(NULL, ".WAV file corrupt.", "Load Failed",
MB_OK|MB_ICONEXCLAMATION);
  return FALSE;
}


// find the format section
secondary.ckid = mmioFOURCC('f','m','t',' ');
if (mmioDescend(hFile, &secondary, &primary, 0))
{
  // no format?  close it.
  mmioClose(hFile,0);
  MessageBox(NULL, ".WAV format corrupt.", "Load Failed",
MB_OK|MB_ICONEXCLAMATION);
  return FALSE;
}
// read WAV format info
if (mmioRead(hFile, (char•)&formatEx, sizeof(formatEx)) != sizeof(formatEx))
{
  // something else is wrong
  mmioClose(hFile,0);
  MessageBox(NULL, "Incorrect FormatEx size.", "Load Failed",
MB_OK|MB_ICONEXCLAMATION);
  return FALSE;
}
// make sure it's PCM format
if (formatEx.wFormatTag != WAVE_FORMAT_PCM)
{
  // so close, and yet so far...
  mmioClose(hFile,0);
  MessageBox(NULL, "Incorrect .WAV format.", "Load Failed",
MB_OK|MB_ICONEXCLAMATION);
  return FALSE;
```

```
}

// we have a format. time to get the data...
if(mmioAscend(hFile,&secondary,0))
{
  // error. here we go again.
  mmioClose(hFile,0);
  MessageBox(NULL, "MMIO ascending error.", "Load Failed",
MB_OK|MB_ICONEXCLAMATION);
  return FALSE;
}

// trolling for data
secondary.ckid = mmioFOURCC('d','a','t','a');

if (mmioDescend(hFile,&secondary,&primary,MMIO_FINDCHUNK))
{
  // no data
  mmioClose(hFile,0);
  MessageBox(NULL, "MMIO descending error.", "Load Failed",
MB_OK|MB_ICONEXCLAMATION);
  return FALSE;
}

// everything is just peachy, read the data.
// allocate memory for the temporary buffer
m_pByte = (void*)malloc(secondary.cksize);

// read the .WAV data
int check = mmioRead(hFile,(char*)m_pByte,secondary.cksize);

// close the file
mmioClose(hFile,0);
//m_pByte = (LPBYTE)tempBuffer;
m_dwLength = secondary.cksize;

// set up the wave format
m_FormatEx = new WAVEFORMATEX;
memset((void*)m_FormatEx, 0, sizeof(WAVEFORMATEX));
memcpy((void*)m_FormatEx, (void*)&formatEx, sizeof(WAVEFORMATEX));
```

```
    return TRUE;
} // end CDSoundWAV::Load
```

We now have a WAVEFORMATEX populated with everything we know from the file and a large buffer full of actual sound data. We can now use all the data we extracted to create our sound buffer so that we can play it in our game.

Using *CreateSoundBuffer*

The first thing we need to do is put our WAVEFORMATEX information into a DSBUFFERDESC so that we can use it to specify the buffer information DirectSound needs. So let's make one. The soundWAV referred to is the class into which we read all the information from the file using MMIO. It knows the length of the file we read that can be accessed using GetDataLength, as well as the WAVEFORMATEX of the file we loaded that we can get using GetWAVFormat.

```
DSBUFFERDESC bufferDesc; // this will be our buffer description
DWORD length;

// first, we allocate enough memory to hold a DSBUFFERDESC
memset(&bufferDesc, 0, sizeof(DSBUFFERDESC));

// next, we ask the class we used to load the file how long the data is
bufferDesc.dwBufferBytes = soundWAV->GetDataLength();

// set up the buffer flags for panning, volume, and frequency control
// also put in the flags to specify that this is a static buffer in software memory
bufferDesc.dwFlags = DSBCAPS_CTRLPAN | DSBCAPS_CTRLVOLUME | DSBCAPS_CTRLFREQUENCY |
    DSBCAPS_STATIC | DSBCAPS_LOCSOFTWARE;

// the size of the buffer will be… the size of the buffer struct, naturally
bufferDesc.dwSize = sizeof(DSBUFFERDESC);

// retrieve the WAVEFORMATEX from the class we loaded it into
bufferDesc.lpwfxFormat = soundWAV->GetWAVFormat();
```

Now that we have our buffer description all set up and ready, let's create the sound buffer. We'll use CreateSoundBuffer, which looks like this:

```
HRESULT CreateSoundBuffer(
    LPCDSBUFFERDESC lpcDSBuffDesc,    // the buffer description we just made
    LPLPDIRECTSOUNDBUFFER lplpDSBuff, // actual sound data
```

```
        IUnknown FAR •pUnkOuter // always NULL
};
```

Once we've created the buffer, we will lock it so that we can copy our sound information into it, and then we'll unlock it so that it can be used. Earlier, we discussed the fact that DirectSound uses circular buffers, which makes things a little more complex than just copying data over. The command to lock the buffer for writing is as follows:

```
HRESULT Lock (
        DWORD dwOffset, // write cursor offset in bytes
        DWORD dwBytes, // number of bytes you want to lock
        LPVOID lpAudioPtr1, // returns a pointer to the first buffer portion
        LPDWORD lpdwAudioBytes1, // bytes in first buffer portion
        LPVOID lpAudioPtr2, // returns a pointer to the second buffer portion
        LPDWORD lpdwAudioBytes2, // bytes in second buffer portion
        DWORD dwFlags // locking flags
);
```

The dwFlags can be either DSBLOCK_FROMWRITECURSOR, which locks the buffer for the value of dwBytes from the write cursor, or DSBLOCK_ENTIREBUFFER, which locks the entire buffer for writing. We aren't streaming, so we can use DSBLOCK_ENTIREBUFFER, which is much easier. The DSBLOCK_ENTIREBUFFER flag will simply ignore the dwBytes value. We will also be making things easier by setting our second buffer portions as NULL because locking the entire buffer makes that portion unnecessary.

Once our buffer is locked and we can write to it, we're going to memcopy the information we got for the sound buffer from the file. Then we need to unlock the buffer (using UnLock) so that we can use it, like this:

```
HRESULT Unlock(
        LPVOID lpAudioPtr1, // first buffer portion from Lock
        DWORD dwAudioBytes1, // bytes in first buffer portion from Lock
        LPVOID lpAudioPtr2, // second buffer portion from Lock
        DWORD dwAudioBytes2, // bytes in second buffer portion from Lock
);
```

So, to populate the buffer using our sound data, we would do the following:

```
// declare the buffer we're making
LPDIRECTSOUNDBUFFER soundBuffer = NULL;
// pointer used to hold the buffer portion pointer
void• lpBuffer = NULL;
DWORD length;
```

```
// create the buffer. lpSound is our LPDIRECTSOUND object
lpSound->CreateSoundBuffer(&bufferDesc, &soundBuffer, NULL);

// find the data length of the buffer we read in previously so we can copy it
length = soundWAV->GetDataLength();

// copy the information into the new buffer
soundBuffer->Lock(0, length, &lpBuffer,
                            &length, NULL, NULL, DSBLOCK_ENTIREBUFFER);
memcpy(lpBuffer, soundWAV->GetWAVData(), soundWAV->GetDataLength());
soundBuffer->Unlock(lpBuffer, soundWAV->GetDataLength(), NULL, 0);
```

Now you can use the sound all you want. Remember, though, that you created this buffer, and you're responsible for it. When you're completely done with the buffer and that sound will no longer be needed, you need to clean up after yourself by releasing the buffer. To release it, merely use the following:

> **CAUTION**
>
> **Keep in mind that this entirely destroys the sound buffer, so only do this when you are sure you won't need the sound again.**

```
soundBuffer->Release();
```

Playing the Secondary Buffers

We went to all the trouble of setting up our secondary buffers; it would be a shame if we didn't actually play them, so let's do so. To play a sound, you use the Play function (imagine that), which looks like this:

```
HRESULT Play (
     DWORD dwReserved1, // reserved, 0
     DWORD dwReserved2, // reserved, 0
     DWORD dwFlags // play flags
);
```

There is only one possible flag, DSBPLAY_LOOPING. As you can guess, it tells DirectSound to play the sound repeatedly until you tell it to stop. For our sound buffer that we set up earlier, if we wanted to play the sound once, we would use the following:

```
soundBuffer->Play( 0, 0, 0 );
```

Simple, isn't it? Let's look at a few other things you might want to do to a sound. For instance, you might want to stop a sound after it's started playing but before it's done, or you might want to stop a sound that you told to loop indefinitely. Simply use the Stop function, which looks like this:

```
HRESULT Stop();
```

Again, it's very simple and to the point. To stop the sound we just started up, we would use:

```
soundBuffer->Stop();
```

If you remember back to when we first set up our buffer, we specified DSBCAPS_-CTRLPAN | DSBCAPS_CTRLVOLUME | DSBCAPS_CTRLFREQUENCY, which means we can control the pan, volume, and frequency of our sounds. These are fun things to play with, so let's look at how to change the values.

DSBCAPS_CTRLPAN lets you pan a sound from left to right. The function for it looks like this:

```
HRESULT SetPan( LONG lPan );
```

The value of lPan can range from −10,000 to 10,000 and indicates the decibel split between the left and the right in hundredths of a decibel. A value of −10,000 would indicate an attenuation of 100dB in the right speaker, whereas a value of 10,000 would indicate an attenuation of 100dB in the left speaker. A 0 in the lPan value indicates that both speakers are at the same attenuation level, so they will be equally at full volume; otherwise, one speaker will be at full volume and the other will be attenuated. An lPan of 3,500 would mean that the right speaker is at full volume, while the left speaker is attenuated by 35.00dB.

DSBCAPS_CTRLVOLUME lets you mess with the volume levels of sound. DirectSound cannot actually amplify sounds for you, so you will need to plan for the fact that you can make sounds softer than full volume but not louder. The function for changing volume is as follows:

```
HRESULT SetVolume( LONG lVolume );
```

The amount of attenuation is specified by lVolume in hundredths of a decibel. This value can range from 0, which is full volume with no attenuation, to −10,000, which is a 100dB attenuation.

DSBCAPS_CTRLFREQUENCY lets you change a sound's frequency. This can give you some great sound variety without needing a bunch of buffers to do it. Changing the frequency of a sound clip of someone speaking can give you a range between "munchkin" and "Jabba the Hut" with minimal effort. To change frequency, use the following:

```
HRESULT SetFrequency( DWORD dwFrequency );
```

The new frequency, in hertz, is the value of dwFrequency. The allowable range is 100 Hz to 100,000 Hz. The higher the frequency, the higher the pitch will be. To set your sound back to the original frequency, use DSBFREQUENCY_ORIGINAL for dwFrequency, and DirectSound will set the buffer back to the frequency it was at when you created it. It's important to note that using this command to change the frequency will not change the format of the sound buffer, and you are not allowed to use SetFrequency on the primary sound buffer.

MIDI with DirectMusic

Now that we have sounds, it's time to add a little music. With DirectMusic, it is very important to cooperate with the DirectSound primary sound buffer. When using DirectMusic, keep in mind that it wasn't introduced to DirectX until version 6.0, which means that Windows NT will not support it. The functionality of DirectMusic is truly massive, but we're going to look at how to simply play a MIDI file using DirectMusic because that's probably what you're going to want to do in your game. The nice thing about DirectMusic is that it uses the Microsoft Software Synthesizer unless you specifically instruct otherwise, which is fantastic because it means your MIDI files are going to be using the same Roland sound fonts regardless of what computer they're on. Finally, musicians can stop stressing about how terrible their MIDIs might sound using the voices on different sound cards!

DirectMusic is the very first pure COM component in DirectX, which means you don't have to worry about any libraries. You do need to know the header files, which are dmkctrl.h, dmusicc.h, dmusicf.h, and dmusici.h.

Like DirectSound, DirectMusic has several important interfaces to consider. The following are the COM interfaces and objects we will be using:

- IDirectMusic This is the main DirectMusic interface, but you won't be directly using it. It will be created by default in the creation of IDirectMusicPerformance, which will be the actual interface you use while manipulating MIDI.

- **IDirectMusicPerformance** This is your main interface. It controls and manipulates all the musical data and creates the default main IDirectMusic object automatically when you create the performance.

- **IDirectMusicLoader** Microsoft was kind enough to give us this interface, which will take care of loading our MIDI files for us so that we won't have to go mucking about with MMIO again.

- **IDirectMusicPort** This is the port at which you direct your MIDI data stream. Usually this will be the Microsoft Software Synthesizer unless you decide to use a hardware-accelerated port found via enumeration.

- **IDirectMusicSegment** This is the actual data chunk from your MIDI file representing the music. We're going to make a structure to contain this and the IDirectMusicSegmentState (along with a few other interesting tidbits of data), so we can make a whole bunch of these for as many MIDI songs as we want to play.

- **IDirectMusicSegmentState** This keeps track of the current status of the data in the segment.

Since DirectMusic is pure COM, we start with a call to CoInitialize(). This goes in the constructor of the DirectMusic class you're making and looks like this:

```
if (FAILED(CoInitialize(NULL)))
{
  MessageBox(NULL, "Initialization of MIDI COM object failed.", "Constructor
  Failed", MB_OK|MB_ICONEXCLAMATION);
  m_bValid = FALSE;
  return;
}
```

That wasn't so bad. Now that COM is initialized, it's time to start using it by creating the DirectMusic performance. I've previously set up a member variable in my DirectMusic class that keeps track of my IDirectMusicPerformance, which was declared as follows:

```
IDirectMusicPerformance •m_Performance;     // primary DirectMusicPerformance object
```

I initialized the m_Performance to NULL in my constructor because we need the CoCreateInstance to give me the pointer it creates for my performance. Keep in mind that when this CoCreateInstance is called, a hidden IDirectMusic interface is also created, but we don't need to worry about it.

```
if (FAILED(CoCreateInstance(CLSID_DirectMusicPerformance, NULL, CLSCTX_INPROC,
  IID_IDirectMusicPerformance, (void••)&m_Performance)))
```

```
{
  MessageBox(NULL, "Failed to create performance.", "Constructor Failed",
  MB_OK|MB_ICONEXCLAMATION);
  m_bValid = FALSE;
  return;
}
```

Initializing the
IDirectMusicPerformance

Now that we have an IDirectMusicPerformance, we need to initialize it. This is the important part if you decide to use DirectMusic and DirectSound together. The Init function looks like this:

```
HRESULT Init(IDirectMusic** ppDirectMusic,
             LPDIRECTSOUND pDirectSound,
             HWND hWnd);
```

We didn't make our own IDirectMusic, so we can pass in a NULL for ppDirectMusic.

Does the LPDIRECTSOUND look familiar? It should because it's the same thing as the DirectSound primary buffer we were working with back in the DirectSound section. If you are using DirectSound and DirectMusic together, you absolutely must set up DirectSound first and keep track of your LPDIRECTSOUND to use it in this Init call. If you aren't using DirectSound and DirectMusic together, pass in a NULL for pDirectSound, and DirectMusic will create an IDirectSound itself.

For our hWnd, we simply use our game's main window as usual.

This is what my Init looks like:

```
if (FAILED(m_Performance->Init(NULL, m_lpPrimaryDSound, m_hWnd)))
{
  MessageBox(NULL, "Failed to init.", "Constructor Failed",
  MB_OK|MB_ICONEXCLAMATION);
  m_bValid = FALSE;
  return;
}
```

The m_lpPrimaryDSound is the DirectSound buffer from the DirectSound section, which I stored previously as a member variable, along with the m_hWnd representing our game's main window.

Creating an *IDirectMusicPort*

Now all we need is to create a port to which to stream our data, and then we can get on with the loading and playing of MIDI files. Creating an IDirectMusicPort is as simple as the other things we've done so far. All we need to do is tell the performance to add a port to itself, as follows:

```
if (FAILED(m_Performance->AddPort(NULL)))
{
  MessageBox(NULL, "Failed to add port.", "Constructor Failed",
  MB_OK|MB_ICONEXCLAMATION);
  m_bValid = FALSE;
  return;
}
```

The NULL specifies the use of a default port instead of one we set up ourselves. You can set up your own port if you'd like using the IDirectMusicPerformance, but if you do you'll need to activate it, assign the block of channels, and (when you're done) remove it. If you use the default port, DirectMusic will take care of that for you.

Setting Up the *IDirectMusicLoader*

We now have all the pieces ready to start working with our MIDI files. Naturally, the first thing we want to do is set up the IDirectMusicLoader so that we can load a MIDI file; otherwise, we'll have nothing to play. To get a loader, we'll need to venture yet again deep into COM territory and make a CoCreateInstance call for it.

I've already set up an IDirectMusicLoader member variable in my class header, as follows:

```
IDirectMusicLoader *m_Loader; // loader for MIDI files
```

As with the performance member variable, I set this one to NULL in the constructor for my MIDI class as well. The CoCreateInstance call looks like this:

```
if (FAILED(CoCreateInstance( CLSID_DirectMusicLoader, NULL, CLSCTX_INPROC,
  IID_IDirectMusicLoader, (void**)&m_Loader)))
{
  MessageBox(NULL, "Failed to create loader.", "Constructor Failed",
  MB_OK|MB_ICONEXCLAMATION);
  m_bValid = FALSE;
  return;
}
```

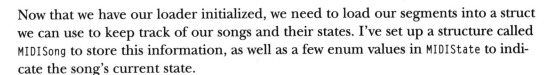

Now that we have our loader initialized, we need to load our segments into a struct we can use to keep track of our songs and their states. I've set up a structure called MIDISong to store this information, as well as a few enum values in MIDIState to indicate the song's current state.

```
enum MIDIState{ MIDI_OPEN, MIDI_LOADED, MIDI_PLAYING };

struct MIDISong
{
  IDirectMusicSegment       *segment;       // the segment containing a complete song
  IDirectMusicSegmentState  *segmentState;  // the state of this segment
  int                        id;            // the id number of this song
  MIDIState                  state;         // the current state of this song
};
```

Loading a Song

Now that we have a MIDISong struct, we can use our loader to load in the information contained in our MIDI file. This is the loading code from my DirectMusic wrapper. As you can see, I have an array for my MIDI segments called m_SongArray. I'm passing in the file name of the MIDI I want to load into an open segment in my array.

```
int CDMIDIWrap::LoadSong( CString fileName )
{
  IDirectMusicSegment* pSegment = NULL;

  int slot = -1;

  // find an open slot
  for (int i = 0; i < NUM_SONGS; i++)
  {
   if (m_SongArray[i].state == MIDI_OPEN)
   {
     slot = i;
     break;
   }
  }

  if (slot == -1)
    return -1;
```

```
// deal with the crazy wide character stuff
WCHAR wideFileName[_MAX_PATH];
MultiByteToWideChar(CP_ACP,MB_PRECOMPOSED,fileName.GetBuffer(0),
 -1,wideFileName,_MAX_PATH);

// set up a description structure
DMUS_OBJECTDESC ddDesc;
//DD_INIT_STRUCT(ddDesc);
ddDesc.dwSize = sizeof(DMUS_OBJECTDESC);
ddDesc.guidClass = CLSID_DirectMusicSegment;
wcscpy(ddDesc.wszFileName, wideFileName);
ddDesc.dwValidData = DMUS_OBJ_CLASS|DMUS_OBJ_FULLPATH;

// set up load object
if (FAILED(m_Loader->GetObject(&ddDesc, IID_IDirectMusicSegment,
          (void**)&pSegment)))
{
  MessageBox(NULL, "Failed loading object.", "Load Failed",
MB_OK|MB_ICONEXCLAMATION);
  return -1;
}

// set segment parameters to standard MIDI
if (FAILED(pSegment->SetParam(GUID_StandardMIDIFile,-1,0,0,(void*)m_Performance)))
{
  MessageBox(NULL, "Failed setting standard parameter.", "Load Failed",
MB_OK|MB_ICONEXCLAMATION);
  return -1;
}

// set download parameter
if (FAILED(pSegment->SetParam(GUID_Download,-1,0,0,(void*)m_Performance)))
{
  MessageBox(NULL, "Failed setting download parameter.", "Load Failed",
MB_OK|MB_ICONEXCLAMATION);
  return -1;
}

m_SongArray[slot].segment = pSegment;
m_SongArray[slot].segmentState = NULL;
```

```
    m_SongArray[slot].state        = MIDI_LOADED;

    return slot;
} // end CDMIDIWrap::LoadSong
```

Playing a Song

Now that we have a MIDI segment loaded and ready to go, it's time to ask DirectMusic to play it for us. To do this, we use IDirectMusicPerformance's PlaySegment, which looks like this:

```
HRESULT PlaySegment(
        IDirectMusicSegment· pSegment, // the segment to play
        DWORD dwFlags, // play flags, which will be 0 most of the time
        _int64 i64StartTime, // when to start playing
        IDirectMusicSegmentState·· ppSegmentState); // tracks the playing state
```

I play the songs in my m_SongArray by passing in the index of the song to play, as follows:

```
BOOL CDMIDIWrap::PlaySong( int songIndex )
{
  // if there is a song playing, shut it off
  if (m_nCurrentSong != -1)
    StopSong();

  // play the desired segment
  m_Performance->PlaySegment(m_SongArray[songIndex].segment, 0, 0,
                          &m_SongArray[songIndex].segmentState);
  m_SongArray[songIndex].state = MIDI_PLAYING;

  // save the index
  m_nCurrentSong = songIndex;

  return TRUE;
} // end CDMIDIWrap::PlaySong
```

As you can see, I make sure that my MIDISong state is set to MIDI_PLAYING to keep track of it. I also keep track of what song I'm playing by keeping track of the index of the song in m_nCurrentSong.

Stopping a Song

Once you start playing a song, you will probably eventually want to make it stop playing. To do so, we use IDirectMusicPerformance's Stop function, which looks like this:

```
HRESULT Stop(
    IDirectMusicSegment• pSegment, // segment to be stopped
    IDirectMusicSegmentState• pSegmentState, // state of the segment
    MUSIC_TIME mtTime, // indicates when to stop it
    DWORD dwFlags); // control flags
```

The dwFlags variable will again usually be 0. The pSegmentState isn't important, so we can pass a NULL. Here is my wrapper's StopSong:

```
BOOL CDMIDIWrap::StopSong( )
{
 m_Performance->Stop(m_SongArray[m_nCurrentSong].segment, NULL, 0, 0);
 m_SongArray[m_nCurrentSong].state = MIDI_LOADED;
 m_nCurrentSong = -1;
 return TRUE;
} // end CDMIDIWrap::StopSong
```

I kept track of the current song playing in m_nCurrentSong, so all I need to do is pass that segment from my m_SongArray to ask that it be stopped. I set my song state back to MIDI_LOADED to indicate that that array slot is loaded but isn't currently playing, and I set my m_nCurrentSong to –1 to indicate that no song is currently being played.

Checking for Play Status

The third thing we might find useful while using MIDI is to check on the current state of a segment. To do this, we use IDirectMusicPerformance's IsPlaying, as follows:

```
if (m_Performance->IsPlaying( m_SongArray[index], NULL) == S_OK)
  // the segment is playing
else
  // the segment is not playing
```

Releasing a Segment

When you are entirely done with a segment and don't intend to play it ever again, you need to release the resources. This is done using IDirectMusicSegment's SetParam to unload the instrument data and then using IDirectMusicSegment's Release to release the interface pointer. The following is my wrapper's UnloadSegment function, which releases the resources by index.

```
BOOL CDMIDIWrap::UnloadSegment( int index )
{
 if (m_SongArray[index].state == MIDI_PLAYING)
   StopSong();

 if (m_SongArray[index].state != MIDI_LOADED)
   return TRUE;

 m_SongArray[index].segment->SetParam(GUID_Unload, -1, 0, 0, (void*)m_Performance);
 m_SongArray[index].segment->Release();
 m_SongArray[index].segment = NULL;

 m_SongArray[index].state = MIDI_OPEN;

 return TRUE;
} // end CDMIDIWrap::UnloadSegment
```

Note that I first check to see if the song is playing, and if so, I stop it. I then unload the instrument data, release the segment, and set my state to MIDI_OPEN to indicate that that array slot is open to have a new song loaded into it.

Conclusion: Shutting Down DirectMusic

When you are entirely done with DirectMusic, you must close down the performance object and loader and any segments you still have loaded. This is my MIDI wrapper destructor, in which I shut everything down.

```
CDMIDIWrap::~CDMIDIWrap()
{
 // stop the currently playing song
 StopSong();

 // shut down the segments
 for (int i = 0; i < NUM_SONGS; i++)
 {
   if (m_SongArray[i].state == MIDI_LOADED)
   {
```

```
    // unload the instruments
    UnloadSegment(i);
  }
}

// shut down the performance
if (m_Performance != NULL)
{
 m_Performance->CloseDown();
 m_Performance->Release();
}

// shut down the loader
if (m_Loader != NULL)
 m_Loader->Release();

// shut down the COM
CoUninitialize();

} // end CDMIDIWrap::~CDMIDIWrap
```

Everything I allocated is released at this point

In this chapter, you learned the techniques necessary to use WAV and MIDI files in the games that you create. Using these basic techniques will add life to your game and get the game player more submerged into your game world. Let's face it, a game simply is not a game without sound and music! So, use the tricks you have learned in this chapter to enhance your games and the players game experience. Trust me, you will be glad that you took the extra time to add this important aspect to your game.

TRICK 9

2-D Sprites

Jeff Wilkerson

Introduction

If you have ever played a video game before (and I'll take the Vegas odds that you have), you in some way, shape, or form have interacted with sprites. It seems nowadays the word sprite is synonymous with 2-D. Since 3-D games are currently the "rage," one might falsely think that they don't need to know or care about sprites. This simply isn't the case. Sprites are used in 2-D and 3-D games alike.

So what exactly is a sprite? Well, in its most basic form, a sprite is an image that moves about the screen. Yep, that's right, a sprite is essentially a piece of artwork. Nothing tricky, nothing fancy, just a 2-D rectangular image. The way sprites typically relate to games is when multiple bitmaps are combined in a sequential fashion to create an animation. Animations are then strung together to create a "character." It is not uncommon to refer to this final "character" as a sprite. I'll be referring to a sprite as an individual image and a character throughout this chapter.

After reading through this chapter and carousing through its source code, you'll have enough knowledge to make your own sprite engine. Then, making a sprite-based game will be a hop, skip, and a jump away.

What You Will Learn

If the title didn't tip you off, this chapter will be about sprites. You can expect to learn the following concepts:

- How to annually load bitmaps
- DirectDraw basics
- Transparency with sprites
- Drawing and moving of sprites
- Basic collision detection with sprites

Image Loading

We know a sprite contains images, so it's kind of important that we know how to load an image. In our case, the image is a 24-bit .bmp file. Windows provides a pretty straightforward Application Programmer's Interface (API) to load .bmp files. We're not going to use it though. Why you ask? In the long run, it gives us a lot more flexibility if we load it ourselves. We'll create a class, `CImage` to handle this loading task for us. Once we have this class in place, we could easily add methods to load other file formats that Windows does not have an API for. Additionally, by loading our own images, we get a pointer to the pixel bits. With a pointer to the pixel bits, we can alter the image at runtime before we give it to DirectDraw if we so desire. If we wanted to load an image and then invert it, we could do this with relative ease. If we just loaded the image using a Win32 API, we'd only get a `HANDLE` to the bitmap and consequently could not directly manipulate the pixel data.

Since our sprite is contained in a 24-bit .bmp file, let's take a look at Figure 9.1 to see what the file layout for a .bmp file looks like:

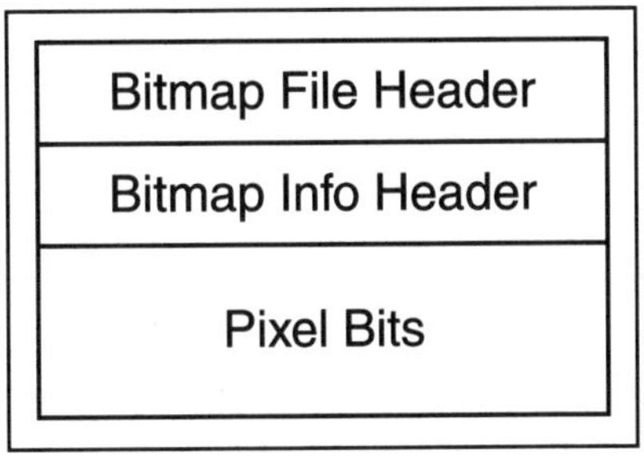

```
┌─────────────────────────────────────┐
│  ┌───────────────────────────────┐  │
│  │     Bitmap File Header        │  │
│  ├───────────────────────────────┤  │
│  │     Bitmap Info Header        │  │
│  ├───────────────────────────────┤  │
│  │                               │  │
│  │        Pixel Bits             │  │
│  │                               │  │
│  └───────────────────────────────┘  │
└─────────────────────────────────────┘
```

Figure 9.1

Bitmap file format

The *bitmap file header* contains the following: file type, size of bitmap in bytes, and an offset into the file where the pixel bits begin.

The *bitmap info header* contains the following: width of image, height of image, number of bits per pixel, and other information that we really don't care about.

Lastly, the *pixel bits* are the actual pixel data. Depending on the bit depth of the image this pixel data will either be indexes into a palette of colors or RGB data. Since our bitmap is 24-bits, it has 24-bits per pixel. That means every pixel in the bitmap has 8-bits (8-bits = 1-byte) for the red component, 8-bits for the green component, and 8 bits for the blue component. Typically, each pixel is thought of as an RGB value where R, G, and B are in the range of 0–255.

The .bmp file format is pretty simple. This is one of the reasons I chose this format for our sprite. Also it is viewable/modifiable in Microsoft Paint, which comes stock on any Microsoft operating system.

Okay, so we know the basics of how a .bmp file is laid out. Now we can talk about how to load one. First we'll create a class, CImage, to handle the loading/creation of 24-bit bitmaps. The class definition looks like this:

```
class CImage {

public:

  CImage(); // Constructor()

  inline int getWidth() const { return width; }
  inline int getHeight() const { return height; }
  inline int getChannels() const { return channels; }
  inline int getStride() const { return stride; }
  inline HDC getHDC() const { return hdc; }

  // Creates a blank CImage of specified width, height and channels
  bool setCImage(int width, int height, int channels);

  // Loads a 24-bit .bmp with specified file_name
  bool loadBitmap(char *file_name);

  // Returns a pointer to the beginning of a line of pixels specified by
  "which_line"
  inline uchar* getLinePtr(int which_line);

  ~CImage(); // Deconstructor()

private:

  int width, height; // Width/Height of CImage
  int channels;// Number of channels in CImage
  int stride; // Number of bytes (including padding) in a line of pixels (DWORD
  aligned)
HBITMAP hbitmap; // Handle to a CImage
  HBITMAP old_bmp; // Handle to "previous bitmap"
  HDC hdc; // Handle to a CImage's device context
  uchar *pixels_bits; // Pointer to the pixel bits

  void freeCImage(); // Releases all memory associated with CImage
};
```

Now that we have our `CImage` class, the next step is reading in the .bmp file data. We need to start at the top of the bitmap, naturally, and read in the bitmap file header and the bitmap file info in that order.

```
BITMAPFILEHEADER bmp_fileheader;

// Read the BITMAPFILEHEADER
fread(&bmp_fileheader, sizeof(BITMAPFILEHEADER), 1, bmp_file);

BITMAPINFOHEADER bmp_infoheader;

// Read the BITMAPINFOHEADER
fread(&bmp_infoheader, sizeof(BITMAPINFOHEADER), 1, bmp_file);
```

Once we have these structures we'll create an "empty bitmap" in memory for us to fill in. This requires a couple of quick definitions of *channels* and *stride*. A bitmap's channels are equal to its bits per pixel divided by 8. So a 24-bit .bmp file has three channels (24÷8 = 3).

The stride of a bitmap is the total length in bytes of one complete line of pixels. In general, the total length of a line of pixels equals the width of the bitmap multiplied by the channels of the bitmap. So an 8×8, 24-bit image would have 24 bytes of information for each line of pixels (each R, G, and B is one byte of information). Refer to the one in Figure 9.2.

	0	1	2	3	4	5	6	7
0	RGB	RGB	RGB	RGB	RGB	RGB	RGB	RGB
1	RGB	RGB	RGB	RGB	RGB	RGB	RGB	RGB
2	RGB	RGB	RGB	RGB	RGB	RGB	RGB	RGB
3	RGB	RGB	RGB	RGB	RGB	RGB	RGB	RGB
4	RGB	RGB	RGB	RGB	RGB	RGB	RGB	RGB
5	RGB	RGB	RGB	RGB	RGB	RGB	RGB	RGB
6	RGB	RGB	RGB	RGB	RGB	RGB	RGB	RGB
7	RGB	RGB	RGB	RGB	RGB	RGB	RGB	RGB

Figure 9.2

Pixel layout

However, Windows forces the .bmp layout to be DWORD aligned (divisible evenly by 4). This means if we have an 11×11 bitmap, Windows adds a padding byte and effectively makes the bitmap 12×11. Therefore, the stride of a bitmap refers to the total length of a line of pixels.

So to create an "empty" bitmap, we first need to create a device context compatible to the one currently being used to draw our window. We will select our newly created bitmap into the compatible device context so it will have the capability of being drawn to the screen.

```
// Create a compatible HDC
hdc = CreateCompatibleDC(NULL);
```

Next we need to decide what the width, height, and channels of our bitmap are going to be. We'll assume the dimensions are being passed in.

```
// Set width, height, and channels
width = w;
height = h;
channels = c;
```

Now we can calculate the stride of bitmap. Remember it must be DWORD aligned.

```
// Calculate the stride of the bitmap.
stride = width * channels;

while((stride % 4) != 0)
    stride++;
```

We've filled in some defining attributes of our bitmap; it's time to actually make it. We'll start by filling a BITMAPINFO structure that stipulates how our bitmap should be created.

```
// BITMAPINFO for filling
BITMAPINFO bmp_info = {0};

// We'll initialize the parameters that we care about
bmp_info.bmiHeader.biSize = sizeof(BITMAPINFOHEADER); // Must be set
bmp_info.bmiHeader.biWidth = width;
bmp_info.bmiHeader.biHeight = height;
bmp_info.bmiHeader.biPlanes = 1; // Must be set
bmp_info.bmiHeader.biBitCount = channels * 8;
bmp_info.bmiHeader.biCompression = BI_RGB; // No compression
```

Once we have our BITMAPINFO filled in, we can make our bitmap.

```
// Create the bitmap aka DIB Section (Device Independent Bitmap Section)
hbitmap = CreateDIBSection(hdc, &bmp_info, DIB_RGB_COLORS, (void**)&pixels_bits, 0,
    0);
```

This function call will return two things: a valid bitmap handle in `hbitmap` and a pointer to the pixel data in `pixel_bits`.

We are almost finished. Lastly, we loop over the pixel data and fill our newly created bitmap.

```
// Calculate the number of pixel bytes per line
unsigned int bytes_per_line = width * channels;

// Calculate the number of "padding" bytes
unsigned int padding = stride - bytes_per_line;

// Loop over all the pixel data
for(int y = 0; y < height; y++)
{
  // Get the current line
  uchar *line_ptr = getLinePtr(y);

  // Read the precise number of bytes that the line requires into the bitmap
  fread(line_ptr, bytes_per_line, 1, bmp_file);

  // Skip over any padding bytes
  fseek(bmp_file, padding, SEEK_CUR);

} // end of for(int y = 0; y < height; y++)
```

After reading all the pixel data we'll be loaded. Now the party can officially start.

DirectDraw Basics

DirectDraw allows us "direct" access to the hardware for drawing (blitting) to the screen. To create a simple DirectDraw application these are the four general steps you follow:

1. Create a DirectDraw interface.

2. Create surfaces to draw on.

3. Create a clipper for the DirectDraw surfaces.

4. Blit to the screen.

Step #1

Creating a DirectDraw interface is pretty straightforward. First we need to create an instance of a "base" DirectDraw object. Upon getting a valid DirectDraw object, we can query it for a DirectDraw interface. This interface is how we will communicate with DirectDraw for creation of our surfaces and clipper.

```
LPDIRECTDRAW lpdd = NULL; // Empty DirectDraw object
```

```
// Creates the DirectDraw object
DirectDrawCreate(NULL, &lpdd, NULL);
```

The first parameter, NULL, is the globally unique identifier (GUID) that represents the display driver to use for our DirectDraw object. By passing in NULL, we are saying, "Use the default display driver." The second parameter is the DirectDraw object that is to be filled. The last parameter is one of Microsoft's famous "expansion parameters" (that never seem to get used). It must be NULL.

Once we have a valid DirectDraw object, we query it for a valid DirectDraw interface. Different versions of DirectDraw allow for creation of different interfaces. However, all interfaces are backwards compatible. Meaning DirectX 7.0 can compile and run DirectX 3.0 but not vice-versa.

Here we query for the interface that we want. The interface will be stored in "lpdd2."

```
lpdd->QueryInterface(IID_IDirectDraw2,(void**)&lpdd2);
```

Now that we received the interface we want, we can get rid of the base DirectDraw object.

```
lpdd->Release(); // It's served its purpose lets get rid of it
```

Lastly, we need to set the cooperative level. The cooperative level answers the question "How is the DirectDraw application going to behave?" We want our application to act like a normal window so will set the cooperative level to "normal."

```
lpdd2->SetCooperativeLevel(hwnd,DDSCL_NORMAL);
```

Step #2

We have our DirectDraw interface, but now we need something to draw on. We are going to create three surfaces. One will be the primary surface. This surface will essentially be the screen. The second surface will be our back buffer. This back buffer will be the surface we do all the drawing of a particular frame to FIRST.

Once the back buffer is filled it will be drawn to the primary buffer. Last we will have a generic "draw" buffer. We will use this to draw each frame of animation of our sprite to.

When creating a surface in DirectDraw, you have to fill out a structure named **DDSURFACEDESC**. This structure describes how you want your surface created. For the primary surface we will do the following:

```
// DirectDraw surface descriptor
DDSURFACEDESC surf_desc = {0};

// Init the fields for the primary surface
surf_desc.dwSize = sizeof(DDSURFACEDESC); // Has to be set
surf_desc.dwFlags = DDSD_CAPS;
surf_desc.ddsCaps.dwCaps = DDSCAPS_VIDEOMEMORY | DDSCAPS_PRIMARYSURFACE;
```

The `dwFlags` parameter says, "These members of the `DDSURFACEDESC` have been filled with valid data." As you can see, we indeed fill the `ddsCaps` member with valid data. The `ddsCaps` variable is itself a set of flags. The two flags we set it to say, "First this surface will be created in video memory (i.e., in display memory). Second, this surface will be a primary surface (i.e., what is drawn to the screen)."

```
// Create the primary surface
lpdd2->CreateSurface(&surf_desc,&pri_surface,NULL);
```

Before we create the back and general draw surfaces, we need to slightly modify our surface descriptor.

```
surf_desc.dwFlags = DDSD_CAPS | DDSD_HEIGHT | DDSD_WIDTH;
surf_desc.dwWidth = width;
surf_desc.dwHeight = height;
surf_desc.ddsCaps.dwCaps = DDSCAPS_VIDEOMEMORY | DDSCAPS_OFFSCREENPLAIN;
```

Once again we set `dwFlags` so that it stipulates what data members of `DDSURFACEDESC` we are going to fill with valid data. This time we will fill the `dwWidth`, `dwHeight`, and `ddsCaps` members with valid information. The `dwWidth` and `dwHeight` variables will be filled with the width and height of our surface. The width and height of our back and draw surfaces will be the same as the width and height of our window. The flags we set the `ddsCaps` to say, "The surface will be created in video memory and it will be a rectangular area of memory (conceptually) for drawing to."

It is important to note that surface creation could fail. If video memory is already full, you won't be able to create new surfaces in it. To create surfaces in system memory change the `DDSCAPS_VIDEOMEMORY` flag to `DDSCAPS_SYSTEMMEMORY`. Now for the sample sprite application provided, it only tries to build the surfaces in video memory. The reason being is that we are only creating three surfaces and they should all easily fit in video memory. When creating a game, however, you'd most likely want to allow creation of any surfaces besides the primary surface in either video or system memory.

Step #3

A DirectDraw clipper object will "clip" our surface(s) to the rectangular area of our window. Creating a clipper only requires a function call.

```
DirectDrawCreateClipper(0,&clipper,NULL);
```

With our clipper created, we can set the clipper to the window we want our surfaces' clipped to.

```
clipper->SetHWnd(0,hwnd);
```

Now that our clipper is set up, we simply assign it to all of our surfaces.

```
pri_surface->SetClipper(clipper);
back_surface->SetClipper(clipper);
draw_surface->SetClipper(clipper);
```

Now all the surfaces should be clipped to the dimensions of our window. Really, you only need a clipper if the application is going to be windowed, but creating a clipper on a full-screen application shouldn't hurt anything. Additionally, the back and draw surfaces should have been created with the windows dimensions and therefore would not need to be clipped. We'll always set all of the surfaces' clippers anyway just to be ultra-safe.

Step #4

Finally, we have our DirectDraw object set up and ready for action. There are two main ways we will draw with our surfaces. The first way will involve getting the surfaces' device context and using standard Win32 functions to draw to it. The second involves drawing from one DirectDraw surface to another.

Getting the device context of a surface is really easy.

```
HDC draw_hdc = NULL;

// Fills draw_dc with the draw_surface's device context
draw_surface->GetDC(&draw_hdc);
```

Once we have a surfaces' HDC, we can draw using any good ole' Win32 function such as BitBlt(). When we complete the drawing process, we need to release the device context.

```
draw_surface->ReleaseDC(draw_hdc);
```

Releasing the device context is a must. Failure to do so could result in your application locking up or things getting drawn in an extremely bizarre fashion.

Now we know how to fill a surface using common Window functions such as BitBlt(). Drawing from surface to surface is not much more complicated.

The first thing we want to do is fill a DDBLTFX structure. This structure simply explains how the blit from surface to surface is to be carried out. The following is how we set up our DDBLTFX when we draw from our draw_surface to our back_surface.

```
DDBLTFX ddbltfx = {0}; // Blit parameters

// Fill the DDBLTFX fields we care about
ddbltfx.dwSize = sizeof(DDBLTFX); // Must always be set
ddbltfx.dwDDFX = DDBLTFX_NOTEARING;
ddbltfx.ddckSrcColorkey = color_key;
```

Setting the dwDDFX to DDBLTFX_NOTEARING, means that when we draw to the screen we never want to tear the image. Tearing is a visual atrocity produced when the screen refresh rate is out of sync with an application's frame rate. The top portion of the current frame is displayed at the same time the bottom portion of the last frame is being displayed resulting in a virtual tear in the screen. So setting this flag prevents this from happening at all costs. Now color_key is our transparency color to use during the blit. I'll talk at a much greater length about transparency colors in the next section of this chapter. We have our DDBLTFX structure filled with the pertinent information so we can actually blit one surface to the other.

```
// Blit the draw_surface to the back_surface
back_surface->Blt(NULL, draw_surface, NULL, DDBLT_WAIT | DDBLT_KEYSRCOVERRIDE,
    &ddbltfx);
```

The first parameter, NULL, is the RECT specifying the destination of the blit. By passing in NULL we're saying use the entire area of the destination surface for the blit. The second parameter, draw_suface, is the source for the blit. It's what we are drawing. The third parameter, NULL, is the RECT specifying the source area for the blit. Again by passing NULL, we are saying use the entire source area for the blit. DDBLT_WAIT and DBLT_KEYSRCOVERRIDE are two flags that govern how the blit should be carried out. They basically say, if we can't blit because the hardware is already drawing, wait until it is done and then blit. Also, when we do get to blit, use the source surface transparency color in the DDBLTFX structure passed in. Lastly, ddbltfx is the structure we filled with the transparency color and the flag stipulating we don't want any tearing.

Those are the four basic steps in creation of a DirectDraw application. It's really quite simple once you get your feet wet. Everything we've talked about here is utilized in the sample source code provided.

Before we move on to transparency colors, we need to make sure you can compile a DirectDraw application. Because everybody has his or her own custom setup, it's impossible to say one way or another why something would compile on one person's machine but not on another's. For a majority of people, the sample source code should compile verbatim. However, if you cannot get the sprite sample to compile, follow these steps:

1. Search for these files on your computer: `ddraw.lib`, `dxguid.lib`, and `ddraw.h`. If you cannot find all three of these files on your computer, you need to download the latest edition of DirectX.

2. Copy each of these files and paste them in the local directory of your project.

3. Change the angled brackets (<>'s) around `ddraw.h` (included in `DDrawObj.h`) to quotation marks. So the line that includes `ddraw.h` should look like this: `#include "ddraw.h."`

That should do it. Recompile and make sure any unresolved externals and other linking errors are resolved. If you are still having compiler problems, there's a 99% chance it has to do with an error other than not being able to link to the needed files for a DirectDraw application.

Transparency with Sprites

Because drawing to the screen requires the use of rectangles, this creates a problem when wanting to make a sprite of nonrectangular shape. To get around this, the artists and/or programmers agree on a color that will be the *transparency color*. A transparency color is an RGB value that does not get displayed when an image is drawn to the screen. Two typical transparency colors are solid black and bright pink. Once you have an image with a transparency color, you can then perform a *transparent blit*. A transparent blit is the rendering of an image to the screen in which all pixels whose color is equivalent to a preset transparency color are skipped and not drawn.

Some confuse transparent blitting with alpha blending. Alpha blending is a technique that uses the alpha channel of an image (only 32-bit images have a true alpha channel) to determine the opacity of the image. Therefore, a pixel with an alpha value of 0 will be drawn completely transparent. A pixel with an alpha value of 255 will be drawn completely opaque. Alpha blending is completely separate from transparent blitting; however, you can achieve transparency using alpha blending, although it's slower.

For our application I picked, RGB (215,0,215) as our transparency color (which happens to be a bright pinkish color). It's extremely easy to see this color compared to the rest of the sprite image. DirectDraw handles transparency by having you set a color key. In Step #4 of the overview of DirectDraw basics, we used a variable color_key to set the transparency color for Blt(). In general, a *color key* is the value to use for transparency during a blit. You declare a color key in DirectDraw by doing the following:

```
DDCOLORKEY color_key; // Transparency color key
```

A DDCOLORKEY contains a low and high value, allowing you to set a range of transparency colors if you so choose. For our purposes, and in general, it's probably best to stick to one transparency color for an entire application. It's also a good idea to have this color be symmetrical (i.e., the red and blue components are the same value).

To set the transparency color we do the following:

```
COLORREF trans_color = RGB(215,0,215);

color_key.dwColorSpaceHighValue = (DWORD)trans_color;
color_key.dwColorSpaceLowValue = (DWORD)trans_color;
```

The compiler expects the high value and low value to be DWORDs, so we have to typecast to keep it happy.

If you have forgotten how to perform a transparent blit in DirectDraw, flip back a few pages and you will find the answers to your questions.

Drawing and Moving Sprites

All right, we've done all the back work and now we're ready for some good old-fashioned sprite-drawing pleasure. First, lets take a look at the CSprite class.

```
class CSprite {

public:

// Constructor
CSprite();

// Data Access Functions *****

  int getDir() const { return dir; }

  int getX() const { return x_pos; }
  int getY() const { return y_pos; }

  int getWidth() const { return width; }
  int getHeight() const { return height; }

  HDC getHDC() const { return image.getHDC(); }

// ***** End of Data Access Functions
// Initializes CSprite data
bool initSpriteData(int init_dir, int x, int y, int init_x_vel, int init_y_vel,

 int desired_fps, char *file_name, int num_frames);

void setDir(int new_dir); // Set direction of CSprite
void setXVel(int new_x_vel); // Set the velocity in the x direction
void setYVel(int new_y_vel); // Set the velocity in the y direction

void move(); // Moves the sprite in its current direction

bool canMove(int dir, const RECT &collide_rect, uchar type = BOUNDARY);

int getSrcX() const; // Returns the x coord of where to blit from in CImage
int getSrcY() const; // Returns the y coord of where to blit from in CImage

private:

CImage image; // The image that contains all "frames" of the CSprite

int dir; // CSprite's direction
```

```
int cur_frame; // Current frame
int max_frames; // Maximum number of frames
float fps; // Number of frames of animation per second to display

int width; // Width of CSprite
int height; // Height of CSprite

int x_pos; // Upper left x coord of CSprite on the screen
int y_pos; // Upper left y coord of CSprite on the screen

int x_vel; // Velocity in the x direction (horizontally)
int y_vel; // Velocity in the y direction (vertically)

void updateFrame(); // Updates to the next frame
bool timeToUpdateFrame(); // Returns true if it's time to update the frame,

 false otherwise


// Returns true if CSprite HAS NOT COLLIDED with the bounding area specified by
// rect (assumes CSprite was initally inside this area), false otherwise
    bool boundsCheck(const RECT &rect, int x, int y);

// Returns true if CSprite HAS NOT COLLIDED with rect, false otherwise
    bool rectAreaCheck(const RECT &rect, int x, int y);

};
```

Hopefully that doesn't look too daunting. I swear it's really easy. Before we get into what each method specifically does, lets talk about our sprite character a little bit. Our sprite is a creature that has four directions it can move in north, west, south, and east. For each direction it can move in, there are four frames of animation. Our sprite is contained in only one image. This means we must be able to parse out the correct frame of animation based upon the sprite's animation state. Our CSprite class provides us with a painless way to do that. The class is quite flexible but there are some rules that must be followed.

1. Animations sequences in the image must be arranged in the following order: north, west, south, and east. However, if you want to add other directions, it's a piece of cake.

2. The CSprite may have only one transparency color.

3. All animation sequences must be comprised of an equal number of animation frames. We'll talk about a simple way to alter this later.

4. Each animation frame should be the same width and height. Although it's not essential for the CSprite class to operate, each animation frame of the sprite should also be contained in the smallest enclosing rectangular area as possible.

Figure 9.3 illustrates our sprite layout.

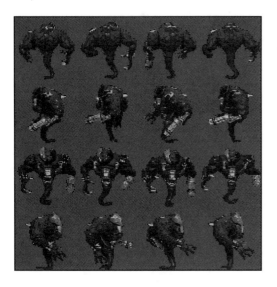

Figure 9.3

A sample sprite page used for animation

As long as we follow those simple rules, the CSprite class will allow us the ability to do quite a few things. With it we can draw sprites, moves sprites around on the screen, cycle through a sprite's animation frames, increase or decrease the velocity at which a sprite moves, increase or decrease the frame rate of the sprite's animations, and check for bounding and box collision.

So without any further ado, let's go through each of the CSprites starting from the top. We'll skip the constructor and data access functions because it's painfully obvious what they do. So, first up is the initSpriteData() method.

```
// Initializes CSprite data
void initSpriteData(int init_dir, int x, int y, int init_x_vel, int init_y_vel, int
    desired_fps, char *file_name, int num_frames);
```

As the name implies, this initializes all the variables of the CSprite. What gets initialized (in order of being passed into the method) is the following: the initial direction the sprite is heading, the starting upper-left x and y coordinates of the sprite, the starting velocities the CSprites move down the x and y axes, the frame rate between sprite animations, the name of the file storing the CSprite image, and last but not least, the number of animation frames for the CSprite.

For our sprite to be displayed correctly, it is imperative that the image is laid out as shown in Figure 9.4.

The sprite image layout can be thought of as the following grid:

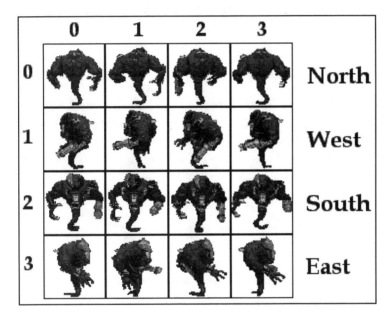

Figure 9.4

A sprite page in grid format

Each animation set (for instance, all the frames that constitute walking north) is a row in the grid. The first frame of animation (starting on the left) corresponds to column zero in the grid. The last frame of animation (ending on the right) corresponds to the third column in the grid. When we reach the last frame of animation, we will wrap around back to the beginning, so the last frame needs to sync up with the first frame of animation.

The three set methods in our CSprite do the following:

```
void setDir(int new_dir); // This sets the direction are sprite is
    facing/traveling in. Valid directions for our sprite are north, west, south and
    east
```

```
void setXVel(int new_x_vel); // This method sets the velocity that our sprite
    for traveling the "x-axis" (horizontally)
```

```
void setYVel(int new_y_vel); // This method sets the velocity that our sprite
    for traveling the "y-axis" (vertically)
```

If you think back to the math class that you frequently skipped to go to the beach, you might recall the notion of velocity. Basically all velocity is, in this context, is how fast or slow we are going to move in a certain direction. So, for instance, the higher our x velocity, the faster the sprite will travel right and left. If either velocity is ever set to a negative value, the controls will reverse. If the CSprite's x velocity is –5, it will push the key to move our sprite to the right.

The next method in the CSprite is the move method.

```
void move(); // Moves the sprite in it's current direction
```

The move method simply moves the CSprite in the direction it's heading by the specified amount of the CSprite's x and y velocities. Let's suppose our CSprite's upper-left coordinate is located at (5,5) and it's x and y velocity are both 2. We press a key to move the CSprite one unit to the right. The CSprite's resulting upper-left position would be (7,5). See, simple algebra is useful.

Continuing down, the next method is canMove().

```
bool canMove(int dir, const RECT &collide_rect, uchar type = BOUNDARY);
```

Let's break down each parameter:

- dir—the direction you want to check (north, west, south, east)
- collide_rect—the rectangular area you want to use for determining if a collision happened or not
- type—the type of collision check you want to perform

So, to sum it up, the canMove() method returns true if the sprite can move in the specified direction using the specified collision RECT, utilizing the specified collision check. Yeah, that's a mouthful all right. The beauty is that you can add your own collision types (for instance, collision with a circle) really quickly and easily. We will talk more about collision later on.

We are down to the final two public methods of our CSprite. These methods' implementation are extremely easy, but absolutely vital to the sprite being displayed correctly.

```
int getSrcX() const; // Returns the x coord of where to blit from in CImage
int getSrcY() const; // Returns the y coord of where to blit from in CImage
```

If you recall, we said the image and its layout that defines our sprite can be thought of as a grid like Figure 9.4.

All animation sequences start at the left (column 0) and end at the right (column 3). Because each sprite is the exact same width and height (64×64) we can easily deduce the upper-left x coordinate by the following equation:

Sprites current frame * width of sprite;

So say we're heading north and we are on frame two of the animation. The equation would give us this as our source x for blitting (see Figure 9.5):

2 *64 (width of sprite) = 128

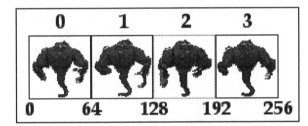

Figure 9.5

Sprite offset example

In a similar fashion, we can easily calculate the upper-left y coordinate to begin blitting from. The equation for this is:

Sprites current direction * height of sprite;

We define the directions our sprite can move as follows:

```
#define NORTH 0
#define WEST 1
#define SOUTH 2
#define EAST 3
```

Notice how that matches exactly the row numbers in the grid layout of our image. Thus, if we were heading south, the equation to obtain the upper-left y coordinate would give us:

2 * 64 (height of sprite) = 128

Hopefully, the reasons we imposed certain rules on the layout of the sprite image are becoming much clearer. It is imperative to set some structure on how the image is laid out or a ton of extra work would have to be done on the programming side of things.

Now it's time to discuss private methods. The `boundsCheck()` and `rectAreaCheck()` get explained in the next section of this chapter so we're only going to talk about `updateFrame()` and `timeToUpdateFrame()` right now.

```
void updateFrame(); // Updates to the next frame
```

The `updateFrame()` function simply updates the current frame count. When the frame count equals the maximum number of frames, it gets set back to zero.

```
// Returns true if it's time to update the frame, false otherwise
bool timeToUpdateFrame();
```

This method is used to determine if it's time to draw the frame or not. It might not seem obvious why we need to have a timer for every frame of animation, so let's go over a quick example of why we do. Say my sprite has four frames of animation. Your final application runs at a solid 30 frames-per-second. That means your animation sequence will run 30/4 times-per-second. That comes out to 7.5 times through the entire animation sequence every second! Chances are that's much faster than what you want. Thus, our `CSprite` has the ability to set the frame rate for advancing to the next animation frame. There's not a set rule for stipulating what the frame rate should be for a sprite. Through a little empirical analysis, I found that having the frame rate equal to the maximum number of frames of the sprite worked best for the look I was going for. You'll just have to play to get the look you want.

That pretty much wraps up the `CSprite` class. Any method we didn't specifically discuss should be self-explanatory. Of course, the full implementation and additional comments are provided in the source code of the CD.

There is one thing that seems to be missing—how in the heck do we draw the sprite? Well, as you've noticed, the `CSprite` class doesn't handle the actual drawing of the sprite. We use our `DDrawObj` for all drawing routines. However, the `CSprite` gives us all the information needed to fill in a `BitBlt()` call when filling the draw surface of our `DDrawObj`. Following is an example of a `BitBlt()` function that draws our sprite to the draw surface.

```
BitBlt(draw_hdc, sprite.getX(), sprite.getY(), sprite.getWidth(), sprite.getHeight(),
    sprite.getHDC(), sprite.getSrcX(), sprite.getSrcY(), SRCCOPY);
```

Let's break this code down by argument:

- `draw_hdc`—The first argument of `BitBlt()` is where we want to draw to. It is our destination device context. For the sprite demo, this is our `DDrawObj`'s draw surface.

- sprite.getX()—The second argument of BitBlt() is the upper-left x coordinate of the rectangular area to draw to. If you look at the definition for CSprite, this is exactly what getX() returns.

- sprite.getY()—The third argument of BitBlt() is the upper-left y coordinate of the rectangular area to draw to. Again, this is exactly what getY() in CSprite returns.

- sprite.getWidth()—The fourth argument of BitBlt() is the width of the destination rectangle for drawing to. The width will always correspond to the width of our sprite.

- sprite.getHeight()—The fifth argument of BitBlt() is the height of the destination rectangle for drawing to. The height will always correspond to the height of our sprite.

- sprite.getHDC()—The sixth argument of BitBlt() is where we want to draw from. It is our source device context. For our sprite demo this will always be the CSprite's HDC.

- sprite.getSrcX()—The seventh argument of BitBlt() is the upper-left x coordinate of where we want to draw from. This vertical offset into the sprite image is determined by the sprite's current animation state. We'll talk more on this later.

- sprite.getSrcY()—The eighth argument of BitBlt() is the upper-left y coordinate of where we want to draw from. This horizontal offset into the sprite image is determined by the sprite's current animation state. Again, more on this later.

- SRCCOPY—The final argument to BitBlt() is the ROP (Raster-Operation Code). This particular ROP means, "Copy the source rectangular area directly to the destination rectangular area."

That wraps up everything necessary for moving and displaying a sprite. Be sure to check out the source code provided so you can see everything we've talked about up to this point in action.

Basic Collision Detection with Sprites

Well, we are able to load a sprite, display a sprite, and move a sprite around the screen. We need one more element in place before we have a great base for a kickin' 2-D side-scroller—collision detection. When you are dealing with sprites, there are two major types of collision detection you work with: *boundary collision detection* and *rectangular area collision detection*. Boundary collision detection is when you have a sprite inside a rectangular boundary and check to make sure that it is still contained within that boundary after a sprite moves. This is a lot easier to implement than it is to articulate in a sentence. The following illustration (Figure 9.6) shows exactly what we are checking for.

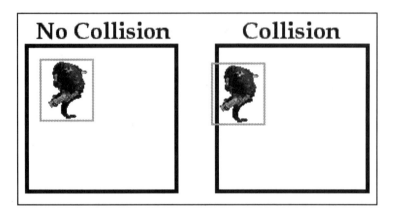

Figure 9.6

Collision detection

Basically we're just keeping a box (the rectangle that defines the sprite) inside another bigger box (the window in our case). The code to do this is completely painless. Assuming rect is the bounding rectangle we are checking, (x,y) is the upper-left corner of the sprite, and width and height are the width and height of the sprite, this is all you have to do:

```
if(x < rect.left) // Check left X coordinate
  return false;

if(x + width > rect.right) // Check right X coordinate
  return false;

if(y < rect.top) // Check top Y coordinate
  return false;

if(y + height > rect.bottom) // Check bottom Y coordinate
  return false;

return true;
```

The other commonly used collision type when dealing with sprites is rectangular area collision. This is also commonly referred to as bounding box collision.

Rectangular area collision occurs when one rectangle (the rectangle that defines the sprite) intersects another rectangular (this could be pretty much anything you want). The following illustration shows what we are checking for:

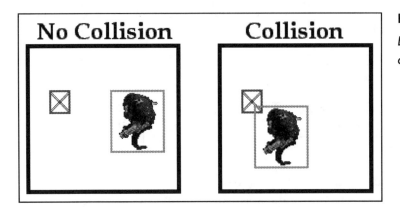

Figure 9.7

Bounding box collision detection

Luckily, just like boundary collision, the code to do this is painless. Assuming rect is the rectangle you want to check collision with, (x,y) is the upper-left corner of the sprite, and width and height are the width and height of the sprite, all you have to do is this:

```
// RECT of CSprite in screen coordinates
RECT sprite_rect = {x, y, x + width, y + height};

RECT temp;

// This handy dandy Win32 function will determine if the RECT's "sprite_rect"
   and "rect"
// collide or not -- Additionally, if there is a collision, "temp" will get
   filled with the
// RECT that defines the area of the collision
if(IntersectRect(&temp,&sprite_rect,&rect))
   return false;

return true;
```

Isn't collision easy with sprites? When you add physics to the equation that's when things get a little more complicated, but basic collision detection is really quite simple. The demo on the CD has the source code to do both boundary and rectangular area collision although it only uses boundary in the application itself.

Summary

Doesn't it feel good to be a sprite guru? Once you begin work on the next great sidescroller, it's good to know some performance results that are obtainable.

The sprite demo provided on the CD produced the following frame rates:

OS	Processor	Ram	Video Card	FPS
Windows 2000	PIII—1 Ghz	256 MB	GeForce2	73
Windows '98 SE	PIII—1.4 Ghz	512 MB	GeForce2	181
Windows 2000	PIII—800 Mhz	256 MB	GeForce3	385

Figure 9.8

Frame rate information per system

Assuming you go on to make a full-fledge sprite-based video game, you can expect your end frame rates to be lower. Additional sprites, collision checks, sound, AI, etc., will eat away at your frame rate.

Chapter Conclusion

In case every last word on the previous pages didn't get etched into your memory, here is a quick summary of the more important points the chapter covered.

- Bitmaps (.bmp files) are comprised of three main parts: the bitmap file header, the bitmap info header, and the bitmap's pixel bits.

- A bitmap's number of channels defines the number of bytes per pixel that bitmap has.

- A bitmap's stride is the total number of bytes contained in one line of pixels. The stride of a bitmap will always be `dword` aligned.

- Loading our own images manually is important. It provides us with the flexibility to load other file types that are not handy and APIs allow us to manipulate the images with code if we so desire.

- There are four main parts to a DirectDraw application: create a DirectDraw interface, create DirectDraw surfaces, create a DirectDraw clipper, and blit to the screen.

- A transparency color is an RGB value that represents a color that will appear transparent (i.e., not drawn to the screen) in an image. This color is also referred to as a color key.

If you yearn for more information (and don't we all?), the following Web sites should help you out:

> **http://gamedev.net/**
>
> **http://www.gametutorials.com/**
>
> **http://www.flipcode.com/**

With the knowledge gathered here and at the aforementioned sites, you should be a 2-D sprite master in no time at all. Happy coding!!!

TRICK 10

Moving Beyond OpenGL 1.1 for Windows

Dave Astle, GameDev.net,
www.gamedev.net

Introduction

Once you've been programming with OpenGL for Windows for a while, you'll probably notice that the headers and libraries you're using are old. Dig around in the gl.h header, and you'll see the following:

```
#define GL_VERSION_1_1                          1
```

This means you're using OpenGL 1.1, which was released in 1996. In the world of graphics, that's ancient! If you've been paying attention, you know that the current OpenGL specification is 1.3 (at the time of this writing). OpenGL 1.4 should be released later this year, with 2.0 following soon after. Obviously, you need to update your OpenGL headers and libraries to something more recent.

As it turns out, the most recent headers and libraries for Windows correspond to . . . OpenGL 1.1. That's right, the files you already have are the most recent ones available.

This, of course, presents a problem. Although you can do some impressive things with OpenGL 1.1, to take full advantage of modern consumer graphics hardware, you're going to need functionality available through more recent versions, as well as features available through extensions (but we'll get to that in a bit). The question, then, is how to access newer features when your headers and libraries are stuck at OpenGL 1.1. The purpose of this chapter is to answer that question.

In this chapter, I will do the following:

- Explain in greater detail why you need to take some extra steps to use anything beyond OpenGL 1.1

- Explain OpenGL's extension mechanism and how it can be used to access OpenGL 1.2 and 1.3 functionality

- Give you an overview of the new options available in OpenGL 1.2 and 1.3 and a look at some of the most useful extensions

- Give you some tips for using extensions while ensuring that your game will run well on a wide range of systems

- Provide a demo showing you how to use the techniques described

The Problem

If you're new to OpenGL or have only needed the functionality offered in OpenGL 1.1, you may be confused about what the problem is, so let's clarify.

To develop for a given version of OpenGL on Windows, you need three things. First, you need a set of libraries (opengl32.lib and possibly others such as glu32.lib) and headers (gl.h, and so on) corresponding to the version you'd like to use. These headers and libraries contain the OpenGL functions, constants, and other things you need to compile and link an OpenGL application. Second, the system on which you intend to run the application needs to have an OpenGL dynamic link library (OpenGL32.dll) or OpenGL runtime library. The runtime needs to be for either the same or a more recent version of OpenGL as the headers and libraries you're using. Ideally, you will also have a third component called an Installable Client Driver (ICD). An ICD is provided by the video card drivers to allow for hardware acceleration of OpenGL features as well as possible enhancements provided by the graphics vendor.

So, let's look at these three things and see why you have to jump through a few hoops to use anything newer than OpenGL 1.1:

- **Headers and libraries.** As I mentioned in the introduction, the latest versions of the OpenGL headers and libraries available from Microsoft correspond to version 1.1. If you look around on the Internet, you may come across another OpenGL implementation for Windows created by Silicon Graphics (SGI). SGI's implementation also corresponds to OpenGL 1.1. Unfortunately, this implementation is no longer supported by SGI. In addition, the Microsoft implementation is based on it, so you really gain nothing by using it. Where does that leave us?

  Well, there is reason to hope that someone will release up-to-date libraries. Although (to my knowledge) no one has committed to doing so, several parties have discussed it. Microsoft is the obvious candidate, and despite years of promising and not delivering, it appears that the company has taken an interest in the recently proposed OpenGL 2.0. Whether that interest will lead to action remains to be seen, but given the large number of graphics workstations running Windows NT and Windows 2000, it's not beyond the realm of possibility.

  Besides Microsoft, there have apparently been discussions among the members of OpenGL's Architectural Review Board (ARB) to provide their own implementation of the headers and libraries. At present, though, this is still in the discussion stage, so it may be a while before we see anything come of it.

- **The runtime.** Most versions of Windows (the first release of Windows 95 being the exception) come with a 1.1 runtime. Fortunately, this isn't really as important as the other elements. All that the runtime does is guarantee a baseline level of functionality and allow you to interface with the ICD.

- **The ICD.** This is the one area where you're okay. Most hardware vendors (including NVIDIA and ATI) have been keeping up with the latest OpenGL standard. For them to be able to advertise that their drivers are compliant with the OpenGL 1.3 standard, they have to support everything included in the 1.3 specification (though not necessarily in hardware). The cool thing about this is that the ICD contains the code to do everything in newer versions of OpenGL, and we can take advantage of that.

The thing that's important to note here is that although the headers and libraries available don't directly enable you to access newer OpenGL features, the features do exist in the video card drivers. You just need to find a way to access those features in your code. You do that by using OpenGL's extension mechanism.

OpenGL Extensions

As you're aware, the graphics industry has been moving at an alarmingly rapid pace for many years now. Today, consumer-level video cards include features that were only available on professional video cards (costing thousands of dollars) a few years ago. Any viable graphics API has to take these advances into account and provide some means to keep up with them. OpenGL does this through extensions.

If a graphics vendor adds a new hardware feature that it wants OpenGL programmers to be able to take advantage of, it simply needs to add support for the feature in its ICD and then provide developers with documentation as to how to use the extension. This is oversimplifying a bit, but it's close enough for our purposes. As an OpenGL programmer, you can then access the extension through a common interface shared by all extensions. You'll learn how to do this in the "Using Extensions" section later in this chapter, but for now let's look at how extensions are identified and what they consist of.

Extension Names

Every OpenGL extension has a name by which it can be precisely and uniquely identified. This is important because hardware vendors frequently introduce extensions with similar functionality but very different semantics and usage. You need to be able to distinguish between them. For example, both NVIDIA and ATI provide extensions for programmable vertex and pixel shaders, but they bear little resemblance to each other. So, if you want to use pixel shaders in your program, it isn't enough to find out whether the hardware supports pixel shaders. You have to be able to specifically ask whether NVIDIA's or ATI's version is supported and then handle each appropriately.

All OpenGL extensions use the following naming convention:

`PREFIX_extension_name`

The `PREFIX` is there to help avoid naming conflicts. It also helps identify the developer of the extension or, as in the case of EXT and ARB, its level of promotion. Table 10.1 lists most of the prefixes currently in use. The `extension_name` identifies the extension. Note that the name cannot contain any spaces. Some sample extension names are `ARB_multitexture`, `EXT_bgra`, `NV_vertex_program`, and `ATI_fragment_shader`.

Table 10.1 OpenGL Extension Prefixes

Prefix	Meaning/Vendor
ARB	Extension approved by OpenGL's Architectural Review Board (first introduced with OpenGL 1.2)
EXT	Extension agreed on by more than one OpenGL vendor
3DFX	3dfx Interactive
APPLE	Apple Computer
ATI	ATI Technologies
ATIX	ATI Technologies (experimental)
HP	Hewlett-Packard

continues

Table 10.1 OpenGL Extension Prefixes *(continued)*

Prefix	Meaning/Vendor
INTEL	Intel Corporation
IBM	International Business Machines
KTX	Kinetix
NV	NVIDIA Corporation
MESA	www.mesa3d.org
OML	OpenML
SGI	Silicon Graphics
SGIS	Silicon Graphics (specialized)
SGIX	Silicon Graphics (experimental)
SUN	Sun Microsystems
SUNX	Sun Microsystems (experimental)
WIN	Microsoft

CAUTION

Some extensions share a name but have a different prefix. These extensions generally are not interchangeable because they may use entirely different semantics. For example, ARB_texture_env_combine is not the same thing as EXT_texture_env_combine. Rather than making assumptions, be sure to consult the extension specifications when you're unsure.

What an Extension Includes

You now know what an extension is and how extensions are named. Next let's turn our attention to the relevant components of an extension. There are four parts of an extension that you need to deal with.

Name Strings

Each extension defines a name string, which you can use to determine whether the OpenGL implementation supports it. By passing *GL_EXTENSIONS* to the `glGetString()` method, you can get a space-delimited buffer containing all the extension name strings supported by the implementation.

Name strings are generally the name of the extension preceded by another prefix. For core OpenGL name strings, this is always GL_ (for example, `GL_EXT_texture_compression`). When the name string is tied to a particular Windows system, the prefix will reflect which system that is (for example, Win32 uses WGL_).

> **NOTE**
>
> Some extensions may define more than one name string. This would be the case if the extension provided both core OpenGL functionality and functionality specific to the Windows system.

Functions

Many (but not all) extensions introduce one or more new functions to OpenGL. To use these functions, you'll have to obtain their entry point, which requires that you know the name of the function. This process is described in detail in the "Using Extensions" section later in this chapter.

The functions defined by the extension follow the naming convention used by the rest of OpenGL, namely `glFunctionName()`, with the addition of a suffix using the same letters as the extension name's prefix. For example, the *NV_fence* extension includes the functions `glGetFencesNV()`, `glSetFenceNV()`, `glTestFenceNV()`, and so on.

Enumerants

An extension may define one or more enumerants. In some extensions, these enumerants are intended for use in the new functions defined by the extension (which may be able to use existing enumerants as well). In other cases, they are intended for use in standard OpenGL functions, thereby adding new options to them. For example, the `ARB_texture_env_add` extension defines a new enumerant, `GL_ADD`. This enumerant can be passed as the *params* parameter of the various `glTexEnv()` functions when the *pname* parameter is `GL_TEXTURE_ENV_MODE`.

The new enumerants follow the normal OpenGL naming convention (that is, `GL_WHATEVER`), except that they are suffixed by the letters used in the extension name's prefix, such as `GL_VERTEX_SOURCE_ATI`.

Using new enumerants is much simpler than using new functions. Usually, you will just need to include a header defining the enumerant, which you can get from your hardware vendor or from SGI. Alternately, you can define the enumerant yourself if you know the integer value it uses. This value can be obtained from the extension's documentation.

Dependencies

Very few extensions stand completely alone. Some require the presence of other extensions, while others take this a step further and modify or extend the usage of other extensions. When you begin using a new extension, you need to read the specification and understand the extension's dependencies.

TIP

Extensions don't need to define both functions and enumerants (though many do), but they'll always include at least one of the two. There wouldn't be much point to an extension that didn't include either!

Speaking of documentation, you're probably wondering where you can get it, so let's talk about that next.

Extension Documentation

Although vendors may (and usually do) provide documentation for their extensions in many forms, one piece of documentation is absolutely essential—the specification. These are generally written as plain text files and include a broad range of information about the extension, such as its name, version number, dependencies, new functions and enumerants, issues, and modifications/additions to the OpenGL specification.

The specifications are intended for use by developers of OpenGL hardware or ICDs and, as such, are of limited use to game developers. They'll tell you what the extension does but not why you'd want to use it or how to use it. For that reason, I'm not going to go over the details of the specification format. If you're interested, Mark Kilgard has written an excellent article about it that you can read at **www.opengl.org**.[1]

As new extensions are released, their specifications are listed in the OpenGL Extension Registry, which you can find at the following URL:

http://oss.sgi.com/projects/ogl-sample/registry/

This registry is updated regularly, so it's a great way to keep up with the newest additions to OpenGL.

For more detailed descriptions of new extensions, your best bet is the Web sites of the leading hardware vendors. In particular, NVIDIA[2] and ATI[3] both provide a wealth of information, including white papers, PowerPoint presentations, and demos.

CAUTION

Including links to Web sites in a book is dangerous because they can change frequently. The links I've included here have remained constant for a while, so I hope they are relatively safe. If you find a broken link, you should be able to visit **www.opengl.org** and find the new location of the information.

NOTE

Extensions that are promoted to be part of the core OpenGL specification may be removed from the Extension Registry. To obtain information about these, you'll have to refer to the latest OpenGL specification.[4]

Using Extensions

Finally, it's time to learn what you need to do to use an extension. In general, there are three steps you need to take:

1. Determine whether or not the extension is supported.

2. Obtain the entry point for any of the extension's functions you want to use.

3. Define any enumerants you're going to use.

Let's look at each of these steps in greater detail.

CAUTION

Before checking for extension availability and obtaining pointers to functions, you *must* have a current rendering context. In addition, the entry points are specific to each rendering context, so if you're using more than one, you'll have to obtain a separate entry point for each.

Querying the Name String

To find out whether or not a specific extension is available, first get the list of all of the name strings supported by the OpenGL implementation. To do this, you just need to call glGetString() using GL_EXTENSIONS, as follows:

```
char• extensionsList = (char•) glGetString(GL_EXTENSIONS);
```

After this executes, extensionsList points to a null-terminated buffer containing the name strings of all the extensions available to you. These name strings are separated by spaces, including a space after the last name string.

To find out whether or not the extension you're looking for is supported, you'll need to search this buffer to see if it includes the extension's name string. I'm not going to go into great detail about how to parse the buffer because there are many ways to do so. It's something that at this stage in your programming career you should be able to do without much effort. One thing you need to watch out for, though, is accidentally matching a sub-

> **NOTE**
>
> I'm casting the value returned by glGetString() because the function actually returns an array of unsigned chars. Since most of the string manipulation functions I'll be using require signed chars, I do the cast once now instead of doing it many times later.

string. For example, if you're trying to use the EXT_texture_env extension and the implementation doesn't support it but does support EXT_texture_env_dot3, then calling something like

```
strstr("GL_EXT_texture_env", extensionsList);
```

is going to give you positive results, making you think that the EXT_texture_env extension is supported when it's really not. The CheckExtension() function in the demo program included on the accompanying CD-ROM shows one way to avoid this problem.

Obtaining the Function's Entry Point

Because of the way in which Microsoft handles its OpenGL implementation, calling a new function provided by an extension requires that you request a function pointer to the entry point from the ICD. This isn't as bad as it sounds.

First of all, you need to declare a function pointer. If you've worked with function pointers before, you know that they can be pretty ugly. If you haven't, here's an example:

```
void (APIENTRY • glCopyTexSubImage3DEXT) (GLenum, GLint, GLint, GLint, GLint, GLint,
    GLint, GLsizei, GLsizei) = NULL;
```

Now that you have the function pointer, you can attempt to assign an entry point to it. This is done using the *wglGetProcAddress()* function:

```
PROC wglGetProcAddress( LPCSTR  lpszProcName );
```

The only parameter is the name of the function for which you want to get the address. The return value is the entry point of the function if it exists; otherwise, it's NULL. Since the value returned is essentially a generic pointer, you need to cast it to the appropriate function pointer type.

Let's look at an example using the function pointer previously declared:

```
glCopyTexSubImage3DEXT   =
    (void (APIENTRY •) (GLenum, GLint, GLint, GLint, GLint, GLint, GLint, GLsizei,
    GLsizei))
    wglGetProcAddress("glCopyTexSubImage3DEXT");
```

And you thought the function pointer declaration was ugly.

You can make life easier on yourself by using typedefs. In fact, you can obtain a header called glext.h that contains typedefs for most of the extensions out there. This header can usually be obtained from your favorite hardware vendor (for example, NVIDIA includes it in its OpenGL SDK) or from SGI at the following URL:

http://oss.sgi.com/projects/ogl-sample/ABI/glext.h

Using this header, the preceding code becomes:

```
PFNGLCOPYTEXSUBIMAGE3DEXTPROC glCopyTexSubImage3DEXT = NULL;
glCopyTexSubImage3DEXT = (PFNGLCOPYTEXSUBIMAGE3DEXTPROC)
    wglGetProcAddress("glCopyTexSubImage3DEXT");
```

Isn't that a lot better?

As long as wglGetProcAddress() doesn't return NULL, you can freely use the function pointer as if it were a normal OpenGL function.

Declaring Enumerants

To use new enumerants defined by an extension, all you have to do is define the enumerant to be the appropriate integer value. You can find this value in the extension specification. For example, the specification for the EXT_texture_lod_bias says that GL_TEXTURE_LOD_BIAS_EXT should have a value of *0x8501*, so somewhere, probably in a header (or possibly even in gl.h), you'd have the following:

```
#define GL_TEXTURE_LOD_BIAS_EXT    0x8501
```

Rather than defining all these values yourself, you can use the glext.h header, mentioned in the preceding section, because it contains all of them for you. Most OpenGL programmers I know use this header, so don't hesitate to use it yourself and save some typing time.

Win32 Specifics

In addition to the standard extensions that have been covered so far, there are some that are specific to the Windows system. These extensions provide additions that are very specific to the windowing system and the way it interacts with OpenGL, such as additional options related to pixel formats. These extensions are easily identified by their use of WGL instead of GL in their names. The name strings for these extensions normally aren't included in the buffer returned by glGetString(GL_EXTENSIONS), although a few are. To get all of the Windows-specific extensions, you'll have to use another function, wglGetExtensionsStringARB(). As the ARB suffix indicates, it's an extension itself (ARB_extensions_string), so you'll have to get the address of it yourself using wglGetProcAddress(). Note that, for some reason, some ICDs identify this as

CAUTION

Normally, it's good practice to check for an extension by examining the buffer returned by glGetString() before trying to obtain function entry points. However, it's not strictly necessary to do so. If you try to get the entry point for a nonexistent function, wglGetProcAddress() will return **NULL**, and you can simply test for that. The reason I'm mentioning this is because to use wglGetExtensionsStringARB(), that's exactly what you have to do. It appears that with most ICDs, the name string for this extension, WGL_ARB_extensions_string, doesn't appear in the buffer returned by glGetString(). Instead, it is included in the buffer returned by wglGetExtensionsStringARB()! Go figure.

wglGetExtensionsStringEXT() instead, so if you fail to get a pointer to one, try the other. The format of this function is as follows:

const char· wglGetExtensionsStringARB(HDC hdc);

Its sole parameter is the handle to your rendering context. The function returns a buffer similar to that returned by glGetString(GL_EXTEN-SIONS), the only difference being that it only contains the names of WGL extensions.

> **NOTE**
>
> Some **WGL** extension string names included in the buffer returned by wglGetExtensionsStringARB() **may also appear in the buffer returned by** glGetString().**This is because those extensions existed before the creation of the** ARB_extensions_string **extension, so their name strings appear in both places to avoid breaking existing software.**

Just as there is a glext.h header for core OpenGL extensions, there is a wglext.h for WGL extensions. You can find it at the following link:

http://oss.sgi.com/projects/ogl-sample/ABI/wglext.h

Extensions, OpenGL 1.2 and 1.3, and the Future

At the beginning of this chapter, I said that OpenGL 1.2 and 1.3 features could be accessed using the extensions mechanism, which I've spent the last several pages explaining. The question, then, is how you go about doing that. The answer, as you may have guessed, is to treat 1.2 and 1.3 features as extensions. When it comes right down to it, that's really what they are because nearly every feature that has been added to OpenGL originated as an extension. The only real difference between 1.2 and 1.3 features and "normal" extensions is that the former tend to be more widely supported in hardware because, after all, they are part of the standard.

> **NOTE**
>
> Sometimes an extension that has been added to the OpenGL 1.2 or 1.3 core specification will undergo slight changes, causing the semantics and/or behavior to be somewhat different from what is documented in the extension's specification.You should check the latest OpenGL specification to find out about these changes.

The next update to OpenGL will probably be 1.4. It most likely will continue the trend of promoting successful extensions to become part of the standard, and you should be able to continue to use the extension mechanism to access those features. After that, OpenGL 2.0 will hopefully make its appearance, introducing some radical changes to the standard. Once 2.0 is released, new headers and libraries may be released as well, possibly provided by the ARB. These will make it easier to use new features.

What You Get

As you can see, using OpenGL 1.2 and 1.3 (and extensions in general) isn't a terribly difficult process, but it does take some extra effort. You may be wondering what you can gain by using them, so let's take a closer look. The following sections list the features added by OpenGL 1.2 and 1.3, as well as some of the more useful extensions currently available. With each feature, I've included the extension you can use to access it.

OpenGL 1.2

3-D textures allow you to do some really cool volumetric effects. Unfortunately, they require a significant amount of memory. To give you an idea, a single 256×256×256 16-bit texture will use 32MB! For this reason, hardware support for them is relatively limited, and because they are also slower than 2-D textures, they may not always provide the best solution. They can, however, be useful if used judiciously. 3-D textures correspond to the EXT_texture3D extension.

BGRA pixel formats make it easier to work with file formats that use blue-green-red color-component ordering rather than red-green-blue. Bitmaps and Targas are two examples that fall in this category. BGRA pixel formats correspond to the EXT_bgra extension.

Packed pixel formats provide support for packed pixels in host memory, allowing you to completely represent a pixel using a single unsigned byte, short, or int. Packet pixel formats correspond to the EXT_packed_pixels extension, with some additions for reversed component order.

Normally, since texture mapping happens after lighting, modulating a texture with a lit surface will "wash out" specular highlights. To help avoid this effect, the *Separate Specular Color* feature has been added. This causes OpenGL to track the specular color separately and apply it after texture mapping. Separate specular color corresponds to the EXT_separate_specular_color extension.

Texture coordinate edge clamping addresses a problem with filtering at the edges of textures. When you select GL_CLAMP as your texture wrap mode and use a linear filtering mode, the border will get sampled along with edge texels, which are the 3-D equivalent to pixels. Texture coordinate edge clamping causes only the texels that are part of the texture to be sampled. This corresponds to the SGIS_texture_edge_clamp extension (which normally shows up as EXT_texture_edge_clamp in the GL_EXTENSIONS string).

Normal rescaling allows you to automatically scale normals by a value you specify. This can be faster than renormalization in some cases, although it requires uniform scaling to be useful. This corresponds to the EXT_rescale_normal extension.

Texture LOD control allows you to specify certain parameters related to the texture level of detail used in mipmapping to avoid popping in certain situations. It can also be used to increase texture transfer performance because the extension can be used to upload only the mipmap levels visible in the current frame instead of uploading the entire mipmap hierarchy. This matches the SGIS_texture_lod extension.

The *Draw Element Range* feature adds a new function to be used with vertex arrays. glDrawRangeElements() is similar to glDrawElements(), but it lets you indicate the range of indices within the arrays you are using, allowing the hardware to process the data more efficiently. This corresponds to the EXT_draw_range_elements extension.

The *imaging subset* is not fully present in all OpenGL implementations because it's primarily intended for image-processing applications. It's actually a collection of several extensions. The following are the ones that may be of interest to game developers:

- *EXT_blend_color* allows you to specify a constant color that is used to define blend weighting factors.
- *SGI_color_matrix* introduces a new matrix stack to the pixel pipeline, causing the RGBA components of each pixel to be multiplied by a 4×4 matrix.
- *EXT_blend_subtract* gives you two ways to use the difference between two blended surfaces (rather than the sum).
- *EXT_blend_minmax* lets you keep either the minimum or maximum color components of the source and destination colors.

OpenGL 1.3

The *multitexturing* extension was promoted to ARB status with OpenGL 1.2.1 (the only real change in that release), and in 1.3, it was made part of the standard. Multitexturing allows you to apply more than one texture to a surface in a single pass; this is useful for many things such as lightmapping and detail texturing. It was promoted from the `ARB_multitexture` extension.

Texture compression allows you either to provide OpenGL with precompressed data for your textures or to have the driver compress the data for you. The advantage of the latter is that you save both texture memory and bandwidth, thereby improving performance. Compressed textures were promoted from the `ARB_compressed_textures` extension.

Cube map textures provide a new type of texture consisting of six 2-D textures in the shape of a cube. Texture coordinates act like a vector from the center of the cube, indicating which face and which texels to use. Cube mapping is useful in environment mapping and texture-based diffuse lighting. It is also important for pixel-perfect dot3 bump mapping, as a normalization lookup for interpolated fragment normals. It was promoted from the `ARB_texture_cube_map` extension.

Multisampling allows for automatic antialiasing by sampling all geometry several times for each pixel. When it's supported, an extra buffer is created that contains color, depth, and stencil values. Multisampling is, of course, expensive, and you need to be sure to request a rendering context that supports it. It was promoted from the `ARB_multisampling` extension.

The *texture add environment mode* adds a new enumerant that can be passed to `glTexEnv()`. It causes the texture to be additively combined with the incoming fragment. This was promoted from the `ARB_texture_env_add` extension.

Texture combine environment modes add a lot of new options for the way textures are combined. In addition to the texture color and the incoming fragment, you can also include a constant texture color and the results of the previous texture environment stage as parameters. These parameters can be combined using passthrough, multiplication, addition, biased addition, subtraction, and linear interpolation. You can select combiner operations for the RGB and alpha components separately. You can also scale the final result. As you can see, this addition gives you a great deal of flexibility. Texture combine environment modes were promoted from the `ARB_texture_env_combine` extension.

The *texture dot3 environment mode* adds a new enumerant to the texture combine environment modes. The dot3 environment mode allows you to take the dot product of two specified components and place the results in the RGB or RGBA components of the output color. This can be used for per-pixel lighting or bump mapping. The dot3 environment mode was promoted from the `ARB_texture_env_dot3` extension.

Texture border clamp is similar to texture edge clamp, except that it causes texture coordinates that straddle the edge to sample from border texels only rather than from edge texels. This was promoted from the `ARB_texture_border_clamp` extension.

Transpose matrices allow you to pass row major matrices to OpenGL, which normally uses column major matrices. This is useful not only because it is how C stores 2-D arrays but because it is how Direct3D stores matrices; this saves conversion work when you're writing a rendering engine that uses both APIs. This addition only adds to the interface; it does not change the way OpenGL works internally. Transpose matrices were promoted from the `ARB_transpose_matrix` extension.

Useful Extensions

At the time of this writing, 269 extensions were listed in the Extension Registry. Even if I focused on the ones actually being used, I couldn't hope to cover them all, even briefly. Instead, I'll focus on a few that seem to be the most important for use in games.

Programmable Vertex and Pixel Shaders

It's generally agreed that shaders are the future of graphics, so let's start with them. First of all, the terms *vertex shader* and *pixel shader* are in common usage because of the attention they received with the launch of DirectX 8. However, the OpenGL extensions that you use for them have different names. On NVIDIA cards, vertex shaders are called vertex programs and are available through the `NV_vertex_program` extension. Pixel shaders are called register combiners and are available through the `NV_register_combiners` and `NV_register_combiners2` extensions. On ATI cards, vertex shaders are still called vertex shaders and are available through the `EXT_vertex_shader` extension. Pixel shaders are called fragment shaders and are available through the `ATI_fragment_shader` extension.

If you're unfamiliar with shaders, a quick overview is in order. Vertex shaders allow you to customize the geometry transformation pipeline. Pixel shaders work later in the pipeline and allow you to control how the final pixel color is determined. Together, the two provide incredible functionality. I recommend that you download NVIDIA's Effects Browser to see examples of the things you can do with shaders.

Using shaders can be somewhat problematic right now due to the fact that NVIDIA and ATI handle them very differently. If you want your game to take advantage of shaders, you'll have to write a lot of special-case code to use each vendor's method. At the ARB's last several meetings, this has been a major discussion point. There is a great deal of pressure to create a common shader interface. In fact, it is at the core of 3D Labs' OpenGL 2.0 proposal. Hopefully, the 1.4 specification will address this issue, but the ARB seems to be split as to whether a common shader interface should be a necessary component of 1.4.

Compiled Vertex Arrays

The *EXT_compiled_vertex_arrays* extension adds two functions that allow you to lock and unlock your vertex arrays. When the vertex arrays are locked, OpenGL assumes that their contents will not be changed. This allows OpenGL to make certain optimizations such as caching the results of vertex transformation. This is especially useful if your data contains large numbers of shared vertices or if you are using multipass rendering. When a vertex needs to be transformed, the cache is checked to see if the results of the transformation are already available. If they are, the cached results are used instead of recalculating the transformation.

The benefits gained by using compiled vertex arrays (CVAs) depend on the data set, the video card, and the drivers. Although you generally won't see a decrease in performance when using CVAs, it's quite possible that you won't see much of an increase either. In any case, the fact that they are fairly widely supported makes them worth looking into.

WGL Extensions

A number of available extensions add to the way Windows interfaces with OpenGL. Here are some of the main ones:

- *ARB_pixel_format* augments the standard pixel format functions (`DescribePixelFormat`, `ChoosePixelFormat`, `SetPixelFormat`, and `GetPixelFormat`), giving you more control over which pixel format is used. The functions allow you to query individual pixel format attributes and allow for the addition of

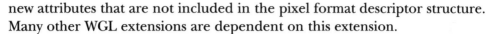

new attributes that are not included in the pixel format descriptor structure. Many other WGL extensions are dependent on this extension.

- *ARB_pbuffer* adds pixel buffers, which are off-screen (nonvisible) rendering buffers. On most cards, these buffers are in video memory, and the operation is hardware accelerated. They are often useful for creating dynamic textures, especially when used with the render texture extension.

- *ARB_render_texture* depends on the pbuffer extension. It is specifically designed to provide buffers that can be rendered to and used as texture data. These buffers are the perfect solution for dynamic texturing.

- *ARB_buffer_region* allows you to save portions of the color, depth, or stencil buffers to either system or video memory. This region can then be quickly restored to the OpenGL window.

Fences and Ranges

NVIDIA has created two extensions, NV_fence and NV_vertex_array_range that can make video cards(based on the NVIDIA chipsets) use vertex data much more efficiently than they normally would.

According to NVIDIA, the vertex array range extension is currently the fastest way to transfer data from the application to the GPU. Its speed comes from the fact that it allows the developer to allocate and access memory that usually can only be accessed by the GPU.

Although not directly related to the vertex array range extension, the fence extension can help make it even more efficient. When a fence is added to the OpenGL command stream, it can then be queried at any time. Usually it is queried to determine whether it has been completed yet. In addition, you can force the application to wait for the fence to be completed. Fences can be used with vertex array range when there is not enough memory to hold all of your vertex data at once. In this situation, you can fill up available memory, insert a fence, and when the fence has completed, repeat the process.

Shadows

There are two extensions, SGIX_shadow and SGIX_depth_texture, that work together to allow for hardware-accelerated shadow-mapping techniques. The main reason I mention these is that there are currently proposals in place to promote these extensions to ARB status. In addition, NVIDIA is recommending that they be included in the OpenGL 1.4 core specification. Because they may change somewhat if they are promoted, I won't go into detail as to how these extensions work. They may prove to be a very attractive alternative to the stencil shadow techniques presently in use.

Writing Well-Behaved Programs Using Extensions

Something you need to be very aware of when using any extension is that it is highly likely that someone will run your program on a system that does not support that extension. It's your responsibility to make sure that, when this happens, your program behaves intelligently rather than crashing or rendering garbage to the screen. In this section, you'll learn several methods to help you ensure that your program will get the best possible results on all systems. The focus is on two areas: how to select which extensions to use and how to respond when an extension you're using isn't supported.

Choosing Extensions

The most important thing you can do to ensure that your program runs on as many systems as possible is to choose your extensions wisely. The following are some factors you should consider.

Do You Really Need the Extension?

A quick look at the Extension Registry will reveal that there are a lot of different extensions available, and new ones are being introduced on a regular basis. It's tempting to try many of them out just to see what they do. If you're coding a demo, there's nothing wrong with this, but if you're creating a game that will be distributed to a lot of people, you need to ask yourself whether the extension is really needed. Does it make your game run faster? Does it make your game use less video memory? Does it improve the visual quality of your game? Will using it reduce your development time? If the answer to any of these is yes, the extension is probably a good candidate for inclusion in your product. On the other hand, if it offers no significant benefit, you may want to avoid it altogether.

At What Level of Promotion Is the Extension?

Extensions with higher promotion levels tend to be more widely supported. Any former extension that has been made part of the core 1.2 or 1.3 specification will be supported in compliant implementations, so they are the safest to use (1.2 more than 1.3 because it's been around longer). ARB-approved extensions (the ones that use the ARB prefix) aren't required to be supported in compliant implementations, but they are expected to be widely supported, so they're the next safest. Extensions using the EXT prefix are supported by two or more hardware vendors and are thus moderately safe to use. Finally, vendor-specific extensions are the most dangerous. Using them generally requires that you write a lot of special-case code. They often offer significant benefits, however, so they should not be ignored. You just have to be especially careful when using them.

> **NOTE**
>
> There are times when a vendor-specific extension can be completely replaced by an **EXT** or **ARB** extension. In this case, the latter should always be favored.

Who Is Your Target Audience?

If your target audience is hardcore gamers, you can expect that they are going to have newer hardware that will support many, if not all, of the latest extensions, so you can feel safer using them. Moreover, they will probably expect you to use the latest extensions; they want your game to take advantage of all the features they paid so much money for!

If, on the other hand, you're targeting casual game players, you'll probably want to use very few extensions, if any.

When Will Your Game Be Done?

As mentioned earlier, the graphics industry moves at an extremely quick pace. An extension that is only supported on cutting-edge cards today may enjoy widespread support in two years. Then again, it may become entirely obsolete, either because it is something that consumers don't want or because it gets replaced by another extension. If your ship date is far enough in the future, you may be able to risk using brand-new extensions to enhance your game's graphics. On the other hand, if your game is close to shipping or if you don't want to risk possible rewrites later on, you're better off sticking with extensions that are already well supported.

What to Do When an Extension Isn't Supported

First of all, let's make one thing very clear. Before you use any extension, you need to check to see if it is supported on the user's system. If it's not, you need to do something about it. What that "something" is depends on a number of things (as we'll discuss here), but you really need to have some kind of contingency plan. I've seen OpenGL code that just assumes that the needed extensions will be there. This can lead to blank screens, unexpected rendering effects, and even crashes. Here are some of the possible methods you can use when you find that an extension isn't supported.

Don't Use the Extension

If the extension is noncritical or if there is simply no alternate way to accomplish the same thing, you may be able to get away with just not using it at all. For example, compiled vertex arrays (EXT_compiled_vertex_array) offer potential speed enhancements when using vertex arrays. The speed gains usually aren't big enough to make or break your program, though, so if they aren't supported, you can use a flag or some other means to tell your program to not attempt to use them.

Try Similar Extensions

Because of the way in which extensions evolve, it's possible that the extension you're trying to use is present under an older name. For example, most ARB extensions used to be EXT extensions or vendor-specific extensions. If you're using a vendor-specific extension, there may be extensions from other vendors that do close to the same thing. The biggest drawback to this solution is that it requires a lot of special-case code.

Find an Alternate Way

Many extensions were introduced as more efficient ways to do things that could already be done using only core OpenGL features. If you're willing to put in the effort, you can deal with the absence of these extensions by doing things the "old way." For instance, most things that can be done with multitexturing can be done using multipass rendering and alpha blending. In addition to the additional code you have to add to handle this, your game will run slower because it has to make multiple passes through the geometry. That's better than not being able to run the game at all, and it's arguably better than simply dumping multitexturing and sacrificing visual quality.

Exit Gracefully

In some cases, you may decide that an extension is essential to your program, possibly because there is no other way to do the things you want to do or because providing a backup plan would require more time and effort than you're willing to invest. When this happens, you should cause your program to exit normally with a message telling the user what she needs to play your game. Note that if you choose to go this route, you should make sure that the hardware requirements listed on the product clearly state what is needed; otherwise, your customers will hate you.

The Demo

I've created a simple demo to show you some extensions in action. As you can see in Figure 10.1, the demo itself is fairly simple—nothing more than a light moving above a textured surface, casting a light on it using a lightmap. The demo isn't interactive at all. I kept it simple because I wanted to be able to focus on the extension mechanism.

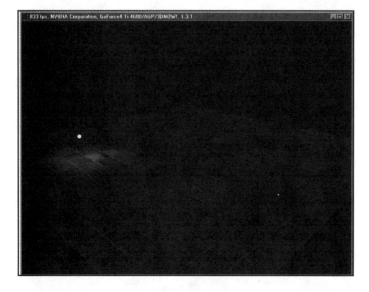

Figure 10.1

Light moving above a textured surface

The demo uses seven different extensions. Some of them aren't strictly necessary, but I wanted to include enough to get the point across. Table 10.2 lists all of the extensions in use and how they are used.

Table 10.2   Extensions Used in the Demo

Extension	Usage
ARB_multitexture	The floor in this demo is a single quad with two textures applied to it: one for the bricks and the other for the lightmap, which is updated with the light's position. The textures are combined using modulation.
EXT_point_parameters	When used, this extension causes point primitives to change size depending on their distance from the eye. You can set attenuation factors to determine how much the size changes, define maximum and minimum sizes, and even specify that the points become partially transparent if they go below a certain threshold. The yellow light in the demo takes advantage of this extension. The effect is subtle, but you should be able to notice it changing size.
EXT_swap_control	Most OpenGL drivers allow the user to specify whether or not screen redraws should wait for the monitor's vertical refresh, or vertical sync. If this is enabled, your game's frame rate will be limited to whatever the monitor refresh rate is set to. This extension allows you to programmatically disable vsync to get to avoid this limitation.
EXT_bgra	Since the demo uses Targas for textures, using this extension allows the demo to use their data directly without having to swap the red and blue components before creating the textures.
ARB_texture_compression	Because the demo only uses two textures, it won't gain much by using texture compression, but since it's easy I used it anyway. I allowed the drivers to compress the data for me rather than doing so myself beforehand.

continues

EXT_texture_edge_clamp	Again, this extension wasn't strictly necessary, but the demo shows how easy it is to use.
SGIS_generate_mipmap	GLU provides a function, gluBuild2DMipMaps, that allows you to specify just the base level of a mipmap chain and automatically generates the other levels for you. This extension performs essentially the same function with a couple of exceptions. First, it is a little more efficient. Second, it will cause all of the mipmap levels to be regenerated automatically whenever you change the base level. This can be useful when using dynamic textures.

The full source code to the demo is included on the accompanying CD-ROM, but there are a couple of functions that I want to look at.

The first is InitializeExtensions(). This function is called at startup, right after the rendering context is created. It verifies that the extensions used are supported and gets the function entry points that are needed.

```
bool InitializeExtensions()
{
  if (CheckExtension("GL_ARB_multitexture"))
  {
    glMultiTexCoord2f = (PFNGLMULTITEXCOORD2FARBPROC)
  wglGetProcAddress("glMultiTexCoord2fARB");
        glActiveTexture = (PFNGLCLIENTACTIVETEXTUREARBPROC)
  wglGetProcAddress("glActiveTextureARB");
    glClientActiveTexture = (PFNGLACTIVETEXTUREARBPROC)
  wglGetProcAddress("glClientActiveTextureARB");
  }
  else
  {
    MessageBox(g_hwnd, "This program requires multitexturing, which is not supported
  by your hardware", "ERROR", MB_OK);
    return false;
  }

  if (CheckExtension("GL_EXT_point_parameters"))
  {
```

```
    glPointParameterfvEXT = (PFNGLPOINTPARAMETERFVEXTPROC)
wglGetProcAddress("glPointParameterfvEXT");
    }


    if (CheckExtension("WGL_EXT_swap_control"))
    {
      wglSwapIntervalEXT = (PFNWGLSWAPINTERVALEXTPROC)
wglGetProcAddress("wglSwapIntervalEXT");
    }


    if (!CheckExtension("GL_EXT_bgra"))
    {
      MessageBox(g_hwnd, "This program requires the BGRA pixel storage format, which
is not supported by your hardware", "ERROR", MB_OK);
      return false;
    }


    g_useTextureCompression = CheckExtension("GL_ARB_texture_compression");
    g_useEdgeClamp = CheckExtension("GL_EXT_texture_edge_clamp");
    g_useSGISMipmapGeneration = CheckExtension("GL_SGIS_generate_mipmap");


    return true;
}
```

As you can see, there are two extensions that the demo requires: multitexturing and BGRA pixel formats. Although I could have provided alternate ways to do both of these things, doing so would have unnecessarily complicated the program. The point parameter and swap control extensions aren't required, so I don't exit if they aren't present. Instead, where they are used, I check to see if the function pointer is invalid (that is, set to NULL). If so, I simply don't use the extension. I use a similar approach with the texture compression, texture edge clamp, and generate mipmap extensions. Since all three of these extensions only introduce new enumrants, I set global flags to indicate whether or not they are supported. When they are used, I check the flag; if they aren't supported, I use an alternate method. For texture compression, I just use the normal pixel format; for texture edge clamp, I use normal clamping instead; and if the generate mipmaps extension isn't supported, I use `gluBuild2DMipmaps()`.

The other function I want to look at is the `CheckExtension()` function, which is used repeatedly by `InitializeExtensions()`.

```
bool CheckExtension(char• extensionName)
```

```
{
    // get the list of supported extensions
    char* extensionList = (char*) glGetString(GL_EXTENSIONS);

    if (!extensionName || !extensionList)
        return false;

    while (extensionList)
    {
        // find the length of the first extension substring
        unsigned int firstExtensionLength = strcspn(extensionList, " ");


        if (strlen(extensionName) == firstExtensionLength &&
            strncmp(extensionName, extensionList, firstExtensionLength) == 0)
        {
            return true;
        }

        // move to the next substring
        extensionList += firstExtensionLength + 1;
    }

    return false;
}
```

This function gets the extensions string and then parses each full extension name string from it, comparing each to the requested extension. Notice that I'm finding each string by looking for the next space to be sure that I don't accidentally match a substring.

This function doesn't check for WGL extensions at all, although it could easily be modified to do so. The code in the demo is not intended to be optimal, nor is it intended to be the "best" way to use extensions. Some people like to make extension function pointers global (as I have done) so that they can be used just like core OpenGL functions anywhere in your program. Others like to put class wrappers around them. Use whatever means you prefer. The demo was intentionally kept as straightforward as possible so that you could easily understand it and take out the parts that interest you.

Conclusion

You've now seen how you can use OpenGL's extensions to use the latest features offered by modern video cards. You've learned what some of these features are and how your game can benefit from them. You've also seen ways in which you can get the most out of extensions without unnecessarily limiting your target audience.

Now that you have a basic understanding of extensions, I encourage you to spend some time researching them and experimenting on your own. You may find that some of them enable you to significantly improve the efficiency and visual quality of your games.

Acknowledgments

I'd like to thank Alexander Heiner and Mark Shaxted for reviewing this chapter and correcting some minor inaccuracies and for suggesting ways to make it more complete. I'd also like to thank my wife, Melissa, for making me look like a better writer than I really am.

References

[1]Mark Kilgard, "All About Extensions," **www.opengl.org/developers/code/ features/OGLextensions/OGLextensions.html**

[2]NVIDIA Corporation, NVIDIA Developer Relations, **http://developer.nvidia.com/**

[3]ATI Technologies, ATI Developer Relations, **www.ati.com/na/pages/resource_ centre/dev_rel/devrel.html**

[4]OpenGL Architectural Review Board, OpenGL 1.3 Specification, **www.opengl.org/developers/documentation/specs.html**

TRICK 11

Creating a Particle Engine

Trent Polack

Introduction

Particle engines are probably the coolest and most useful tools in a programmer's special effects toolbox. Using a well-designed particle engine, a programmer can create fire, smoke, vapor trails, explosions, colored fountains, and an infinite number of other possibilities. The hard part is designing a simple, easy-to-use, and flexible particle engine that can create these effects with almost no effort on the user's part. That is our goal for this chapter.

I'm going to assume that you know C and some simple C++ and are familiar with vectors. The sample programs will all use OpenGL, but I made sure to minimize the amount of calls needed, therefore making it easier to port to other APIs. I am also using Microsoft Visual C++ 6.0.

What You Will Learn from This Fun-Filled Particle Adventure

We will be designing and implementing what looks to be two different particle engines; the first will be something similar to the Particle System API[1], and the "second" will be a wrapper over our API. The Particle System API will have very OpenGL-like syntax and is a pretty low-level way of creating several particle effects (using an emission function or using a per-particle creation function). The wrapper will be a class that encases all of the Particle System API's functionality and makes it more object-oriented (for those who absolutely loathe straight C). When I'm explaining both the API and the wrapper (the API mostly, though), it may seem like I'm just teaching you how to use my Particle System API, but that's not really the intent. I'm teaching you how I went about creating it, so if you want to do something like it, you will know my thought process when I created each function. I will *not* be providing the source code to most of the functions later on in the text; that's a lot of code, and I'm not really a huge fan of code dumps.

Sounds Great . . . What's a Particle Engine?

I'm guessing it's kind of hard to create a particle engine without knowing exactly what one is, so just in case you do not know, let's go over the history of where they came from and what exactly they do. If you'd like to see a good particle simulator, check out Richard Benson's "Particle Chamber" demo[2]. If you are already a particle veteran, feel free to skip to the section "Designing the Particle System API" later in this chapter. The next few sections are a complete introduction to particle engines.

The whole idea behind particle engines started back in 1982. The person we have to thank for all of our particle goodness is a man by the name of William T. Reeves.[3] He wanted to come up with an approach to render "fuzzy" things, such as explosions and fire, dynamically. The following is a list of what Reeves said needs to be done to implement such a thing:

- New particles are generated and placed into the current particle engine.
- Each new particle is assigned its own unique attributes.
- Any particles that have outlasted their life span are declared "dead."
- The current particles are moved according to their scripts.
- The current particles are rendered.

This is exactly how we are going to make our particle engine. And now, I'll describe what a particle engine actually is. A particle engine is a "manager" of several individual *particles*, which in our case are very small objects that have a certain set of attributes (which we'll get to in a second). A particle is emitted from an *emitter*, which is a certain location or boundary in 3-D space, and the particle moves in a set path unless acted on by an outside force (like gravity) from its conception to its "death." (All of this can be seen visually in Figure 11.1). The particle engine manages an emitter (or group of emitters) and all the particles that are currently alive. (Why would you want to waste processing power on a dead particle?)

By now, I bet you're asking yourself, "But what does it all mean?" I'll answer that question momentarily, but for now, we need to continue on with a bit more about the individual particles. Each particle possesses a set of attributes that will define how it acts and looks. Let's make a little list about the attributes we want each particle to have:

- **Life span.** How long the particle will live
- **Current position.** The particle's current position in 2-D/3-D space

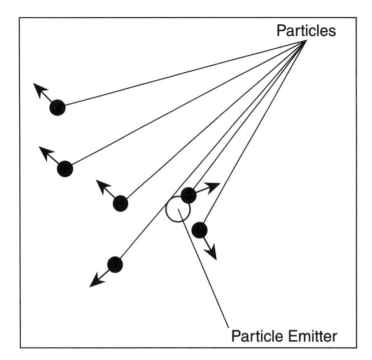

Particles

Particle Emitter

Figure 11.1

The relationship between particles and a particle emitter

- **Velocity.** The particle's direction and speed
- **Mass.** Used to accurately model particle motion
- **Color.** The current color of the particle (RGB triplet)
- **Translucency.** The current transparency, alpha, value of the particle
- **Size.** The particle's visual size
- **Air resistance.** The particle's susceptibility to friction in the air

Each of these attributes is pretty obvious in its meaning, but you may be a little confused as to why we have mass and then also have size. Well, the mass of the particle is used to accurately calculate the particle's momentum (we also use the particle's current velocity in this calculation), whereas the size is the actual visual size of the particle (height, width, and depth). We also want the simulation to *look* physically realistic, and a particle under normal conditions would not be immune to friction while traveling through the air—hence, the air resistance variable.

Now let's do a simple implementation. We first need to set up our data structures. We also need the individual particle structure and the particle engine (manager of particles). The particle structure should be easy enough to design, and I'll let you figure that out on your own (or if you need a bit of guidance, check out the first sample program and code), but I'll guide you through the creation of the actual engine.

First, we are going to need an array of particles. (For simplicity's sake, I'm not making the array dynamic . . . at least not yet! *evil maniacal laughter*) Once we have the array of particles, we need to make a copy of all the attributes for a particle and put the copies in the engine class. We do this so that, when we create a new particle, we have a value to which to set the particle's matching attribute. Get it? If you don't, you will soon. Here is our engine class, as of right now:

```
class CPARTICLE_ENGINE
{
    private:
        SPARTICLE p_particles[NUM_PARTICLES];
        int       p_iNumParticlesOnScreen;

        //engine attributes
        CVECTOR p_vForces;

        //base attributes
        float p_fLife;
        CVECTOR p_vPosition;

        float p_fMass;
        float p_fSize;

        CVECTOR p_vColor;
        float p_fFriction;
};
```

Notice that I left out the alpha variable; I did that because, right now, we are just basing the particle's translucency on the particle's life. If the particle has just started out, it is opaque; as it slowly nears its end, it will become more translucent.

Now we need to create some functions for our class. Since our array is preallocated, we really do not need any initiation functions to find out how many particles the user wants in his system, and we really do not need a shutdown function either. (We will need both later on, though.) All we need is a function to create a single particle, an update function, a rendering function, and some attribute customization functions. The customization functions are pretty self-explanatory, so I will not waste the space here to show them. (You can just check them out in the first demo's code.) That means we only need to create three functions.

First, let's look at the particle creation function. We are going to have the user pass the particle's velocity, and the function will create it. At the outset of the function, we are going to loop through all of the particles and try to find out if it is alive; if we cannot, we exit the function. If a particle is found, it is created. It's so simple that it's almost scary. Here is the function's code:

```
l_iChoice= -1;

for(i=0; i<NUM_PARTICLES; i++)
{
    if(p_particles[i].pu_fLife<=0.0f)
    {
        l_iChoice= i;
        break;
    }
}

if(l_iChoice==-1)
    return;

p_particles[l_iChoice].pu_fLife= p_fLife;

p_particles[l_iChoice].pu_vPosition= p_vPosition;

p_particles[l_iChoice].pu_vVelocity.Set(a_fVelX, a_fVelY, a_fVelZ);

p_particles[l_iChoice].pu_vColor= p_vColor;
p_particles[l_iChoice].pu_fAlpha= 1.0f;

p_particles[l_iChoice].pu_fSize= p_fSize;
p_particles[l_iChoice].pu_fMass= p_fMass;

p_particles[l_iChoice].pu_fFriction= p_fFriction;
```

Now we'll move on to the update function. In this function, we need to update each particle from the last frame. First we need to subtract the particle's life by one (since one frame has gone by), and then we'll check to make sure it's not dead. If it's dead, there's no point in updating that particle. If the particle is alive, we need to move the particle's position based on the particle's momentum (which is the particle's velocity multiplied by the particle's mass). Then we need to update the alpha value (the particle's current life divided by the class's base/max life). Finally, we are going to update the velocity, and take into account friction and gravity. Check out the following code:

```
for(i=0; i<NUM_PARTICLES; i++)
{
    p_particles[i].pu_fLife-= 1;

    if(p_particles[i].pu_fLife>0.0f)
    {
        l_vMomentum= p_particles[i].pu_vVelocity * p_particles[i].pu_fMass;

        p_particles[i].pu_vPosition+= l_vMomentum;

        p_particles[i].pu_fAlpha= p_particles[i].pu_fLife/p_fLife;

        //Now it's time for the external forces to take their toll
        p_particles[i].pu_vVelocity*= 1-p_particles[i].pu_fFriction;
        p_particles[i].pu_vVelocity+= p_vForces;
    }
}
```

Now it's time for rendering. I won't show the exact code for the rendering process because I want this explanation to remain API independent, but all we are going to do for the first demo is render the particle as a single-colored, nontextured, alpha-blended pixel. You will want to turn off depth testing for this, by the way; otherwise, your results will not look as good as they could—or they may be just plain ugly. That's all there is to rendering . . . for now.

Okay, I know I said we only needed to work on those three functions, but I lied. We need one more function to make something worth looking at. What we are going to do is create a function that will create an explosion of particles. Check out the following:

```
while(--a_iNumParticles>0)
{
    l_fYaw  = RANDOM_FLOAT*PI*2.0f;
    l_fPitch= DEG_TO_RAD(RANDOM_FLOAT*(rand()%360));

    vCreateParticle((cosf(l_fPitch))*a_fMagnitude,
                    (sinf(l_fPitch)*cosf(l_fYaw))*a_fMagnitude,
                    (sinf(l_fPitch)*sinf(l_fYaw))*a_fMagnitude);
}
```

Okay, that's it! You are well on your way to becoming a particle master. Go witness the fruit of your labor in the first particle demo (press E to see the explosion of particles) or just check out Figure 11.2, which is a screenshot of the demo we just worked to create.

Figure 11.2

Particles being rendered as alpha-blended pixels (from ParticleDemo_1)

The next step is to add texture support to your particle engine. Getting the particles textured is easy, but it means we have to switch from rendering single pixels to rendering two triangles per particle. This change comes with two small problems. The first and most important problem is that two triangles are far more processor-intensive (slower), which will hurt your overall frame rate. The second problem is that you need to align the textured squares to coincide with the viewer's point of view; this is called billboarding and is discussed in the next section.

Billboarding

Billboarding is when you need to align a two-dimensional object (like a square) so that it will always face the user. To do this, you need to get the current matrix from the rendering API and extract the Up vector and Right vector from it. I'm assuming that the matrix is 4×4, and I'm also assuming that you are putting it in a single array of 16 floating-point variables. (Since this is what OpenGL needs, you would need to adapt this to another API if you are not using OpenGL.) Figure 11.3 shows how you would extract the correct information for the vectors.

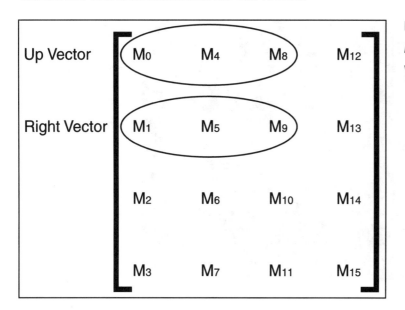

Figure 11.3

Extracting the Up and Right vectors from a matrix (in 1D array form)

Here it is in code form:

```
up Vector= (matrix[0], matrix[4], matrix[8])
right Vector= (matrix, matrix[5], matrix[9])
```

Now you need to apply the Up and Right vectors to our square's four points, as follows:

```
BillboardedTopRight    = ((RightVector+UpVector)   *
                          ParticleSize)+ParticlePosition;

BillboardedTopLeft    = ((UpVector    -RightVector)*
                          ParticleSize)+ParticlePosition;

BillboardedBottomRight= ((RightVector-UpVector)    *
                          ParticleSize)+ParticlePosition;

BillboardedBottomLeft = ((RightVector+UpVector)    *-
                          ParticleSize)+ParticlePosition;
```

It's as easy at that. Now all you have to do is texture it like you would a normal quad, and you'll have textured particles that always face the viewer. Go ahead and check out the second demo (see Figure 11.4) to see what the particles look like now. (Again, press E to see the explosion of particles.)

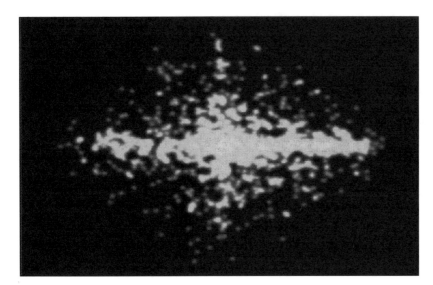

Figure 11.4

Particles being rendered as alpha-blended, textured, triangle strips (from ParticleDemo_2)

Pretty spiffy, eh? As cool looking as the particles might be, though, we still have a couple more things to cover: variable interpolation and time-based movement and updating.

Interpolation and Time-Based Movement

Interpolation, as used here, is when we take a current value and slowly change it to a certain end value. For instance, you may want a particle to start out being pure orange, but as it grows older, you may want it to turn more reddish (like fire flames). You also may want to have a particle start out at a relatively small size but expand as it ages (like smoke). The possibilities are endless.

First we need to add a few "counter" variables to the particle structure for the size, color, and alpha variables. These are the variables that will combine with the current color/size/alpha every frame to slowly produce the ending value. Once the counter variables have been added, we need to edit the base attributes within the engine class, and instead of what we had before, we need to make starting size/color/alpha variables and ending ones. What we are going to be doing is setting the particle's initial size/color/alpha to the engine's starting equivalent, and then we are going to figure out the counter variable with the following equation:

```
Counter= (EndValue-CurrentValue)/ParticlesLife;
```

Then all you have to do is add the counter to the particle's current value (size/color/alpha), and the particle's starting value will slowly change over to the ending value. Finally, the last item in our informational tour of the world of particles is time-based movement. All we have to do is add an argument to our update function that represents a *time step*, which is how far to advance the simulation per frame. (You can make this variable based on the number of frames per second so that, no matter how slow things get, the simulation will continue as if nothing happened; it just will not look as smooth.) In this case, 1 represents a single frame. Here is our new update function:

```
for(i=0; i<NUM_PARTICLES; i++)
{
    p_particles[i].pu_fLife-= 1;

    if(p_particles[i].pu_fLife>0.0f)
    {
        l_vMomentum= p_particles[i].pu_vVelocity * p_particles[i].pu_fMass;

        p_particles[i].pu_vPosition+= l_vMomentum*a_fTimeStep;

        p_particles[i].pu_vColor+= p_particles[i].pu_vColorCounter*a_fTimeStep;
        p_particles[i].pu_fAlpha+= p_particles[i].pu_fAlphaCounter*a_fTimeStep;

        p_particles[i].pu_vSize+= p_particles[i].pu_vSizeCounter*a_fTimeStep;

        //Now it's time for the external forces to take their toll
        p_particles[i].pu_vVelocity*= 1-p_particles[i].pu_fFriction;
        p_particles[i].pu_vVelocity+= p_vForces*a_fTimeStep;
    }
}
```

Notice that all addition operations are affected by the time step. Also notice, however, that I did not change the friction operation because multiplying that by the time step variable will screw things up big time. (For an experiment, multiply the friction by the time step anyway and see what happens.) Now, if you check out particle demo number three (see Figure 11.5), you will see our old green explosion turn into smoke as time goes on. I also changed the speed of the whole simulation a bit, by passing 2 to the update function instead of the default of 1. This will make the simulation play out twice as fast as normal. Now, just for fun, look again at the screenshots from the first couple of demos and then look at Figure 11.5. See how far you've advanced in just a few pages?

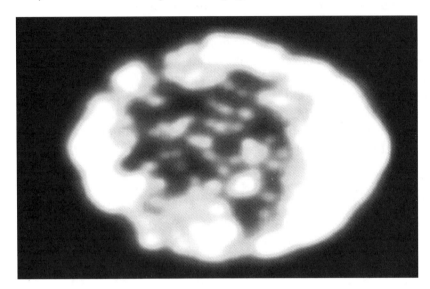

Figure 11.5

Particles being rendered as alpha-blended, textured, triangle strips, along with value interpolation (from ParticleDemo_3)

Designing the Particle System API

Now that you are a particle expert, we can get to the really fun stuff. First we will design the Particle System API (since we need it done before we can write a wrapper over it). The idea came to me late, late, late one night that it would be cool if people could call a few quick functions (like OpenGL's immediate calls: glVertex, glColor, and so on) that would customize, render, and update a particle engine with ease. After coding a very rough implementation of the Particle System API, a few guys told me that it had already been done (which did not make me too happy—I thought I was being completely original!).[4] This did not stop me from working on the Particle System API night and day, though, and even now it still is not done. (Well, maybe it is, but I wanted to leave some stuff for you guys to mess around with and add.) It is extremely powerful and incredibly fun to just play around with. So, without further interruption, let's design!

We're going to start with a simple flowchart (see Figure 11.6). The chart will show how we'd like the user to be able to use the API (and the wrapper later on, for that matter). Things like initiation and shutdown will be done at the start/end of the program (respectively), and the rest of the operations will be in real time.

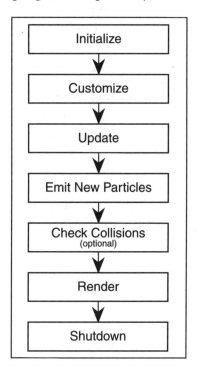

Figure 11.6

An API flowchart

First I created the particle structure as something to build off of (I like to start small and build up), and the particle structure is exactly the same as it was in the third particle demo, except with a new name: SPAPI_PARTICLE. Next I created the general particle engine structure. (Remember that we are designing the Particle System API using C-style syntax, which means no classes.) It looks like this:

```
typedef struct SPAPI_ENGINE_TYP
{
    unsigned int pu_uiID;

    //Particles
    SPAPI_PARTICLE* pu_pParticles;
    Int             pu_iMaxParticles;
    int             pu_iNumParticlesOnScreen;
} SPAPI_ENGINE, *SPAPI_ENGINE_PTR;
```

I'm betting that right about now you are wondering what the point of the ID variable is. Well, it's a very simple and nifty little concept, if I do say so myself. I wanted to make things as easy as possible for the user, so instead of the user having any access to the variables of this structure, I made a little layer of abstraction over it. I predefined a certain number of engines (PAPI_MAX_ENGINES) that will be put into a global array for the Particle System API to access in its routines. Then I did this:

```
typedef unsigned int PAPI_ENGINE;
```

PAPI_ENGINE is the variable that the user will be using to create, bind (select as the current particle engine), and destroy various engines. If you are familiar with OpenGL's way of handling textures, this should start feeling like familiar territory. Knowing OpenGL's texture system will make this explanation easier, but either way, it's still not a hard concept. Let me take a bit of time to explain how engine creation will function within our API. First you would call a creation function (in our case, pGenEngine) and supply the amount of particles you would like to create and a pointer to your engine instance. If we wanted to create a PAPI_ENGINE named pEngine and have it contain 1,000 particles, all we would have to do is this:

```
pGenEngine(1000, &pEngine);
```

Simple enough! Now that engine is filled with memory for 1,000 particles. Within that function, we are allocating memory for our particle buffer using new/delete, which is very handy. (Yes, I know I'm using C++ in C-oriented code, but hey, I make my code as easy as possible to understand, and if that means using an odd mixture of C and C++, so be it.) After doing this, the Particle System API will make PAPI_ENGINE equal to the current engine number, and from then on, PAPI_ENGINE refers to that engine in the global engine array. When you call pBindEngine, you are actually just setting the global "current engine" variable to your engine ID. We also need a function to clean up the memory that we previously allocated (for the particles), so I created pDeleteEngine. All it does is clear the particle buffer memory and set the engine's members so that it can be used for a new particle engine later on. I also created some helpful functions to retrieve the current engine ID, to reset the maximum number of particles in the current engine, and to see how many particles are currently being rendered (the number of particles onscreen).

Next we need to create a series of customization functions. These functions will be like OpenGL's immediate calls, and if you are unfamiliar with those, let me give you a very brief explanation. OpenGL has immediate calls that you can use to customize things about the current polygon being rendered. For instance, calling glColor4f(. . .) will set the API's current color values to the color values passed in the function, and every polygon rendered (considering that the function is never called again) will be that color. That is what our "immediate mode" functions will be doing. We will make a "current attribute" structure, create a global instance of that, and our customization functions will edit its members.

```
typedef struct SPAPI_ATTRIBUTES_TYP
{
    float pu_fLife1;
    float pu_fLife2;

    CVECTOR pu_vVelocity1;
    CVECTOR pu_vVelocity2;
    float pu_fMass1;
    float pu_fMass2;

    CVECTOR pu_vStartColor1;
    CVECTOR pu_vStartColor2;
    CVECTOR pu_vEndColor1;
    CVECTOR pu_vEndColor2;

    CVECTOR pu_vStartSize1;
    CVECTOR pu_vStartSize2;
    CVECTOR pu_vEndSize1;
    CVECTOR pu_vEndSize2;

    float pu_fStartAlpha1;
    float pu_fStartAlpha2;
    float pu_fEndAlpha1;
    float pu_fEndAlpha2;

    CVECTOR pu_vGravity;

    float pu_fFriction1;
    float pu_fFriction2;

    CVECTOR pu_vEmitterLightColor;
    int     pu_iEmitterLight;

    int pu_iMaxParticleLightsAllowed;

    bool pu_bEmitterLighting;
} SPAPI_ATTRIBUTES, *SPAPI_ATTRIBUTES_PTR;
```

I'd go through what each individual member means, but we already did that in the history segment, so I'll just go through the new ones. First of all, you are probably wondering why there are two copies of each variable. These two copies are used as a min/max boundary (that the user sets) so that, if the user wants, no two particle will ever be alike; needless to say, this is very cool indeed.

All of the new variables are for particle emitter lighting. What you could do for this is create lighting routines using some type of lighting algorithm. I have things set up for an emitter light (this is very easy to handle), but for a *much* more realistic effect, you would set a light not to the emitter but to each individual particle (which is how it would be if this was a completely real simulation). Alas, that would absolutely kill our speed.

To make the customization functions, we need to provide two sets of arguments: The first set will be the minimum value set, and the second set will be the maximum value set. Inside the function, we will assign our global attribute instance to the corresponding function arguments. Here is a sample function that will set the lifespan of our particles:

```
void pLife(float a_fLife1, float a_fLife2)
{
    g_PAPIAttribs.pu_fLife1= a_fLife1;
    g_PAPIAttribs.pu_fLife1= a_fLife2;
}
```

And that's how all of the customization functions will look (basically). Probably a couple of the most important functions of the whole API are the vertex and emission functions. The pEmit function relies heavily on the pVertex function, so let's cover the vertex function first.

The pVertex function creates a particle (with the previously customized attribute instance) at the coordinates that the user provides. Although this is a very nice way to handle the particle and can be used to create almost any effect imaginable, it's not what the user will be using. This function creates every aspect of a particle, and the next function (the emission function) uses it to create particles with a specific geometry in mind, so let's go there.

The pEmit function, while it looks large, is incredibly easy to use and is very nice. The user specifies a geometry type from one of the following basic primitives. (These are not the names that the API uses.) The primitives that the API actually has code for have a slight description as to how to provide the arguments, but most of the primitives are going to be left up to an exercise for the reader.

- A single point: A single ordered triplet is needed.
- A line: Two ordered triplets are needed, one for each of the line's endpoints.
- A plane
- A triangle
- A rectangle: Two ordered triplets are needed, one for the minimum boundary and one for the maximum.
- A circle
- A sphere
- A cylinder

As an example, here is how you would go about creating seven particles using a line-shaped emitter, with one endpoint at (0, –7, –25) and one endpoint at (0, –3, –25):

```
pEmit(PAPI_LINE, 5, 0.0f, -7.0f, -25.0f, 0.0f, -3.0f, -25.0f);
```

Next on our ultrafun list of things to do is the update function. This function is very simple; none of the code in it is much different than what we discussed earlier in the chapter. The only argument that the function takes is a time-step function to make frame-rate dependent motion possible. (The argument has a default value of 1.0f.) All you have to do is call the function, and all of the particles in the currently binded system will be updated. It's that simple. If you feel like murdering a bunch of newly born particles, there is a function to kill all particles immediately.

Next we need a simple function that will handle particle collision. I wanted something powerful yet flexible that had support for collision with a ton of primitives (though I only included collision source for a few primitives; the rest is yet another exercise for the reader). This function is pCollide, and it's very similar to the emission function. It has support for the exact same primitives and the exact same arguments for each primitive. What happens is that when the function is called, it checks every particle for a collision with the selected primitive (which is defined by the arguments). If there is a collision, the function performs appropriate collision response. (I'm not going to go through the physics for this.) Particle demo 4 shows this in action (along with the rest of the Particle System API), and the final argument in the collision function (in the demo) controls the bounciness of the particles when they collide with the surface.

Finally, we can perform the rendering of the particles. Two rendering functions are available for use. In one, you pass an OpenGL display list (so, if you feel the need, you could render the particles as a bunch of 3-D models), and in the other, you select a shape from the following primitives:

- A single pixel
- A line (the length of which depends on the particle's speed; the faster the speed, the longer the line)
- A triangle strip (a quad)

And that's all there is to it! You can now check out the sample demo in Figure 11.7 (ParticleDemo_4). The demo is now a particle fountain, with the particles colliding against an unseen surface directly below the lowest possible emission point.

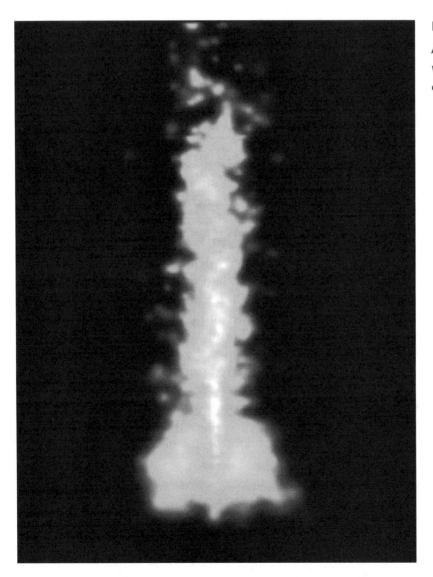

Figure 11.7

A particle fountain with full particle collision

Designing the Particle Wrapper

We are almost done with our complete coverage of particles. Now all that's left is to design a wrapper around our previously created Particle System API. This wrapper is very nice to have around, especially if you're interested in integrating a particle engine into your game engine; it's also nice if you just do not like straight C-style code.

What we want to do first (after we set up a class skeleton for CPARTICLE_ENGINE, or whatever you want to call the class) is duplicate the attribute structure from the Particle System API and put the attribute structures as private variables in the class. This may seem stupid, but there is a method to my madness. First, we'd have to bind the engine for every customization function that is called. That's okay, but it's something we would prefer to stay away from. Second, there is a large chance that the user will have no idea what is going on in the background, so he may customize one class's particle engine and then customize about five other classes' particle engines before updating, rendering, emitting, and so on. This would completely screw up the attributes, so I decided that each class needed to have its own variables. You know what that means—you have to make even more customization functions. So, I'll pause a moment while you sigh and get to work. *long pause*

Most of the work for the class involves just copying functions from the Particle System API and making a nice little wrapper around them. For example, check out the wrapped rendering function:

```
void CPARTICLE_ENGINE::
        vRender(_pAPIprimitiveENUM a_primitive)
{
        pBindEngine(p_engine);
        pRenderEnginep(a_primitive);
}
```

That's all that there is to most of the functions. For the update function, you're going to want to include a call to pGravity because the update function needs those values to update the particles. You need to make a call to all of the customization functions (the Particle System API ones) inside the emission function so that the newly created particles will have all of the correct attributes. Besides that, all you have to do is copy the functions from the Particle System API and put them inside the class. Then, in the function definition, you just have to bind the engine and make the corresponding function call using the Particle System API. That's mostly all there is to it.

Now you can just go crazy with your newly created wrapper and make it much more easy to use from within your game engine. For fun, I created a rainbow effect (which was very simple to do) and made it a predefined color scheme. Check it out in Figure 11.8 (ParticleDemo_5). Look how much you've learned to do in just a few simple pages!

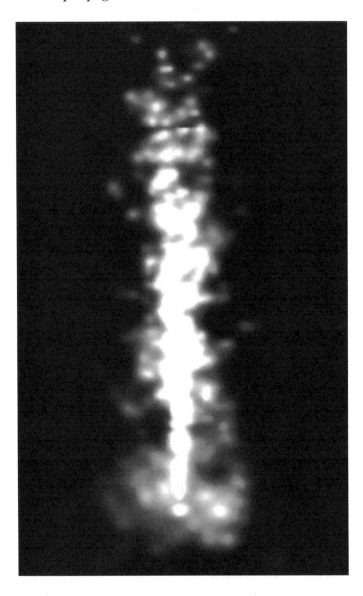

Figure 11.8

A rainbow fountain with full particle collision

Summary: Reminiscing About Our Little Particles

We certainly have gotten quite a lot of work done in such a small amount of time! We started out with a complete introduction to particle engines and then created our own simple pixel-plotting engine. We then advanced that engine to support billboarding and texturing. We even advanced the engine by creating a value interpolation system and time-based movement. After that fun run-through of particle engines, we started designing and implementing our own C-style particle engine, which I called the Particle System API (a very original name). We then went on to create an object-oriented wrapper over our API.

Going Further: How to Get More in Touch with Your Inner Particle

Now that you have completed two different styles of particle engine (well, they are *sort of* different), where do you go from here? If you just want to get used to particle physics, you can mess around with the demos I've provided, or the demo I have listed as reference [2], changing function arguments around and such. If you want to go a bit deeper but still are not ready to completely design your own engine, you can add more functionality to the Particle System API and then add support for the new material inside the wrapper.

If you are convinced that all of this is too simple, you can get into creating very advanced particle effects and code. Here are some ideas:

- Create a realistic lightning simulator (using only particles).
- Figure out how to create realistic model liquids using particles. (Although this has been done before, it has not been done real-time, so how is that for a challenge?)
- Code your own particle routines from scratch.
- Add realistic lighting (not to be confused with lightning) systems.
- Create a scripting system so that the user can define how the particle engine will act by using an editor or editing the parameters in a text file.

The possibilities are endless! Just be creative and you will no doubt have fun.

Conclusion: The End Is Here

This has been a very interesting chapter covering almost everything related to particle effects. You started off learning the very basics and slowly got more advanced until you created two completely cool pieces of code (the Particle System API and its object-oriented wrapper). I have provided you with a list of things you can work on if you really liked this chapter, and the following resources are very interesting and will give you even more information on particle systems. Once you have the basics down, your imagination is the limit, so quit reading this right now and go have some fun!

Trent Polack (ShiningKnight)

Game programmer

ShiningKnight7@hotmail.com

References

[1]McAllister, David K. "The Design of an API for Particle Systems."

[2]Benson, Richard. "Particle Chamber."
    www.dxcplusplus.co.uk/DemoVault/ParticleChamber.zip

[3]Reeves, William T. "Particle Systems—A Technique for Modeling a Class of Fuzzy Objects." *ACM Transactions on Graphics*, vol. 2, no. 2, pp. 91-108, April 1983.

[4]Watt, Alan and Fabio Policarpo. *3D Games: Real-Time Rendering and Software Technology*. Boston: Addison-Wesley, 2001.

TRICK 12

S1MPLE
GAME
SCR1PT1NG

ALEX VARANESE,
ALEX@XENONSTUD1OS.COM

Introduction

In recent years, scripting has gone from being an esoteric feature of high-end game engines and applications to one of the most in-demand techniques for game developers of all classes and skill levels. Whether they're working for Nintendo and developing for next-generation console systems or working for McDonald's and developing for their Pentium II at home, everyone seems to want to know more about how scripting engines are designed and implemented.

Although this does have the word "fad" written all over it, scripting is anything but a mindless trend that people will forget about in six months. It's a powerful technique that allows game content to be separated entirely from the underlying engine. No longer will the details of your plot, characters, and other in-game elements like weapons and items have to be hard-coded into and compiled with your game's source code. Scripting enables these higher-level, game-related entities to be programmed exclusively in their own separately compiled language that is used "inside" your game engine rather than running directly on the CPU. In other words, game logic can be just as modular and swappable as more traditional forms of media like art, music, and sound, as seen in Figure 12.1.

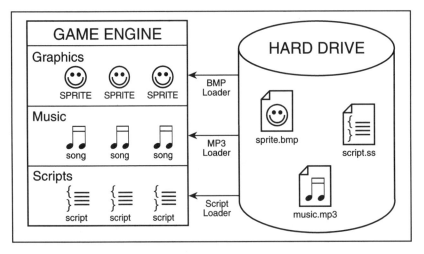

Figure 12.1

Game logic can be just as flexible and as easily swapped in and out as other forms of media such as graphics and sound when a scripting system is in place

Ideally, a scripting language should be just as high level and flexible as the language used to write the game itself. This usually means that, to develop a scripting system, you'll need to understand the details behind implementing entire languages like C and C++. This is a massive job, and it is well beyond the scope of the single chapter we have to work with here—you'd need an entire book at least to do the subject justice. So we're going to simplify things just a bit and instead focus on implementing a simple, lower-level scripting language with syntax based loosely on Intel's 80×86 assembly language. The syntax may be more awkward than a pure High-Level Language (HLL), but it'll be capable of just about anything, and this will make it applicable to virtually any game project for which you may need it.

The final product will be compiled with our own homemade compiler to a binary, *bytecode* format that can be executed quickly by a runtime environment we'll design as well. This runtime environment will be easy to integrate with any game project, allowing for simple but surprisingly flexible scripting.

In the following pages, we'll . . .

- Design a low-level but free-form scripting language with a syntax and layout based primarily on Intel assembly, offering typeless variables that can contain integers, floats, and strings. One-dimensional arrays will be supported as well.

- Build a compiler capable of reducing any script written in our language to a compact, binary version that can be loaded by the game engine and executed quickly.

- Design and implement a runtime environment capable of executing compiled scripts and providing an interface to the game engine itself, allowing its functions to be called and data to be shared easily.

- Test our scripts on a script runtime console I've put together that provides a simple game programming API. As a final test of our language's capabilities, we'll write an entire game with it and run it on this console.

- Cover a detailed list of ways to improve and expand the finished product to increase its power and flexibility.

Designing the Language

The natural place to start with a project like this is coming up with the language itself. The language is obviously a vital piece of the puzzle. Not only do we need to understand it to write scripts with it in the first place, the compiler must understand it as well to translate the scripts to an executable format.

As previously mentioned, implementing a high-level language like C or C++ is a huge job and would be far too much to cover here. High-level languages are complex, to say the least, and writing a compiler sophisticated enough to understand and translate them would take a considerable amount of time. The advantage, however, would be an incredibly flexible and easy-to-use scripting system that would provide a language almost identical to the one used to code the engine and that would thus be the least amount of headache for the programmer in the end.

We'll compromise a bit, however, and decide to base our language on something a little simpler. Intel 80×86 assembly language provides the model for a simple but effective language that provides all the major constructs and features of basic high-level programming—variables, arrays, conditional logic, and iteration—but with an extremely fine-grained, simplistic syntax.

To get an idea of what we're in for and to get your feet wet a bit if you don't have any experience with assembly, let's look at an example. Consider the following block of C code:

```
int Y = 32;
for ( int X = 0; X < 16; ++ X )
        Y += X;
```

In a nutshell, we've declared an integer variable called Y and initialized it to 32. We then used a for loop and a variable called X to add the numbers 0 through 15 to it. This is naturally a trivial thing to do with a high-level language like C. In fact, it's pretty easy to do in an assembly-like language as well, but you'll notice a stark contrast in the syntax and layout of the program:

```
Mov                 32, Y
        Mov             0, X
LoopStart:
        Add             X, Y
        Inc             X
        Cmp             X, 16
        JL              LoopStart
```

Quite a difference, eh? If you have no idea what I'm doing here, the preceding is basically an Intel assembly language version of the original block of C. Notice that the main difference between assembly code and high-level code is that assembly only performs one action per line. Each line usually consists of two things: *instructions* and *operands*. These are almost analogous to function calls in that instructions are like the name of the function and operands are like its parameters. Each instruction performs a specific task, such as moving memory from one place to another (Mov), adding two values (Add), or comparing a set of values (Cmp). With this in mind, let's examine it line by line.

The first thing I did was use Mov to put the value 32 into Y. I then set X to 0 with another Mov instruction to prepare the loop counter. The next line is a bit different; it's a line label just like the ones offered in C (much to the dismay of computer science teachers). This is where the loop will begin (which is why I called it LoopStart), and it gives us a place to jump back to after each iteration of the loop executes. The code following the line label is the code that will execute each time through the loop. All we really need to do is add X to Y and increment our loop counter (with the Inc instruction). Then, to actually implement the loop logic itself, we simply need to compare X to 16 (using Cmp) and jump back to LoopStart if it's less than 16. This is what JL does; it "Jumps if Less than" to the specified line label.

It should now be pretty clear that you can do anything in assembly that you can do in C; it's just a bit more work sometimes. The syntax is definitely alien, and you have to approach algorithms and logic with a slightly different mindset, but everything you need is in there somewhere. The advantage, however, is that the preceding code we looked at is *much* easier to compile than C. As you'd probably imagine, it's really just a matter of extracting the instruction and the value of each operand.

This is more or less what our language will be like. We'll determine the minimum set of instructions we need to create a versatile and reasonably powerful language, and from there it'll just be a matter of implementing them. Once we have the capability to move data around and perform basic arithmetic, conditional logic, and branching, as well as the capability to call game engine functions from within running scripts, we'll have enough functionality to do pretty much anything.

Fortunately, I've done the work for us. I've basically come up with a set of 18 instructions that provides just enough functionality to do anything. It's not the most convenient or lavish set of instructions in the world, but it's clean, orthogonal, and straightforward. Once you've implemented them, you'll easily be able to add as many other instructions as you want to create an epic masterpiece of a language.

Before I list the instructions, however, let's nail down exactly what we want to do with this language. We've already just about covered it, but before we get hip deep in the nitty-gritties, let's formally state our objectives:

- The language needs enough instructions to roughly emulate the functionality of a higher-level language like C. This means we need the ability to assign values to variables (in other words, move memory around) and perform basic arithmetic. We'll also need instructions for handling conditional logic and branching (jumping) to other parts of the script.

- We'd like our variables to be typeless or at least somewhat so. *Typeless* variables are variables that don't have a strict data type. In other words, you can assign any value to any variable at any time, whether it's a string value, an integer, or whatever.

- A wider selection of basic data types would be nice. To cover all the bases, we'll make sure to include support for integer, floating-point, and string values. Strings will be loosely defined and can have any number of characters. Finally, we'll throw in one-dimensional arrays just to be complete. As you'll see, this is easier than you might think.

- As a last major feature of the language, we need to be able to communicate with the game engine. As you can imagine, not having this ability would make the entire scripting system pretty much useless. Basically, we need to be able to somehow make function calls from the script to the engine and allow the engine to return values.

- For simplicity's sake, we'll allow variables to be used without first being declared. BASIC users might like this. Arrays will need to be explicitly declared, however, since the compiler will need to know how many elements they contain.

So there it is, our fledgling language in a nutshell. Now that we understand exactly what we need to do, the instruction set I've picked out should make sense.

Basic Instructions

```
Mov        Source, Destination
```

Mov, short for "Move," is perhaps the most fundamental and commonly used instruction and is responsible for moving memory around (like the assignment operator in higher-level languages like C and C++). Mov moves the contents of Source into Destination. Source can be anything: a memory reference like a variable or array index, or any immediate value like an integer, string, or float. Destination must be a memory reference.

Arithmetic

```
Add        Source, Destination
Sub        Source, Destination
Mul        Source, Destination
Div        Source, Destination
```

These are the arithmetic instructions, and they basically work exactly like Mov. The only difference is that rather than simply copying the data into Destination, they perform some basic arithmetic function. They're pretty self-explanatory: Add adds Source to Destination, Sub subtracts Source from Destination, and so on. The same rules that apply to Mov's operands apply to these. Also, anyone familiar with Intel 80×86 assembly language will notice that these Mul and Div instructions are much friendlier.

String Processing

```
Concat          Source, Destination
GetSubStr       Souce, Index0, Index1, Destination
```

I've really whittled down string processing to the two most basic operations. We've basically got Concat, which concatenates (combines) two strings, and GetSubStr, which returns a substring of a larger string. You can almost think of these as the string-processing equivalent of addition and subtraction (more or less). The point is that virtually any other string-processing operation can be derived from these two. Concat's Source operand must either be a variable containing a string value or an immediate string value. Destination must be memory location. The same holds for GetSubStr, but Index0 and Index1 can be either immediate integer values or memory locations.

Branching

```
Jmp         Destination
JG          Op0, Op1, Destination
JL          Op0, Op1, Destination
JGE         Op0, Op1, Destination
JLE         Op0, Op1, Destination
JE          Op0, Op1, Destination
JNE         Op0, Op1, Destination
```

This rather large collection of instructions provides everything we'll need for conditional logic and branching. The first thing I should mention is that anyone who's familiar with Intel 80×86 assembly will find these to be a bit strange. Essentially, these jump instructions provide built-in comparison. In other words, you give the instruction the two operands you want to compare and the destination of the jump to make if the comparison evaluates to true.

The two operands can be anything, although only certain combinations will make sense. For example, comparing a string value to an integer or float doesn't make a whole lot of sense, so the string will automatically be cast to an integer value of 0. This won't produce meaningful results, so such comparisons aren't recommended. The last operand, Destination, is unlike any operand we've dealt with so far. Rather than being an immediate value or memory reference, it must be a line label. The label can be defined anywhere in the code before the jump instruction or after, but it must be defined somewhere. Also, unlike the 80×86, there are no limits on the range of a jump. (There's no need to worry about near and far jump targets.) So, as an example, if you want to jump to the label MyLabel if X is greater than or equal to Y, you'd use the following line of code:

```
JGE             X, Y, MyLabel
```

Simple, eh? The actual jump instructions are as follows: Jmp unconditionally jumps to the destination, so you'll want to use this whenever you absolutely must move to another part of the script in all cases. JG and JL jump if Op0 is greater than Op1 and if Op0 is less than Op1, respectively. JGE and JLE mean "jump if greater than or equal to" and "jump if less than or equal to," respectively. Lastly, JE and JNE round out the group with "jump if equal" and "jump if not equal."

Host API

```
CallHost        FunctionIndex, Param0, Param1, Param2, …
GetRetVal       Destination
```

These two functions are designed to interface with the game engine, or the *host*. The host is the program that's actually running the script, and the functions it provides for interfacing with it are called the *Host API*. We'll get to the details of how the host actually exposes functions to the scripting system later on, but for now all we need to know is that CallHost calls a host API function based on a *function index*, which is simply an integer value that corresponds to one of the host's functions (again, just go along with it for now), as well as a variable number of parameters that can be any type of operand (except line labels). FunctionIndex can be either an integer immediate value or a memory reference.

The only other real issue when calling host functions is how to handle return values. In C, for example, return values are simply handled by preceding the function call with the assignment operator, like this:

```
X = MyFunc ( Y );
```

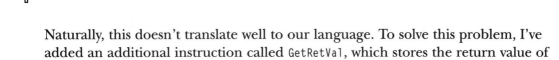

Naturally, this doesn't translate well to our language. To solve this problem, I've added an additional instruction called `GetRetVal`, which stores the return value of the most recently called function in `Destination`, which must be a memory reference. `GetRetVal` can be called any time after a function is called.

Miscellaneous

```
Pause       Delay
Exit
```

The last two instructions in our language are completely unrelated, but I've grouped them together just to make things easier. `Pause` suspends the script for `Delay` milliseconds but is only accurate within about 55 milliseconds due to the way I've implemented it. (This will only affect us in practice, and depending on the platform for which you develop or the API you use, this might not be an issue at all.) `Exit` is probably the simplest instruction of them all and causes the script to unconditionally terminate. Just throw it in there whenever you know for a fact that the script should exit at that point. `Exit` is not required at the end of a script, however. The runtime environment will interpret a lack of any further instructions as a sign that the script has terminated.

Directives

With the instruction set out of the way, the next part of the language is its *directives*. Directives are instructions for the compiler that help control the code it outputs, but they are not present at runtime and have no further effect. Our language will only need one directive, which will be used for declaring arrays. The syntax will look like this:

```
Array Identifier [ Size ]
```

This directive creates an array called `Indentifier` with `Size` elements. `Size` must be an immediate integer value; variables and noninteger values are illegal array sizes. To refer to an array index in your code (which counts as a memory reference, just like variables), use the typical C-style array syntax. For example:

```
Mov         X, MyArray [ 3 ]
```

Variables can also be used as array indices:

```
Mov         10, X
```

```
Mov             Y, MyArray [ X ]
```

Comments

The last thing to cover is commenting. Continuing with our trend of using Intel 80×86 assembly as a basic model for our language, we'll use its comment style as well. The semicolon (;) denotes a comment and causes anything following it to be ignored by the compiler. It functions exactly like the // comments in C++.

```
; This is a comment!
Mov             X, Y        ; So is this!
```

So there you have it. Our language is fully designed, and we're ready to get started with the implementation. While our ultimate goal is, of course, to write scripts in this language and run them, the first step toward doing this is compiling them down to bytecode. Therefore, our next task is writing a compiler that can understand these instructions and produce the executable format that our runtime environment will accept.

Building the Compiler

Building a compiler of any sort is a formidable task, and it's for this reason that we've designed our language the way we have. Without the recursively defined expressions and structures of higher-level languages to worry about, we won't have too much trouble getting our compiler to understand the simple instruction-and-operand format that our scripts will be written in.

I should also mention up front that we'll be designing our compiler entirely by hand. Compiler construction tools like *lex* and *yacc*, despite their widespread use in the implementation of more sophisticated language translators and processors, are almost overkill for a language like this. Besides, we'll learn a lot more by doing everything ourselves.

Before we go any further, it's also important that we fully understand *why* we're going to be compiling our script code in the first place. It'd definitely be possible to write a runtime environment that could interpret uncompiled code in real time, and it'd save us the hassle of writing the compiler altogether. So why bother?

The first and most important reason is that for a piece of software to read and understand code that looks like this:

```
Mov             20, X
```

```
          Add              Y [ Z ], Q
          JLE              X, Q, Label
          Add              1, Z
          Div              Y [ Z ], Q
Label:
          Concat           String0, String1
```

It has to perform a tremendous amount of string processing and comparisons. Since strings are inherently more complicated and simply larger than primitive data types like integers, this is a huge waste of processing power. The end result is a scripting system that slows down the game engine and therefore makes it far more prohibitive to speed-critical applications (and what game isn't speed critical?).

When we compile code, we replace all of those extraneous string values with integer codes (hence the term *bytecode*) that represent them in a more compact format. Instructions are enumerated, mapping each instruction string (like Mov and GetRetVal), which is called a *mnemonic*, to a numeric value (like 0, 1, and so on), called an *opcode* (see Figure 12.2). The term "opcode" is an abbreviation of "operation code," which should make sense—it's a code that represents the operation performed by the instruction to which it's mapped. So, if you can imagine a compiler simply looping through the source code of a script and replacing each instruction mnemonic with its opcode, you can already see how the result would be easier to process.

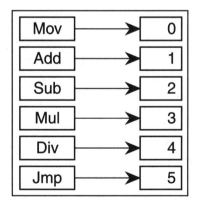

Figure 12.2

A compiler maps instruction mnemonics to opcodes

Furthermore, there's the issue of errors in the source code. What if you accidentally forget to include one of the operands of a given instruction or misspell Mov as Mpv? If the runtime environment has to deal with these mistakes and typos, it means the game itself will come to a screeching halt. It also means you'll have a less-than-convenient testing ground for errors in your code. Debugging code is enough of a hassle, and you'll only add insult to injury by forcing yourself to have to play through the game itself just to invoke the errors in the first place. Compilers enable you to immediately validate your code, highlighting compile-time errors with helpful information like the line number of the offending code as well as a description of what's wrong. The runtime environment can then assume that the compiled script has been validated beforehand, can save even more processing power by not having to worry about checking for code mistakes, and can focus solely on executing it as quickly as possible.

There are also other benefits, like the fact that compiled code is much smaller than uncompiled code and thus takes less memory to store, both on the hard drive and in RAM at runtime. Additionally, uncompiled code is very easy to hack—game players can hijack human-readable scripts effortlessly, screwing up your game and reflecting a less-than-polished image. Compiled scripts are simply binary data; without a translator of some sort, the average gamer will have no way to make meaningful changes.

The fact is, there are a million reasons why you should compile your scripts, so now that you're convinced, let's get on with actually doing it!

An Overview of Script Compilation

We're almost ready to get started, so just like we did with our language, we should state our objectives for what we want the compiler to do. The most general goal is simply to reduce handwritten, human-readable code to a purely numeric format that can be processed quickly and easily by our runtime environment. In a nutshell, this means that everything we would write as a string in a script, such as the name of an instruction (Mov, Div, GetSubStr) or the identifier used for a variable or array (MyVar or MyArray), needs a numeric equivalent that represents the same thing.

The compiled script will be composed of a number of major parts. The first and most important is the *instruction stream,* which is a series of compiled instructions and their operands. The next is the *symbol table,* which maintains information about all of the arrays and variables a script may need. In addition to variables, we'll also need the *string table,* which stores every immediate string value used in the script (this will make more sense later). Lastly, the *label table* keeps track of the targets of branching instructions based on the labels to which they point (which are really just reduced to indices into the instruction stream).

Compiling a Basic Instruction Stream

We'll get started by generating the basics of the instruction stream. The first order of business here is to simply assign every instruction a numeric index (in other words, its corresponding opcode) that we can use to store it internally. This can be expressed as a table and looks like Table 12.1:

Table 12.1 Opcode-Instruction Mappings

Opcode	Instruction
0	Mov
1	Add
2	Sub
3	Mul
4	Div
5	Concat
6	GetSubStr
7	Jmp
8	JG
9	JL
10	JGE
11	JLE
12	JE
13	JNE
14	CallHost
15	GetRetVal
16	Pause
17	Exit

This means that the first and most basic thing our compiler will do is simply scan through this table every time it reads a new instruction, find the opcode to which it maps, and write that as an integer value out to the executable file. Doing this alone would give us a stream of bytecode, a series of opcodes that perform the same overall operations as the original script but in a much smaller and convenient format.

In fact, this would be a complete compiler if not for the operands. Naturally, the opcodes themselves are only so useful—with the exception of the Exit instruction, every opcode needs to be followed by its operands. Without them, we wouldn't know what to do with it at runtime.

So let's think about this for a second. What we really need to figure out now is every possible form that an operand can take. Once we know these, we can figure out how to translate them. Speaking in high-level terms, we can expect the following types of operands:

- Integer immediate values (8, 64, 32768)
- Floating-point immediate values (3.14159, 2.7828)
- String immediate values ("Hello, world!", "256", "_l33th4x0r_")
- Variable memory reference (X, Y, MyVar)
- Array memory reference with immediate index (MyArray [16])
- Array memory reference with variable index (MyArray [MyVar])
- Labels (MyLabel)

All counted, our language supports seven possible operand types. If you combine this with what we already know about instructions, we can assume that almost every line of a given script will take on the following form (although the operand count will certainly vary):

```
Instruction Operand0, Operand1, Operand2
```

I say almost every line because certain lines won't be instructions; they might be array declarations, line labels, or even extraneous stuff like whitespace and comments. We'll worry about these special cases in a little bit; for now, let's think about what we want to convert these operands into exactly.

Integer operands are dead simple. There's really nothing we can do to reduce or simplify their format; they're already numbers and that's that. Integer operands are written exactly as they are to the executable file. (Of course, they'll initially be read from the source file as a string, so we'll need to convert them to true integer values before writing them out, but that's simply accomplished with a call to atoi ().)

Floating-point operands are fairly easy as well. Once we read them in their string form from the source file, we'll use atof () to convert them to true float values and write them directly out to the executable. All we need to do is pass fwrite () a pointer to the floating-point value and its size, which looks like this:

```
fwrite ( & fFloat, sizeof ( float ), 1, pFile );
```

fFloat and pFile are the floating-point value and the pointer to the file out stream, respectively.

We haven't yet discussed the precise format of the instruction stream, however, as it will appear in the executable file. Before continuing, it'd be a good idea to work this out.

We already know that as each instruction is read, its opcode is determined with a lookup table. Each instruction in the stream is headed by an opcode. Although you can use any integer data type you'd like for this (a character, word, double word, or whatever), we'll just use the standard 32-bit int. Some would call this wasteful, but our scripts in the context of this chapter won't be particularly large to begin with, and you're free to change this to whatever you want in your own implementation. I'm just sticking to ints for pretty much everything to keep things uniform and simple. We'll use them as our basic unit of data in a compiled script and will thus refer to them as *words* from now on.

The true meaning of "word"

The term "word" has gained something of a double meaning over the years. The technical definition refers to the width of the processor's data bus, which is 32-bits in the context of the average Pentium. So technically, it's correct for us to refer to our basic 32-bit integer values as "words." However, due primarily to the backward compatibility of the Intel 80X86 platform, which used to be exclusively 16-bit in the days of real mode, "word" is also frequently used to refer to 16-bit values, while 32-bit values are known as "double words."

The next issue to consider is how the runtime environment, which is what will ultimately read the instruction stream, will know where one instruction begins and another ends. The simple solution to this problem is to immediately follow the instruction word with another word that contains the number of operands that will follow. This will allow the runtime environment to read an opcode and immediately know how far to read until the next opcode is to be expected.

This is only part of the puzzle, however. While it's important to know how many operands will follow an opcode, it's just as important that we store information regarding the *type* of each operand as well. This is important for two reasons. First, the runtime environment needs to know how many bytes to physically read to extract the entire operand. Second, it needs to know what to do with the extracted data. Obviously, an integer is stored in RAM much differently than a float, so this needs to be taken into account.

Including the opcode and operands themselves, this means that each instruction in the instruction stream will consist of four pieces of data, as illustrated in Figure 12.3:

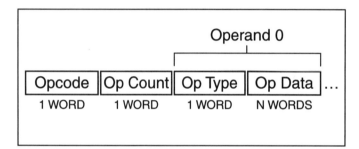

Figure 12.3

A compiled instruction will contain an opcode word, an opcode count word, and a variable number of operands, each of which will consist of an operand type word and the operand data itself

So far, we've just copied the operand data in its almost exact form from the source file and dumped it into the executable file. Although we've yet to actually cover the implementation details of this process, we've essentially formed a theoretical compiler on paper that can compile instructions and operands with integer or floating-point immediate values. Not a bad start. This rounds out the basics of the instruction stream, so let's move on to the more complex operand types.

Compiling Strings

With the basics of the instruction stream in place, we can move on to the more complex operand types, which will also introduce us to the remaining parts of the compiled script such as the string and symbol tables.

The next type of operand to consider is string immediate values. These are handled in almost the same fashion as integers and floats in the sense that there's no real conversion to be done; a string will appear in the compiled script in the same way that it will appear in the uncompiled source code. The difference, however, is where it will be stored. Rather than cluttering up the instruction stream with potentially huge strings, we'll store all immediate string values in a separate area known as the *string table*. Each string will be placed into the table in the order in which it's encountered in the script. Every time a string is added to the table, its index will be calculated (which just means incrementing the index of the previous string), and this value will be written out to the instruction stream, rather than to the string itself. This way, instructions need only deal with an index into the string table rather than the string itself. The end result is that all instructions, regardless of their operand types, will only consist of a handful of words. Extraneous and bulky data like string values will be stored elsewhere, and the implementation will be cleaner overall (see Figure 12.4).

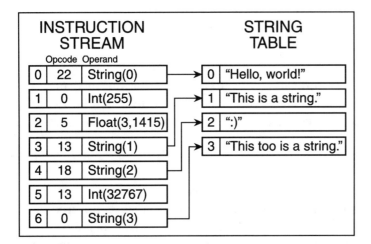

Figure 12.4

The string table separates the potential clutter of string literal data from the instruction stream

The string table itself will be implemented in the compiler as a linked list. We need to do this since we have no idea how many strings a script may present, and any arbitrary limit would probably end up being too restrictive. The string table will thus consist of two basic data structures. One represents the table itself, keeping track of things like pointers to the head and tail of the list and the number of strings it currently holds. There will also be a structure representing a string table node, which will contain the string itself and its index.

Let's have a look at the string table structure:

```
typedef struct _StringTable
{
        int iStringCount;           // Current number of strings in table
        StringTableNode * pHead,    // Pointer to head string node
        * pTail;                    // Pointer to tail string node
}
        StringTable;
```

It's pretty basic. iStringCount simply tells us how many strings the table currently has, while pHead and pTail point to the head and tail nodes of the list. Here's the node structure:

```
typedef struct _StringTableNode
{
        _StringTableNode * pPrev,        // Pointer to previous string node
                         * pNext;            // Pointer to next string node

        char * pstrString;               // Pointer to string itself
        int iIndex;                      // Index into the table
}
        StringTableNode;
```

It's also very straightforward. pPrev and pNext point to the previous and next nodes in the list. pstrString is the string value itself, and iIndex tells us to which index the string is mapped. The last step is declaring a global string table for the program to refer to:

```
StringTable g_StringTable;
```

We now need a few functions to manage the list. The main operations we'll concern ourselves with will be initializing the list when the compiler starts up, freeing it when the compiler shuts down, adding strings and retrieving their associated index, and writing the string table to the executable file. Let's look at initialization first:

```
void InitStringTable ()
{
        g_StringTable.iStringCount = 0;
        g_StringTable.pHead = NULL;
        g_StringTable.pTail = NULL;
}
```

This one's a no brainer. Simply reset the string count to 0 and nullify the head and tail pointers. Let's knock out the deallocation routine as well while we're at it:

```
void FreeStringTable ()
{
        StringTableNode * pCurrString = g_StringTable.pHead,
                        * pNextString;
        for ( int iCurrStringIndex = 0;
        iCurrStringIndex < g_StringTable.iStringCount;
        ++ iCurrStringIndex )
```

```
            {
            pNextString = pCurrString->pNext;
            free ( pCurrString->pstrString );
            free ( pCurrString );
            pCurrString = pNextString;
            }
}
```

The list is freed in a loop that runs from the head pointer to the tail pointer, using the string count to determine how far to go. At each iteration of the loop, the pointer to the next node in the list is saved, and the string and node structures are freed from memory. The saved pointer is then used to traverse to the next node, and the process continues.

Now that we can initialize and free our string table, let's take a look at what's perhaps the most complex operation, adding a string to the table and returning its index:

```
int AddStringToStringTable ( char * pstrString )
{
        int iIndex = g_StringTable.iStringCount;
        // Is this the first string in the table?
        if ( ! g_StringTable.iStringCount )
        {
                g_StringTable.pHead = ( StringTableNode * ) malloc ( sizeof (
   StringTableNode ) );
                g_StringTable.pTail = g_StringTable.pHead;
                    g_StringTable.pHead->pNext = NULL;
                g_StringTable.pHead->pPrev = NULL;
                g_StringTable.pHead->pstrString = ( char * ) malloc ( strlen (
   pstrString ) + 1 );
                strcpy ( g_StringTable.pHead->pstrString, pstrString );
                g_StringTable.pHead->iIndex = iIndex;
        }
        // If not, add it to the tail of the list
        else
        {
                StringTableNode * pOldTail = g_StringTable.pTail;
                g_StringTable.pTail = ( StringTableNode * ) malloc ( sizeof (
   StringTableNode ) );
                g_StringTable.pTail->pNext = NULL;
                g_StringTable.pTail->pPrev = pOldTail;
                g_StringTable.pTail->pstrString = ( char * ) malloc ( strlen (
```

```
      pstrString ) + 1 );
            strcpy ( g_StringTable.pTail->pstrString, pstrString );
            g_StringTable.pTail->iIndex = iIndex;
            pOldTail->pNext = g_StringTable.pTail;
      }
      ++ g_StringTable.iStringCount;
      return iIndex;
}
```

Although this is a simple function overall, there are two particular cases we should discuss. If the string is the first in the list, we need to make sure to line up the pointers properly by assigning both the head and tail members of the string table structure. Otherwise, we need to use the table's tail pointer to find out where to insert the new string. Space for the node structure itself is first allocated, and the string passed to the function is copied to it. The index of the string is simply determined by checking the current string count. The string count is then incremented and the function returns, passing the index back to the caller. This general process can be seen in Figure 12.5.

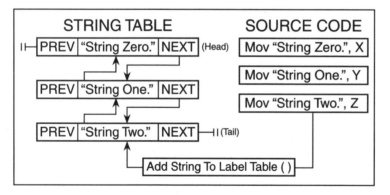

Figure 12.5

Adding a string found in the source code to the string table

Before wrapping up, let's quickly cover the last and perhaps most important string table operation: writing the entire table out to the executable file. It's a pretty simple function, and it looks like this:

```
void WriteStringTableToExec ()
{
      // Write the string count first
      WriteIntToBinFile ( g_StringTable.iStringCount, g_pExecFile );
      // Write each string length, followed by the string itself
      StringTableNode * pCurrString = g_StringTable.pHead;
      for ( int iCurrStringIndex = 0;
```

```
        iCurrStringIndex < g_StringTable.iStringCount;
        ++ iCurrStringIndex )
        {
                WriteIntToBinFile ( strlen ( pCurrString->pstrString ),
  g_pExecFile );
                for ( unsigned int iCurrCharIndex = 0;
iCurrCharIndex < strlen ( pCurrString->pstrString ); ++ iCurrCharIndex )
WriteCharToBinFile (
pCurrString->pstrString [ iCurrCharIndex ], g_pExecFile );
                pCurrString = pCurrString->pNext;
        }
}
```

The first step is writing a word containing the string count. The contents of the table themselves are then written out, starting from the head node and traversing the list until the tail is reached. At each step, a word containing the length of the string is written out, followed by the string itself (which is written character by character).

To sum things up, the string table is just a linked list of strings that are read from the script table and added in the order they're encountered. Whenever a string is added to the table, its index is returned to the caller.

OPTIMIZATION TIP

Although I haven't implemented it here, the string table could be optimized for memory by checking all incoming strings against the existing strings in the table. If the string to be added is already present, the original string's index could be returned to the caller, and the new string could be discarded. There's no need to keep multiple copies of the same string. The only question to ask, of course, is how often you expect this to happen. If you find yourself writing scripts with the same string immediate values being used often, it might be worth considering.

That wraps up the implementation of the string table. With the table in place, we can now easily solve the problem of compiling immediate string variables. All that's necessary is a call to AddStringToStringTable () every time a new string is found in the source, and then you write the returned index to the instruction stream.

Things are moving along pretty well. We've now reached a point at which our theoretical compiler can process instructions as well as operands of all three immediate data types. The last major piece of the puzzle is the processing of memory references and labels, so let's get to it.

Compiling Memory References— Variables and Arrays

With the exception of handling branching instructions, the last major problem to work out is how to process memory references. Memory references can be a rather complicated part of compiler construction, but we'll take a fairly simplified route and handle variables and arrays with relative ease.

To get things started, let's talk about basic variables. A variable in our language, as previously mentioned, is completely typeless. This means that there's no such thing as an integer variable, a string variable, or whatever. All variables can be assigned all data types and that's that. To further simplify things, we won't even require our scripts to contain variable declarations. Variables are brought into existence immediately as they're used, which makes things easier for the script writer and even for us in a few ways.

The first thing we need to understand about variables is how they're going to be stored in compiled scripts and what that compiled information will mean to the runtime environment. At runtime, when our scripts are being executed, the memory that variables refer to will be a large, contiguous region known as the *heap*. All variables and arrays will be stored here, and therefore any given variable is really just a symbolic name for an index into the heap, as you can see in Figure 12.6. Each element of the heap has enough memory to contain any of the possible data types that a variable can have. This is an advantage for us. Since typeless variables are all the same size, it means we can maintain a simple counter to track the index in the heap to which each variable maps.

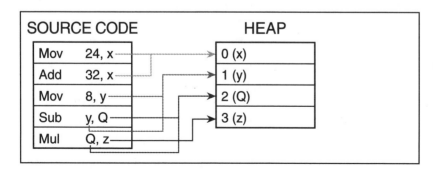

Figure 12.6

Variables are really just symbolic names for the indices

In other words, think of it like this. The following block of script code would declare three variables: X, Y, and Z.

```
Mov          16, X
Mov          32, Y
Mov          64, Z
```

As our compiler reads through the source code, it will encounter these variables in the order they were used. It'll find X first, Y second, and Z third. This means that if we start at the first index of the heap, index zero, and increment the index after every new variable is found, X will point to the first heap element, Y will point to the second, and Z will point to the third. We can then throw away the variable name itself and simply write the heap index out to the executable file. At runtime, the environment will use these indices to interact with the heap as our executable code performs various operations like arithmetic and moving memory around. So now, even though we write code that looks like this:

```
Mov          16, X
Mov          32, Y
Add          Y, X
Mov          2, Z
Div          Z, X
```

Our compiler will produce code that looks like this (assume that any number inside the brackets is a heap index):

```
Mov          16, [ 0 ]
Mov          32, [ 1 ]
Add          [ 1 ], [ 0 ]
Mov          2, [ 2 ]
Div          [ 2 ], [ 0 ]
```

We can think of the overall logic like this:

- Move the value of 16 into heap index 0 (X).
- Move the value of 32 into heap index 1 (Y).
- Add heap index 1 (Y) to heap index 0 (X).
- Move the value of 2 into heap index 2 (Z).
- Divide heap index 0 (X) by heap index 2 (Z).

To stack or not to stack, that is the question

Anyone familiar with traditional compiler construction and the general structure of how programs are executed may be wondering where the stack is. Since our language doesn't support functions of its own (its only interaction with functions is calling the host API, which is obviously different), there's no need for a stack. All code runs at the same level, and thus a central heap from which all variables and arrays can be indexed makes more sense.

Now that we understand how variables become heap indices, it's clear that we're going to need a data structure similar to the string table to hold them. This structure will perform nearly the same operations—we'll pass it a variable identifier that it'll add to the table, returning the heap index. It's known as the *symbol table* because it stores information regarding the program's symbols ("symbol" being a synonym for "identifier"). The only major difference between this and the string table is that we *must* check every addition to the table against all previous entries to determine whether or not this is the first time the identifier has been encountered. Remember that the first time the memory reference is detected we add it to the table, but any subsequent encounters shouldn't be added. Rather, the Add () function should simply note that the identifier has already been added and return the heap index it's associated with. If we fail to do this, the following code would technically contain two separate variables called X and would not behave as expected:

```
Mov        32, X
Add        Y, X
```

We're almost ready to see the implementation of the symbol table, but before we get into it, we should first address the issue of array references. Arrays themselves are really just variables that take up more space; an array of 16 elements can be thought of as 16 variables or, in other words, 16 consecutive heap indices. This is illustrated in Figure 12.7. The only thing that complicates matters is indexing the array. When an array index is used as an operand, we can expect one of two things: The index will be expressed either as an integer immediate value or as a variable. In the first case, all we have to do is send the array identifier to the symbol table and retrieve its index. This is known as the *base index* and lets us know where the array begins in the heap. We then add the integer immediate value, known as the *relative index*, to this base index to retrieve the *absolute index*, which is the actual value we want. So, for example, imagine we declare an array of 16 elements . . .

```
Array MyArray [ 16 ]
```

. . . and reference it with an integer immediate as follows:

```
Mov           MyArray [ 8 ], Y
```

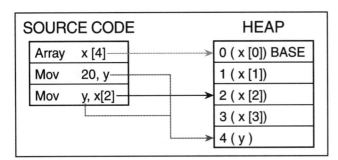

Figure 12.7

An array is just a linear series of variables collectively referred to with a single name

MyArray would be added to the heap at some offset, which we'll call X. The supplied index was 8, which means that the final index into the heap that we want to move into Y is X + 8. This is the value we'll write out to the instruction stream. (Of course, the value of X will be known, so this will be resolved to a single integer value.)

Things get slightly more complicated, however, when a variable is used to index an array. In this case, we have two heap indices to add: the base index of the offset and the index of the variable. The problem with this is that there's no way to tell at compile time to what value that second index will point. We know that the first index will always be the base index of the array, but the value of the variable is simply an element in the heap, which is only known at runtime. Thus, we won't be able to put a completely resolved index into the instruction stream at compile time. Rather, operands that involve an array indexed with a variable will be compiled down to the base index and the index of the variable that's being used for indexing. Then, at runtime, the environment will extract the base index, use the variable index to look up an element in the heap, and add that value to determine the final index. Phew!

Now that we've got everything sorted out, let's take a look at the implementation of the symbol table. The actual data structures will be nearly identical to that of the string table, save for a few added fields.

> We'll end up developing a number of structures that are all based on
> similar linked lists. C++ users may want to instead base them on a sin-
> gle, generic, linked-list implementation such as one provided by the
> STL. C users can certainly derive these from a more generic set of
> structures and functions as well. I've taken the more redundant path
> for readability but would highly recommend a more streamlined
> approach in your own projects.

As with the symbol table, we'll have both symbol nodes and a general table structure, as follows:

```
typedef struct _SymbolTableNode
{
        _SymbolTableNode * pPrev,          // Pointer to previous symbol node
                         * pNext;              // Pointer to next symbol node
        char * pstrIdent;          // Identifier
        int iIndex;                // Index into the table
        int iSize;                 // Size ( used for arrays )
}
        SymbolTableNode;
```

Basically, all you need to pay attention to is the string member that contains the
identifier (symbol) itself, the index into the heap that it maps to, and the size. As I
mentioned, all variables are the same size due to their typeless nature, but since
arrays are treated more or less as collections of simple variables, they make use of
the field.

```
typedef struct _SymbolTable
{
        int iSymbolCount;          // Current number of symbols
        SymbolTableNode * pHead,   // Pointer to head symbol node
                        * pTail;   // Pointer to tail symbol node
}
        SymbolTable;
```

This is even more inconsequential. Virtually nothing has changed from the string
table with the exception of the names of each field. Obviously, iSymbolCount is now
the number of symbols in the table.

The initializing and freeing of the symbol table is handled in pretty much the exact same way as the string table, so there's no need to examine these functions as well. To recap the process, however, initialization simply sets the symbol count to 0 and the head and tail pointers to NULL. Freeing loops through each symbol in the table frees both the identifier string and the node structure itself.

Things get interesting when we add to the symbol table. Once again, the process is nearly identical to adding to the string table, but we first need to make sure that the identifier being added doesn't already exist somewhere. If it does, we simply return that index; otherwise, we add the new one and return the new index.

Let's take a look at the code:

```
int AddSymbolToSymbolTable ( char * pstrIdent,
                             int iSize, int * iTableIndex )
{
        // Check for pre-existing record of symbol
        SymbolTableNode * pSymbolNode;
        if ( pSymbolNode = GetSymbolNode ( pstrIdent ) )
        {
                if ( iTableIndex )
                        * iTableIndex = pSymbolNode->iIndex;
                return 0;
        }
        // It's a new addition, so determine its index
        int iIndex = 0;
        // Add symbol to table
        if ( ! g_SymbolTable.iSymbolCount )
        {
                g_SymbolTable.pHead = ( SymbolTableNode * )
malloc ( sizeof ( SymbolTableNode ) );
                g_SymbolTable.pTail = g_SymbolTable.pHead;
                g_SymbolTable.pHead->pNext = NULL;
                g_SymbolTable.pHead->pPrev = NULL;
                g_SymbolTable.pHead->pstrIdent =
( char * ) malloc ( strlen ( pstrIdent ) + 1 );
                strcpy ( g_SymbolTable.pHead->pstrIdent, pstrIdent );
                g_SymbolTable.pHead->iIndex = iIndex;
                g_SymbolTable.pHead->iSize = iSize;
        }
        else
        {
```

```
                iIndex = g_SymbolTable.pTail->iIndex + g_SymbolTable.pTail->iSize;
                SymbolTableNode * pOldTail = g_SymbolTable.pTail;
                g_SymbolTable.pTail = ( SymbolTableNode * )
malloc ( sizeof ( SymbolTableNode ) );
                g_SymbolTable.pTail->pNext = NULL;
                g_SymbolTable.pTail->pPrev = pOldTail;
                g_SymbolTable.pTail->pstrIdent = ( char * )
malloc ( strlen ( pstrIdent ) + 1 );
                strcpy ( g_SymbolTable.pTail->pstrIdent, pstrIdent );
                g_SymbolTable.pTail->iIndex = iIndex;
                g_SymbolTable.pTail->iSize = iSize;
                pOldTail->pNext = g_SymbolTable.pTail;
        }
        // Increment the symbol count and return the index
        ++ g_SymbolTable.iSymbolCount;
        if ( iTableIndex )
                iTableIndex = iIndex;
        return 1;
}
```

As previously mentioned, the first step is to make sure the identifier isn't already present in the table. If it is, its index is simply returned to the caller and the function exits early. Otherwise, the typical process is followed for adding a new node, and the newly created index is returned.

The next detail to cover regarding arrays is the directive for declaring them. As we just saw, our language accepts array declaration with the following syntax:

```
Array Identifier [ Size ]
```

The size of the array must be an immediate value; variables are not allowed. Also, we'll add a rule stating that all arrays must be declared before the code begins. Although we could easily get around this, it's sometimes good to enforce certain coding practices. It's only going to lead to clutter if scripts can define arrays arbitrarily within the code blocks.

Whenever a new Array directive is found, the identifier and the size are passed to AddSymbolToSymbolTable (). The heap index will then be incremented by the size of the array (instead of by one), so the next symbol added to the table, whether it's another array or a variable, will index into the heap after all of the array's elements. So if you write a script that looks like this:

```
Array MyArray0 [ 256 ]
```

```
Array MyArray1 [ 512 ]
Mov           72, X
```

MyArray0 will occupy heap indices 0 to 255, MyArray1 will take 256 to 767, and Y will point to heap element 768. Another subtle advantage of forcing array declarations to precede code, which is really just a superficial thing, is that all arrays will be contiguous and start from the bottom of the heap. All variables will then be added to the heap afterward, leading to a more organized heap overall.

The last detail to mention about the symbol table is how it's written out to the executable file. It's funny because this will probably end up being the easiest part of the entire compilation process. Believe it or not, the only thing we need to store in the executable is a word containing the final size of the heap after all variables and arrays have been counted. In other words, there's no "table" to store at all.

The reason for this is simple. Since all variables are typeless and arrays are simply treated as contiguous groups of variables, there's no real information to store. The only information we need to retain about each specific variable is the heap index to which it's mapped, but those have already been stored in the instruction stream and will be handled automatically by the runtime environment. In other words, if we define 3 variables, we'll have a heap size of 3. Each variable will be indexed in the script, so heap indices 0 to 2 will be passed as operands to the instructions that the runtime environment processes and that'll be that. Simple, eh? All the runtime environment needs to know is to make room for three variables, and it takes it on faith that all indices will be used for something throughout the lifespan of the script.

Compiling Label Declarations and Branch Instructions

The last aspect of our theoretical compiler (which, by the way, will be implemented in reality soon enough, so just sit tight) is the compilation of label declarations and branch instructions.

Branching and labels manifest themselves in two forms in source code. First, certain lines simply

> **NOTE**
>
> You'll notice that even though writing the symbol "table" to the executable file is simply a matter of writing a single word, I've stored it in a function called WriteSymbolTableToExec () anyway. This is simply so you can expand it further in the future if need be. If you end up supporting more sophisticated variables or data types, you might need to end up storing a table of variable information after all. You may even want to make your language typed, in which case a description of each variable in the script may come in handy.

declare labels. Second, certain instructions (in the case of our language, only the branching J* instructions) actually accept line labels as operands. Much like strings and identifiers, a third table will be constructed to keep track of labels as they're found in the source. Each entry in the table will require two major pieces of information: the label string and its index into the instruction stream.

Compiling labels is a mostly straightforward job. When a new label is found, it's added to the label table along with its place in the instruction stream. Of course, the actual label itself is discarded during the compilation phase since there's no need for it at runtime. Instead, each label is assigned to an index (again, just like strings and symbols) that maps it to various jump instructions. This table is then written to the executable file along with the other tables we've been maintaining.

The one kink, however, is what to do about label operands. In many cases it's no big deal; you simply find the label in the label table and write its instruction index to the instruction stream. This only works in cases in which the label was defined *before* the operand that referred to it, however. What are we going to do if a label is defined 10 lines down from where it's used as an operand in a jump instruction, as shown in Figure 12.8?

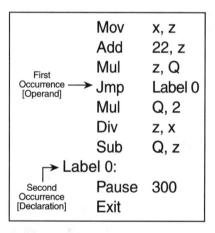

Figure 12.8

A jump instruction may present a given label as an operand before it gets defined

Although this is perfectly legal (and necessary for a number of forms of iterative techniques and algorithms), it does make things a bit trickier for the compiler. We certainly can't prohibit scripts from doing this; being able to jump forward in code is a necessity. Fortunately, the solution is simple. Every time a label is encountered as our compiler scans through the source code, whether it's a declaration or an operand, it's added to the label table. However, its instruction index is only added to the table when it's found in the form of a declaration. If a label is initially encountered as an operand, its instruction index field is left blank until the declaration is found. Then, when the declaration finally pops up, the Add () function for the label table informs us that the label has already been found and that all we need now is the instruction index of the declaration. By the time the entire source file has been scanned, we'll have matched up every label with its instruction index. The only two things to watch for are multiple definitions of the same label and labels that are referred to as operands but never defined. Both of these will result in compile-time errors.

As you can see, labels and jumps aren't particularly hard to deal with. The only thing to remember is that labels can be defined anywhere relative to the operands by which they may be referred to, so we have to think in parallel when scanning the source file. At any time, we could find either a label declaration or an operand, and we need to be prepared to handle each.

Let's finish this section up by taking a look at the code behind the label table. Again, we use a linked list to dynamically store our list of labels as we progress through the source code. First up is the node structure:

```
typedef struct _LabelTableNode
{
        _LabelTableNode * pPrev,          // Pointer to previous label node
                        * pNext;          // Pointer to next label node
        char * pstrLabel;                 // Pointer to label
        int iInstrOffset;                 // Instruction the label points to
        int iIndex;                       // Index into the label table
        int iFoundType;                   // How was this label found?
}
        LabelTableNode;
```

You'll notice that the final implementation has four major data members. pstrLabel is obviously the label string. iInstrOffset is the offset into the instruction stream, which will tell our runtime environment where to reroute the program when jump instructions are executed. iIndex is the index that will be used to map jump operands to the label. iFoundType will require a bit of explanation, however. As previously mentioned, labels can appear in any order, either as their formal declaration or as operands in jump instructions. Although both cases involve adding the label to the table, we need to keep track of how the label was found the last time we saw it. iFoundType can thus be assigned one of two values: FOUND_AS_DEF, which means it was found as a definition, or FOUND_AS_OP, which means it was found as an operand. The reason for this is that if a label is found as a definition, we need to make sure this is the first time. If a label is added to the table as a definition and iFoundType already equals FOUND_AS_DEF, a label redefinition error has occured.

The label table structure is again exactly like that of the string and symbol tables. It simply manages the current number of labels stored in the table, as well as pointers to the head and tail nodes of the list. The same goes for the initialization and freeing of the table; it's the same routine as the string and symbol tables.

Let's now shift our focus to the only really complicated part of dealing with labels—the AddToLabelTable () function.

```
int AddToLabelTable ( char * pstrLabel, int iInstrOffset, int iFoundType )
{
        LabelTableNode * pCurrLabel = g_LabelTable.pHead;
        // First look for a previous entry of the label
        for ( int iCurrLabelIndex = 0; iCurrLabelIndex < g_LabelTable.iLabelCount; ++
  iCurrLabelIndex )
        {
                if ( stricmp ( pCurrLabel->pstrLabel, pstrLabel ) == 0 )
                {
                        // If the label is found, set its instruction
                        // offset. Return whether or not it's been found as
                        // a definition
                        if ( iInstrOffset != -1 )
                                pCurrLabel->iInstrOffset = iInstrOffset;
                        if ( iFoundType == FOUND_AS_DEF )
                                if ( pCurrLabel->iFoundType == FOUND_AS_DEF )
                                        return -1;
                                else
                                        pCurrLabel->iFoundType = FOUND_AS_DEF;
                        return pCurrLabel->iIndex;
                }
                pCurrLabel = pCurrLabel->pNext;
        }
        // Otherwise, add it to the table
        int iIndex = g_LabelTable.iLabelCount;
        if ( ! g_LabelTable.iLabelCount )
        {
                g_LabelTable.pHead = ( LabelTableNode * ) malloc ( sizeof (
  LabelTableNode ) );
                g_LabelTable.pTail = g_LabelTable.pHead;
                g_LabelTable.pHead->pNext = NULL;
                g_LabelTable.pHead->pPrev = NULL;
                g_LabelTable.pHead->pstrLabel = ( char * ) malloc ( strlen (
```

```
pstrLabel ) + 1 );
                strcpy ( g_LabelTable.pHead->pstrLabel, pstrLabel );
                g_LabelTable.pHead->iInstrOffset = iInstrOffset;
                g_LabelTable.pHead->iIndex = iIndex;
                g_LabelTable.pHead->iFoundType = iFoundType;
        }
        else
        {
                LabelTableNode * pOldTail = g_LabelTable.pTail;
                g_LabelTable.pTail = ( LabelTableNode * ) malloc ( sizeof (
LabelTableNode ) );
                g_LabelTable.pTail->pNext = NULL;
                g_LabelTable.pTail->pPrev = pOldTail;
                g_LabelTable.pTail->pstrLabel = ( char * ) malloc ( strlen (
pstrLabel ) + 1 );
                strcpy ( g_LabelTable.pTail->pstrLabel, pstrLabel );
                g_LabelTable.pTail->iInstrOffset = iInstrOffset;
                g_LabelTable.pTail->iIndex = iIndex;
                g_LabelTable.pTail->iFoundType = iFoundType;
                pOldTail->pNext = g_LabelTable.pTail;
        }
        ++ g_LabelTable.iLabelCount;
        return iIndex;
}
```

Much like the Add () functions for symbol and string tables, the real brunt of the
function is simply a matter of adding the label to the table, and the code is pretty
much the same. The only part worth noting is the first block of code in the function; it determines how the label has been found in the source code and how to
process the parameters it's been passed. It starts off by looping through each label
until the label in question is found. It then checks the value of the passed instruction offset. If it's not –1, it's interpreted as a valid offset and is written to the label's
instruction offset member. It then determines whether or not a label redefinition
has occurred by comparing the passed iFoundType to the one currently stored in the
label's node.

The last function to cover handles the writing of the table to the executable file
and looks like this:

```
void WriteLabelTableToExec ()
{
        // Write label count
```

```
        WriteIntToBinFile ( g_LabelTable.iLabelCount, g_pExecFile );
        // Write each label index and offset
        LabelTableNode * pCurrLabel = g_LabelTable.pHead;
        for ( int iCurrLabelIndex = 0; iCurrLabelIndex < g_LabelTable.iLabelCount; ++
    iCurrLabelIndex )
        {
              if ( pCurrLabel->iInstrOffset == -1 && pCurrLabel->iFoundType ==
    FOUND_AS_OP )
              {
                    char pstrErrorMssg [ 1024 ];
                    sprintf ( pstrErrorMssg, "Undefined label '%s'", pCurrLabel-
    >pstrLabel );

                    ExitOnSourceError ( pstrErrorMssg, 0, 0, -1 );
              }
              WriteIntToBinFile ( pCurrLabel->iIndex, g_pExecFile );
              WriteIntToBinFile ( pCurrLabel->iInstrOffset, g_pExecFile );
              pCurrLabel = pCurrLabel->pNext;
        }
    }
```

The function really just writes out each label index and its offset into the instruction stream. The runtime environment then uses the indices to map jump instruction operands to instruction stream offsets, but we'll learn more about that later on.

Putting It All Together

The last step in working out the details of our theoretical compiler is basically putting together everything we've covered so far. So let's summarize everything we've discussed up to this point and pin down the exact format of the executable format we've pieced together.

Although I've presented the generation of the instruction stream as a "first step" of sorts, it's really a constant task that lasts through the entire process of compilation. The string, symbol, and label tables are all created during the generation of the instruction stream, not after (as can be seen in Figure 12.9). Everything is really happening in parallel. The only time we can make distinctions in terms of what comes before what is in the order of these four blocks of information as they are written out in the executable file. So let's have a look at that.

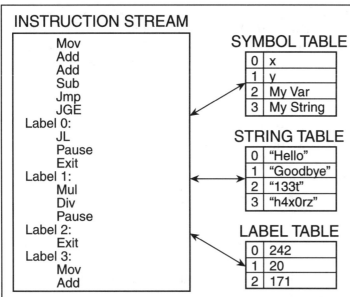

Figure 12.9

The instruction stream, symbol table, string table, and label table

The format for our compiled scripts will be extremely simple. It'll start with the instruction stream, followed by the symbol table, then the string table, and finally the label table.

The instruction table will begin with a single word that tells us how many instructions are in the stream, followed by the stream itself. Each instruction in the stream consists of an opcode, an operand count word, and then the operands themselves. Each operand is composed of an operand type word and the operand's data. As we saw earlier, there are seven different types of operands. The value of the operand type word can be any of the following constants:

```
OP_TYPE_INT
OP_TYPE_FLOAT
OP_TYPE_STRING
OP_TYPE_MEMORY
OP_TYPE_ARRAY_INDEX_IMMEDIATE
OP_TYPE_ARRAY_INDEX_VARIABLE
OP_TYPE_LABEL
```

After the operand type word is the operand data itself. This is equally simple in most cases. Integer operands (OP_TYPE_INT) are simply a word containing the integer value. Floating-point values (OP_TYPE_FLOAT) are pretty much the same thing; the 4 bytes that make up the float data type (depending on your platform) are simply written out as binary data. Strings (OP_TYPE_STRING) are also single words; they exist as operands only in the form of indices into the string table. Labels (OP_TYPE_LABEL) are the same thing, just single-word indices into the label table. Rounding out the simpler operands are variables (OP_TYPE_MEMORY); they're just single words containing an index into the heap.

Arrays are more involved. Arrays with integer immediate values as their indices (OP_TYPE_ARRAY_INDEX_IMMEDIATE) are stored as two words. The first is the base index (an index into the heap that points to the start of the array), and the second is the relative index (an integer value that is added to the base index to point out a specific array element). Both indices could actually be added together at compile time and written to the file as a single value, but I decided against this to keep things more readable.

Arrays with variables as their indices (OP_TYPE_ARRAY_INDEX_VARIABLE) are also stored as two words, both of which are heap indices. The first is the array's base index; the second points to the relative index, which at runtime must be added to it to find the absolute index.

This is everything we need to know about the instruction stream. As previously mentioned, the symbol table immediately follows the stream. As we learned, however, all we really need to keep track of is the heap size, so the next step in writing the executable file is just a matter of writing a single word containing the heap size after the last word of the stream.

The string table isn't such a free ride. The first word of the table is the number of strings that will follow. The string data immediately follows this word, composed of two members: a single word containing the length of the current string and a character stream making up the string itself.

The last information in the executable is the label table, which is composed of a single word that contains the number of labels in the table, followed by a series of index-offset pairs. The index of the pair is a single word that is used to map its offset to operands in jump instruction operands. The offset is another single word, the value of which determines to which instruction the runtime environment should jump to reach the location the label represents.

That's everything. At this point our theoretical compiler is complete, and you should understand (for the most part) all of the major steps involved in converting human-readable script code to a more compact and efficient bytecode format.

The next step, finally, is discussing the actual real-world implementation of the compiler. Fortunately for us, the knowledge we've armed ourselves with in the last few sections will prepare us well for constructing the actual program.

Implementing the Compiler

It's been easy to discuss the conversion of our script code to executable code in high-level terms, but there's a big difference between saying something like "First read the instructions and then read each operand" and actually *doing* it. Now that we've seen the overview of our strategy for compiling script code, we're going to learn how the breakdown, analysis, and extraction of the information our script code is trying to convey will actually be implemented.

The first thing to understand is that the entire script file can be thought of as one big string. From the perspective of a piece of software, it's simply an arbitrary stream of characters that could just as likely be the script to the behavior of an enemy in the second dungeon of your RPG as it could be an excerpt from *The Age of Spiritual Machines*. It's our job, then, to make our compiler understand how to break up this incoming stream of text and make sense of it. This, of course, will ultimately lead to the ability to translate it.

The upshot to all of this is that we've got a significant amount of string processing ahead of us. Virtually every individual operation required to compile our scripts will involve processing string data and attempting to analyze and transform its contents. This means that our first order of business will be putting together a small library of string-handling functions. While the standard C libraries do provide a decent number of routines for this task, we'll need a few more and will end up rewriting a few of the simpler ones just for consistency with other functions we'll write.

A Small String-Processing Library

In this section, we'll put together a small but useful library of string-processing routines. We're building them now because we'll need them to construct our compiler later, but unfortunately, this means not every function we code now will make immediate sense. I'm going to do my best to explain why each is necessary as we cover them, but don't worry too much if you can't understand just yet why something is necessary. Everything will be explained somewhere down the line.

One common operation we'll find ourselves performing time and time again is determining whether or not a given character or string is of a certain type (that is, whether or not it's numeric, alphanumeric, whitespace, or whatever). So let's start off by writing a few functions that will allow us to determine the type of a given chararacter.

First up will be a simple function called `IsCharWhitespace ()`. This will return 1 if the given character is a space, a tab, or a new line:

```
int IsCharWhitespace ( char cChar )
{
        if ( cChar == ' ' || cChar == '\t' || cChar == '\n' )
                return 1;
        else
                return 0;
}
```

Since our language will be *free form*, we'll allow the user to put any amount of whitespace between relevant characters and strings like commas, identifiers, values, and so on. This means that the following line of code [...]

```
Mov           X, 10
```

[...] is considered equivalent to this:

```
Mov X                  ,10
```

`IsCharWhitespace ()` will help us easily skip over this whitespace, allowing us to focus instead on the stuff we're really after. Next up is `IsCharNumeric ()`, which will tell us whether or not a given character is a numeral between 0 and 9.

```
int IsCharNumeric ( char cChar )
{
        if ( cChar >= '0' && cChar <= '9' )
                return 1;
        else
                return 0;
}
```

When reading numeric values in from the source file, we'll make heavy use of this function to ensure that each character forming the number is valid.

In addition to numbers, however, we'll also be reading in identifiers, which can be strings consisting of underscores, characters, and numerals. Any character that can fall into one of these three groups is considered a valid identifier character, according to the function IsCharIdent ():

```
int IsCharIdent ( char cChar )
{
        if ( ( cChar >= '0' && cChar <= '9' ) ||
             ( cChar >= 'A' && cChar <= 'Z' ) ||
             ( cChar >= 'a' && cChar <= 'z' ) ||
              cChar >= '_' )
             return 1;
        else
             return 0;
}
```

A third type of entity to watch for when parsing source code is delimiters, which are usually single characters that denote either the beginning or the end of a certain type of data. Examples of delimiters include the brackets surrounding array indices and the commas that separate operands. IsCharDelimiter () helps us determine whether or not a given character is a delimeter:

```
int IsCharDelimiter ( char cChar )
{
        if ( cChar == ':' || cChar == ',' || cChar == '"' ||
             cChar == '[' || cChar == ']' ||
           IsCharWhitespace ( cChar ) )
                return 1;
        else
                return 0;
}
```

This wraps up the functions we'll need for testing individual characters. With that out of the way, let's have a look at some functions for processing full strings.

When dealing with source code, it's often convenient to be able to easily strip a given string of its whitespace. As you're probably starting to suspect, whitespace will be frequently dealt with as our compiler is built. TrimWhitespace () will help us out by removing the spacing on either side of a given string and returning the trimmed version.

```
void TrimWhitespace ( char * pstrString )
{
        unsigned int iStringLength = strlen ( pstrString );
        unsigned int iPadLength;
```

```
            unsigned int iCurrCharIndex;
            if ( iStringLength > 1 )
            {
                    // First determine whitespace quantity on the left
                    for ( iCurrCharIndex = 0; iCurrCharIndex < iStringLength;
++ iCurrCharIndex )
                            if ( ! IsCharWhitespace ( pstrString [ iCurrCharIndex ] ) )
                                    break;
                     // Slide string to the left to overwrite whitespace
                    iPadLength = iCurrCharIndex;
                    if ( iPadLength )
                       {
                    for ( iCurrCharIndex = iPadLength;
iCurrCharIndex < iStringLength; ++ iCurrCharIndex )
                                pstrString [ iCurrCharIndex - iPadLength ]
= pstrString [ iCurrCharIndex ];

for ( iCurrCharIndex = iStringLength - iPadLength;
iCurrCharIndex < iStringLength;
++ iCurrCharIndex )
                                        pstrString [ iCurrCharIndex ] = ' ';
                    }

                    // Terminate string at the start of right hand whitespace

                    for ( iCurrCharIndex = iStringLength - 1;
iCurrCharIndex > 0;
- iCurrCharIndex )
                    {
                            if ( ! IsCharWhitespace
( pstrString [ iCurrCharIndex ] ) )
                            {
                                    pstrString [ iCurrCharIndex + 1 ] = '\0';
                                    break;
                            }
                    }
            }
}
```

The function works by scanning through the string from left to right to determine where the beginning of the string's content is (in other words, the location of the first nonwhitespace character). Once found, it then runs through the remaining characters, one by one, and slides them over, effectively overwriting the extraneous whitespace. It then scans through the string again, this time from the right to left, and writes a null terminating character ('\0') just after the first nonwhitespace character it finds.

Next let's look at IsStringWhitespace (), which scans through a string with IsCharWhitespace () to determine whether or not it's composed entirely of whitespace:

```
int IsStringWhitespace ( char * pstrString )
{
if ( ! pstrString )
            return 0;

        if ( strlen ( pstrString ) == 0 )
            return 1;

        for ( unsigned int iCurrCharIndex = 0;
iCurrCharIndex < strlen ( pstrString );
++ iCurrCharIndex )
                if ( ! IsCharWhitespace ( pstrString [ iCurrCharIndex ] ) )
                    return 0;

        return 1;
}
```

While we're at it, we'll make full-string versions of all our character analysis functions. To start things off, let's build a function that can determine whether or not a string is an identifier around IsCharIdent (). The function's called IsStringIdent () and looks like this:

```
int IsStringIdent ( char * pstrString )
{
if ( ! pstrString )
            return 0;

        if ( strlen ( pstrString ) == 0 )
            return 0;

        if ( pstrString [ 0 ] >= '0' && pstrString [ 0 ] <= '9' )
        return 0;
```

```
            for ( unsigned int iCurrCharIndex = 0;
iCurrCharIndex < strlen ( pstrString );
++ iCurrCharIndex )
                if ( ! IsCharIdent ( pstrString [ iCurrCharIndex ] ) )
                    return 0;

        return 1;
}
```

All it does is loop through each character in the string and make sure it's a valid identifier character. Before doing so, however, it makes sure that the first character in the string isn't a number, which would render the identifier invalid.

We'll want some functions for determining whether or not a string is a numeric value as well, but when we're dealing with full strings, we have a few more situations to look out for. We'll need to differentiate between integers and floating-point values, so we'll make two different routines. First let's look at the integer version:

```
int IsStringInteger ( char * pstrString )
{
if ( ! pstrString )
                return 0;

        if ( strlen ( pstrString ) == 0 )
                return 0;

        unsigned int iCurrCharIndex;

for ( iCurrCharIndex = 0;
iCurrCharIndex < strlen ( pstrString );
++ iCurrCharIndex )
                if ( ! IsCharNumeric ( pstrString [ iCurrCharIndex ] )
&& ! ( pstrString [ iCurrCharIndex ] == '-' ) )
                    return 0;

        for ( iCurrCharIndex = 1;
iCurrCharIndex < strlen ( pstrString );
++ iCurrCharIndex )
                if ( pstrString [ iCurrCharIndex ] == '-' )
                    return 0;
```

```
        return 1;
}
```

The function starts by scanning through the string and making sure every character is a valid character in an integer (which simply means being either a digit or a possible negative sign). It then checks every character in the string past the first to make sure it's not a negative sign since this can only occur at the first character. Validating floating-point values isn't much harder; it's really just a matter of adding a check for the radix point:

```
int IsStringFloat( char * pstrString )
{
        if ( ! pstrString )
                return 0;

        if ( strlen ( pstrString ) == 0 )
                return 0;

        // First make sure we've got only numbers and radix points

        unsigned int iCurrCharIndex;

        for ( iCurrCharIndex = 0;
iCurrCharIndex < strlen ( pstrString );
++ iCurrCharIndex )
                if ( ! IsCharNumeric ( pstrString [ iCurrCharIndex ] ) &&
        ! ( pstrString [ iCurrCharIndex ] == '.' ) &&
                ! ( pstrString [ iCurrCharIndex ] == '-' ) )
                        return 0;

        // Make sure only one radix point is present

        int iRadixPointFound = 0;

        for ( iCurrCharIndex = 0;
iCurrCharIndex < strlen ( pstrString );
++ iCurrCharIndex )
                if ( pstrString [ iCurrCharIndex ] == '.' )
                        if ( iRadixPointFound )
                                return 0;
                        else
```

```
                                    iRadixPointFound = 1;

        for ( iCurrCharIndex = 1;
iCurrCharIndex < strlen ( pstrString );
++ iCurrCharIndex )
                if ( pstrString [ iCurrCharIndex ] == '-' )
                        return 0;

if ( iRadixPointFound )
        return 1;
        else
                return 0;
}
```

The logic is really the same here as it was in `IsStringInteger ()`; the only major difference is that the initial scan through the string considers radix points valid. It then performs another scan through the string to determine that no more than one radix point is present.

That's everything we'll need in the way of string processing. As long as we're here, however, we might as well throw in a few more basic helper functions.

File I/O Functions

Just to round out our little library, we'll throw in some really quick file I/O functions that will make it a bit easier to write primitive data types to files:

```
int WriteCharToBinFile ( char cChar, FILE * pFile )
{
        fwrite ( & cChar, sizeof ( char ), 1, pFile );
        return sizeof ( char );
}


int WriteIntToBinFile ( int iInt, FILE * pFile )
{
        fwrite ( & iInt, sizeof ( int ), 1, pFile );
        return sizeof ( int );
}


int WriteFloatToBinFile ( float fFloat, FILE * pFile )
{
        fwrite ( & fFloat, sizeof ( float ), 1, pFile );
```

```
        return sizeof ( float );
}
```

These should all be pretty self-explanatory. Each simply writes a given primitive data type to a file and returns the size of the written data in bytes. (The reasons for this will become clear later.)

Program Structure of the Compiler

Now that we've got our library of helper functions out of the way, we can finally start thinking about how we're going to lay out the compiler as a program. The first thing to consider is the program's general flow, which fortunately will be relatively simple.

I'll be implementing the compiler as a basic Win32 console application, although it could just as easily be written in DOS or Linux since command-line utilities are pretty much all the same and use the same standard C library. The user will tell the compiler which source file he wants to compile by passing its file name as a command-line argument.

The flow of the program more or less will work out like this:

1. A "logo" will be printed to the screen, containing the title of the program and credit information (just to make it look official).

2. The program will check to see if a command-line argument has been passed. If so, this will be interpreted as the file name of the script that the user wants to compile. If no command-line arguments are present, some simple usage information will be printed explaining how to interact with the program, and the program will exit.

3. As long as the command line contained at least one argument, its value will be considered the source file name. The file name will first be checked to determine whether or not the user included a file extension. Our compiler will accept script files with an .ss extension (meaning source script) and produce compiled scripts with an .es extension (meaning executable script). If a file extension is found, the source file is opened. If not, the proper extension is appended. The source file will be opened for ASCII reading, while the executable file will be opened (or, more accurately, created) for binary writing. The name of the executable file is always the same as the source file name, with the proper extension. If the file name is invalid, a file I/O error is reported to the user and the program exits.

4. The instruction set list will be initialized for use by the parser. Basically, at this point we're going to build a list of each instruction our compiler will recognize, along with relevant information such as the number of operands each instruction takes as well as what type these operands must be. You'll learn more about this later.

5. The symbol, string, and label tables will be initialized. We've already seen how this works.

6. The compilation process will begin. Each line of the source file will be read from the file, stripped of all extraneous whitespace as well as its comments, and compiled. As we've learned, this step can also involve additions to the symbol, string, and label tables. During this step, compile-time errors may occur and will be reported to the user, causing the program to abort. As each line of code is processed, it's written out to the file, thus generating the instruction stream.

7. With the fully compiled instruction stream now generated and written out to the executable file, the symbol, string, and label tables will also be written out.

8. Finally, some basic statistics will be printed to the screen, listing the number of lines processed and the number of instructions, variables, strings, and labels found. A success message will be printed as well, letting the user know the file name of the executable script that is now ready to use.

9. The program will close the file handles of both the source file and the executable and will finally exit.

If all goes well, we should have ourselves a finished script by the time this process exits. At this point, we've seen the source behind our modest library of helper functions and the full implementations of the symbol, string, and label tables. Now we're going to move through the entire implementation of the compiler from start to finish, using the general process previously outlined as something of a guide to keep us on track.

Printing the Logo and Usage Information

This step obviously has nothing to do with compiler implementation per se, but it's a good place to start since there's nothing to it. First let's take a look at the top of the compiler's main () function:

```
main ( int argc, char * argv [] )
{
        PrintLogo ();

        // If no command line arguments are present,
// show usage screen and exit

        if ( argc < 2 )
        {
                PrintUsage ();
                return 0;
        }
...
```

As previously stated, the program prints out its logo and then checks to see if the source file name was included. If not, it prints the usage information and exits. The logo and usage functions look like this:

```
void PrintLogo ()
{
        printf ( "Mini Script Compiler v1.0\n" );
        printf ( "Copyright (C) 2002 Paper Street Soap Company\n" );
        printf ( "All rights reserved.\n" );
        printf ( "\n" );
}

void PrintUsage ()
{
        printf ( "Usage: Compiler [ Filename ]\n" );
        printf ( "\n" );
        printf ( "Notes\n" );
        printf ( "\t- Extension is optional on filenames.\n" );
}
```

With that out of the way, we can move on to the rest of main ():

```
        ...

// Initialize the instruction list
InitInstrList ();

// Open up the source and executable files and compile
if ( ! OpenFiles ( argv [ 1 ] ) )
```

```
        ExitOnError ( "File I/O error" );
else
        CompileSourceScript ();

// Close everything up and shut down
CloseFiles ();

        return 0;
}
```

For now we're going to skip InitInstrList (), so let's move on to the call to
OpenFiles (). When passed the file name of the source script, this function will do a
number of things for us such as validating the presence of a file extension, deriving
the file name of the executable, opening both files in the proper modes, and
returning an error status. Let's have a look:

```
int OpenFiles ( char * pstrFilename )
{
        // Validate filenames ( append file extensions if necessary )
        strupr ( pstrFilename );
        strcpy ( g_pstrSourceFilename, pstrFilename );

        if ( ! strstr ( g_pstrSourceFilename, SCRIPT_SOURCE_EXT ) )
        {
                strcat ( g_pstrSourceFilename, SCRIPT_SOURCE_EXT );
                strcpy ( g_pstrExecFilename, pstrFilename );
                strcat ( g_pstrExecFilename, SCRIPT_EXEC_EXT );
        }
        else
        {
                for ( int iCurrCharIndex = strlen ( pstrFilename ) - 1;
iCurrCharIndex > 0;
-- iCurrCharIndex )
                {
                        if ( pstrFilename [ iCurrCharIndex ] == '.' )
                                break;
                }

                strncpy ( g_pstrExecFilename, pstrFilename,
                        iCurrCharIndex );
                g_pstrExecFilename [ iCurrCharIndex ] = '\0';
```

```
            strcat ( g_pstrExecFilename, SCRIPT_EXEC_EXT );
    }

    // Open files
    g_pSourceFile = fopen ( g_pstrSourceFilename, "r" );
    if ( ! g_pSourceFile )
            return 0;

    g_pExecFile = fopen ( g_pstrExecFilename, "wb" );
            if ( ! g_pExecFile )
                    return 0;

    return 1;
}
```

When this function returns, we check its error status and proceed if everything went okay. If not, however, we need to print out a fatal I/O error report and exit. This brings up the need for our first error-handling function, the rather simple ExitOnError ():

```
void ExitOnError ( char * pstrErrorMssg )
{
    printf ( "\n" );
    printf ( "Fatal Error: %s.\n", pstrErrorMssg );
    printf ( "\n" );
exit ( 0 );
}
```

Simply pass it the error message, and it'll print it to the screen and exit. If OpenFiles () succeeds, however, we start our journey into the belly of the beast by calling the mammoth, awe-inspiring CompileSourceScript (). This large function is responsible for nearly the entire compilation process, so we're going to step through it in chunks rather than looking at it all at once. We'll also make a number of stops along the way to check out some other functions.

In fact, there's so much going on in CompileSourceScript () that we're going to take a quick detour and learn about the first and most basic capability of the compiler: a process called *tokenization*.

Tokenization

Tokenization is the process of breaking up a stream of text into its constituent parts, known as *tokens*. For example, consider the phrase "Hello, world!" When written out normally, it looks like this:

```
Hello, world!
```

However, when tokenized (a process that our brain does automatically when reading), each chunk of the sentence is isolated and can be expressed like this:

```
Hello

,

world

!
```

This means that there are four tokens in the phrase: the two words ("Hello" and "world"), a comma, and an exclamation point. Notice that the whitespace wasn't included. This is because whitespace isn't considered a token of its own; rather, it's a simple way to separate tokens. Since its only purpose is to delimit pieces of information, it carries no relevant information of its own and is thus ignored. This is why free-form languages like C, C++, and even ours allow such flexible use of whitespace—because it's not relied on for anything other than a separation of elements.

Anyway, you'll notice that the four tokens we extracted each provided a small piece of information. In the context of sentences and speech, "Hello" tells us that the following sentence is going to be a greeting, the comma tells us to pause slightly, "world" tells us to whom the greeting is directed, and the exclamation point implies a certain sense of friendly enthusiasm. This information is gathered not only from the tokens themselves but also the order in which they were presented. Note that the following wouldn't make quite as much sense, even though the same tokens were used:

```
world ,! Hello
```

Now, to finally answer a question that was raised earlier in the chapter, this is precisely *how* we can extract specific things from a line of code, such as the instruction and individual operands. All of these things—instructions, integer values, strings, variables, everything—are tokens and are separated by other tokens (and whitespace). So, for example, imagine the following line of code:

```
Mov              "This is a string", MyArray [ 63 ]
```

When broken down into its constituent tokens, it'd look like this:

```
Mov
"
This is a string
"
,
MyArray
[
63
]
```

Let's analyze each token like we did with the preceding sentence. The first token is the instruction, which tells us that we are not processing an array declaration or a line label. We know it's an instruction for two reasons: The token ahead of it is not a colon, which would indicate a line label, and the token itself is not Array, which would indicate an array declaration. By the process of elimination, we can be sure that an instruction is the only other thing this line could be.

Whatever the next token is, it must be either the first operand or part of the first operand (assuming that this particular instruction requires an operand, which Mov certainly does). This is confirmed by reading the next token, which, indeed, is a quote. This tells us that we're dealing with a string, so we know that the next token is the string value itself, and the token after that is the closing quote. Once we've finished the string, we know that the first operand is finished, so a comma must come next. It indeed does, and once we've read that, we know the next operand is on the way.

The second operand consists of four tokens: an identifier, an opening bracket, an integer value, and a closing bracket. By the time we've read the first token, we know that we're dealing with a memory reference because it's an identifier. We still don't know it's an array, though. Until we read the next token, we'll probably think it's just a variable. The next token in the stream, however, is an open bracket, so we know for sure that an array index is in the works. Once we know this, we can read the next two tokens and expect the first to be either an integer index (as it is) or a variable index. We can expect the next token in either case to be the closing bracket. After that, we'll attempt to read another token and be told that we've reached the end of the line. This is fine and simply means that we're done and can proceed to the next line in the script.

The process we just glossed over is essentially the secret to building a simple compiler like ours. In a nutshell, the idea is to read a token and attempt to determine what sort of code you're processing based on that token's type. This, in turn, gives you an idea of what to expect from future tokens as well as what information exactly is being carried on those tokens. The more tokens you read, the less guess-work you have to do, and the surer you can be of what you're dealing with. Tokens also provide an elegant and simple way to handle compile-time errors. If the closed bracket after the 63 token wasn't found, we'd easily know that the array index was malformed and could provide a reasonably useful error for the user.

Something to note, however, is that tokenization isn't quite as easy as you might think. It's a bit more complicated than simply breaking up the line based on the whitespace; for example, recall the string token in the preceding example, which looked like this:

```
This is a string
```

Notice that there are three separate spaces within this token, but the tokenizer was smart enough to know not to cut the token off at the first one. This is because it knew, based on the previous token (which was a quotation mark), that it was deal-ing with a string, and it read every character until the closing quote was found. These sorts of details can make tokenization a tricky process.

With that said, let's solidify our understanding of tokenization by going over the process from start to finish.

Implementing the Tokenizer

Tokenization is indeed a tricky process, as previously mentioned. While at first glance it seems like a simple issue of splitting up a string at each space, it is indeed far more complicated. Our tokenizer needs to understand every supported token type and be prepared for all of the possible ways in which tokens can be separated from one another. As you'll see, this isn't always a simple matter of whitespace.

Token Types

The first thing we should do, as always, is identify what we're working with. Specifically, let's consider all of the possible types of tokens that our tokenizer needs to be able to process.

```
TOKEN_TYPE_INT
```

These are simple integer values—in other words, any string of digits with an optional negative sign in front.

```
TOKEN_TYPE_FLOAT
```

These are floating-point values, which follow the same rules as integer tokens except they can contain one radix point.

```
TOKEN_TYPE_STRING
```

String tokens are special cases because a string, as we know it, requires three separate tokens to properly express. Since this single token cannot also include the quotation mark tokens that surround it, a string token is defined as simply a string of characters. All characters are valid in strings, including whitespace and special delimiters such as brackets and colons.

```
TOKEN_TYPE_IDENT
```

Identifiers are defined as strings of alphanumeric characters and underscores, although they cannot begin with a number.

```
TOKEN_TYPE_COLON
```

```
TOKEN_TYPE_OPEN_BRACKET
```

```
TOKEN_TYPE_CLOSE_BRACKET
```

```
TOKEN_TYPE_COMMA
```

```
TOKEN_TYPE_QUOTE
```

These are the single-character tokens, and they are usually used as delimiters for other larger tokens. They're pretty self-explanatory in terms of what they consist of, but let's quickly review their function. Colons always follow line label definitions, opening and closing brackets are used for array declarations as well as indexing, commas are used to separate instruction operands, and quotes always surround string tokens.

As you can see, this means we have nine different types of tokens to prepare for.

Tokenizer Basics

So now let's think about how tokenization will actually work. At each iteration of the main loop of the compiler, the next line of code will be fetched from the source script, and tokens will be requested from it. This means our tokenizer, given a single line of code, needs to be able to break it down into its constituent parts, taking all nine of our established token types into account.

To get started, let's consider an extremely basic tokenizer job. Assume you're given the following string and are asked to break it up into tokens:

```
Token0 Token1 Token2
```

This is simply a matter of scanning through the line and breaking it up at each space. The end result provides the following tokens:

```
Token0
Token1
Token2
```

A pseudocode example of such a simple tokenizer might look like this:

```
function GetNextToken ( string SourceLine )
{
static int Index = 0;
string Token = "";
char Char;

while ( TRUE )
{
Char = SourceLine [ Index ];
++ Index;
if ( Char != ' ' )
strcat ( Token, Char );
else
return Token;
}
}
```

This simple function starts by defining a few variables. The static integer Index is a pointer to the current character in the source string. It's static so that the function can be called multiple times and still keep track of its position in SourceLine. A blank token string is then defined as well as a character that will be used to hold the current character.

The function then loops through the string, starting from Index and continuing until a space is found. Each time it loops, it checks the current character to see if it's a space, and if it's not, the character is appended to the token. If it is, the token is returned and the function exits. It should be clear that this function will indeed identify and return the three tokens properly.

Now that we understand a basic example of tokenization, let's kick things up a notch and see how our current tokenizer implementing holds up. Imagine that we now want to tokenize strings that contain variable amounts of whitespace, such as the following:

```
Token0      Token1               Token2 Token3
```

There are only four tokens, but the string is rather long due to a large number of spaces. Free-form languages allow exactly this, however, so we'll certainly need to know how to handle it. If you think the current tokenizer is up for the job, you're wrong. While the first token (Token0) will be returned properly, every space character following it will be returned as well, considered by the function to be a valid token. As we've learned, this is unacceptable; whitespace is never considered a token but rather a simple means to separate them.

So why does our tokenizer screw up? More importantly, why does it only screw up after the first token is read? To understand why, let's look again at the main loop of the function:

```
while ( TRUE )
{
Char = SourceLine [ Index ];
++ Index;
if ( Char != ' ' )
strcat ( Token, Char );
else
return Token;
}
```

Notice that as soon as the first character is read, we immediately check to see whether or not it was a space. After the first token is read, there exists a number of spaces between it and the next token, which means that each of these spaces will immediately cause the tokenizer to return as they're read. Thus, the tokenizer will step through each space, compare it to ' ', and return it, thinking its job is done.

Naturally, this is a problem. We need to refine our tokenizer to understand one thing—that tokens may often be preceded by an indefinite amount of whitespace. In other words, the tokenizer needs to read all the way through the following string (quotes added to illustrate the presence of whitespace):

```
"      Token1"
```

To process the second token correctly, we can add another loop to our function, like this:

```
function GetNextToken ( string SourceLine )
{
static int Index = 0;
string Token = "";
char Char;
```

```
while ( TRUE )
{
Char = SourceLine [ Index ];
++ Index;
if ( ! IsCharWhitespace ( Char ) );
break;
}

while ( TRUE )
{
Char = SourceLine [ Index ];
++ Index;
if ( Char != ' ' )
strcat ( Token, Char );
else
return Token;
}
}
```

This simple addition makes all the difference in the world. Now, whenever GetNextToken () is called, it first scans through all preceding whitespace until it runs into its first nonwhitespace character. When it does, it knows that the actual token itself is now ready to be processed and terminates the loop. The second loop can then scan through all of the nonwhitespace characters, assembling the token, and once again return when the next whitespace character is encountered.

The output of our second implementation of the tokenizer on the spaced-out string will look like this:

```
Token0
Token1
Token2
Token3
```

Now we're making some progress! We now understand how to tokenize strings of variable amounts of whitespace. The problem is, what do we do when two tokens aren't separated by any whitespace at all? For example, consider the following line of script code:

```
Mov             X, Y                              .
```

Our current tokenizer would produce the following output:

```
Mov
X,
Y
```

X and the comma have been lumped together into a single token. While we understand that commas are considered to be their own tokens and should not be combined with any of their neighbors, this erroneous result shouldn't come as a
surprise. Our current tokenizer is only designed to recognize whitespace as a token
delimiter. It doesn't have any clue that the comma can also mean the current token
has ended, so how do we fix this?

Well, we could simply do this to our main loop:

```
while ( TRUE )
{
Char = SourceLine [ Index ];
++ Index;
if ( Char != ' ' && Char != ',' )
strcat ( Token, Char );
else
return Token;
}
```

Although the output would be different, it still wouldn't be correct:

```
Mov
X
Y
```

The token is no longer a part of the X, but that's because it's gone altogether.
Although the token may not provide us with a huge amount of information, we still
need to ensure that it was present in the code, and therefore our current implementation of GetNextToken () is unacceptable. This isn't the only problem, however.
Imagine we then passed the tokenizer this line:

```
Mov             X, Y[Q]
```

Or this even-more-condensed line:

```
Mov             X,Y[Q]
```

We've now got six tokens lined up next to each other without a single space.
Although we could start adding all of these delimiting characters to our main loop,
we'll simply use one of our handy string-processing helper functions from earlier:

```
while ( TRUE )
```

```
{
Char = SourceLine [ Index ];
++ Index;
if ( ! IsCharDelimiter ( Char ) )
strcat ( Token, Char );
else
return Token;
}
```

This slick little function now lets us test for all possible delimiters as well as more intelligent whitespace (since it includes tabs and new lines as whitespace characters). Our tokenizer is now capable of intelligently isolating tokens regardless of how they're separated, but we still have one problem, which is illustrated in the following line of code:

```
Mov             X, Y
```

Even with our latest GetNextToken () implementation, the output is still:

```
Mov
X
Y
```

Where does that comma keep running off to? The answer is simple: We increment the index after every character is read, whether or not that character becomes part of the token. The problem is that after X is read, the tokenizer hits the comma and exits. Before doing so, however, it increments the index, and the next time the function is called, it's already on the Y. The end result is that the comma is never even considered, and we get a missing token. This isn't just a problem with commas. All one-character tokens, including one-character identifiers, numeric values, and so on, are susceptible to this issue. Simply put, the solution is to only increment the index when the character is added to the token:

```
while ( TRUE )
{
Char = SourceLine [ Index ];
if ( ! IsCharDelimiter ( Char ) )
{
strcat ( Token, Char );
++ Index;
}
else
return Token;
```

```
}
```

Of course, the results will be correct now:

```
Mov
X
,
Y
```

Our tokenizer is now almost working properly, but there are still a few features to add and a handful of kinks to work out. For example, what if we wanted to tokenize the following line:

```
Mov                "This is a string!", MyString
```

Our current tokenizer would produce the following results:

```
Mov
"
This
is
a
string
"

,
MyString
```

Whoa! Where'd all those extra tokens come from? `This is a string` is just one token—a string token—right? Not according to the rules we've programmed into our current tokenizer. Unfortunately, there's simply no extra rule we can add to it to tell it whether or not the current token is a string since a string is allowed to contain the very characters we use to delimit tokens in the first place.

The only way to solve this problem is to add a currently missing feature: the capability to not only extract a token but to determine its type. After a token is read, we'd like to send not only the string itself back to the caller, but also a variable that is set to whatever type of token that string contains.

The problem of determining a token's type is not particularly difficult to address, and it'll end up helping us figure out how to manage string tokens. In fact, with the exception of strings, tokens are quite easy to analyze and identify. Once the token is complete, a few elementary checks will answer the question nicely.

The first thing to ask is whether or not the token is a single character. If it is, a simple switch statement will tell us which delimiting character it is (if any), and we can consider our job complete:

```
if ( strlen ( Token ) == 1 )
{
switch ( Token )
{
        case ':':
                TokenType = TOKEN_TYPE_COLON;
                return;

case '[':
        TokenType = TOKEN_TYPE_OPEN_BRACKET;
        return;

case ']':
        TokenType = TOKEN_TYPE_CLOSE_BRACKET;
        return;

case ',':
        TokenType = TOKEN_TYPE_COMMA;
        return;

case '"':
        TokenType = TOKEN_TYPE_QUOTE;
        return;
}
}
```

Easy, huh? This immediately knocks out five token types. The rest of the tokens will fall through the switch and be subject to further checks. With the single-character tokens out of the way, the next step is to identify the longer, more complex tokens. Fortunately, our string-processing helper functions once again come to the rescue. The following block of code should be pretty much self-explanatory:

```
if ( IsStringInteger ( Token ) )
{
        TokenType = TOKEN_TYPE_INTEGER;
        return;
}
```

```
if ( IsStringFloat ( Token ) )
{
        TokenType = TOKEN_TYPE_FLOAT;
        return;
}

if ( IsStringIdent ( Token ) )
{
TokenType = TOKEN_TYPE_IDENT;
return;
}
```

As you can see, it's simply a matter of passing the token string to our various
IsString* () functions. If it passes any of these tests, it's clearly a string of that type
and therefore a token of that type as well. Now, being that this is pseudocode, the
exact nature of the TokenType is somewhat ambiguous. In practice, this would have
to be global for the caller to access it, of course. And since we're now returning two
variables to the caller (both the token and the token type), we might as well wrap
them up in a struct of some sort and create a global instance of it. We'll come back
to this in a second. First let's see if we can't budge that string token issue a bit.

There's still no good way to check for a string token based on the contents of the
token alone. There's no way to tell from within the tokenizer whether or not a
delimiting character is actually separating tokens, or simply another character in a
string that we don't realize we're tokenizing. To solve the problem, we need to be
able to check the type of the *previous* token. Why? Because if the previous token was
a quotation mark, we can be sure that we're dealing with a string. We then enter a
different loop than usual, one that adds every character to the current token until
another quotation mark, and *only* another quotation mark, is found. We then set
the token type for TOKEN_TYPE_STRING and presto.

The only problem is, how do we know what the last token was? That information
isn't currently saved anywhere, so it's lost by the time the next call to GetNextToken
() is made. This brings us back to the idea of creating a global struct that maintains
all sorts of data on the current status of the tokenizer. It might look something like
this:

```
struct Tokenizer                        // The current state of the tokenizer
{
string Token;               // The token itself
int Type;                   // The type of the token
int Index;                      // The token's index into the source line
```

```
}
```

```
Tokenizer g_Tokenizer;              // Declare a global instance
```

In addition to keeping track of the current token and token type, it could also keep track of the previous token and its respective type. Then our tokenizer can simply refer to this previous token information when processing the current one to determine whether or not it should attempt to process a string token. We might then create two data structures—one to represent a token and the other to represent the tokenizer itself—like this:

```
struct Token                        // Describes a single token
{
string Token;           // The token itself
int Type;                   // The type of the token
int Index;                      // The token's index into the source line
}

struct Tokenizer                        // Current tokenizer
{
Token CurrentToken,         // Current and previous tokens
PreviousToken;
}
```

The only problem is the issue of RewindTokenStream (), which is a function that essentially moves the tokenizer back to the previous token. This function hasn't been introduced yet, but we'll learn about it in the next section. Until then, just take it on faith that the capability to move back to the previous token in the stream is necessary at times. This function works by moving the information on the previous token into the current one. In other words:

```
CurrentToken.Token = PreviousToken.Token;
CurrentToken.Type = PreviousToken.Type;
CurrentToken.Index = PreviousToken.Index;
```

The problem is that even after rewinding the token stream, we may want to check the status of the previous token. Unfortunately, the previous token of the previous token won't exist. To better explain this, consider tokenizing the following line of sample code:

```
Ident 256 3.14159
```

There are three tokens here: an identifier, an integer, and a float. After the first call to GetNextToken () is made, our tokenizer will look like this:

```
g_Tokenizer.CurrentToken.Token = "Ident";
g_Tokenizer.CurrentToken.Type = TOKEN_TYPE_IDENT;
g_Tokenizer.PreviousToken.Token = NULL;
g_Tokenizer.PreviousToken.Type = 0;
```

After the second pass of the tokenizer, the first token will become the previous token, and the next token will become the current one:

```
g_Tokenizer.CurrentToken.Token = "256;
g_Tokenizer.CurrentToken.Type = TOKEN_TYPE_INTEGER;
g_Tokenizer.PreviousToken.Token = "Ident";
g_Tokenizer.PreviousToken.Type = TOKEN_TYPE_IDENT;
```

After yet another pass, the first token will be lost entirely, and the second token will become the previous token:

```
g_Tokenizer.CurrentToken.Token = "3.14159;
g_Tokenizer.CurrentToken.Type = TOKEN_TYPE_FLOAT;
g_Tokenizer.PreviousToken.Token = "256";
g_Tokenizer.PreviousToken.Type = TOKEN_TYPE_INTEER;
```

So far, this isn't a problem. But what happens if we suddenly need to rewind the token stream? The previous token would be moved into the current token's slot, but what would happen to the previous token slot? With no data to move into it, it'd simply be nullified:

```
g_Tokenizer.CurrentToken.Token = "256;
g_Tokenizer.CurrentToken.Type = TOKEN_TYPE_INTEGER;
g_Tokenizer.PreviousToken.Token = NULL;
g_Tokenizer.PreviousToken.Type = 0;
```

This will pose a serious problem if we need to check the previous token for any reason. The solution here is to maintain an array of three tokens that will allow us to rewind the token stream a single time and be assured that both the current and previous tokens will be valid. To reiterate, this will only allow us to rewind the token stream once (but as we'll see in the next few sections, this is all we need).

So here's the final psuedocode version of the tokenizer struct:

```
struct Tokenizer
{
string CurrentLine;
int CurrentLineNumber;
int CurrentInstruction;
Token Tokens [ 3 ];
}
```

You'll notice that in addition to adding an array of three tokens, I've also added three new members. They hold the current line itself, the current line number, and the type of the current instruction. These will all come in handy later and help group things better.

So, with the three-token array in place, we've got enough information to handle string tokens. The idea is that *before* the next token is processed, we check the "current" token (which is actually the last token since a new call to GetNextToken () has already begun, it just hasn't moved the tokens back yet) to see if it's a quotation mark. If it is and the "previous" token is not a string, it can only mean that the token we're about to process is the string.

The next step is to "advance" the token stream, which pushes every token in our three-token array back by one. This frees up the CurrentToken slot, which will of course be filled after the tokenizer finishes its work. With that said, let's have a look at the final strategy for our tokenizer:

```
function GetNextToken ()
{
        // Determine whether or not we're dealing with a string

int TokenType = -1;

if ( g_Tokenizer.Tokens [ 2 ].Token == '"' &&
     g_Tokenizer.Tokens [ 1 ].Type == TOKEN_TYPE_STRING )
        TokenType == TOKEN_TYPE_STRING;

// Advance the token stream

g_Tokenizer.Tokens [ 0 ] = g_Tokenizer.Tokens [ 1 ];
g_Tokenizer.Tokens [ 1 ] = g_Tokenizer.Tokens [ 2 ];

// Scan through potential initial whitespace

int Index;
char Char;
string Token;

while ( TRUE )
{
        Index = g_Tokenizer.Tokens [ 2 ].Index;
Char = g_Tokenizer.CurrentLine [ Index ];
```

```
if ( ! IsCharWhitespace ( Char ) ) );
break;
++ g_Tokenizer.Tokens [ 2 ].Index;
}

        // Process a string token

        if ( TokenType == TOKEN_TYPE_STRING )
{
while ( TRUE )
{
        Index = g_Tokenizer.Tokens [ 2 ].Index;
Char = g_Tokenizer.CurrentLine [ Index ];
if ( Char != '"' )
strcat ( Token, Char );
else
return Token;
}
}

// Process a nonstring token

else
{
while ( TRUE )
{
        Index = g_Tokenizer.Tokens [ 2 ].Index;
Char = g_Tokenizer.CurrentLine [ Index ];
if ( ! IsCharDelimiter ( Char ) )
strcat ( Token, Char );
else
return Token;
            }
}

g_Tokenizer.Tokens [ 2 ].Token = Token;

// Identify the token type

// If it's a string we can exit immediately
```

```
if ( TokenType == TOKEN_TYPE_STRING )
{
        g_Tokenizer.Tokens [ 2 ].Type = TOKEN_TYPE_STRING;
        return;
}

// Check single-character tokens

if ( strlen ( Token ) == 1 )
{
switch ( Token )
{
        case ':':
                g_Tokenizer.Tokens [ 2 ].Type
= TOKEN_TYPE_COLON;
                return;

case '[':
g_Tokenizer.Tokens [ 2 ].Type
= TOKEN_TYPE_OPEN_BRACKET;
        return;

case ']':
g_Tokenizer.Tokens [ 2 ].Type
= TOKEN_TYPE_CLOSE_BRACKET;
        return;

case ',':
        g_Tokenizer.Tokens [ 2 ].Type
= TOKEN_TYPE_COMMA;
        return;

case '"':
        g_Tokenizer.Tokens [ 2 ].Type
= TOKEN_TYPE_QUOTE;
        return;
}
}

// Finally, check longer tokens
```

```
if ( IsStringInteger ( Token ) )
{
g_Tokenizer.Tokens [ 2 ].Type
      = TOKEN_TYPE_INTEGER;
      return;
}

if ( IsStringFloat ( Token ) )
{
g_Tokenizer.Tokens [ 2 ].Type
= TOKEN_TYPE_FLOAT;
      return;
}

if ( IsStringIdent ( Token ) )
{
g_Tokenizer.Tokens [ 2 ].Type
= TOKEN_TYPE_IDENT;
return;
}
}
```

To sum it all up, our finished tokenizer first starts by checking previous token information to determine whether or not a string is currently being processed. It then advances the token stream by pushing each token in the three-token array back by one, making room for the next token. The initial whitespace is then scanned through to allow for free-form code, at which point we scan in the token itself. If the token is a string, we read unconditionally until a quotation mark is encountered. Otherwise, we read until the next delimiting character of any sort. Finally, the complete token is identified. If we already know it's a string, we can exit immediately; otherwise, we have to perform a series of simple checks and set the token type based on the results.

That's pretty much everything we'll need to know about tokenization, so let's move on to the next level of our compiler.

Parsing

As previously mentioned, we can think of the source code as one big string or one big stream of characters. With the help of the tokenizer, though, we'll now be able to think of it in slightly higher-level terms. In other words, we can now think of the source file as a *token stream* (see Figure 12.10). At any time, we can request the next token by making a call to GetNextToken (), and the token itself as well as its type will be returned.

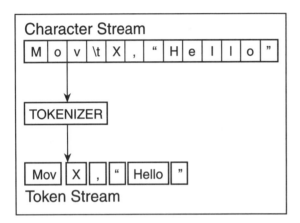

Figure 12.10

A character stream is abstracted to a token stream with the help of a tokenizer

This allows us to parse the incoming source code easily. A token stream allows us to quickly and easily scan the source file and attempt to understand it, and by "understand," I mean make sense of the tokens as they're read. The process of reading in tokens and attempting to interpret their meaning is called *parsing* and is the real secret to building a simple compiler like the one we need for our language.

In addition to GetNextToken (), I've also provided a helper function for each type of token:

```
int ReadInteger ();
int ReadNumeric ();
int ReadIdent ();
int ReadColon ();
int ReadOpenBracket ();
int ReadCloseBracket ();
int ReadComma ();
int ReadQuote ();
```

These simple functions attempt to read a specific type of token and return 1 if they succeed or 0 if either the token stream runs out (in other words, if the end of the line has been reached) or the read token was not of the desired type. Obviously, call `ReadInteger ()` when you want to read an integer token from the stream, call `ReadColon ()` when you want to read a colon from the stream, and so on. As an example of working with these functions, let's look at some pseudocode for reading an array in terms of its tokens:

```
if ( ! ReadIdentifier () ) Error ();
if ( ! ReadOpenBracket () ) Error ();
if ( ! ReadNumeric () && ! ReadIdentifier () ) Error ();
if ( ! ReadCloseBracket () ) Error ();
```

Simply put, we first attempt to read the array's identifier, then the open bracket, then either a numeric index or a variable index, and finally the closed bracket. At each point, if the proper token is not found, a compile-time error is reported. The preceding code can be used to validate array references and will intelligently point out any errors it finds, at the proper location. If we apply this to every possible piece of data we can expect to find in a script, we'll have built a piece of software fully capable of understanding our scripting language. Cool, huh?

As mentioned, our compiler will occasionally have to look ahead in the token stream to get a better idea of what it's dealing with. This is simple; it's just a matter of making another call to either `GetNextToken ()` or one of the `Read* ()` helper functions. The problem, though, is that you'll often want to move the token stream back to where it was after looking ahead. For example, if you've just read an identifier and want to know if it's an array or a variable, you'd look ahead one token by calling `ReadOpenBracket ()`. If the function returns 1, the identifier is for an array, and you can proceed to read out the rest of its tokens. If you don't find an open bracket, however, it means that the identifier was for a variable, and you now need to somehow restore things to the way they were to continue your work. To do this, simply call `RewindTokenStream ()`, which will do exactly that—move the stream back by one token again.

Parsing is the real work behind compilation and is ultimately how we're going to interpret and validate the code as we compile scripts. In fact, to understand the actual code behind the compiler, we must first familiarize ourselves with the parsing process of each major element of code that our scripts can present. These "elements" are the three different types of code lines we accept:

- Array declarations
- Labels
- Instructions

Array declaration and label lines follow the exact same format in all cases, but instruction lines can assume many forms. Specifically, there can be any number of operands, and the actual form of each operand differs wildly, as we've seen when discussing them. Since our language supports seven types of operands, there are ultimately 10 elements of code we need to plan for when thinking about the design of our parser.

To get things started, let's first look at the parsing of an array declaration. Array declarations always take on the following form:

```
Array <Identifier> [ <Integer> ]
```

The <> signs mean that the term they surround will be replaced by an actual value or string in practice. This means that in all array declarations, the first token is the string Array, the second is the identifier that names the array, the third is the opening bracket, the fourth is an integer value that describes the size of the array, and the fifth is the closing bracket. Therefore, pseudocode for parsing an array would look like this:

```
GetNextToken ();
if ( Token == "Array" )
{
GetNextToken ();
Ident = Token;
if ( ! IsStringIdent ( Token ) )
Error ( "Invalid identifier." );
        if ( ! ReadOpenBracket () )
                Error ( "[ expected." );

        if ( ! ReadInteger () )
                Error ( "Invalid array size." );
        Size = atoi ( Token );

        if ( ! ReadCloseBracket () )
                Error ( "] expected." );

        AddSymbol ( Ident, Size );
}
```

Let's assume, by the way, that Token is a global string variable that is updated with each call to GetNextToken () to contain the current token. As you can see, parsing can be rather simple, at least in this case. The tokenizer makes it incredibly easy to grab the information we need—like the array's identifier (`Ident`) and it's size (`Size`)—to pass to the symbol table.

Line labels are even easier and look like this:

```
<Identifier>:
```

It's simply an identifier followed by a colon. The actual parser looks like this:

```
GetNextToken ();
Label = Token;
if ( ReadColon () )
AddLabel ( Label );
else
RewindTokenStream ();
```

Label processing is possible entirely because of the capability to rewind the token stream after looking ahead. After reading a token, it's saved temporarily in `Label` in the event that we are in fact dealing with a line label. We can test this by attempting to read a colon with a call to `ReadColon ()`. If the next token is in fact a colon, we're obviously dealing with a token and can add the label to the label table. If a colon is not read, we're clearly dealing with a token of some other sort and must rewind the token stream to perform other token checks.

This leaves one last type of code line to parse, but it's the most complex by far. Instructions can take on a number of forms, most of which are rather detailed, so let's start with the basics and move slowly. First let's attempt to define the general form of an instruction:

```
<Instruction> <Operand0>, <Operand1>, <Operand2>
```

Of course, there can be any number of operands, so an instruction could just as easily look like one of the following:

```
<Instruction> <Operand>
<Instruction>
<Instruction> <Operand0>, <Operand1>
```

So far, this seems reasonably simple to parse. Just read in the instruction and then attempt to read in any operands. If the token stream ends just after the instruction, it means the instruction didn't take any operands. If it ends after an operand (but not after a comma), it means that the last operand read was the final one accepted by the instruction. The problem, though, is that there are seven different types of operands. Before we can hope to parse instructions, we'll have to understand how to parse them individually.

The first and simplest operands are integer and floating-point immediate values, which are both single-token operands and look like this:

```
<Integer>
<Float>
```

IsStringInteger () and IsStringFloat () are all we'll need to validate them. A single call to ReadNumeric (), which attempts to read either an integer or float token, will suffice. Next up are string operands, which consist of three tokens:

```
"<String>"
```

Remember that both the opening and closing quotes are tokens of their own. Any character that lies between the two quotes is considered part of the string token. Our tokenizer will have to be smart enough to know that only the closing quote can terminate this token, not whitespace or a delimiting character like an opening bracket. Here's how to parse string operands:

```
if ( ! ReadQuote () )
        Error ( "\" expected." );
GetNextToken ();
String = Token;
if ( ! ReadQuote () )
        Error ( "\" expected." );
AddString ( String );
```

Remember that all string immediate values are added to the string table. Next in line are variable operands, which are almost as easy as integers and floats since they only consist of a single token:

```
<Identifer>
```

Thus, they can be read with a single call to GetNextToken (), so let's have a look:

```
GetNextToken ();
if ( ! IsStringIdent ( Token ) )
        Error ( "Invalid identifier." );
Ident = Token;
AddSymbol ( Ident, 1 );
```

Notice that after validating the identifier, it's added to the symbol table with a size of 1. This is because, if you recall, all variables are typeless and are thus the same size. Only arrays can take on sizes larger than a single variable.

Speaking of arrays, they form the next two operand types we need to handle and look like this:

```
<Identifier> [ <Integer> | <Identifier> ]
```

Notice the use of the | symbol, which means "or." In the case of this description of array operands, it means that the index can be either an integer or a variable, as we've learned throughout our discussion of our language's semantics. This description can be implemented like this:

```
GetNextToken ();
if ( ! IsStringIdent ( Token ) )
        Error ( "Invalid identifier." );
Ident = Token;
if ( ! ReadOpenBracket () )
        Error ( "[ expected." );
GetNextToken ();
if ( IsStringInteger () )
        ArrayIndex = atoi ( Token );
else if ( IsStringIdent () )
        HeapIndex = AddSymbol ( Token, 1 );
else
        Error ( "Invalid array index." );
if ( ! ReadCloseBracket () )
        Error ( "] expected." );
```

It's definitely a slightly more complicated operand to parse, but it's still nothing we can't handle. In fact, the worst of the operands is most definitely over because parsing label operands is almost criminally easy:

```
<Identifier>
```

In fact, the description of this particular operand is really the same as variable operands, so the parsing can't be much more complex:

```
GetNextToken ();
if ( ! IsStringIdent () )
        Error ( "Invalid label." );
AddLabel ( Token, FOUND_AS_OP );
```

Remember that we have to tell the label table that the label was found as an operand as opposed to a declaration. This will be very important when it comes time to write the label table to the executable and we have to make sure that all labels are properly declared.

Now that we understand how to parse each operand, there's the matter of applying it to our instruction parser. I'd also like to point out once again that this is pseudocode we're dealing with here, so a lot of the function names I've been using are not the ones we'll see in the actual code. They're just simple approximations. Let's have a look the general breakdown of instruction parsing:

```
GetNextToken ();
if ( ! IsInstruction ( Token ) )
        Error ( "Invalid instruction." );
else
        for ( each operand )
{
if ( the current operand is not the first )
if ( ! ReadComma () )
        Error ( ", expected." );

                GetNextToken ();
                switch ( Token.Type )
                {
                        case TOKEN_TYPE_INTEGER:
                                // Read integer operand

                        case TOKEN_TYPE_FLOAT:
                                // Read float operand

                        case TOKEN_TYPE_STRING:
                                // Read string operand

                        case TOKEN_TYPE_IDENT:
                                // Read label, variable or array
                                // operand
}
}
```

Since we've already seen how each operand is parsed, I've left them out of the preceding source code to make things easier to follow. Essentially, it works like this: First a token is read, and we perform some test to determine whether or not it's in fact a valid instruction. (We'll create a list of instructions later on that we can search to determine this.) Once we know we've got a valid instruction, the next step is to read its operands. At each iteration of the operand-reading loop, we first check to see whether or not we're parsing the first operand. If we aren't, we know that a comma must be the next token since commas are used as operand delimiters but only appear after the first. Once we've validated that the comma is present (if necessary), we get the next token and consider this the first piece of the operand itself. If this token turns out to be numeric, we know we've got an integer or float-ing-point immediate value and can immediately process it. If we read a quote, we then read the next two tokens. The first token of the two is the string itself, whereas the second should be the closing quote. (We saw this just a moment ago in our string operand parser.) Finally, we check for an identifier token, which implies that we've got either a memory reference (variable or array index) or a label to parse.

A Generic Instruction Parsing Loop

So those are the basics of parsing an instruction. You may have noticed a few loose ends, however. Namely, how do we know how many operands a given instruction requires and, worse still, what each operand type is? We need to know this to prop-erly flag compile-time errors; otherwise, bizarre code like this would slip right through:

```
Mov
Add 16, 8
Exit MyLabel
```

Naturally, the preceding code doesn't make any sense, but without some way to vali-date both the number types of the operands following an instruction, we'd have no way to stop it. Also, we clearly need to determine whether the instruction itself is valid, and we also somehow need to determine its opcode. We don't seem to have any of this information readily available as our compiler is laid out thus far.

We do have everything we need to fully parse an instruction and its operands, so you may be wondering why we don't just hard-code each instruction into the main parsing loop. The end result would basically look like this:

```
Parsing Loop
{
        switch ( Current Instruction )
{
case "Mov":
Read Source Operand;
Read Destination Operand;

                case "Jmp":
                        Read Destination Label Operand;
```

```
        case "GetSubStr":
                Read Source String Operand
                Read Index0 Operand
                Read Index1 Operand
                Read Destination String Operand


        case "Exit":
}
}
```

This would certainly work, but the code will end up being rather redundant, and it'll be considerably awkward to make changes to the language after the compiler is finished. Adding or removing instructions, or even changing the format of existing ones, will involve direct changes that must be made to the main loop. I personally can't stand coding this way and have opted for a more generic solution.

Rather than hard-coding each instruction into the compiler itself, we'll simply create a generic loop that can parse and validate *any* instruction by referring to a list or table that describes the language. This way, the language can be easily modified later by simply adding, removing, or changing existing entries in this data structure, and the parsing code itself can remain generic and unchanged.

To do this, we must first determine exactly what information we'll need to know to describe a given instruction and then create a data structure based on that description. Finally, an array of these structures will be created, and our instruction list will be ready to work with.

When we compile an instruction, the most important pieces of information are as follows:

- The number of required operands
- Whether or not optional, extra operands are accepted
- The data type of each required operand
- The opcode to write to the executable

So basically, if we can create an array of instructions, each defined with this structure, our generic parsing loop will simply use this list to validate the contents of the incoming source file. Let's take a look at the structure we'll use to describe an instruction:

```
#define MAX_INSTR_COUNT                     32
#define MAX_INSTR_MNEMONIC_LENGTH      16
#define MAX_OP_COUNT                          8
```

```
typedef struct _Instr
{
char pstrInstrMnemonic [ MAX_INSTR_MNEMONIC_LENGTH ];
int iOpCount;
int iExtraOpsAllowed;
int iOpType [ MAX_OP_COUNT ];
}
        Instr;
```

```
Instr g_InstrList [ MAX_INSTR_COUNT ];
```

pstrInstrMnemonic contains the actual instruction string itself; this is used to match up the current instruction token with the proper index of the list. iOpCount simply tells us how many operands the instruction requires. iExtraOpsAllowed tells us whether or not extra operands are allowed, and iOpType is an array that contains a bit field for each operand. The bitfield is a series of flags that relate to specific data types, so each element of the array contains all of the data types that the operand it relates to can accept.

To really make this list useful, however, we need a simple interface for adding entries to it. This will boil down to a function called SetInstr (), which sets an instruction's mnemonic, operand count, and whether or not it accepts extra operands. Here's an example for the Mov instruction:

```
SetInstr ( INSTR_MOV, "Mov", 2, 0 );
```

INSTR_MOV is a constant containing Mov's opcode (which is 0). Mov is obviously the instruction mneomonic, 2 is the number of its required parameters (source and destination in this case), and 0 states that no extra operands are necessary.

SetInstr () looks like this (not surprisingly):

```
void SetInstr ( int iInstr, char * pstrInstrMnemonic, int iOpCount,
                    int iExtraOpsAllowed )
{
strcpy ( g_InstrList [ iInstr ].pstrInstrMnemonic,
   pstrInstrMnemonic );
        g_InstrList [ iInstr ].iOpCount = iOpCount;
        g_InstrList [ iInstr ].iExtraOpsAllowed = iExtraOpsAllowed;
}
```

Once the instruction is set, we need to also tell the instruction list what sort of data types are acceptable for each operand. Since these are stored as bitfields, it's simply a matter of performing a bitwise or operation on a number of the following constants (which we've seen before):

```
#define OP_TYPE_INT                        1
#define OP_TYPE_FLOAT                   2
#define OP_TYPE_STRING              4
#define OP_TYPE_MEMORY          8
#define OP_TYPE_LABEL                16
```

So, in the case of Mov, which accepts a source operand of any type other than label and a destination operand that must be a memory reference, we'd set it's operand data types with the following code:

```
g_InstrList [ INSTR_MOV ].iOpType [ 0 ] = OP_TYPE_INT |
OP_TYPE_FLOAT | OP_TYPE_STRING | OP_TYPE_MEMORY;

g_InstrList [ INSTR_MOV ].iOpType [ 1 ] = OP_TYPE_MEMORY;
```

With that in mind, let's take a look at the first few instructions defined in InitInstrList (), a function called by main () to initialize this instruction list before compilation begins.

```
void InitInstrList ()
{
        // --- Main --------------

        // Mov                       Source, Destination

        SetInstr ( INSTR_MOV, "Mov", 2, 0 );
g_InstrList [ INSTR_MOV ].iOpType [ 0 ] = OP_TYPE_INT |
OP_TYPE_FLOAT | OP_TYPE_STRING | OP_TYPE_MEMORY;
        g_InstrList [ INSTR_MOV ].iOpType [ 1 ] = OP_TYPE_MEMORY;

        // --- Arithmetic ----------

        // Add                       Source, Destination

        SetInstr ( INSTR_ADD, "Add", 2, 0 );
        g_InstrList [ INSTR_ADD ].iOpType [ 0 ] = OP_TYPE_INT |
OP_TYPE_FLOAT | OP_TYPE_MEMORY;
        g_InstrList [ INSTR_ADD ].iOpType [ 1 ] = OP_TYPE_MEMORY;
```

```
        // Sub                     Source, Destination

        SetInstr ( INSTR_SUB, "Sub", 2, 0 );
        g_InstrList [ INSTR_SUB ].iOpType [ 0 ] = OP_TYPE_INT |
OP_TYPE_FLOAT | OP_TYPE_MEMORY;
        g_InstrList [ INSTR_SUB ].iOpType [ 1 ] = OP_TYPE_MEMORY;


        // Mul                     Source, Destination

        SetInstr ( INSTR_MUL, "Mul", 2, 0 );
        g_InstrList [ INSTR_MUL ].iOpType [ 0 ] = OP_TYPE_INT |
OP_TYPE_FLOAT | OP_TYPE_MEMORY;
        g_InstrList [ INSTR_MUL ].iOpType [ 1 ] = OP_TYPE_MEMORY;


        // And so on...
```

This, of course, continues until all 18 of our instructions have been defined. With these definitions in place, we can now implement an intelligent, generic, instruction-parsing loop that simply refers to these values to determine how to parse the incoming token stream. But before we get to that, let's take a moment and discuss something that might currently have you confused.

We've mentioned "extra operands" quite a few times in the last few pages in regards to this instruction list. This property of an instruction is quite simple; it means that after the required operands have all been read in, there can exist 0–N extra operands, which can be of any data type. Why is this feature useful? Well, consider the CallHost instruction. It's designed to allow scripts to call the host API to execute game-engine functions. These functions require parameters, however, and we don't know anything about their parameter lists at compile time. So CallHost accepts one required operand—the function index that you want to call—and the rest of the operands it finds are considered parameters for whatever that function happens to be. They can be of any type and in any order. It doesn't matter to us. The runtime environment will be responsible for putting these parameters to use; all we need to do is keep track of them.

Getting back to our instruction-parsing loop, we now have enough information to plot out its general structure. At each iteration of the main parsing loop, a new line of script code is read from the source file. Once the possibility of an array declaration, line label declaration, or whitespace is ruled out, we know we have an instruction on our hands and will basically follow this strategy:

```
- Write a null word (zero)
int InstructionCount = 0;
Main Parsing Loop
{
        // Get next line of script

        g_Tokenizer.CurrentLine = GetNextSourceLine ();

        // Strip comments

        StripComments ( g_Tokenizer.CurrentLine );
        TrimWhitespace ( g_Tokenzier.CurrentLine );

        // Handle array declarations, line label declarations, as well as
        // whitespace and comments here (not shown)

        // Get the instruction mnemonic

        GetNextToken ();
        String Instruction = g_Tokenizer.Tokens [ 2 ].Token;

        // Get the index of the instruction

        Index = GetInstructionIndex ( Instruction );
        if ( Index == -1 )
                Error ( "Invalid instruction." );

        - Write instruction index (opcode) to instruction stream

        // Find out how many operands are required and what their
        // types are

        int OpCount = g_InstrList [ Index ].iOpCount;
        int ExtraOpsAllowed = g_InstrList [ Index ].iExtraOpsAllowed;

        - Write operand count to instruction stream
        - If extra parameters are allowed, write a zero

        int ExtraOpCount = 0;

        Loop through each operand
```

```
{
            - If this operand is the second or later, read a comma
    - Read operand tokens using parsing techniques discussed
    - If operand is not extra, validate its data type
    - Write value to instruction stream

    ++ ExtraOpCount;
}


    - If extra parameters were allowed, scan file pointer back
      and overwrite operand count word.

    ++ InstructionCount;
}


    - Scan the file pointer back to the start of the file
    and write the instruction count
```

The logic here is simple. First the next line of source is read out, and its comments and extraneous whitespace are trimmed. The slightly refined line of code is then tokenized (by first reading the instruction mnemonic) and then each operand. After the first operand, every subsequent operand must be preceded with a comma token. After reading an operand, its data type must be validated (unless it's extra) since extra operands are not validated by the compiler. Lastly, its value is written to the instruction stream.

There are a few tricky situations, however. First of all, we agreed earlier that the instruction stream should be preceded by a word containing the number of instructions in the stream. The problem is that we don't know how many instructions are in the stream until *after* they've been written, at which point we can no longer write the beginning of the file. The solution is to first write a null word to the executable, then move the file pointer back to the beginning of the file after the instructions have been counted, and finally overwrite the zero with this value.

This problem manifests itself in another form with operands. Normally, we know how many operands an instruction will require because we've decided ahead of time and have stored this information in the instruction list. However, instructions that can optionally accept extra operands won't have a predetermined amount, and therefore, we need to keep a running count of these operands as they're parsed. In this case, we use the same solution: Write a zero out where you'd like the value to eventually be, parse all of the operands and write them to the instruction stream while keeping track of the operand count, and finally, rewind the file pointer to the null word and overwrite it with this new value.

For the most part, this is everything. You've now seen how a stream of raw character data is converted to a more structured stream of tokens and how those tokens are then parsed to form coherent language structures like declarations, instructions, and values.

We've also studied the necessity, structure, and implementation of the various data structures that accompany the compiled instruction stream—namely, the symbol, string, and label tables. We learned how to add to these tables during the compilation process, how to replace strings and other human-readable elements with pure binary data, and ultimately, how to form an infinitely more efficient stream of byte-code and compiled symbol and string data. We also learned how to add finishing touches like intelligent error handling that not only displays the offending line but also points out the specific character. All in all, we've seen precisely how script source code becomes an executable.

To finalize what we've discussed, I suggest you take a look at the script compiler I've included on the accompanying CD-ROM. It's a finished, working implementation of everything we've discussed, and although the code is quite a bit more involved (since it's more of a real-world application than a demo), it's definitely worth exploring a bit. Try writing simple scripts with the instructions we've come up with to see how the process works. Then test the compiler's error-handling capabilities by purposely screwing up various things just to get a feel for its robustness.

With the compiler figured out, we now need a place to take these executable files we've spent so much time creating. This is what the runtime environment is for.

The Runtime Environment

As important as the compiler is, an executable script by itself isn't much good. To truly bring our system to life, we need to provide an environment in which scripts can interact with memory and execute code. The combination of the CPU and the operating system on your computer provides this very same environment for your OS executables (EXEs and DLLs under Win32, for example).

We can trust that the contents of the executable script files are error checked because this is one of the compiler's primary objectives. That being said, it's really just a matter of unpacking its contents back into memory and deriving some sort of logic from them.

To understand how this works, let's think back to the original compilation process of the instruction stream. If you recall, instruction mnemonics like Mov and Add were replaced with numeric opcodes, which, as we learned, specify a certain action. For example, Mov's opcode is a code that says "move the source operand into the destination operand," whereas Exit's opcode says "terminate the script." So what this really all means is that the runtime environment's most fundamental and important responsibility is to simply run through the instruction stream and perform whatever operation the current opcode specifies.

When these instructions are processed in sequence in real time, the end result is full execution of our code's logic, which is our goal exactly. So the first thing we need to understand is how to organize the contents of an executable in memory so that it can be most easily processed in sequence.

Fundamental Components of the Runtime Environment

Just as our compiler was composed of a few large modules (the tokenizer and the parser) and data structures (the symbol, string, and label tables), the runtime environment is best described in terms of a handful of major components as well.

On the most basic level, the contents of an executable script can be broken down into two categories: code and data. Code is, of course, the instruction stream and describes the logic of whatever action the script is designed to perform. Data is equally recognizable as the heap, where all of our variables and arrays are stored. In addition to the heap is the string table, which contains all of the program's string literal values. Together, these two segments of the script provide all the information necessary to execute the exact intentions of the script writer.

Execution of the instruction stream works by maintaining a pointer to the current instruction, which I call the *instruction pointer*, or IP (although the term *program counter*, or PC, is popular as well). The instruction pointer is incremented after each instruction is executed so that, at every pass through the runtime environment's main loop, a new instruction is executed. Although the program is usually in a state of linear progression through the sequence of opcodes, the branching (J*) instructions are designed specifically to cause the IP to move around in more intelligent ways. Loops, for example, are implemented by causing IP to move back to a position it's already been, thereby executing the same code over again.

The other major aspect of executing code is the actual implementation of the instructions themselves. This is most commonly handled with a relatively large switch block. At each iteration of the main loop, the current instruction is executed as one of many possible cases. Basically, the code is something like this:

```
switch ( CurrentInstruction )
{
case INSTR_MOV:
// Implement Mov
break;

case INSTR_ADD:
// Implement Add
break;

case INSTR_GETSUBSTR:
// Implement GetSubStr
break;

case INSTR_PAUSE:
        // Implement pause
break;

        case INSTR_EXIT:
                // Terminate the script
                break;
}
```

This simple solution allows each instruction to be given its own block of code that will be run whenever it passes through the instruction stream. Adding instructions to the runtime environment's supported language then becomes as easy as adding a new case to the switch block.

The data-oriented side of things is handled primarily by a data structure called the heap. The heap is a contiguous region of memory that is indexed like an array by variables and array indices in the script's code. Each element, or "index," of the heap is a special data structure called a Value, which looks like this:

```
typedef struct _Value              // Represents a value
{
```

```
        int iType;                      // Type of value

        struct
        {
                int iInt;               // Integer value
                float fFloat;       // Float value
                int iHeapIndex;         // Index into the heap
int iHeapOffsetIndex;        // Index into the heap pointing to
// an array offset variable
                int iStringIndex;       // Index into the string table
                int iLabelIndex;        // Index into the label table
        };
}
        Value;
```

This structure is what enables the typeless nature of our language. Since every index in the heap contains every possible data type, as well as the iType member to let us determine what specific type is currently in use, any variable in any script can be given any value without the need for special conversion or casting.

Although this structure should be mostly self-explanatory, let's take a second to cover it anyway. iInt and fFloat are the two primitive data types; they store integer and float immediate values, respectively. iHeapIndex is a base pointer into the heap. In the case of single variables, this is all you need to determine the variable's value. In the case of arrays, this is the array's base pointer—in other words, the index into the heap at which the array begins. If the array was indexed with an integer immediate in the original source code, this will be added to iHeapIndex, and this, as with variables, is the only member you'll need to index the array element. The final case, however, in which an array is indexed with both the base index and a relative index stored in a variable, requires two heap indices. One points to the base of the array; the other points to the variable in which you'll find the relative index, which can be added to the base to produce the absolute index.

Storing a Script in Memory

We have to load a script into memory before we can execute it. While this may seem trivial at first, it's actually a fairly intricate operation. A given script file contains a wide range of different types of data, all of which is tightly packed into variable-size fields. This means there will be a significant amount of dynamic allocation to store them in memory.

A script file contains the following pieces of information (shown in Figure 12.11):

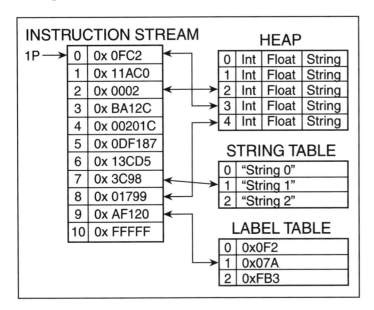

Figure 12.11

A script laid out in memory

- The instruction stream
- The symbol table (which is really just the size of the heap)
- The string table
- The label table

This means we'll have four major data structures to prepare before loading scripts. First up is the instruction stream, which will be the most complex by far. Each instruction in the stream needs to store a number of pieces of information, which we'll wrap up into the Instr structure:

```
typedef struct _Instr          // Describes an instruction
{
        int iOpcode;                   // Instruction opcode
        int iOpCount;                  // Number of operants
        Op * pOpList;                  // Operand list
}
        Instr;
```

iOpcode is, of course, the opcode itself, in which iOpCount stores the number of operands. The operands themselves are stored in a dynamic array of Op's called pOpList. So let's take a look at the Op structure:

```
struct _Op
{
Value Value;
}
        Op;
```

Our basic implementation won't need any more information for a given operand than its Value, but I've wrapped this in a larger structure to allow for easier expansion since a more complex scripting system may require more per-operand data.

Moving on, our next objective is the heap. Just as it was when writing the heap to the executable, "loading" the heap is a pretty easy job since there's nothing to actually load in the first place. The compiler's only output regarding the symbol table is the size of the heap that will be necessary to facilitate the number and size of the script's variables and arrays. This means all we have to do is read the heap size word from the executable file and use it to allocate an array of that many Values.

Next up is the string table. At first, we may be tempted to simply store the string table as an array of char pointers. After all, we already know how many strings the script requires and their sizes. Unfortunately, our two string-processing operands, Concat and GetSubStr, can both modify existing strings in the string table and add new strings altogether. When GetSubStr is called, it's creating a new string based on the substring of another; this substring will need to be stored somewhere. As a result, the string table will be a linked list, just as it was in the compiler. Here are its node and table structs:

```
typedef struct _StringTableNode
{
        _StringTableNode * pPrev,      // Pointer to previous string node
                         * pNext;      // Pointer to next string node

        char * pstrString;             // Pointer to string itself
        int iIndex;                    // Index into the table
}
StringTableNode;

typedef struct _StringTable
{
```

```
int iStringCount;              // Current number of strings in
// table
       StringTableNode * pHead,       // Pointer to head string node of
// the list
                       * pTail;       // Pointer to tail string node of
// the list
}
       StringTable;
```

Everything here should be self-explanatory. The last structure to deal with is the label table, which stores both the index of its destination instruction and a label index to which the operands of branch instructions map:

```
typedef struct _Label
{
       int iIndex;                        // Label index
       int iInstrOffset;                  // Offset of the target instruction
}
Label;
```

With all of our individual structures decided on, we need to declare them. We could simply make a number of global pointers that will hold each of these dynamic arrays, but I prefer grouping them into a larger structure called Script. This not only will provide a more logical naming convention, it will also leave things open for expansion (such as augmenting the system to run multiple scripts at once, which I describe at the end of this chapter). Script looks like this:

```
typedef struct _Script
{
       Instr * pInstrStream;          // Instruction stream
       int iInstrCount;               // Number of instructions in the
// stream

       Value * pHeap;                 // Heap
       int iHeapSize;                 // Size of the heap

       StringTable StringTable;       // String table

       Label * pLabelTable;           // Label table
       int iLabelCount;               // Number of labels in the table

Value ReturnValue;                 // Return value from last host
```

```
// function call

        int iCurrInstr;                     // Current instruction

        int iIsPaused;                      // Determines whether or not the
// script is currently paused
        unsigned int iPauseEndTime;         // Time at which the pause will end

        int iIsRunning;                     // Whether or not the script is
// running
}
        Script;
```

In addition to the array pointers themselves, you'll notice that they're also accompanied by fields that contain their size, such as iInstrCount (the number of instructions in the stream) and iHeapSize. There are also a few new fields entirely.

ReturnValue is a single Value that holds whatever the most recently called host API function called. iCurrInstr is our instruction pointer and always lets us know what the current instruction is. iIsPaused is a flag that keeps track of whether or not the script is paused due to use of the Pause instruction, and iPauseEndTime is the time at which the current pause will end. Finally, iIsRunning is a simple flag that determines whether or not the script is currently being executed.

Loading the Script

So we've designed the data structures that will hold a script in memory. Let's now think about the actual process of transferring script data from the executable file to these structures. Naturally, this will be done in the same order as the scripts were written. First we'll extract the instruction stream, then the symbol table, and so on. A more exact depiction of an executable script file can be seen in Figure 12.12.

Just as its data structure is the most complex, the instruction stream is also the most work to load. The general process is outlined in the following steps:

1. Read the first word of the file; it contains the number of instructions in the stream. Then allocate an array of Instrs and assign it to the instruction stream pointer in g_Script. Also, set the iInstrCount field of g_Script to the number of instructions we just read.

2. For each instruction in the stream, first read the opcode and then the operand count. Use the operand count to allocate an array of Ops and assign

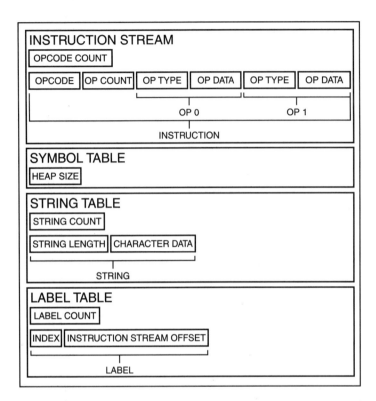

Figure 12.12

A more exact depiction of the script file format

the pointer to this array to the current Instr in the array we just allocated. Then read through each operand.

3. For each operand, first read the operand type word. This will tell us how to load the following data. Use a switch to handle the different types of operands. For integers, floats, and string and label table indices, read them directly into their corresponding fields in the Value structure for this operand.

For variable operands, read a single word and store it in iHeapIndex. For array references with an integer index, read the first word and store it in iHeapIndex and then read the second word and add it as well. This will calculate the absolute address of the array element. Finally, for array references with variable indices, read the first word and store it in iHeapIndex. Read the second word and store that in iHeapOffsetIndex.

After reading each operand, set the proper value for the Value structure's iType field. Use the operand type constants we established earlier for this:

OP_TYPE_INT

```
OP_TYPE_FLOAT
OP_TYPE_STRING
OP_TYPE_MEMORY
OP_TYPE_LABEL
```

Next we have the symbol table. All that's necessary here is to read a single word from the executable and allocate a dynamic array of this many Values. It's now a done deal. Remember to also set the size of the heap in g_Script to the appropriate value.

Following the symbol table is the string table, which is stored in the executable file as raw string data separated by size headers. The first word in the string table tells us how many strings are present, so read this first. Store this value in the iStringCount field of the StringTable structure. Then loop through each string in the table and read a single word. This word tells us how many characters follow (in other words, the length of the string). Allocate a new string table node followed by a new string of the specified length and copy the character data from the executable file to it. (By the way, the string table in the runtime environment uses the same functions as the one in the compiler, so I'm just assuming they're available here. You can simply copy them from your compiler's code and use them in your runtime environment.)

The final block of data to read from the executable is the label table. To start, read a single word. This word tells us how many labels to make room for, so allocate an array of Labels of this size and set g_Script.iLabelCount to this value. Next, for each label following, read two words. The first is the label index, and the second is the offset into the instruction stream that this label corresponds to. Store each in its appropriate field in the Label structure.

That's all there is to it. We've now extracted all of the data from the executable file and loaded it into a well-defined set of structures, so we're ready to roll. Now let's see how we make it run.

Overview of Script Execution

Scripts are executed in the same way your CPU executes machine code, albeit in a much more simplified fashion. Starting from the first instruction in our compiled instruction stream, it executes each opcode and then moves on to the next. Along the way it will move memory around, perform arithmetic, or even jump to other, nonsequential opcodes in the stream. All of these actions are performed because of the value of the opcodes themselves. It is in this way that our script finally achieves execution and is brought to life. Figure 12.13 shows the runtime execution steps.

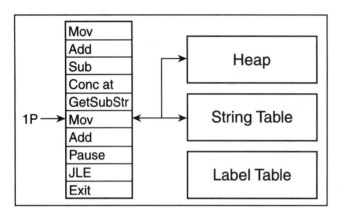

Figure 12.13

The runtime environment steps through the instruction stream and executes each opcode

The opcodes and operands have been loaded, the heap is prepared, and the string table is full. Since the only real logic of the runtime environment itself is to loop through each instruction of the stream, the real work lies in the implementation of each individual opcode. For example, the runtime environment itself doesn't know how to move values around in memory, add numbers, concatenate strings, or anything really. All it knows how to do is move to the next opcode and use that as the criteria for a giant `switch` construct, the `cases` of which contain the code that causes its individual instruction to function. The pseudocode for our runtime environment thus looks like this:

```
IP = 0;
while ( 1 )
{
switch ( InstructionStream [ IP ] )
{
        case MOV:
                // Implement Mov

        case ADD:
                // Implement Add

        case CALLHOST:
                // Implement CallHost

        case EXIT:
                return;
```

```
}
++ IP;
if ( IP > InstructionCount )
        return;
}
```

This surprisingly simple model is really all that's necessary to execute the compiled code of our scripts. The IP starts at zero, is evaluated at every iteration of the main loop to execute the current opcode, and is then incremented so that the next iteration will execute the next instruction. Finally, we also check to make sure we haven't passed the last opcode in the stream; if we have, we take this as a sign to terminate the script (as if the Exit instruction were encountered.)

The only thing left to understand about building a runtime environment is the implementation of the opcodes themselves.

Implementing Opcodes

As our runtime environment scans through the instruction stream, it'll use the current opcode as the criteria of a switch block, which will route execution to a block of code designed to handle that specific instruction. These blocks of code are the very heart of the runtime environment itself. Without these opcode implementations, our scripts wouldn't be functional in any way.

Generally speaking, there are a few major things that almost all instructions must do. First and foremost, they need to access the values of their operands. This is analogous to a function referencing its parameters. They also need to access, modify, and add values to the heap and string table (especially since their operands are likely to point to such values). Some operands may also need the capability to move the instruction pointer around.

I don't have the room to cover the implementation of all 18 opcodes in our scripting system, so I'll instead just cover a few. Figure 12.14 provides a visual interpretation of their basic functionality as well. Fortunately, the functionality of almost all of these opcodes is relatively simple, so you shouldn't have much trouble filling in the rest on your own. To get started, let's take a look at what is probably the most common and fundamental instruction: Mov.

Mov works by moving the value of a source operand into a destination operand. The easy part about this is that the destination operand is *always* a memory reference.

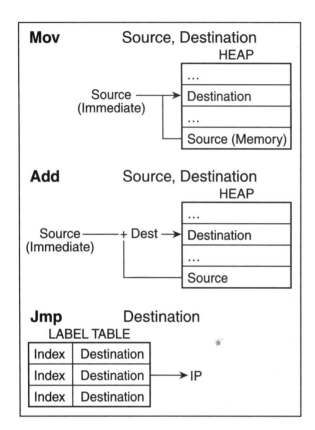

Figure 12.14

Various opcodes, expressed visually

(Nothing else would make sense. Immediate values are constants, and constants, by their name alone, can't be changed.) This means that once we know where the destination operand is pointing, we just need to determine exactly what the value of the source operand is and move it there.

Resolving the heap index of the destination operand is easy. The operand is most likely going to be a simple variable, so all you'll usually need to do is read the iHeapIndex member of the operand's Value structure. The same goes for array references with integer indices (although to be honest, we won't even know from our perspective since an array index is treated the same as a variable by the runtime environment). The only other case is array references with variable indices, in which case we must read from the heap to produce the final, absolute heap index we want. The first thing we do is read the operand's iHeapIndex member, which is the array's base index. We then read iHeapOffsetIndex and use this value as an index into Heap, from which we read the corresponding Value structure. We then take this value and add it to the value we read from iHeapOffsetIndex.

We're going to end up doing this quote often since almost every instruction can accept memory references as operands, so let's put it all into a function:

```
int ResolveMemoryOp ( Op Op )
{
        int iHeapIndex = Op.Value.iHeapIndex;

        if ( Op.iType == OP_TYPE_ARRAY_INDEX_VARIABLE )
                iHeapIndex += g_Script.pHeap [ Op.Value.iHeapOffsetIndex ].iInt;

        return iHeapIndex;
}
```

ResolveMemoryOp () is a simple function that accepts an Op and returns the fully resolved, absolute index to which it points.

Getting back to the Mov operand itself, we now need to think about how to move the value of the source operand into its destination. In the case of immediate values like integers, floats, and string indices, we can simply copy the source operand's Value member directly into the heap index we got from the destination operand:

```
DestIndex = ResolveMemoryOp ( DestOp );
```

```
case OP_TYPE_INT:
case OP_TYPE_FLOAT:
case OP_TYPE_STRING:
{
g_Script.Heap [ DestIndex ] = SourceOp.Value;
}
break;
```

> **NOTE**
>
> In practice, the operands will not be named SourceOp and DestOp. Rather, they'll be indices in an operand array associated with the current instruction's Instr structure.

Simple, huh? The other case to consider is when the source operand is a memory operand. In this case, we need to once again resolve a memory operand and use that heap index to retrieve a Value structure and assign it to the destination heap index.

```
default:
{
        Value = g_Script.Heap [ ResolveMemoryOp ( SourceOp ) ];
g_Script.Heap [ DestIndex ] = Value;
}
```

And that's how Mov works. The cool thing about the instructions is that they're also the basis for all of the arithmetic instructions work, like Add and Mul. The only difference, of course, is that they also apply a binary operator of some sort rather than just assigning the value of the source to the source. Also, there are issues of casting to worry about. For example, while we specifically do not allow addition of strings and numerics, what would happen if the script tried adding a float to an integer? Surely this needs to be supported, but some manual casting will need to be done beforehand to make sure the proper data types are being used when the arithmetic operation takes place.

Let's shift our focus now to the branching instructions. For simplicity's sake, we'll take a look at the Jmp instruction, which unconditionally jumps to the destination label.

The logic for Jmp is really quite simple: First read the single operand it accepts, which is a line label. Use its value (which is a label index) to find the label in the label table and set IP to point to this new instruction index. Here's an example:

```
LabelIndex = Op.Value.LabelIndex;
DestInstr = GetLabelByIndex ( LabelIndex );
g_Script.iCurrInstr = DestInstr;
```

The only missing part here is GetLabelByIndex (), but this is yet another simple function, so let's just check it out real fast:

```
int GetLabelByIndex ( int iIndex )
{
        for ( int iCurrLabelIndex = 0;
    iCurrLabelIndex < g_Script.iLabelCount;
    ++ iCurrLabelIndex )
                if ( g_Script.pLabelTable [ iCurrLabelIndex ].iIndex
== iIndex )
                        return g_Script.pLabelTable
[ iCurrLabelIndex ].iInstrOffset;

return NULL_INDEX;
}
```

This function loops through each label in the label table until it matches up the supplied index. It then returns the value of the label, which is an offset into the instruction stream.

As you can see, branching is nothing more than changing the value of the instruction pointer, at least in the case of `Jmp`. Combine this with our knowledge of how `Mov` works, and we've got enough understanding to move memory around and perform conditional branching, which is the very foundation of programming to begin with. Well, we almost do, that is.

The only other aspect of branching is, of course, the comparison itself, which is how logic works in the first place. This is a simple addition to the logic in `Jmp`'s implementation, however. For example, if you want to implement `JGE`, the logic is the same as it was behind an unconditional jump, except that the jump is only executed if a given comparison evaluates to true. In the case of `JGE`, it'd look like this:

```
if ( Op0.Value.iInt >= Op1.Value.iInt )
        // Jump
```

The other branch instructions are just different Boolean expressions, so that's all you need to keep in mind when implementing them. There is one other detail, however. Like `Mov`, this function will require some level of casting to properly compare similar but not identical data types like integers and floats.

This should be enough basic understanding of instruction implementation to put together the rest. Just about everything can be broken down into terms of moving memory around and jumping based on conditional logic, so the things we've learned here should help you out when fleshing out our language with the rest of our 18 opcodes. Now that we've got that under control, let's move on to what really makes this whole script system worth building in the first place—the interface to the game engine and the host API.

Communication with the Game Engine

Despite the complexities of the compiler and the runtime environment, the truth of the matter is that the only reason any of us are involved in all this to begin with is so we can script *games*. As a result, the game engine itself is really the most important figure in this whole situation when you think about it, so naturally, the interface between it and the scripting system is extremely important.

Without such an interface, what would our scripts be capable of? They'd be quite mute—perfectly capable of "thinking" and executing within their own little world but totally unable to communicate with anyone or anything around them. The game engine would never know they were there, nor would the players. So to justify the amount of work we've put in so far, we must certainly provide a way for game-engine functions to be called from within the script and return values.

This is a tricky problem, however. I mean, after all, how would the runtime environment have any idea what a function's name is? If we declare a function in the game engine like this . . .

```
void MyFunc ()
{
// Whatever
}
```

. . . and somehow try to call that function from within a script, perhaps by passing the function name as an operand to CallHost like this . . .

```
CallHost              MyFunc
```

. . . how is the implementation for the CallHost instruction going to use the function name to make anything happen? Function names aren't retained at runtime, so there's not much that it *can* do. We're therefore going to need some other way to specify a game engine function from within the script that can be resolved by the runtime environment, as in Figure 12.15.

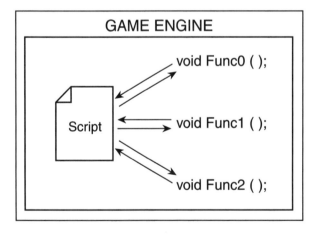

Figure 12.15

Scripts call the game engine's host API functions and receive return values

One simple way to do this is with an array of function pointers. The game engine "registers" a function with the script runtime environment by adding a pointer to it to this array. An integer value is then sent as the single required operand to CallHost, which is used as an index into the array. The function pointer at that particular array element is then invoked, and the function originally specified in the script is ultimately executed. This is a simple and straightforward solution that is easy to implement and reasonably easy to use.

This does bring with it some downsides, however. First, each function that the game engine registers with the script system must have the same signature, meaning that it accepts the same parameters and returns the same value (which will have to be void; you'll learn more about how to return values in a moment). However, this can be overcome easily by passing each function an array of Values. The typeless nature of the Value structure allows values and memory references from the script to be easily passed to the host API function. The array is then unpacked from within the function, and the parameters are used just like normal. This process is illustrated in Figure 12.16

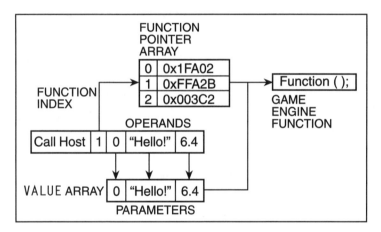

Figure 12.16

Calling a game engine function from a script

Return values are an equally easy hack. Since we can't use the built-in return keyword to return a value directly to a script, we can instead make a macro that wraps return and sets the value of g_Script's ReturnValue member. The GetRetVal instruction will then simply assign ReturnValue to a given memory location, and the return value problem will be solved.

So let's look at some code. First of all, let's look at how this function pointer array will actually be coded:

```
typedef struct _HostFunc
{
        void ( * HostFunc )( Value * ParamList,
  int iParamCount );
}
        HostFunc;
```

I've simply wrapped the appropriate function pointer in a struct called HostFunc (which you can expand later on if you like). An array of these structures will then be declared:

```
HostFunc g_HostAPI [ MAX_HOST_API_SIZE ];
```

Any value can be used for MAX_HOST_API_SIZE as long as it's not too restricting. I use 128, which is probably complete overkill, but you never know.

Notice that the function pointer accepts two parameters: a pointer to an array of parameters and the number of parameters in the array. This is strikingly similar to the way console applications pass command-line parameters to the program, so it should look familiar.

Next we're going to need a function that the game engine can call to register one of its own host API functions:

```
int AddFuncToHostAPI ( void ( * HostFunc )
Value * pParamList, int iParamCount ) )
{
        for ( int iCurrHostFuncIndex = 0;
iCurrHostFuncIndex < MAX_HOST_API_SIZE;
++ iCurrHostFuncIndex )
        {
                if ( ! g_HostAPI [ iCurrHostFuncIndex ].HostFunc )
                {
                        g_HostAPI [ iCurrHostFuncIndex ].HostFunc = HostFunc;
                        return iCurrHostFuncIndex;
                }
        }

        return -1;
}
```

This function scans through the host API array and finds the first NULL pointer. Upon finding it, it sets the value to the function pointer passed and returns the index (not that it's of much use to the game engine). It returns −1 if there wasn't room to add the new function.

So now we can add and store the functions that make up the game engine's host API. The only real challenges left are how to call these functions from the script and pass them parameters, and the details of how to write the host API functions themselves so that they can properly interact with the runtime environment.

First let's think about how the CallHost instruction is going to work. Really, this is a simple process. We read the first operand, which is an index into the array of function pointers, and find out what function we need to call. After the first operand should be a word that tells us how many extra operands follow. Since each host API function can conceivably accept any number of parameters (including none), we need to allocate this array dynamically. To do this, we simply allocate one Value for each extra operand.

We then loop through the operands, adding them to the newly allocated Value array. Then we call the function using the supplied function pointer and pass it both a pointer to the Value array and the number of elements (parameters) in the array. Here's the basic idea:

```
ParamCount = Instr.OpCount;

if ( ParamCount > 1 )
{
ParamList = ( Value * ) malloc ( ParamCount * sizeof ( Value ) );
for ( Op = 0; Op < ParamCount; ++ Op )
        ParamList [ Op - 1 ] = Ops [ Op ]
}
HostFunc = Ops [ 0 ];
if ( g_HostAPI [ HostFunc ].HostFunc )
        g_HostAPI [ HostFunc ].HostFunc ( ParamList, ParamCount );

if ( ParamList )
        free ( ParamList );
```

The block of code starts by determining how many operands there are. Since any call to CallHost must at least contain one operand (the host function index), we know that the operand count is actually the parameter count plus one. We then loop through each parameter and store it in the new array. The function pointer is then called, we free the parameter list, and by this point, the game engine function has already run and returned.

Returning values is easy. The host API function will set g_Script.ReturnValue itself, leaving it up to the script to use GetRetVal to retrieve it. As previously mentioned, this instruction is really just mov except that it always moves a specific memory reference into the destination. As a result, there's no need to cover it again.

Rounding off our discussion on calling the host API, we should take a look at exactly how such a function is written. Since our usual methods of parameter referencing and return values have been effectively limited, we must instead write our own code to simulate these facilities. Although there's nothing particularly hard about referencing an index of the pParamList array, I've created a few helper macros to make it seem even more transparent. Each is used to extract a parameter of a given data type based on a specified index:

```
#define GetIntParam( iParamIndex )                    \
pParamList [ iParamIndex ].iInt

#define GetFloatParam( iParamIndex )        \
        pParamList [ iParamIndex ].fFloat

#define GetStringParam( iParamIndex )        \
        GetStringByIndex ( pParamList [ iParamIndex ].iStringIndex )
```

As you can see, the integer and floating-point macros aren't the most useful things in the world, but the string macro definitely helps since it masks the function call to GetStringByIndex.

Returning values is just as simple. Three functions were written, each for returning a separate data type. They look like this:

```
void _ReturnInt ( int iInt )
{
        g_Script.ReturnValue.iType = OP_TYPE_INT;
        g_Script.ReturnValue.iInt = iInt;
}

void _ReturnFloat ( float fFloat )
{
        g_Script.ReturnValue.iType = OP_TYPE_FLOAT;
        g_Script.ReturnValue.fFloat = fFloat;
}

void _ReturnString ( char * pstrString )
{
        g_Script.ReturnValue.iType = OP_TYPE_STRING;
        g_Script.ReturnValue.iStringIndex =
AddStringToStringTable ( pstrString );
}
```

These functions work simply by setting the value and type of the ReturnValue member, with the exception of _ReturnString, which also has to create a new string for the string table and put the index into the return value member. You'll notice I preceded each of these three functions with underscores. This is because the functions themselves are not intended to be used. Rather, they should be called by the following three macros:

```
#define ReturnInt( iInt )          \
{                                       \
        _ReturnInt ( iInt );       \
        return;                    \
}


#define ReturnFloat( fFloat )               \
{                                               \
        _ReturnFloat ( fFloat );        \
        return;                             \
}


#define ReturnString( pstrString )          \
{                                               \
        _ReturnString ( pstrString );       \
        return;
}
```

The problem with the original functions is that they didn't cause their calling function to return, so you'd have to type this every time you used one:

```
_ReturnInt ( MyInt );
return;
```

This is just corny. With this method, however, the following [...]

```
ReturnInt ( MyInt );
```

[...] is all that's necessary. So let's take a look at some of these helper functions in action. To demonstrate, I'll code a simple function that can add two integers and return the result:

```
void Add ( Value * pParamList, int iParamCount )
{
int X = GetIntParam ( 0 ),
    Y = GetIntParam ( 1 );
```

```
int Sum = X + Y;

ReturnInt ( Sum );
}


AddFuncToHostAPI ( Add );
```

It's simple but very cool. This function can then be called from the script like this:

```
Mov              Op0, 128
Mov              Op1, 256
CallHost         0, Op0, Op1
GetRetVal        Sum
```

If all goes well, Sum should equal 384. And that, my friends, is what communication with the game engine is all about.

Timeslicing

The last thing we should think about with regard to the runtime environment is exactly how it will run alongside the game engine. Since the ultimate goal of a script is usually to provide control over a given in-game entity, we need scripts to somehow run at the same time as the game engine without intruding.

Although there are a number of ways to do this, including a true multithreaded approach in which the scripting system runs in one thread and the game engine runs in another, we'll go with something a bit simpler and simulate threads of our own.

Naturally, any game is going to be based around a main loop of some sort, and this is even truer if you've designed your game in terms of a finite state machine. So, obviously, whatever we do to wedge our scripting system into the game engine, it's going to have something to do with the main loop. The question, though, is exactly how.

One very simple way is to write scripts designed to be run entirely at each iteration of the loop. In other words, the script provides an "extension" to the loop that allows it to do its own thing after the game engine has done whatever it's interested in for that frame. The problem with this approach, though, is that it's a bit rigid. Scripts must be written in a certain way and become *part* of the main game loop rather than existing in their own space and being able to create a main loop of their own.

To solve this problem, we're going to use a technique called *timeslicing*. Timeslicing is commonly used in operating systems and multitasking/multithreading kernels in general. The idea is that, given a number of different tasks or threads that must all run concurrently, the only real way to simulate this is to run each of them for a very brief period of time over and over. This is more or less what we'll do for our scripts. At each iteration of the main game loop, a function will be called that executes the currently loaded script for a given number of milliseconds. The end result will appear to be handling both the game engine and the script simultaneously (see Figure 12.17).

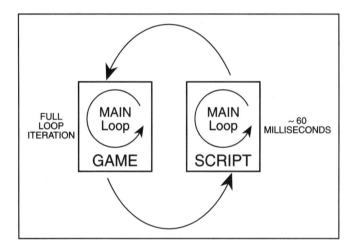

Figure 12.17

Round-robin-style timeslicing can make the game engine and script appear to be running concurrently

The actual implementation of this technique is very simple and only requires a timer function of some sort be available. (I'm using the Win32 API's GetTickCount ().) Now let's assume you currently have a function called RunScript () that runs the script from start to finish when called. Obviously, this won't work as-is. We need to somehow integrate this with the game engine's main loop, and running the entire script every time isn't going to work. So we'll expand RunScript () a bit to accept a parameter now: a duration, expressed in milliseconds, that will tell the function how long it should execute the script before returning. The key, of course, is that the IP and heap are not reset after each call to the function; rather, they gradually advance through the script over the course of multiple function calls.

RunScript () will, of course, execute script code by performing a loop that handles opcodes and increments the instruction pointer. The only real change that needs to be made to support timeslicing is a comparison of the current tick count to the tick count at which the function must return. Here's some pseudocode:

```
void RunScript ( int Duration )
```

```
{
int ExitTime = GetTickCount () + Duration;

while ( 1 )
{
if ( GetTickCount () > ExitTime )
break;
switch ( Instructions [ IP ] )
{
// Implement opcodes
}
        ++ IP;

}
}
```

The main game loop would then look something like this:

```
main ()
{
        Init ();
while ( 1 )
{
// Handle game logic
HandleFrame ();
// Run script timeslice
RunScript ( TIMESLICE_DURATION );
}

ShutDown ();

return;
}
```

Presto! Instant timeslicing. The actual value of TIMESLICE_DURATION is up to you, so experiment with different durations and see what suits you. I personally use around 60 milliseconds, which works out since GetTickCount () is only accurate to about 55 milliseconds or so. Your implementation may be more accurate, so feel free to try something more precise if this is the case.

With that, we're more or less finished. The compiler compiles, the runtime environment runs, and now we've taken a quick look at how to integrate it all with a game engine. I now suggest you take the time to flip through the source to my included runtime environment. Like the compiler, it's quite a bit more complex and dense overall, but it's a working implementation that may prove useful.

The Script Runtime Console

Finally, we have a finished language, compiler, and runtime environment! This is certainly a considerable accomplishment, but we really won't be sure it's complete until we've had a chance to thoroughly test it. Although we could make a small console application that provides some sort of functional API for our runtime environment library and run test scripts with it, I have something slightly more interesting in mind.

The whole point of building this language was to provide a scripting system for our games, so I've come up with something a bit more appropriate for game programmers. While I can't provide a full game engine to script, I have constructed a small Windows application that provides a basic game programming API (see Figure 12.18). In a nutshell, the program is a loop that blits a back buffer to the window at each iteration. Just before blitting, it draws a full-screen background to the back

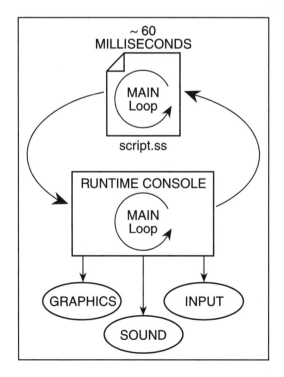

Figure 12.18

The runtime console and its interface

buffer as well as a number of sprites. Finally, each iteration of the loop ends by allowing a loaded script to run for a brief timeslice.

The functions that the program exposes to the script are as follows:

```
API_LoadBG ( String Filename )
```

This loads a 512×384 .bmp file that will be drawn to the back buffer each frame as a full-screen background.

```
API_LoadSprite ( Sting Filename, Integer XSize, Integer YSize );
```

This loads a .bmp file of the supplied dimensions (XSize × YSize) and returns a handle to bitmap.

```
API_SetSprite ( Integer SpriteHandle, Integer BitmapHandle )
```

This assigns the given bitmap to the specified sprite. The bitmap handle is returned from LoadSprite (), while the sprite handle is up to the script.

```
API_MoveSprite ( Integer SpriteHandle, Integer X, Integer Y )
```

This moves the specified sprite to X, Y. Since the runtime console automatically updates the game window, MoveSprite () immediately takes effect when it's called.

```
API_SetSpriteVisibility ( Integer SpriteHandle, Integer IsVisible )
```

This sets the specified sprite's visibility. A 1 means make the sprite visible, and 0 means make the sprite invisible. All sprites are invisible by default, so any sprites that the script creates must be manually turned on with this function.

```
API_IsKeyDown ( Integer ScanCode )
```

This returns 1 if the specified key is down; otherwise, it returns 0.

```
API_LoadSample ( String Filename )
```

This loads the specified .wav file and returns a handle to the sample.

```
API_PlaySample ( Integer Handle )
```

This plays the specified sample.

As you can see, the API is pretty basic, but it's enough to put together some cool little demos. A script can use these functions to load and manipulate graphics and sound. Since the runtime console automatically runs the script and updates the screen in parallel, you can write an entire game by coding its logic as a looping script. The two loops will execute alongside one another, and the end result will be an interactive game demo, albeit a rather simplistic one.

To illustrate this concept, I've written a paddleball game in our language (see Figure 12.19). It wasn't a particularly difficult job, and the end result is really quite cool. Here's the source, followed by a brief explanation.

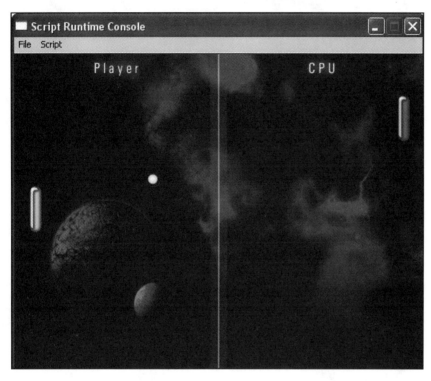

Figure 12.19

Paddleball in action!

```
; Project.
;         Paddleball
; Abstract.
;         Remake of the arcade game of unmentioned name.
; Date Created.
;         4.23.2002
; Author.
;         Alex Varanese

        ; — Give the functions symbolic constants

        Mov             0, LoadBG
        Mov             1, LoadSprite
        Mov             2, SetSprite
        Mov             3, MoveSprite
```

```
Mov                 4, SetSpriteVisibility
Mov                 5, IsKeyDown
Mov                 6, LoadSample
Mov                 7, PlaySample

; — Set up some basic constants

Mov                 200, KEY_UP
Mov                 208, KEY_DOWN

Mov                 511, SCREEN_X_MAX
Mov                 383, SCREEN_Y_MAX

Mov                 480, CPU_X0
Mov                 495, CPU_X1
Mov                 20, PLAYER_X0
Mov                 35, PLAYER_X1

; — Load background

CallHost        LoadBG, "gfx/bg.bmp"

; — Load sprites

CallHost        LoadSprite, "gfx/player_paddle.bmp",
15, 56
GetRetVal        PlayerPaddleHandle
CallHost        LoadSprite, "gfx/cpu_paddle.bmp", 15, 56
GetRetVal        CPUPaddleHandle
CallHost        LoadSprite, "gfx/ball.bmp", 16, 16
GetRetVal        BallHandle

; — Load samples

CallHost        LoadSample, "sound/bounce.wav"
GetRetVal        BounceHandle
CallHost        LoadSample, "sound/buzzer.wav"
GetRetVal        BuzzerHandle
```

```
        ; — Set up sprites

    Mov             192, PlayerY
    Mov             192, CPUY

    Mov             256, BallX
    Mov             192, BallY
    Mov             1, BallVelX
    Mov             1, BallVelY

    Mov             0, PlayerSpriteHandle
    Mov             1, CPUSpriteHandle
    Mov             2, BallSpriteHandle

    CallHost        SetSprite, PlayerSpriteHandle, PlayerPaddleHandle
    CallHost        SetSprite, CPUSpriteHandle, CPUPaddleHandle
    CallHost        SetSprite, BallSpriteHandle, BallHandle

    CallHost        MoveSprite, PlayerSpriteHandle, PLAYER_X0, PlayerY
    CallHost        MoveSprite, CPUSpriteHandle, CPU_X0, CPUY
    CallHost        MoveSprite, BallSpriteHandle, BallX, BallY

    CallHost        SetSpriteVisibility, PlayerSpriteHandle, 1
    CallHost        SetSpriteVisibility, CPUSpriteHandle, 1
    CallHost        SetSpriteVisibility, BallSpriteHandle, 1

        ; — Main game loop

LoopStart:

        ; — Move ball

        Add             BallVelX, BallX
        Add             BallVelY, BallY
        CallHost        MoveSprite, BallSpriteHandle, BallX, BallY

        ; — Handle ball collision detection

        Mov             BallX, TempBallX        ; Take the ball's
size into account
        Mov             BallY, TempBallY
```

```
        Add               16, TempBallX
        Add               16, TempBallY


        ; — Check to see if it hit a paddle

        JL                BallX, PLAYER_X0, SkipPlayerHit
        JG                BallX, PLAYER_X1, SkipPlayerHit
        Mov               PlayerY, PlayerY0
        Sub               23, PlayerY0
        Mov               PlayerY, PlayerY1
        Add               23, PlayerY1
        JL                TempBallY, PlayerY0, SkipPlayerHit
        JG                BallY, PlayerY1, SkipPlayerHit
        Mov               BallVelX, Temp
        Mov               0, BallVelX
        Sub               Temp, BallVelX
        CallHost          PlaySample, BounceHandle
SkipPlayerHit:

        JL                TempBallX, CPU_X0, SkipCPUHit
        JG                TempBallX, CPU_X1, SkipCPUHit
        Mov               CPUY, CPUY0
        Sub               23, CPUY0
        Mov               CPUY, CPUY1
        Add               23, CPUY1
        JL                TempBallY, CPUY0, SkipCPUHit
        JG                BallY, CPUY1, SkipCPUHit
        Mov               BallVelX, Temp
        Mov               0, BallVelX
        Sub               Temp, BallVelX
        CallHost          PlaySample, BounceHandle
SkipCPUHit:


        ; — Check to see if it made it past a paddle

        JG                TempBallX, SCREEN_X_MAX, RestartGame
        JL                BallX, 0, RestartGame
        Jmp               SkipRestartGame


RestartGame:
        CallHost          PlaySample, BuzzerHandle
```

```
        Mov                256, BallX
        Mov                192, BallY
        Mov                1, BallVelX
        Mov                1, BallVelY
        Pause              800
        Jmp                LoopStart
SkipRestartGame:

        ; — Check to see if it hit the top or bottom of screen

        JGE                BallY, 0, SkipClipBallYMin
        Mov                BallVelY, Temp
        Mov                0, BallVelY
        Sub                Temp, BallVelY
        CallHost           PlaySample, BounceHandle
SkipClipBallYMin:

        JLE                TempBallY, SCREEN_Y_MAX, SkipClipBallYMax
        Mov                BallVelY, Temp
        Mov                0, BallVelY
        Sub                Temp, BallVelY
        CallHost           PlaySample, BounceHandle
SkipClipBallYMax:

        ; — Handle player input

        CallHost           IsKeyDown, KEY_UP
        GetRetVal          KeyState
        JNE                KeyState, 1, SkipMovePlayerUp
        Sub                2, PlayerY
        JGE                PlayerY, 0, SkipMovePlayerUp
        Mov                0, PlayerY
SkipMovePlayerUp:

        CallHost           IsKeyDown, KEY_DOWN
        GetRetVal          KeyState
        JNE                KeyState, 1, SkipMovePlayerDown
        Add                2, PlayerY
        JLE                PlayerY, 327, SkipMovePlayerDown
        Mov                327, PlayerY
SkipMovePlayerDown:
```

```
                ; — Move CPU paddle

        Mov              BallY, CPUY
        Sub              23, CPUY

        JGE              CPUY, 0, SkipClipCPUUp
        Mov              0, CPUY
  SkipClipCPUUp:

        JL               CPUY, 327, SkipClipCPUDown
        Mov              327, CPUY
  SkipClipCPUDown:

                ; — Update paddle positions

        CallHost         MoveSprite, PlayerSpriteHandle,
PLAYER_X0, PlayerY
        CallHost         MoveSprite, CPUSpriteHandle, CPU_X0, CPUY

    Jmp LoopStart
```

The script starts by assigning function indices to variables to allow us to refer to them symbolically. You'll find this to be a rather useful technique as you write scripts of your own.

It then proceeds to load all of the graphics and sound with LoadBG (), LoadSprite (), and LoadSample (), facilitated by the CallHost instruction. The three sprites needed by the game—the two paddles and the ball—are then initialized and assigned their respective bitmaps. Some basic variables are initialized as well, such as the position of each paddle and the ball as well as the ball's horizontal and vertical velocity.

The main game loop then begins. It starts by moving the ball by adding its velocity to its X, Y location. Collision detection is then handled, which is a somewhat involved process. First, ball-paddle collisions are checked, which means comparing the top and bottom corners of the ball to the sides of each paddle. If it's within this rectangular region, the ball is bounced in the opposite direction. If the ball has moved too far past either paddle, the ball is reset, a buzzer sound is played, and a new game begins automatically. The last check for collision detection is with the top and bottom of the screen, which simply causes it to bounce in a new vertical direction.

The player's input is handled with a few calls to IsKeyDown (), and the position of the player's paddle is updated accordingly. The CPU paddle's "AI," if you can even call it that, is simply to follow the ball's vertical position, thus making it impossible to defeat. This particular game, it seems, is less about victory and more about survival.

Finally, an unconditional jump is made back to the start of the loop, allowing the game to run indefinitely. We don't need to worry about exiting the script since the runtime console gives the user plenty of ways to do this.

I definitely suggest that you check out the console, which is included on the accompanying CD-ROM. Check out the included paddleball executable, paddle.es, as well as the source file, paddle.ss. Try making changes to the game and see how it works. (Maybe you can actually give it some decent AI.)

Summary

Phew! Was that a long road or what? In only one chapter, we've learned enough about basic scripting to completely implement a low-level language of our own design by creating a functional compiler and runtime environment. We saw how instructions and operands work together in low-level languages, how to implement three basic data types (as well as variables and arrays), how tokenization and simple parsing can be used to interpret and understand human-readable script code, and of course, how to reduce this code to a binary bytecode format that can be quickly executed by the runtime environment.

We also learned the all-important lesson of interfacing our scripting system's runtime environment with the game engine itself, allowing the two to communicate via function calls. Our runtime environment was able to load executable scripts of our own format and execute them by implementing 18 basic opcodes that allowed us to approximate anything we could do in a higher-level language like C.

Finally, we took our system out for a spin with the script runtime console I provided, and we saw how an entire game could be written using our new language alone. Obviously, if it's capable of implementing a nearly complete version of paddleball, it can certainly provide enough functionality to script our games. The only question left is, what now?

Where to Go from Here

While our finished product is indeed impressive and will undoubtedly prove useful when applied to real-world game projects, I have tried to stress as much as possible that this is an extremely basic implementation. I only had so much room to cover the full design and implementation of this bad boy, so there was quite a lot I had to leave out. Fortunately, I've got a list of instructions to share with you in the hopes that you'll be inspired to implement them yourself.

New Instructions

While the 18 instructions we've implemented so far are certainly useful and provide the core functionality we need to perform basic logic, there are countless other instructions we could add to make the language even more powerful and convenient.

First of all, consider adding a set of bitwise instructions that would allow basic bitwise operations to be performed on integer values. You never know when these might come in handy.

It should also not be forgotten that we have what is perhaps the most basic set of string-processing instructions imaginable. As a result, you may want to flesh it out a bit. To get the ball rolling, try implementing two new string instructions: `GetChar` and `SetChar`. These return and set the value of individual string characters, respectively. The functionality of both of these instructions can be emulated now but is far less convenient.

Games are loaded with data of all sorts, so you may want to consider adding to our arsenal of arithmetic instructions. To get your gears turning, start off by adding the following: `Inc` and `Dec`, which increment and decrement values, respectively; `Neg`, which negates a value (positive numbers become negative and vice versa); and `Exp`, which performs exponents.

New Data Types

Although the three data types we currently support certainly cover the major bases, it'd be nice to add a few extras, like Boolean. With a Boolean data type, `TRUE` and `FALSE` constants would be directly understood by the compiler, allowing you to use them instead of 1 and 0 (which are far less intuitive). Consider the following:

```
CallHost          SetSpriteVisibility 0, 1
```

or

```
CallHost                SetSpriteVisiblity, 0, TRUE
```

It's pretty safe to say that the latter reads better. The trick to adding this new type is adding a few new tokens such as `OP_TYPE_BOOL`, which can be further broken down into `OP_TYPE_TRUE` and `OP_TYPE_FALSE`. Of course, the instruction list should also accept Boolean as an operand data type.

Script Multitasking

Currently, the runtime environment only allows one script to be loaded at once. This works fine for small demos like the runtime consoles, but large-scale games can often have tens or even hundreds of entities all alive and kicking at the same. If each of these entities is scripted, we certainly need the ability to load and run *N* number of scripts at once.

You'll notice that I designed our runtime environment with this in mind ahead of time. The entire script is encapsulated in the global structure `g_Script`, which means that the first step toward allowing multiple scripts to exist in memory at once is to make this an array of `Scripts` rather than just a single instance.

Once you can load multiple scripts, your best bet for running them concurrently would be to allow `RunScript ()` to accept another parameter that tells it from which script in the array to work. By following the example set in the script runtime console (the source for which can be found on the accompanying CD-ROM), simply take a round-robin approach and run every currently loaded script for a brief number of milliseconds every time your game's loop executes. This is illustrated in Figure 12.20.

Higher Level Functions/Blocks

Although our scripting language is indeed low level, there are plenty of easy ways to make it seem a bit higher level without redesigning it completely. Namely, you could try adding the functionality of functions or blocks, which can then be called by name from other parts of the script. An example might look like this:

```
Function SayHello
{
CallHost                PrintText, "Hello!"
}
Mov             8, Counter
LoopStart:

        Call            SayHello
```

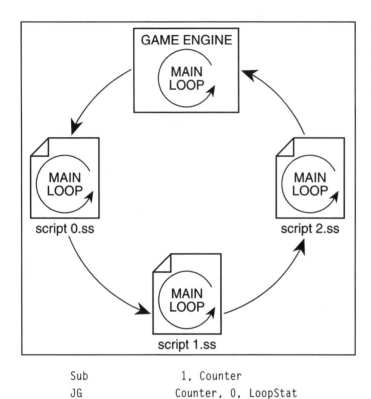

Figure 12.20

Running multiple scripts at once is similar to running a single script alongside the game engine

```
    Sub              1, Counter
    JG               Counter, 0, LoopStat
```

This simple example creates a function called SayHello that is called using a new instruction called Call, eight times in a loop. Assuming the host has provided a function called PrintText () that prints a string of text to the screen or console, this script would produce the following output:

```
Hello!
Hello!
Hello!
Hello!
Hello!
Hello!
Hello!
Hello!
```

Naturally, the Call instruction simply moves IP to point to the first instruction in the specified function. Of course, before doing so, it would have to somehow preserve the current instruction pointer so that, when the called function terminated, execution could resume where it left off. This is known as a *return address*. This is all fine and good when only one function is called, but what if another function is called from the first function? How would we manage multiple return addresses? The answer is what is known as a *call stack*, which maintains a list of return addresses in the form of a stack. Whenever a function is called, a new return address is pushed on to the top of the call stack. When a function exits, it pops the top address off and uses this to find its way back. This allows for all sorts of interesting function-related behavior, including recursion. This might be considered a somewhat advanced idea for extending the language, however, and I unfortunately can't go into much more detail here.

The list of ideas goes on and on, too. In addition to simply allowing blocks of code to be grouped by name and called from other parts of the script, you can also add functionality to allow both parameters and return values to be passed to and from functions. This involves placing more data on the call stack, making things quite a bit more complicated, but the end result will get you ever closer to a C-style language.

Finally, consider the idea of registering script-defined functions with the host program in the same way that the host registers functions with the script. This would allow the host to call specific parts of the script, which is known as a *callback*. This can come in handy in event-based programming when individual script functions are assigned specific events to which to react.

Block Comments

The ; comments we currently use get the job done, but they aren't the friendliest thing in the world when you want to jot down a large, multiline comment (like credits and title information) at the top of your script. To solve this, consider adding block comments like the /* Comment */ notation used in C and C++.

A Preprocessor

Although this is a rather large job, the results can be incredible. A preprocessor could be added to your script system that would function much like the one we know and love in C. Most notably, it could be used to combine various files at compile time by way of an Include directive of some sort.

To understand how useful this can be, consider the technique I showed you in the paddleball script of assigning host API function indices to variables. Imagine now that you've got 20 script files for your game, all of which use these same functions and thus declare the same variables. You've now got 20 copies of the same code floating around, which will make it very difficult to make changes. Imagine if you suddenly want to add or remove a function from the host API. You'll have to make the change in 20 places.

With a preprocessor, you can isolate the variable declarations you want to share among your 20 scripts in a separate file called FunctionSymbols.ss that might simply contain this:

```
Mov                 0, MovePlayer
Mov                 1, PrintText
Mov                 2, PlaySoundFX
```

You can include it in each of the 20 files using a preprocessor directive that might look like this:

```
Include "FunctionSymbols.ss"

CallHost            MovePlayer, 10, 20
CallHost            PlaySoundFX GUNSHOT
```

Not only does this save you the typing of having to declare your variables in 20 different files, it also just looks cleaner. At compile time, the preprocessor will scan through the source file, looking for instances of the Include directive. Whenever it finds one, it'll extract the file name, open the contents of that file, and replace the Include line with those contents. The compiler will never know the difference, but you'll gain quite a bit of organization as a result.

Escape Characters

Currently, strings are defined as three tokens: opening and closing quotation marks and the string itself. But what happens if you want to create a string value that contains a quotation mark? How will the compiler know that it's part of the string rather than the end of it? The answer is to implement *escape characters*, which allow the script writer to tell the compiler specifically that a given character should be ignored by the tokenizer.

Imagine that you want to assign a variable the following string variable:

```
Mov             "He screamed, "NOOO!!!"", MyString
```

The problem is that you need to use quotation marks within the string, but the tokenizer won't be able to tell which quotes are part of the string value itself and which delimit the operand's beginning and end. With escape characters, however, a special character is recognized by the tokenizer when tokenizing strings that basically says, "The character immediately following me should be ignored." In C and many other high-level languages, this special character is the backslash (\\). So, using escape characters, we can rewrite the preceding line like this . . .

```
Mov             "He screamed, \"NOOO!!!\"", MyString
```

[...] and everything will compile just fine. The reason is that, when the tokenizer is parsing the string, it's on the lookout for the backslash. When it finds it, it ignores the next character, effectively preventing it from being tripped up by it. The backslashes themselves are not considered part of the string, so you don't have to worry about them being visible if the string in question is printed by the host program to the screen or whatever. Rather, they simply serve as notes to the tokenizer to help it parse your string more intelligently.

The last detail, however, is what to do about backslashes themselves. They may be useful in letting us denote special uses of the quotation mark to the compiler, but what do we do if we actually want to put a real backslash into our string? For example, imagine the following line of code if the compiler supported escape sequences:

```
Mov             "D:\Graphics\Image.BMP", Filename
```

Characters G and I would be treated like escape characters, and the backslashes themselves would be ignored. This obviously wouldn't work well if we tried using this variable to load a file. The answer is to repeat the backslash twice everywhere you want to use it once. The first backslash is the escape character as usual, but the tokenizer knows that if another backslash is found immediately after it, we're trying to tell it that we just want to use the second one. So, the preceding line of code would be rewritten as follows and work just as expected:

```
Mov             "D:\\Graphics\\Image.bmp", Filename
```

Read Instruction Descriptions from an External File

This is a simple but highly useful improvement to consider for our scripting system. As things stand currently, the only way to change the language that our compiler understands is to change the code that populates the instruction list. This works well enough and is certainly easy to do, but it does require a full recompile for the changes to take effect.

A more elegant solution would be to store these instructions in a separate file that the compiler reads in when it starts up. This would allow us to change the language as frequently as we wanted without ever recompiling the compiler itself. One detail to note, however, is that you might want to consider storing the instruction list in a linked list as opposed to an array since the compiler won't know how many instructions the file will define.

Forcing Variable Declarations

Currently, only arrays need be defined so that the compiler can immediately tell how much space to allocate for them. We purposely did not impose this convention for variables, however, because coders often find it convenient to simply imply the declaration of a variable by immediately using it, especially when writing smaller scripts and test code.

Problems can arise from this, however. Since the compiler doesn't require any mention of a variable before its use, a subtle typo could cause a bizarre logic error that would be incredibly difficult to track down. Consider the following code:

```
Mov             16, MyValue
Add             32, MyValue
Mul             2, MyValue
Mov             32, MyOtherValue
Add             MyVolue, MyOtherValue
```

The error here may be hard to spot, but it's definitely there. In the last line, we add MyVolue to MyOtherValue, which is obviously a misspelling of the real variable, MyValue. Although the outcome of this script is expected to be that MyOtherValue is set to 128, it will actually remain at 32 since the final line will declare a new variable called MyVolue, immediately initialize it to zero, and add it to MyOtherValue.

I can say from extensive experience with a number of languages that allow immediate use of nondeclared variables that logic errors involving identifier typos can be a nightmare and are extremely frustrating when they're finally solved. However, the ease of use of these languages still has its advantages.

As a result, I suggest that you add the option to force all variables to be declared. Perhaps this could be another compiler directive called something like ForceDeclar. Any program that contains this directive would force all variables to be declared with another directive, perhaps called Var. Thus, our preceding script would look like this:

```
ForceDeclar

Var MyValue
Var MyOtherValue

Mov             16, MyValue
```

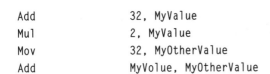

```
Add             32, MyValue
Mul             2, MyValue
Mov             32, MyOtherValue
Add             MyVolue, MyOtherValue
```

The last line would then be caught by the compiler, calmly alerting you that you've used an undeclared variable and saving you hours, days, or maybe even weeks of frustrating debugging sessions:

```
Error: Line 10
Undeclared identifier 'MyVolue'

Add             MyVolue, MyOtherValue
                   ^
```

Slick, huh?

This is pretty much everything I can think of off the top of my head, but it should be plenty to keep you busy. In addition to the ideas I've listed here, I certainly encourage you to try coming up with your own improvements and expansions as well. As you use your scripting system, you'll undoubtedly notice ways in which it could be improved or redesigned to better fit your games, and it's important that you take these details seriously. As long as you keep your script system in a constant state of evolution, you'll keep your efficiency and productivity at the maximum and eventually will create the perfect language for your needs, truly making it an invaluable part of your gamedev arsenal.

One Last Improvement

Well, there is one last thing I should mention. Throughout this chapter, I've made numerous references to higher-level, C-like scripting languages. We've learned that they're extremely powerful but also extremely sophisticated internally and thus difficult to develop at best. Although this is true, I think everyone should learn how they work at some point or another because the lessons learned in their development can be applied to countless other forms of programming. Besides, creating your own high-level language is a huge accomplishment and allows you to do all sorts of amazing things.

If you'd like to pursue this, you might be interested to know that I've also written a separate book dedicated to the topic of developing scripting systems called *Game Scripting Mastery* (part of the Premier Press Game Development Series, just like this one). It's a comprehensive, step-by-step guide to the process of creating your own

C-style language from the ground up. If you've found the work we've done in this chapter interesting, you'll probably find quite a lot to like in *Game Scripting Mastery*. You may even find that a lot of what we've learned here will be directly applicable.

SECTION 3

Advanced Game Programming Tricks

If you are reading this then you are probably quite the game programmer! Do you think you have learned everything you need to know? I hope not because Part III gets into some heavy-duty topics that any elite game programmer must know! Have you ever wondered how to creating a scripting language that can be used in your games? How about increasing the load time of your resource files? Part III covers these topics and much more! In this section you will learn how to make your character creations smarter by implementing fuzzy logic AI. You will also learn how to create game environments that are so realistic that you will forget that it is computer generated. These are just a few of the many topics covered in this section.

I have tried to add an element of surprise to each section and this section is no different. The last section contained a rare look into how to create text-based adventure games. Now, I have seen some books that cover Assembly Language and I've even seen some books cover the use of Assembly Language in games. But I don't recall ever seeing a book that covered pure Assembly Language game programming! In fact, once you are done reading that chapter, you will have created a fully functional game! And it will be in pure Assembly Language!

With the tricks in this section, you will be able to say that you are on your way to becoming a member of the elite group of game programmers. So, what are you waiting for? Read on to get started!

TRICK 13

High-Speed Image Loading Using Multiple Threads

Mason McCuskey, Spin Studios,
www.spin-studios.com

Introduction

Most of the games I've seen have insanely long loading screens that occur fairly frequently throughout the game. Don't get me wrong—I understand that there's a price to pay for the jaw-dropping visuals and stunning sound effects. But I don't want to wait any longer than I have to. Unfortunately, some developers inadvertently release games with needlessly long load times because they don't understand the power of multithreading.

This chapter will look at how to speed up load times by using multiple threads. You'll learn the basic concepts of multithreading, how to create threads, how to ensure that your code is thread safe, and most importantly, how to reduce the time it takes that little progress bar to move from left to right.

Thread Basics

Before you start coding the optimized loading functions, you need to understand the basics of working with multiple threads. That's what this section is for. Keep in mind that I don't have the space in this chapter to cover everything you could possibly do with the thread, so I'm only explaining what you'll need to understand the optimized loading code.

What's a Thread?

Simply put, a *thread* is a path of execution through your program. Let me explain this with an analogy. Imagine your program is a recipe for donuts (yum, donuts). The cook who "runs" that recipe to create the donuts is like a thread. He starts at the top of your recipe (your main function or *thread entry point*) and uses the ingredients he has as he follows your directions for making donuts. The path he takes through your recipe is his path of execution.

What Is Multithreading?

In the old days, everything was single threaded—there was only one cook in the kitchen. In a multithreaded program, there are several cooks in the kitchen. Each cook is following a central copy of your recipe. They all have their own ingredients, and they're all doing exactly the same thing because they're all reading off the same recipe.

"That's all fine and good," you say, "but how is this beneficial?" Imagine that there's a line in the donut recipe that says, "Deep fry for 10 minutes." The cook follows exactly what's in the recipe, so he plops the donuts into the oil and waits for 10 minutes. During this time, the entire productivity of the kitchen comes to a complete standstill. The only thing happening is that the donuts are frying, even though it's entirely possible that something else could be done in the meantime.

I've just given you an analogy for a single-threaded program. When the CPU encounters an instruction that takes a long time to execute (for example, reading a whole bunch of bytes off the hard drive), it stops, and your entire computer waits for those bytes to move off the drive and into RAM.

Now here's an analogy for a multi-threaded program. Everything's pretty much the same; the cooks are still dumb, but now there are two of them. So, while one's sitting around waiting for the donuts to fry, the other can still progress with his recipe as usual. Of course, if both cooks need the oven, there's a problem, and you'll learn how to deal with that later. But assuming that one cook is slightly behind the other, that cook can work while the

TIP

There is a disadvantage to multithreading: You're using more memory. You have to load the entire file into memory before you start processing it, whereas in a single-threaded model you could process the data as you read it.

It's important to keep in mind here that hard drives, when compared to CPUs, are wicked slow. This means that in the time it takes to read one byte from the drive, you could process several bytes in memory.

That's why multithreading is useful, and it's why multithreaded game-loading code will go faster than its single-threaded counterpart. Single-threaded code wastes time by not doing something while the bytes are being read, whereas multithreaded code can keep working as the bytes trickle in from the drive.

Of course, unless you have two CPUs, you're not really doing two things at once. Internally, the OS is alternating very quickly between the two threads. The OS also knows when one thread is waiting on something (like a byte to come in from a drive), and it is smart enough to ignore the waiting thread and concentrate on other threads until the byte comes in.

other is waiting, and more work in the kitchen can be accomplished in the same amount of time.

Loading resources from a disk into a game involves two distinct steps: getting the bytes off the hard drive and converting them into a format the game likes. For example, a texture in memory must be in a certain color depth, whereas on disk it might be arranged differently and might even contain a different color depth. Loading that image requires getting it from the disk and then performing any color depth or other processing on it.

Starting a Thread

Enough theory. Let's look at some actual multithreaded source code.

Multithreaded source code has one thing that single-threaded source code does not: a call to the `CreateThread` Win32 API function. To get multiple threads running, simply call `CreateThread` with a pointer to a function that the new thread should start running. For example:

```
// create first thread
threadhandle = CreateThread(
  NULL,          // security attributes, NULL = default
  0,             // stack size, 0 = default
  MyThreadProc,  // function thread starts in
  NULL,          // parameter for the function
  0,             // flags
  &tid1);        // where to put the new thread's ID
```

The preceding code creates a new thread that begins running the function `MyThreadProc`. `MyThreadProc` looks like this:

```
DWORD WINAPI MyThreadProc(LPVOID param)
{
  /* do something */
  return(0); // thread exit code = 0
}
```

This is a normal function that returns a `DWORD` and takes as input a void pointer. The `WINAPI` is just a synonym for `__stdcall`, which tells the compiler the calling convention for this function. You need `WINAPI`; otherwise, the compiler will complain about you trying to give `CreateThread` a pointer to a non `__stdcall` function.

As you can see, MyThreadProc returns zero. When the thread hits this line, it dies in exactly the same way that a single-threaded program dies when it gets to the end of main(). The return value from MyThreadProc becomes the thread's exit code, which other threads can look up.

The single parameter to MyThreadProc is automatically set to the same value given in the call to CreateThread. If you want to pass more than one parameter to a thread entry point, you'll need to make a class that contains whatever you need and then pass the address of that class as the LPVOID parameter. Inside the thread function, you can reinterpret_cast the LPVOID back into a pointer to the class and extract what you need.

If the thread is successfully created, CreateThread gives you back a HANDLE that you can use to identify the thread later.

TIP

Most of the time, C++ programmers will want a thread to start at a certain member function of a certain object. This is easy—just pass the this **pointer to the class you want and have the thread entry point function immediately call a certain method using that pointer. For example:**

```
class CFoo
{
  public:
  /* other stuff goes here */
  DWORD ThreadStart() { /* do multithreaded stuff!
  */ }
  void Start();
  unsigned long m_tid; // thread ID
};
DWORD WINAPI FooEntryPoint(LPVOID param)
{
  CFoo *foo = reinterpret_cast<CFoo *>(param);
  return(foo->ThreadStart());
}
void CFoo::Start() {
  CreateThread(NULL, 0, FooEntryPoint, this, 0,
  &m_tid);
}
void main(void)
{
  CFoo foo;
  foo.Start();
}
```

In this snippet, you can see how the code passes this **as the parameter to the thread starting function** FooEntryPoint. FooEntryPoint **then casts the void pointer back to a** CFoo **pointer and calls the** ThreadStart **method of that pointer. Presto, multithreaded objects!**

Waiting for a Thread to Finish

Once your main thread creates all the different subthreads, it's very common to want that main thread to just wait until all the other threads have finished.

You could implement this using a while loop and the Sleep API call, as follows:

CAUTION

It's vital that you close the handle that CreateThread gives you when you're done using it. Many programmers assume that the system will automatically clean up a thread handle when you return from the thread's entry point. This is incorrect. You need to explicitly close (via CloseHandle) all threads that you create; otherwise, your application will leak thread handles, which could eventually cause a system crash.

```
// create thread
HANDLE threadhandle = CreateThread(NULL, 0, ThreadProc, this, 0, &tid);
// the child thread sets the m_ThreadDone
// variable to true when it's finished
while (!m_ThreadDone) {
  Sleep(100);
}
```

There are a couple of serious problems with this, however. For starters, your program could potentially pause for close to 100 milliseconds if the child thread completes right after the main thread checks the m_ThreadDone variable. This could lead to incredibly slow programs if this thread wait code is in a loop that runs many times. Second, the main thread is burning CPU cycles doing nothing, CPU cycles that the child thread(s) could use to complete their work faster.

Here's a better way to do the same thing:

```
// create thread
HANDLE threadhandle = CreateThread(NULL, 0, ThreadProc, this, 0, &tid);
WaitForSingleObject(threadhandle, INFINITE);
// close thread
CloseHandle(threadhandle);
```

This code uses the WaitForSingleObject Win32 API call. WaitForSingleObject doesn't return until the thread whose handle you gave it terminates. The INFINITE parameter is actually a timeout in milliseconds. In this case, the code is prepared to wait forever, but you could also wire it so that WaitForSingleObject returns after a certain number of milliseconds. You can check the return value of `WaitForSingleObject` to determine whether it returned because the thread whose handle you gave died or because the timeout was hit—consult your MSDN documentation.

This is better because, here, you're telling the OS explicity, "Pause this thread until the other thread finishes." This allows the OS to ignore that thread and give more CPU cycles to the child thread. The OS knows when the child thread finishes and at that point restores your main thread.

There's also a `WaitForMultipleObjects` API call that takes an array of handles instead of just one:

```
// create 3 threads
HANDLE threadhandles;
threadhandles[0] = CreateThread(NULL, 0, ThreadProc, this, 0, &tid);
threadhandles[1] = CreateThread(NULL, 0, ThreadProc, this, 0, &tid);
threadhandles = CreateThread(NULL, 0, ThreadProc, this, 0, &tid);
// wait for all 3 threads to finish
WaitForMultipleObjects(3, threadhandles, true, INFINITE);
// close all 3 threads
CloseHandle(threadhandles[0]);
CloseHandle(threadhandles[1]);
CloseHandle(threadhandles);
```

Here you give `WaitForMultipleObjects` the size of your handle array, the handle array itself, and a boolean specifying whether you want the function to return when all threads die (true) or when any one thread dies (false). Again, you can check the return value to determine exactly why it returned.

> **TIP**
>
> **You can also use** `WaitForSingleObject` **and** `WaitForMultipleObjects` **to wait for things other than threads dying. You'll see how to use it for semaphores later in this chapter.**

Race Conditions

Before you get much further, you need to understand what race conditions are and how to prevent them from occurring. Race conditions are the bane of the multi-threading programmer's existence. They are what cause random crashes that are incredibly difficult to debug. So let's learn how to avoid creating them. After all, the only code that's truly bug free is the code that doesn't exist!

To learn what a race condition is, fire up the RaceCondition sample program on the accompanying CD-ROM. The idea behind the sample program is very simple:

to output alternating pound signs (#) and dots (.). The program has a problem, however, and doesn't do what you'd expect it to.

Here's the source that the threads in the RaceCondition sample program use:

```
char g_lastchar = '#';
DWORD WINAPI UnprotectedThreadProc(LPVOID param)
{
  int count=0;
  while (count < 1000) {
    if (g_lastchar == '.') {
      printf("#");
      g_lastchar = '#';
    }
    else {
      printf(".");
      g_lastchar = '.';
    }
    count++;
  }
  return(0);
}
```

The RaceCondition sample program has two threads running the preceding code. As you can see, the code tries to print alternating pound/dot characters using two threads. You'd expect to end up with a bunch of characters alternating, like this:

#.

Unfortunately, this isn't what happens. Run the program, and you'll instead see output like this:

#.#.#.#..#.#.#.##.#.#.#.#..#.#..#.##.#.##.#.#.#.#.#.##.#.#.#.#

The pattern is interrupted by random occurrences of two dots or two pound signs. What's going on here?

The problem is that g_lastchar can change in between the time the code tests it and the time sets it again.

For example, see Figure 13.1. The two threads both test g_lastchar at the same time, which causes the second thread to output a dot even though the first thread has already output a dot.

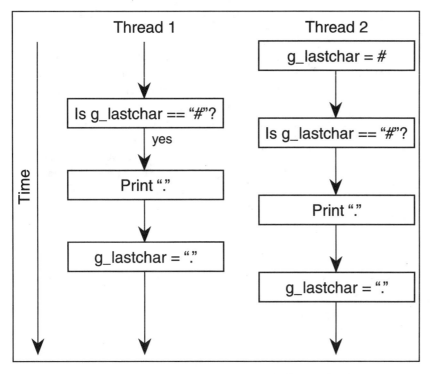

Figure 13.1

An example of a race condition

The preceding code isn't thread safe—it won't always work as you expect it to. Programmers refer to this situation as a race condition.

Formally defined, a *race condition* exists when the output of your program depends on the execution order of your threads (that is, if your program relies on threads entering or exiting functions at a certain time or changing variables at a certain time). For the preceding code to work consistently, the threads must never enter at precisely the same time.

Atomic Operations

To get the code to work, what you really need is a way to say, "Hold on, thread 2. Thread 1 is currently doing something and can't be interrupted." You want each thread to wait until the other thread has flip-flopped the g_lastchar variable.

In other words, you need a certain segment of code (an "operation") to be "atomic." A yawn is a good example of an atomic operation. Once you start one, it can't be interrupted until it's done. (Sorry if I made you yawn just then.) Atomic operations are a way to guarantee that once you start something, all other threads are going to wait for you to finish, thus avoiding chaos.

Critical Sections

One of the most common ways to deal with a race condition is to use a critical section. A *critical section*, simply put, allows you to make anything you want into an atomic operation. Simply mark the beginning and end of the critical section of code, and the OS makes sure that only one thread is within that critical section at any given time.

TIP

Quite frequently in multithreaded programming, you need to be able to increment and decrement variables (and test their values) atomically. This is the foundation upon which all of the other multithreaded mechanisms (critical sections, semaphores, and so on) are based. If you're doing serious multithreaded programming, you need to understand these atomic increment/decrement functions (`InterlockedIncrement` and `InterlockedDecrement`).

This is sort of like reducing a highway from four lanes to one. Just as only one car can move through that section of highway at a time, you're mandating that only one thread can move through that section of code at a time. The other threads will wait until it's their turn.

Returning to the pound and dot example, here's how you would use a critical section to get the pattern you want:

TIP

You should only use critical sections where you absolutely need them. The more you use them, the more you cut into the benefits provided by multithreading. Make your one-lane highways as short as possible.

```
DWORD WINAPI ProtectedThreadProc(LPVOID param)
{
  int count=0;
  while (count < 1000) {
    ::EnterCriticalSection(&g_CriticalSection);
    if (g_lastchar == '.') {
      printf("#");
      g_lastchar = '#';
    }
    else {
      printf(".");
      g_lastchar = '.';
    }
    ::LeaveCriticalSection(&g_CriticalSection);
    count++;
  }
  return(0);
}
```

This `ProtectedThreadProc` is identical to the `UnprotectedThreadProc` in the previous section, with the exception of the `EnterCriticalSection` and `LeaveCriticalSection` API calls. Together, these two functions define the critical section of code. The OS keeps track (using atomic increment/decrement) of whether there's a thread inside the critical section. The `EnterCriticalSection` function won't return until the thread that called it can enter the critical section.

Also, it's important to note that once you're in a critical section, the only way out is to call `LeaveCriticalSection`. A critical section lives on even if you return from a function, throw an exception, or even end a thread!

You might be wondering why the code passes `g_CriticalSection` into the `EnterCriticalSection` and `LeaveCriticalSection` calls. Without going into too much detail, `g_CriticalSection` is the variable that the OS is using to keep track of whether there's a thread in the critical section. It's a global variable, defined as follows:

> ## CAUTION
>
> Imagine what would happen if you entered a critical section and then never left it. One thread could get in, but all other threads in your program would be locked out at the front gates, and your program would hang. Thankfully, it'd be a "nice" hang. It wouldn't be using any CPU power because all of its threads would be stuck (blocked) at the critical section.
>
> By the way, programs that have all their threads blocked, with no opportunity to get them unblocked, are called *zombies*. They truly are like the living dead.

```
CRITICAL_SECTION
    g_CriticalSection;
```

The `CRITICAL_SECTION` type is defined by Win32. It's a structure that contains some internal variables that the OS needs, things like the handle to the thread that's currently inside the critical section, how many times it's recursed in there, and so on.

There's a subtle difference that you should be aware of, however: `g_CriticalSection` is *not* a critical section. A critical section is a segment of code guarded by enter and leave calls. The `g_CriticalSection` variable is a structure, and that structure has a somewhat misleading name. If it were up to me, I would have called it `CRITICAL_SECTION_TRACKING_INFO` or something because it's really a collection of things that the OS uses to track what thread is inside a critical section.

It is possible to use `g_CriticalSection` to keep track of two completely different critical sections of code. You can't do it if the code blocks nest or if there's a chance that two different threads can run inside the two different critical sections at the same time, so it's risky behavior. Programmers therefore tend to only use a given CRITICAL_SECTION structure to keep track of one specific critical section.

You must initialize this structure (by calling the InitializeCriticalSection Win32 API call) before you attempt to enter a critical section using it:

```
InitializeCriticalSection(&g_CriticalSection);
```

Similarly, you must use another Win32 API call to delete the structure when you're done using it:

```
DeleteCriticalSection(&g_CriticalSection);
```

> **TIP**
>
> Cool programmers use C++ critical section objects because they make initialization, usage, and cleanup a snap. The constructor initializes the critical section and then immediately enters it; the destructor leaves the critical section and then deletes it.
>
> This allows you to declare critical section objects statically and have their scope automatically become a critical section. For example:
>
> ```
> void MyFunction(void)
> {
>   /* do some non-critical-section stuff */
>   {
>     CCriticalSection mysection;
>     // critical section initialized and entered!
>     /* do some critical section stuff */
>     // critical section is left and deleted when
>     // mysection goes out of scope
>   }
>   /* do more non-critical-section stuff */
> }
> ```

Producers and Consumers

You're on a roll. You understand what a critical section is and know when and where to use one. Now let's look at a different type of multithreading problem: the producer/consumer problem.

I used donuts for the last example, so here's a new setting: a grocery store on Saturday morning. For those of you who don't know, in American grocery stores, Saturday morning is when the free samples come out. Customers can grab samples of specific brands of bread, cheese, sausage, and so on, from plates scattered throughout the store. If you walk around long enough, you could free sample your way to a pretty decent breakfast.

Zoom in on the bakery and specifically the plate of free cookies on the counter. On one side of the counter are the producers—the grocery store staff tasked with making sure that there are always cookies on the plate. On the other side are the consumers—the customers looking to snag an early morning treat.

Returning to code, the cookie plate itself can be represented by an STL vector of CCookie objects:

```
std::vector<CCookie> m_CookiePlate;
```

Okay, that's easy enough. Now let's say there are three producers and 20 consumers (because grocery stores are always chronically understaffed). The producers might have code that looks like this:

```
DWORD WINAPI ProducerThread(LPVOID param)
{
  std::vector<CCookie> *pCookiePlate =
    reinterpret_cast<std::vector<CCookie> *>(param);
  while (StoreIsOpen()) {
    if (pCookiePlate->size() < 12) {
      // Make a new cookie and put it on the plate.
      pCookiePlate->push_back(CCookie());
    }
  }
  return(0);
}
```

In the preceding code, you can see what the producers are trying to do. Whenever the plate contains less than 12 cookies, they put a new cookie on the plate.

The customers might have a brain like this:

```
DWORD WINAPI ConsumerThread(LPVOID param)
{
  std::vector<CCookie> *pCookiePlate =
    reinterpret_cast<std::vector<CCookie> *>(param);
  while (Hungry()) {
```

```
    if (pCookiePlate->size() > 0) {
      // there's a cookie on the plate!  Grab it
      CCookie mycookie = pCookiePlate[pCookiePlate->size()-1];
      // pull the cookie off the plate
      pCookiePlate->pop_back();
    }
  }
  return(0);
}
```

These are greedy customers. If there is a cookie on the plate, they take it. Of course, the action of taking the cookie is not very realistic. The code doesn't really take the cookie; instead, it makes a copy of it and deletes the original.

These two thread functions look okay on the surface, but they hide a bunch of serious problems. For starters, give yourself extra credit if you noticed that there's no critical section ensuring that only one thread can mess with the cookie vector at one time. Imagine if a producer pushed a cookie onto the vector at the exact same time a customer was pulling one off. Who knows what weird memory errors you'd get!

Here's another problem: Both the producer and the consumer can burn CPU cycles doing nothing. If there are already a dozen cookies on the plate, the producer code does nothing but loop around an empty "while loop," taking CPU cycles away from the consumers. Conversely, if there are no cookies in the vector, the consumer is burning cycles.

Here's the most insidious problem, however: Imagine what happens when two consumers both try to grab for the last cookie. This is a horrible race condition. In real life, humans automatically compensate for this sort of thing: Your eyes see another person's hand make off with the treat, and you abort your grab process. But threads don't have eyes. There's no way for one consumer to know whether another consumer thread has grabbed the last cookie, so there's the possibility for both threads to grab the same C++ object and begin messing with the same areas of memory. This is a recipe for disaster.

Semaphores to the Rescue

What the code needs is a semaphore. A *semaphore*, like a critical section, is a device you can use to keep the threads of your program under control. Semaphores are used to count things. Specifically, they're used to count how many things are currently available.

There are two things that you can tell a semaphore to do. First, you can tell it to add a certain amount to its count. Producers do this—when the producer code creates a new cookie, it adds one to the semaphore's count.

Conversely, you can also tell a semaphore to decrease its count. This is a little different, though. For starters, you can only decrease by one. Also, the decrease operation performs the following logic:

```
// if the current count of this semaphore > 1,
  // subtract one and return
// else
  // wait until it is at least 1
  // subtract one and return
// endif
```

So the Subtract function is more like a "Subtract one if you can; otherwise, wait until there's something to subtract and then subtract that" function.

Are you starting to see how semaphores are useful? Essentially, the producers add to the semaphore, and the consumers do the subtract-if-you-can-but-wait-if-you-can't logic. Of course, the logic of the semaphore is an atomic operation, so there's no chance of one thread modifying a variable at the wrong time.

Programming Semaphores

The only question left then is "How do I put semaphores into my code?"

Creating Semaphores

To start out, create a semaphore using the Win32 API call CreateSemaphore:

```
HANDLE hSemaphore = CreateSemaphore(
  NULL, // security attributes
  0,    // initial count
  10,   // maximum count
  NULL  // name (if sharing between processes)
);
```

Every semaphore has a maximum allowable value. Continuing with the cookie example, this maximum value is akin to the maximum number of cookies on the plate. If you try to add more when the semaphore's at its maximum, the API call fails.

If you plan on sharing a semaphore between programs, you can also specify a unique name for it (since the handle variables won't go across process boundaries).

Destroying Semaphores

To get rid of a semaphore, simply close its handle:

```
CloseHandle(hSemaphore); // buh-bye!
```

Releasing a Semaphore (Adding to It)

The naming conventions get somewhat tricky here. When you want to add a certain amount to the semaphore, it's called *releasing* a semaphore. You can remember this by thinking of it this way: Whenever you add value to a semaphore, you potentially release other threads from their wait-until-the-semaphore-is-greater-than-zero status.

The Win32 API call is named `ReleaseSemaphore`:

```
bool result = (ReleaseSemaphore(hSemaphore, 1, NULL) != 0);
```

As you can see, `ReleaseSemaphore` returns nonzero if the specified amount was added successfully (that is, if the semaphore didn't hit its maximum value); otherwise, it returns false. The three parameters to the API call are the semaphore handle, the amount to add, and an optional pointer to a `long int` that receives the old value of the semaphore. Most of the time, you don't care about this and can leave the last parameter as `NULL`, as in the preceding example.

> **TIP**
>
> In the semaphore release example line, notice the trick to convert an `int` to a `bool`:
>
> ```
> int someinteger = 5;
> bool badbool = someinteger; // issues a compiler
>     warning
> bool goodbool = (someinteger != 0); // no warning
> ```
>
> If you just assign an `int` to a `bool`, the compiler will issue a warning. After all, a `bool` isn't the same as an `int`. A clever trick is to test the `int` against zero and put the result of that test (which is either true or false) into a `bool`.

Subtracting One from a Semaphore (Wait for It!)

Now that you can add, let's learn how to taketh away. Believe it or not, you subtract one from a semaphore by using the `WaitForSingleObject` or `WaitForMultipleObjects` API call explained earlier. These API calls magically know (based on the handles you give them) if something's a semaphore and will automatically subtract one from the semaphore.

CProducerConsumerQueue

As you can see, there is a bit of work you must do to ensure that a producer/consumer system behaves in a thread-safe manner. Fortunately, you can create a class that contains that work.

All of the additional things you must do come into play when you're putting elements into or pulling them out of a queue. So it makes sense to make a special queue class. Also, since you want this queue class to be able to handle any data type, it makes sense to templatize it:

```
template <class Type>
class CProducerConsumerQueue {
  /* fun stuff here */
};
```

This section will walk you through filling in the `fun stuff here` comment. There are essentially four core operations that this class needs: initializing the queue, adding and removing elements, and shutting down the queue.

Initializing the Queue

The queue doesn't need much in the way of initialization. It uses one critical section to control access to the underlying STL queue object and uses an event to tell the threads when it is being shut down (more on that in the next section).

Here's the code from the constructor:

```
CProducerConsumerQueue(int maxcount) {
  ::InitializeCriticalSection(&m_cs);
  m_Handle[SemaphoreID] = ::CreateSemaphore(NULL, 0, maxcount, NULL);
  m_Handle[TerminateID] = ::CreateEvent(NULL, TRUE, FALSE, NULL);
}
```

You should notice two things here. First, the constructor expects a single parameter, maxcount. This is akin to the maximum number of cookies that can be on the plate. It's the starting value of our semaphore. As consumers pick off items from the queue, the semaphore value will decrease until it hits zero, and then threads will have to start waiting.

TIP

Coming up with a good initial value for your queue semaphore involves estimating whether your producers will generally be faster than your consumers or vice versa. Assume that producers are faster than consumers. In this case, it makes sense to choose a large semaphore value so that your producers have room to keep the array full. Of course, it doesn't have to be terribly big. Even if a consumer takes the last value from the queue, you can probably produce another one in short order. However, a large value can give you buffer protection.

Incidentally, it's for this same reason that portable CD players used to advertise how big their antishock buffers were. A CD player can read bytes much faster than speakers can play them, meaning the CD's "producer" (the laser) is much faster than its "consumer" (the speaker). Big buffers give the laser more time to recover when it loses track of where it is, and this increases the odds of it being able to right itself and fill the queue back up before the speaker ever runs out of data to play.

Conversely, if it takes longer to produce than to consume, you can go with a pretty small value because the odds are good that you'll never be able to fill your queue anyway. Unless the consumers stall for some reason, there will generally always be a consumer ready and waiting to take a newly produced object.

In a resource loader, usually the producer is much slower than the consumer because the producer has to read from disk. There can be exceptions (if the process of interpreting a certain file type takes a long time), but in general, I've found that a small value (four or five) works well.

Adding an Element to the Queue

Here's the code that handles adding elements onto the end of the queue:

```
bool AddToBack(Type type) {
  ::EnterCriticalSection(&m_cs);

  m_Queue.push(type);
  bool result = (::ReleaseSemaphore(
    m_Handle[SemaphoreID], 1, NULL) != 0);

  if(!result) {
    OutputDebugString(\nWarning, queue full!");
    m_Queue.pop();
  }
  else {
    char str[256];
    _snprintf(str, 256,
      "\nItem Added! Items in queue: %d", m_Queue.size());
    OutputDebugString(str);
  }
  ::LeaveCriticalSection(&m_cs);

  return result;
}
```

The whole method is protected by a critical section. The code starts by pushing the object onto the back of the STL queue. Next it calls ReleaseSemaphore to raise the count of the semaphore by one. If ReleaseSemaphore fails, it means that the semaphore is already at its maximum value. If this happens, to keep the semaphore and queue size in sync, the object that was just added must be removed from the STL queue.

Next the method uses the Win32 API function OutputDebugString to output a debug message. Debug messages are cool because they go directly to the Visual Studio Debug Output Window, so you can see the queue filling up in real time.

Finally, the code leaves the critical section and returns whether or not the object was added successfully.

Removing an Element from the Queue

Here's the code that pulls an element off the front of the queue:

```
bool RemoveFromFront(Type &t) {
  ProducerConsumerQueueIDs result =
    (ProducerConsumerQueueIDs)WaitForMultipleObjects(2,
    m_Handle, FALSE, INFINITE);
  if (result == SemaphoreID) {
    bool result=true;
    ::EnterCriticalSection(&m_cs);
    try {
      if (m_Queue.size()) {
        t = m_Queue.front();
                  m_Queue.pop();
      }
      else {
        result = false;
      }
    } catch(...) { }
    char str[256];
    _snprintf(str, 256, "\nItem Removed! Items in queue: %d",
        m_Queue.size());
    OutputDebugString(str);
    ::LeaveCriticalSection(&m_cs);
    return result;
  }
  return(NULL);
}
```

This code is a little more complex than AddToBack, but it's still nothing terribly complex. First the code waits for two handles: the semaphore handle and the terminate event handle. When either of these handles is ready (that is, if the semaphore has a count of at least one or the terminate event handle is set), WaitForMultipleObjects returns, and the code checks the return value to determine which handle caused WaitForMultipleObjects to come back.

If WaitForMultipleObjects came back because of the semaphore, the code enters a critical section, pops the frontmost object off the queue, and assigns it to the reference given to it. Remember that WaitForMultipleObjects automatically decrements the semaphore count, so things stay in sync.

The code then outputs a debug message, leaves the critical section, and returns whether or not it was able to grab an object.

Notice the importance of the terminate event here. Without the terminate event, the only way to get `RemoveFromFront` to return after you called it would be to add an object to the queue and increment (release) the semaphore. This isn't optimal. However, by using the terminate handle, we can force `RemoveFromFront` to bail out without having to mess with the semaphore.

Shutting Down the Queue

The `Terminate` function is the one responsible for setting the terminate event:

```
void Terminate() {
  ::SetEvent(m_Handle[TerminateID]);
}
```

Hasta la vista, baby! When `m_Handle[TerminateID]` is set, it frees up all consumer threads potentially stuck waiting for the semaphore to rise above zero. This, combined with some logic on the consumer side that tells them to quit when they don't get any more objects back, allows us to cancel the whole producer/consumer setup at any time.

CProducerConsumerQueue Wrapup

What I've described for you here is the basic core of a virtual cookie plate. There are many other things you can add onto this class, and I encourage you to spend time adding the features that you think are worthwhile.

Having a class such as this in your "programmer's toolbox" can really come in handy. Since most multithreaded problems involve some variant of the producer/consumer algorithm, this class could quickly become one of your most treasured multithreaded weapons.

Introducing *CResourceLoader*

Whew! That was a whirlwind tour of threading and producer/consumer queues, but it gave you everything you need to understand this next section, in which you learn how to implement a multithreaded (and wicked fast!) resource loader.

The Big Idea

The design of the resource loader is relatively straightforward, although it does involve several small classes. At the core of the whole system is the idea that there's a loader (CResourceLoader) that operates on tasks (CResourceLoaderTask). Each task contains all the information needed to load one resource from disk. Specifically, each task contains the file name of the item to load as well as a pointer to a base-class object that knows how to read it and where to put it in memory.

This base class is what allows the resource loader to work on any type of file. All of the details about what the file is and how to interpret it go inside the "loadable object" base class, CLoadableObject. CLoadableObject is simply an interface; it contains nothing except pure virtual functions. To load a specific type of resource, you need to derive a new class from this base class and fill in the functions (see Figure 13.2).

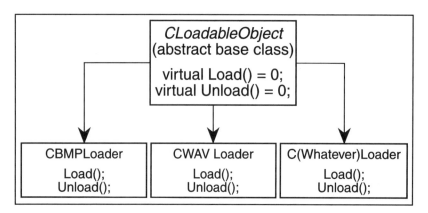

Figure 13.2

Deriving different types of loaders from a common CLoadableObject *base class*

Each task also contains a variable that indicates what the loader is currently doing to the task:

```
enum eResourceLoaderTaskState {
  TASKSTATE_QUEUED = 0,
  TASKSTATE_LOADING,
  TASKSTATE_LOADED,
  TASKSTATE_FAILED
};
```

The valid values here are TASKSTATE_QUEUED, which means the bytes from the file haven't been read yet; TASKSTATE_LOADING, which means the bytes have been read and are currently being interpreted; and TASKSTATE_LOADED, which means the resource is ready to go. Of course, if something happens while loading or interpreting the file, there's always TASKSTATE_FAILED.

The loader works in a two-phase process. In the first phase, you repeatedly call AddTask to give it a big list of all the stuff you want loaded. Once you've given the loader all your tasks, you say go, and the second phase begins. In this phase, the loader goes through your task list and loads the resources.

Tasks

The CResourceLoaderTask object is pretty dumb, as objects go. It's really more like a structure that only CResourceLoader can manipulate. This is because all of its data members are protected, but it declares CResourceLoader as a friend:

```
class CResourceLoaderTask
{
public:
  friend class CResourceLoader;
  CResourceLoaderTask() { m_State = TASKSTATE_QUEUED; }

  CResourceLoaderTask(string filename, CLoadableObject *obj) {
                m_State = TASKSTATE_QUEUED;
                m_Filename = filename;
                m_Object = obj;
  }
  virtual ~CResourceLoaderTask() { }

protected:
  eResourceLoaderTaskState m_State;
  string m_Filename;
  CLoadableObject *m_Object;
  CByteBlock m_Data;
};
```

As you know, in C++, a "friend" class has access to protected and private members and methods. Here we use the friend mechanism to ensure that the only thing that can manipulate a CResourceLoaderTask is a CResourceLoader.

A couple of other things are worthy of notice as well. Each task object contains a CByteBlock called m_Data. A CByteBlock is essentially a memory-mapped file. It's responsible for loading a file from disk and storing its contents. This allows you to separate loading data and interpreting data into two distinct operations. Load the data into the byte block and then give that byte block to another function that interprets it somehow (creates a texture, or a sound effect, and so on).

The m_Object member of CResourceLoaderTask is a pointer to an object that knows how to interpret the byte block and where to put it. For example, if you wanted to load a texture, m_Object would point to your texture class, which would contain a pointer to the texture memory that would be filled in when your texture class's load function was called.

Queuing Up Tasks

The first thing you'll want to do with this loader is give it some things to load. You do this through the AddTask function:

```
void CResourceLoader::AddTask(CResourceLoaderTask &task)
{
  ::EnterCriticalSection(&m_Tasks_cs);

  m_Tasks.push_back(task);
  ::LeaveCriticalSection(&m_Tasks_cs);
}
```

This is fairly straightforward. The code uses a critical section to ensure that only one thread is accessing the task's array.

Beginning the Loading Process

Once all tasks have been added, the user of the code calls BeginLoading to start the loading process. Here's what BeginLoading looks like:

```
void CResourceLoader::BeginLoading()
{
  ResetEvent(m_EverythingDoneEvent);
  // start producer & consumer threads
  if (NULL == ::CreateThread(NULL, 0,
    LoaderThreadStartProc, (LPVOID)this, 0,
    &m_LoaderThreadID)) {
    throw("can't create loader thread!");
  }
  if (NULL == ::CreateThread(NULL, 0,
    ProcessorThreadStartProc, (LPVOID)this, 0,
    &m_ProcessorThreadID)) {
    throw("can't create processor thread!");
  }
}
```

As you can see, this is where the producer and consumer threads are started. Before they're started, however, the code resets an event handle called m_EverythingDoneEvent. To understand why that's there, we need to look at another method: WaitUntilFinished.

```
void CResourceLoader::WaitUntilFinished()
{
  WaitForMultipleObjects(1, &m_EverythingDoneEvent, FALSE, INFINITE);
}
```

When the loading is in full swing, there are actually three threads running amok in our process: the consumer and producer threads and also the main thread of the application (the thread that called BeginLoading). Different games may want to do different things with their main thread. Some might prefer to have the main thread keep pumping out frames or possibly display a progress bar.

Other games might not want to do anything with their main thread while things are being loaded. If there are only a couple of megabytes to load, it really isn't worth your time to put up a load screen and progress bar. For those situations, you can call the WaitUntilFinished function.

WaitUntilFinished does just that—it pauses the main thread until everything's loaded. It knows when everything's loaded when the m_EverythingDoneEvent is set (by the consumer thread). This is thread communication (or synchronization) at its most basic.

TIP

It's very easy to tell when you need to use a synchronization object (such as an event) to communicate between threads. You probably need one whenever you find yourself tempted to write something like this:

```
while (ready == false) { Sleep(1000); }
```

Never use the dreaded while loop wait (also known as a busy wait). Always use thread synchronization objects (events, semaphores, and so on) instead.

The Secondary Threads

At this point, you should be fairly comfortable with the organization of CResourceLoader. Now let's take a peek at how the producer and consumer threads work.

The producer thread's job is simple: get the bytes off the drive and store them in the task object. Here's how the code looks:

```
void CResourceLoader::LoaderThread_Entry()
{
  for (int q=0; q < GetNumTasks(); q++) {
    CResourceLoaderTask *task = &m_Tasks[q];
    if (!task->m_Data.Load(task->m_Filename)) {
      task->m_State = TASKSTATE_FAILED;
    }
    else {
      task->m_State = TASKSTATE_LOADING;
      m_Queue.AddToBack(task);
    }
  }
  m_Queue.Terminate();
}
```

There's nothing terribly complex here. The loader thread loops through each and every task in the m_Tasks array. It tells the CByteBlock object of each task to load the data off the drive. If that works, it sets the state of the task to TASKSTATE_LOADING because, at this point, the task is about halfway loaded (if you pretend that the two steps to loading are "load from disk" and "interpret"). It then puts the task on the CProducerConsumerQueue so that the consumer thread can pick it off when it's ready.

If something goes wrong, the thread sets the task's state to TASKSTATE_FAILED and doesn't add it to the queue.

Now turn your attention to the consumer:

```
void CResourceLoader::ProcessorThread_Entry()
{
  CResourceLoaderTask *task = NULL;
  while (m_Queue.RemoveFromFront(task)) {
    if (task) {
      task->m_Object->Load(task->m_Data);
      task->m_State = TASKSTATE_LOADED;
    }
  }
  SetEvent(m_EverythingDoneEvent);
}
```

This thread picks things off the front of the producer/consumer queue. It calls the Load method of the m_Object abstract base class to interpret the data and sets the task's state to TASKSTATE_LOADED when it's done. When all objects have been interpreted, it sets the "everything's done" event.

The Payoff

After all this work, you no doubt want to see the system in action. This section explains how to write a good test program so that you can see for yourself why you went to all this multithreading trouble. If you like, follow along by firing up the ResourceLoader test program in your IDE.

Simulating Work

The first question you need to answer is, "What kind of things should I load in my test application?" You could decide to load all sorts of nifty files: textures, sounds, levels, whatever. For the purposes of the ResourceLoader test program, though, I decided to keep things simple and create a "dummy" object so that I wouldn't have to write any code to actually interpret data files.

```
class CDummyResource : public CLoadableObject {
public:
  bool Load(CByteBlock &data);
  bool Unload() { m_Data.resize(0); return(true); }
protected:
  vector<unsigned char> m_Data;
};
bool CDummyResource::Load(CByteBlock &data)
{
  // this is a dummy loader, so let's just increment each byte then store
  // it in our array.
  //m_Data.reserve(data.GetSize());
  for (int q=0; q < data.GetSize(); q++) {
    unsigned char c = 0;  data.ReadByte(c);
    m_Data.push_back(c);
  }
  Sleep(50);
  return(true);
}
```

This is about as dumb as one can get and still have a worthwhile test bed to see how the multithreading performs. I derive a CDummyResource class from CLoadableObject. My dummy class pretends to interpret a byte block by copying memory in a very slow way. Also, to simulate all the other processing that may occur during interpretation of data, I made my dummy resource sleep for 50 milliseconds. I figured this was fairly realistic.

The Evils of Cache When Evaluating Disk Performance

Sometimes our modern operating systems make writing simple benchmarking programs a real pain. In this case, I wanted to simulate the worst possible case when it came to loading game data. I wanted to pretend that this was the very first time the game had been loaded so that no data files were already inside the operating system's disk cache.

This was easier said than done. By default, Windows caches any file you read or write. This completely skewed the results of my testing! So I had to implement a version of CByteBlock's Load method that explicitly told Windows not to cache the data it was reading. This meant using the relatively low-level CreateFile and ReadFile API calls and specifying the FILE_FLAG_NO_BUFFERING flag, which tells Windows not to cache the data.

Of course, it didn't stop there. It turns out that to use FILE_FLAG_NO_BUFFERING, you must follow a couple of rules: Your reads must be memory aligned on multiples of the drive's sector size, and you can only read in multiples of the drive's sector size. I eliminated some of this pain by making my sample data files exactly 1MB in size, but I still had to use the Win32 VirtualAlloc and VirtualFree API calls to allocate memory that was aligned properly. What a drag!

Anyway, the upshot to all this is that you probably should not use CByteBlock as written in a real game. It's optimized for the special case of testing the worst possible loading situation. A real byte block load method would want disk caching, so it could be much simpler.

Catching Performance Data

Once the dummy resource and the specialized CByteBlock were written, it was time to fire the whole thing up and start capturing some performance data.

Figure 13.3 shows a graph I captured using Windows XP's performance monitor application.

This graph shows how active my hard drive was when I was running the single-threaded segment of the test program. I loaded about 100MB of data using a single thread, alternatively calling CByteBlock's Load method (to get the bytes off the disk) and CDummyResource's Load method (to interpret the bytes).

As you can see, the hard drive stays fairly busy, but it's not pegged at 100 percent. This is because I'm only using a single thread, so the hard drive has to wait every so often while my one thread is interpreting the data. This is bad because it's telling us that we're not reading data from the drive as quickly as we can.

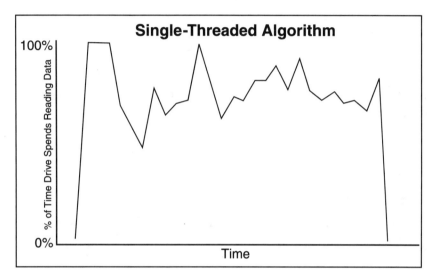

Figure 13.3

Disk read performance with a single-threaded loading algorithm

Compare that graph to Figure 13.4, which shows how the drive behaves in the multithreaded producer/consumer algorithm.

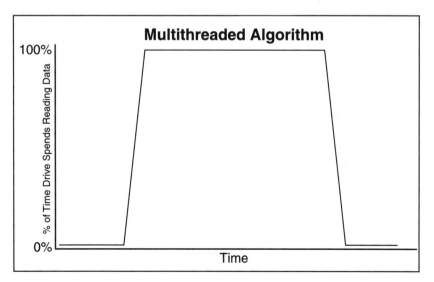

Figure 13.4

Disk read performance with a multithreaded loading algorithm

Here you can see that the drive is constantly busy throughout the load process. In this situation, the bottleneck is truly the speed of the drive. We have ample time to process data "in the background" on another thread.

The end result is significantly faster load times. In my tests, my single-threaded test took roughly 26 seconds, whereas my multithread code did the same job in 18 seconds—8 seconds less or about 30 percent faster. Before you start rushing out to implement multithreaded loads, though, realize that my tests exemplify the worst-case scenario. It's quite possible that a multithreaded load function would be just as slow as—and potentially slightly slower than—a single-threaded counterpart.

You should test things out for yourself, but in most cases, you'll find that multi-threading is the way to go.

Conclusion (Where to Go from Here)

Congratulations, you now know the basics. Of course, what I've provided in this chapter is a very simple loader. There are several enhancements you could make to it:

- You could add functions that would report back how many tasks are complete so that you could display an accurate progress bar.

- You could add a function that would reload everything. This is useful when you're using DirectX because if the user switches to another program, some of your resources could get lost.

- You could add a function that would immediately stop the loading process. This would let you put a Cancel button up for players in case they accidentally hit something that causes a lengthy load process.

- You could use this object as a basis for a truly background loader (that is, a loader that reads resources as they are needed). This would allow you to create huge levels because you could load in segments of the level as the player traveled to them.

Remember to always try to keep your load times as short as possible. You'll have more fun writing fast code, and your players will have more fun since they won't have to wait for unoptimized load code!

TRICK 14

Space Partitioning with Octrees

Ben Humphrey, GameTutorials,
www.GameTutorials.com

Introduction

In the last decade, 3-D games have captivated gamers of all ages. With the eye-popping effects and realistic worlds that gamers crave and expect, developers are always pushing the limits of real-time rendering. There are numerous genres, such as first-person shooters, 3-D adventures, and real-time strategy games, to name a few, that demand huge, elaborate worlds to roam around and discover. Currently, there is absolutely no way you can pass all the level data down your 3-D pipeline at the same time and expect to get anything over two frames per second, and that doesn't even include rendering your characters or the AI going on in the background. You need some way of only rendering the data your camera can see. There are a few ways of doing this, and many factors suggest that you should use one technique or another, or perhaps even a mixture of several.

The technique discussed in this chapter is an octree. An *octree* is a way of subdividing 3-D space, also known as *space partitioning*. It allows you to only draw the part of your world/level/scene that is in your frustum (camera's view). It can also be used for collision detection. Usually, an octree is implemented with an outside scene, whereas a *Binary Space Partitioning* (BSP) tree seems to be more appropriate for indoor levels. Some engines incorporate both techniques because parts of their worlds consist of both indoor and outdoor scenes.

Let me reiterate why space partition is necessary. Assume you created a world for your game, and it was composed of more than 200,000 polygons. If you did a loop and passed in every one of those polygons—on top of your characters' polygons each time you render the scene—your frame rate would come to a crawl. If you had a nice piece of hardware such as a new Geforce card, it might not be as horrible. The problem is that you just restricted anyone from viewing your game that doesn't have a $300+ graphics card. Sometimes, even though you have a really nice video card, the part that slows down your game a considerable amount is the loop you use to pass in that data. Wouldn't it be great if there were a way to render only the polygons that the camera was looking at? This is the beauty of an octree. It allows you to quickly find the polygons that are in your camera's view and draw only them, ignoring the rest.

What Will Be Learned/Covered

This chapter will further explain what an octree is, how it's created, when to stop subdividing, how to render the octree, and frustum culling. It also will provide some ideas on collision detection once we have the world partitioned. With the examples and source code given, you should be able to understand what an octree is and how to create your own. We will be using a terrain model created in 3D Studio Max to demonstrate the space partitioning. The terrain's data is stored as just vertices, which are stored in an ASCII text file (terrain.raw) like so:

```
// This would be the first point/vertex in the triangle (x, y, z)

-47.919212 -0.990297 47.910084

// This would be the second point/vertex in the triangle (x, y, z)

-45.841671 -1.437729 47.895947

// This would be the third point/vertex in the triangle (x, y, z)

-45.832878 -1.560482 45.789059

etc...


// The next vertex would be the first one of the second triangle in the list
```

Instead of writing some model-loading code, I chose to simply read in straight vertices so that anyone can understand what is going on in the source code. This also cuts the code virtually in half and makes it easier to follow. The file was created by loading a 3DS file into one of my loaders and then using fprintf() instead of glVertex3f() in the rendering loop to save the vertex data to a file. After the first frame, I quit the program. Most likely, you would not model the terrain; you have a height map instead. That way, you can use terrain-rendering techniques to more efficiently render what you need to. With that aside, it seemed like a good example to show space partitioning with a less complicated world.

We will create two different applications that build off of one another. The first one will simply load the terrain, create the octree from the given vertices, and then draw everything. There will be no frustum culling because this will be added to the next application. For those of you who aren't familiar with the term "frustum culling," it refers to checking whether something is in our 3-D view (the camera's view). If it is, we draw it; otherwise, we ignore it. This is a fundamental part of the octree. You'll learn more about this later in the chapter.

The source code provided is in C++, using Win32 and OpenGL as the API. It's assumed that you are comfortable with the Win32 API or at least OpenGL. If you haven't ever programmed in Win32, don't stress. The octree code has nothing to do with it, other than the fact that our application uses it to create and handle the window. You should be able to put Octree.cpp and Octree.h independently in your own C++ framework, though the source code is intended to teach rather than be a robust class. Since we are working with OpenGL, the axis referred to when pointing up will be the Y-axis. This chapter is considered to be somewhat of an advanced topic; therefore, it is assumed that the reader has a basic grasp of 3-D math and concepts. This includes understanding vectors, matrices, and standard linear algebra equations. Before we dive into the code, let's get a basic understanding of how octrees work.

How an Octree Works

An octree works in *cubes*, eight cubes to be exact. Initially, the octree starts with a root node that has an axis-aligned cube surrounding the entire world, level, or scene. Imagine an invisible cube around your whole world (see Figure 14.1). A node in an octree is an area defined by a cube, which references the polygons that are inside of that cube. This is how we keep track of partitions. When we refer to a cube's minimum and maximum boundaries, we are indirectly talking about the region of 3-D space that the polygons reside in.

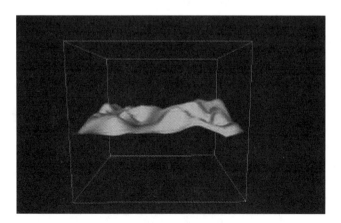

Figure 14.1

The bounding box around the world, which is also the root node in the octree

This root node now stores all the polygons in the world. Currently, this wouldn't do us much good because it will draw the whole thing. We want to subdivide this node into eight parts (hence the word *oct*ree). Once we subdivide, there should be eight cubes inside the original root node's cube. That means four cubes on top and four on the bottom. Take a look at Figure 14.2. Keep in mind that the yellow lines outlining each node would not be there. The lines were added to provide a visual idea of the nodes and subdivisions.

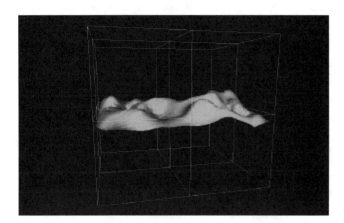

Figure 14.2

The first subdivision in the octree tree

We have now divided the world into eight parts with just one subdivision. Can you imagine how effective this would be if we had two, three, or four subdivisions? Well, now what? We subdivided the world, but where does that leave us? Where does the speed come from that I mentioned? Let's say the camera is in the middle of the world, looking toward the back-right corner (see Figure 14.3). If you look at the lines, you will notice that we are only looking at four of the eight nodes in the octree. These nodes include the two back-top and -bottom nodes. This means we

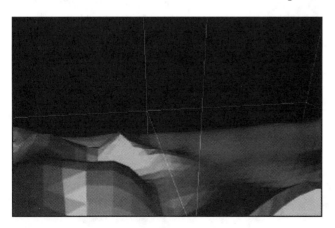

Figure 14.3

We only need to draw the nodes that our camera can see

would only need to draw the polygons stored in those nodes. How do we check which nodes are in our view? This is pretty easy if you have frustum culling.

Describing the Frustum

In 3-D, you have a camera with a *field of view* (FOV). This determines how far you can see to the left and right of you. The camera also has a near and far clipping plane. This means that the camera can only see what is between the near and far clipping planes and between the side planes created by the FOV. These six created planes are what is known as our *frustum planes*. A frustum can best be understood by imagining an infinite pyramid (see Figure 14.4). The pyramid is created from the field of view perspective. The eye of the camera is at the tip of the bottomless pyramid. Now imagine the near and far clipping planes inserted into the pyramid, creating a polyhedron (see Figure 14.5).

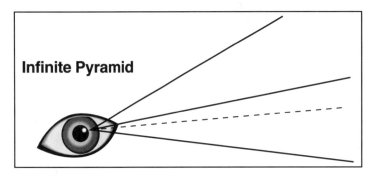

Figure 14.4

The infinite pyramid created from the camera's field of view

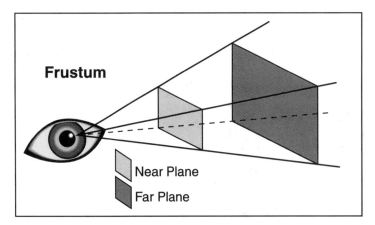

Figure 14.5

The frustum is the camera's field of view, sliced by the near and far clipping planes

The region inside of this object is our frustum. Anything outside of that region is not visible to our camera. This is the area in 3-D that we will be checking to see if any of the nodes in our octree intersect it. If a node is partially or fully inside this space (in our viewing frustum), all of its associated polygons are drawn. We check to see if a node intersects the frustum by its invisible cube that surrounds it. Instead of checking whether each polygon is in the frustum, we just need to check the cube that surrounds the polygons. This is where the speed is. The math for collision between two boxes is easy and fast. Once we know that a node is in our view, we can render it. One thing that hasn't been mentioned is that the node must be an end node. That means the node does not have any children nodes assigned to it. Only end nodes hold polygonal data.

In Figure 14.3, we basically just cut down the amount we need to draw by 50 percent. Remember that this was just one subdivision of our world. The more subdivisions, the more accuracy we will achieve (to a point). Of course, we don't want too many nodes because it could slow us down a bit with all that recursion. Looking back at Figure 14.3, even though we aren't looking at every polygon in the top-back nodes, we still would render them all. Each subdivision gets us closer to a better approximation of which polygons are really in our frustum, but there will be a few hitchhikers that straggle in. Our job is to eliminate as many of those as we can without compromising the overall efficiency when rendering the octree. Hopefully, this is starting to make sense. Let's subdivide yet another level. Take a look at Figure 14.6.

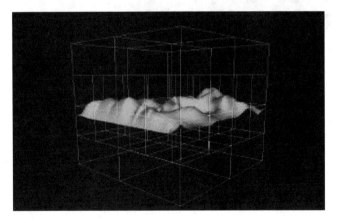

Figure 14.6

The second subdivision of the terrain only creates nodes that contain vertices

You'll notice something different about Figure 14.6 from the last subdivision. This level of subdivision didn't create eight cubes inside of each of the original eight cubes. The top and bottom parts of the original eight nodes aren't subdivided. This is where we get into the nitty-gritty of the octree-creation process. You always try to subdivide a node into eight more nodes, but if there are no triangles stored in that area, we disregard that node and don't allocate any memory for it. This way, we don't create a node that has no data in it. The further we subdivide, the more the nodes shape the original world. If we went down another level of subdivision, the cubes would form a closer resemblance to the scene.

To further demonstrate this, take a look at Figure 14.7. There are two spheres in this scene but on completely opposite sides. Notice that in the first subdivision (left), it splits the world into only two nodes, not eight. This is because the spheres only reside in two of the nodes. If we subdivide two more times (right), it more closely forms over the spheres. This shows that nodes are only created where they need to be. A node will not be created if there are no polygons occupying its space.

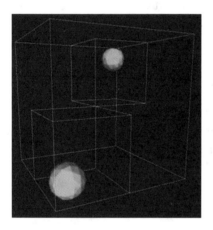 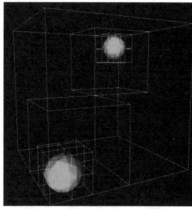

Figure 14.7

When subdividing, only nodes that have vertices stored in their cube's dimensions are created

When to Stop Subdividing

Now that we understand how the subdivision works, we need to know how to stop it so that it doesn't recur forever. There are a few ways in which we can do this:

- We can stop subdividing the current node if it has a triangle (or polygon) count that is less than a max triangle count that we define. Let's say, for instance, we choose 100 for the max. That means that before we subdivide the node, it will check to see if the total amount of triangles it has contained in its area is less than or equal to the max triangle count on which we decided. If it is less than or equal to the max, we stop subdividing and assign all those triangles to that node. This node is now considered to be an end node. Note that we never assign any triangles to a node unless it's the end node. If we subdivide a node, we do not store the triangles in that node; instead, we store them in its children's nodes, or their children's nodes, or even their children's, and so on. This will make more sense when we go over how we draw the octree.

- Another way to check whether we want to stop subdividing is if we subdivide past a certain level of subdivisions. We could create a max subdivision level like 10, and if we recurse above that number, we stop and assign the triangles in the cube's area to that node. When I say "above that number," I mean 11 levels of subdivision.

- The last check we can perform is to see if the nodes exceed a max node variable. Let's say we set this constant variable to 500. Every time we create a node, we increment the "current nodes created" variable. Then, before we create another node, we check whether our current node count is less than or equal to the max node count. If we get to 501 nodes in our octree, we should not subdivide that node; instead, we should assign its current triangles to it.

I personally recommend the 1st and 2nd methods.

How to Draw an Octree

Once the octree is created, we can then draw the nodes that are in our view. The cubes don't have to be all the way inside our view, just a little bit. That is why we want to make our triangle count in each node somewhat small, so that if we have a little corner of a node in our frustum, it won't draw thousands of triangles that aren't visible to our camera. To draw the octree, you start at the root node. We have a center point stored for each node and a width. This is perfect to pass into a function, as follows:

```
// This takes the center point of the cube (x, y, z) and its size (width / 2)
bool CubeInFrustum( float x, float y, float z, float size );
```

This will return `true` or `false`, depending on whether the cube is in the frustum. If the cube is in the frustum, we check all of its nodes to see if they are in the frustum; otherwise, we ignore that whole branch in the tree. Once we get to a node that is in the frustum but does not have any nodes under it, we want to draw the vertices stored in that end node. Remember that only the end nodes have vertices stored in them. Take a look at Figure 14.8 to see a sample run-through of the octree. The shaded nodes are the ones that were in the frustum. The white cubes are not in the frustum. This shows the hierarchy of two levels of subdivision.

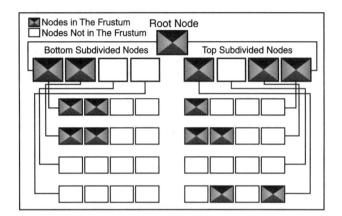

Figure 14.8

*The hierarchy of two levels of subdivision
in the terrain*

Examining the Code

By now, you should have a general idea of what an octree is and how it works in theory. Let's explore the code that will create and use an octree. In the first sample application, we will demonstrate how to create the octree from a list of vertices and then draw every single node. There will not be any frustum culling added so that we can focus on the actual creation and basic rendering process. Here is the prototype for the octree class we will be using:

```
// This is our octree class
class COctree
{

public:

    // The constructor and deconstructor
    COctree();
    ~COctree();

    // This returns the center of this node
    CVector3 GetCenter() { return m_vCenter; }

    // This returns the triangle count stored in this node
    int GetTriangleCount() { return m_TriangleCount; }

    // This returns the width of this node (A cube's dimensions are the same)
    float GetWidth() { return m_Width; }
```

```
// Returns true if the node is subdivided, possibly making it an end node
bool IsSubDivided() { return m_bSubDivided; }

// This sets the initial width, height and depth for the whole scene
void GetSceneDimensions(CVector3 *pVertices, int numberOfVerts);

// This subdivides a node depending on the triangle and node width
void CreateNode(CVector3 *pVertices,
                int numberOfVerts, CVector3 vCenter, float width);

// This goes through each node and then draws the end node's vertices.
// This function should be called by starting with the root node.
void DrawOctree(COctree *pNode);

// This frees the data allocated in the octree and restores the variables
void DestroyOctree();

private:

// This initializes the data members
void InitOctree();
// This takes in the previous nodes center, width and which node ID that
// will be subdivided
CVector3 GetNewNodeCenter(CVector3 vCenter, float width, int nodeID);

// Cleans up the subdivided node creation process, so our code isn't HUGE!
void CreateNewNode(CVector3 *pVertices, vector<bool> pList,
                   int numberOfVerts,   CVector3 vCenter,  float width,
                   int triangleCount,   int nodeID);

// This Assigns the vertices to the end node
void AssignVerticesToNode(CVector3 *pVertices, int numberOfVerts);

// This tells us if we have divided this node into more subnodes
bool m_bSubDivided;

// This is the size of the cube for this current node
float m_Width;

// This holds the amount of triangles stored in this node
int m_TriangleCount;
```

```
// This is the center (X, Y, Z) point for this node
CVector3 m_vCenter;

// This stores the triangles that should be drawn with this node
CVector3 *m_pVertices;

// These are the eight child nodes that branch down from this current node
COctree *m_pOctreeNodes[8];
};
```

Let me explain the member variables in the class first. m_bSubDivided tells us whether the node has any children. We query this boolean when we are drawing to let us know whether its data needs to be rendered or whether we should recurse further and render its children's data. The width of our node is stored in m_Width. This is used in conjunction with the center of the node, m_vCenter, to determine whether the node intersects the viewing frustum. When looping through our vertices to render the octree, we query m_TriangleCount for the amount of vertices we have. We say that 3 * m_TriangleCount = the number of vertices since we are using triangles as our polygons. The CVector3 data type is our simple vector class that has the + and − operators overloaded with member variables:

```
float x, y, z;
```

Notice that we create an array of eight COctree pointers. This array will hold pointers to each of the node's children. Not all nodes have eight children or any children for that matter. All nodes are created on a need-to-subdivide basis.

The member functions are pretty straightforward, but I will give a brief description of the important ones. GetSceneDimensions() is called before we create the octree. This goes through and finds the center point and width of the entire scene/level/ world. Once we find the initial center point and width of the world, we can then call CreateNode(), which recursively creates the octree.

By now, the octree should be created (assuming the world as we know it didn't collapse and you are in a pit of lava), so we can call DrawOctree() in our render loop. Starting at the root node, DrawOctree() recurses down the tree of nodes and draws the end nodes. Eventually, this will use frustum culling but not until later. Last but not least, we use DestroyOctree() to free and initialize the data again. Usually you wouldn't use this function as the client, but in this application, we can manipulate some of the octree variables on-the-fly, such as g_MaxTriangles and g_MaxSubdivisions. Once we change these, we need to re-create the tree from the new restrictions.

You'll learn more about these variables later, but before I move into discussing the function definitions, I would like to brush by one more class for our debug lines:

```
// This is our debug lines class to view the octree visually
class CDebug
{

public:

    // This adds a line to our list of debug lines
    void AddDebugLine(CVector3 vPoint1, CVector3 vPoint2);

    // Adds a 3-D box with a given center, width, height and depth to our list
    void AddDebugBox(CVector3 vCenter, float width, float height, float depth);

    // This renders all of the lines
    void RenderDebugLines();

    // This clears all of the debug lines
    void Clear();

private:

    // This is the vector list of all of our lines
    vector<CVector3> m_vLines;
};
```

This class was designed to visualize the octree nodes. It's frustrating if you can't see what is going on. As you can see, it just draws lines and boxes. I won't go into the details of these functions because they aren't vital to our understanding of the octree, but the source code is commented well enough if you care to peruse it.

Getting the Scene's Dimensions

Looking back at Figure 14.1, you'll see the root node's dimensions represented by a yellow, wireframe cube. Let's explore how we calculated these initial dimensions in GetSceneDimensions(). For the full source code, refer to Octree.cpp of the first application.

```
void COctree::GetSceneDimensions(CVector3 *pVertices, int numberOfVerts)
{
```

We pass in the list of vertices and the vertex count to get the center point and width of the whole scene. Later, we use this information to subdivide our octree. Depending on the data structures you use to store your world data, this will vary. In the following code, the center point of the scene is calculated. All you need to do is add *all* the vertices and then divide that total by the number of vertices added up to find the average for x, y, and z. If you can determine the average test score of a list of high school students' grades, it works the same way. So all the x's get added together, and then y's, and so on. This doesn't mean you add them to form a single number, but three separate floats (totalX, totalY, totalZ).

Notice that we are adding two CVector3's together, m_vCenter and pVertices[i]. If you look in the CVector3 class, I overloaded the + and – operators to handle these operations correctly. It cuts down on code instead of adding the x, and then the y, and then the z separately. At the end of GetSceneDimensions(), there will be no return values, but we will be setting the member variables m_Width and m_vCenter.

```
// Go through all of the vertices and add them up to find the center
for(int i = 0; i < numberOfVerts; i++)
{
    // Add the current vertex to the center variable (operator overloaded)
    m_vCenter = m_vCenter + pVertices[i];
}

// Divide the total by the number of vertices to get the center point.
// We could have overloaded the / symbol but I chose not to because we
// rarely use it in the code.
m_vCenter.x /= numberOfVerts;
m_vCenter.y /= numberOfVerts;
m_vCenter.z /= numberOfVerts;
```

Now that we have the center point, we want to find the farthest distance from it. We can subtract every vertex from our new center and save the farthest distance in width, height, and depth (in other words x, y, and z). Once we get the farthest width, height, and depth, we then check them against each other. Whichever one is higher, we use that value for the cube width of the root node.

```
// Go through all of the vertices and find the max dimensions
for(i = 0; i < numberOfVerts; i++)
{
    // Get the current dimensions for this vertex. abs() is used
    // to get the absolute value because it might return a negative number.
    int currentWidth = abs(pVertices[i].x - m_vCenter.x);
```

```
    int currentHeight = abs(pVertices[i].y - m_vCenter.y);
    int currentDepth = abs(pVertices[i].z - m_vCenter.z);

    // Check if the current width is greater than the max width stored.
    if(currentWidth > maxWidth) maxWidth = currentWidth;

    // Check if the current height is greater than the max height stored.
    if(currentHeight > maxHeight) maxHeight = currentHeight;

    // Check if the current depth is greater than the max depth stored.
    if(currentDepth > maxDepth) maxDepth = currentDepth;
}
```

Once the max dimensions are calculated, we multiply them by two because this will
give us the full width, height, and depth. Otherwise, we just have half the size since
we are calculating from the center of the scene. After we find the max dimensions,
we want to check which one is the largest so that we can create our initial cube
dimensions from it. First we check if the maxWidth is the largest and then maxHeight;
otherwise, it must be maxDepth. It won't matter if any of them are equal since we use
the >= (greater than or equal to) logical operand. If the maxWidth and maxHeight were
equal yet larger than maxDepth, the first if statement would assign maxWidth as the
largest:

```
// Get the full width, height, and depth
maxWidth *= 2; maxHeight *= 2; maxDepth *= 2;

// Check if the width is the highest and assign that for the cube dimension
if(maxWidth >= maxHeight && maxWidth >= maxDepth)
    m_Width = maxWidth;

// Check if height is the highest and assign that for the cube dimension
else if(maxHeight >= maxWidth && maxHeight >= maxDepth)
    m_Width = maxHeight;

// Else it must be the "depth" or it's the same value as the other ones
else
    m_Width = maxDepth;
}
```

After finding the root node width, we can now start to actually create the octree.
From the client side, this just takes one call of the CreateNode() function.

Creating the Octree Nodes

This is our main function that creates the octree. We will recurse through this function until we finish subdividing. This is because we either subdivided too many levels or divided all of the triangles up. The parameters needed for this function are the array of vertices, the number of vertices, and the center point and width of the current node.

```
void COctree::CreateNode(CVector3 *pVertices,
                         int numberOfVerts, CVector3 vCenter, float width)
{
```

When calling CreateNode() for the first time, we will pass in the center and width of the root node. That is why we need to call GetSceneDimensions() before this function, so that we have the initial node's data to pass in. In the opening of this function, some variables need to be set. We create a local variable to hold the numberOfTriangles, and we set the member variables m_Width and m_vCenter to the data passed in. Though in the beginning the root node will already have the width and center set, the other nodes won't.

```
    // Create a variable to hold the number of triangles
    int numberOfTriangles = numberOfVerts / 3;

    // Initialize the node's center point. Now we know the center of this node.
    m_vCenter = vCenter;

    // Initialize the node's cube width. Now we know the width of this node.
    m_Width = width;
```

To get a visual idea of what is going on in our octree, we add the current node's cube data to our debug box list. This way, we can now see this node as a cube when we render the boxes. Since it's a cube, we can pass in the node's width for the width, height, and depth parameters for AddDebugBox(). g_Debug is our global instance of the CDebug class.

```
    g_Debug.AddDebugBox(vCenter, width, width, width);
```

Before we subdivide anything, we need to check whether we have too many triangles in this node and haven't subdivided above our max subdivisions. If not, we need to break this node into potentially eight more nodes. Both of the given conditions must be true to subdivide this node. Initially, g_MaxSubdivisions and g_CurrentSubdivisions are 0, which means that the if statement will be false until we increase g_MaxSubdivisions. While running the octree application, we can increase/decrease the levels of subdivision by pressing the + and – keys. This is great because it allows us to see the recursion happening in real time. To increase/decrease the maximum number of triangles in each node, we press the F5 and F6 keys.

```
if( (numberOfTriangles    > g_MaxTriangles  ) &&
    (g_CurrentSubdivision < g_MaxSubdivisions) )
{
```

Since this node will be subdivided, we set its m_bSubDivided member variable to true. This lets us know that this node does not have any vertices assigned to it, but its nodes have vertices stored in them (or their nodes, and so on). Later in DrawOctree(), this variable will be queried when the octree is being drawn.

```
        m_bSubDivided = true;
```

A dynamic list will need to be created for each new node to store whether a triangle should be stored in its triangle list. For each index, it will be a true or false to tell us if that triangle is in the cube of that node. The Standard Template Library (STL) vector class was chosen as the list data type because of its flexibility. I hope it's obvious in the following code that I chose not to display all eight lines of code for the list initialization. Refer to the source code that accompanies this book for the remaining code.

```
        // Create the list of booleans for each triangle index
        vector<bool> pList1(numberOfTriangles); // TOP_LEFT_FRONT node list
        vector<bool> pList2(numberOfTriangles); // TOP_LEFT_BACK node list
        vector<bool> pList3(numberOfTriangles); // TOP_RIGHT_BACK node list
        // Etc... up to pList8
        ...

        // Create a variable to cut down the thickness of the code below
        CVector3 vCtr = vCenter;
```

If you are uncomfortable with STL, you can dynamically allocate the memory yourself with a pointer to a bool. For example:

```
        bool *pList1 = new bool [numberOfTriangles];
        // Etc...
```

You'll notice in the comments that we have constants such as TOP_LEFT_FRONT and TOP_LEFT_BACK. These belong to the eOctreeNodes enum, which was created to assign an ID for every section of the eight subdivided nodes, which also happens to be an index into the m_pOctreeNodes array. Looking at numbers like 0, 1, 2, 3, 4, 5, 6, and 7 hardly creates readable code. Keep in mind that these enum constants are assuming that we visualize being in front of the world and looking down the −z axis, with positive y going up and positive x going to the right.

```
enum eOctreeNodes
{
    TOP_LEFT_FRONT,          // 0
    TOP_LEFT_BACK,           // 1
    TOP_RIGHT_BACK,          // etc...
    TOP_RIGHT_FRONT,
    BOTTOM_LEFT_FRONT,
    BOTTOM_LEFT_BACK,
    BOTTOM_RIGHT_BACK,
    BOTTOM_RIGHT_FRONT
};
```

Following the creation of our eight lists, the next step will be to check every vertex passed in to see where its position is according to the center of the current node. (That is, if it's above the center to the left and back, it's the TOP_LEFT_BACK.) Depending on the node, the node's pList* index is set to true. This will tell us later which triangles go to which node.

You might catch that this will produce doubles in some nodes. Some triangles will intersect more than one node, right? You generally have two options in this situation. Either you can split the triangles along the node's plane they are intersecting, or you can ignore it and assume there will be some hitchhikers that won't be seen when rendering. Each of these choices has its own benefits and drawbacks. When splitting the triangles, you create more polygons in your world. Depending on how the world is set up, the split could increase your polygons in your scene by a disastrous number. You will also need to recalculate the face and UV coordinate information for each new polygon created. Some splits will just create one new triangle, whereas others will create two. See Figure 14.9 for examples of different splits along a plane.

You can imagine that it will create two new triangles more often than one. In many cases, the split will create a four-sided polygon, which means you will need to triangulate it to make two triangles from the quad. Of course, this assumes that you only want to deal with triangles. To me, this makes perfect sense for a BSP tree, but it's not completely necessary for an octree.

Instead of splitting the polygons, we just save the indices in a vertex array in our list. This completely eliminates the need to recalculate any face or UV data, and it

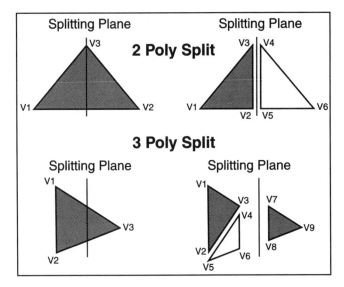

Figure 14.9

When splitting a polygon over a plane, it's more likely that three polygons will be created rather than two

cuts out a big chunk of code for splitting and triangulating polygons. The problem with this method is that it can potentially draw two of the same triangles at the same time, which will cause pointless overlapping of triangles.

For this last method, when passing the world data into our CreateNode() function to be subdivided, we could store the world model information in the root node and pass a pointer to it down to each node when drawing the octree. This would allow us to free the model that was passed in after creating the octree, or we could instead not free the model after creating the octree and pass down a pointer to the world model through DrawOctree(), which could be potentially error prone, along with needing constant access to that model. Since we do not deal with any face information besides the vertices of our terrain, our octree code simply copies the vertices to each end node, allowing us to free the terrain data immediately after creating the octree if so desired. Another benefit of storing face indices is that it allows you more easily to render the octree using vertex arrays.

The following "for" loop will be used in checking each vertex to see in which section it lies, according to the current node's center. You'll notice that we divide the current vertex index i by 3 because there are three points in a triangle. If the vertex indexes 0 and 1 are in a node section, both 0 / 3 and 1 / 3 are 0, which will set the 0th index of the pList*[] to true twice, which doesn't hurt. When we get to index 3 of pVertices[], we will then be checking index 1 of the pList*[] array (3 / 3 = 1). We do this because we want a list of the triangle indices in each child node list, not the vertex indices. This is most likely better understood by looking at the code. In a nutshell, we just store the index to the triangle in the pList* versus the index of the vertices. Later, in `CreateNewNode()`, we will use this data to extract the vertices into a new list to check in the newly created child node, of course, only if any triangles are in that node's section.

```
for(int i = 0; i < numberOfVerts; i++)
{
    // Create a variable to cut down the thickness of the code
    CVector3 vPt = pVertices[i];

    // Check if the point lines within the TOP LEFT FRONT node
    if( (vPt.x <= vCtr.x) && (vPt.y >= vCtr.y) && (vPt.z >= vCtr.z) )
        pList1[i / 3] = true;

    // Check if the point lines within the TOP LEFT BACK node
    if( (vPt.x <= vCtr.x) && (vPt.y >= vCtr.y) && (vPt.z <= vCtr.z) )
        pList2[i / 3] = true;

    // Check if the point lines within the TOP RIGHT BACK node
    if( (vPt.x >= vCtr.x) && (vPt.y >= vCtr.y) && (vPt.z <= vCtr.z) )
        pList3[i / 3] = true;

    // Etc... up to pList8
    ...
}
```

Right before this node is subdivided, we need to add up how many triangles we found in each section. With a simple for loop to go through the total number of triangles, this is very easy. If the current index in the `pList*[]` is true, we simply increase the triangle count stored in a local variable for each list. This could obviously be optimized if needed by incorporating it into the previous code, but it provides a bit more clarity down here.

```
// Create a variable for each list that holds how many triangles
// were found for each of the 8 subdivided nodes.
int triCount1 = 0; int triCount2 = 0;
 int triCount3 = 0; int triCount4 = 0;
int triCount5 = 0; int triCount6 = 0;
 int triCount7 = 0; int triCount8 = 0;

// Go through each of the lists and increase the
// triangle count for each node.
for(i = 0; i < numberOfTriangles; i++)
```

```
        {
            // Increase the triangle count for each
            // node that has a "true" for the index i.
            if(pList1[i]) triCount1++; if(pList2[i]) triCount2++;
            if(pList3[i]) triCount3++; if(pList4[i]) triCount4++;
            if(pList5[i]) triCount5++; if(pList6[i]) triCount6++;
            if(pList7[i]) triCount7++; if(pList8[i]) triCount8++;
        }
```

Next comes the dirty work. We need to set up the new node and pass in the triangles that are in its area, along with the new center point and width. Through recursion, we subdivide this node into eight more nodes but only if triCount* is greater than 0. It would be pointless and a waste of memory to allocate a new node if there were no triangles stored in that space. I created a function called CreateNewNode() that handles all the setup work since it needs to happen eight times.

The data passed in to CreateNewNode() is the initial list of vertices to this node, the newly created list of triangle indices, the number of initial vertices, the center point, the width, the triangle count of the associated pList* that we just calculated, and finally, the ID for this node's section. Remember that the IDs are from the eOctreeNodes enum stored in octree.h. The ID acts as the index into the m_pOctreeNodes array.

```
        // Create the subdivided nodes if necessary and then
        // recurse through them. The information passed into CreateNewNode() is
        // essential for creating the new nodes. We pass in one of the 8 ID's
        // so it knows how to calculate it's new center.
        CreateNewNode(pVertices, pList1, numberOfVerts,
                    vCenter,    width,  triCount1,    TOP_LEFT_FRONT);
        CreateNewNode(pVertices, pList2, numberOfVerts,
                    vCenter,    width,  triCount2,    TOP_LEFT_BACK);
        CreateNewNode(pVertices, pList3, numberOfVerts,
                    vCenter,    width,  triCount3,    TOP_RIGHT_BACK);
        // Etc... up to pList8
        ...
    }
```

If there was no need to subdivide this node and the check proved false, we skip all the recursive code and just assign the vertices to this current node. The AssignVerticesToNode() function handles this procedure. The required parameters are the array of vertices and the vertex count.

```
    else
```

```
    {
        // Assign the vertices to this node since we reached an end node
        AssignVerticesToNode(pVertices, numberOfVerts);
    }
}
```

Setting Up New Nodes for Recursion

This function helps us set up the new node being created. We only want to create a new node if there were triangles found in its area of 3-D space. If no triangles were found in this node's cube, we ignore it and don't create a node. First we check whether triangleCount is greater than zero before continuing; otherwise, we return from the function. Once we know that there are triangles to use, memory can be allocated for an array of CVector3's that will hold the vertices found in this node's 3-D region.

```
void COctree::CreateNewNode(CVector3 *pVertices, vector<bool> pList,
                            int numberOfVerts,  CVector3 vCenter, float width,
                            int triangleCount,  int nodeID)
{
```

To fill in the new array of vertices, we create a loop that checks every vertex to see if its triangle index was set to true. The triangle index is calculated by taking the current vertex index i and dividing it by 3. A separate counter is held to store the current index into the pNodeVertices[] array. Each time a new vertex is found in the region, it's assigned to the pNodeVertices[] array and the index counter is increased by 1. As you can see, once a triangle index is found to be in the node's list, the next three vertices will be assigned in a row, which make up the triangle found.

```
    // Check if the first node found some triangles in it, else, return
    if(triangleCount <= 0) return;

    // Allocate memory for the triangles found in this node
    CVector3 *pNodeVertices = new CVector3 [triangleCount * 3];

    // Create a counter to count the current index of the new node vertices
    int index = 0;

    // Go through all the vertices and assign the vertices to the node's list
    for(int i = 0; i < numberOfVerts; i++)
```

```
    {
        // If this current triangle is in the node, assign its vertices to it
        if(pList[i / 3])
        {
            pNodeVertices[index] = pVertices[i];
            index++;
        }
    }
}
```

Now comes the initialization of the node. First we allocate memory for our new node and then get its center point. Depending on the nodeID, GetNewNodeCenter() knows which center point to pass back from a simple switch statement.

```
// Allocate a new node for the octree
m_pOctreeNodes[nodeID] = new COctree;

// Get the new node's center point depending on the nodeID
// (nodeID: meaning, which of the 8 subdivided cubes).
CVector3 vNodeCenter = GetNewNodeCenter(vCenter, width, nodeID);
```

Before and after we recurse further down into the tree, we keep track of the level of subdivision we are in. This way, we can restrict it. When creating your own octree, this isn't necessary. I threw this in to help us visualize the octree by being able to change the max levels of subdivision. Now we are ready to recurse.

With a call to CreateNode(), we step down another level of subdivision in our tree. The new parameters passed in are the new vertices, the total number of vertices (triangleCount * 3), and the new center and width of the newly created node. The width / 2 is passed in because we just cut in half our region we are dealing with. Once we return from subdividing this current node, we can delete the vertices passed in because they are no longer needed. In the function AssignVerticesToNode(), new memory is allocated to store the assigned vertices to each node. The initial vertices passed in from our world are not deleted in the octree code but can be released once the octree is created.

```
// Increase the current level of subdivision
g_CurrentSubdivision++;

// Recurse through this node and subdivide it if necessary
m_pOctreeNodes[nodeID]->CreateNode(pNodeVertices, triangleCount * 3,
                                    vNodeCenter,   width / 2);

// Decrease the current level of subdivision
```

```
g_CurrentSubdivision--;

// Free the allocated vertices for the triangles found in this node
delete [] pNodeVertices;
}
```

Getting a Child Node's Center

Previously in CreateNewNode(), we called GetNewNodeCenter() to obtain the new nodes center. This function takes an enum ID and returns the new subdivided nodes center, depending on the center and width of its parent node, passed in as vCenter and width. The node ID is given to a switch statement to determine how the new center should be calculated. Once the new node's center is found, we return it at the bottom.

```
CVector3 COctree::GetNewNodeCenter(CVector3 vCenter, float width, int nodeID)
{
```

Calculating the new center is fairly simple. First you want to get the distance that the new center is from the original center. To do this, just divide the current center by 4. Now, if we want to find the TOP_LEFT_BACK node's center, we would say:

```
vNodeCenter ={vCenter.x - distance, vCenter.y + distance, vCenter.z - distance}
```

Figure 14.10 shows an example of this in 2-D, assuming the parent node has a width of 100. If we divide the width by 4 we get 25, which is the distance from the center

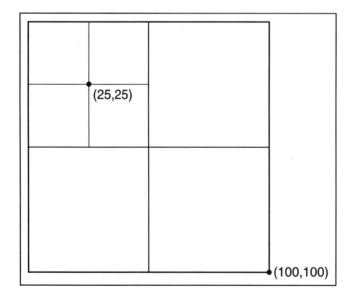

Figure 14.10

To find the center point of a new child node, we divide the width of the current node by 4 and then add or subtract that result from the center, depending on the desired child node

point to the new node. Since we are dealing with the TOP_LEFT_BACK, we subtract that distance from the center's x, add the distance to the center's y, and then subtract the distance from the center's z to get the 3-D position for the new node's center.

```
// Initialize the new node center
CVector3 vNodeCenter(0, 0, 0);

// Create a dummy variable to cut down the code size
CVector3 vCtr = vCenter;

// Store the distance the new node center will be from the center
float distance = width / 4.0f;

// Switch on the ID to see which subdivided node we are finding the center
switch(nodeID)
{
    case TOP_LEFT_FRONT:
        // Calculate the center of this new node
        vNodeCenter = CVector3(vCtr.x - distance,
                               vCtr.y + distance, vCtr.z + distance);
        break;

    case TOP_LEFT_BACK:
        // Calculate the center of this new node
        vNodeCenter = CVector3(vCtr.x - distance,
                               vCtr.y + distance, vCtr.z - distance);
        break;

    case TOP_RIGHT_BACK:
        // Calculate the center of this new node
        vNodeCenter = CVector3(vCtr.x + distance,
                               vCtr.y + distance, vCtr.z - distance);
        break;

    // Etc... up to BOTTOM_RIGHT_FRONT
    ...
}

    // Return the new node center
    return vNodeCenter;
}
```

Assigning Vertices to the End Node

Until now, we have just been playing hot potato by passing off the vertices to everyone else. When an end node is determined and we don't need to subdivide any more, the vertices can then be assigned. Once again, end nodes are determined in our CreateNode() function by the following test:

```
if( (numberOfTriangles    > g_MaxTriangles) &&
    (g_CurrentSubdivision < g_MaxSubdivisions) )
{
    // This node must not be an end node, so subdivide it further...
    // ...
}
else
{
    // An end node is found, so assign the vertices to it.
    // ...
}
```

In the "else" scope, the function AssignVerticesToNode() is called. As the function suggests, the end node is put in charge over its vertices. This is one of our smallest functions in the octree class, but let's go over what it's doing.

```
void COctree::AssignVerticesToNode(CVector3 *pVertices, int numberOfVerts)
{
```

All that's going on here is we are setting our m_bSubDivided flag to false, setting our m_TriangleCount member variable to the number of triangles that will be stored, allocating memory for the new vertices, and then doing a memcopy() to copy all the vertex data into the newly allocated memory. New memory is allocated (instead of just having m_pVertices point to the vertex data passed in) so that we are not dependent on the memory of the original vertex data loaded in at the beginning. We will free the memory of the original vertices but have the end nodes keep their own memory. This is done so that each node is responsible for its own memory; otherwise, we could be freeing the same memory twice later on.

Note that instead of the end nodes storing the actual vertices, another way of doing this is to have them just store indices into an array of vertices and face data. This way, we won't have to cut up the information, which makes you have to recalculate the face indices for your world/level. This was discussed earlier in the CreateNode() function definition.

```
    // Since we did not subdivide this node we want to set our flag to false
    m_bSubDivided = false;

    m_TriangleCount = numberOfVerts / 3;

    // Allocate enough memory to hold the needed vertices for the triangles
    m_pVertices = new CVector3 [numberOfVerts];

    // Initialize the vertices to 0 before we copy the data over to them
    memset(m_pVertices, 0, sizeof(CVector3) * numberOfVerts);

    // Copy the passed in vertex data over to our node vertex data
    memcpy(m_pVertices, pVertices, sizeof(CVector3) * numberOfVerts);

    // Increase the amount of end nodes created (Nodes with vertices stored)
    g_EndNodeCount++;
}
```

Drawing the Octree

Partitioning the octree was the hard part, but now you get to see how easily the
nodes are drawn. The DrawOctree() function was created just for this purpose. Using
recursion, the octree is drawn starting at the root node and then working down
through the children until the end nodes are reached. These are the only nodes
that have vertices assigned to them; therefore, they are the only nodes to be rendered. In this version of DrawOctree(), every single end node is drawn, regardless of
whether it's inside or outside the frustum. This will be changed when we cover frustum culling.

```
void COctree::DrawOctree(COctree *pNode)
{
```

We should already have the octree created before we call this function. This goes
through all nodes until it reaches their ends and then draws the vertices stored in
those end nodes. Before we draw a node, we check to make sure it is not a subdivided node (from m_bSubdivided). If it is, we haven't reached the end and need to
keep recursing through the tree. Once we get to a node that isn't subdivided, we
draw its vertices.

```
    // Make sure a valid node was passed in; otherwise go back to the last node
    if(!pNode) return;
```

```
// Check if this node is subdivided. If so, then we need to draw its nodes
if(pNode->IsSubDivided())
{
    // Recurse to the bottom of these nodes and draw
    // the end node's vertices, Like creating the octree,
    // we need to recurse through each of the 8 nodes.
     DrawOctree(pNode->m_pOctreeNodes[TOP_LEFT_FRONT]);
     DrawOctree(pNode->m_pOctreeNodes[TOP_LEFT_BACK]);
     DrawOctree(pNode->m_pOctreeNodes[TOP_RIGHT_BACK]);
     DrawOctree(pNode->m_pOctreeNodes[TOP_RIGHT_FRONT]);
     DrawOctree(pNode->m_pOctreeNodes[BOTTOM_LEFT_FRONT]);
     DrawOctree(pNode->m_pOctreeNodes[BOTTOM_LEFT_BACK]);
     DrawOctree(pNode->m_pOctreeNodes[BOTTOM_RIGHT_BACK]);
     DrawOctree(pNode->m_pOctreeNodes[BOTTOM_RIGHT_FRONT]);
}
 else
 {
    // Make sure we have valid vertices assigned to this node
    if(!pNode->m_pVertices) return;

    // Since we can hit the left mouse button and turn wire frame on/off,
    // we store a global variable to hold if we draw lines or polygons.
    // g_RenderMode will either be GL_TRIANGLES or GL_LINE_STRIP.
    glBegin(g_RenderMode);

    // Turn the polygons green
    glColor3ub(0, 255, 0);

    // Store the vertices in a local pointer to keep code more clean
    CVector3 *pVertices = pNode->m_pVertices;

    // Go through all of the vertices (the number of triangles * 3)
    for(int i = 0; i < pNode->GetTriangleCount() * 3; i += 3)
    {
```

Before we render the vertices, we want to calculate the face's normal of the current polygon. That way, when lighting is turned on, we can see the definition of the terrain more clearly. In reality, you wouldn't do this in real time. To calculate the face normal, we use the cross product on two of the current triangles sides, which returns an orthogonal vector, and then we normalize this vector to find the desired normal of that face.

```
        // Here we get a vector from two sides of the triangle
        CVector3 vVector1 = pVertices[i + 1] - pVertices[i];
        CVector3 vVector2 = pVertices[i + 2] - pVertices[i];

        // Then we need to get the normal by the 2 vector's cross product
        CVector3 vNormal = Cross(vVector1, vVector2);

        // Now we normalize the normal so it is a unit vector (length of 1)
        vNormal = Normalize(vNormal);

        // Pass in the normal for this triangle for the lighting
        glNormal3f(vNormal.x, vNormal.y, vNormal.z);

        // Render the first point in the triangle
        glVertex3f(pVertices[i].x, pVertices[i].y, pVertices[i].z);

        // Render the next point in the triangle
        glVertex3f(pVertices[i + 1].x,
                pVertices[i + 1].y, pVertices[i + 1].z);

        // Render the last point in the triangle to form the triangle
        glVertex3f(pVertices[i + 2].x,
                pVertices[i + 2].y, pVertices[i + 2].z);
    }

    // Quit Drawing
    glEnd();
  }
}
```

Destroying the Octree

With C++, freeing the octree is easy. In our COctree class, we call DestroyOctree() in
the deconstructor. When the root node goes out of scope or is destroyed manually,
DestroyOctree() will be called. Inside of this function, we go through all the eight
potential children associated with the dying node. If the child has allocated memory, we "delete" it. This in turn calls the child node's deconstructor, which repeats
the process on the node's children. In a way, this creates its own type of recursion
to go through all the nodes until we reach the end nodes and then frees the

memory from the bottom up. The root node will not leave DestroyOctree() until all of its subdivided children have been destroyed.

```
void COctree::DestroyOctree()
{
    // Free the triangle data if it's not NULL
    if( m_pVertices )
    {
        delete m_pVertices;
        m_pVertices = NULL;
    }

    // Go through all of the nodes and free them if they were allocated
    for(int i = 0; i < 8; i++)
    {
        // Make sure this node is valid
        if(m_pOctreeNodes[i])
        {
            // Free this array index. This will call the deconstructor,
            // which will free the octree data correctly. This allows
            // us to forget about a complicated clean up
            delete m_pOctreeNodes[i];
            m_pOctreeNodes[i] = NULL;
        }
    }

    // Initialize the octree data members
    InitOctree();
}
```

Until now, we have explained the very basics of what it takes to create an octree. In the next section, we will tackle the awe and mystery of implementing the frustum culling.

Implementing Frustum Culling

An octree without frustum culling is about as useful as a Corvette without a gas pedal. Sure, the outside looks all nice and pretty. It even gives you the image that you can use it to cruise down the highway at great speeds. Only after you turn it on and shift into first do you realize that you aren't going anywhere. It is now determined that there is no way to move the car, and as a matter of fact, the experience leaves you a bit disgruntled. This is how it is without that one function call that checks the octree's end nodes against the frustum. The increase in vertices drawn even makes the rendering of the world a bit slower. Moving on to the next application, we will add the metaphorical gas pedal to our car.

Though the code needed to handle frustum culling is small, it requires that you understand a bit of math. Since we are dealing with planes, the plane equation will be instrumental in calculating frustum intersection. More of the math will be explained later, but let me first introduce you to our frustum class. The frustum code is stored in Frustum.cpp and Frustum.h in the second octree sample application accompanying this book.

```
// This will allow us to create an object to keep track of our frustum
class CFrustum {

public:

    // Call this every time the camera moves to update the frustum
    void CalculateFrustum();

    // This takes a 3-D point and returns TRUE if it's inside of the frustum
    bool PointInFrustum(float x, float y, float z);

    // This takes a 3-D point and a radius and returns TRUE if the sphere is inside
    of the frustum
    bool SphereInFrustum(float x, float y, float z, float radius);

    // This takes the center and half the length of the cube.
    bool CubeInFrustum( float x, float y, float z, float size );

private:

    // This holds the A B C and D values for each side of our frustum.
    float m_Frustum[6][4];
};
```

The CFrustum class stores an array of 6 by 4 and of type float for its only member variable. The dimensions are such that we have six sides of our frustum, with an A, B, C, and D for each side's plane equation. Instead of storing 3-D points for our frustum, we just describe it by its planes. Initially, we need to calculate the frustum by calling CalculateFrustum(). If the camera moves, the frustum must once again be recalculated to reflect the new frustum planes. Either you can make sure this function is called when the user has any movement, or in the case of a first-person shooter, it's rare that the camera will not be moving, so you could decide to just ignore the checks and calculate it every frame. Though it's not a CPU hog to calculate the frustum, it does have some multiplication, division, and square root operations that can be avoided if it's not necessary to do so.

Once the frustum is calculated, we are all set from there. We can now start querying potential points, spheres, and cubes in the frustum. To check if a point lies in the frustum, we could make a call to the following:

```
// (x, y, z) being the potential point
bool bInside = g_Frustum.PointInFrustum(x, y, z);
```

To check if a sphere is inside of the frustum, we call our sphere function as follows:

```
// (xyz) being the center of the sphere and (radius) being the sphere's radius
bool bInside = g_Frustum.SphereInFrustum(x, y, z, radius);
Finally, to check if a cube lies inside of the frustum, we use:
// (x, y, z) being the cube's center and also the cube's width / 2
bool bInside = g_Frustum.CubeInFrustum(x, y, z, cubeWidth / 2);
```

To make the code more clear, two enums are created for each index of the rows and columns of the m_Frustum member variable. The first enum, eFrustumSide, is associated with each index into the sides of the frustum; the second, ePlaneData, corresponds to the four variables needed to describe each side's plane using the plane equation.

```
// Create an enum of the sides so we don't have to call each side 0, 1, 2, ...
// This way it makes it more intuitive when dealing with frustum sides.
enum eFrustumSide
{
    RIGHT    = 0, // The RIGHT side of the frustum
    LEFT     = 1, // The LEFT side of the frustum
    BOTTOM   = 2, // The BOTTOM side of the frustum
    TOP      = 3, // The TOP side of the frustum
    BACK     = 4, // The BACK side of the frustum
    FRONT    = 5  // The FRONT side of the frustum
};


// Instead of using a number for the indices of A B C and D of the plane, we
// want to be more descriptive.
enum ePlaneData
```

```
{
    A    = 0, // The X value of the plane's normal
    B    = 1, // The Y value of the plane's normal
    C    = 2, // The Z value of the plane's normal
    D    = 3  // The distance the plane is from the origin
};
```

The Plane Equation

If the mention of the plane equation has confused you, we will address this right now. What is the plane equation? What is it used for? Why do we need it for frustum culling? These might be some of the questions you are asking yourself. In most collision detection, besides the basic 2-D bounding rectangle or sphere-to-sphere collision, you need to use the plane equation. The plane equation is defined as follows:

$$Ax + By + Cz + D = 0 \qquad \text{meaning} \qquad A*x + B*y + C*z + D = 0$$

Vector (A, B, C) represents the plane's normal, where (x, y, z) is the point on the plane. D relates to the distance the plane is from the origin. The result is a single number, such as a double or float. The preceding equation is basically saying that by the plane's normal and its distance from the plane, the point (x, y, z) lies on that plane. The right-hand result is the distance that the point (x, y, z) is from the plane. Since it's 0, that means it is on that plane. If the result were a positive value, that would tell us that the point is in front of the plane by that positive distance; if it were a negative number, the point would be behind the plane by that negative distance. How do we know what is the front and back of the plane? Well, the front of the plane is the side from which the normal is pointing out.

As a simple example of the usage of the plane equation, let's go over how we would check whether a line segment intersects a plane. If we have a plane's normal and its distance from the origin, plus the two points that make up the line segment, we should be fine. Simply check the distance that the first point of the line is from the described plane and then check the distance that the second point of the line is from the plane. If both of the distances from the plane are positive or negative, the line did not intersect because they are both either in front of or behind the plane. If the distances have opposite signs, however, there was a collision. For example, let's say we have the normal of the plane being described as (0, 1, 0), with a distance of 5 from the origin. So far, our equation is as follows:

$$0*x + 1*y + 0*z + 5 = ???$$

The only thing left is to fill in the (x, y, z) point that we are testing against the plane. Just looking at the equation so far, we know that the polygon is pointing straight up and that the x and z values of the point will be superfluous in determining which side the point is on. For our line segment, we will use the points (–3, 6, 2) and (1, –6, 2) to demonstrate some actual values (see Figure 14.11).

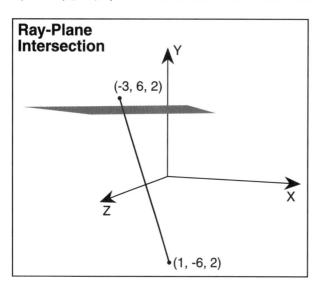

Figure 14.11

Demonstrating the plane equation when calculating the collision with a line segment and a plane

Take a look at the equation now:

distance1 = 0*–3 + 1*6 + 0*2 +5
distance1 = 11

Point 1 of the line segment has a distance of 11 from the plane (in front of the plane).

distance2 = 0*1 + 1*–6 + 0*2 +5
distance2 = –1

Point 2 of the line segment has a distance of –1 from the plane (behind the plane).

Once we have the two distances, to check whether the line segment collided with the plane, we can multiply them. If the result is greater than zero, there was no collision. This is because there must be a negative distance, indicating that one of the points is on the opposite side of the other point. We might also have a distance of 0, which tells us that our point lies on the plane. When distance1 * distance2 is computed, we get –11. The result is not greater than zero, so there is an intersection of the given line segment and plane. If you understand these concepts, you will be able to understand how the intersection tests against the frustum work as well.

Calculating the Frustum Planes

Your initial feelings about calculating the frustum might be that it is complicated and crazy math. This is not so. The math is simple, but it does require knowledge of matrices. First let's answer some of the basic questions that might arise.

What constitutes our frustum?

To do frustum culling, we don't need the coordinates that make up our frustum. All we need is the six planes for each side of the frustum box. This box is created from our field of view and perspective, along with the near and far clipping planes sliced into that view. The area in between these planes is our frustum. For our purposes, we just need the normals of each plane, including the distance each plane is from the origin. With this information, it allows us to fill in the plane equation.

What information do I need to calculate the frustum planes?

The information needed is the current model view and projection matrix. In OpenGL, this is easily obtained by a call to glGetFloatv() with the appropriate parameters passed in. Let us review what the purpose of these two matrices is. The model view matrix holds the camera orientation. When you rotate or translate your camera with calls to glRotatef() and glTranslatef(), you are affecting the model view matrix. A call to gluLookAt() allows you to manually set this matrix with a position, view, and up vector.

When rendering your scene, unless you specify otherwise, the model view matrix usually is loaded as the affected matrix. If you want to go to orthographic mode or change your perspective, the projection matrix needs to be loaded. To get a better understanding of these matrices, let's relate them to a real-life example. Imagine yourself holding a handheld camera. Whenever you walk, kneel, or rotate the camera, you are affecting the model view matrix. The point at which you start messing around with the buttons on your camera—such as the field of view, focal length, or perhaps you pop on a fish-eye lens—this effects the projection matrix.

What do I do with the model view and projection matrices once I get them?

Once you have the model view and projection matrices, you multiply them. We will call this resultant matrix M. Matrix M is now defined as follows:

$$
M = \begin{bmatrix} m0 & m1 & m2 & m3 \\ m4 & m5 & m6 & m7 \\ m8 & m9 & m10 & m11 \\ m12 & m13 & m14 & m16 \end{bmatrix}
$$

The next step is then to multiply M against the six OpenGL clipping coordinate planes. This matrix will be called P. The OpenGL specifications say that clipping is done in clip coordinate space. Geometry is given to OpenGL in object coordinates, and OpenGL transforms them by the model view matrix into eye space, where it performs some operations such as lighting and fog. These coordinates are then transformed by the projection matrix into clip coordinates. OpenGL clips all geometry in this coordinate space. The volume used for clipping is defined by these six planes:

$$
\begin{array}{cccc}
A & B & C & D \\
[\,-1 & 0 & 0 & 1\,] \ \text{Right Plane} \\
[\ 1 & 0 & 0 & 1\,] \ \text{Left Plane} \\
[\ 0 & -1 & 0 & 1\,] \ \text{Top Plane} \\
[\ 0 & 1 & 0 & 1\,] \ \text{Bottom Plane} \\
[\ 0 & 0 & -1 & 1\,] \ \text{Front Plane} \\
[\ 0 & 0 & 1 & 1\,] \ \text{Back Plane}
\end{array}
$$

P =

These are the clip coordinate planes that OpenGL actually uses for clipping. This happens before doing the perspective division and the view port transformation, followed by scan conversions into the frame buffer. The result of matrix M and P concatenated will be called F, which will hold the object coordinate clipping planes (or in other words, our frustum). Matrix F will store the A, B, C, and D values for each side of the frustum. To simplify F, we don't actually need to do the full matrix multiplication. Taking into account that much of the multiplication will be cancelled out due to the 1s, –1s, and 0s in matrix P, there is no reason to do it in the first place. This saves us quite of bit of cycles on the CPU. For example, take the calculations needed for the first element in F:

A = –1 * m0 + 0 * m1 + 0 * m2 + 1 * m3

Watch as we break this down:

A = –1 * m0 + 0 * m1 + 0 * m2 + 1 * m3
A = –1 * m0 + 1 * m3
A = –m0 + m3
A = m3 – m0

As you can see, the multiplication was completely eliminated from our equation. This goes for all the calculations. Some elements will be addition, and some will be subtraction. Matrix F can then be defined as follows:

$$
\begin{array}{cccc}
[\ m3 - m0 & m7 - m4 & m11 - m8 & m15 - m12\ ] \\
[\ m3 + m0 & m7 + m4 & m11 + m8 & m15 + m12\ ] \\
[\ m3 - m1 & m7 - m5 & m11 - m9 & m15 - m13\ ]
\end{array}
$$

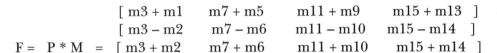

$$\begin{array}{cccc}
[\ m3 + m1 & m7 + m5 & m11 + m9 & m15 + m13\ ] \\
[\ m3 - m2 & m7 - m6 & m11 - m10 & m15 - m14\ ] \\
[\ m3 + m2 & m7 + m6 & m11 + m10 & m15 + m14\ ]
\end{array}$$

$$F = P * M = \begin{array}{cccc}
[\ m3 + m2 & m7 + m6 & m11 + m10 & m15 + m14\ ]
\end{array}$$

To get a better understanding of what is going on, I recommend going through each element and seeing for yourself the simplification in action. That way, when you see the code, it won't be confusing why it's doing what it is doing. There is one final thing we need to do for us to correctly define our frustum, and that is normalize the frustum planes we receive. Our NormalizePlane() function was created just for this purpose. Enough theory, let's move into the code.

```
void CFrustum::CalculateFrustum()
{
    float prj[16];      // This will hold our projection matrix
    float mdl[16];      // This will hold our model view matrix
    float clip[16];     // This will hold the clipping planes

    // glGetFloatv() is used to extract information about our OpenGL world.
    // Below, we pass in GL_PROJECTION_MATRIX to get the projection matrix.
    // It then stores the matrix into an array of [16].
    glGetFloatv( GL_PROJECTION_MATRIX, prj );

    // Pass in GL_MODELVIEW_MATRIX to abstract the current model view matrix.
    // This also stores it in an array of [16].
    glGetFloatv( GL_MODELVIEW_MATRIX, mdl );
```

Now that we have our model view and projection matrix, if we combine these two matrices, it allows us to extract the clipping planes from the result. To combine two matrices, we multiply them. Usually you would have your matrix class do this work for you, but instead of creating one just for this instance, I chose to do the matrix multiplication out in the open. The result is stored in our clip[] array.

```
clip[ 0] = mdl[ 0] * prj[ 0] + mdl[ 1] * prj[ 4] +
           mdl[ 2] * prj[ 8] + mdl[ 3] * prj[12];

clip[ 1] = mdl[ 0] * prj[ 1] + mdl[ 1] * prj[ 5] +
           mdl[ 2] * prj[ 9] + mdl[ 3] * prj[13];
clip[ 2] = mdl[ 0] * prj[ 2] + mdl[ 1] * prj[ 6] +
           mdl[ 2] * prj[10] + mdl[ 3] * prj[14];
clip[ 3] = mdl[ 0] * prj[ 3] + mdl[ 1] * prj[ 7] +
           mdl[ 2] * prj[11] + mdl[ 3] * prj[15];
```

```
clip[ 4] = mdl[ 4] * prj[ 0] + mdl[ 5] * prj[ 4] +
           mdl[ 6] * prj[ 8] + mdl[ 7] * prj[12];
clip[ 5] = mdl[ 4] * prj[ 1] + mdl[ 5] * prj[ 5] +
           mdl[ 6] * prj[ 9] + mdl[ 7] * prj[13];
clip[ 6] = mdl[ 4] * prj[ 2] + mdl[ 5] * prj[ 6] +
           mdl[ 6] * prj[10] + mdl[ 7] * prj[14];
clip[ 7] = mdl[ 4] * prj[ 3] + mdl[ 5] * prj[ 7] +
           mdl[ 6] * prj[11] + mdl[ 7] * prj[15];

clip[ 8] = mdl[ 8] * prj[ 0] + mdl[ 9] * prj[ 4] +
           mdl[10] * prj[ 8] + mdl[11] * prj[12];
clip[ 9] = mdl[ 8] * prj[ 1] + mdl[ 9] * prj[ 5] +
           mdl[10] * prj[ 9] + mdl[11] * prj[13];
clip[10] = mdl[ 8] * prj[ 2] + mdl[ 9] * prj[ 6] +
           mdl[10] * prj[10] + mdl[11] * prj[14];
clip[11] = mdl[ 8] * prj[ 3] + mdl[ 9] * prj[ 7] +
           mdl[10] * prj[11] + mdl[11] * prj[15];

clip[12] = mdl[12] * prj[ 0] + mdl[13] * prj[ 4] +
           mdl[14] * prj[ 8] + mdl[15] * prj[12];
clip[13] = mdl[12] * prj[ 1] + mdl[13] * prj[ 5] +
           mdl[14] * prj[ 9] + mdl[15] * prj[13];
clip[14] = mdl[12] * prj[ 2] + mdl[13] * prj[ 6] +
           mdl[14] * prj[10] + mdl[15] * prj[14];
clip[15] = mdl[12] * prj[ 3] + mdl[13] * prj[ 7] +
           mdl[14] * prj[11] + mdl[15] * prj[15];
```

Next we can find the sides of the frustum, being defined by a normal and a distance. To do this, we take the resultant matrix from the preceding and multiply it by the six clipping coordinate planes. Remember that the multiplication cancels itself out. This means we can just avoid it and use the simplified equation generated without the multiplication. The frustum planes extracted will be stored in the m_Frustum member variable.

```
// This will extract the RIGHT side of the frustum
m_Frustum[RIGHT][A] = clip[ 3] - clip[ 0];
m_Frustum[RIGHT][B] = clip[ 7] - clip[ 4];
m_Frustum[RIGHT][C] = clip[11] - clip[ 8];
m_Frustum[RIGHT][D] = clip[15] - clip[12];

// This will extract the LEFT side of the frustum
```

```
m_Frustum[LEFT][A] = clip[ 3] + clip[ 0];
m_Frustum[LEFT][B] = clip[ 7] + clip[ 4];
m_Frustum[LEFT][C] = clip[11] + clip[ 8];
m_Frustum[LEFT][D] = clip[15] + clip[12];

// This will extract the BOTTOM side of the frustum
m_Frustum[BOTTOM][A] = clip[ 3] + clip[ 1];
m_Frustum[BOTTOM][B] = clip[ 7] + clip[ 5];
m_Frustum[BOTTOM][C] = clip[11] + clip[ 9];
m_Frustum[BOTTOM][D] = clip[15] + clip[13];

// This will extract the TOP side of the frustum
m_Frustum[TOP][A] = clip[ 3] - clip[ 1];
m_Frustum[TOP][B] = clip[ 7] - clip[ 5];
m_Frustum[TOP][C] = clip[11] - clip[ 9];
m_Frustum[TOP][D] = clip[15] - clip[13];

// This will extract the BACK side of the frustum
m_Frustum[BACK][A] = clip[ 3] - clip[ 2];
m_Frustum[BACK][B] = clip[ 7] - clip[ 6];
m_Frustum[BACK][C] = clip[11] - clip[10];
m_Frustum[BACK][D] = clip[15] - clip[14];

// This will extract the FRONT side of the frustum
m_Frustum[FRONT][A] = clip[ 3] + clip[ 2];
m_Frustum[FRONT][B] = clip[ 7] + clip[ 6];
m_Frustum[FRONT][C] = clip[11] + clip[10];

m_Frustum[FRONT][D] = clip[15] + clip[14];
```

After the A, B, C, and D values for each side of the frustum have been stored, we want
to normalize that normal and distance. The function NormalizePlane() was created
to take in the frustum data and the index into the side that needs to be
normalized.

```
NormalizePlane(m_Frustum, RIGHT);
NormalizePlane(m_Frustum, LEFT);
NormalizePlane(m_Frustum, TOP);
NormalizePlane(m_Frustum, BOTTOM);
NormalizePlane(m_Frustum, FRONT);
NormalizePlane(m_Frustum, BACK);
}
```

Our NormalizePlane() function is defined as follows:

```
void NormalizePlane(float frustum[6][4], int side)
{
```

Here we calculate the magnitude of the normal to the plane (point A B C). Remember that (A, B, C) is that same thing as the normal's (X, Y, Z). To calculate the magnitude, you use the equation magnitude = sqrt(x^2 + y^2 + z^2).

```
    float magnitude = (float)sqrt( frustum[side][A] * frustum[side][A] +
                                   frustum[side][B] * frustum[side][B] +
                                   frustum[side][C] * frustum[side][C] );

    // Divide the plane's values by its magnitude.
    frustum[side][A] /= magnitude;
    frustum[side][B] /= magnitude;
    frustum[side][C] /= magnitude;
    frustum[side][D] /= magnitude;
}
```

The remaining code enables us to make checks within the frustum. For example, we could check to see if a point, a sphere, or a cube lies inside of the frustum. Due to the fact that all of our planes point inward (the normals are all pointing inside the frustum), we can then state that if a portion of our geometry is in *front* of all of the planes, it's inside the area of our frustum.

If you have a grasp of the plane equation (A*x + B*y + C*z + D = 0), the rest of this code should be quite obvious and easy to figure out yourself. The first check we will cover is whether a given point is inside of our frustum. The algorithm is to find the distance from the point to each of the six frustum planes. If any of the distances returned a result that is less than or equal to zero, the point must be outside of the frustum. Since the distance formula returns a positive number when we are in front of a plane and all of our frustum planes face inward, it is impossible to be behind or on one of the planes and be inside. The point is defined by (x, y, z).

```
bool CFrustum::PointInFrustum( float x, float y, float z )
{
    // Go through all the sides of the frustum
    for(int i = 0; i < 6; i++ )
    {
        // Calculate the plane equation and check if
        // the point is behind a side of the frustum
        if(m_Frustum[i][A] * x + m_Frustum[i][B] * y +
            m_Frustum[i][C] * z + m_Frustum[i][D] <= 0)
```

```
        {
            // The point was behind a side, so it ISN'T in the frustum
            return false;
        }
    }


    // The point was inside of the frustum
    return true;
}
```

Checking if a sphere is inside of a frustum is almost identical to checking a point, except now we have to deal with a radius around that point. The point being tested is the center of the sphere. The point might be outside of the frustum, but it doesn't mean that the rest of the sphere is. It could be half and half. Instead of checking whether the distance is less than 0, we need to add on the radius to the 0. Let's say the equation produced –2, which means the center of the sphere is the distance of 2 behind the plane. Well, what if the radius was 5? The sphere is still inside, so we would say if(-2 < -5), we are outside. In that case, it's false, so we are inside of the frustum by a distance of 3. The sphere is defined by its center point (x, y, z) and it's radius.

```
bool CFrustum::SphereInFrustum( float x, float y, float z, float radius )
{
    // Go through all the sides of the frustum
    for(int i = 0; i < 6; i++ )
    {
        // If the sphere's center is farther away from
        // the plane than the size of the radius
        if( m_Frustum[i][A] * x + m_Frustum[i][B] * y +
            m_Frustum[i][C] * z + m_Frustum[i][D] <= -radius )
        {
            // The distance was greater than the radius
            // so the sphere is outside of the frustum
            return false;
        }
    }


    // The sphere was inside of the frustum!
    return true;
}
```

Testing a cube against the frustum is a bit more work, but it's not too much more complicated. Basically, what is going on is that we are given the center of the cube and half the length. Think of it like a radius. Next we check each point of the cube and see if it is inside the frustum. If a point is found in front of a side, we skip to the next side. If we get to a plane that does *not* have a point in front of it, it will return false.

Note that this will sometimes say that a cube is inside the frustum when it isn't. This happens when all the corners of the cube are not behind any one plane. This is rare and shouldn't affect the overall rendering speed. To make this completely accurate, you would have to test the eight corners of the frustum against the six planes that make up the sides of the bounding box. If the bounding box is axis aligned, you can forget the box's planes and perform simple greater-than or less-than tests for each corner of the frustum. Since our octree cubes are axis aligned, this would be a good place for some optimization. The cube being passed in is defined with the center point being (x, y, z) and half of its width as the size.

```cpp
bool CFrustum::CubeInFrustum( float x, float y, float z, float size )
{
    // Go through the frustum planes and make sure that at
    // least 1 point is in front of each plane
    for(int i = 0; i < 6; i++ )
    {
        if(m_Frustum[i][A] * (x - size) + m_Frustum[i][B] * (y - size) +
            m_Frustum[i][C] * (z - size) + m_Frustum[i][D] > 0)
            continue;
        if(m_Frustum[i][A] * (x + size) + m_Frustum[i][B] * (y - size) +
            m_Frustum[i][C] * (z - size) + m_Frustum[i][D] > 0)
            continue;
        if(m_Frustum[i][A] * (x - size) + m_Frustum[i][B] * (y + size) +
            m_Frustum[i][C] * (z - size) + m_Frustum[i][D] > 0)
            continue;
        if(m_Frustum[i][A] * (x + size) + m_Frustum[i][B] * (y + size) +
            m_Frustum[i][C] * (z - size) + m_Frustum[i][D] > 0)
            continue;
        if(m_Frustum[i][A] * (x - size) + m_Frustum[i][B] * (y - size) +
            m_Frustum[i][C] * (z + size) + m_Frustum[i][D] > 0)
            continue;
        if(m_Frustum[i][A] * (x + size) + m_Frustum[i][B] * (y - size) +
            m_Frustum[i][C] * (z + size) + m_Frustum[i][D] > 0)
            continue;
        if(m_Frustum[i][A] * (x - size) + m_Frustum[i][B] * (y + size) +
            m_Frustum[i][C] * (z + size) + m_Frustum[i][D] > 0)
            continue;
```

```
    if(m_Frustum[i][A] * (x + size) + m_Frustum[i][B] * (y + size) +
        m_Frustum[i][C] * (z + size) + m_Frustum[i][D] > 0)
            continue;

    // If we get here, there was no point in the cube that was in
    // front of this plane, so the whole cube is behind this plane
    return false;
    }

    // By getting here it states that the cube is inside of the frustum
    return true;
}
```

This completes the frustum class. Though we won't be using the point and sphere tests, it doesn't hurt to include them for a greater understanding of frustum culling. The next step is to incorporate the frustum culling with our octree.

Adding Frustum Culling to Our Octree

To add frustum culling to our octree, we need to jump back to Octree.cpp and center our attention around the DrawOctree() function. We left the code like this:

```
void COctree::DrawOctree(COctree *pNode)
{
    // Make sure a valid node was passed in; otherwise go back to the last node
    if(!pNode) return;
    // Check if this node is subdivided. If so, then we
    // need to recurse and draw it's nodes
    if(pNode->IsSubDivided())
    {
        // Subdivide farther down the octree
        ...
    }
    else
    {
        // Render the end node
        ...
    }
}
```

Without frustum culling, the octree was drawing every single end node. Let's fix this problem.

```
void COctree::DrawOctree(COctree *pNode)
{
    // Make sure a valid node was passed in; otherwise go back to the last node
    if(!pNode) return;
    // Make sure its dimensions are within our frustum
    if(!g_Frustum.CubeInFrustum(pNode->m_vCenter.x, pNode->m_vCenter.y,
                                pNode->m_vCenter.z, pNode->m_Width / 2))
    {
        return;
    }
    // If this node is subdivided, then we need to recurse and draw its nodes
    if(pNode->IsSubDivided())
    {
        // Subdivide farther down the octree
        ...
    }
    else
    {
        // Render the end node
        ...
    }
}
```

With a simple addition to our code, the effects are exponentially positive. The code just implemented assures us that an end node's vertices will only be drawn when its cube's dimensions lie partially or fully inside the planes of our frustum. A global instance of the CFrustum class, g_Frustum, is created in our Main.cpp to allow the octree to access the current frustum information. Calling our CubeInFrustum() function, we pass in the end node's center (x, y, z), along with half of its width. This width is then used in conjunction with the center point to find the cube's eight points.

Assuming our test returned a true, the end node's assigned vertices would be passed into OpenGL to be rendered. Remember that this will only work if the frustum has been calculated prior to this test. If we move our attention to Main.cpp, we can see where this is being done. Instead of calculating the frustum only when the camera moves, I ignore this optimization and throw it in the main RenderScene() function. All it takes is a simple call to CalculateFrustum() from our global g_Frustum variable. It's important to note that this must be done after we position the camera. In this case, the frustum is calculated after `gluLookAt()`, which is used to manipulate the model view matrix (camera orientation matrix).

```
void RenderScene()
{
    // Clear The Screen And The Depth Buffer
    // and initialize the model view matrix
    glClear(GL_COLOR_BUFFER_BIT | GL_DEPTH_BUFFER_BIT);
    glLoadIdentity();

    // Position our camera's orientation
    gluLookAt(g_Camera.m_vPosition.x,
              g_Camera.m_vPosition.y, g_Camera.m_vPosition.z,
              g_Camera.m_vView.x, g_Camera.m_vView.y, g_Camera.m_vView.z,
              g_Camera.m_vUpVector.x,
              g_Camera.m_vUpVector.y, g_Camera.m_vUpVector.z);

    // Each frame we calculate the new frustum. Really, you
    // only need to calculate the it when the camera moves
    g_Frustum.CalculateFrustum();
```

After the frustum is calculated for the current camera orientation, we are free to check geometry against it. This is exactly what will need to happen when drawing our octree. In the following, a global instance of the `COctree` class makes a call to `DrawOctree()`. Due to the recursive nature of the function, it passes an address to the global octree object as the root node, which will be the first node checked to see if there is a collision. Lastly, the debug lines are drawn to visualize the octree nodes, and then the back buffer is flipped to the foreground to update the screen.

```
    // Draw the octree, starting with the root node and recursing down.
    // When we get to the end nodes we will draw the vertices assigned to them.
    g_Octree.DrawOctree(&g_Octree);

    // Render the cubed nodes to visualize the octree (in wire frame mode)
    g_Debug.RenderDebugLines();

    // Swap the back buffers to the foreground with our global hDC
    SwapBuffers(g_hDC);
    ...
}
```

When discussing the DrawOctree() code earlier in the chapter, it was mentioned that the octree obviously must be created before attempting to draw it, but where does this happen? At the top of Main.cpp, our Init() function is defined. This is defined as follows:

```
void Init(HWND hWnd)
{
    // Initialize OpenGL
    ...

    // This loads the vertices for the terrain
    LoadVertices();
```

Before the octree is created, it is essential to find the bounding box of the scene. The bounding box will actually be a cube dimension, described by its width. This way, we just store a cube width for each node. A list of vertices and the vertex count need to be passed in to determine the surrounding cube, which is set in LoadVertices(). In our case, the terrain vertices (g_pVertices) and vertex count (g_NumberOfVerts) are simply stored in a global variable that is initialized from LoadVertices(). Ideally, this information would come from the scene object that holds the loaded world/level.

Most likely, you will want to just pass in the scene object for CreateNode() and GetSceneDimensions() instead of vertices. Following the calculation of the scene's dimension, we can then create the octree by using our CreateNode() function. Through recursion, this will prepare our octree to be drawn. Notice that we pass in the center and width of the root node. This center and width will be the starting point to then subdivide from.

```
    // Calculate the surrounding cube width from the center of our scene
    g_Octree.GetSceneDimensions(g_pVertices, g_NumberOfVerts);

    // Here we pass in the information to create the root node. This will then
    // recursively subdivide the root node into the rest of the nodes.
    g_Octree.CreateNode(g_pVertices, g_NumberOfVerts, g_Octree.GetCenter(),
    g_Octree.GetWidth());

    ...
}
```

When creating your own octree class according to your data structures that are being used for the scene, here are more appropriate function parameters for CreateNode():

```
void CreateNode(COctree *pCurrentNode, CModel *pModel);
```

This way, you just need to pass in the current node that is being subdivided, along with the scene or model object. Once again, I would like to reiterate that this octree class was created to help understand the concept of an octree. A more useful class will need to be tailored to the data structures you are working with. No complex scene stores just vertices. There are UV coordinates, texture maps, normals, and a bit more data that needs to be subdivided along with the vertices. Once again, storing just face vertices will eliminate the need to cut up the model's data and will make it easy for rendering the octree with vertex arrays.

Summary and Review

Well, this pretty much covers the octree code. Let's briefly review everything that has been discussed. We learned that an octree is used to divide a world/level/scene into sections. The reason we do this is to have a way to draw only what is necessary. It allows us to check these sections against our frustum. We also learned that a frustum is a region in space that represents what our camera can see.

A frustum has six sides that are created from our field of view, sliced by our perspective near and far planes. This usually is graphically displayed as a tapered box. These six planes can be calculated by multiplying our projection and model view matrices and then multiplying this resultant matrix by OpenGL's clipping coordinate planes. Each node in the octree will have a cube width and center point to pass into our CubeInFrustum() function. This will determine whether that node is indeed inside of our frustum and has data that needs to be drawn. Remember that the frustum needs to be calculated at least every time the camera moves; otherwise, the frustum culling won't work correctly.

The octree is created by first finding out the initial scene's dimensions and then calling CreateNode() to recursively subdivide the polygon data from the starting center and width of the root node. There are a few options to choose from when sectioning off the data to different nodes. The first option is to check whether any of the vertices in a triangle reside in the node being tested; if so, pass a copy of that polygon's data to store in that node or the node's children. A second approach is not to simply copy the polygon's data to be stored in that node, but to split that polygon across the node's planes and then possibly triangulate the new pieces. The third choice is to only store face indices in the end nodes, which index into the original model's face array. This seems to be the easiest technique to manage the octree, yet each method has its benefits and drawbacks. It is up to you to choose which one works best for you.

When subdividing our world, we need to know when to stop. This can be controlled with a constant number of max polygons that can be stored in each end node. For instance, if we chose to have a maximum of 1,000 polygons in each end node, the nodes would then continue to be subdivided as long as there were more than 1,000 in that node. Once the current node contained less than or equal to 1,000 polygons, it would then become an end node, and no more subdivision would take place for that child.

To draw the octree with frustum culling, we simply start with the root node as the current node. First we check to see if the current node's cube dimensions intersect our frustum. If the node is in our camera's view, we check to see if it has any children. If they exist, the node's children are also checked against the frustum; otherwise, it must be an end node, which stores the polygon data to be drawn. This data can either be actual polygonal information or indices into the original scene object's face arrays.

Cleaning up the octree is quite simple. If a deinitialization function is created to go through each of the node's children and free them, it can be called in the node's deconstructor. This in effect handles the recursive memory deallocation for us.

Where to Go from Here

An octree isn't just for rendering; it can be used for collision detection as well. Since collision detection varies from game to game, you will want to pick your own algorithm for checking whether your character or object collided with the world. A sample method might be to create a function that allows you to pass in a 3-D point with a sphere radius into your octree. This function would return the vertices that are found around that point with the given radius. The point you would pass in could be the center point of your character or object. Once you get the vertices that are in that area of your character or object, you can do your more intense collision calculations.

Octrees don't have to be just for collision in large worlds; they can be quite useful when testing collision against high poly objects that don't conform nicely to a bounding box or sphere. Suppose you are creating a game in outer space that includes high poly spaceships. When you shoot a missile at the ship, you can minimize the polygons tested against the missile by assigning an octree to the ship. Of course, for optimum speed, the missile and ship would test their surrounding spheres until there was a collision between the two spheres, at which time the octree would come into play to get greater precision.

Though space partitioning is vital knowledge when it comes to real-time rendering, it is hard to find much information on it besides the famous BSP tree technique. With first-person shooters being quite popular, the BSP tree method seems to be the most prevalent technique discussed.

If you want to see if you grasp the concept of creating an octree, try making a simple application that allows you to load a scene with texture information from any popular 3-D file format and then subdivide it. It should be obvious that you would not use function calls such as glVertex3f() to render the data but should pass the data through vertex arrays and displays lists. This will increase your rendering speed drastically as your worlds get bigger.

Conclusion

Hopefully, this chapter has been effective in explaining the concepts and benefits of space partitioning with octrees. Although the theory and implementation of an octree are somewhat straightforward, it helps to have a reference to test your own assumptions as to how it can be done. On a side note, I would like to thank Mark Morley and Paul Martz for their help with the frustum culling.

In addition to my day job as a game programmer, I also am the co-Web host of **www.GameTutorials.com**. Our site has well over 200 tutorials that teach C or C++ from the ground up, all the way to advanced 3-D concepts. You can even find a few tutorials on octrees there as well. The last octree tutorial demonstrates loading a world from a .3ds file and partitioning it. This code was too huge to fit into this chapter, but it is still a great example of a real-world implementation. When you visit the site, it will be little wonder why it gets around a million hits a month.

Serialization Using XML Property Bags

Mason McCuskey, Spin Studios, www.spin-studios.com

Introduction

After spending last year writing about game programming instead of *doing* game programming, I decided it was time for me to get back to what I really love: making video games. To better facilitate that, I decided to spend some time enhancing my game engine. One of the things I wanted to do was improve the file format in which I stored sprite and animation data. The current format worked, but over time I had built up a wish list for a truly flexible and easily extendible file format. My wish list included things like the following:

- The file format must be human readable, and editable with a text editor. That way, I could quickly tweak animation speeds and such without having to rely on a custom editing program.

- The file format must be expandable. If I finish coding the base file format and then I realize that I've forgotten something, I want the capability to quickly add the missing part back in while still maintaining backwards compatibility.

- The file format must be able to contain a wide variety of data types. Animation data can consist of integers as well as color data, rectangles, x/y offsets, 3-D vectors, and so on. I want a file format that can handle all of these without trouble.

- The file format must be able to support an unlimited number of properties, organized into an unlimited number of categories and subcategories. In other words, I want something like the Windows Registry, where you can create as many folders and subfolders as you want and can store as many things as you want in each folder.

One idea that was especially interesting to me was to use an XML-like format for storing my animation data. The goals of XML are closely related to my wish list, so it made sense to capitalize on the design of the XML standard, even if I didn't follow it to the letter.

What Is XML?

XML (an acronym for eXtensible Markup Language) is quickly gaining popularity among software developers as a standard for data serialization (that is, the saving and loading of data). XML can be used in software in any industry; in this chapter, we're going to take a peek at how it can be used in game development.

XML, as its name implies, is a markup language (similar to HTML) that is capable of being extended in many different ways. A really simplistic way of thinking of an XML file is as a beefed-up INI file. An INI file stores program settings and configuration data in the form of key=value pairs organized under [section] headings. XML also stores data but in a style similar to HTML: The data is squished between <start> and </start> delimiters (see Figure 15.1).

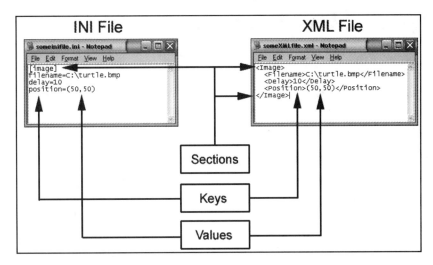

Figure 15.1

INI and XML files formats

To use XML, you need to write what is known as an XML *parser*. The job of the parser is to read an XML file (also called an XML document) and convert it to a data structure that the program can actually use. Parsers come in two main flavors: validating and nonvalidating. A *validating parser* makes sure that the given XML document is valid for the specific context at hand. Let's say you have two XML documents. One contains baseball stats; the other holds accounting data. If your accounting program has a validating parser, it knows when you try to feed it baseball stats and issues an error message. Even though the baseball stats document has the correct XML syntax, it's not the right type of data for the situation at hand. The validating parser realizes this when it reads the file, and it errors out.

Nonvalidating parsers, on the other hand, don't know or care about what the document contains. As long as the document has the correct XML syntax, a nonvalidating parser is happy. Of course, when your accounting program asks for a data element called the "year-to-date interest" and no such data element exists in the baseball file, errors will occur. The difference is that with a validating parser you can detect errors like this immediately when the document is loaded. A nonvalidating parser can't do this. It doesn't know that anything is wrong until another part of the code asks for something that does not exist.

We're going to concentrate on nonvalidating parsers, in part because they're easier to write and in part because I decided that I didn't need the strength of a full-fledged validating parser for my video games.

A Sample Data File

Here's an example of a file I wanted to use to store my animation data:

```
<AnimSeq1.00>
            <Name>Turtle (Test!)</Name>
            <Loop>Forward</Loop>
            <Defaults>
                        <Image>
                                    <ColorKey>&RGB(0,0,0)</ColorKey>
                                    <DrawOffset>&xy(0,0)</DrawOffset>
                        </Image>
                        <Delay>20</Delay>
                        </Defaults>
            <Frame>
                        <Image>
                                    <File>turtle_01.bmp</File>
                                    <ColorKey>&RGB(255,0,255)</ColorKey>
                        </Image>
                        <Delay>20</Delay>
            </Frame>
            <Frame>
                        <Image>
                                    <File>turtle_02.bmp</File>
                        </Image>
                        <Delay>20</Delay>
            </Frame>
</AnimSeq1.00>
```

In this file, you can see several things. The first thing you should notice is that it looks a lot like HTML. We have named tags, `<Image>`, and corresponding end tags, `</Image>`, arranged in a hierarchy. `<Name>` is a child of `<AnimSeq1.00>`, and `<Image>` is a child of `<Defaults>`. All of these elements serve to group individual pieces of data. For example, the name of the bitmap file for an image is embedded inside a `<File>` tag. Together with the `<ColorKey>` and `<DrawOffset>` tags, the `<File>` tag forms an `<Image>` element.

Another thing you should notice is that tag names can be duplicated. This data file represents an animation with two frames, so it contains two `<Frame>` elements. This will be important later on when you learn what STL structure to use for this.

A Bag Is Born

I once played a wizard in Advanced Dungeons & Dragons (AD&D), so my design was inspired by the very useful Bag of Holding that any good wizard can't be without. A Bag of Holding is a special pouch that can hold anything your wizardly heart desires (even other Bags of Holding, although one night we lost many minutes debating whether this is true). Since `CBagOfHolding` was difficult to type, I decided to name my class `CPropBag` instead. The remainder of this chapter teaches you how to implement and use `CPropBags`.

One of the first things you need to decide when implementing your bag is what data types it will store. Of course, you'll probably want it to store the basics: strings, ints, and floats. But you might also have more advanced data types such as 3-D vectors, rectangles, colors, (x,y) coordinates, and so on.

> **TIP**
>
> You're going to be using the STL throughout this article. If you're unfamiliar with it, STL is an abbreviation for Standard Template Library (STL). STL provides several data-structure classes as well as several general-purpose classes and functions. Think of it as a C++ extension to the C runtime library.

You first need to figure out how you're going to store all of these elements. After all, if you don't know how to store a single rectangle on disk, you'll be lost when it comes to storing a whole bag full of rectangles.

Programmers know that almost anything can be stored inside a string. For example, assume you have a `CRect` class that you use to store rectangles. `CRect` contains four members—m_x1, m_y1, m_x2, and m_y2—representing the four corner points of the rectangle. Given that, you could easily store a rectangle into a string by doing something like the following:

```
class CRect {
public:
  int m_x1, m_y1, m_x2, m_y2;

  string ToString() {
    stringstream stream;
    stream << "&rect(" << m_x1 << "," << m_y1 << ","
                       << m_x2 << "," << m_y2 << ")";
    return(stream.str());
  }
};
```

Here you can see how a C++ stringstream object makes short work of formatting the rectangle's elements into a string. You let the stringstream do all the dirty work and then just convert it to a string on its way out of the method. You end up with a string that looks like this:

```
&rect(50,75,125,225);
```

When you need the original rectangle back, you could just as easily parse the string and read the four original data elements:

```
class CRect {
  . . .
  bool FromString(string str) {
    vector<string> tokens;
    MakeUpperCase(str); // establishes case-insensitivity
    Tokenize(str, tokens, "(,)");
    if (tokens[0] == "&RECT") {
      m_x1 = atoi(tokens.c_str());
      m_y1 = atoi(tokens.c_str());
      m_x2 = atoi(tokens.c_str());
      m_y2 = atoi(tokens[4].c_str());
      return(true);
    }
    return(false);   // unknown format
  }
};
```

TIP

If stringstream freaks you out, there are several other alternatives you can use, including the tried and true sprintf. You should use snprintf instead of sprintf, however, so you can ensure that you never overflow your string buffer.

The heart of this `FromString` method is the `Tokenize` call. `Tokenize` splits a single string into a vector of strings based on any number of delimiters (in this case, the opening and closing parentheses and the comma). If you're curious about how the `Tokenize` function works, trace through the sample program in the debugger. It's not hard to figure out.

The point is, using that sort of code, you can reduce practically anything into a string. If you do this for all the other primitive data elements, you can reduce the complexity of the property bag a great deal. For example, you could store (x,y) values and colors like this:

```
&xy(10,20)
&rgb(200,0,100)
```

Instead of worrying about ints, floats, colors, vectors, and so on, now there are just two types of properties: single string properties and property bags (which we'll look at in a moment).

> **TIP**
>
> If you're an experienced C++ programmer, you may want to use the streaming operators, << and >>, instead of explicitly making `ToString` and `FromString` methods.

STL Multimaps

Now that you know how to make essentially anything into a string and get it back again, you're almost ready to start coding the bag class. However, you first need to decide on a data structure that will hold the bag's contents. Underneath the hood, will the bag store things in an array (STL `vector`)? How about an STL `list` or STL `deque`?

As it turns out, there is one STL data structure that's particularly well suited to our bag. That data structure is called a *hash*, or STL map. A map, as its name implies, "maps" one thing to another. For example, imagine you have a list of books (represented by a `CBook` class) and a list of authors (represented by STL strings). You could use an STL map to map the authors to their books. Similarly, we can use an STL map to associate tags with data.

STL maps come in two flavors: `std::map` and `std::multimap`. The difference between the two is that in an `std::map`, each key can be mapped to only one value. In an `std::multimap`, each key can be associated with several values (see Figure 15.2). In the author/book example, an `std::multimap` would be more appropriate. Since the same author can write more than one book, you'd want each author name to be able to map to more than one book class.

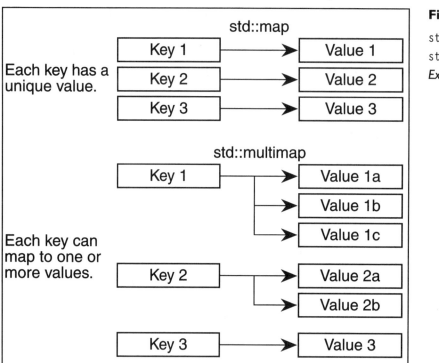

Figure 15.2

std::map *and*
std::multimap
Examples

If you look back at the sample data file, you can see that it has multiple values for one tag (in particular, `<Frame>`). To get this functionality, you'll need to use an `std::multimap`.

Implementing the Bag

You now know that the bag will use a `multimap` under the hood, and you know that you'll be mapping tags (which are strings) to the values they contain. So you know the data type for the keys in your map: strings. But what data type do you use for the values? Since you just learned that practically anything can be stored in a string, you might be tempted to use strings for the values. However, there's a more powerful way that involves polymorphism.

You can use polymorphism to cleanly store any type of property in an STL map. We know that the value of any given tag will be either a primitive element (which we can store in a string) or an entire bag. So let's make a base class and derive a couple of classes from it:

```
class CPropItem
{
public:
  . . .
};
class CPropString : public CPropItem
{
  . . .
};
class CPropBag : public CPropItem
{
  . . .
};
```

In this code, you can see that I've created a CPropItem base class and have derived from it two other classes: CPropString and CPropBag. This makes it really easy for a CPropBag to store both individual properties (CPropItem) as well as other CPropBags because, to the STL map, they look exactly the same.

Now you're ready to set up the STL map, as in the following code:

```
typedef multimap<string, CPropItem **> PropertyMap;
```

This line of code tells the compiler that a PropertyMap is an STL multimap of strings to CPropItem pointers. This means that our keys are strings, and our values are pointers to CPropItem classes.

Okay, now that you've set up the class hierarchy, it's time to think about what pure virtual functions are common to both CPropBag and CPropString. In other words, what do both CPropBag and CPropString do but do differently?

For starters, they can both save themselves to a string. This is easier for CPropString than for CPropBag. So you can make a Save function:

```
virtual string Save(int indentlevel=0) const = 0;
```

You'll learn about this function later. For now, it's enough to know that both CPropString and CPropBag have it. This means that saving an entire bag is simple; all you need to do is loop through and call Save for each CPropItem in the bag. Polymorphism hides the fact that CPropString and CPropBag save differently.

While you're at it, go ahead and add a couple of equality operators, too. Equality operators will be useful to programs that use CPropBag, and unfortunately, you can't rely on the default equality operators provided by the compiler because the

> ## CAUTION
>
> You must use pointers when storing several different derived classes in an STL map (and really, in any STL data structure). If we used CPropItems instead of CPropItem pointers, every object we put inside the map would be "sliced" down into a CPropItem object. We wouldn't be able to tell which things in the map were CPropStrings and which were CPropBags. Everything would be a CPropItem.
>
> With pointers, however, we can use runtime type identification (RTTI) to determine whether a given CPropItem pointer is really a CPropString or a CPropBag:
>
> ```
> CPropItem **data = /** something, we dunno. **/;
> CPropBag **bag = dynamic_cast<CPropBag **>(data);
> CPropString **str = dynamic_cast<CPropString **>(data);
> if (NULL != bag) { /** it's a bag! **/ }
> if (NULL != str) { /** it's a string! **/ }
> ```
>
> In the preceding code, the one thing that makes it all happen is the dynamic_cast. Dynamic casting is a new C++ way of casting. Instead of brute forcing the cast (using something like bag = (CPropBag **)data), dynamic casting says, "Hey, Mr. Compiler, if this object is really a pointer to a bag, then cast it; otherwise, put **NULL** in my pointer." In the preceding code, if data really is a bag, the compiler will set the bag pointer equal to the data pointer. If data isn't a bag, the compiler will set bag equal to **NULL**.
>
> You can't do this unless you have a CPropItem pointer to begin with, so remember that whenever you want to store several different kinds of objects (all derived from a common base) in an **STL** container, you must use pointers to ensure that the objects don't get sliced on their way in.

compiler will just compare raw memory, and raw memory will always be different because your pointers will always point to different things. Here are the pure virtual equality operators:

```
virtual bool operator==(const CPropItem &r) = 0;
bool operator!=(const CPropItem &r) { return(!((*.this) == r)); }
```

As you can see, writing an inequality operator is easy—just call the equality operator and negate the result. However, the equality operator is a little more complex, so you'll learn the specifics of that later. For now, just realize that it's there.

Adding Data Elements

Now that you know how the classes are organized, I'll bet you're anxious to start adding elements. To do that, you need some new CPropBag methods:

```
class CPropBag : public CPropItem
{
public:
  /** other stuff snipped! **/
  void Add(string key, string data, bool convert = true);
  void Add(string key, int data);
  void Add(string key, float data);
  void Add(string key, CRGB data);
  void Add(string key, CRect data);
  void Add(string key, CXY data);
  void Add(string key, CPropBag &data);
};
```

CPropBag now contains overloaded functions for all the different data types you can add. In practice, there are many more than just these, but these will serve to show you the overall pattern.

You'll learn how to add strings first because they're the easiest:

```
void CPropBag::Add(string key, string data, bool convert)
{
  CPropString **newprop = new CPropString(data, convert);
  newprop->SetName(key);
  m_Data.insert(make_pair(key, newprop));
}
```

This is fairly easy. The code takes a tag name (key) and a value for that tag (data) and puts it in the map. It does this by making a new CPropString out of the given data string, telling that CPropString its name, and then adding it to our STL multimap.

If you haven't used STL maps before, you may not have encountered the make_pair function. The make_pair function is part of STL, and it simply takes any two things and returns an object that contains both of them. STL maps, contrary to what you might expect, don't store separate key and value lists. Instead, they package both keys and values together into one object and then store a list of those objects (see Figure 15.3).

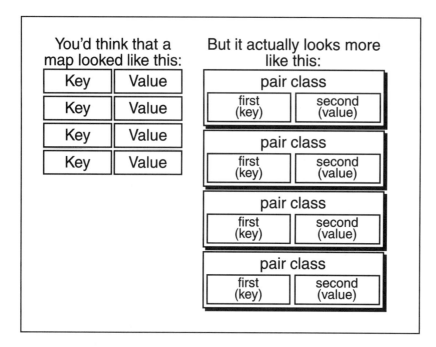

You'd think that a map looked like this:

Key	Value
Key	Value
Key	Value
Key	Value

But it actually looks more like this:

pair class

| first (key) | second (value) |

pair class

| first (key) | second (value) |

pair class

| first (key) | second (value) |

pair class

| first (key) | second (value) |

Figure 15.3

A view into an STL map

Translating Special Characters

The only thing that does any work here is the constructor of `CPropString`. Before you learn about it, however, you should know that there's one caveat to adding data elements—you need to translate special characters. You are using three special characters: the ampersand (&) character, which you use to denote the start of a specific data type (as in `&rgb` or `&rect`), and the left and right chevrons (< and >, also known as the greater than and less than signs), which you use to denote the beginning and end of key names.

Because these three characters mean specific things, you can't have them floating around inside your data. For example, consider the following lines:

```
<math>7 & 8 are > 6</math>
<playername>Joe Hac|<er</playername>
```

Both of these keys are attached to data that contains your special characters. It wouldn't be good if the game crashed on Joe because your property file loader accidentally interpreted his cool hacker "K" as the beginning of another key.

So you need to somehow deal with special characters. For example, you could use the HTML standard &amp in place of an ampersand character and the &lt and &gt strings in place of the chevrons:

```
<math>7 &amp 8 are &gt 6</math>
<playername>Joe Hac|&lter</playername>
```

Using these codes, you've ensured that < and > will never appear in raw data and that, whenever an & appears, it will be followed either by "amp" (to denote itself) or by some other characters that identify a data type (like &rgb or &rect). Of course, this only works if your code remembers to convert to and from these codes correctly.

Now that you have a plan of attack, here's the CPropString constructor:

```
class CPropString {
  /** other stuff left out **/
  CPropString(string data, bool convert = true) {
    SetData(data, convert);
  }
  void SetData(string d, bool convert) {
    if (convert) MakeStringSafeForPropBag(d);
    m_Data = d;
    m_Converted = convert;
  }
};
```

The real work here is accomplished by SetData, which is called by the constructor. Notice that there's a boolean parameter, convert. This parameter tells SetData whether or not it should convert the <, >, and & characters to their respective codes. You need this because some methods of CPropBag need to manipulate the strings of their bag, and if conversion were always on, these methods would be needlessly complex. By having a boolean (with a default true value), you help yourself use the CPropString class correctly while still maintaining flexibility for special situations.

The only thing interesting about the code for SetData itself is the MakeStringSafeForPropBag method. (Hey, laugh at the long name if you want, but realize also that you already know exactly what the method does!)

Here are the details of MakeStringSafeForPropBag:

```
void CPropString::MakeStringSafeForPropBag(string &str)
{
```

```
// replace all &'s with &amp;
Replace(str, string("&"), string("&amp;"));
// replace all <'s with &lt;
Replace(str, string("<"), string("&lt;"));
// replace all >'s with &gt's
Replace(str, string(">"), string("&gt;"));
}
```

This code relies heavily on a function called `Replace`. Since STL doesn't provide a very good string-replacement function, I had to augment it by writing my own `Replace` function, which you can find inside `PrimitiveDataElements.cpp`. I'm not going to talk about `Replace` here except to say that it looks through the first parameter (which is a reference) and replaces all instances of the second parameter with the third parameter. The `MakeStringSafeForPropBag` method is using it to convert <, >, and & into their respective codes.

Of course, you also need the other function—the one that converts the codes back into characters. Here it is:

```
void CPropString::RestoreOrigFromSafeString(string &str)
{
  // replace all &amp; with &
  Replace(str, string("&amp;"), string("&"));
  // replace all &lt; with <
  Replace(str, string("&lt;"), string("<"));
  // replace all &gt; with >
  Replace(str, string("&gt;"), string(">"));
}
```

Nothing special is going on here. This code is just doing the opposite of what `MakeStringSafeForPropBag` did. Using these methods, you're able to ensure that special characters are handled correctly.

TIP

You could make your bag more robust by enhancing the `MakeStringSafeForPropBag` **and** `RestoreOrigFromSafeString` **methods so that they dealt with non-ASCII characters (perhaps by converting them to their hex-code equivalents). This would allow your bag to store binary data, which might be cool for storing encrypted passwords and whatnot inside property files.**

Adding Nonstring Elements

Whew! Now that you know how to deal with special characters, you can learn how to store other, nonstring data elements. Here's how to store an integer:

```
void CPropBag::Add(string key, int data)
{
  stringstream stream;
  stream << data;
  Add(key, stream.str());
}
```

Nothing to it! This code just streams the int into a string and then calls the Add overload for strings we just wrote.

Here's a rectangle, which is a little more complex:

```
void CPropBag::Add(string key, CRect data)
{
  CPropString **newprop = new CPropString(data.ToString(), false);
  newprop->SetName(key);
  m_Data.insert(make_pair(key, newprop));
}
```

Notice that this code is calling the rectangle's ToString method that you learned about earlier. Notice also that the code specifies false for the CPropString constructor's conversion parameter. Think about this for a moment—the string that the rectangle gives back to you looks something like &rect(10,20,50,70). If you didn't supply false to the constructor, it would take that string and convert the ampersand to &amp, giving you &amprect(10,20,50,70). This would later screw up the rectangle's FromString method because it would be looking for &rect, not &amprect. This is why you need the capability to turn off special-character conversion.

TIP

In fact, the various Add overloads are so similar that you might consider writing a template for them.

Other data types play out in essentially the same way.

Adding Bags

Adding a bag is different than adding a string element:

```
void CPropBag::Add(string key, CPropBag &data)
{
```

```
CPropBag **newbag = new CPropBag();
**newbag = data;
m_Data.insert(make_pair(key, newbag));
}
```

Here the code is relying on the bag's overloaded assignment operator (which you'll learn about in a few sections) to make a copy of the bag and then add that to its internal m_Data map. The assignment operator makes a copy of all the contents of the bag, so that one simple assignment operator could generate a lot of work.

TIP

Notice that this Add overload takes a CPropBag reference to the data instead of just a CPropBag. If the code didn't take a reference, you'd need to write a copy constructor that behaved identically to the assignment operator. The compiler would use this copy constructor to make a copy of the bag as you entered the Add method. This is wasteful. That bag copy is a temporary variable and is only going to live until you return from the method, so it doesn't make sense to copy it. Be careful—C++ programs can lose a lot of speed like this. A simple optimization is to go through your methods and make any parameter that's currently an object be a reference to an object instead. If you wanted to get really fancy, you could make them const references, which would prevent the methods from modifying the referenced objects in any way.

Getting Elements

At this point, you can add virtually anything you want to a CPropBag, but you still need to learn how to retrieve the elements you've added. It's time to take a look at CPropBag's Get overloads, starting with the string overload.

Getting Strings

The following code snippet demonstrates how to retrieve string information.

```
bool CPropBag::Get(string key, string &dest, int instance)
{
  if (m_Data.find(key) == m_Data.end()) return(false);
  PropertyMap::iterator iter = m_Data.lower_bound(key);
  for (int q=0; q < instance; q++) iter++;
```

```
  dest = iter->second->Save();
  return(true);
}
```

The parameters for the Get function are pretty much what you'd expect. There's key, also known as the stuff in between the < >'s, and dest, a reference to a string that Get puts the value into. (Remember that this is the string overload—other Gets will have different dests.) The final parameter, instance, is only useful if you have two or more keys with the same name. It tells the function which instance of the key you want.

The first thing the code does is a sanity check. If no key with the given name exists, the method returns false. If it does exist, the code moves on and grabs the first key with the given name. (That's what the lower_bound method of multimap does—look it up in the docs for more details.)

The next line moves the iterator received from the lower_bound function to the requested instance of key. Now, it would be great if you could just write the following:

```
PropertyMap::iterator iter = m_Data.lower_bound(key)+instance;
```

Unfortunately, STL multimaps don't support this because of the way they store their data internally. Instead, you can use a for loop to "bounce along" the map until you land at the instance you want. This is what's going on here.

Remember that make_pair function? It takes any two things and makes a class out of them. The class has two members: first, which is the first thing, and second, which is the second thing. In this case, first is a string (the key), and second is a pointer to a CPropItem (the value). Once the iterator lands on the requested instance of the requested key, it simply calls the Save method of second. Polymorphism takes care of the rest. If this thing that the iterator's on is a CPropString, you get that string; if it's a bag, the bag saves itself to a string and gives that to you. Cool, isn't it?

Getting Other Data Types

The other Get overloads build on the string overload you just learned about. Here's a floating point example:

```
bool CPropBag::Get(string key, float &dest, int instance)
{
  string str;
  if (!Get(key, str, instance)) return(false);
```

```
dest = atof(str.c_str());
return(true);
}
```

As you can see, all of the real work is done by the string overload of Get. The function gets the key as a string and then calls the C runtime library function atof to convert that string to a float. Nothing to it!

TIP

There are more C++ ways to convert a string to a float—for example, through stringstream—but I grew up in C, and sometimes you've just got to return to your old-school roots. Besides, adding a string stream would needlessly complicate things. All we need is one float, not several separated by whitespace!

Getting Bags

Now it's time to look at the third type of Get overload. Here's how to pull one bag out from another:

```
bool CPropBag::Get(string key, CPropBag &dest, int instance)
{
  if (m_Data.find(key) == m_Data.end()) return(false);
  PropertyMap::iterator iter = m_Data.lower_bound(key);
  for (int q=0; q < instance; q++) iter++;
  CPropBag **bag = dynamic_cast<CPropBag **>(iter->second);
  if (NULL == bag) return(false);
  dest = **bag;
  return(true);
}
```

This method's a close cousin to the string overload with one exception: the dynamic_cast that happens once the iterator points to the correct value. You've learned about a method that can convert a bag to a string (Save), but there's no method that can convert a string to a bag (or at least, I didn't see a need to write one). So we need to explicitly check that the given key really does map to a CPropBag and not a CPropString. If it does, all is well. The code makes the given reference point at that bag and returns true. If it's not a CPropBag, it returns false.

TIP

You might consider adding a method that will turn a string into a bag. This would give you the capability to eliminate a layer of tags for elements that only contain one value. This might be handy in certain situations.

Saving and Loading Bags

Of course, none of the techniques you've learned so far will do any good if you can't save and load CPropBags. Let's start with the Save function since it's the easier of the two.

Saving Bags

Here's the code that saves our bag to disk:

```
string CPropBag::Save(int indentlevel) const
{
  string out;
  string indent(indentlevel, '\t');
  for (PropertyMap::const_iterator i = m_Data.begin();
    i != m_Data.end(); i++) {
    CPropItem **data = (**i).second;
    string key = (**i).first;
    string line, dataformat;
    CPropBag **bag = dynamic_cast<CPropBag **>(data);
    line = data->Save((bag) ? indentlevel+1 : indentlevel);
    stringstream withname;
    if (bag) {
      withname << indent << "<" << key << ">" << endl
        << line << indent << "</" << key << ">" << endl;
    }
    else {
            withname << indent << "<" << key << ">" << line
        << "</" << key << ">" << endl;
    }
    out += withname.str();
  }
  return(out);
}
```

There's a bit of recursion at play here. First, the code uses the only parameter, indentlevel (which defaults to zero), and creates a string that indents by that number of tabs.

> **TIP**
>
> The STL string has a handy constructor that allows you to construct a string that's nothing but a single character. For example, the following line creates a string that contains "***************":
>
> ```
> string stars(10, '*');
> ```
>
> Impress your friends with this silly STL trick!

Next the bag begins to loop through each of the elements in its m_Data multimap. For each element, it determines whether it's a CPropBag or a CPropString. Then it calls the elements Save method. If it's a bag, the code increments the indent level on the way in.

This is where the recursion lives. If the CPropItem in question is actually a CPropBag, the code will recurse down into that bag and start the whole thing over, only with an additional level of indentation. This is powerful, and it's important that you understand how this works. If you're confused, trace through it in the debugger using a simple bag until you understand it.

Save gives back a string representation of the element. The next few lines take the element's key and the string representation and format them. If the element is a bag, it puts the key and the string representation on different lines, like this:

```
<key>
  [string representation of data]
</key>
```

If the element is a CPropString, it puts everything on one line, like this:

```
<key>[string representation of data]</key>
```

Finally, after it has done this for each of its data elements, the bag returns the finished string.

The Save function for CPropString is considerably more simple:

```
string CPropString::Save(int indentlevel)
  const { return(m_Data); }
```

Gotta love that it's a one-liner! Since the CPropString's data is already in string format, it doesn't have to do anything to Save it.

TIP

Bonus! The bag saved out its contents in alphabetical order, even though you never explicitly told it to. An STL map is a template class, and one of its template arguments specifies how to sort its contents. Sorting the contents as they are added actually makes looking up a value for a particular key wicked fast. Under the hood, the STL map is using a tree structure, and that requires a sorting function to balance the tree. The default template argument for sorting is an alphabetical sort, so the map automatically alphabetizes the key/value pairs as you add them. This is nifty, but if for some reason you want to sort a different way, you can override the template arguments when you declare the map and make it use a different built-in mechanism, or you can roll your own from scratch.

Loading Bags

Loading is more complex than saving and requires a flowchart (see Figure 15.4).

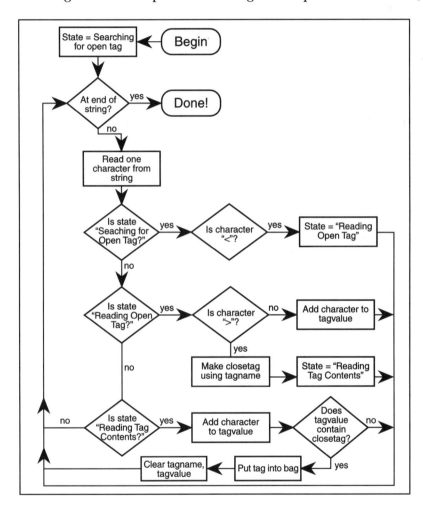

Figure 15.4

A "Loading" flowchart

Here's how the flowchart looks in code:

```
bool CPropBag::LoadFromString(string data)
{
  m_Data.clear();
  enum eElanPropBagReadState {
    SearchingForOpenTag = 0,
    ReadingOpenTag = 1,
    ReadingTagContents = 2,
```

```
    } curstate = SearchingForOpenTag;
    string tagname, tagvalue, closetag;

    for (string::iterator iter = data.begin();
          iter != data.end(); ++iter) {
      unsigned char b = **iter;
      switch(curstate) {
      case SearchingForOpenTag:
        if (b == '<') {
          // we've found our open tag!
          curstate = ReadingOpenTag;
        }
        break;
      case ReadingOpenTag:
        if (b == '>') {
          // end of tag
          curstate = ReadingTagContents;
          closetag = string("</") + tagname + string(">");
        }
        else tagname += b;
        break;
      case ReadingTagContents:
        tagvalue += b;
        if (tagvalue.find(closetag) != string::npos) {
          Replace(tagvalue, closetag, string(""));
          PutTagIntoBag(tagname, tagvalue);
          curstate = SearchingForOpenTag;
          tagname = ""; tagvalue = "";
        }
        break;
      }
    }
    return(true);
}
```

This code takes a string and converts it to a CPropBag. The Load code is based on a state machine with three states: SearchingForOpenTag, ReadingOpenTag, and ReadingTagContents. This means that as the code loops through each character of the string it was given, it can be searching for an opening tag (a <), reading a key name, or reading the data that goes with a key.

The code starts in the SearchingForOpenTag state. The only thing that the case statement for this state cares about is whether the current character is a <. If it is, the code moves to the ReadingOpenTag state. If not, it does nothing, and the character is discarded. This lets you put as much whitespace between tags as you need.

Once it gets to the ReadingOpenTag state, the code starts paying attention to the characters, adding each character to a tagname variable. If it finds a >, it knows that the opening tag is over. It also knows what the closing tag will look like because the closing tag is always in the form </opentag>. Finally, it moves to the ReadingTagContents state. The opening tag is complete; now it's time to start reading the data.

The ReadingTagContents state just puts each character into another variable, tagvalue. It does this until the entire close tag gets put in tagvalue. If it finds the closing tag in tagvalue, it's time for the real work to start. It now knows both the key (tagname) and its associated value (tagvalue), so it can add that element to the m_Data multimap. The PutTagIntoBag function accomplishes this. Once it does, the code clears out the tagname and tagvalue variables and goes back to the SearchingForOpenTag state. This continues until the entire string is parsed.

The only remaining piece to this puzzle is the PutTagIntoBag method. Here's how it looks:

```
bool CPropBag::PutTagIntoBag(string tagname, string tagvalue)
{
  // a < and > mean it's a bag within a bag
  if (tagvalue.find("<") != string::npos &&
      tagvalue.find(">") != string::npos) {
    // it's a bag.
    CPropBag **newbag = new CPropBag;
    newbag->LoadFromString(tagvalue);
    m_Data.insert(make_pair(tagname, newbag));
  }
  else {
    // it's a primitive data type.
    CPropString **newstr = new CPropString(tagvalue, false);
    newstr->SetName(tagname);
    m_Data.insert(make_pair(tagname, newstr));
  }
  return(true);
}
```

This code gets a `tagname` and a `tagvalue`—the key and value for the new data element. The first thing it does is determine whether the `tagvalue` is another bag. If there are any < or > characters in the `tagvalue`, the code knows it's a bag. (Remember that any < or > in the actual data should be converted to their &gt or &lt codes.) If the code finds < or >, the recursion happens: The code calls the `LoadFromString` method of a newly created `CPropBag`, and the whole thing starts all over for the data inside `tagvalue`.

If there are no < or > characters, the code knows it's not a bag, and things are easier. It creates a new `CPropString` from the `tagvalue` and inserts it into the `m_Data` multimap. Notice that, again, we turn off the special character conversion because we don't want any &gt, &lt, or &amp codes that already exist in `tagvalue` to get turned into &ampgt, &amplt, or &ampamp.

Other Operations

Now that you have the basics mastered, you can round out your property bag with a few useful, although not unconditionally needed, methods. In this section, you'll learn how to compare bags, merge them, and copy them.

Testing for Equality

Testing for equality is fairly easy, but like most other bag operations, it involves a bit of recursion. Recall that when you wrote the class declarations for `CPropItem`, `CPropString`, and `CPropBag`, you declared a virtual `operator==` method. Now you'll learn how to implement that method, starting with the implementation for `CPropString`:

```
class CPropString : public CPropItem
{
  /** other stuff omitted **/
  bool operator==(const CPropItem &r) {
    try {
      const CPropString &rStr = dynamic_cast<const CPropString &>(r);
      return(m_Data == rStr.m_Data);
    } catch(...) { return(false); }
  }
};
```

That's fairly painless. At the core, all you do is compare the data members of the two `CPropStrings`. However, the whole thing is wrapped by a try/catch handler. This is because of `dynamic_cast`. Recall that `dynamic_cast` sets your pointer to NULL if it isn't of the type to which you're casting. This works for pointers, but in C++, you can't have a reference that points to NULL. So, instead of setting your reference to NULL, `dynamic_cast` throws an exception. We need to catch that exception because it can crash the system if it goes uncaught. Here, if the code catches an exception, it can infer that r, the thing to which it's comparing itself, isn't a `CPropString`, so it returns false.

Now take a peek at `CPropBag`'s equality operator:

```
class CPropBag : public CPropItem
{
  /** other stuff omitted **/

  bool operator==(const CPropBag &r);
  bool operator==(const CPropItem &r) {
    try {
      const CPropBag &rBag = dynamic_cast<const CPropBag &>(r);
      return((**this) == rBag);
    } catch(...) { return(false); }
  }
};
```

As you can see, there are two equality operators: one that compares the bag to a `CPropItem` and one that compares the bag to another `CPropBag`. The `CPropItem` overload is virtually identical to the `CPropString` equality operator, except that it `dynamic_casts` to a `CPropBag` instead of a `CPropString`. Here's the other overload:

```
bool CPropBag::operator==(const CPropBag &r)
{
  if (r.m_Data.size() != m_Data.size()) return(false); // that was easy
  PropertyMap::const_iterator riter = r.m_Data.begin();
  PropertyMap::const_iterator liter = m_Data.begin();
  for (; riter != r.m_Data.end() && liter != m_Data.end();
        ++riter, ++liter) {
        if ( (liter->first) !=   (riter->first))  return(false);
        if (**(liter->second) != **(riter->second)) return(false);
  }
  return(true);
}
```

This starts easy. The code says, "If my multimap isn't the same size as his multimap, we're obviously different," and returns false. From there, it gets more complex. The code needs to loop and compare each element in its multimap against the element at that same position in the other bag's multimap. Since the two multimaps have the same alphabetical sort mechanism, this is safe. The instant it finds two elements whose keys or values don't equal each other, it returns false. If it makes it all the way through its contents, it knows that it's equal to the other guy and returns true. Notice that this code uses the CPropString equality operator you just learned.

> **TIP**
>
> Notice the use of const_interator in the operator== method. Since the code has been handed a reference to a const CPropBag, it can't use a normal iterator because doing so might break the "constness" of the parameter (because standard iterators allow you to read as well as change the data to which they point). The const_iterator, on the other hand, provides read-only access, so you can use it on const objects.

An Assignment Operator and a Copy Constructor

Pun alert: Another useful thing to have in our bag of tricks is the capability to copy a bag—that is, to be able to assign one bag to another by overloading the equals operator:

```
CPropBag emptybag;
CPropBag fullbag;
// add some stuff...
fullbag.Add("item1", "data1");
fullbag.Add("item2", "data3");
fullbag.Add("item3", "data3");
// make empty bag full!
emptybag = fullbag;
```

By default, C++ will provide you with an equals operator for every class you create. The "default" assignment operator simply treats your class as a struct and copies the memory:

```
// the C++ operator= does this.  Not good!
memcpy(&emptybag, &fullbag, sizeof(CPropBag));
```

On the surface this may look fine, but it's not. Because the bag class contains pointers to other things, you can't simply copy the pointer values. All of a sudden two bags would point to the same thing, and when one bag deleted the memory to which the pointer pointed, the other bag's pointer would become invalid. In effect, the first bag would have pulled the rug out from under the second bag, and the second bag would not access any data when it tried to do anything with the pointer because it would be trying to access memory that had already been freed.

So you need to write code for what's known as a *deep copy*. Instead of just copying memory "on the surface," a deep copy makes a copy of everything that a class contains.

It might also be useful to give your CPropBags a copy constructor. Here's how to kill both those requirements with one method:

```
class CPropBag : public CPropItem
{
  /** other stuff omitted **/
public:
  CPropBag(const CPropBag &r) { Init(); Copy(r); }
  CPropBag &operator=(const CPropBag &r) { Copy(r); return(**this); }
private:
  // stuff that's common to all constructors goes here
  void Init() { }
  void Copy(const CPropBag &r);
};
```

This code illustrates a common C++ trick—using a common Copy method as the brains for both the copy constructor and the assignment operator. And now, here's Copy:

```
void CPropBag::Copy(const CPropBag &r)
{
  Clear(); // empty this bag
  string rsave = r.Save();
  LoadFromString(rsave);
}
```

Were you expecting more recursion? No need! Your bags already know how to save themselves to a string and how to load themselves from a string, so the easiest way to copy one bag to another is to save the old bag to a string and load that string back into the new bag. Nifty!

Merging

When I wrote the first version of my animation sequence file, I made it very simple: For every frame, I specified an image file, a color key, and a delay. When I went to use this in a real game, however, I realized pretty quickly that my animation sequence files were needlessly large. For example, I tended to use the same color key for all the frames of an animation. Why was I explicitly specifying the color key on each and every frame?

I realized that a better way would be to specify defaults for the animation frames up front and write the code so that it used those defaults unless I explicitly provided a different value. If you look back to the sample file, you can see that I have a <Defaults> section that contains the same keys as each individual <Frame>. Individual <Frame> tags only contain keys that deviate from the defaults inside the <Defaults> tag.

Implementing this in code requires a method that will merge one bag with another. Once you have that method, it's easy to merge each <Frame> tag with the <Defaults> tag and then send the merged bag off to the Image Loading Code (see Figure 15.5). For the cost of writing one method, you gain a tremendous amount of flexibility.

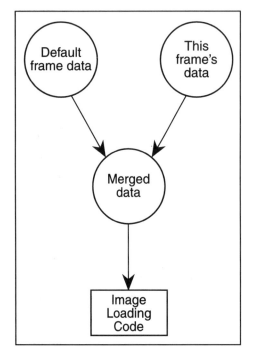

Figure 15.5

Sending data to the image loading code

The Merge method looks like this:

```
void CPropBag::Merge(const CPropBag &newstuff, bool overwrite)
{
  for (PropertyMap::const_iterator newiter = newstuff.m_Data.begin();
       newiter != newstuff.m_Data.end(); ++newiter) {
    CPropString **pStr = dynamic_cast<CPropString **>(newiter->second);
    CPropBag **pBag = dynamic_cast<CPropBag **>(newiter->second);
    if (pStr) {
      // if it doesn't already exist here, or if overwrite is set,
      if (m_Data.find(newiter->first) != m_Data.end() || overwrite) {
        // add it to this bag
        Remove(newiter->first);
        Add(newiter->first, pStr->GetData(), false);
      }
    }
    if (pBag) {
      // if it doesn't exist, just add the bag (easy!)
```

Table 15.1   Merge Method Logic

Old Element	New Element	Overwrite	Action
string	string	T	Replace old string with new string
string	string	F	Do nothing
string	bag	T	Remove the old string, put in the new bag
string	bag	F	Do nothing
bag	string	T	Remove the old bag, put in the new string
bag	string	F	Do nothing
bag	bag	T	Recurse
bag	bag	F	Recurse

```
      PropertyMap::iterator origbagiter = m_Data.find(newiter->first);
      if (origbagiter == m_Data.end()) Add(newiter->first, **pBag);
      else {
        // it exists, so we need to recurse into the subbag
        CPropBag **origbag =
          dynamic_cast<CPropBag **>(origbagiter->second);
        if (origbag) origbag->Merge(**pBag, overwrite);
        else {
          // it's a string, and we have a bag...
          // if we should overwrite, do so.
          if (overwrite) {
            Remove(newiter->first);
            Add(newiter->first, **pBag);
          } // if
        } // else (!origbag)
      } // else (origbagiter != m_Data.end())
    } // if pBag
  } // for loop
}
```

This code takes as input a bag to merge in and a boolean specifying whether to overwrite any keys that may already be present. It loops on each element of the given bag newstuff and takes different action based on whether that element is a CPropString or a CPropBag (see Table 15.1).

If it's a string, it looks at the overwrite flag and determines whether it should add the string. If so, it calls Add to add the element (specifying that special codes should not be converted).

If the element is a bag, two things can happen. If the corresponding bag is not already here, Merge simply adds the new bag by calling the bag overload of Add. If, however, the bag already exists, Merge calls itself (whoo-hoo, more recursion!). You don't want to completely replace the original bag with the bag in newstuff. You want to Merge it, so you need the recursion.

Now for the final case. Let's say the original bag contains a <test> key with a string for its data. Now say that newstuff contains a <test> key that's a bag. In this situation, the code checks overwrite. If it's true, it removes the old value (in this example, the string) and puts in the new value (in this example, the bag).

Processing continues like this for each element until all elements have been merged.

Conclusion:_OK, But Is This Really XML?

You now know how to do essentially everything you need to do with property bags, but you may be asking yourself, "Self, did I just write a nonvalidating XML parser?" The answer is "yes and no" or, more precisely, "not a complete one." XML has features above and beyond what you've coded here (for example, the capability to specify a NULL element using <Keyname/>). However, what you've written should do nicely for most game-programming tasks.

If you feel you need to add the other features of XML, I encourage you to do so.

Enhancements and Exercises

The way to property bag nirvana that I've just described isn't the only way; it was simply the best way given my design constraints. Since your design constraints are undoubtedly different, I encourage you to come up with your own design to accomplish the same functionality. Here are a few things you can try:

- Use templates. Most of the Add and Get methods of CPropBag are identical except for the data type on which they operate. See if you can figure out how to use templates to eliminate the large chunks of cut-and-pasted code present in the sample program.

- Use copy-on-write. Recall that our assignment operator copies the entire contents of one bag to another and that the compiler will implicitly call our bag's copy constructor when we pass bags (not bag references) to methods. You might consider implementing a copy-on-write mechanism; instead of copying the bag contents right then and there, the assignment operator would set a flag saying, "Hey, if anything tries to modify this bag, you need to make a copy first." Copy-on-write is a great technique that professional C++ programmers use, mainly so that they can use objects, instead of references of objects, as parameters.

- Implement a derivative of `CPropBag` that doesn't allow multiple keys. It isn't that hard.

- Implement the complete XML feature set, making the property bag code a complete implementation of the XML standard.

- Last but not least, feel free to use property bags in your own games to reduce the chore of saving and loading data.

TRICK 16

INTRODUCTION TO FUZZY LOGIC

ANDRÉ LAMOTHE,
CEO@XGAMES3D.COM

Introduction

So what is fuzzy logic? Fuzzy Logic is a method of analyzing sets of data such that the elements of the sets can have partial inclusion. Most people are used to *Crisp Logic* where something is either included or it isn't in any particular set. For example, if I were to create the sets *child* and *adult,* I would fall into the adult category and my 7-year-old nephew would be part of the child category. That is crisp logic.

Fuzzy logic on the other hand, allows objects to be contained within a set even if they aren't totally in the set. For example, I might say that I am 10% part of the child set and 100 percent part of the adult set. Similarly, my nephew might be 2% included in the adult set and 100% included in the child set. These are fuzzy values. Also, you'll notice that the individual set inclusions don't have to add up to 100%. They can be greater or less since they don't represent probabilities, but rather are included in different classes. However, when we are talking about probabilities, the probability of an event or state in different classes must add to 1.0 for all the events that make up that class.

The cool thing about Fuzzy Logic is that it allows you to make decisions that are based on fuzzy, error, or noise-ridden data. These decisions are usually correct and much better than possible with crisp logic. With a crisp logic system you can't even begin to think about doing this since every function I have ever seen in C/C++ or any other language has a specific number of inputs and outputs. If you're missing a variable or input, then it won't work, but with fuzzy systems, the system can still function and function well, just like a human brain. I mean, how many decisions do you make each day that feel fuzzy to you? You don't have all the facts, but you're still fairly confident of the decision?

Well, that's the 2-cent tour of fuzzy logic and its applications to Artificial Intelligence (AI) are obvious in the areas of decision making, behavioral selections, and input/output filtering. With that in mind, let's take a look at the various ways fuzzy logic is implemented and used.

Standard Set Theory

A standard set is simply a collection of objects. To write a set, use a capital letter to represent it and then place the elements contained in the set between braces and separated by commas. Sets can consist of anything: names, numbers, colors, whatever. Figure 16.1 illustrates a number of standard sets. For example, set $A=\{3,4,5,20\}$ and set $B=\{1,3,9\}$. Now there are many operations that we can perform on these sets, as shown below:

- **Element of "∈"**: When talking about a set, you might want to know if an object is contained within the set? This is called set inclusion. Hence, if you wrote $3 \in A$, reads; "3 an element of A" that would be true, but $2 \in B$ is not.

- **Union "∪"**: This operator takes all the objects that exist in both sets and adds them into a new set. If an object appears in both sets initially, then it is only added to the new set once. Hence, $A \cup B = \{1,3,4,5,9,20\}$.

- **Intersection "∩"**: This operator takes only the objects that are in common between the two sets. Therefore, $A \cap B = \{3\}$.

- **Subset of "⊂"**: Sometimes you want to know if one set is wholly contained in another? This is called set inclusion or subset of. Therefore, $\{1,3\} \subset B$, which reads "the set $\{1,3\}$ is a subset of B. However, $A \not\subset B$, which reads "A is not a subset of B".

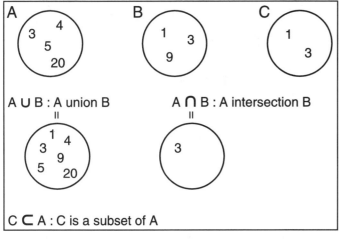

Figure 16.1

Some simple sets

Ok, that's a little set theory for you. Nothing complicated, just some terminology and symbols. Everyone works with set theory every day—they just don't know it. However, the one thing I want you to get from this section is that standard sets are exact. Either "it's a fruit or it's not," "either 5 is in the set, or it's not." This is not the case with fuzzy set theory.

TIP

Usually a slash "/" or prime " ' "symbol means "NOT" or "complement," "invert," etc.

Fuzzy Set Theory

The problem with computers is that they are exact machines and we continually use them to solve inexact or fuzzy problems—or at least try to. In the 1970s, computer scientists started applying a technique of mathematics called *Fuzzy Logic* or *Uncertainty Logic* to software programming and problem solving. Hence, the fuzzy logic that we are talking about here is really the application of fuzzy set theory and its properties. Therefore, let's take a look at the fuzzy version of everything we just learned about with standard set theory.

First, when talking about fuzzy set theory, we don't focus so much on the objects in the set any more. This means that the objects *are* in the set, but we focus on the *degree of membership* any particular object has within a certain class. For example, let's create a fuzzy class or category (see Table 16.1)called "Computer Special FX." Then, let's take a few of our favorite movies (mine at least) and estimate how much each of them is in the fuzzy class "Computer Special FX."

Table 16.1   Degree of Membership for Killer Movies

Movie	Degree of Membership in Class
Antz	100%
Forrest Gump	20%
Terminator	75%
Aliens	50%
The Matrix	90%

Do you see how fuzzy this all is? Although "The Matrix" had some really killer computer-generated FX, the entire movie "Antz" was computer-generated, so I have to be fair. However, do you agree with all these? If "Antz" is totally computer-generated and has a running time of two hours, but "Forrest Gump" has only five minutes total of mixed real life and computer-generated imagery. Hence, is it fair to rate it at 20%? I don't know. That's why we are using fuzzy logic. Anyway, we write each fuzzy degree of membership as an ordered pair of the form:

{candidate for inclusion, degree of membership}

Therefore, for our movie example we would write:

{Antz, 1.00}

{Forrest Gump, 0.20}

{Terminator, 0.75}

{Aliens, 0.50}

{The Matrix, 0.9}

Finally, if we had the fuzzy class "Rainy," what would you include "today" as? Here it is: *{today, 0.00}*—blue skies and bikinis in California!

Now, we can add a little more abstraction and create a full fuzzy set. A fuzzy set (in most cases) is an ordered collection of the *degrees of membership* (DOM) of a set of objects in a specific class. For example, in the class "Computer Special FX" we have the set composed of the degrees of membership:

A={1.0, 0.20, 0.75, 0.50, 0.90}

One entry for each movie respectively—each of the variables represents the DOM of each of the movies as listed in Table 16.1, so order counts! Now, suppose that we have another set of movies that all have their own degrees of membership as:

B={0.2, 0.45, 0.5, 0.9, 0.15}.

Now, let's apply some of our previously learned set operations and see the results. However, before we do there is one caveat—since we are talking about fuzzy sets which represent degrees of membership or fitness vectors of a set of objects, then many set operations must have the same number of objects in each set. This will become more apparent when you see what the set operators do below.

- **Fuzzy Union "∪":** The union of two fuzzy sets is the MAX of each element from the two sets. For example, with fuzzy sets:

  A={1.0, 0.20, 0.75, 0.50, 0.90}

  B={0.2, 0.45, 0.5, 0.9, 0.15}

  The resulting fuzzy set would be the max of each pair:

  $A \cup B$ = {MAX(1.0,0.2), MAX(0.20,0.45), MAX(0.75,0.5), MAX(0.90,0.15)}

  = {1.0,0.45,0.75, 0.90}

- **Fuzzy Intersection "∩":** The intersection of two fuzzy sets is just MIN of each element from the two sets. For example, with fuzzy sets:

  A={1.0, 0.20, 0.75, 0.50, 0.90}

  B={0.2, 0.45, 0.5, 0.9, 0.15}

  $A \cap B$ = {MIN(1.0,0.2), MIN(0.20,0.45), MIN(0.75,0.5), MIN(0.90,0.15)}

  = {0.2,0.20,0.5, 0.15}

Subsets and elements of fuzzy sets have less meaning than with standard sets, so I'm skipping them; however, the *complement* of a fuzzy value or set is of interest. The complement of a fuzzy variable with degree of membership x is (1–x), thus, the complement of A written A' is computed as:

A = {1.0, 0.20, 0.75, 0.50, 0.90}

Therefore,

A' = {1.0 – 1.0, 1.0 – 0.20, 1.0 – 0.75, 1.0 – 0.50, 1.0 – 0.90}

= {0.0, 0.8, 0.25, 0.5, 0.1}

I know this is killing you, but bear with me.

Fuzzy Linguistic Variables and Rules

Alrighty then! Now that you have an idea of how to refer to fuzzy variables and sets, let's take a look at how we are going to use them in game AI? Ok, the idea is that we are going to create an AI engine that uses fuzzy rules and then applies fuzzy logic to inputs and then outputs fuzzy or crisp outputs to the game object being controlled. Take a look at Figure 16.2 to see this graphically.

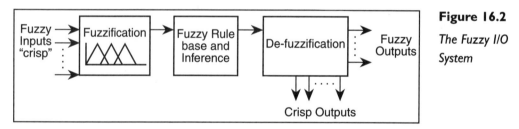

Figure 16.2

The Fuzzy I/O System

Now, when you put together normal conditional logic, you create a number of statements or a tree with propositions of the form:

```
if X AND Y then Z
```

or

```
if X OR Y then Z
```

The *(X, Y)* variables, if you recall, are called the *antecedents* and *Z* is called the *consequence*. However, with fuzzy logic, *X* and *Y* are *Fuzzy Linguistic Variables* or FLVs. Furthermore, *Z* can also be an FLV or a crisp value. The key to all this fuzzy stuff is that *X* and *Y* represent fuzzy variables and, hence, are not crisp. Fuzzy propositions of this form are called Rules and ultimately are evaluated in a number of steps. We don't evaluate them like this:

```
if EXPLOSION AND DAMAGE then RUN
```

And just do it if *EXPLOSION* is *TRUE* and *DAMAGE* is *TRUE*. Instead, with fuzzy logic the rules are only part of the final solution, the *fuzzification* and *de-fuzzification* is what gets us our final result. It's shades of truth we are interested in.

FLVs represent fuzzy concepts that have to do with a range. For example, let's say that we want to classify the distance from the player and AI object with 3 different fuzzy linguistic variables (names basically). Take a look at Figure 16.3; it's called a *Fuzzy Manifold* or surface and is composed of three different triangular regions which I have labeled as follows:

>**NEAR:**   Domain range (0 to 300)
>
>**CLOSE:**   Domain range (250 to 700)
>
>**FAR:**   Domain range (500 to 1000)

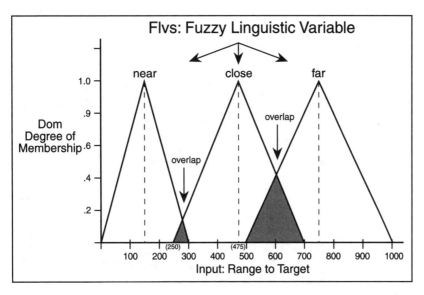

Figure 16.3

A Fuzzy Manifold composed of range FLVs

The input variable is shown on the X-axis and can range from 0 to 1000; this is called the *Domain*. The output of the fuzzy manifold is the Y-axis and ranges from 0.0 to 1.0 always. For any input value x_i (which represents range to player in this example), you compute the degree of membership (DOM) by striking a line vertically as shown in Figure 16.4 and computing the Y value(s) at the intersection(s) with each fuzzy linguistic variable's triangular area.

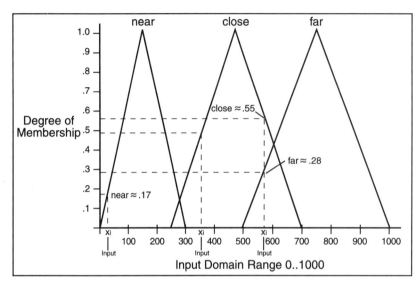

Figure 16.4

Computing the degree of membership of a domain value in one or more FLVs

Each triangle in the fuzzy surface represents the area of influence of each fuzzy linguistic variable (NEAR, CLOSE, FAR). In addition, the regions all overlap a little—usually 10–50 percent. This is because when NEAR becomes CLOSE and CLOSE becomes FAR, I don't want the value to instantly switch. There should be a little overlap to model the fuzziness of the situation. This is the idea of fuzzy logic.

So, let's recap here for a moment. We have rules that are based on fuzzy inputs from the game engine, environment, etc. These rules may look like normal conditional logic statements, but must be computed using fuzzy logic since they are really FLVs that classify the input(s) with various degrees of membership.

NOTE

You have already seen something like this kind of technique used to select states in a previous FSM example; the range to a target was checked and forces the FSM to switch states, but in the example with FSMs, we used crisp values without overlap or fuzzy computations. There was an exact range that the crisp FSM AI switches from *EVADE* to *ATTACK* or whatever, but with fuzzy logic, it's a bit blurry.

Furthermore, the final results of the fuzzy logic process may be converted into discrete crisp values such as: "fire phasers," "run," "stand still," or converted into continuous values such as a power level from 0–100. Or you might leave it fuzzy for another stage of fuzzy processing.

Fuzzy Manifolds and Membership

It's all coming together— just hang in there. All right, now we know that we are going to have a number of inputs into our fuzzy logic AI system. These inputs are going to be classified into one or more (usually more) fuzzy linguistic variables (that represent some fuzzy range). We are then going to compute the degree of membership for each input in each of the FLV's ranges. In general, at range input x_i, what is the degree of member in each fuzzy linguistic variable *NEAR*, *CLOSE*, and *FAR*?

Thus far, the fuzzy linguistic variables are areas defined by symmetrical triangles. However, you can use asymmetrical triangles, trapezoids, sigmoid functions, or whatever. Take a look at Figure 16.5 to see other possible FLV geometries. In most cases, symmetrical triangles (symmetrical about the Y-axis) work fine. You might want to use trapezoids though if you need a range in the FLV that is always 1.0. In any case, to compute the degree of membership (DOM) for any input x_i in a particular FLV, you take the input value x_i and then project a line vertically and see where it intersects the triangle (or geometry) representing the FLV on the Y-axis, and this is the DOM.

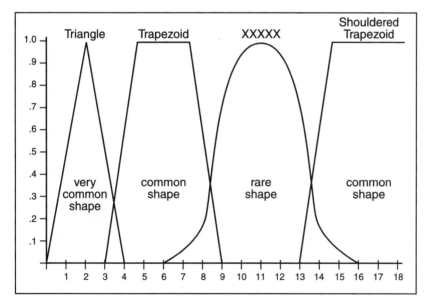

Figure 16.5

Typical fuzzy linguistic variable geometries

Computing this value in software is easy. Let's assume that we are using a triangular geometry for each FLV with the left and right starting points defining the triangle labeled *min_range, max_range* as shown in Figure 16.6. Then to compute the DOM of any given input x_i the following algorithm can be used:

```
// first test if the input is in range
if (xi >= min_range && xi <= max_range)
  {
  // compute intersection with left edge or right
  // always assume height of triangle is 1.0

  float center_point = (max_range + min_range)/2;

  // compare xi to center
  if (xi <= center_point)
    {
    // compute intersection on left edge
    // dy/dx = 1.0/(center - left)
    slope = 1.0/(center_point - min_range);

    degree_of_membership = (xi - min_range) * slope;

    } // end if
  else
    {
    // compute intersection on right edge
    // dy/dx = 1.0/(center - right)
    slope = 1.0/(center_point - max_range);

    degree_of_membership = (xi - max_range) * slope;
```

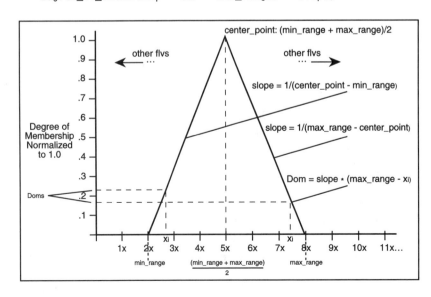

Figure 16.6

The details of computing degree of membership (DOM) for a FLV

```
  } // end else

  } // end if
else // not in range
  degree_of_membership = 0.0;
```

Of course, the function can be totally optimized, but I wanted you to see what was going on. If we had used a trapezoid instead, then there would be three possible intersection regions to compute rather than two: the left edge, the plateau, and the right edge.

In most cases, you should have at least three fuzzy linguistic variables. If you have more, try to keep the number odd so there is always one variable that is centered; otherwise, you might have a "trough" or hole in the center of the fuzzy space. In any case, let's take a look at some examples of computing the degree of membership of our previous fuzzy manifold shown in Figure 16.3. Basically, for any input x_i, you project a line vertically and determine where it intersects each of the FLVs in the fuzzy manifold; however, the line might intersect more than one FLV and this needs to be resolved, but first let's get some DOMs.

Assume that we have input ranges $x_i = \{50, 75, 250, 450, 550, 800\}$ as shown in Figure 16.7, then the degrees of membership for each FLV; NEAR, CLOSE, FAR, can be computed with the algorithm or read off graphically and are in Table 16.2.

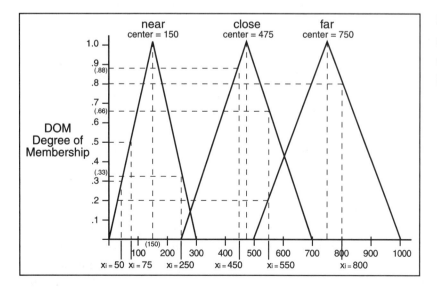

Figure 16.7

Our range manifold with a number of inputs

Table 16.2   Computations of Degree of Membership for "Range" Manifold

Input "Range to target" xi	DOMs	NEAR	CLOSE	FAR
50		0.33	0.0	0.0
75		0.5	0.0	0.0
250		0.33	0.0	0.0
450		0.0	0.88	0.0
550		0.0	0.66	0.20
800		0.0	0.0	0.80

Studying the values, there are a number of interesting properties. First, note that for any input value x_i the results of membership don't add up to 1.0. Remember, these are degrees of membership, not probabilities, so this is alright. Secondly, for some x_i's the degree of membership falls within one or two different fuzzy variables. There could have as easily been cases that an input fell into all three regions (if I made the triangles big enough). The process of selecting the size (range) of each triangle is called "tuning" and sometimes you may have to do this repeatedly to get the results you want. I tried to pick ranges that worked out nice for examples, but in real life you may need more than three FLVs and they may not have nice end points that are all multiples of 50!

> **NOTE**
>
> This step is called the fuzzification process.

As an example of creating a fuzzy manifold for some input and a number of FLVs check out FUZZY01.CPP|EXE on the CD-ROM; it allows you to create a number of fuzzy linguistic variables, that is, categories for some input domain. Then you can input numbers and it will give you the degree of membership for each input. It's a console application, so compile appropriately. Furthermore, the data printed for membership is also normalized to 1.0 each time. This is accomplished by taking each DOM and dividing by the sum of DOMs for each category.

At this point we know how to create a fuzzy manifold for an input x_i that is composed of a number of ranges that each are represented by a fuzzy linguistic variable. Then we select an input in the range and compute the degree of membership for each FLV in the manifold to come up with a set of numbers for that particular input. This is called fuzzification. Now, the real power of fuzzy logic comes into play when we fuzzify two or more variables then connect them with "if" rules and see the output. To accomplish this step in our example, we have to first come up with another input to fuzzify—let's call it the "power level" of the AI bot that we are moving around. Figure 16.8 shows the fuzzy manifold for the power level input. The fuzzy linguistic variables are:

WEAK: Domain Range (0.0 to 3.0)

NORMAL: Domain Range (2.0 to 8.0)

ENERGIZED: Domain Range (6.0 to 10.0)

Notice that this fuzzy variable domain is from 0–10.0 rather than 0–1000 as is the range to player. This is totally acceptable. In addition, I could have added more than three FLVs, say five, but three makes the problem symmetric. To process both fuzzy variables we need to construct a rule base and then create a fuzzy associative matrix. Let's talk about that next.

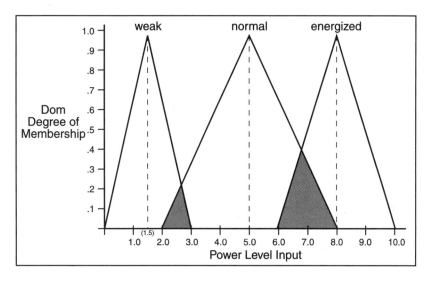

Figure 16.8

The fuzzy manifold for the power level

Fuzzy Associative Matrices

Fuzzy associative matrices or FAMs are used to "infer" a result from two or more fuzzy inputs and a given rule base and output a fuzzy or crisp value. Figure 16.9 shows this graphically. In most cases, FAMs deal with only two fuzzy variables since this can be laid out in a 2-D matrix; one variable represents each axis, and each entry in the matrix is the logical proposition of the form:

```
if Xi AND Yi then Zi
```

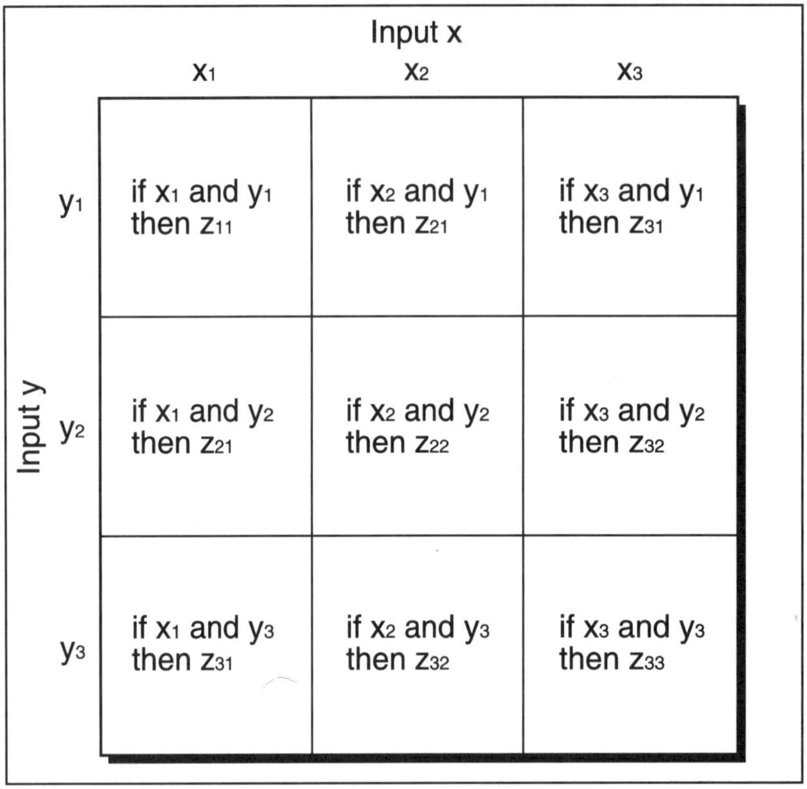

Figure 16.9

Using a fuzzy associative matrix

Or,

```
if Xi OR Yi then Zi
```

where Xi is the fuzzy linguistic variable on the X-axis, Yi is the fuzzy linguistic variable on the Y-axis, and Zi is the outcome—which may be a fuzzy variable or crisp value.

So, to build the FAM, we need to know the rules and the outputs to put in each one of the matrix entries. Hence, we need to make a rule base and decide on an output variable that is either crisp or linear. A crisp output would be:

{"ATTACK", "WANDER", "SEARCH"}

while a linear output might be a thrust level from 0 to 10. Obtaining both is relatively the same. In either case, we will have to defuzzify the output of the FAM and find the output.

We're going to cover examples of both a crisp singular output and an example that outputs a value in a range. However, much of the setup is the same. Anyway, let's do the example that computes a range as the final output first.

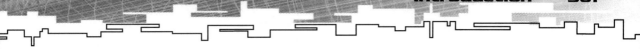
Step 1: Select your inputs and define the FLVs and build your manifolds.

The inputs to our fuzzy system are the range to the player and the power level of the AI controlled bot.

> **Input X:** Range to player.
>
> **Input Y:** Powel level of self.

Referring back to Figures 16.3 and 16.8, these are the fuzzy manifolds that we are using.

Step 2: Create a rule base for the inputs that tie them to an output.

The rule base is nothing more than a collection of logical propositions of the form *"if X AND Y then Z"* or *"if X OR Y then z."* This makes a difference when computing the FAM outputs though. A logical *AND* means "minimum of the set" while a logical *OR* means "maximum of the set" when dealing with fuzzy set theory. For now, we will use all *ANDs*, but I'll explain how to use *ORs* later.

In general, if you have two fuzzy inputs and each input has m FLVs, then the fuzzy associative matrix will have dimension mxm. And since each element represents a logical proposition this means we need 9 rules (3×3 = 9) that define all possible logical combinations and the output for each. However, this is not necessary. If you only have 4 rules, then the other outputs are just set to 0.0 in the FAM. Nevertheless, I will use up all 9 slots in our example to make it more robust. For an output I'm going to use the fuzzy output "thrust level" which I'm going to make a fuzzy variable that is made up of the following fuzzy categories (FLVs):

> **OFF:**   Domain Range (0 to 2)
>
> **ON HALF:**   Domain Range (1 to 8)
>
> **ON FULL:**   Domain Range (6 to 10)

The fuzzy manifold is shown for these FLVs in Figure 16.10. Note that the output could have more categories, but I decided to pick three.

Here are my somewhat arbitrary rules for the fuzzy manifold:

> Input 1: Distance to Player.
>
> > NEAR
> >
> > CLOSE
> >
> > FAR
>
> Input 2: Power Level of Self.

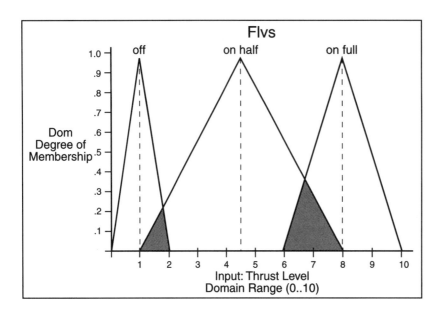

Figure 16.10

The output of fuzzy manifold for the thrust level

WEAK

NORMAL

ENERGIZED

Output: Internal navigational thrust level, i.e, speed.

OFF

ON HALF

ON FULL

Rules: These aren't necessarily functional, just examples.

```
if NEAR AND WEAK then ON HALF
if NEAR AND NORMAL then ON HALF
if NEAR AND ENERGIZED then ON FULL
if CLOSE AND WEAK then OFF
if CLOSE AND NORMAL then ON HALF
if CLOSE AND ENERGIZED then ON HALF

if FAR AND WEAK then OFF
if FAR AND NORMAL then ON FULL
if FAR AND ENERGIZED then ON FULL
```

These rules are heuristic in nature and impart knowledge from an "expert" about what he wants the AI to do in these conditions. Although they may seem somewhat contradictory, I did think about them for about two minutes, so there was actual thought put into this example! Seriously, now that we have the rules, we can finally fill the fuzzy associative matrix in completely as shown in Figure 16.11 and we are ready to rock and roll.

Input 1 : Distance to Player

Input 2 : Power Level of Self	near	close	far
weak	and on half	and off	and off
normal	and on half	and on half	and on full
energized	and on full	and on half	and on full

Figure 16.11

The FAM, complete with all the rules

Processing the FAM with the Fuzzified Inputs

To use the FAM you do the following:

Step 1: Get the crisp inputs for each fuzzy variable and fuzzify them by computing their DOM for each FLV. For example, say that we have the following inputs:

Input 1: Distance to player = 275

Input 2: Power level = 6.5

To fuzzify these, you input them into the two fuzzy manifolds and compute the degree of membership for each fuzzy variable for each input. See Figure 16.12.

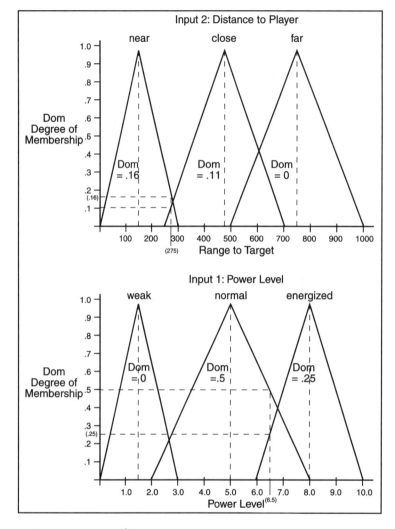

Figure 16.12

Some inputs plugged into the fuzzy variables

For Input 1 = 275, the degree of membership of each FLV is:

    NEAR: 0.16
    CLOSE: 0.11
    FAR: 0.0

For Input 2 = 6.5, the degree of membership of each FLV is:

    WEAK: 0.0
    NORMAL: 0.5
    ENERGIZED: 0.25

At this point, we refer to the fuzzy associative matrix and test the rule in each cell to see what its output value is based on the above fuzzy values. Of course, many of the FAM's cells will be 0.0 since two of the FLVs (one from each input) are 0.0. Look at Figure 16.13. It depicts our FAM, along with all the cells that have non-zero outputs shaded in. Now, here comes the tricky part.

	Input 2 = 275		
	near = .16	close = .11	far = 0
weak = 0	0 and .16 = 0 0 ∧ .16 = 0 min (0, .16) = 0 output: on half value: 0	0 and .11 = 0 0 ∧ .11 = 0 min (0, .11) = 0 output: off value: 0	0 and 0 = 0 0 ∧ 0 = 0 min (0, 0) = 0 output: off value: 0
normal = .5	.5 and .16 = .16 .5 ∧ .16 = .16 min (.5, .16) = .16 output: *on half value: .16	.5 and .11 = .11 .5 ∧ .11 = .11 min (.5, .11) = .11 output: *on half value: .11	.5 and 0 = 0 .5 ∧ 0 = 0 min (.5, 0) = 0 output: on full value: 0
energized = .25	.25 and .16 = .16 .25 ∧ .16 = .16 min (.25, .16) = .16 output: *on full value: .16	.25 and .11 = .11 .25 ∧ .11 = .11 min (.25, .11) = .11 output: *on half value: .11	.25 and 0 = 0 .25 ∧ 0 = 0 min (.25, 0) = 0 output: on full value: 0

Input 2 = 6.5 (left axis label)

* – means this rule fire s

Figure 16.13

The fuzzy associative matrix showing active cells and their values

Each one of those cells in the FAM represents a rule. For example, the upper left-hand cell represents:

```
if NEAR AND WEAK then ON HALF
```

So to evaluate this rule, we take the antecedents and test them using a *MIN()* rule for the logical *AND*. In this case, we have that *NEAR = 0.16* and *WEAK = 0.0*, hence:

```
if (0.16) AND (0.0) then on HALF
```

which is computed using the *MIN()* function as:

```
(0.16) ∧ (0.0) = (0.0)
```

Thus, the rule doesn't fire at all. On the other hand, let's take a look at the rule:

```
if CLOSE AND ENERGIZED then ON HALF
```

That really means:

```
if (0.11) AND (0.25) then ON HALF
```

Computed using the *MIN()* function is:

$$(0.11) \wedge (0.25) = (0.11)$$

Ah hah! The rule "ON HALF" fires at a level of 0.11, so we place that value in the FAM associated with the rule "ON HALF" at the intersection of *CLOSE* and *ENERGIZED*. We continue this process for the whole matrix until we have found all nine entries. This is shown in Figure 16.13.

At this point, we are finally ready to defuzzify the FAM. This can be accomplished in a number of ways. Basically, we need a final crisp value that represents the thrust level from (0.0 to 10.0). There are two main ways to compute this: We can use the disjunction or MAX() method to find the value or we can use an averaging technique based on the *"fuzzy centroid."* Let's take a look at the *MAX()* method first.

Method 1: The MAX Technique

If you look at the FAM data, basically we have the following fuzzy outputs:

OFF:	(0.0)
ON HALF:	{0.16, 0.11, 0.16}, use sum which is 0.43
ON FULL:	(0.16)

Note that the rule ON HALF has fired within three different outputs; thus, we have to make a decision what we want to do with the results. Should we add them, average them, or max them? It's really up to you. For this example, let's take sum: 0.16 + 0.11 + 0.16 = 0.43.

This is still fuzzy, but looking at the data, it looks like ON HALF has the strongest membership, so it makes sense to just go with that, or mathematically:

output = MAX(OFF, ON HALF, ON FULL)

= MAX(0.0, 0.43, 0.16) = 0.43

or using the disjunction operator $\vee$:

$$(0.0) \vee (0.43) \vee (0.16) = (0.43)$$

And that's it. We simply multiply (0.43) times the scale of the output and that's the answer:

$(0.43) \times (10) = (4.3)$

Final Output: Set the thrust to (4.3).

The only problem with this method is that even though we are taking the variable that has the most membership, its total "area of influence" in the fuzzy space may be very small. For example, a 40 percent *NORMAL* is definitely stronger than a 50 percent *WEAK*. See my point? Hence, it might be better to plug some of the values into the output fuzzy manifold for (OFF, ON HALF, ON FULL), compute the area of influence and then compute the centroid of the whole thing and use that as the final output?

Method 2: The Fuzzy Centroid

To find the fuzzy centroid you do the following: Take the fuzzy values for each FLV in the output.

OFF: (0.0)
ON HALF: (0.43) {**note:** could also use average value of .14}
ON FULL: (0.16)

Then plug them into the Y-axis of the FLV diagram and fill in the area for each. This is shown in Figure 16.14. Then you add the areas up and find the centroid of the resulting geometric shape. As you can see there are two ways to add the areas up: overlap and additive. Overlapping loses a bit of information, but is easier sometimes. The Additive technique is more accurate. The centroids of each method have been computed on the bottom half of Figure 16.14. That's great, but the computer isn't a piece of graph paper, so how do you compute the centroid?

Basically, we need to perform a numerical integration (that's a calculus term). All it means is that we want to find the center of area of this fuzzy area object, we need to sum up each piece of the object and its contribution to the total and then divide by the total area. Or mathematically, we want to do this:

$$\frac{\sum_{i}^{\text{Domain}} d_i * \text{dom}_i}{\sum_{i}^{\text{Domain}} \text{dom}_i}$$

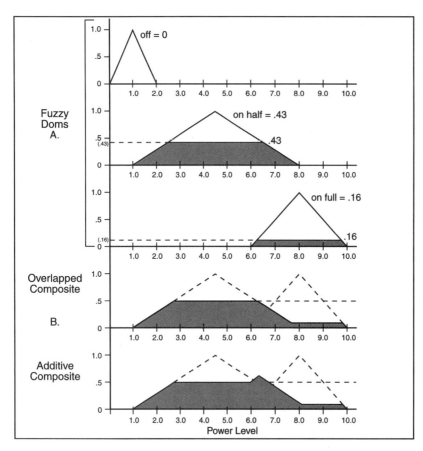

Figure 16.14

Finding the area and the centroids graphically in the fuzzy manifold

where d_i is the input value for the domain and dom_i is the degree of membership of that value. This is much easier to explain with a real example. In our example, the output domain is from 0.0 to 10.0. This represents the thrust level. Ok, so we need a loop variable d_i that loops from 0 to 10. Then, at each interval of the loop, we are going to compute the degree of membership that particular d_i is in the merged geometry, shown in Figure 16.15. However, since each triangle has a certain height now that was cut off by the original values:

OFF: (0.0)

ON HALF: (0.14)

ON FULL: (0.16)

We have to compute the degree of membership with a trapezoid rather than a triangle, but that's not too bad. So here's the pseudocode:

```
sum    = 0.0;
```

```
total_area = 0.0;

for (int di = 0; di<=10; di++)
  {
  // compute next degree of membership and add to
  // total area
  total_area = total_area + degree_of_membersip(di);

  // add next contribution of the shape at position di
  sum = sum + di * degree_of_membership(di);

  } // end for

// finally compute centroid
centroid = sum/total_area;
```

And the thing to remember is that the function degree_of_membership() is taking the generic values (0..10) and plugging them into the merged output fuzzy manifold that is a result of plugging the fuzzy values:

OFF: (0.0)
ON HALF: (0.14)
ON FULL: (0.16)

into the output variable and finding the area of influence of each one. Finally, reading off Figure 16.15, we see the output is approximately 5.6. If we compare this to the previous *MAX()* method of 4.3, they are almost identical. The 5.6 is probably "more" correct, but it's not worth the work in most cases. As you can see, using the MAX() method sure is a lot easier and most of the time works just as well as the centroid.

As far as computing a crisp value rather than a linear value for the final output that's easy. Just use the MAX() method and pigeonhole the output. Or you could select the output domain to be 0,1,2,3,4 and have exactly five crisp output commands. It's all about scale.

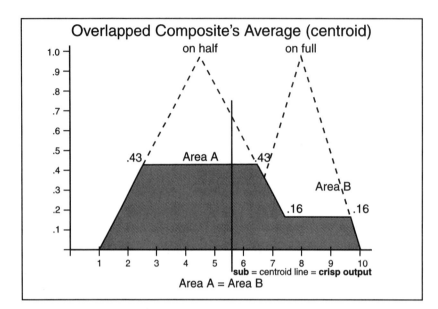

Figure 16.15

Computing the final crisp output from the fuzzy centroid

Conclusion = {.1 beginning, .5 middle, .99 end}

Well, that about wraps it up concerning fuzzy logic. This has already turned out a lot longer than I wanted, but the idea of fuzzy logic is simple; it's the actual implementation that is detailed. Anyway, no demo this time, but look on the CD-ROM in the AI subdirectories for a commercial fuzzy logic demo program.

TRICK 17

Introduction to Quaternions

by André LaMothe,
ceo@xgames3d.com

Introduction

Quaternions were invented in the 1800s by the mathematician William Rowan Hamilton (if you study graph theory you should be familiar with Hamiltonian Paths). Quaternions weren't specially designed for 3-D graphics (obviously), but they have found their application in a couple of areas of 3-D graphics that are well suited for 3-D camera control, and smooth 3-D interpolation; in addition, they can be stored very compactly. In this chapter, we are going to cover the basics of quaternions and their applications to 3-D games. The following topics will be addressed:

- General complex number theory
- Hyper complex numbers and quaternions
- Basic mathematical operations using quaternions
- 3-D rotation using quaternions
- A simple quaternion math library
- Building a quaternion lab

Complex Number Theory

Quaternions are based on *complex numbers* that are a bit abstract to understand. And, of course, they don't really mean anything in the real world, they only exist mathematically. However, complex numbers are a tool that can be used to represent mathematical ideas that don't work with real numbers. With that in mind, first we are going to take a look at basic complex number theory and then move on to quaternions and their mathematical properties. We'll also look at how quaternions are applied in computer graphics and games. With that in mind, let's begin . . .

The set of real numbers R consists of all numbers in the interval $[-\infty, +\infty]$. Easy enough, but take a look at these equations.

```
x = sqrt(4) = 2
x = sqrt(1) = 1
x = sqrt(-1) = ???
```

The third equation is the problem. We don't have a number in the set of real numbers for the square root of –1 since there is no number that, when multiplied by itself, is equal to –1. You might say, –1? But –1 × –1 = 1, so that's not correct. We need a new number to solve this problem that has the property we are looking for.

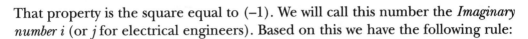
That property is the square equal to (–1). We will call this number the *Imaginary number i* (or *j* for electrical engineers). Based on this we have the following rule:

```
let i=sqrt(-1).
```

And then,

```
i*i = -1
```

So now we can compute things like *sqrt(-4)*, which would be:

```
sqrt(-4) = 2*i
```

since,

```
(2*i)*(2*i) = 4*i² = 4*-1 = -4
```

Now, the cool thing about the imaginary number *i* is that you can think of it as a variable or coefficient. All the rules of standard algebra still hold. You just pretend *i* is a variable like "x" and do what you would normally do, then, at some point, whenever you see i^2 terms you can convert them to (–1)'s if you wish to simplify. For example, look at the following sum:

```
3 + 5*i + 3*i² - 10 + 6*i
```

Collecting terms we get,

```
= 3*i² + 5*i + 6*i + 3 - 10
= 3*i² + 11*i - 7
= 3*(-1) + 11*i - 7
= -3 + 11*i - 7
= -10 + 11*i
```

Nothing unordinary there. But, the imaginary number by itself is pretty boring, so mathematicians came up with the concept of a *complex number*, which is the sum of a real number and an imaginary one. Mathematically, a complex number looks like this:

```
z = (a + b*i)
```

a is called the *Real Part (RP)*, and *b* is called the *Imaginary Part (IM)*. Since *a* and *b* can never be added together due to the imaginary coefficient of *b*, you can also think of complex numbers as points in the Complex-Plane as shown in Figure 17.1.

As a convention, most people call the x-axis the real part and the y-axis the imaginary part. Thus, we have a geometrical interpretation of complex numbers based on the vector basis:

```
z = a*(1,0) + b*(0,i)
```

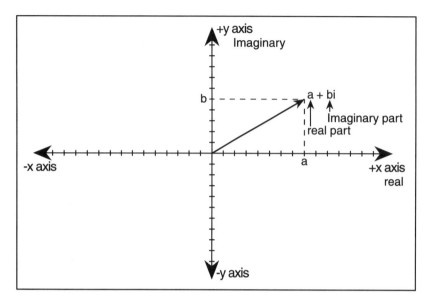

Figure 17.1

The complex plane

Now, I want to come back to this concept a little later, so keep it in mind. However, let's look at the operations on complex numbers and see how to add, subtract, multiply, and divide.

Complex Scalar Multiplication/Division

Multiplication of a scalar and a complex number is performed on a component by component basis as follows:

Given,

```
z₁ =(a+b*i)
k*z₁ = k*(a+b*i) = (k*a + (k*b)*i)
```

Example:

```
3*(2+5*i) = (6 + 15*i)
```

That is, the scalar simply distributes over the complex number. Division, of course is similar, since you can think of it as multiplication by the inverse.

Complex Addition and Subtraction

To add or subtract complex numbers, you simply add or subtract the real and the imaginary parts separately as follows:

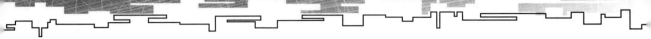
Given,

z_1 =(a+b*i)
z_2 =(c+d*i)
z_1 + z_2 = (a+b*i) + (c+d*i) = ((a+c) + (b+d)*i)

Example:

(3 + 5*i) + (12 - 2*i) = (15 + 3*i)

Complex Additive Identity

Also, the *additive identity* in complex numbers, that is, the complex number that when added to any other complex number is that number, is (0+0*i) since:

(0+0*i) + (a+b*i) = (0+a + (0+b)*i) = (a+b*i)

Complex Additive Inverse

The complex additive inverse, that is, the number that when added to any other complex number is the additive identity (0 + 0*i) is z^*=(–a – b*i), for any complex number z=(a + b*i) since:

(a + b*i) + (-a - b*i) = (a-a) + (b-b)*i) = (0 + 0*i)

Complex Multiplication

Now for the fun part! Multiplying complex numbers is actually very easy. Let's do it and pretend that *i* is a variable, as we have before.

z_1 = (a+b*i)
z_2 = (c+d*i)
z_1*z_2 = (a+b*i) * (c+d*i)
       = (a*c + a*d*i + b*c*i + b*d*i^2)

Noting that i^2= –1 and collecting terms,

= (a*c + (a*d+b*c)*i + b*d*(-1))

Collecting terms once again,

= ((a*c-b*d) + (a*d+b*c)*i)

Therefore, we see that the real part equals (a*c – b*d), and the imaginary part equals (a*d + b*c). Let's do an example:

Example:

```
(1+2*i) * (-3 + 3*i) = ((-3-6) + (-6+3)*i) = (-9 - 3*i)
```

Complex Division

Division of complex numbers can be accomplished using brute force; for example, we can compute the quotient of two complex numbers z_1/z_2 in the following way:

```
z₁ = (a+b*i)
z₂ = (c+d*i)
```

$$z_1/z_2 = \frac{(a+b*i)}{(c+d*i)}$$

If c=0 or d=0, then the division is trivial, but if neither c nor d is equal to 0, then we are at a bit of an impasse. The question is how to perform the division, so that the result is in the form (a + b*i) once again. The trick is to clear the denominator first and turn it into a pure scalar; this way we can simply divide the scalar into the real part and imaginary part of the numerator. To turn the denominator into a pure scalar, we must multiply by the *complex conjugate*, usually denoted by superscript asterisk "*".

The complex conjugate of z=(a + b*i) is z^*=(a – b*i). When we multiply a complex number and its conjugate the result is always a pure real number. Take a look:

Given,

```
z=(a+b*i)
```

Then,

```
z * z* =
(a+b*i) * (a-b*i) = (a² + a*b*i - a*b*i - b²*i²)
                  = (a² + b²)
```

Cool huh? Now with this trick we can convert the quotient problem into a more palatable form.

Given the quotient of two complex numbers,

$$\frac{(a+b*i)}{(c+b*i)}$$

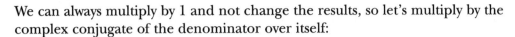

We can always multiply by 1 and not change the results, so let's multiply by the complex conjugate of the denominator over itself:

$$\frac{(a+b*i)}{(c+d*i)} * \frac{(c-d*i)}{(c-d*i)}$$

Lot's of steps go here . . .

$$= \left(\frac{(a*c+b*d)}{(a^2 + b^2)} + \frac{((b*c-a*d)*i)}{(a^2 + b^2)} \right)$$

Ugly as it may seem, rest assured it's of the form (a+b*i).

Multiplicative Inverse

The last mathematical object we need to make complex numbers a closed set is a *multiplicative inverse*. That is, a complex number that when multiplied by another results in "1," where "1" in complex numbers is equal to (1+0*i). If you think about it long enough, you will definitely see that we can use the complex conjugate in some way. Let's just try the obvious and write an equation to see what happens. We want the following:

$$(a+b*i) * (c+d*i) = (1+0*i)$$

Amazingly, the multiplicative inverse of **z**=(a+b*i) is just:

$$1/\mathbf{z} = \frac{1}{(a+b*i)}$$

But, the problem is that we no longer have something in the form (real_part + imaginary_part*i). We have the inverse of the form, so we need to reform the previous function so it's of the form (a + b*i). We can use the multiplication by the complex conjugate to find them resulting in:

$$\frac{1}{(a+b*i)} \frac{(a-b*i)}{(a-b*i)} = \frac{a}{(a^2 + b^2)} + \frac{b}{(a^2 + b^2)} * i$$

Gnarly huh? So what this means is that if you are given the complex number (a+b*i), it's inverse is 1/(a+b*i), but if you need the real part and imaginary part, then you need to use the equation above.

Complex Numbers as Vectors

Last but not least, I want to revisit the representation of complex numbers and show you another way of thinking of them (if you haven't already figured it out). Complex numbers can also be thought of as vectors in a 2-D plane. If you take a look at Figure 17.2, we plotted an imaginary number on a 2-D Cartesian plane with the real part as the x-coordinate and the imaginary part as the y-component. So there's no reason why we can't think of imaginary numbers as vectors with the basis:

```
z = a*(1,0) + b*(0,i)
```

Or more compactly,

```
z = <a,b>
```

where a is the real part and b is the imaginary part. Figure 17.2 shows our new representation in vector form.

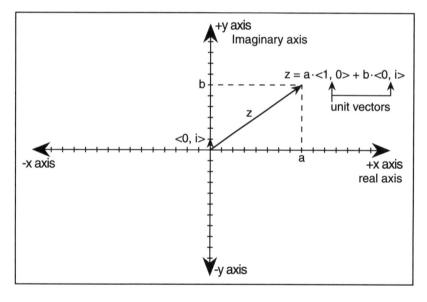

Figure 17.2

Complex numbers in a unit vector form

The cool thing about representing complex numbers as vectors is that we can transform them as vectors with the results turning out all perfectly valid. Moreover, representing complex numbers as vectors allows us to better visualize an abstract mathematical notion such as complex numbers and to thus "see" relationships that might otherwise elude us in their pure mathematical form.

Norm of a Complex Number

Many times we want to know the length of the vector represented by a complex number or the magnitude, in other words. Of course, this doesn't make much sense in a purely mathematical sense, but when we think of complex numbers as vectors in space, it's very natural and easy to understand. Anyway, the *norm* of a complex number can be computed in the following ways:

Given,

$$z = a + b*i$$

Then,

$$|z| = \text{sqrt}(a^2 + b^2)$$

Also, take a look at the product of any complex number and its conjugate:

Given,

$$z = a + b*i, \quad z^* = a - b*i$$

Then,

$$z * z^* = a^2 + b*i - b*i + b^2 = a^2 + b^2$$

Therefore, the norm is also equal to,

$$|z| = \text{sqrt}(z * z^*)$$

Equation 17.1

Hyper Complex Numbers

Quaternions are nothing more than *hyper complex* numbers. Hyper complex numbers can really mean anything mathematically, but usually it means a complex number that has more than one imaginary component. In our case, we are going to refer to hyper complex numbers with one real part and three imaginary parts—otherwise known as *Quaternions.*

A quaternion can be written in many ways, but in general it's of the form:

$$q = q_0 + q_1*\mathbf{i} + q_2*\mathbf{j} + q_3*\mathbf{k}$$

Or

$$q = q_0 + \mathbf{q}_v, \text{ where } \mathbf{q}_v = q_1*\mathbf{i} + q_2*\mathbf{j} + q_3*\mathbf{k}$$

Equation 17.2

The form of a quaternion

And $i=<1,0,0>$, $j=<0,1,0>$, $k=<0,0,1>$ and $<q_0,q_1,q_2,q_3>$ are all real numbers and $<i,j,k>$ are all imaginary numbers and form the vector basis of the quaternion q. Moreover, q_0 is real and has no imaginary coefficient.

Also, the imaginary basis $<i,j,k>$ has some interesting properties. It can be thought of as a 3-D mutually perpendicular set of unit vectors in an imaginary coordinate system that locates points in $<i,j,k>$ space as shown in Figure 17.3. But, the interesting thing about $<i,j,k>$ is the following relationship:

$$i^2 = j^2 = k^2 = -1 = i*j*k$$

Equation 17.3

The quaternion basis products

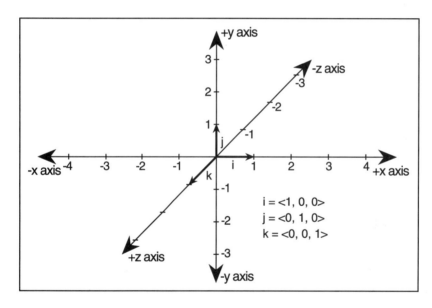

Figure 17.3

The hyper complex basis interpreted as a 3-D system

ICON MATH: Note that I am bolding the imaginary basis **i, j, k**; thus, we would think they are vectors, and they are, but they can also be thought of as variables. The point is, they have a dualism to them and sometimes it's appropriate to think of them in their vector form, but sometimes it's not. The point is, I may switch back and forth especially when I am using the i,j,k alone and showing relationships among them.

Which seems almost reasonable, the " = **i*j*k**" part takes a little getting used to, but it's correct. And of course, you can manipulate the relationship to arrive at the following:

Given,

$$i^2 = j^2 = k^2 = -1 = i*j*k$$

Therefore,

$$i = j*k = -k*j$$

$$j = k*i = -i*k$$

$$k = i*j = -j*i$$

This intuitively seems right since the cross product of any two perpendicular vectors in an orthonormal basis should be perpendicular to the vectors themselves or the third vector in a 3-D orthonormal basis. And, if we invert the order of multiplication, then we should see (and we do see that) an inversion or sign flip.

At this point, I want to lay down some conventions about writing quaternions; otherwise, we are going to get caught up in notation. Many people like to write quaternions using lowercase letters to represent them, but break them up into real and imaginary parts where they represent the imaginary part as a vector like this:

$$\mathbf{q} = q_0 + \mathbf{q_v}$$

where,

$$\mathbf{q_v} = q_1*\mathbf{i} + q_2*\mathbf{j} + q_3*\mathbf{k}$$

So q_0 is the real part, $\mathbf{q_v}$ is the imaginary part, and $\mathbf{q}$ is a vector $<q_1, q_2, q_3>$. That's cool, but I don't like the fact that $\mathbf{q}$, the quaternion itself, is non-bold. It's confusing since it's a 4-tuple itself, so we are going to use the notation that quaternions are represented in lowercase bold and the vector part is also in lowercase bold. Here's an example:

$$\mathbf{a} = -1 + 3*i + 4*j + 5*k$$

Which in pure vector form is:

$$\mathbf{a} = <-1, 3, 4, 5>$$

Or in real-vector form is:

$$\mathbf{a} = q_0 + \mathbf{q_v}$$

Where $q_0 = -1$, and $\mathbf{q_v} = <3,4,5> = 3*i + 4*j + 5*j$.

The point is that we are obviously going to use arrays to represent quaternions in real life and the first number will always be the real part and the remaining three numbers will always be the imaginary coefficients of $<i,j,k>$. Moreover, from now on, I want to start getting you into the habit of representing quaternions in the format:

> **NOTE**
>
> Note that we are taking advantage of the vector property of $<i,j,k>$.

```
q = q₀ + x*i + y*j + z*k
```

Or in another way,

```
q = q₀ + <x,y,z> . <i,j,k>
```

That is simply referring to the real part as q_0 and the imaginary part as $\mathbf{q_v} = <x,y,z>$ which gives us a little more to grasp onto when relating quaternions to 3-D space. But, depending on what we are doing, we may flip from one representation to another, but I think you get the point.

Now, the cool thing about quaternions or any hyper complex number system is that the mathematics of addition, multiplication, inverses, etc., are all the same as in standard complex number theory, but with more elements. Hence, we really already know how to do this stuff, but we just have to take into consideration that we now have three imaginary components rather than 1 as we did with basic complex numbers or complex numbers of "rank 1."

Now let's take a look at the basic operations that we might need to perform on quaternions when doing calculations—I'm going to go fast since this should all be obvious at this point.

Quaternion Addition & Subtraction

Addition or subtraction of quaternions is accomplished by adding or subtracting the real part and the imaginary part just as with normal complex numbers.

Example:

```
q = q₀ + qᵥ
p = p₀ + pᵥ

q + p = (q₀+p₀) + (qᵥ+pᵥ)
```

Example:

```
q = 3  + 4*i + 5*j + 6*k = <3,4,5,6> in vector form.
p = -5 + 2*i + 2*j - 3*k = <-5,2,2,-3> in vector form.

q + p = (3 + -5) + ( (4 + 2)*i + (5 + 2)*j + (6 + -3)*k)
     = -2 + 6*i + 7+j + 3*k
```

As you can see, the writing of the imaginary coefficients is getting rather tedious, and we could have just written:

```
<3,4,5,6> + <-5,2,2,-3> = <-2,6,7, 3>.
```

However, we have to be careful since this works for addition and subtraction, but for multiplication we need to recall that the last three components are complex and we do have to watch out for oversimplification. Therefore, keep the quaternions in a form that at least keeps the real and imaginary parts separate.

Additive Inverse and Identity

The additive inverse of any quaternion q is the number that when added to q results in 0; this is surprisingly just $-q$. That is:

Given,

$q = q_0 + q_v$

The additive inverse is just:

$-q = -q_0 - q_v$

Since,

$q - q = (q_0-q_0)+ (q_v- q_v) = 0 + 0*i + 0*j + 0*j$

And the additive identity or "0" in quaternion math must be:

$q = 0 + 0*i + 0*j + 0*k = <0,0,0,0>.$

Quaternion Multiplication

Addition and subtraction are always easy, huh? It's multiplication that ruins the party every time! And this is no exception! However, since quaternions are nothing more than hyper complex numbers based on real numbers with imaginary coefficients, we should be able to just multiply them out, taking into consideration the imaginary coefficients in the products and keeping track of them. Let's just try it and see what happens?

Given,

$$p = p_0 + p_1*i + p_2*j + p_3*k = p_0 + \mathbf{p_v}$$
$$q = q_0 + q_1*i + q_2*j + q_3*k = q_0 + \mathbf{q_v}$$

Then,

$$p*q = (p_0 + p_1*i + p_2*j + p_3*k) * (q_0 + q_1*i + q_2*j + q_3*k)$$
$$= p_0*q_0 +$$
$$p_0*q1*i + p_1*q_2*j + p_2*q_3*k +$$
$$p_1*i*q_0 + p_1*i*q_1*i + p_1*i*q_2*j + p_1*i*q_3*k +$$
$$p_2*j*q_0 + p_2*j*q_1*i + p_2*j*q_2*j + p_2*j*q_3*k +$$
$$p_3*k*q_0 + p_3*k*q_1*i + p_3*k*q_2*j + p_3*k*q_3*k$$

If you have a good eye, you should see some structure to this product—maybe a cross product here and there, and a dot product? Keep that in mind while we collect terms and use Equation 17.4 to simplify the imaginary product terms:

$$= p_0*q_0 +$$
$$p_0*q_1*i + p_1*q_2*j + p_2*q_3*k +$$
$$p_1*q_0*i + p_1*q_1*i^2 + p_1*i*q_2*j + p_1*i*q_3*k +$$
$$p_2*j*q_0 + p_2*q_1*j*i + p_2*q_2*j^2 + p_2*q_3*j*k +$$
$$p_3*q_0*k + p_3*q_1*k*i + p_3*q_2*k*j + p_3*q_3*k^2$$

Given,	**Equation 17.4**
$$\mathbf{p} = p_0 + p_1*i + p_2*j + p_3*k = p_0 + \mathbf{p_v}$$ $$\mathbf{q} = q_0 + q_1*i + q_2*j + q_3*k = q_0 + \mathbf{q_v}$$ Then, $$\mathbf{r} = \mathbf{p}*\mathbf{q} = (p_0*q_0 - (\mathbf{p_v} \cdot \mathbf{q_v})) + (p_0*\mathbf{q_v} + q_0*\mathbf{p_v} + \mathbf{p_v} \times \mathbf{q_v})$$ $$= r_0 + \mathbf{r_v}$$	*Formula for quaternion products*

At this point there are a lot of ways to format these products, but I will stop here and show you this equation:

And since dot products always result in scalars and cross-products in vectors, the first term $(p_0*q_0 - (\mathbf{p_v} \cdot \mathbf{q_v}))$ is the real part r_0 and the term $(p_0*\mathbf{q_v} + q_0*\mathbf{p_v} + \mathbf{p_v} \times \mathbf{q_v})$ is the vector or imaginary part $\mathbf{r_v}$. I have to admit that quaternion multiplication is a very ugly thing in mathematics!

NOTE

The "×" operator is the standard vector cross-product and is calculated on the vector imaginary part of the quaternion as if the imaginary part was a standard 3-tuple vector.

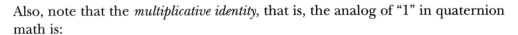

Also, note that the *multiplicative identity*, that is, the analog of "1" in quaternion math is:

$q_1 = 1 + 0*i + 0*j + 0*k$

This is true since any $q * q_1 = q = q_1 * q$.

Quaternion Conjugate

Computing the conjugate of a quaternion q, q^* is accomplished in the same manner as with complex numbers; you simply invert the sign of the imaginary component q_v.

Given,

$q = q_0 + q_1*i + q_2*j + q_3*k = q_0 + q_v$

The complex conjugate is computed by inverting the sign of the imaginary part:

$q^* = q_0 - q_1*i - q_2*j - q_3*k = q_0 - q_v$

Equation 17.5

Computation of complex conjugate

And take a look at the product of q and q^*; it's rather interesting (using Equation 17.4 to perform the multiplication):

$$q * q^* = (q_0 + q_v) * (q_0 + (-q_v))$$
$$= q_0*q_0 - (q_v \cdot (-q_v)) + q_0*q_v + q_0*(-q_v) + (q_v \times (-q_v))$$
$$= q_0^2 + q_1^2 + q_2^2 + q_3^2 + (q_0*q_v - q_0*q_v) + (0)$$
$$= q_0^2 + q_1^2 + q_2^2 + q_3^2$$

Equation 17.6

The quaternion-conjugate product

Interestingly, the product is simply the square of each term. This property will come in handy when we deal with computing the norm and inverse of a quaternion.

Norm of a Quaternion

The norm of a quaternion is computed in the same manner as a complex number is:

Given,

$$\mathbf{q} = q_0 + q_1{}^*\mathbf{i} + q_2{}^*\mathbf{j} + q_3{}^*\mathbf{k} = q_0 + \mathbf{q}_v$$

Then,

$$|\mathbf{q}| = sqrt(q_0{}^2+q_1{}^2+q_2{}^2+q_3{}^2) = sqrt(\mathbf{q} * \mathbf{q}^*)$$

And of course,

$$|\mathbf{q}|^2 = (q_0{}^2 + q_1{}^2 + q_2{}^2 + q_3{}^2) = (\mathbf{q} * \mathbf{q}^*)$$

Equation 17.7

Norm of a quaternion

Multiplicative Inverse

The multiplicative inverse of a quaternion is of special importance to us since it can be used to simplify quaternion rotation. In fact, everything we have learned up until now is going to come to the single focus of rotating a vector using quaternions, and the inverse is needed for this operation. So put on your thinking cap and check it out.

> **NOTE**
> Note that $(q * q^*) = (q^* * q)$ is the product of a quaternion and its conjugate is order-independent, but in general $q^*p \ \pi \ p^*q$. Also, note that $q + q^* = 2^*q0$.

Given a quaternion $\mathbf{q}$, we want to find another quaternion $\mathbf{q}^{-1}$ such that the following statement is true:

$q^*q^{-1} = 1 = q^{-1}{}^*q$

Now, don't blink and watch this:

Let's multiply each side by the complex conjugate $\mathbf{q}^*$:

$(q \star q^{-1}) \star q^*= 1 = (q^{-1} \star q) \star q^* = q^*$

Since the products in parentheses are 1, we know that 1 multiplied by the conjugate and the conjugate multiplied by 1 are both the conjugate, so we haven't changed anything or created a false statement. Alright, now's the cool part. Let's stare at this a minute and see if we can figure out what the inverse is. Do you see it? Let's look at the right side alone that is:

$(q^{-1} \star q) \star q^* = q^*$

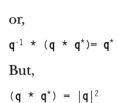

or,

$q^{-1} * (q * q^*) = q^*$

But,

$(q * q^*) = |q|^2$

So the final result is:

$$q^{-1} = q^*/|q|^2$$

Equation 17.8a

Inverse of a quaternion

Furthermore, if q is a unit quaternion, then $|q|^2 = 1$, we can further simplify the inverse to this:

$$q^{-1} = q^*$$

Equation 17.8b

Inverse of a unit quaternion

Pretty cool, huh? The above equation is the whole reason that makes using quaternions to perform rotations even thinkable. Thus, most of the time we will assume that all quaternions are unit quaternions, so we can use the above equation without a problem.

Applications of Quaternions

After all that work learning about quaternions, they probably seem just like interesting mathematical objects with little or no real use to us. However, the fact is that quaternions are very useful for a couple functions in 3-D graphics: rotation and interpolation of rotations from one to another, as shown in Figure 17.4. Referring to the figure, you see two camera directions defined by two set of angles relative to the x-y-z axis $camera_1 = (\alpha_1, \phi_1, \theta_1)$ and $camera_2 = (\alpha_2, \phi_2, \theta_2)$. How we point the camera in those directions is unimportant, but what if we wanted to smoothly interpolate from the orientation of camera1 to camera2? Could we linearly interpolate based on the angles? A number of problems can occur when you do this, such as jerky motion and loss of a degree of freedom when the camera happens to align on an axis.

Quaternions, by their 4-D nature, can handle this problem much more elegantly than standard angles and rotation matrices; however, they are a bit slower, but

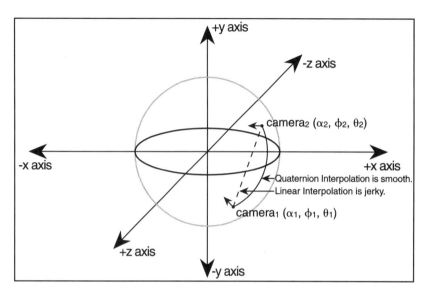

Figure 17.4

Interpolation from one orientation to another

worth it. The technique is usually called SLERP (spherical linear interpolation). That is interpolating from one quaternion to another where the initial and end points of the interpolation are camera1, and camera2, as shown in Figure 17.4. But, we are getting way ahead of ourselves; first we need to learn how to perform rotations with quaternions.

Quaternion Rotation

Alright, at some point you might wonder which operators can be represented by quaternion transformations; in other words, can they do anything interesting? The answer is yes; one of those interesting and useful operations is the ability to rotate a vector **v**. The math in unimportant to arrive at the results, just algebra really, but in the end we get something like given a vector **v**=<x,y,z> which in quaternion form we will call $\mathbf{v}_q$=<0,x,y,z> in 3-D (we use a dummy 0=q_0, so that we can use **v** as a quaternion), and a unit quaternion **q**, the following operations will rotate $\mathbf{v}_q$:

Right Handed System

a. $\mathbf{v}_q' = \mathbf{q}^* * \mathbf{v}_q * \mathbf{q}$, clockwise rotation

b. $\mathbf{v}_q' = \mathbf{q} * \mathbf{v}_q * \mathbf{q}^*$, counterclockwise rotation

Left Handed System

c. $\mathbf{v}_q' = \mathbf{q} * \mathbf{v}_q * \mathbf{q}^*$, clockwise rotation

d. $\mathbf{v}_q' = \mathbf{q}^* * \mathbf{v}_q * \mathbf{q}$, counterclockwise rotation

Equation 17.9

Quaternion rotation

So $\mathbf{v}_q$ is a vector encoded in a quaternion with $q_0=0$, and $\mathbf{q}$ is a quaternion, but what exactly does $\mathbf{q}$ represent? Meaning, what's its relationship to the x-y-z axis and $\mathbf{v}_q$? You're going to love this—$\mathbf{q}$ defines both the axis of rotation and the angle θ to rotate about the axis!

> **NOTE**
>
> We can use q* in this operator only for unit quaternions, otherwise, you must use the full inverse of q.

Of course, the result $\mathbf{v}_q'$ is technically a 4-D vector or a quaternion, but the first component, q_0 will always be zero, thus, we just throw it away and think of the last 3 elements as just a vector in 3-D representing the original vector $\mathbf{v}$ after rotation.

If you have ever tried to rotate a 3-D object around an arbitrary axis, you know it's not that easy, it takes a lot of work to figure it out, but now it's very easy. The axis that the quaternion $\mathbf{q}$ defines along with the angle isn't that obvious, but it's not that bad. Referring to Figure 17.5, we see that for a given unit quaternion $\mathbf{q} = q_0 + \mathbf{q}_v$, the axis of rotation is just the line defined by the vector part $\mathbf{q}_v$ and the angle of rotation θ is encoded in q_0 using the following transforms:

$$\mathbf{q} = \cos(q/2) + \sin(q/2)*\mathbf{v}_q$$

Thus,

$$q_0 = \cos(q/2) \text{ and } \mathbf{q}_v = \sin(q/2)* \mathbf{v}_q$$

Equation 17.10

Conversion of axis and angle to quaternion

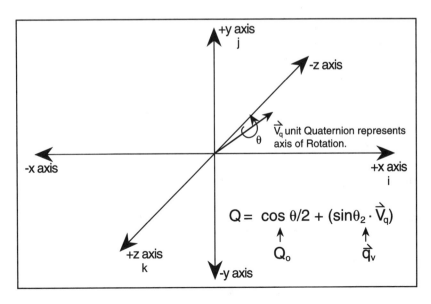

Figure 17.5

A geometrical interpretation of a rotation quaternion

Now, what if you don't have a vector that you want to rotate around, but have the standard Euler rotation angles? Then you can create a quaternion from the angles by generating one of the products:

> **NOTE**
>
> Of course, qv must be a unit vector itself, so that q remains a unit quaternion.

$$
\begin{aligned}
\mathbf{q}_{final} \quad &= \mathbf{q}_{xq}{}^{*}\mathbf{q}_{yq}{}^{*}\mathbf{q}_{zq}\\
&= \mathbf{q}_{xq}{}^{*}\mathbf{q}_{zq}{}^{*}\mathbf{q}_{yq}\\
&= \mathbf{q}_{yq}{}^{*}\mathbf{q}_{xq}{}^{*}\mathbf{q}_{zq}\\
&= \mathbf{q}_{yq}{}^{*}\mathbf{q}_{zq}{}^{*}\mathbf{q}_{xq}\\
&= \mathbf{q}_{zq}{}^{*}\mathbf{q}_{xq}{}^{*}\mathbf{q}_{yq}\\
&= \mathbf{q}_{z\theta}{}^{*}\mathbf{q}_{y\theta}{}^{*}\mathbf{q}_{x\theta} \quad \text{<-most common transform.}
\end{aligned}
$$

Where x_q refers to the *pitch* (angle parallel to the x-axis), y_q refers to the *yaw* (angle parallel to the y-axis), and z_q refers to the *roll* (angle parallel to the z-axis) as shown in Figure 17.6. Most people use the last transform most commonly in 3-D engines, but all are just as valid. In any case, once you have the order of transforms, then you can plug in the following formulas for the quaternions $\mathbf{q}_{xq}$, $\mathbf{q}_{yq}$, $\mathbf{q}_{zq}$ and perform the multiplication to arrive at $\mathbf{q}_{final}$:

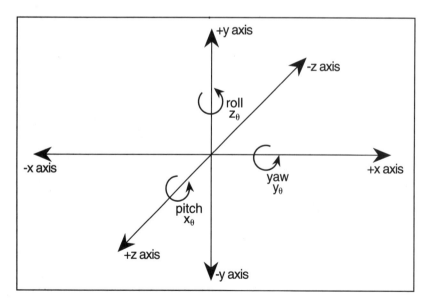

Figure 17.6

Yaw, pitch, and roll

$$\mathbf{q}_{xq} = \cos(x_q/2) + \sin(x_q/2)*\mathbf{i} + 0*\mathbf{j} + 0*\mathbf{k}$$
$$q_0 = \cos(x_q/2),\ \mathbf{q}_v = <\sin(x_q/2),\ 0,\ 0>$$
$$\mathbf{q}_{yq} = \cos(y_q/2) + 0*\mathbf{i} + \sin(y_q/2)*\mathbf{j} + 0*\mathbf{k}$$
$$q_0 = \cos(y_q/2),\ \mathbf{q}_v = <0,\ \sin(y_q/2),\ 0>$$
$$\mathbf{q}_{zq} = \cos(z_q/2) + 0*\mathbf{i} + 0*\mathbf{j} + \sin(z_q/2)*\mathbf{k}$$
$$q_0 = \cos(z_q/2),\ \mathbf{q}_v = <0,0,\sin(z_q/2)>$$

Equation 17.11

Euler angles to quaternion

So to rotate a vector **v** using the Euler form, you are really doing this for the example of roll, yaw, pitch:

$$\mathbf{v}_q'(0,x',y',z') = (\mathbf{q}_{zq}*\mathbf{q}_{yq}*\mathbf{q}_{xq})*\ \mathbf{v}_q\ *\ (\mathbf{q}_{zq}*\mathbf{q}_{yq}*\mathbf{q}_{xq})^*$$

Where $\mathbf{v}_q = <0,x,y,z>$, the initial vector or point we want to rotate cast into quaternion form.

Of course, you only need to compute the product in parentheses once. And since each of the factors $\mathbf{q}_{xq}$, $\mathbf{q}_{yq}$, $\mathbf{q}_{zq}$, is of the form:

$$\mathbf{q}_{(i,j,k)} = \cos(\theta/2) + \sin(\theta/2)*(\mathbf{i},\mathbf{j},\mathbf{k})$$

The product of terms of this form have a lot of cancellations, thus the product $\mathbf{q}_{z\theta}*\mathbf{q}_{y\theta}*\mathbf{q}_{x\theta}$, for example, ends up looking like:

$$q_0 = \cos(_{z\theta/2})*\cos(_{y\theta/2})*\cos(_{x\theta/2}) + \sin(_{z\theta/2})*\sin(_{y\theta/2})*\sin(_{x\theta/2})$$
$$q_1 = \cos(_{z\theta/2})*\cos(_{y\theta/2})*\sin(_{x\theta/2}) - \sin(_{z\theta/2})*\sin(_{y\theta/2})*\cos(_{x\theta/2})$$
$$q_2 = \cos(_{z\theta/2})*\sin(_{y\theta/2})*\cos(_{x\theta/2}) + \sin(_{z\theta/2})*\cos(_{y\theta/2})*\sin(_{x\theta/2})$$
$$q_3 = \sin(_{z\theta/2})*\cos(_{y\theta/2})*\cos(_{x\theta/2}) - \cos(_{z\theta/2})*\sin(_{y\theta/2})*\sin(_{x\theta/2})$$

NOTE

Note that each quaternion in the products can be thought of as an individual rotation operation, but it takes much less work to multiply quaternions than matrices. Therefore, if you find yourself doing a lot of matrix multiplies in a loop, you might be able to optimize it by converting to quaternions, doing all the matrix operations in quaternion form and then converting back.

Building a Simple Quaternion Engine

The next thing we are going to do is create a set of library functions to manipulate quaternions and implement basic quaternion rotation at the very least, so you can see how to rotate a point in 3-D space using quaternions. The only problem is that we need a few support data structures and functions, but of course we don't have room or time to cover vectors and the functions for them, hence, you will have to refer to the listings on the CD for the vector functions. However, there's nothing that isn't blatantly obvious when you look at the names of the functions in the code listings that make up the quaternion functions. Nevertheless, at the very least, here's the *VECTOR3D* structure that we use in the functions:

```
typedef struct VECTOR3D_TYP
{
union
    {
    float M[3]; // array indexed storage
    // explicit names
    struct
        {
        float x,y,z;
        }; // end struct
    }; // end union
} VECTOR3D, POINT3D, *VECTOR3D_PTR, *POINT3D_PTR;
```

With that in mind, let's agree on a quaternion representation next. Basically, all we need to do is track four values: one real, and three imaginary; let's call them $q0$, $q1$, $q2$, $q3$, thus, we can write any quaternion as the sum:

$$\mathbf{q} = q_0 + q_1 * \mathbf{i} + q_2 * \mathbf{j} + q_3 * \mathbf{k}$$

Or

$$\mathbf{q} = q_0 + \mathbf{q}_v, \text{ where } \mathbf{q}_v = q_1 * \mathbf{i} + q_2 * \mathbf{j} + q_3 * \mathbf{k}$$

So basically we need to keep track of four floating point numbers. Additionally, we might like to access them in different ways to optimize our algorithms. The data structure *QUAT* below implements this functionality with a number of unions:

```
typedef struct QUAT_TYP
{
union
```

```
    {
    float M[4]; // array indexed storage w,x,y,z order

    // vector part, real part format
    struct
        {
        float    q0;   // the real part
        VECTOR3D qv;   // the imaginary part xi+yj+zk
        };
    struct
        {
        float w,x,y,z;
        };
    }; // end union
} QUAT, *QUAT_PTR;
```

With this structure we can access the quaternion as an array, as a real and a vector, and as four unique identifiers. This makes writing various algorithms a snap! Anyway, let's take a look at all the functions I have written to help you in your quest of quaternion domination:

Function Prototype

```
void VECTOR3D_Theta_To_QUAT(QUAT_PTR q, VECTOR3D_PTR v, float theta);
```

Functional Listing

```
void VECTOR3D_Theta_To_QUAT(QUAT_PTR q, VECTOR3D_PTR v, float theta)
{
// initializes a quaternion based on a 3-D direction vector and angle
// note the direction vector must be a unit vector
// and the angle is in rads

float theta_div_2 = (0.5)*theta; // compute theta/2

// compute the quaternion, note this is from Chapter 4
// pre-compute to save time
float sinf_theta = sinf(theta_div_2);

q->x = sinf_theta * v->x;
q->y = sinf_theta * v->y;
q->z = sinf_theta * v->z;
```

```
q->w = cosf( theta_div_2 );

} // end VECTOR3D_Theta_To_QUAT
```

Purpose

void VECTOR3D_Theta_To_QUAT() creates a rotation quaternion based on a direction vector *v*, and an angle *theta*. Referring back to Figure 17.5 see this construction. This function is primarily used to create quaternions for rotations of points. Note that the direction vector *v* must be a unit vector.

Example

```
// create the vector to rotate about
// in this case the diagonal of the unit cube
// for octant 1
VECTOR3D v={1,1,1};
QUAT qr;
// normalize v
VECTOR3D_Normalize(&v);
float theta = DEG_TO_RAD(100); // 100 degrees
// create a rotation quaternion about v
// with angle theta
VECTOR3D_Theta_To_QUAT(&q, &v,theta);
```

Function Prototype

```
void EulerZYX_To_QUAT(QUAT_PTR q, float theta_z, float
theta_y, float theta_x);
```

Functional Listing

```
void EulerZYX_To_QUAT(QUAT_PTR q, float theta_z, float theta_y, float theta_x)
{
// this function initializes a quaternion based on the zyx
// multiplication order of the angles that are parallel to the
// zyx axis respectively, note there are 11 other possibilities
// this is just one, later we may make a general version of the
// the function

// precompute values
float cos_z_2 = 0.5*cosf(theta_z);
float cos_y_2 = 0.5*cosf(theta_y);
```

```
float cos_x_2 = 0.5*cosf(theta_x);

float sin_z_2 = 0.5*sinf(theta_z);
float sin_y_2 = 0.5*sinf(theta_y);
float sin_x_2 = 0.5*sinf(theta_x);

// and now compute quaternion
q->w = cos_z_2*cos_y_2*cos_x_2 + sin_z_2*sin_y_2*sin_x_2;
q->x = cos_z_2*cos_y_2*sin_x_2 - sin_z_2*sin_y_2*cos_x_2;
q->y = cos_z_2*sin_y_2*cos_x_2 + sin_z_2*cos_y_2*sin_x_2;
q->z = sin_z_2*cos_y_2*cos_x_2 - cos_z_2*sin_y_2*sin_x_2;

} // EulerZYX_To_QUAT
```

Purpose

void EulerZYX_To_QUAT() creates a rotation quaternion based on the Euler angles parallel to the z,y, and x axes, respectively. This is your basic camera transform. Of course there are a total of six ways (permutations = 3!) to multiply x*y*z together, but this is the most common. Use this function to convert your Euler rotation angles to a quaternion.

Example

```
QUAT qzyx;

// create rotation angles
float theta_x = DEG_TO_RAD(20);
float theta_y = DEG_TO_RAd(30);
float theta_z = DEG_TO_RAD(45);

// create rotation quaternion
EulerZYX_To_QUAT(&qzyx,theta_z,theta_y,theta_x);
```

Function Prototype

```
void QUAT_To_VECTOR3D_Theta(QUAT_PTR q, VECTOR3D_PTR v, float *theta);
```

Functional Listing

```
void QUAT_To_VECTOR3D_Theta(QUAT_PTR q, VECTOR3D_PTR v, float *theta)
{
// this function converts a unit quaternion into a unit direction
// vector and rotation angle about that vector
```

```
// extract theta
*theta = acosf(q->w);

// pre-compute to save time
float sinf_theta_inv = 1.0/sinf(*theta);

// now the vector
v->x     = q->x*sinf_theta_inv;
v->y     = q->y*sinf_theta_inv;
v->z     = q->z*sinf_theta_inv;

// multiply by 2
*theta*=2;

} // end QUAT_To_VECTOR3D_Theta
```

Purpose

void QUAT_To_VECTOR3D_Theta() converts a unit rotation quaternion into a unit 3-D vector and a rotation angle theta about that vector. This function is basically the opposite of *VECTOR3D_Theta_To_QUAT()*.

Example

```
QUAT q;
// assume q now has a unit rotation quaternion in it

// storage for the vector and angle
float theta;
VECTOR3D v;

// now convert the quat to a vector and an angle
QUAT_To_VECTOR3D_Theta(&q, &v, &theta);
```

Function Prototype

```
void QUAT_Add(QUAT_PTR q1, QUAT_PTR q2, QUAT_PTR qsum);
```

Purpose

void QUAT_Add() adds the quaternions *q1* and *q2* and stores the sum in *qsum*.

Example

```
QUAT q1 = {1,2,3,4}, q2 = {5,6,7,8}, qsum;
// add em
QUAT_Add(&q1, &q2, &qsum);
```

Function Prototype

```
void QUAT_Sub(QUAT_PTR q1, QUAT_PTR q2, QUAT_PTR qdiff);
```

Purpose

void QUAT_Sub() subtracts the quaternion *q2* from *q1* and stores the difference in *qdiff.*

Example

```
QUAT q1 = {1,2,3,4}, q2 = {5,6,7,8}, qdiff;
// subtract em
QUAT_Sub(&q1, &q2, &qdiff);
```

Function Prototype

```
void QUAT_Conjugate(QUAT_PTR q, QUAT_PTR qconj);
```

Purpose

void QUAT_Conjugate() computes the conjugate of the quaternion *q* and returns in *qconj.*

Example

```
QUAT q = {1,2,3,4}, qconj;
// compute conjugate
QUAT_Conjugate(&q, &qconj);
```

Function Prototype

```
void QUAT_Scale(QUAT_PTR q, float scale, QUAT_PTR qs);
```

Purpose

void QUAT_Scale() scales the quaternion *q* by the factor *scale* and stores the result in *qs.*

Example

```
QUAT q = {1,2,3,4}, qs;
// scale q by 2
QUAT_Scale(&q, 2,  &qs);
```

Function Prototype

```
void QUAT_Scale(QUAT_PTR q, float scale);
```

Purpose

void QUAT_Scale() scales the quaternion *q* by the factor *scale* in place, that is, modifies *q* directly.

Example

```
QUAT q = {1,2,3,4};
// scale q by 2
QUAT_Scale(&q, 2);
```

Function Prototype

```
float QUAT_Norm(QUAT_PTR q);
```

Purpose

float QUAT_Norm(QUAT_PTR q) returns the norm the quaternion *q*, that is, its length.

Example

```
QUAT q = {1,2,3,4};

// whats the length of q?
float qnorm = QUAT_Norm(&q);
```

Function Prototype

```
float QUAT_Norm2(QUAT_PTR q);
```

Purpose

float QUAT_Norm2(QUAT_PTR q) returns the norm squared of the quaternion *q*, that is, its length squared. This function is useful since many times we need norm of a quaternion squared, thus, calling *QUAT_Norm2()* rather than calling

QUAT_Norm() and then squaring the return value saves us both a *sqrt()* call and a multiply.

Example

```
QUAT q = {1,2,3,4};

// whats the length of q*q?
float qnorm2 = QUAT_Norm2(&q);
```

Function Prototype

```
void QUAT_Normalize(QUAT_PTR q, QUAT_PTR qn);
```

Purpose

void QUAT_Normalize() normalizes the quaternion *q* and sends the result back in *qn*.

> **NOTE**
> Remember, all rotation quaternions must be unit quaternions.

Example

```
QUAT q = {1,2,3,4}, qn;

// normalize q
QUAT_Normalize(&q, &qn);
```

Function Prototype

```
void QUAT_Normalize(QUAT_PTR q);
```

Purpose

void QUAT_Normalize() normalizes the quaternion *q* in place, that is, modifies *q* itself.

Example

```
QUAT q = {1,2,3,4};
// normalize q in place
QUAT_Normalize(&q);
```

Function Prototype

```
void QUAT_Unit_Inverse(QUAT_PTR q, QUAT_PTR qi);
```

Purpose

void QUAT_Unit_Inverse() computes the inverse of the quaternion *q* and returns the result in *qi*. However, *q* must be a unit quaternion for the function to work since the function is based on the fact that the inverse of a unit quaternion is its conjugate.

Example

```
QUAT q = {1,2,3,4}, qi;
// normalize q first
QUAT_Normalize(&q);
// now compute inverse
QUAT_Unit_Inverse(&q, &qi);
```

Function Prototype

```
void QUAT_Unit_Inverse(QUAT_PTR q);
```

Purpose

void QUAT_Unit_Inverse() computes the inverse of the quaternion *q* in place modifying *q*. However, *q* must be a unit quaternion for the function to work since the function is based on the fact that the inverse of a unit quaternion is its conjugate.

Example

```
QUAT q = {1,2,3,4};

// normalize q first
QUAT_Normalize(&q);

// now compute inverse
QUAT_Unit_Inverse(&q);
```

Function Prototype

```
void QUAT_Inverse(QUAT_PTR q, QUAT_PTR qi);
```

Purpose

void QUAT_Inverse() computes the inverse of a general non-unit quaternion *q* and returns the result in *qi*.

Example

```
QUAT q = {1,2,3,4}, qi;

// now compute inverse
QUAT_Inverse(&q, &qi);
```

Function Prototype

```
void QUAT_Inverse(QUAT_PTR q);
```

Purpose

void QUAT_Unit_Inverse() computes the inverse of a general non-unit quaternion *q* in place modifying *q*.

Example

```
QUAT q = {1,2,3,4};

// now compute inverse
QUAT_Inverse(&q);
```

Function Prototype

```
void QUAT_Mul(QUAT_PTR q1, QUAT_PTR q2, QUAT_PTR qprod);
```

Functional Listing

```
void QUAT_Mul(QUAT_PTR q1, QUAT_PTR q2, QUAT_PTR qprod)
{
// this function multiplies two quaternions

// this is the brute force method
//qprod->w = q1->w*q2->w - q1->x*q2->x - q1->y*q2->y - q1->z*q2->z;
//qprod->x = q1->w*q2->x + q1->x*q2->w + q1->y*q2->z - q1->z*q2->y;
//qprod->y = q1->w*q2->y - q1->x*q2->z + q1->y*q2->w - q1->z*q2->x;
//qprod->z = q1->w*q2->z + q1->x*q2->y - q1->y*q2->x + q1->z*q2->w;

// this method was arrived at basically by trying to factor the above
// expression to reduce the # of multiplies

float prd_0 = (q1->z - q1->y) * (q2->y - q2->z);
float prd_1 = (q1->w + q1->x) * (q2->w + q2->x);
```

```
float prd_2 = (q1->w - q1->x) * (q2->y + q2->z);
float prd_3 = (q1->y + q1->z) * (q2->w - q2->x);
float prd_4 = (q1->z - q1->x) * (q2->x - q2->y);
float prd_5 = (q1->z + q1->x) * (q2->x + q2->y);
float prd_6 = (q1->w + q1->y) * (q2->w - q2->z);
float prd_7 = (q1->w - q1->y) * (q2->w + q2->z);

float prd_8 = prd_5 + prd_6 + prd_7;
float prd_9 = 0.5 * (prd_4 + prd_8);

// and finally build up the result with the temporary products
qprod->w = prd_0 + prd_9 - prd_5;
qprod->x = prd_1 + prd_9 - prd_8;
qprod->y = prd_2 + prd_9 - prd_7;
qprod->z = prd_3 + prd_9 - prd_6;

} // end QUAT_Mul
```

Notice that at first, I was using the brute force method of multiplying the quaternions by the definition of multiplication (16 multiplies, 12 additions), then with some algebra, I simplified the multiplication to 9 multiplies and 27 additions. Normally, you might think this is better, but on floating point processors, that may not be the case.

Purpose

void QUAT_Mul() multiplies the quaternion *q1*q2* and stores the result in *qprod*.

Example

```
QUAT q1={1,2,3,4}, q2={5,6,7,8}, qprod;

// multiply q1*q2
QUAT_Mul(&q1, &q2, qprod);
```

Function Prototype

```
void QUAT_Triple_Product(QUAT_PTR q1, QUAT_PTR
   q2, QUAT_PTR q3, QUAT_PTR qprod);
```

CAUTION

The product *q1*q2* is not equal to *q2*q1* unless *q1* or *q2* is the multiplicative identity. Hence, multiplication is non-commutative for quaternions in general.

Purpose

void QUAT_Triple_Product() multiplies the three quaternions *q1*q2*q3* and stores the result in *qprod*. This function is useful for rotating points since the transform

$(q^*)*(v)*(q)$ and $(q)*(v)*(q^*)$ are triple products that rotate vectors or points. This function is very useful in performing rotation as shown in the example.

Example

```
// lets rotate the vector/point (5,0,0)
// around the z-axis 45 degrees

// Step 1: create the rotation quaternion
VECTOR3D vz = {0,0,1};

QUAT qr, // this will hold the rotation quaternion
    qrc; // this will hold its conjugate

// create the rotation quaternion
VECTOR3D_Theta_To_QUAT(&qr, &vz, DEG_TO_RAD(45));

// now its conjugate
QUAT_Conjugate(&qr, &qrc);

// now create a point to rotate with the q0
// element equal to 0 and the x,y,z as the point
QUAT qp={0,5,0,0};

// now we do the rotation which will rotate
// p about the z-axis 45 degrees, of course
// the rotation axis could have been anything
QUAT_Triple_Product(&qr, &qp, &qrc, &qprod);

// now the result will still have q0=0,
// so we can just extract the point from the
// x,y,z elements of the quaternion
```

Function Prototype

```
void QUAT_Print(QUAT_PTR q, char *name);
```

Purpose

void QUAT_Print() prints out a quaternion with the given name to the error file.

Example

QUAT_Print(&q);

As a demo of some of the quaternion functions check out QUATERNION01.CPP|
EXE. Figure 17.7 shows a screen shot of the application running; basically, you can
input a couple of quaternions, and vectors, and then manipulate them with the
library functions. Try entering in a rotation quaternion along with a vector and
then rotate the vector and see if the results are correct!

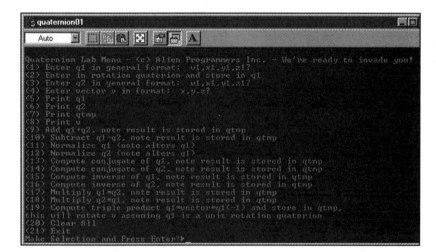

Figure 17.7

*A quaternion lab in
all its glory*

Conclusion

At this point, you should have a good working knowledge of quaternions, what they
are, and how they can be applied to operations, such as rotation. Of course, the
real power of quaternions comes into play when we use them to represent camera
operations, taking advantage of the fact that a quaternion can hold both a direction and rotation angle around that direction.

Terrain Collision with Quadtrees

By Richard Benson,
rbenson@earthlink.net

Introduction

Modern 3-D video games are always pushing the limits of today's computer hardware. The environments that we play in are using more and more polygons in order to achieve as much realism as possible. This is especially true of games that take place outdoors with large sections of terrain for the player to explore. Given the nature of terrain being organic and non-uniform, it takes a large number of polygons to represent it accurately. While high polygon counts can make the environments look great, they can really stress the hardware that the game is running on. The cost of rendering high polygon count environments can be assisted greatly by modern 3-D video cards. This doesn't mean that we don't need to worry about the costs of rendering all those polygons; it's just not the focus of this chapter. Our main focus for this chapter is how we go about doing accurate collision detection with these environments without bringing the system to a crawl.

The problem is that most 3-D video games are real-time applications. That means that we have to maintain 30–60 frames per second to keep the game flowing smoothly. In order to maintain 30 frames per second, all of our calculations and renderings have to be finished in approximately 33.3 milliseconds. And 60 frames per second would only give you half of that time: approximately 16.6 milliseconds. Combine that with the high polygon count environments and you've got a challenge ahead of you. Here's an extreme example of the problem. Let's say your environment has 150,000 polygons and you're trying to maintain 60 frames per second. Even with only one player in the game, you'll have to check 9,000,000 polygons to see if the player has collided with them. On average, only half of the polygons will have to be checked before a collision is found. This means that on average we're still checking 4,500,000 polygons per second. That's insane! What we need is a way to quickly rule out polygons that the player has no chance of colliding with before the costly collision detection calculation is performed.

One of the available solutions is an organizational technique called *spatial partitioning*. Spatial partitioning works by dividing space into discrete regions. This makes it easy to disregard polygons before the costly collision detection tests are performed on them. For this chapter, we'll be discussing a specific type of spatial partitioning known as the quadtree.

What Will Be Covered

This chapter will explain what a quadtree is and why the quadtree is the spatial partition of choice for outdoor environments. You will learn how to build a quadtree from a set of polygons, how to quickly find polygons in the vicinity of where you're checking and how to find an intersection point within those polygons. We will go over various design decisions associated with quadtrees, including the choices that were made for the quadtree implementation described in this chapter. Also, let me state that this quadtree implementation has been purposely simplified to make the material accessible to someone who's never dealt with quadtrees or any spatial partitioning techniques, for that matter. Also the terms *polygons* and *triangles* will be used interchangeably in this chapter since we only support three-sided polygons (triangles).

For this chapter, we will be using the right-handed coordinate system shown in Figure 18.1. The x and y axes make up the ground plane and the positive z axis is up.

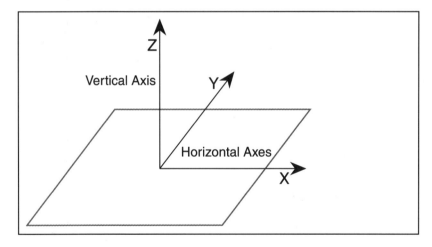

Figure 18.1

The coordinate system used for this chapter

Introduction to Trees

As mentioned previously, a quadtree is a specific type of spatial partitioning. Most of the techniques for spatial partitioning use data structures that are often referred to as *trees*.

A *tree*, for our needs, is defined as a collection of *nodes*. Just think of each node as a container. The contents of the nodes are irrelevant for right now. Usually, the tree starts off with one node that is called the *root*. The way the tree is organized is that every node has links to other nodes. These links are often referred to as *branches*. For the most part, branches can only be traversed in one direction. In reference to Figure 18.2, the branches would align top to bottom. When a node has branches to other nodes below it, it is often called the *parent node*. Consequently, the nodes it links to are known as its *child nodes* or *children*. If a node doesn't have any child nodes, it is called a *leaf node*. If for every node in the tree, there are an equal number of nodes below it, then the tree is said to be *balanced*. Balanced trees produce the fastest search times. This is because as you go down farther into the tree, you are decreasing the remaining nodes exponentially.

One last term associated with trees is *depth*. Every time you follow a branch deeper into the tree, your depth increases by one. For example, the leaf nodes in Figure 18.2 at the bottom are all at a depth of two. Okay, that should be enough information about trees to get you through the rest of the chapter. Let's get back to spatial partitioning.

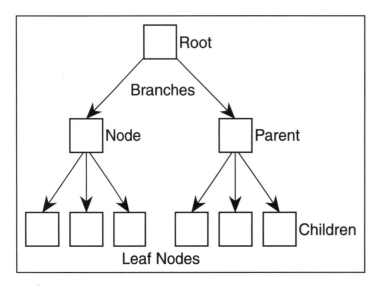

Figure 18.2

An abstract representation of a tree

Spatial Partitioning

The term *Spatial Partitioning* describes a technique for organizing objects in 3-D space by their location. Three of the most popular forms of spatial partitioning are BSP (*Binary Space Partition*) trees, octrees, and quadtrees. Each of these techniques works by collecting all of the objects in the world (whether they're game objects or polygons) and then recursively putting the objects in smaller regions until some limit is reached. For BSP trees, this limit is usually that we don't have any more polygons to sort. For octrees and quadtrees, the limiting factor is often that the tree has reached a maximum depth or that each node has a minimal amount of objects.

BSP Trees

The word binary can be defined as "consisting of two parts." This holds true for a BSP because it recursively splits the world into two half spaces. It starts by picking one plane that will divide the world into two half spaces. One half space is on the positive side of the plane and one half space is on the negative side of the plane. Then for each half space, we pick a new plane that divides it into two half spaces, and so on. Note that in Figure 18.3, Plane D has been chosen as the first splitting plane of the BSP tree. That left us with two sets of planes remaining, ABC and EFG. For each one of those sets, we pick the plane that best divides in half. As you can see by the BSP tree on the right side of Figure 18.3, we chose B to split ABC and F to split EFG.

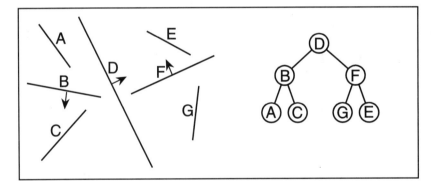

Figure 18.3

An overhead view of polygons before BSP tree is built

A visual representation of the tree is also shown. In practice, BSP trees are much more complex than shown here, but this will do for the sake of instruction. Indoor environments often use BSP trees since the walls of the environment can be used as the splitting planes for the tree.

Octrees

Octrees usually start with a cube that contains all the objects in the world. To build the octree, we divide the first cube into eight equally sized cubes. Then for each one of the new eight cubes, we split the cube into eight octants as necessary.

Since octrees cover all three dimensions equally, they are a good general method for spatial partitioning 3-D objects and/or geometry. We'll see in a second why quadtrees are a better choice for when the environment is mostly terrain (see Figure 18.4).

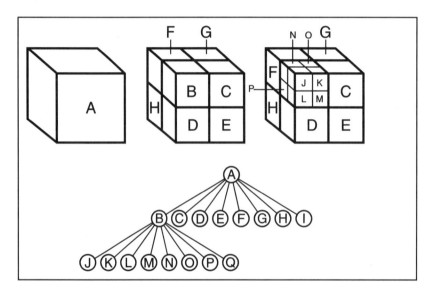

Figure 18.4

This is how an octree gets divided

Quadtrees

Similarly to octrees, quadtrees start with a region that contains all the objects in the environment. The way that quadtrees differ from octrees is that quadtrees use a 2-D square instead of a 3-D cube as their bounding region. To build a quadtree you start with the bounding region (see Figure 18.5) and split it into four equally sized regions. Then you recursively split each of the squares into four equally sized squares (quadrants) as needed.

Refer to Figure 18.6, which is an overhead view of a piece of terrain. Since typical terrain has no overlapping polygons, there is only one contact point for a given x,y coordinate. This is a perfect candidate for a quadtree.

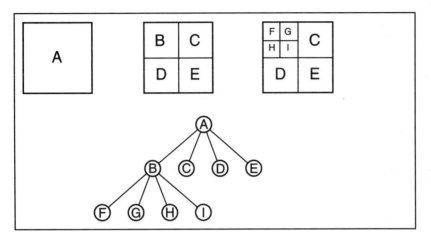

Figure 18.5

This is how a quadtree gets divided; the corresponding quadtree is also shown

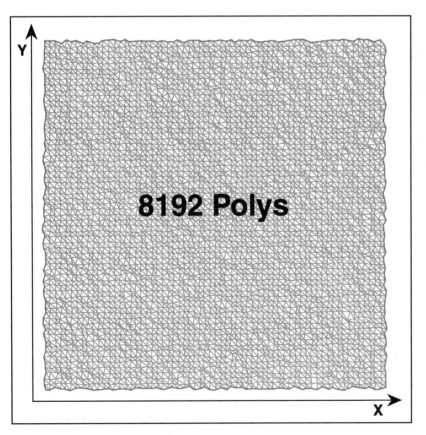

Figure 18.6

Overhead view of a sample piece of terrain

The Quadtree

The best way to think of the quadtree is from a top-down perspective. Look at Figure 18.7. In our demo, our terrain has 8,192 polygons (triangles). We use a 64 by 64 grid and each grid section has two polygons: $64 \times 64 \times 2 = 8192$. Imagine yourself at the top of our quadtree that contains 8,192 polygons. Now given the x and y coordinates you want to test, you move down the tree one level by comparing the x and y coordinates with the midpoint of the current node (the root). Let's say you calculate that you need to go down to the upper-left quadrant. The amazing thing is that you just reduced the polygons you have to test to 2,048. That's a reduction of 75 percent! That's the magic of a quadtree. The deeper you go down in the tree, the more you are narrowing your search.

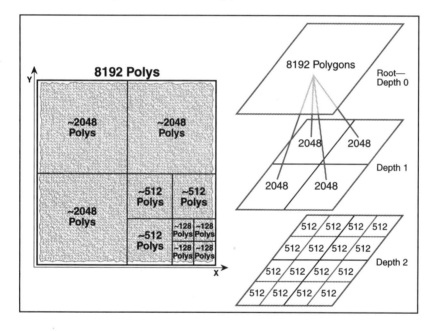

Figure 18.7

The lower we go down in the tree, the less polygons we have to interact with

The *CQuadtree* Class

Let's begin this section by taking a look at the CQuadtree class.

```
class CQuadtree
{
public:
        CQuadTree(float minX, float maxX, float minY, float maxY);
        ~CQuadTree();
```

```
        void AddFace(CVector3& v0, CVector3& v1, CVector3& v2);
        bool Intersect(float x, float y, float& height, CVector3& normal);

private:
        CQuadTreeNode* m_root;
};
```

This is our quadtree class. As you can see there's not much to it. Its main purpose is really just an interface for CQuadtreeNode, which we will discuss shortly. The most important element is m_root, which is the link that connects us to the entire tree. Let's look at the constructor for CQuadtree.

```
CQuadtree::CQuadtree(float minX, float maxX, float minY, float maxY)
{
    // Create a root node that covers the extents of the quadtree.
    // Note that the last parameter is the depth of the node. Since
    // it's the root node, we set the depth to zero.
    m_root = new CQuadTreeNode(minX, maxX, minY, maxY, 0);

    // verify that our allocation worked
    assert(m_root);
}
```

The only way to create an instance of CQuadtree is by passing the extents of the area that the quadtree will cover. We create a new node and assign it to our m_root pointer.

At this point the quadtree is ready to be used. We have one node that encompasses the extents of the quadtree. What we'll do then is split that node into smaller nodes as we add polygons to the tree. Note that the last parameter of the CQuadtreeNode constructor is the depth of the node being created. Since we are creating the root node, we tell it to set its depth to 0.

```
// verify that our allocation worked
assert(m_root);
```

Since the rest of the code assumes that m_root is a valid pointer, we need to stop executing if the allocation of the root node fails. This is what the assert() is for. If m_root is NULL after we try and create a new CQuadtreeNode instance, our code will stop execution. Let's move on to the CQuadtreeNode class.

The *CQuadtreeNode* Class

Now let's examine the CQuadtreeNode class.

```
class CQuadtreeNode
{
    // CQuadtree needs access to our data and functions.
    friend class CQuadtree;

private:
    // Constructor / Destructor.
    CQuadtreeNode(float minX, float maxX, float minY, float maxY);
    ~CQuadTreeNode();

    // Intersect will find the polygon that intersects the
    // x,y coordinate given.
    bool Intersect(float x, float y, float& height, CVector3& normal);
    // AddFace adds the polygon described by the three vertices to
    // the quadtree.
    void AddFace(CVector3& v0, CVector3& v1, CVector3& v2);

    // STL List of pointers to TreeFace data.
    // This is the polygon data contained in this CQuadtreeNode.
    list<TreeFace*>  m_PolyList;

    // x,y extents of this node
    float       m_minX;
    float       m_minY;
    float       m_maxX;
    float       m_maxY;

    // pointers to our four children
    CQuadtreeNode*    m_pChild_UL;
    CQuadtreeNode*    m_pChild_UR;
    CQuadtreeNode*    m_pChild_LL;
    CQuadtreeNode*    m_pChild_LR;

    // The depth of this quadtree node within the quadtree
    // We'll need this since we're always going to add polygons
    // to the bottom-most quadtree nodes.
```

```
    int        m_depth;
};
```

The `CQuadtreeNode` class is the heart of our quadtree implementation. This is where we have all the data that we're storing in the nodes, as well as the information that allows us to traverse them quickly. At the top, you'll notice that we've declared `CQuadtree` as a friend class. This will give the main quadtree access to the nodes of the tree and keep the code from being filled with lots of accessory routines. `m_PolyList` is a Standard Template Library (STL) list of pointers to our poly information. This is where we will store any polygons that belong to this `QuadtreeNode`.

> **NOTE**
>
> STL is the Standard Template Library. It is a portable, fast, and efficient set of common routines and data structures. We use the List template as a means to store pointers to polygon data in each quadtree node. The List template is a linked list implementation which allows us to easily add and remove nodes as well as making it easy to access the polygon data for a given quadtree node.

Then we have `m_minx`, `m_minY`, `m_maxX` and `m_maxY`. These are the min and max values that describe the extents of this node in the x,y plane. We will use these extents to determine the sizes and locations of our children. We will also be using these extents to quickly traverse the quadtree, looking for the quadtree node that contains the point we're checking. The four pointers to the children of this quadtree node are declared as four separate pointers; one to each quadrant. This makes the code a little easier to follow. It's perfectly valid for these pointers to be NULL, so we'll need to check their validity before we try and access them at runtime. Figure 18.8 shows a visual representation of a quadtree node.

```
CQuadtreeNode* m_pChild_UL; // Upper Left
CQuadtreeNode* m_pChild_UR; // Upper Right
CQuadtreeNode* m_pChild_LL; // Lower Left
CQuadtreeNode* m_pChild_LR; // Lower Right
```

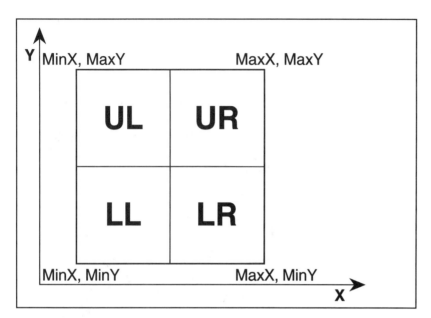

Figure 18.8

A visual representation of CQuadTreeNode

Building Up the Quadtree

Once we've declared an instance of the quadtree, we can start adding polygons to it. We start by passing the three vertices of the triangle to the AddFace() method of our quadtree.

```
void CQuadTree::AddFace(CVector3& v0, CVector3& v1, CVector3& v2)
{
    // calculate the min and max extents for this triangle
    float minX = __min( v0.x(), __min( v1.x(), v2.x()));
    float maxX = __max( v0.x(), __max( v1.x(), v2.x()));

    float minY = __min( v0.y(), __min( v1.y(), v2.y()));
    float maxY = __max( v0.y(), __max( v1.y(), v2.y()));

    // verify that the vertices all fit within the extents of the quadtree
    assert( (minX >= m_root->m_minX) && (maxX <= m_root->m_maxX) &&
        (minY >= m_root->m_minY) && (maxY <= m_root->m_maxY) );

    m_root->AddFace(v0, v1, v2);
}
```

First, we need to determine if the triangle fits entirely in the quadtree's root node. Remember when we called the constructor for CQuadtree, we told it how big to make the quadtree. So as long as the size was calculated correctly for the set of polygons in the environment, every polygon should fit. Checking to see if every polygon fits in the quadtree's root node before adding it is overkill but I thought it would help for someone who was trying out the quadtree code for the first time. This way instead of the quadtree not working, they'll get an assert if they try to add any polygons that don't fit.

Once the quadtree calls `AddFace()` for the root node, we start passing the polygon down through the tree, creating new nodes as necessary until we find the node where we want to store it. One problem we have to deal with when adding polygons to the quadtree is what to do when a polygon doesn't fit exactly within a quadtree node. For example, in Figure 18.9, the polygon touches all four quadtree nodes. We have three options to choose from:

1. Split the polygon into smaller polygons that fit entirely within the quadtree nodes. This option creates more polygons and is more complicated than the other two.

2. Leave the polygon in the current node and don't pass it down farther in the tree. Using this option will often leave a lot of the polygons in the root node and will decrease the benefits of storing the polygons in a quadtree.

3. Add the polygon to every quadtree node that it touches. This method is simple but will waste some memory and computer processing unit time. In order to keep things as simple as possible, we will use this method.

In order to simplify the process of determining which quadrants to add the polygon to, we calculate a bounding box that surrounds the polygon. We then call the root node's `AddFace()` method, which if you'll remember is the node that is as big as the entire tree. Then what `AddFace()` will do is figure out from the bounding box which quadrants the polygon is touching and pass the polygon down to them.

It should be noted that this method has its flaws and will sometimes add a polygon to a quadtree node that it

> **NOTE**
> A fourth option is often used when the quadtree is used to store game objects. That option entails using loose boundaries for the quadtree nodes.[1] The best way to visualize this is to think of adding the game object to the quadrant that it's closest to fitting in or the quadrant that most of the object is in. Using loose boundaries, the edges of the quadrants overlap and therefore are no longer discrete or separate from each other.

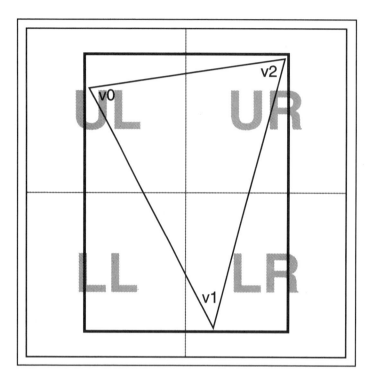

Figure 18.9

This is the bounding box that enclosves the triangle; using the bounding box, we can determine which quadrants to insert the triangle into

shouldn't, but it simplifies the code enough that I thought it was better to use this method. To see this problem better, refer to Figure 18.9. You can see that if v0 and v1 were moved over to the right a little, the triangle would not intersect the LL quadrant at all. But in that case, the bounding box of the triangle would still intersect quadrant LL and as such the polygon would be added to LL. The only problems this causes is a waste of memory and some wasted Computer Processing Unit (CPU) time if we're testing polygons that aren't in our quadrant. Now that we know how we figure out which nodes to pass the polygon to, let's see what happens from there.

CQuadtreeNode::AddFace()

Moving right along, let now examine CQuadtreeNode::AddFace().

```
void CQuadtreeNode::AddFace(CVector3& v0, CVector3& v1, CVector3& v2)
{
    // The depth of this node is as deep as we want to go
    // Add the poly to this node and return.
    if (m_depth >= MAX_DEPTH)
    {
```

```
    TreeFace* newFace = new TreeFace(v0, v1, v2);
    m_PolyList.push_back(newFace);
    return;
}


float minX = __min( v0.x(), __min( v1.x(), v2.x()));
float maxX = __max( v0.x(), __max( v1.x(), v2.x()));

float minY = __min( v0.y(), __min( v1.y(), v2.y()));
float maxY = __max( v0.y(), __max( v1.y(), v2.y()));

// determine which quadrants are touched by a bounding box
// surrounding the triangle.
// Upper Left
bool UL = ((minX < halfX) && (minY < halfY));
// Upper Right
bool UR = ((maxX > halfX) && (minY < halfY));
// Lower Left
bool LL = ((minX < halfX) && (maxY > halfY));
// Lower Right
bool LR = ((maxX > halfX) && (maxY > halfY));

// only create a child if the bounding box of the poly touches it
if (UL)
{
  if (!m_pChild_UL)
  {
     m_pChild_UL = new CQuadTreeNode(m_minX, halfX, m_minY, halfY,
                     m_depth+1);
     assertt(m_pChild_UL);
   }
   m_pChild_UL->AddFace(v0, v1, v2);
}

if (UR)
{
  if (!m_pChild_UR)
  {
     m_pChild_UR = new CQuadTreeNode(halfX, m_maxX, m_minY, halfY,
```

```
                            m_depth+1);
            assert(m_pChild_UR);
        }
        m_pChild_UR->AddFace(v0, v1, v2);
    }

    if (LL)
    {
        if (!m_pChild_LL)
        {
            m_pChild_LL = new CQuadTreeNode(m_minX, halfX, halfY, m_maxY,
                            m_depth+1);
            assert(m_pChild_LL);
        }
        m_pChild_LL->AddFace(v0, v1, v2);
    }

    if (LR)
    {
        if (!m_pChild_LR)
        {
            m_pChild_LR = new CQuadTreeNode(halfX, m_maxX, halfY, m_maxY,
                            m_depth+1);
            assert(m_pChild_LR);
        }
        m_pChild_LR->AddFace(v0, v1, v2);
    }

    return;
}
```

The first thing we do is check to see if we are at the maximum depth of the tree. The maximum depth is a predetermined value that will vary for different environments. For the purposes of our implementation, I decided to add polygons to the bottom of the tree because the terrain we're dealing with is fairly uniform. This will maximize the effectiveness of the quadtree by keeping it fairly balanced. If the terrain you're dealing with isn't uniform, you may benefit by maintaining a polygon limit per quadtree node. Then if you overflow that node, you can pass polygons down to your children.

If we're not at the maximum depth of the tree, then we continue on and calculate which child quadtree nodes we will pass this polygon down to. We calculate the bounding region of the triangle as shown in Figure 18.9. Then we perform a series of tests to see which quadrants the bounding box touches. We store a Boolean value for each quadrant. Once we've done this we start looking at the Boolean values to determine which child quadtree nodes to send this polygon down to. If the Boolean value for a quadrant is true, then we test to see if we already have a valid pointer to this child. If we don't have a valid pointer, then this is the first time we've attempted to add a polygon to this child and so we create a new CQuadtreeNode and assign our pointer to that child.

You'll notice that I've placed assert() calls in every location where we try to create new quadtree nodes. If for some reason we can't allocate a new CQuadtreeNode for this quadrant, then the code will assert and we'll know something has gone wrong.

Once we've added all of our polygons to the quadtree, we can start to use it for its intended use, terrain collision.

Finding an Intersection

So we have a quadtree that will allow us blazingly fast access to the polygon data of the terrain. Here's our first attempt at putting it to use. A typical need for a quadtree that contains terrain data is for it to tell us the height at a specific coordinate in the x,y plane.

While we're at it, we'll have the quadtree tell us the normal of the surface at the point of intersection. That way we can do things like determine if the terrain is too steep for a player to climb, accurately model the velocity of an object sliding on the terrain, etc. The function that we call to get all this information is CQuadtree::Intersect(). It returns a Boolean value to tell us whether or not it found a polygon below the given x,y coordinate. If it returns true, then height will be the z coordinate of intersection and normal will contain the surface normal of the polygon at the point of intersection. Here's the implementation:

```
bool CQuadTree::Intersect(float x, float y, float& height, CVector3& normal)
{
    // Verify that our quadtree covers the coordinate they're looking for.
    // This doesn't guarantee that there is a poly at this coordinate, it
    // just makes the rest of the code simpler since we know it's in our
    // range.
    if ((x < m_root->m_minX) || (x > m_root->m_maxX)) return false;
```

```
    if ((y < m_root->m_minY) || (y > m_root->m_maxY)) return false;

    return m_root->Intersect(x, y, height, normal);
}
```

CQuadtree::Intersect() starts by checking to see if the x,y coordinate we passed in is inside the extents of the quadtree. If the x,y coordinate is not inside the extents of the root quadtree node, then we return false which tells us that there is no polygonal data below that x,y coordinate. Once CQuadTree::Intersect() determines that the coordinate we're checking is within its extents, it calls CQuadtreeNode::Intersect() which will start a recursive chain of node traversals.

```
bool CQuadTreeNode::Intersect(float x, float y, float& height,
                CVector3& normal)
{
    float halfX = (m_minX + m_maxX) * 0.5f;
    float halfY = (m_minY + m_maxY) * 0.5f;

    // Upper
    if (y < halfY)
    {
        // Upper Left
        if (x < halfX)
        {
            if (m_pChild_UL)
                return m_pChild_UL->Intersect(x, y, height, normal);
        }
        // Upper Right
        else
        {
            if (m_pChild_UR)
                return m_pChild_UR->Intersect(x, y, height, normal);
        }
    }
    // Lower
    else
    {
        // Lower Left
        if (x < halfX)
        {
            if (m_pChild_LL)
```

```
            return m_pChild_LL->Intersect(x, y, height, normal);
    }
    // Lower Right
    else
    {
        if (m_pChild_LR)
            return m_pChild_LR->Intersect(x, y, height, normal);
    }
}


// We need to pick a starting location for our trace.
// The Z value doesn't matter. RayIntersectTriangle() can handle
// the case where the polygon is above the start of the ray.
CVector3 start(x, y, 0);
// A vector straight down
CVector3 dir(0, 0, -1);

// no children, look within our own list of tris
list<TreeFace*>::iterator it = m_PolyList.begin();

CVector3 v0, v1, v2;
for ( /* no init */; it != m_PolyList.end(); ++it )
{
    v0 = (*it)->v0;
    v1 = (*it)->v1;
    v2 = (*it)->v2;

    if ( RayIntersectTriangle( start, dir, v0, v1, v2, height, normal) )
        return true;
}

    return false;
}
```

Now that `CQuadTree` has temporarily handed off control to us, let's start walking the tree. Since every node breaks up into quadrants, we pre-calculate the middle of our node in x and y. Now we can easily determine which quadrant the search coordinate is in. First we check the y coordinate to see if we're looking in the upper or lower half. Once we determine that, we only have two choices, left or right. When we've determined the quadrant the point is in, we try and traverse the child node for that quadrant. If we don't have a child node for that quadrant, then this is as deep in the tree as we can go. Now we need to look at all the triangles that we are responsible for and see if any of them intersect the coordinate being searched for. For our tests we will use a Ray–Triangle intersection test as shown in Figure 18.10.

A Ray has a starting point and a direction, but no endpoint. It continues on from its starting point indefinitely.

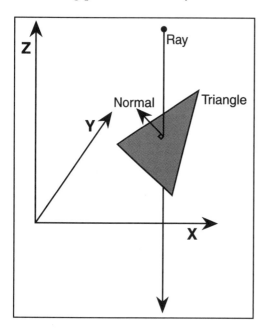

Figure 18.10

An example of a successful Ray–Triangle intersection test

The Ray needs a starting location and a direction. The x and y coordinates for the starting location are simple, in fact they were given to us. The question is, what z value do we choose? You'll be happy to know that for the algorithm we use, it doesn't matter. I'll explain this shortly when we talk about the algorithm for Ray–Triangle intersection.

Explanation of *RayIntersectTriangle()*

The following source code will aid in the explanation of the RayIntersectTriangle().

```
bool RayIntersectTriangle(CVector3& P, CVector3& Dir, CVector3& v0,
CVector3& v1, CVector3& v2, float& height, CVector3& normal)
{
    // Compute two edges from the three vertices passed in.
    CVector3 edge1(v1 - v0), edge2(v2 - v0);
```

```
// Compute normal of triangle by crossing two edges
// Note: we'll need to normalize this before exit
//
// The caret symbol ^ is the cross product for our CVector3 class.
normal = CVector3(edge1 ^ edge2);
normal.Normalize();

// Ray equation
// Q = P + t*Dir
//
// Plane equation
// Ax + By + Cz + D = 0
//
// normal.Q + D = 0
// normal.(P + t*Dir) + D = 0
// normal.P + t*normal.Dir + D = 0
//
// t = -(D + normal.P)
//    ----------
//     normal.Dir
//
// For any plane, D is the distance from the origin to the plane.
// By definition, D can be computed by calculating the negative
// of the normal dotted with any vertex on the plane.
// D = -normal.vertex0
//
// The pipe symbol | is the dot product for our CVector3 class.
float D = -normal | v0;

// denominator = Normal.Dir
float denominator = normal | Dir;

// Check if ray is parallel with the plane of the triangle
// Keep in mind the denominator can't be zero or extremely close to zero
// or when we divide numerator by denominator we could get division
// by zero or exceeed the limits of float.
if (fabs(denominator) < 0.0001f)
   return false;
```

```
    // numerator = -(Normal.P + D)
    float numerator = -((normal | P) + D);


    // t tells us how far from P along Dir we intersect the plane of the
    // triangle. Note that t can be negative if the intersection point
    // is behind P from the perspective of Dir.
    float t = numerator / denominator;


    // Start at P and move along t units in the direction of Dir to
    // find the intersection point Q.
    //
    // Q = P + t * Dir
    CVector3 Q = P + Dir.Scale(t);


    // Calculate the edges of our triangle in the correct order
    // for our winding.
    CVector3 e1(v1-v0), e2(v2-v1), e3(v0-v2);


    // Now that we have Q and we know it's on the plane of the triangle
    // let's test to see if it's on the inside edge of each side.


    // calculate a normal for edge e1
    CVector3 edgeNormal = e1 ^ normal;


    // Determinant = N.(Q-Vertex of Edge)
    // Determinant > 0 : Q is on the outside of the current edge.
    // Determinant = 0 : Q is on the current edge.
    // Determinant < 0 : Q is on the inside of the current edge.
    Determinant = edgeNormal | (Q - v0);


    // if Q is outside of any of the edge planes, we are done.
    if (Determinant > 0.001f) return false;


    // Q is on the inside of edge E1, now check E2
    edgeNormal = E2 ^ normal;
    Determinant = edgeNormal | (Q - v1);


    // if Q is outside of any of the edge planes, we are done.
    if (Determinant > 0.001f) return false;
```

```
// Q is on the inside of edge E2 and E1, now check E3
edgeNormal = E3 ^ normal;
Determinant = edgeNormal | (Q - v2);

// if Q is outside of any of the edge planes, we are done.
if (Determinant > 0.001f) return false;

// Q is on inside of all three edges of triangle.

// Now that we're sure that Q is an intersection with this triangle,
// set the height value we return to the z value of Q
height = Q.z();

return true;
}
```

Let me start by saying that this implementation of a Ray versus Triangle Intersection test is by no means the fastest or cleanest version available. I chose this method since the code is very straightforward and easy to explain. Given a starting location, a direction, and a triangle, this function can tell us if there was an intersection with the triangle. It will also store the height and normal at the point of intersection in the variables we passed in if an intersection is found.

The first part of the function is really just a Ray–Plane intersection test.[2] We first test to make sure that the ray and the plane aren't parallel. If they are parallel, then an intersection will never occur and we return `false`. If they aren't parallel, then we calculate Q, which is the point at with the ray intersects the plane of the triangle. Let me reiterate that Q isn't guaranteed to be on the triangle (as shown in Figure 18.11), it's only guaranteed to be in the same plane as the triangle. Once

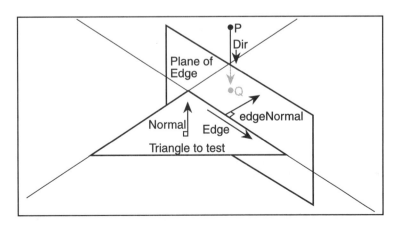

Figure 18.11

Check to see if a point on the plane of a triangle is actually within the triangle

we've calculated Q, we then have to test to see if it falls within the triangle we're testing. We again reference the plane equation. For each edge of the triangle, we calculate the plane that has a normal perpendicular to the normal of the triangle. This can be seen as the "Plane of Edge" in Figure 18.11.

If we calculate a vector from Q to a point on this edge plane and dot it with the normal of the plane, we have the determinant. The determinant is really just the distance from Q to the edge plane. If the determinant is zero, then Q on the edge plane is therefore on the edge of the triangle. If the determinant is greater than zero, then the point is on the positive side of the edge plane and is not inside the triangle. Finally, if the determinant is less than zero, then the point is on the inside of the edge plane. In Figure 18.11, Q will have a determinant greater than zero when tested with the right edge of the pictured triangle and will be rejected. If Q is on the inside of each edge plane, then Q is guaranteed to be inside the triangle.

Now, let's talk about how we go about cleaning up the quadtree after we're done with it.

Cleaning Up

The following is a code snippet of a destructor that will help us with the cleanup process for a CQuadtree.

```
CQuadtree::~CQuadTree()
{
    delete m_root;
}
```

When we delete the pointer to a CQuadtree or when it goes out of scope, the destructor for CQuadtree will be called. All we have to do at this point is delete the root node, which starts a recursive chain reaction that will clean up the entire tree and all the geometry data it holds. This is possible due to the recursive nature of the tree and some elegant coding in the destructor for CQuadtreeNode.

```
CQuadtreeNode::~CQuadtreeNode()
{
    // we need an iterator to the first element in our PolyList so that
    // we can delete them in order.
    list<TreeFace*>::iterator it = m_PolyList.begin();

    // keep deleting until our iterator is at the end of the list
    while (it != m_PolyList.end())
```

```
    {
        // *it gives us the pointer that we allocated in AddFace()
        // Since we created it, we are responsible for deleting it.
        delete *it;
        // The erase() method of an STL List has the benefit that
        // it gives you an iterator to the node after the one
        // you're deleting.
        it = m_PolyList.erase(it);
    }
    // Every node is only responsible for its children.
    // Deleting our children will cause them to delete their children
    // and so on. Verify each pointer isn't NULL before deleting.
    if (m_pChild_UL) delete m_pChild_UL;
    if (m_pChild_UR) delete m_pChild_UR;
    if (m_pChild_LL) delete m_pChild_LL;
    if (m_pChild_LR) delete m_pChild_LR;
}
```

As far as cleanup goes, the destructor for CQuadtreeNode is the workhorse of it all. It walks through the list of polygons and deletes them; nothing too fancy there. Now we get to the recursive nature of the cleanup process. In order to fully understand how the cleanup works, it's important to keep in mind that each node is only responsible for deleting its children and the geometry data it holds. So when a node deletes one of its children, that child node's destructor is called. Then the child node deletes its children and this happens till we get all the way down to the last node without children. It's situations like this that make recursion seem elegant. You code a few simple rules and execute them and all of a sudden the entire tree has been deleted and all memory returned back to the system.

Design Decisions and Performance

Now let's talk about some of the various decisions that need to be made before you decide how to use a quadtree for your terrain.

Square Quadtree Nodes

Most quadtree implementations force the quadtree nodes to be square and for their dimensions to be powers of two. Keeping the quadtree nodes square helps keep the distribution even among the x and y axes which helps performance. Also, if the quadtree nodes are square, you don't have to do as much work to determine the extents of each node (since the width and height are the same size). I decided not to force the quadtree nodes to be square for our implementation since it puts limitations on the shape of the environments that the quadtree will fit. However, you don't want the width and height of the quadtree node to differ by too much though or performance will start to suffer slightly. If you have environments that aren't close to being square, then you may want to consider using multiple quadtrees to partition it.

Copying Polygon Data Versus Pointing to Polygon Data

It's up to you to decide how you want the quadtree to reference the polygon data that it contains. Some implementations choose to store pointers to the polygon data. This will save memory and also allow a few other benefits. As you'll see later in the demo, if you store pointers to the vertex data, then your tree will still be valid even if the z values of your polygons change. This can be quite useful for a surface like water where you change the height values of the vertices in real time to simulate the motion of the water.

Another option is to copy the polygon data to the quadtree nodes. The benefit of doing this is that you can separate the quadtree from the actual geometry. If you wanted to, you could copy all your data to the quadtree nodes and then get rid of the original polygon data. Now you can have your quadtree render your geometry for you. More benefits of this will become clearer later when we discuss frustum culling.

Cache Misses

It should be noted that although quadtrees usually increase our performance, they can have performance issues of their own if not profiled on a per application basis. One reason for this is that traversing the branches of the tree and accessing those pointers can cause cache misses. Cache misses can hurt performance on hardware that really depends on the cache performance to keep things going fast. Always test your code to find out what your bottlenecks are.

If cache misses are a problem for you, another option is a method called *Direct Access QuadtreeLlookup*.[3] This will only work if the nodes of the quadtree were allocated as a contiguous array of nodes and if the tree is full and perfectly balanced.

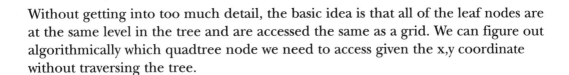

Without getting into too much detail, the basic idea is that all of the leaf nodes are at the same level in the tree and are accessed the same as a grid. We can figure out algorithmically which quadtree node we need to access given the x,y coordinate without traversing the tree.

Depth Versus Breadth

Another way to make the quadtrees performance better is to keep the depth of the nodes as small as possible. So instead of our example where we always add the polygons at the same depth of the tree, we would add polygons to the deepest quadtree node that completely contained them and not push them down to a lower level unnecessarily. This works well for terrain where you have a large variation in the size of the polygons. The large polygons can be stored higher up in the tree and as such we can often find the polygons we're looking for sooner.

Non-uniform Splitting

One last option I'd like to mention is non-uniform splitting. Notice that when we split the quadtree node into four smaller quadrants, we always split it into four equally sized regions. This is done by splitting it in half both vertically and horizontally. If the polygons or objects you're partitioning in your quadtree aren't distributed uniformly, you may not get optimal performance. Remember from earlier that we like to keep things balanced. So what you can do is find a center point that splits the objects or polygons so that there is an equal amount in each quadrant.

Other Uses for Quadtrees

One important thing to understand about quadtrees is the relationship between the parent and child nodes. Since the child nodes of a parent are just small regions within the parent, the parent's extents surround all of its children. Whether you realize it or not we've been using that property to our advantage for our collision detection scheme in this chapter. If you can't collide with a parent node (by checking its extents), then you can't collide with any of its children. The same property can be taken to visibility determination schemes as well. By using a technique called *frustum culling* with a quadtree, you can greatly minimize the number of elements you have to draw.

Frustum Culling

Frustum culling is a technique whereby you throw away anything that the camera can't see. Frustum is the volume that contains everything the camera can see and culling is a term that means, "Something picked out from others. . .". 3-D engines usually use frustum culling on an object-by-object basis. But since we've organized all of our polygons into a quadtree, we can frustum cull our quadtree nodes and save a lot of unnecessary computation.

In Figure 18.12, you can see the camera is located in the upper-right corner. The light gray triangle is an overhead view of the camera's view frustum. This represents everything that the camera can see. All of the white quadtree nodes aren't visible to the camera's view frustum and so we don't have to draw any of the polygons associated with them.

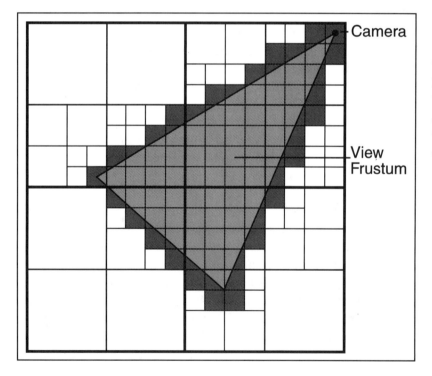

Figure 18.12

Overhead view of a quadtree; a camera's frustum which shows which quadtree nodes would be visible and which wouldn't

Camera

View Frustum

Frustum culling with quadtrees has another benefit as well. Similarly to not having to draw any polygons whose quadtree node isn't visible, any polygons whose quadtree node is completely visible won't have to be clipped to the view frustum. Actually with our current quadtree implementation we would still have to check polygons with the top and bottom planes of the view frustum since our quadtree nodes have no notion of height. However, if you added a minimum and maximum height value to each quadtree node, you could get away without checking the top and bottom frustum planes as well. Just remember that this benefit is only available for quadtree nodes that are completely visible to the camera's view frustum and so no edge of the quadtree node can intersect it.

The Demo

The demo for this chapter, shows a quadtree in action. In the demo, a green ball is supported by a large piece of terrain. A few interesting things to note are that the z values of the vertices are changing in real time similar to waves in water. This doesn't affect the organization of the quadtree since we only care about the location of the vertices in the x,y plane.

The reason that the tree maintains accurate height information for the terrain while it's moving is that for the demo, I chose to have the quadtree store pointers to the vertex data of the terrain instead of copying it. That way, any changes that are made to the vertices of the terrain will be detectible by the quadtree. Of course we can't change the location of the vertices in the x,y plane or we will invalidate the entire quadtree and it will be useless.

The white boxes that you see are the extents of the quadtree nodes that are "touched" as we find the intersection point of the ball with the terrain. You'll notice that there is one large white square which surrounds all of the terrain; this is the root node. The smaller white squares within the root node are the rest of the quadtree nodes we traverse while going deeper into the tree. The most important thing to note is that only the polygons beneath the smallest white square (the polygons of the leaf nodes) are being checked for collision against the location of the ball. In Figure 18.13, the green ball is slightly up and to the right of the center of the terrain. Notice that there are eight triangles below the smallest quadtree node.

For the purposes of the demo, the terrain is built up algorithmically at runtime. The vertices are created and stored in a vertex list. Then a face list is built up that references the vertices from the face list. Then after all the vertices and faces are constructed, the faces (triangles) are added to the quadtree one by one. If you don't like the idea of building the quadtree at runtime, you can build the quadtree offline and save it out to a file. Then your application can load up your quadtree from the file during startup.

Compiling the Demo

The source code for the demo should compile fine with Visual C++ 6.0. The demo uses OpenGL as the renderer for the terrain, quadtree nodes, etc. To compile the demo simply start Visual C++, open the "GL Quadtree" workspace, and hit F7.

Running the Demo

To run the demo, double-click the .exe file or use the Run option in Windows. Your machine will have to have OpenGL support for the application to run, but this should be standard for any machine running Windows 98, Windows ME, Windows 2000, or Windows XP. Once you choose to run full screen or windowed, the demo will start. The keys that are available during the demo are these:

A,Z	Camera zoom in and out
E,D	Shove the ball along the Y axis
S,F	Shove the ball along the X axis
Space	Causes the ball to jump if it's on the ground.
Left, Right:	Moves the camera along the X axis
Up, Down:	Moves the camera along the Z axis
Home, End:	Pitches the camera up and down
Esc:	Exits the demo

I'd like to take this time to thank NeHe for his terrific OpenGL tutorials and for his NeHeGL 1 Basecode that was used for this demo. NeHe's OpenGL site is located at

http://nehe.gamedev.net

Summary and Review

So we can now show that for terrain data with no overlap in the horizontal plane, the quadtree is a perfect way to minimize the time it takes to test for collisions. We've seen that quadtrees are simple to work with, but at the same time have many options to give them diversity. You've learned how to build a quadtree from a set of triangles and how to find where you've collided with them given an overhead x,y coordinate. Also, I've shown how to find the intersection point of a ray and a triangle as well as the normal at the intersection point.

Where to Go from Here

There are many other uses for quadtrees and countless variations in how they are implemented. Try a quick search on **www.google.com** using "quadtree" as the search criteria to further explorer the possibilities of the quadtree.

Also, there are some good tutorials on quadtrees online. Here are a few places I know of.

http://www.vterrain.org
www.flipcode.com
www.gamedev.net

Conclusion

As long as games keep pushing the limits of the hardware they run on, we'll always need ways to simplify the data we work with. I hope this article has shown you the simplicity, elegance, and usefulness of the quadtree for dealing with terrain data. Even though collision detection was the main focus of this chapter, I hope my brief mention of frustum culling helps you to see that there are many more ways to benefit from using quadtrees.

References

[1]Ulrich, "Loose Octrees," *Game Programming Gems*, Charles River Media, 2000, pp. 444–453.

[2]Eric Lengyel, *Mathematics for 3D Game Programming & Computer Graphics*, Charles River Media, 2002, pp. 117–118.

[3]Matt Pritchard, "Direct Access Quadtree Lookup," *Game Programming Gems 2*, Charles River Media, 2001, pp. 394–401.

TRICK 19

RENDERING SKIES

DAVE ASTLE, GAMEDEV.NET,
DAVE@GAMEDEV.NET

Introduction

If you've ever thought about creating an outdoor environment in your game, a potential problem may have occurred to you: How do you create an infinite world with finite geometry? If the player has a clear view of his surroundings, he should be able to see things off in the distance such as hills, mountains, the ocean, and other elements making up a sort of background. If the player can fly or otherwise attain a high elevation, a much larger area may be visible. In another kind of outdoor environment—in space—the player should be able to see extremely distant objects such as stars and nebulas.

One solution to this problem would be to make your world extremely big. Unfortunately, this would be very expensive in terms of both performance and the time required by your artists to populate the world. Unless you're going to allow the player to explore this much bigger area (which usually isn't the case), the additional expense isn't worth it.

A good solution in many cases is to use a skybox or one of its variations. A skybox provides you with a way to fake distant scenery by using static images that are texture mapped to a cube completely surrounding the player. This is somewhat of a hack, but as my graphics professor used to say, everything in graphics is a hack. The only thing that matters is that the final results look good and believable.

Many commercial games have used skyboxes very effectively, as shown in Figures 19.1 and 19.2.

What You Will Learn

This chapter will show you how to make your outdoor setting look more "real" through the use of skyboxes and related approaches. Specifically, this chapter will cover:

- Skyboxes
- Skydomes
- Skyplanes
- Other variations of skyboxes

Figure 19.1

A skybox of a cityscape from The Cranes map in Unreal Tournament

Figure 19.2

An outdoor skybox from the demo of Serious Sam: The Second Encounter

- Creating or otherwise obtaining textures for your skybox
- Improvements to add realism

Most of the information covered here will be API independent, but because the demo provided for this chapter uses OpenGL, I will cover some OpenGL-specific details. Most of the concepts should be easily portable to DirectX Graphics or any other API you may be using.

Skyboxes

Of all the sky representations covered in this chapter, skyboxes are the easiest to implement and understand. They also have a lot in common with the other methods covered, so let's start with them.

What Is a Skybox?

A skybox is a cube that completely surrounds the player and appears to completely surround the game world. Typically, a distant scene is projected onto the skybox using texture mapping. To maintain the illusion, the following criteria are necessary:

- The player should never be able to get close to the skybox, much less pass through it.
- The skybox shouldn't be clipped by the near or far clipping planes.

Now that you have a conceptual understanding of what a skybox is, let's look at the details involved with implementing one.

Representing a Skybox

Skyboxes are typically represented as a cube that's aligned with the world's coordinate axes, as shown in Figure 19.3. There are several popular naming conventions for the faces of the cube. The most common is to use *front, back, left, right, up,* and *down* (or *top* and *bottom*). The only drawback to this scheme is that the names can be ambiguous since the concepts of front, back, left, and right are relative to the player's orientation (up and down may be as well). To avoid this problem, another common practice is to name each face according to the world coordinate axis it corresponds to, meaning x_{pos}, x_{neg}, y_{pos}, y_{neg}, z_{pos}, and z_{neg}. In this chapter and in the included demo program, I'll use the former convention with the assumption that "front" corresponds to the negative z-axis.

Each face of the cube is represented as either a quad or triangle pair. The sides of the cube provide surfaces to which six texture maps are applied. The textures, of course, must be specifically created for use in a skybox. In addition to portraying

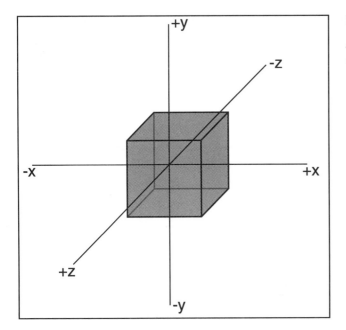

Figure 19.3

A skybox cube centered on and aligned with the world coordinate axes

distant scenery, the textures must be designed so that they smoothly transition into each other when arranged on the inside of the cube. Otherwise, seams between the textures will appear, destroying the illusion. This is one of the reasons why it's important to agree on a naming convention early on and stick to it. As long as you and the person creating the textures are using the same names, you should have no problem aligning the textures as intended.

The quality of your skybox depends entirely on the quality of the textures you use. However, no matter how good your textures are, they are going to look bad if they are stretched or shrunk. This happens whenever the projected size of a texel is not equal to the size of one screen pixel. To minimize this effect, you can determine in advance how big your textures should be using the following formula:

skybox texture width = screen width / tan (field of view angle / 2)

This is also displayed visually in Figure 19.4.

So, for example, if the screen resolution is 800×600 with a 75-degree field of view, the preceding formula becomes:

800 / tan (60 / 2)

This evaluates to about 1,042. Since textures need to have dimensions that are a power of 2, this could be dropped to 1,024.

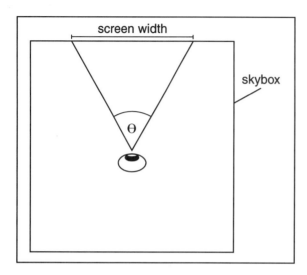

Figure 19.4

Determining the optimum texture size based on the screen width and field of view

It should be immediately obvious, though, that using an ideal resolution won't always be possible. In the example just given, you'd need six 1024×1024 textures. Using 32-bit textures, you'll need 24MB to store those textures in video memory. It gets worse as the resolution gets higher. At 1600×1200 with a 60-degree field of view, you'd need textures that are 2048×2048, consuming 96MB. Even if you reduce these amounts by using 8- or 16-bit textures and by using texture compression, all but the newest cards would have a hard time keeping all of those textures in video memory. And as if that's not bad enough, you have to account for the fact that most games allow players to change the resolution to whatever their video card supports, and many games allow players to change the field of view, such as by zooming with a sniper rifle. To get the best results at all possible resolution/field-of-view combinations, you'd have to have many different skybox texture sizes available. This is starting to sound ugly.

In reality, it's usually not practical to attempt to obtain the best results all of the time. Most games will simply use the largest skybox texture size possible given the game's requirements. Therefore, the formula provided works best as a loose guide. Texture sizes of 512×512 or 256×256 seem to offer the best combination of quality and size, at least on current hardware.

Orienting a Skybox

For a skybox to create a convincing illusion, it must be correctly placed in the world. It needs to be positioned so that the player and the world are both completely contained within it, and it needs to respond correctly to the camera orientation.

Position

One approach to ensure that the entire world is contained within the skybox is to create it as a bounding box for the world, centered on the world origin. However, there are some problems with this approach. First, as the player moves closer to the edge of the world, it will become apparent that the skybox is flat, destroying the illusion. Second, unless the player is relatively close to the skybox, the far clip plane will clip it. There are ways to get around these problems (such as setting the far clip plane to infinity), but there is a better way.

As it turns out, the skybox doesn't really have to contain the world. It just has to *look* like it contains the world. To accomplish this, the skybox can be drawn as a box centered on the camera. The size of the box doesn't matter as long as it's big enough to not get clipped by the near clip plane and small enough to not get clipped by the far clip plane.

By doing this, you ensure that the skybox completely encloses the player and that the player can never get close to the skybox. It is, in essence, infinitely far away from the player. The problem, of course, is that it doesn't appear to contain the entire world yet. Only a small portion of the world is inside the skybox. The rest of the world is actually blocked out by it—not what you wanted!

This problem is easy to fix. The skybox is blocking out the rest of the world because the values written to the depth buffer because of it are closer than most of the world. All you have to do to prevent this is turn off depth buffer writes while rendering the skybox. Doing so will make it impossible for the skybox to occlude anything else in the world. Problem solved.

Rotation

Although the position of the skybox should remain fixed with respect to the camera, it should respond normally to rotations. There are several ways to accomplish this. One option is to position the skybox after setting up the camera, in which case the skybox must be translated by the camera's position to keep it centered on the camera. A second option is to position the skybox before setting up the camera, in which case you have to rotate it according to the camera's orientation. A slight modification of the latter would be to simply push the modelview matrix stack, set up the appropriate rotations, and then pop the matrix stack, in which case it doesn't matter whether you set the camera up before or after the skybox. All of these approaches are valid, so use whichever method you prefer. The demo program included with this chapter uses the first method.

Rendering a Skybox

With the skybox properly positioned and oriented, the next step is to render it. The skybox will normally be rendered before everything else, though this isn't always a requirement. There are several important steps involved with the rendering of the skybox that should be followed for the best results.

Disable States

When rendering the skybox, there are several states that should be turned off, some because they are required for the skybox to work correctly and some because they aren't necessary.

The one state that definitely has to be turned off is depth buffer writes. If the skybox is not the first thing rendered, you also must disable the depth test. Even if your skybox is the first thing rendered (which is recommended when possible), turning off the depth test may give a slight performance boost.

Depending on how your game engine is structured, other states may be enabled that aren't necessary for the skybox. Some of these states may produce undesirable visual results, and even if they don't, they can incur a performance hit. This list of unnecessary states includes lighting, alpha blending, and fog. There may be others, depending on your game. Unless your game engine is structured in such a way that you can be sure none of these states is enabled when entering your skybox rendering routine, you should disable them prior to rendering.

TIP

Because a skybox completely encloses the scene, there is no longer a need to clear the color buffer every frame. The skybox effectively clears it for you. Don't waste processor cycles doing redundant work.

Set Texture States

The next step is to be sure that your textures are set up correctly. Most of the setup actually occurs during texture creation and not within the rendering function, but I'll cover everything here for convenience.

During setup, an appropriate filtering mode must be chosen. Point sampling only works well if the texture size is always a close match for the screen resolution, and as pointed out earlier, this is not often possible. At the other end of the scale, mipmapping produces good results, but it's overkill. The textures will always be about the same distance from the camera, so only one mipmap level will ever be used. Why waste video memory? That leaves bilinear filtering, which is almost always the right choice.

When using bilinear filtering, the texture wrap mode must be set correctly to prevent seams from appearing at the edges of the skybox. This can happen because when sampling pixels at the edge of the texture, two pixels are taken from the edge, and two pixels are taken from somewhere else. What does "somewhere else" mean? It depends on the texture wrap mode. If the texture repeats, those two pixels come from the opposite edge. If the texture just clamps, the samples will come from the border color. Neither is desirable since both will result in colors being added to the edge that aren't supposed to be there, usually resulting in visible seams.

OpenGL provides a texture wrap mode called `GL_CLAMP_TO_EDGE` that provides the needed behavior. It causes samples taken at the edge to only use colors on that edge. The only downside to this mode is that it was introduced in OpenGL 1.2, and thus it has to be treated as an extension (at least on Windows). That said, it seems to be fairly widely supported, so use it whenever possible.

An alternative approach would be to set your texture coordinates slightly inside the edge of the texture. So if your texture is 512×512, instead of using 0.0 and 1.0 for texture coordinates, use 1/512 and 511/512. This method was used in Quake 2. The only catch is that because the skybox textures are designed to smoothly transition between neighbors, this method can also produce seams (though not quite as visible). To prevent this, you can simply generate skybox textures that are two pixels smaller (for example, 510×510) and then create a one-pixel border that repeats the edge.

The last texture state you need to worry about is the texture environment mode. Because the texture doesn't need to be combined with the surface of the cube in any way, the environment mode can be set to replace.

Render Texture-Mapped Cube

Once all of the rendering states are set up, rendering the skybox is easy. You just need to render the six quads (or the equivalent) with texture coordinates applied. For each quad, you enable the appropriate texture and then draw the quad. The quads are drawn centered on the world origin, each parallel to one of the coordinate planes and at a distance placing it anywhere between the near and far clipping planes. That's all there is to it.

Restore State Settings

Before rendering the skybox, you disabled many states including lighting, fog, depth buffer writes, and so on. Once rendering is complete, you should restore all of these state settings to their previous values. You could simply enable everything that you disabled, but this can introduce bigger problems since you could enable states that aren't needed or wanted by other portions of your game.

One solution would be to save all of the old state settings and then restore them to their previous values when you're done. If you're using OpenGL, this is a good time to take advantage of the attribute stack. At the beginning of your rendering routine, before modifying any states, call `glPushAttribs()` with the appropriate flags set. Once the rendering is complete, call `glPopAttribs()` and you're done.

Of course, the best solution would be to build some kind of state management into your engine. State changes are often expensive, so whenever possible you should avoid making unnecessary ones. The discussion of a state management component is well beyond the scope of this chapter, but it's something to think about.

TIP

Try placing your skybox rendering code inside a display list. You should be able to see a small performance improvement because of all the state changes. Vertex arrays, on the other hand, aren't likely to help due to the limited amount of geometry.

Putting It All Together

Let's review the steps involved in using a skybox. At initialization, you'd do something like the following:

1. Create and load six textures.

2. For each texture, set the texture wrap mode to clamp to edge.

3. For each texture, set the texture filter to bilinear.

When rendering, the following steps should be followed:

1. Set up the camera.

2. Translate by the camera's position.

3. Save the current state settings.

4. Disable lighting, fog, blending, and everything else you don't need.

5. Disable the depth test.

6. Set the texture combine mode to replace.

7. Render the six sides of the cube using the appropriate textures.

8. Restore the old state settings.

These steps can be easily converted into code. Because the steps for the other methods are almost identical to these, they won't be repeated.

Skydomes

Skydomes are perhaps the most popular alternative to skyboxes. A skydome is similar to a skybox in concept, except that a sphere (or, more commonly, a hemisphere) is used instead of a cube, as shown in Figure 19.5. Skydomes are often more convenient to use when an animated background is used (such as a sun or clouds moving across the sky) since the transition across the surface of a sphere is easier to make smooth.

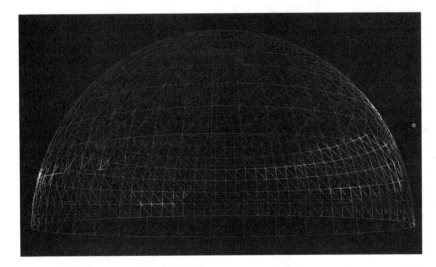

Figure 19.5

The outside wireframe view of a skydome

Creating the Skydome

The fundamental component of the skydome is, of course, the sphere itself. There are a number of algorithms to choose from to create your sphere, so use whichever you prefer. I'm not going to cover any of them in detail in this chapter, but the demo program includes a method that has worked well for me.

Regardless of which method you choose, you will usually create your sphere once at the beginning of your game and then reuse that data rather than re-creating it every frame. In addition, there are several parameters you should be able to control:

- **Resolution.** Because the sphere will be unlit, textured, and viewed from the inside, the triangles it's made up of can be relatively large with little or no loss in visible quality. Still, you'll want to be able to control the number of triangles and use it for your needs with a resolution parameter. The resolution can be described as a single parameter or as one for the latitude and one for the longitude (such as the stacks and slices parameters in several of the GLU quadrics routines).

- **Radius.** As with skyboxes, the radius of the sphere doesn't matter. It just needs to fall between the near and far clip planes.

- **Horizontal sweep.** This value ranges from 0 to 180 degrees and determines the range of the sphere in the horizontal direction. For example, a value of 90 degrees would produce a hemisphere.

Skydome Textures

As with a skybox, textures play a key role in a skydome's quality. However, texturing a sphere is a bit more complicated than texturing a cube. The two most common methods are using cube maps and using a single texture that may be repeated. Let's look at each method in detail.

Cube Maps

Cube maps consist of six different textures that are treated as a single texture. They are most commonly used in environment mapping. Cube map texture coordinates use three components (called s, t, and r) that represent a vector starting at the center of the object and passing through the point being textured. This vector is used to find a point on the cube map texture, which essentially encloses the object to which the texture is being applied.

Using a cube map for a skydome is a natural choice. Because the skydome is a sphere centered on the camera origin, the texture coordinates can easily be generated just by using the coordinates of each vertex making up the sphere. In addition, the textures made for skyboxes work perfectly as cube map textures, with one catch. Normally, cube map textures are applied to the outside of an object. For the skydome, the textures will be viewed from the inside. As a result, they will be mirrored. To compensate, either the s-coordinate or the r-coordinate must be inverted.

Single Texture

For a simpler background, such as basic animated clouds, using a single texture can often be a better solution. This texture may even be repeated. The only challenge involved with using a single texture is that you must generate texture coordinates for each point on the sphere yourself.

Rendering a Skydome

Other than the fact that the geometry itself is a bit more complex, rendering a skydome follows the same steps as rendering a skybox. After the camera is set up, the skydome is translated to the camera's position, all unnecessary states are disabled, and then the skydome is rendered. Because the skydome will use many more triangles than the skybox, it makes sense to render it using triangle strips and/or vertex arrays.

Skyplanes

Skyplanes provide a nice alternative to skydomes and skyboxes because they are remarkably easy to animate. In truth, a skyplane is not a true plane because it is not flat. Instead, it is represented as a plane with the corners pulled down, as shown in Figure 19.6. Note that because skyplanes do not completely surround the camera, they can only be used when some kind of ground plane is present.

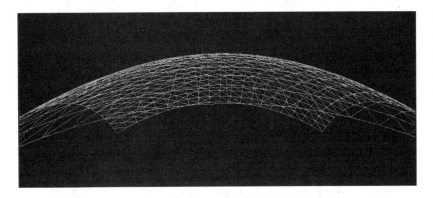

Figure 19.6

The outside wireframe view of a skyplane

Creating the Skyplane

As with a skydome, the geometry for a skyplane should be created at startup and saved for use later. In concept, creating a skyplane is much like creating a plane. However, because the corners are pulled down, the height at each point must be lowered by an amount that's dependent on the distance from the center of the plane. In most cases, you'll want to be able to control the exact shape of the skyplane. Here are some of the properties you may want to control:

- The resolution of the mesh representing the skyplane.
- The number of times to repeat the texture over the skyplane.
- The radius of the circle completely enclosing the skyplane.
- The height of the top, or peak, of the skyplane.
- The height of the middle of the edges of the skyplane. For lack of a better name, this will be referred to as the *horizon height*.

The importance of the last of these properties might not be obvious. Because the skyplane doesn't completely enclose the camera, you need to be sure that whatever portion of the background isn't filled by the skyplane is filled by the ground, mountains, or whatever else you're using. Since you generally know the minimum height of the ground or mountains, you can set the horizon height to be equal to or lower than this to ensure that no gaps appear between the ground and the sky.

With these properties in mind, let's look at the steps involved in the creation of the skyplane.

First, use the radius to determine the size of the skyplane. This can easily be obtained using the Pythagorean theorem. The size of the plane can then be divided by the resolution to determine the distance between each vertex in the plane. Using this information, a mesh containing (resolution + 1) * 2 vertices is created. Texture coordinates can generally be created as if the skyplane were flat, although this can lead to distortion if there is a high degree of curvature.

When generating vertex coordinates, the x- and z-coordinates are easy since the vertices are evenly spaced in the x and z directions. The y-coordinates are a little trickier because they need to take into account the desired peak and horizon heights. To generate the y-coordinate, the following formula can be used:

y = peak height – (peak height [–] horizon height) / (_ plane size)^2 * (x^2 + z^2)

Rendering the Skyplane

Not surprisingly, other than the fact that the geometry itself is different, rendering a skyplane is no different from rendering a skydome or skyplane. Of course, if you're going to animate the skyplane, this is where you'd do it. See the "Animation" section later in this chapter for details.

Other Variations

Although skyboxes, skydomes, and skyplanes are the most popular ways to create a backdrop for your world, there are other methods you can use such as skycylinders and hybrids (that is, a skybox with an intersecting skyplane for animated clouds). Although I'm not going to cover any of these alternate methods in detail, the point you should take away is that if one of the given methods doesn't satisfy your needs, you should be able to modify the basic principles described here to create your own solution.

Improvements

The methods discussed so far are straightforward, and despite being fairly simple, they can produce results that are very good looking. As you'd expect, though, many things can be done to improve your skyboxes. I'll cover a few of them here.

Animation

One of the biggest drawbacks in using skyboxes is that no matter how good they look, they are static. Eventually, the player will notice that the background doesn't change, and the illusion you've created will become weaker. Adding some form of animation to your skybox can help prevent this. Let's look at a few animation examples.

Dynamic Clouds

Skyboxes commonly include clouds, and since clouds in the real world move, yours should, too. If you are using a skyplane or a single texture on a skydome, you can easily make your clouds move by modifying the texture matrix stack. In each frame, when rendering your skybox, select the texture matrix stack and translate by a small amount. Alternatively, if you're using a skydome, you could rotate the dome instead.

For an even greater degree of realism, the cloud texture itself can be dynamically generated using your favorite noise algorithm. That way, the clouds not only are moving, they're changing in shape and size over time—just like real clouds!

Celestial Bodies

Having the sun or moon move across the sky is another effective method of adding realism. Rather than changing the base texture, a separate texture is created and combined with the background using multitexturing as it moves across the sky. This method generally works best with skydomes or skyplanes.

Multiple Layers

Instead of using a single skybox, several layers can be used to create a greater illusion of depth. Each layer is centered on the same point, but they are drawn from the outside in at slightly decreasing distances, with the results blended together. This method is especially useful in creating multilayer, animated clouds.

Sliding

All of the methods discussed so far assume that the skybox is centered on the camera. This is done to ensure that the player is never able to get close to or pass through the skybox. The only downside to this approach is that it requires that the scenery depicted on the skybox be fairly distant. Otherwise, the players will begin to notice that no matter how far they move, their position relative to distant objects doesn't change.

An alternative to this is to use sliding skyboxes. The skybox is still attached to the camera, but as the player moves, the skybox's position relative to the camera also moves slightly. For this to work correctly, you need to know the maximum extents to which the player can move in the world to be sure that the player can never pass through the sides of the skybox.

This method can also be combined with multiple layers to create a sort of 3-D parallax scrolling.

Generating Skybox Textures

One of the keys to having a good-looking sky-box is to have a great set of textures. This section will cover the ways in which these textures can be obtained and will provide a tutorial for creating your own using Terragen.

> **NOTE**
>
> If you're using anything other than standard skyboxes, you may want to create a plug-in to help make your artist's life easier by automatically compensating for distortion.

Have the Artist Make Them

If you're working as part of a team, the artists will almost certainly create the sky-box textures. Programs like 3D Studio Max and Bryce have support for skybox texture creation built in since they are essentially cubic environment maps. Unfortunately, I don't have the space to cover the details of skybox texture creation with these programs, but if your artist is familiar with the software, he or she should be able to produce them fairly easily.

Find Preexisting Textures

Because popular games like Quake 2, Quake 3, Unreal, and Half-Life have used sky-boxes, many Web sites catering to the mod community contain archives of skybox textures. A few of the better sites are listed at the end of this chapter. Although these textures are often free to use (even in commercial projects), it may be difficult to find exactly what you need for your game. They work quite well for demos, though, and if nothing else, they can give you a good idea of what skybox textures look like.

Create Them Using Terragen

Terragen is a tool used for creating terrain. It's free for use in noncommercial projects and is inexpensive otherwise. It also provides a way to create your own skybox textures from scratch with little or no artistic ability. Because it's so easy to use, I'm going to provide a brief tutorial of the steps required to create skybox textures using Terragen.

Installing Terragen

I've included a copy of Terragen (the most recent version available at the time of publication) on the accompanying CD-ROM for this book. You can see if there's an even more recent version at the Terragen home page at **www.planetside.co.uk/ terragen/**.

Installation is a quick and painless process. Once you're done, you're ready to start creating skybox textures.

Generating Terrain

When Terragen starts, you'll see a screen that looks something like Figure 19.7.

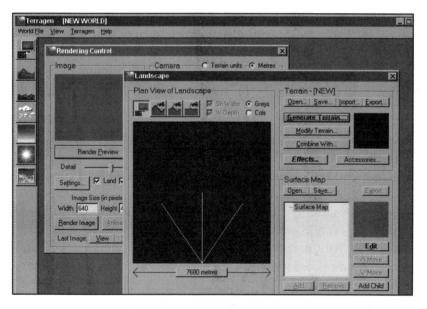

Figure 19.7

Terragen: An inexpensive tool used for creating terrains

The first thing to do is click on the Generate Terrain button in the Landscape window. This will bring up the Terrain Genesis window, which looks like Figure 19.8.

This is where you set the parameters that control how the terrain is generated. For the purposes of this tutorial, the default settings will be used, so I'm not going to go into detail about what each of them does. In fact, because Terragen provides a wide range of settings, I'm not going to be able to cover most of them in this tutorial. I'm just going to focus on the ones that are absolutely necessary for skybox tex-

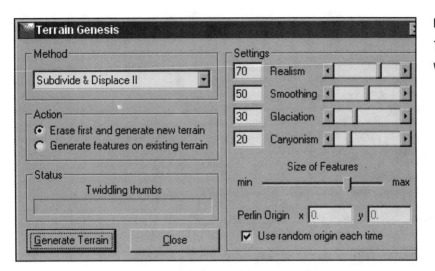

Figure 19.8

The Terrain Genesis window

ture generation. To get the most out of Terragen, read the documentation and do some experimentation.

Go ahead and click on the Generate Terrain button in the Terrain Genesis window. You'll see the heightmap produced in the Landscape window. If you want a different heightmap, click on Generate Terrain again, changing the settings as desired. When you're satisfied, close the Terrain Genesis window and return to the Landscape window.

At this point, you can further adjust your terrain by using one of the sculpting tools, combining it with another terrain, or applying a surface map. If you like, feel free to try some of these things before moving to the next step.

Rendering the Textures

You're now ready to render the skybox textures, so select the Rendering Control window shown in Figure 19.9. Click on the Render Preview button to get an idea of what the final image will look like.

The next step is to set the size and quality of your rendering in the Rendering Control window. First, move the Detail slider all the way to the right to ensure the highest quality. Then click on the Settings button and set the Cloud and Atmosphere sliders to high accuracy. Finally, set the image size. Since the image will be used as a square texture, I suggest that you set both dimensions to the same power of two. The resolution you pick depends on the requirements of your game or demo. Larger textures will look better but consume more video memory. Either 256×256 or 512×512 will work well in most situations.

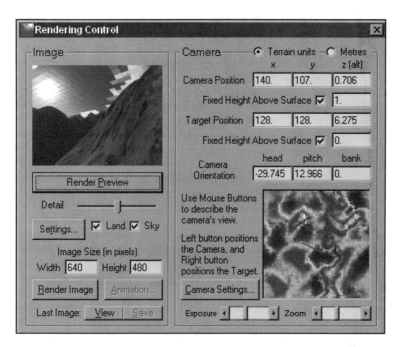

Figure 19.9

The Rendering Control window

The last step is to set up the camera. First, click on the Camera Settings button, set the Zoom/Magnification level to 1, and then click on the Close button. This will ensure a 90-degree field of view. Next, set the head, pitch, and bank Camera Orientation settings to 0. The camera is now pointing in the forward direction of your skybox, and you're ready to render.

Now that everything is set up, the first texture can be rendered. Click on Render Image. The terrain will start rendering in a new window. Once the image is complete (which may take several minutes), save the image and move on to the next view. The only thing that needs to be changed to get the other views is the Camera Orientation. Be careful not to change anything else; otherwise, your textures won't line up. To get the left, back, and right textures, set the head angles to 90, 180, and 270, respectively, and leave the pitch and bank at 0. When generating the top and bottom textures, the pitch angle must be set to 90 and –90, respectively. It doesn't matter what the head angle is set to as long as it's a multiple of 90, but the value you pick will affect the way in which your game orients the top and bottom textures, so be consistent.

TIP

Generating multiple skybox textures this way can get tedious. Although I don't have the space to cover it here, Terragen provides a scripting language in which you can automate the process and ease the pain.

When you're done, your set of textures should look something like Figure 19.10.

Figure 19.10

A set of skybox textures

The Demo

The accompanying CD-ROM for this book includes a program (shown in Figure 19.11) that demonstrates the major principles covered in this chapter. It includes an implementation for a skybox, a skydome, and a skyplane with an animated texture. The program allows you to change between the three modes, view them in wireframe mode, and remove the terrain to get an unobstructed view. Full source code, written in C++ using OpenGL, is included. Instructions for the demo are included on the CD-ROM.

I encourage you to take the demo program and improve it by using some of the ideas suggested in this chapter or by using ideas you come up with on your own.

What You've Learned

In this chapter, you learned about three common methods for generating backgrounds for your 3-D world. You should now be comfortable with using skyboxes, skydomes, and skyplanes. You know where to go to find textures to use with your skyboxes, and you can even generate them on your own. You almost certainly have ideas for improving on the ideas presented here.

Figure 19.11

Real-time skies from an upcoming game (image courtesy of Virtual Tales Entertainment)

Where to Go Now

The following papers, Web sites, and articles provide additional information on sky-boxes and related issues that you may find interesting:

Sky Domes, Luis R. Sempé, October 2001, available online at **www.spheregames.com**

Sky Domes, Tim Smith, September 1999, available online at **www.flipcode.com**

Sky and Atmospheric Rendering resources at **www.vterrain.org/Atmosphere/index.html**

In addition, an advanced series on sky-rendering techniques should appear soon on GameDev.net as part of the Hardcore Game Programming column. Be sure to look for it.

Conclusion

This chapter has provided enough foundational material to enable you to begin experimenting on your own. The methods discussed here provide excellent results and have been used in many commercial games, but improvements can always be made. Here are some things to try:

- Combine skyboxes with dynamic cloud generation using Perlin noise.
- Integrate your skyboxes with other effects such as lens flares, planetary boies moving across the sky (and possibly affecting the lighting of the world), and atmospheric effects like rain or lightning.
- Investigate ways to improve performance, such as performing some kind of occlusion testing on the skydome or skyplane.

Sky rendering is a very active area of research in computer graphics, and this chapter has only scratched the surface of the techniques currently being used and researched. Games will soon include amazingly realistic skies created dynamically in real time, such as the one shown in Figure 19.11. An animated sky can add greatly to the realism of your outdoor game, so I encourage you to do some research and experimentation in this area.

TRICK 20

Game
Programming
Assembly
Style

Chris Hobbs

WIN32 ASM—PART 1

Introduction

This section contains an updated version of the article series that appeared on GameDev and in GIG News. The series followed the development of a game in pure assembly language, of all things, and has been updated for this book. I know all of you are as excited about this as I am, so I will try to keep the introductory phase brief. Instead of laying every single thing out to you in black and white, I will try to answer the questions that are asked most often, and the details will appear as we—and the game—progress. Feel free to follow along with the source code provided on the accompanying CD-ROM.

What Is This All About?

This is about the development of a complete game, SPACE-TRIS, in 100-percent assembly language. We will be covering numerous aspects of game development and examining their implementation in assembly language under Windows . . . from design and code framework to graphics and sound.

Who Is the Target Audience?

This section is meant for anybody who wants to learn something they may not have known before. Since the game is a relatively simple Tetris clone, it is great for the beginner. Also, given that not many people are even aware that it is possible to write for Windows in assembly language, this section is also great for the more advanced developers out there.

What Do I Need?

The only requirement is the ability to read. However, if you want to assemble the source code and experiment with changes to the game, you need a copy of MASM 6.12+. You can download a package called MASM32 that will have everything that you need and then some. Here is the link: **www.movsd.com**.

Why Assembly Language?

Many of you are probably wondering why anybody in his right mind would write in pure assembly language—especially in the present, when optimizing compilers is the "in" thing and everybody knows that VC++ is bug free, right? What about those myths about assembly language being hard to read, nonportable, and extremely difficult to learn? In the days of DOS, these arguments were very valid ones. In Windows, though, they are simply myths left over from the good old days of DOS, and I might as well address them one at a time.

First, assembly language is, in fact, hard to read. But for that matter so is C or even Visual Basic. The readability results from the skill of the programmer and her thoroughness in commenting the code. This is especially true of C++. Which is easier to read: assembly code that progresses one step at a time (for example, move a variable into a register, move a different variable into another register, multiply) or C++ code that can go through multiple layers of virtual functions that were inherited? No matter what language you are in, commenting is essential. Use it and you won't have any trouble reading source code in any language. Remember, just because you know what it means doesn't mean that everybody else does also.

Second, the portability issue is quite often raised as a supposedly valid argument against assembly. Well, assembly language is not portable to other platforms. However, there is a way around this that allows you to write for any x86 platform, but that is way beyond the scope of this chapter. Besides, a good 80 to 90 percent of the games written are for Windows anyway. This means that the majority of your code is specific to DirectX or the Win32 API; therefore, you won't be porting without a huge amount of work anyway. If you want a truly portable game, don't bother writing for DirectX at all. Go get a decent multiplatform development library.

Finally, there is the issue of assembly language being extremely difficult to learn. Although there is no real way for me to prove to you that it is easy, I can offer you the basics—in just a few pages—that have helped many people learn it, even those who had never seen a line of assembly language before. Writing Windows assembly code, especially with MASM, is very easy. It is almost like writing some C code. If you give it a chance, I am certain you won't be disappointed.

Win32 ASM Basics

If you are already familiar with assembly language in the Windows platform, you may want to skip this section. For those of you who aren't, this may be a bit boring but hang with it—this is very important stuff. To save time and space, I will presume that you are at least familiar with the x86 architecture. There aren't very many instructions that you will be using often, so I will simply cover the ones we care about for this project.

MOV Instruction

This instruction moves a value from one location to another. You can only move from register to register, memory to register, or register to memory. You cannot move from one memory location to another memory location directly; it must be placed in a register first.

Examples:

```
MOV        EAX, 30
MOV        EBX, EAX
MOV        my_var1, EAX
MOV        DWORD PTR my_var, EAX
MOV        EBX, EAX
MOV        my_var1, EAX
MOV        DWORD PTR my_var1, EAX
```

The first example moves the value 30 into the EAX register. The second example moves the current value in EAX into the EBX register. The third example moves the value of EAX into the variable my_var1. The fourth example moves the value of EAX into the ADDRESS pointed to by my_var1. We need to use the DWORD specifier so that the assembler knows how much memory to move: 1 byte (BYTE), 2 bytes (WORD), or 4 bytes (DWORD).

ADD and SUB Instructions

These two instructions perform addition and subtraction. Their use is quite intuitive. Remember, however, you cannot operate on two memory locations at the same time.

Examples:

```
MOV        EAX, 30
MOV        EBX, EAX
MOV        my_var1, EAX
ADD        EAX, 30
SUB        EBX, EAX
```

The first example adds 30 to the current value in the EAX register. The second example subtracts the value in the EAX register from the value in the EBX register.

MUL and DIV Instructions

These two instructions perform integer multiplication and integer division. Their use is a little more complicated than the other instructions.

Examples:

```
MOV        EAX, 30
MOV        EBX, EAX
MOV        my_var1, EAX
MOV        EAX, 10
MOV        ECX, 30
MUL        ECX
XOR        EDX, EDX
MOV        ECX, 10
DIV        ECX
```

The preceding examples first load EAX with 10 and ECX with 30. EAX is always the default multiplicand, and you get to select the other multiplier. When performing a multiplication, the answer is stored in EAX:EDX. It only goes into EDX if the value is larger than the EAX register. When performing a divide, you must first clear the EDX register. This can be done with the XOR instruction. This instruction performs an Exclusive OR and, if done on itself, will zero the register. After the divide, the answer is in EAX, with the remainder in EDX (if any exists).

Of course, there are many more instructions, but those should be enough to get you started. We will probably only be using a few others, but they're fairly easy to figure out once you have seen the main ones.

Next we need to deal with the calling convention. We will be using the Standard Call calling convention because that is what the Win32 API uses. This means that we will push parameters onto the stack in right-to-left order, but we aren't responsible for clearing the stack afterward. Everything will be completely transparent to you, however, because we will be using the pseudo-op INVOKE to make our calls. Calling convention knowledge is a good detail to have. Research it more if you feel inclined, although we won't need that detail for this project.

The final thing I need to inform you about is the high-level syntax that MASM provides. These are constructs that allow you to create If-Then-Else and For loops in assembly, with C-like expressions. They are easiest to illustrate once we have some code; therefore, you won't see them just yet. But they are there . . . and they make life infinitely easier.

These are enough basics to get you going. The rest will come together as we take a look at the source code and see how assembly can be applied to game programming topics. Now that we have that out of the way, we can work on designing the game and creating a code framework for it.

The Design Document

Now it's time for something a lot more fun—designing the game. This process is often neglected simply because people want to start writing code as soon as they have an idea. Although that approach can work for some people, it often does not. And if it does work, you often end up recoding a good portion of your game because of a simple oversight. Therefore, we will cover exactly how to create a design document that you will be able to stick to and that will end up helping you with your game.

To begin, you need to have an idea of what you want the game to be and how you want the game played. In our case, this is a simple Tetris clone, so there isn't too much we need to cover in the way of game play and such. In many cases, though, you will need to describe the game play as thoroughly as possible. This will help you to see if your ideas are feasible or if you are neglecting something important.

The easy part is finished, so now we need to come up with as many details as possible. Are we going to have a scoring system? Are we going to have load/save game options? How many levels are there? What happens at the end of a level? Is there an introductory screen? These are the kinds of questions you should be asking yourself as you work on the design of the game. Another thing that might help you is to storyboard or flow chart the game on a piece of paper or your computer. This will allow you to see how the game is going to progress at each point, and this is especially helpful for adventure-type games.

Once you have all of the details complete, it is time to start sketching the levels out. How do you want the screens to appear? What will the interfaces look like? This doesn't have to be precise just yet, but it should give you a realistic idea of what the final versions will look like. I also tend to break out my calculator and estimate pixel coordinates at this point. I have actually run out of room while creating the menu screen before. It was my own fault for not calculating the largest size that my text could be, and it took a few hours to redo everything. The moral is to plan ahead.

The final stage is just sort of a cleanup phase. I like to go back and make sure that everything is the way I want it to be. Take a few days' break from your game beforehand. This will give you a fresh viewpoint when you come back to it later. Oftentimes, you will stare at the document for so long that something extraordinarily simple will be glanced over and not included in your plan, such as how many points everything is worth or the maximum number of points users can fit in their score (not that I have ever found out halfway through the game that the player could obtain more points than the maximum score allowed or anything like that).

Whether you choose to use the process I have outlined or one of your own making, it is imperative that you complete this step. I have never been one for wasted effort. I do it right the first time if possible and learn from my mistakes and the mistakes of others. If this weren't necessary, I wouldn't do it. So do yourself a favor and complete some type of design document, no matter how simple you think your game is going to be.

Code Framework

The final preparation step is something that I like to call code framework. This is where you lay out your blank source code modules and fill them with comments detailing the routines that will go into them and the basic idea behind how they operate. If you think you are perfect and have gotten every detail in your design document, you can probably skip this step. For those of you who are cautious like me, give this phase a whirl. It helps you see how all of the pieces will fit together and more importantly if something has been neglected or mistakenly included. Then, if something needs to be adjusted, you won't have to deal with the possibility of ruining code while rearranging things. I have found this to be a great trick to keep things ordered and interfaces well thought out.

Here is an example of the framework I am speaking about for the SPACE-TRIS example. You can see that nothing much goes into it, just an overview of the module more or less. These things get slightly more complex when developing modules with specific interfaces because those interfaces should be well documented.

> **TIP**
>
> **Any line that starts with a semicolon is a comment in assembly language.**

```
;##############################################################################
;##############################################################################
; ABOUT SPACE-TRIS:
;
;        This is the main portion of code. It has WinMain and performs all
;        of the management for the game.
;
;                - WinMain()
;                - WndProc()
;                - Main_Loop()
;                - Game_Init()
;                - Game_Main()
;                - Game_Shutdown()
;
;
;##############################################################################
;##############################################################################


;##############################################################################
;##############################################################################
; THE COMPILER OPTIONS
;##############################################################################
;##############################################################################

        .386
        .MODEL flat, stdcall
        OPTION CASEMAP :none    ; case sensitive
```

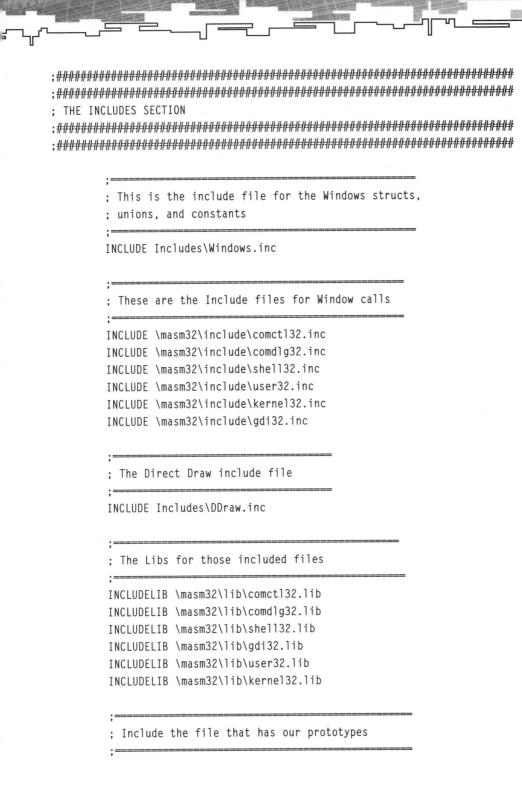

```
;###############################################################################
;###############################################################################
; THE INCLUDES SECTION
;###############################################################################
;###############################################################################


            ;=====================================================
            ; This is the include file for the Windows structs,
            ; unions, and constants
            ;=====================================================
            INCLUDE Includes\Windows.inc


            ;=====================================================
            ; These are the Include files for Window calls
            ;=====================================================
            INCLUDE \masm32\include\comctl32.inc
            INCLUDE \masm32\include\comdlg32.inc
            INCLUDE \masm32\include\shell32.inc
            INCLUDE \masm32\include\user32.inc
            INCLUDE \masm32\include\kernel32.inc
            INCLUDE \masm32\include\gdi32.inc


            ;=====================================================
            ; The Direct Draw include file
            ;=====================================================
            INCLUDE Includes\DDraw.inc


            ;=====================================================
            ; The Libs for those included files
            ;=====================================================
            INCLUDELIB \masm32\lib\comctl32.lib
            INCLUDELIB \masm32\lib\comdlg32.lib
            INCLUDELIB \masm32\lib\shell32.lib
            INCLUDELIB \masm32\lib\gdi32.lib
            INCLUDELIB \masm32\lib\user32.lib
            INCLUDELIB \masm32\lib\kernel32.lib


            ;=====================================================
            ; Include the file that has our prototypes
            ;=====================================================
```

```
        INCLUDE Protos.inc

;#######################################################################
;#######################################################################
; LOCAL MACROS
;#######################################################################
;#######################################################################

        szText MACRO Name, Text:VARARG
                LOCAL lbl
                JMP lbl
                Name DB Text,0
                lbl:
        ENDM

        m2m MACRO M1, M2
                PUSH                    M2
                POP                     M1
        ENDM

        return MACRO arg
                MOV         EAX, arg
                RET
        ENDM

        RGB MACRO red, green, blue
                XOR         EAX,EAX
                MOV         AH,blue
                SHL         EAX,8
                MOV         AH,green
                MOV         AL,red
        ENDM

        hWrite MACRO handle, buffer, size
                MOV         EDI, handle
                ADD         EDI, Dest_index
                MOV         ECX, 0
                MOV         CX, size
                ADD         Dest_index, ECX
                MOV         ESI, buffer
                movsb
```

```
        ENDM

        hRead MACRO handle, buffer, size
                MOV         EDI, handle
                ADD         EDI, Spot
                MOV         ECX, 0
                MOV         CX, size
                ADD         Spot, ECX
                MOV         ESI, buffer
                movsb
        ENDM
```

```
;###############################################################################
;###############################################################################
; Variables we want to use in other modules
;###############################################################################
;###############################################################################


;###############################################################################
;###############################################################################
; External variables
;###############################################################################
;###############################################################################


;###############################################################################
;###############################################################################
; BEGIN INITIALIZED DATA
;###############################################################################
;###############################################################################


        .DATA

;###############################################################################
;###############################################################################
; BEGIN CONSTANTS
;###############################################################################
;###############################################################################
```

```
;###################################################################
;###################################################################
; BEGIN EQUATES
;###################################################################
;###################################################################


            ;================
            ;Utility Equates
            ;================
FALSE               EQU         0
TRUE                EQU         1



;###################################################################
;###################################################################
; BEGIN THE CODE SECTION
;###################################################################
;###################################################################


    .CODE

start:

;###############################################################
; WinMain Function
;###############################################################



;###############################################################
; End of WinMain Procedure
;###############################################################



;###############################################################
; Main Window Callback Procedure — WndProc
;###############################################################
```

```
;###############################################################################
; End of Main Windows Callback Procedure
;###############################################################################




;===============================================================================
;===============================================================================
; THE GAME PROCEDURES
;===============================================================================
;===============================================================================


;###############################################################################
; Game_Init Procedure
;###############################################################################


;###############################################################################
; END Game_Init
;###############################################################################



;###############################################################################
; Game_Main Procedure
;###############################################################################


;###############################################################################
; END Game_Main
;###############################################################################



;###############################################################################
; Game_Shutdown Procedure
;###############################################################################
```

```
;###############################################################################
; END Game_Shutdown
;###############################################################################

;######################################
; THIS IS THE END OF THE PROGRAM CODE #
;######################################
END start
```

Conclusion

This ends the preparation phase. At this point, we are ready to start looking at some code in the next section. Feel free to scour the Internet and find more resources relating to the Win32 assembly language basics I have introduced here. More information is not needed, however, to follow along with the development of SPACE-TRIS. I will be teaching everything that's needed as we progress, but a more extensive knowledge of the instructions in the x86 architecture will be useful for experimenting on your own (which I definitely recommend).

WIN32 ASM—PART 2

So far, we've discussed many basics of Win32 ASM programming, introduced you to the game we will be creating, and guided you through the design process. Now it is time to take it a few steps further. First, I will cover in depth the high-level constructs of MASM that make it extremely readable (at generally no performance cost) and that make it as easy to write as C expressions. Then, once we have a solid foundation in our assembler, we will take a look at the game loop and the main Windows procedures in the code. With that out of the way, we will take a peek at Direct Draw and the calls associated with it. Once we understand how DirectX works, we can build our Direct Draw library. After that, we will build our bitmap file library. Finally, we will put it all together in a program that displays our loading game screen and exits when you hit the Esc key.

It is a tall order, but I am pretty sure we can cover all of these topics in this chapter. Remember: If you want to compile the code, you need the MASM32 package (or at the very least a copy of MASM 6.11+).

If you are already familiar with high-level MASM syntax, I would suggest skipping the next section. However, those of you who are rusty or who have never even heard of it should head on to the next section. There you will learn more than you will probably ever need to know about this totally cool addition to our assembler.

MASM HL Syntax?

I am sure many of you have seen an old DOS assembly language listing. Take a moment to recall that listing and picture the code. Scary? Well, 9 times out of 10 it was scary. Most ASM programmers wrote very unreadable code simply because that was the nature of their assembler. It was littered with labels and JMPs and all sorts of other mysterious things. Try stepping through it with your mental computer. Did you crash? Yeah, don't feel bad. It's just how it is. Now, that was the 9 out of 10 . . . what about that 1 out of 10? What's the deal with that one? Well, those are the programmers who coded macros to facilitate high-level constructs in their programs.

For once, Microsoft did something incredibly useful with MASM 6.0. It built the HL macros that smart programmers had devised into MASM as pseudo-ops.

If you aren't aware of what this means, I will let you in on it. Assembly code in MASM is now just as readable and as easy to write as C. This, of course, is just my opinion, but it is an opinion shared by thousands and thousands of ASM coders. So now that I have touted its usefulness, let's take a look at some C constructs and their MASM counterparts.

IF-ELSE IF-ELSE

C Version:

```
if( var1 == var2 )
{
    // Code goes here ...
}
else
if( var1 == var3 )
{
    // Code goes here ...
}
else
{
    // Code goes here ...
}
```

MASM Version:

```
                MOV        my_var1, EAX
.if ( var1 == var2 )
    ; Code goes here ...
.elseif ( var1 == var3 )
    ; Code goes here ...
.else
    ; Code goes here ...
.endif
```

DO-WHILE

C Version:

```
do
{
    // Code goes here ...
```

```
}while( var1 == var2 );
```

MASM Version:

```
                MOV         my_var1, EAX
    .repeat
        ; Code goes here ...
    .until ( var1 == var2 )
```

WHILE

C Version:

```
    while( var1 == var2 )
    {
        // Code goes here ...
    }
```

MASM Version:

```
                MOV         my_var1, EAX
    .while ( var1 == var2 )
        ; Code goes here ...
    .endw
```

These are the constructs we can use in our code. As you can see, they are extremely simple and allow for nice, readable code—something assembly language has long been without. There is no performance loss for using these constructs, at least none that I've found. They typically generate the same JMP and CMP code that a programmer would if he were writing it manually. So feel free to use them in your code as you see fit—they are a great asset.

There is one other thing we should discuss, and that is the psuedo-ops that allow us to define procedures/functions easily: PROTO and PROC. These allow us to write functions without having to deal with the stack issues normally associated with assembler programming. Using them is really simple. To begin with, just as in C, you need to have a prototype. In MASM, this is done with the PROTO keyword. Here are some examples of declaring prototypes for your procedures:

```
;====================================
; Main Program Procedures
;====================================
WinMain PROTO               :DWORD,:DWORD,:DWORD,:DWORD
WndProc PROTO               :DWORD,:DWORD,:DWORD,:DWORD
```

The preceding code tells the assembler that it should expect a procedure by the name of WinMain and one by the name of WndProc. Each of these has a parameter list associated with it. They both happen to expect four DWORD values to be passed to them. For those of you using the MASM32 package, you already have all of the Windows API functions prototyped; you just need to include the appropriate include file. But you need to make sure that any user-defined procedure is prototyped in this fashion.

Once we have the function prototyped, we can create it. We do this with the PROC keyword. Here is an example:

```
;#############################################################
; WinMain Function
;#############################################################
WinMain PROC    hInstance       :DWORD,
                hPrevInst       :DWORD,
                CmdLine         :DWORD,
                CmdShow         :DWORD


        ;=============================
        ; We are through
        ;=============================
        return msg.wParam


WinMain endp
;#############################################################
; End of WinMain Procedure
;#############################################################
```

By writing our functions in this manner, we can access all passed parameters by the name we give to them. The preceding function is WinMain without any code in it. You will see the code in a minute. For now, though, pay attention to how we set up the procedure. Also notice how it allows us to create much cleaner-looking code, just like the rest of the high-level constructs in MASM.

Getting a Game Loop Running

Now that we all know how to use our assembler and some of the useful features contained in it, let's get a basic game shell up and running.

The first thing we need to do is get set up to enter into WinMain(). You may be wondering why the code doesn't start at WinMain() like in C/C++. The answer is that in C/C++ it doesn't start there either. The code we will write is generated for you by the compiler; therefore, it is completely transparent to you. We will most likely do it differently than the compiler, but the premise will be the same. So here is what we will code to get into the WinMain() function:

```
.CODE

start:
        ;=================================
        ; Obtain the instance for the
        ; application
        ;=================================
        INVOKE GetModuleHandle, NULL
        MOV    hInst, EAX


        ;=================================
        ; Is there a commandline to parse?
        ;=================================
        INVOKE GetCommandLine
        MOV    CommandLine, EAX


        ;=================================
        ; Call the WinMain procedure
        ;=================================
        INVOKE WinMain,hInst,NULL,CommandLine,SW_SHOWDEFAULT


        ;=================================
        ; Leave the program
        ;=================================
        INVOKE ExitProcess,EAX
```

The only thing that may seem a little confusing is why we MOV EAX into a variable at the end of an INVOKE. The reason is that all Windows functions (and C functions, for that matter) place the return value of a function/procedure in EAX. So we are effectively doing an assignment statement with a function when we move a value from EAX into something. This preceding code is going to be the same for every Windows application that you write. At least, I have never had need to change it. The code simply sets everything up and ends it when we are finished. Also notice that we use the start label to tell the assembler where processing should begin, and everything is placed in the .code section.

If you follow the code, you will see that it calls WinMain() for us. This is where things can get a bit confusing, so let's have a look at the code first.

```
;###############################################################################
; WinMain Function
;###############################################################################
WinMain PROC      hInstance         :DWORD,
                  hPrevInst         :DWORD,
                  CmdLine           :DWORD,
                  CmdShow           :DWORD


            ;===================
            ; Put LOCALs on stack
            ;===================
            LOCAL wc               :WNDCLASS


            ;==============================================
            ; Fill WNDCLASS structure with required variables
            ;==============================================
            MOV     wc.style, CS_OWNDC
            MOV     wc.lpfnWndProc,OFFSET WndProc
            MOV     wc.cbClsExtra,NULL
            MOV     wc.cbWndExtra,NULL
            m2m     wc.hInstance,hInst    ;<< NOTE: macro not mnemonic
            INVOKE GetStockObject, BLACK_BRUSH
            MOV     wc.hbrBackground, EAX
            MOV     wc.lpszMenuName,NULL
            MOV     wc.lpszClassName,OFFSET szClassName
            INVOKE LoadIcon, hInst, IDI_ICON ; icon ID
            MOV     wc.hIcon,EAX
            INVOKE LoadCursor,NULL,IDC_ARROW
            MOV     wc.hCursor,EAX


            ;================================
            ; Register our class we created
            ;================================
            INVOKE RegisterClass, ADDR wc
```

```
;=======================================
; Create the main screen
;=======================================
INVOKE CreateWindowEx,NULL,
              ADDR szClassName,
              ADDR szDisplayName,
              WS_POPUP OR WS_CLIPSIBLINGS OR \
              WS_MAXIMIZE OR WS_CLIPCHILDREN,
              0,0,640,480,
              NULL,NULL,
              hInst,NULL


;=======================================
; Put the window handle in for future uses
;=======================================
MOV     hMainWnd, EAX


;=======================================
; Hide the cursor
;=======================================
INVOKE ShowCursor, FALSE


;=======================================
; Display our Window we created for now
;=======================================
INVOKE ShowWindow, hMainWnd, SW_SHOWDEFAULT


;=======================================
; Intialize the Game
;=======================================
INVOKE Game_Init


;=======================================
; Check for an error if so leave
;=======================================
.IF EAX != TRUE
        JMP     shutdown
.ENDIF
```

```
;=================================
; Loop until PostQuitMessage is sent
;=================================
.WHILE TRUE
        INVOKE  PeekMessage, ADDR msg, NULL, 0, 0, PM_REMOVE
        .IF (EAX != 0)
                ;=================================
                ; Break if it was the quit message
                ;=================================
                MOV     EAX, msg.message
                .IF EAX == WM_QUIT
                        ;=====================
                        ; Break out
                        ;=====================
                        JMP     shutdown
                .ENDIF

                ;=================================
                ; Translate and Dispatch the message
                ;=================================
                INVOKE  TranslateMessage, ADDR msg
                INVOKE  DispatchMessage, ADDR msg

        .ENDIF

        ;=================================
        ; Call our Main Game Loop
        ;
        ; NOTE: This is done every loop
        ; iteration no matter what
        ;=================================
        INVOKE Game_Main

.ENDW

shutdown:

;=================================
; Shutdown the Game
;=================================
INVOKE Game_Shutdown
```

```
;==============================
; Show the Cursor
;==============================
INVOKE ShowCursor, TRUE

getout:
;==============================
; We are through
;==============================
return msg.wParam


WinMain endp
;###############################################################################
; End of WinMain Procedure
;###############################################################################
```

This is quite a bit of code and is rather daunting at first glance. But let's examine it a piece at a time. First we enter the function. Notice that the local variables (in this case, a WNDCLASS variable) get placed on the stack without you having to code anything. The code is generated for you; you can declare local variables like in C. Thus, at the end of the procedure, we don't need to tell the assembler how much to pop off of the stack. It is done for us also. Then we fill in this structure with various values and variables.

Next we make some calls to register our window class and create a new window. Then we hide the cursor. You may want the cursor, but for our game we do not. Now we can show our window and try to initialize our game. We check for an error after calling the Game_Init() procedure. If there were an error, the function would not return true, and this would cause our program to jump to the shutdown label. It is important that we jump over the main message loop. If we do not, the program will continue executing. Also, make sure you do not just return out of the code; there still may be some things that need to be shut down. It is good practice in ASM, as in all other languages, to have one entry point and one exit point in each of your procedures. This makes debugging easier.

> **NOTE**
>
> Note the use of m2m. This is because, in ASM, you are not allowed to move a memory value to another memory location without placing it in a register or on the stack first. So this macro pushes it onto the stack and then pops it into the desired register.

Now for the meat of WinMain(): the message loop. For those of you who have never seen a Windows message loop before, here is a quick explanation. Windows maintains a queue of messages that the application receives, whether from other applications, user-generated, or internal. To do *anything*, an application must process messages. These tell you that a key has been pressed, that the mouse button has been clicked, or that the user wants to exit your program. If this were a normal program and not a high-performance game, we would use GetMessage() to retrieve a message from the queue and act on it.

The problem, however, is that if there are no messages, the function *waits* until it receives one. This is totally unacceptable for a game. We need to be constantly performing our loop, no matter what messages we receive. One way around this is to use PeekMessage() instead. PeekMessage() will return zero if it has no messages; otherwise, it will grab the current message off the queue.

What this means is that, if we have a message, it will get translated and dispatched to our callback function. Furthermore, if we do not have a message waiting, the main game loop will be called instead. Now here is the trick: By arranging the code just right, the main game loop will be called—even if we process a message. If we don't do this, Windows could process thousands of messages while our game loop wouldn't execute once!

Finally, when a quit message is passed to the queue, we will jump out of our loop and execute the shutdown code. And that is the basic game loop.

Connecting to Direct Draw

Now we are going to get a little bit advanced, but only for this section. Unfortunately, there is no cut-and-dry way to view DirectX in assembly, so I am going to explain it briefly, show you how to use it, and then forget about it. This is not that imperative to know about, but it helps if you at least understand the concepts.

The very first thing you need to understand is the concept of a *virtual function table*. This is where your call really goes, to be blunt about it. The call offsets into this table and from it selects the proper function address to jump to. What this means to you is that your call to a function is actually a call to a simple lookup table that is already generated. In this way, DirectX (or any other type library such as DirectX) can change functions in a library without you ever having to know about it.

Once we have gotten that straight, we can figure out how to make calls in DirectX. Have you guessed how yet? The answer is that we need to mimic the table in some way so that our call is offset into the virtual table at the proper address. We start by simply having a base address that gets called, which is a given in DirectX libraries. Then we make a list of all functions for that object, appending the size of their parameters. This is our offset into the table. Now we are all set to call the functions.

Calling these functions can be a bit of work. First you have to specify the address of the object on which you want to make the call. Then you have to resolve the virtual address and finally push all of the parameters onto the stack, including the object, for the call. Ugly, isn't it? For that reason, a set of macros is provided that will allow you to make calls for these objects fairly easily. I will only cover one since the rest are based on the same premise. The most basic one is DD4INVOKE. This macro is for a Direct Draw 4 object. It is important to have different invokes for different versions of the same object. If we didn't, wrong routines would be called since the virtual table changes as it adds/removes functions from the libraries.

The idea behind the macro is fairly simple. First you specify the function name, then the object name, and then the parameters. Here is an example:

```
;========================================
; Now create the primary surface
;========================================
        DD4INVOKE CreateSurface, 1pdd, ADDR ddsd, ADDR 1pddsprimary, NULL
```

The preceding line of code calls the CreateSurface() function on a Direct Draw 4 object. It passes the pointer to the object, the address of a Direct Draw Surface Describe structure, the address of the variable to hold the pointer to the surface, and finally NULL. This call is an example of how we will interface to DirectX in this chapter. Now that we have seen how to make calls to DirectX, we need to build a small library for us to use. This will be covered in the next section.

Our Direct Draw Library

We are now ready to start coding our Direct Draw library routines. The logical starting place would be to figure out what kinds of routines we will need for the game. Obviously, we want an initialization and shutdown routine, and we are going to need a function to lock and unlock surfaces. Also, it would be nice to have a function to draw text, and since the game is going to run in 16bpp mode, we will want a function that can figure out the pixel format for us. It also would be a good idea to have a function that creates surfaces, one that loads a bitmap into a surface, and a function to flip our buffers for us. That should cover it, so lets get started.

The first routine we will look at is the initialization routine. This is the most logical place to start, especially since the routine has just about every type of call we will be using in Direct Draw. Here is the code:

```
;###############################################################################
; DD_Init Procedure
;###############################################################################
DD_Init PROC    screen_width:DWORD, screen_height:DWORD, screen_bpp:DWORD

        ;==================================================
        ; This function will setup DD to full screen exclusive
        ; mode at the passed in width, height, and bpp
        ;==================================================


        ;===============================
        ; Local Variables
        ;===============================
        LOCAL   lpdd_1              :LPDIRECTDRAW

        ;==========================
        ; Create a default object
        ;==========================
        INVOKE DirectDrawCreate, 0, ADDR lpdd_1, 0

        ;==========================
        ; Test for an error
        ;==========================
        IF EAX != DD_OK
                ;====================
                ; Give err msg
                ;====================
                INVOKE MessageBox, hMainWnd, ADDR szNoDD, NULL, MB_OK

                ;====================
                ; Jump and return out
                ;====================
                JMP     err

        .ENDIF
```

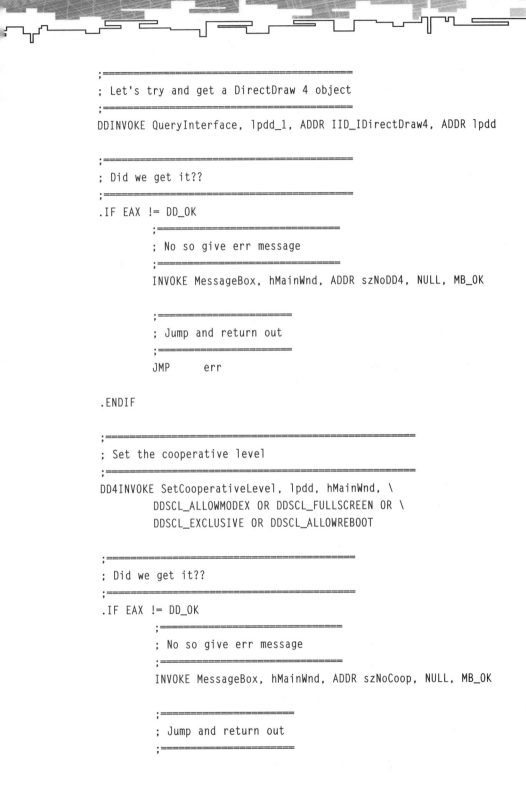

```
;==================================
; Let's try and get a DirectDraw 4 object
;==================================
DDINVOKE QueryInterface, lpdd_1, ADDR IID_IDirectDraw4, ADDR lpdd


;==================================
; Did we get it??
;==================================
.IF EAX != DD_OK

        ;==================================
        ; No so give err message
        ;==================================
        INVOKE MessageBox, hMainWnd, ADDR szNoDD4, NULL, MB_OK


        ;==================================
        ; Jump and return out
        ;==================================
        JMP     err

.ENDIF

;========================================
; Set the cooperative level
;========================================
DD4INVOKE SetCooperativeLevel, lpdd, hMainWnd, \
        DDSCL_ALLOWMODEX OR DDSCL_FULLSCREEN OR \
        DDSCL_EXCLUSIVE OR DDSCL_ALLOWREBOOT


;========================================
; Did we get it??
;========================================
.IF EAX != DD_OK

        ;==================================
        ; No so give err message
        ;==================================
        INVOKE MessageBox, hMainWnd, ADDR szNoCoop, NULL, MB_OK


        ;==================================
        ; Jump and return out
        ;==================================
```

```
            JMP     err

.ENDIF


;=============================================
; Set the Display Mode
;=============================================
DD4INVOKE SetDisplayMode, lpdd, screen_width, \
        screen_height, screen_bpp, 0, 0


;=============================================
; Did we get it??
;=============================================
.IF EAX != DD_OK
        ;=============================================
        ; No so give err message
        ;=============================================
        INVOKE MessageBox, hMainWnd, ADDR szNoDisplay, NULL, MB_OK

        ;=============================================
        ; Jump and return out
        ;=============================================
        JMP     err

.ENDIF


;=============================================
; Save the screen info
;=============================================
m2m     app_width, screen_width
m2m     app_height, screen_height
m2m     app_bpp, screen_bpp


;=============================================
; Setup to create the primary surface
;=============================================
DDINITSTRUCT OFFSET ddsd, SIZEOF(DDSURFACEDESC2)
MOV     ddsd.dwSize, SIZEOF(DDSURFACEDESC2)
MOV     ddsd.dwFlags, DDSD_CAPS OR DDSD_BACKBUFFERCOUNT;
MOV     ddsd.ddsCaps.dwCaps, DDSCAPS_PRIMARYSURFACE OR \
                DDSCAPS_FLIP OR DDSCAPS_COMPLEX
```

```
MOV     ddsd.dwBackBufferCount, 1


;=========================================
; Now create the primary surface
;=========================================
DD4INVOKE CreateSurface, lpdd, ADDR ddsd, ADDR lpddsprimary, NULL


;=========================================
; Did we get it??
;=========================================
.IF EAX != DD_OK

        ;=========================================
        ; No so give err message
        ;=========================================
        INVOKE MessageBox, hMainWnd, ADDR szNoPrimary, NULL, MB_OK


        ;=========================================
        ; Jump and return out
        ;=========================================
        JMP     err

.ENDIF

;=========================================
; Try to get a backbuffer
;=========================================
MOV     ddscaps.dwCaps, DDSCAPS_BACKBUFFER
DDS4INVOKE GetAttachedSurface, lpddsprimary, ADDR ddscaps, \
        ADDR lpddsback


;=========================================
; Did we get it??
;=========================================
.IF EAX != DD_OK

        ;=========================================
        ; No so give err message
        ;=========================================
        INVOKE MessageBox, hMainWnd, ADDR szNoBackBuffer, NULL, MB_OK
```

```
        ;======================
        ; Jump and return out
        ;======================
        JMP      err

    .ENDIF

        ;==========================================
        ; Get the RGB format of the surface
        ;==========================================
        INVOKE DD_Get_RGB_Format, lpddsprimary

done:
        ;====================
        ; We completed
        ;====================
        return TRUE

err:
        ;====================
        ; We didn't make it
        ;====================
        return FALSE

DD_Init ENDP
;###############################################################################
; END DD_Init
;###############################################################################
```

This code is fairly complex, so let's see what each individual section does.

The first step is that we create a default Direct Draw object. This is nothing more than a simple call with a couple of parameters.

Also notice how we check for an error right afterward. This is very important in DirectX. In the case of an error, we merely give a message and then jump to the error return at the bottom of the procedure. It's not the most advanced error handling, but it will work for our purposes.

NOTE

Since the DirectDraw is *not* based on an already-created object, the function is not a virtual one. Therefore, we can call it like a normal function using invoke.

The second step is that we query for a Direct Draw 4 object. (You can query for a higher version if you like.) If this succeeds, we then set the cooperative level and the display mode for our game. Nothing major, but don't forget to check for errors.

The next step is to create a primary surface for the object we have. If that succeeds, we create the back buffer. The structure that we use in this call—and other DirectX calls—needs to be cleared before using it. This is done in a macro, DDINITSTRUCT, that is included in the DDraw.inc file.

The final thing we do is call the routine that determines the pixel format for our surfaces. All of these pieces fit together in initializing our system for use.

The next routine we will look at is the pixel format obtainer. This is a fairly advanced routine, so I wanted to make sure to cover it. Here is the code:

```
;###############################################################
; DD_Get_RGB_Format Procedure
;###############################################################
DD_Get_RGB_Format        PROC      surface:DWORD


        ;=================================================
        ; This function will setup some globals to give us info
        ; on whether the pixel format of the current display mode
        ;=================================================


        ;==================================
        ; Local variables
        ;==================================
        LOCAL   shiftcount       :BYTE


        ;==================================
        ; get a surface description
        ;==================================
        DDINITSTRUCT ADDR ddsd, sizeof(DDSURFACEDESC2)
        MOV       ddsd.dwSize, sizeof(DDSURFACEDESC2)
        MOV       ddsd.dwFlags, DDSD_PIXELFORMAT
        DDS4INVOKE GetSurfaceDesc, surface, ADDR ddsd


        ;==================================
        ; fill in masking values
        ;==================================
```

```
m2m      mRed, ddsd.ddpfPixelFormat.dwRBitMask          ; Red Mask
m2m      mGreen, ddsd.ddpfPixelFormat.dwGBitMask        ; Green Mask
m2m      mBlue, ddsd.ddpfPixelFormat.dwBBitMask         ; Blue Mask


;===============================================
; Determine the pos for the red mask
;===============================================
MOV      shiftcount, 0
.WHILE (!(ddsd.ddpfPixelFormat.dwRBitMask & 1))
         SHR      ddsd.ddpfPixelFormat.dwRBitMask, 1
         INC      shiftcount
.ENDW
MOV      AL, shiftcount
MOV      pRed, AL


;===============================================
; Determine the pos for the green mask
;===============================================
MOV      shiftcount, 0
.WHILE (!(ddsd.ddpfPixelFormat.dwGBitMask & 1))
         SHR      ddsd.ddpfPixelFormat.dwGBitMask, 1
         INC      shiftcount
.ENDW
MOV      AL, shiftcount
MOV      pGreen, AL


;===============================================
; Determine the pos for the blue mask
;===============================================
MOV      shiftcount, 0
.WHILE (!(ddsd.ddpfPixelFormat.dwBBitMask & 1))
         SHR      ddsd.ddpfPixelFormat.dwBBitMask, 1
         INC      shiftcount
.ENDW
MOV      AL, shiftcount
MOV      pBlue, AL


;===============================================
; Set a special var if we are in 16 bit mode
;===============================================
.IF app_bpp == 16
```

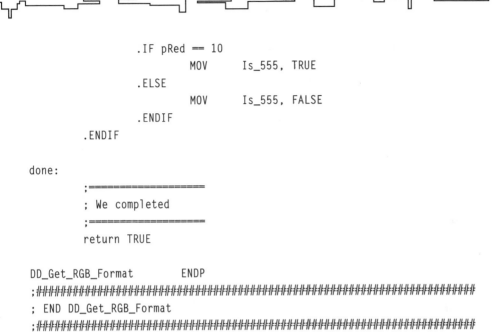

```
              .IF pRed == 10
                      MOV      Is_555, TRUE
              .ELSE
                      MOV      Is_555, FALSE
              .ENDIF
      .ENDIF


done:

      ;====================
      ; We completed
      ;====================

      return TRUE


DD_Get_RGB_Format        ENDP
;################################################################
; END DD_Get_RGB_Format
;################################################################
```

First we initialize our description structure and make a call to get the surface description from Direct Draw. We place the masks that are returned in global variables because we will want to use them in all kinds of places. A *mask* is a value that you can use to set or clear certain bits in a variable/register. In our case, we use them to mask off the unnecessary bits so that we can access the red, green, or blue bits of our pixel individually.

The next three sections of code are used to determine the number of bits in each color component. For example, if we had set the mode to 24bpp, there would be 8 bits in every component. The way we determine the number of bits it needs to be moved is by shifting each mask to the right by 1 and ANDing it with the number 1. This allows us to effectively count all the bits we need to shift by to move our component into its proper position. This works because the mask is going to contain a 1 where the bits are valid. So by ANDing it with the 1, we are able to see if the bit was turned on or not because the number 1 will leave only the first bit set and turn all others off.

Finally, we set a variable that tells us whether the video mode is 5-5-5 or 5-6-5. This is extremely important since 16bpp mode can be either, and we do not want our pictures to have a green or purple tint on one machine and look fine on another!

The last function I want to cover in our Direct Draw library is the text drawing function. This uses GDI, so I figured I should at least give it a small explanation.

```
;############################################################################
; DD_Draw_Text Procedure
;############################################################################
DD_Draw_Text PROC              surface:DWORD, text:DWORD, num_chars:DWORD,
                               x:DWORD, y:DWORD, color:DWORD


            ;========================================================
            ; This function will draw the passed text on the passed
            ; surface using the passed color at the passed coords
            ; with GDI
            ;========================================================


            ;========================================================
            ; First we need to get a DC for the surface
            ;========================================================
            DDS4INVOKE GetDC, surface, ADDR hDC


            ;========================================================
            ; Set the text color and BK mode
            ;========================================================
            INVOKE SetTextColor, hDC, color
            INVOKE SetBkMode, hDC, TRANSPARENT


            ;========================================================
            ; Write out the text at the desired location
            ;========================================================
            INVOKE TextOut, hDC, x, y, text, num_chars


            ;========================================================
            ; release the DC we obtained
            ;========================================================
            DDS4INVOKE ReleaseDC, surface, hDC

done:
            ;==================
            ; We completed
            ;==================
            return TRUE


DD_Draw_Text    ENDP
```

```
;##############################################################
; END DD_Draw_Text
;##############################################################
```

Following this code is relatively simple. First we get the device context (DC) for our surface. In Windows, drawing is typically done through these DCs. Thus, if you want to use any GDI function in Direct Draw, the first thing you have to do is get the DC for your surface. Then we set the background mode and text color using basic Windows GDI calls. Now we are ready to draw our text; again, we just make a call to the Windows function `TextOut()`. There are many others; this is just the one that I chose to use. Finally, we release the DC for our surface.

The rest of the Direct Draw routines follow the same basic format and use the same types of calls, so they shouldn't be too hard to figure out. The basic idea behind all of the routines is the same: We want to encapsulate the functionality we need into some services that still allow us to be flexible. Now it's time to write the code to handle our bitmaps that go into these surfaces.

Our Bitmap Library

We are now ready to write our bitmap library. We will start like the Direct Draw library by determining what we need. As far as I can tell right now, we should be good with two simple routines: a bitmap loader and a draw routine. Since we will be using surfaces, the draw routine should draw onto the passed surface. Our loader will load our special file format, which I will cover in a moment. That should be it; there isn't that much that is needed for bitmaps nowadays. DirectX is how most manipulation occurs, especially since many things can be done in hardware. With that in mind, we will cover our unique file format.

Normally, creating your own file format is a headache and isn't worth the trouble. In our case, however, it greatly simplifies the code, and I have provided the conversion utility with the package on the accompanying CD-ROM. This format is probably one of the easiest you will ever encounter. It has five main parts: `Width`, `Height`, `BPP`, `Size of Buffer`, and `Buffer`. The first three give information on the image. I have our library set up for 16bpp only, but implementing other bit depths would be fairly easy. The fourth section tells us how large of a buffer we need for the image, and the fifth section is that buffer. Having our own format not only makes the code we need to write a lot easier, it also prevents other people from seeing our work before they are meant to see it! Now, how do we load this crazy format?

```
;###############################################################
; Create_From_SFP Procedure
;###############################################################
Create_From_SFP PROC     ptr_BMP:DWORD, sfp_file:DWORD, desired_bpp:DWORD


        ;=======================================================
        ; This function will allocate our bitmap structure and
        ; will load the bitmap from an SFP file. Converting if
        ; it is needed based on the passed value.
        ;=======================================================


        ;=======================================
        ; Local Variables
        ;=======================================
        LOCAL   hFile           :DWORD
        LOCAL   hSFP            :DWORD
        LOCAL   Img_Left        :DWORD
        LOCAL   Img_Alias       :DWORD
        LOCAL   red             :DWORD
        LOCAL   green           :DWORD
        LOCAL   blue            :DWORD
        LOCAL   Dest_Alias      :DWORD


        ;===============================
        ; Create the SFP file
        ;===============================
        INVOKE CreateFile, sfp_file, GENERIC_READ,FILE_SHARE_READ, \
                NULL,OPEN_EXISTING, FILE_ATTRIBUTE_NORMAL,NULL
        MOV     hFile, EAX


        ;===========================
        ; Test for an error
        ;===========================
        .IF EAX == INVALID_HANDLE_VALUE
                JMP err
        .ENDIF


        ;===============================
        ; Get the file size
        ;===============================
        INVOKE GetFileSize, hFile, NULL
```

```
        PUSH    EAX


        ;====================================
        ; test for an error
        ;====================================
        .IF EAX == -1
                JMP     err
        .ENDIF


        ;=============================================
        ; Allocate enough memory to hold the file
        ;=============================================
        INVOKE GlobalAlloc, GMEM_FIXED, EAX
        MOV     hSFP, EAX


        ;======================================
        ; test for an error
        ;======================================
        .IF EAX == 0
                JMP     err
        .ENDIF


        ;======================================
        ; Put the file into memory
        ;======================================
        POP     EAX
        INVOKE ReadFile, hFile, hSFP, EAX, OFFSET Amount_Read, NULL


        ;======================================
        ; Test for an error
        ;======================================
        .IF EAX == FALSE
                ;========================
                ; We failed so leave
                ;========================
                JMP     err

        .ENDIF
```

```
;===================================
; Determine the size without the BPP
;===================================
MOV     EBX, hSFP
MOV     EAX, DWORD PTR [EBX]
ADD     EBX, 4
MOV     ECX, DWORD PTR [EBX]
MUL     ECX
PUSH    EAX


;=====================================
; Do we allocate a 16 or 24 bit buffer
;=====================================
.IF desired_bpp == 16

        ;=========================
        ; Just allocate a 16-bit
        ;=========================
        POP     EAX
        SHL     EAX, 1
        INVOKE GlobalAlloc, GMEM_FIXED, EAX
        MOV     EBX, ptr_BMP
        MOV     DWORD PTR [EBX], EAX
        MOV     Dest_Alias, EAX


        ;=====================================
        ; Test for an error
        ;=====================================
        .IF EAX == FALSE

                ;========================
                ; We failed so leave
                ;========================
                JMP     err


        .ENDIF

.ELSE
        ;=====================================
        ; This is where code for 24 bit would go
        ;=====================================
```

```
                ;===========================
                ; For now just return an err
                ;===========================
                JMP      err

        .ENDIF


        ;===================================
        ; Setup for reading in
        ;===================================
        MOV      EBX, hSFP
        ADD      EBX, 10
        MOV      EAX, DWORD PTR[EBX]
        MOV      Img_Left, EAX
        ADD      EBX, 4
        MOV      Img_Alias, EBX


        ;===================================
        ; Now let's start converting values
        ;===================================
        .WHILE Img_Left > 0
                ;===================================
                ; Build a color word based on
                ; the desired BPP or transfer
                ;===================================
                .IF desired_bpp == 16
                        ;===========================================
                        ; Read in a byte for blue, green and red
                        ;===========================================
                        XOR      ECX, ECX
                        MOV      EBX, Img_Alias
                        MOV      CL, BYTE PTR [EBX]
                        MOV      blue, ECX
                        INC      EBX
                        MOV      CL, BYTE PTR [EBX]
                        MOV      green, ECX
                        INC      EBX
                        MOV      CL, BYTE PTR [EBX]
                        MOV      red, ECX
```

```
;============================
; Adjust the Img_Alias
;============================
ADD      Img_Alias, 3


;============================
; Do we build a 555 or a 565 val
;============================
.IF Is_555 == TRUE
        ;============================
        ; Build the 555 color word
        ;============================
        RGB16BIT_555 red, green, blue
.ELSE
        ;============================
        ; Build the 565 color word
        ;============================
        RGB16BIT_565 red, green, blue

.ENDIF

;============================
; Transfer it to the final buffer
;============================
MOV      EBX, Dest_Alias
MOV      WORD PTR [EBX], AX

;============================
; Adjust the dest by 2
;============================
ADD      Dest_Alias, 2

.ELSE
        ;============================
        ; This is where code for 24 bit would go
        ;============================


        ;============================
        ; For now just return an err
        ;============================
```

```
                    JMP      err

            .ENDIF

            ;====================
            ; Sub amount left by 3
            ;====================
            SUB      Img_Left, 3

        .ENDW

            ;====================================
            ; Free the SFP Memory
            ;====================================
            INVOKE GlobalFree, hSFP

done:

            ;====================
            ; We completed
            ;====================
            return TRUE

err:

            ;====================================
            ; Free the SFP Memory
            ;====================================
            INVOKE GlobalFree, hSFP


            ;====================
            ; We didn't make it
            ;====================
            return FALSE

Create_From_SFP ENDP
;####################################################################
; END Create_From_SFP
;####################################################################
```

The code starts out by creating the file (which, in Windows, is how you open it) and then retrieves the file size. This allows us to allocate enough memory to load in our entire file. The process of reading in the file is fairly simple; we just make a call. As usual, the most important parts are those that check for errors.

Once the file is in memory, we compute the size of the desired image based on the width and height in our header and the desired_bpp level that was passed in to the function. Then we allocate yet another buffer with the information we calculated. This is the buffer that is kept in the end.

The next step is the heart of our load function. Here we read in 3 bytes (since our pictures are stored as 24-bit images) and create the proper color value (5-6-5 or 5-5-5) for the buffer. We then store that value in the new buffer we just created. We loop through all pixels in our bitmap and convert each to the desired format. The conversion is based on a predefined macro. You could also implement the function by using the members we filled when we called the function to get the pixel format. This second way would allow you to have a more abstract interface to the code, but for our purposes, it was better to see what was really happening to the bits.

At the completion of our loop, we free the main buffer and return the address of the buffer with our converted pixel values. If an error occurs at any point, we jump to our error code, which frees the possible buffer we could have created. This is to prevent memory leaks. And . . . that's it for the load function.

Once the bitmap is loaded into memory, we need to be able to draw it onto a Direct Draw surface. Whether we are loading it in permanently or just drawing a quick picture onto the back buffer should not matter. Let's look at a function that draws the passed bitmap onto our passed surface. Here is the code:

```
\;##############################################################################
; Draw_Bitmap Procedure
;##############################################################################
Draw_Bitmap PROC          surface:DWORD, bmp_buffer:DWORD, lPitch:DWORD,
                          bpp:DWORD

    ;=====================================================================
    ; This function will draw the BMP on the surface.
    ; the surface must be locked before the call.
    ;
    ; It uses the width and height of the screen to do so.
    ; I hard-coded this in just 'cause ... okay.
    ;
    ; This routine does not do transparency!
    ;=====================================================================
```

```
;==========================
; Local Variables
;==========================
LOCAL    dest_addr        :DWORD
LOCAL    source_addr      :DWORD


;==========================
; Init the addresses
;==========================
MOV      EAX, surface
MOV      EBX, bmp_buffer
MOV      dest_addr, EAX
MOV      source_addr, EBX


;==========================
; Init counter with height
;
; Hard-coded in.
;==========================
MOV      EDX, 480


;================================
; We are in 16 bit mode
;================================


copy_loop1:
;==========================
; Setup num of bytes in width
;
; Hard-coded also.
;
; 640*2/4 = 320.
;==========================
MOV      ECX, 320


;==========================
; Set source and dest
;==========================
MOV      EDI, dest_addr
MOV      ESI, source_addr
```

```
;===================================
; Move by DWORDS
;===================================
REP      movsd


;===================================
; Adjust the variables
;===================================
MOV      EAX, lPitch
MOV      EBX, 1280
ADD      dest_addr, EAX
ADD      source_addr, EBX


;===================================
; Dec the line counter
;===================================
DEC EDX


;===================================
; Did we hit bottom?
;===================================
JNE copy_loop1


done:

         ;=================
         ; We completed
         ;=================
         return TRUE

err:

         ;=================
         ; We didn't make it
         ;=================
         return FALSE


Draw_Bitmap      ENDP
;############################################################################
; END Draw_Bitmap
;############################################################################
```

This function is a little bit more advanced than some of the others we have seen, so pay close attention. We know, as assembly programmers, that if we can get everything into a register, things will be faster than if we have to access memory. In that spirit, we place the starting source and destination addresses into registers.

We then compute the number of WORDS in our line. We can divide this number by 2 so that we have the number of DWORDS in a line. I have hard-coded this number since we will always be in 640×480×16 for our game. This number is placed in the ECX register. The reason for this is that our next instruction MOVSD can be combined with the REP label. This will move a DWORD, decrement ECX by 1, compare ECX to ZERO, if not equal, then MOVE A DWORD, and so on, until ECX is equal to zero. In short, it is like having a "For" loop with the counter in ECX. As we have the code right now, it is moving a DWORD from the source into the destination until we have exhausted the number of DWORDS in our line. At that point, it does this over again until we have reached the number of lines in our height (480 in our case).

These are our only two functions in the bitmap module. They are short and sweet. More importantly, now that we have our bitmap and Direct Draw routines coded, we can write the code to display our loading game screen!

A Game . . . Well, Sort Of

The library routines are complete, and we are now ready to plunge into our game code. These are the routines that control the main setup, shutdown, the flow of the game, and the windows messages—in other words, all of the core logic needed for your game. We will start by looking at the initialization function since it is called first in our code.

```
;#################################################################
; Game_Init Procedure
;#################################################################
Game_Init        PROC

        ;=================================================
        ; This function will setup the game
        ;=================================================


        ;=================================================
        ; Initialize Direct Draw — 640, 480, bpp
        ;=================================================
```

```
        INVOKE DD_Init, 640, 480, screen_bpp


        ;=================================
        ; Test for an error
        ;=================================
        .IF EAX == FALSE
                ;=========================
                ; We failed so leave
                ;=========================
                JMP     err

        .ENDIF


        ;=================================
        ; Read in the bitmap and create buffer
        ;=================================
        INVOKE Create_From_SFP, ADDR ptr_BMP_LOAD, ADDR szLoading, screen_bpp


        ;=================================
        ; Test for an error
        ;=================================
        .IF EAX == FALSE
                ;=========================
                ; We failed so leave
                ;=========================
                JMP     err

        .ENDIF


        ;=================================
        ; Lock the Direct Draw back buffer
        ;=================================
        INVOKE DD_Lock_Surface, lpddsback, ADDR lPitch


        ;=========================
        ; Check for an error
        ;=========================
        .IF EAX == FALSE
                ;=================
                ; Jump to err
                ;=================
```

```
            JMP      err

.ENDIF

;==================================
; Draw the bitmap onto the surface
;==================================
INVOKE Draw_Bitmap, EAX, ptr_BMP_LOAD, lPitch, screen_bpp


;==================================
; Unlock the back buffer
;==================================
INVOKE DD_Unlock_Surface, lpddsback


;==================================
; Check for an error
;==================================
.IF EAX == FALSE
            ;====================
            ; Jump to err
            ;====================
            JMP      err

.ENDIF


;====================================
; Everything okay so flip displayed
; surfaces and make loading visible
;====================================
INVOKE DD_Flip


;==================================
; Check for an error
;==================================
.IF EAX == FALSE
            ;====================
            ; Jump to err
            ;====================
            JMP      err

.ENDIF
```

```
done:
        ;====================
        ; We completed
        ;====================
        return TRUE

err:
        ;====================
        ; We didn't make it
        ;====================
        return FALSE   .

Game_Init      ENDP
;###############################################################
; END Game_Init
;###############################################################
```

This function plays the most important part in our game so far. In this routine, we make the call to initialize Direct Draw. If this succeeds, we load in our loading game bitmap file from disk. After that, we lock the back buffer. This is very important to do since we will be accessing the memory directly. After it is locked, we can draw our bitmap onto the surface and then unlock it. The final call in our procedure is to flip the buffers. Since we have the bitmap on the back buffer, we need it to be visible. Therefore, we exchange the buffers. The front goes to the back, and the back goes to the front. At the completion of this call, our bitmap is now visible onscreen. One thing that may be confusing here is why we didn't load the bitmap into a Direct Draw surface. The reason is that we will only be using it once, so there was no need to waste a surface.

Next on our list of things to code is the Windows callback function itself. This function is how we handle messages in Windows. Anytime we want to handle a message, the code will go in this function. Take a look at how we have it set up currently.

```
;###############################################################
; Main Window Callback Procedure — WndProc
;###############################################################
WndProc PROC    hWin    :DWORD,
                uMsg    :DWORD,
                wParam  :DWORD,
                lParam  :DWORD
```

```
.IF uMsg == WM_COMMAND

        ;==========================
        ; We don't have a menu, but
        ; if we did this is where it
        ; would go!
        ;==========================


.ELSEIF uMsg == WM_KEYDOWN

        ;========================================
        ; Since we don't have a Direct Input
        ; system coded yet we will just check
        ; for escape to be pressed
        ;========================================
        MOV     EAX, wParam
        .IF EAX == VK_ESCAPE

                ;==========================
                ; Kill the application
                ;==========================
                INVOKE PostQuitMessage,NULL

        .ENDIF


        ;==========================
        ; We processed it
        ;==========================
        return 0

.ELSEIF uMsg == WM_DESTROY

        ;==========================
        ; Kill the application
        ;==========================
        INVOKE PostQuitMessage,NULL
        return 0

.ENDIF


;========================================================
; Let the default procedure handle the message
;========================================================
INVOKE DefWindowProc,hWin,uMsg,wParam,lParam
```

```
RET

WndProc endp
;###############################################################
; End of Main Windows Callback Procedure
;###############################################################
```

The code is fairly self-explanatory. So far, we only deal with two messages: the WM_KEYDOWN message and the WM_DESTROY message. We process the WM_KEYDOWN message so that the user can hit Esc and exit our game. We will be coding a Direct Input system, but until then we needed a way to quit the game. The one thing you should notice is that any messages we do not deal with are handled by the default processing function: DefWindowProc(). This function is defined in Windows already. You just need to call it whenever you do not handle a message.

We aren't going to look at the game's main function simply because it is empty. We haven't added any solid code to our game loop yet. Everything is prepared, however, so that next time we can get to it. That leaves us with the shutdown code:

```
;###############################################################
; Game_Shutdown Procedure
;###############################################################
Game_Shutdown    PROC


            ;==================================================
            ; This shuts our game down and frees memory we allocated
            ;==================================================


            ;=========================
            ; Shutdown DirectDraw
            ;=========================
            INVOKE DD_ShutDown


            ;=========================
            ; Free the bitmap memory
            ;=========================
            INVOKE GlobalFree, ptr_BMP_LOAD

done:
            ;==================
            ; We completed
            ;==================
```

```
        return TRUE

err:

        ;==================
        ; We didn't make it
        ;==================
        return FALSE

Game_Shutdown    ENDP
;###########################################################################
; END Game_Shutdown
;###########################################################################
```

Here we make the call to shut down our Direct Draw library, and we also free the memory we allocated earlier for the bitmap. We could have freed the memory elsewhere, and maybe next time we will. Things are a bit easier to understand, however, when all of your initialization and cleanup code is in one place.

As you can see, there isn't that much game specific code in our game source code. The majority resides in our modules, such as Direct Draw. This allows us to keep our code clean, and any changes we may need to make later on are much easier since things aren't hard-coded inline. Anyway, the end result of what you have just seen is a loading screen that is displayed until the user hits the Esc key. And that—primitive though it may be—is our game so far.

Conclusion

We covered a lot of material in this section. We now have a bitmap library and a Direct Draw library for our game. These are core modules that you should be able to use in any game of this type. By breaking up the code like this, we are able to keep our game code separate from the library code. You do not want any module to be dependent on another module. Furthermore, the way we designed these modules will carry over into our other modules. Consistency in code is a very good thing.

Next we continue our module development with Direct Input and the creation of a menu system. These two things should keep us busy.

WIN32 ASM—PART 3

Now, if I remember correctly, which I do, the preceding section completed our loading game screen for SPACE-TRIS. This means we have a Direct Draw library and a bitmap library but not much else. We had to use the WM_KEYDOWN message to process our input, and we just got the privilege of looking at a loading game screen. That was it.

Well, that's about to change. First, we are going to get a Direct Input library developed. After that, we will code some advanced timing routines and develop the menu code. Finally, we will take a look at the new game loop and how it had to be changed.

We will be covering *a lot* of code in this part of the chapter, so you may want to review the basic concepts in earlier sections if you are new to Win32 ASM programming. Otherwise, keep plugging along, and we will get started with our Direct Input routines.

Direct Input Is a Breeze

Are you ready? Good. For all intents and purposes, Direct Input code has the same basic format as our Direct Draw code. The more you use DirectX, the more you will notice that it's all the same, just with different parameters. Anyway, we will want to put together an initialization routine and a shutdown routine. We also are going to look at the coding of a routine to handle reading the keyboard. The accompanying code has routines for the mouse in it as well, but because we don't care about the mouse in our game, I won't be covering it. It is there, however, so feel free to use it if you'd like.

To start with, I guess you are going to want to see the Direct Input initialization routine.

```
;###############################################################
; DI_Init Procedure
;###############################################################
```

```
DI_Init PROC

        ;==================================================
        ; This function will setup Direct Input
        ;==================================================


        ;===============================
        ; Create our direct Input obj
        ;===============================
        INVOKE DirectInputCreate, hInst, DIRECTINPUT_VERSION, ADDR lpdi,0


        ;===========================
        ; Test for an error creating
        ;===========================
        .IF EAX != DI_OK
                JMP     err
        .ENDIF


        ;===========================
        ; Initialize the keyboard
        ;===========================
        INVOKE DI_Init_Keyboard


        ;===========================
        ; Test for an error in init
        ;===========================
        .IF EAX == FALSE
                JMP     err
        .ENDIF


        ;===========================
        ; Initialize the mouse
        ;===========================
        INVOKE DI_Init_Mouse


        ;===========================
        ; Test for an error in init
        ;===========================
        .IF EAX == FALSE
                JMP     err
        .ENDIF
```

```
done:
                ;===================
                ; We completed
                ;===================
                return TRUE

err:
                ;===================
                ; Give the error msg
                ;===================
                INVOKE MessageBox, hMainWnd, ADDR szNoDI, NULL, MB_OK


                ;===================
                ; We didn't make it
                ;===================
                return FALSE


DI_Init ENDP
;#################################################################################
; END DI_Init
;#################################################################################
```

This code isn't very complex at all. It starts by creating the main Direct Input object. This is the object you use to derive all of the device objects and such. Just a single call is all it takes. We pass it the address of the variable, the version of Direct Input to use, and the instance of our application. Then we call routines to set up our keyboard and mouse. Thus, we need to take a peek at the routine that initializes the keyboard.

```
;#################################################################################
; DI_Init_Keyboard        Procedure
;#################################################################################
DI_Init_Keyboard          PROC

                ;==================================================
                ; This function will initialize the keyboard
                ;==================================================


                ;===============================
                ; Now try and create it
                ;===============================
```

```
        DIINVOKE CreateDevice, lpdi, ADDR GUID_SysKeyboard, ADDR lpdikey, 0


        ;==============================
        ; Test for an error creating
        ;==============================
        .IF EAX != DI_OK
                JMP     err
        .ENDIF


        ;==============================
        ; Set the coop level
        ;==============================
        DIDEVINVOKE SetCooperativeLevel, lpdikey, hMainWnd, \
                DISCL_NONEXCLUSIVE OR DISCL_BACKGROUND


        ;==============================
        ; Test for an error querying
        ;==============================
        .IF EAX != DI_OK
                JMP     err
        .ENDIF


        ;==============================
        ; Set the data format
        ;==============================
        DIDEVINVOKE SetDataFormat, lpdikey, ADDR c_dfDIKeyboard


        ;==============================
        ; Test for an error querying
        ;==============================
        .IF EAX != DI_OK
                JMP     err
        .ENDIF


        ;==================================
        ; Now try and acquire the keyboard
        ;==================================
        DIDEVINVOKE Acquire, lpdikey
```

```
        ;==========================
        ; Test for an error acquiring
        ;==========================
        .IF EAX != DI_OK
                JMP     err
        .ENDIF

done:
        ;==================
        ; We completed
        ;==================
        return TRUE

err:
        ;==================
        ; We didn't make it
        ;==================
        return FALSE


DI_Init_Keyboard            ENDP
;###############################################################################
; END DI_Init_Keyboard
;###############################################################################
```

The first thing this code does is attempt to create the keyboard device. Remember that, like the Direct Draw object, the Direct Input object is generic, and other things must be created off of it (such as keyboard devices). Once you have created the object, you will need to set the cooperative level on it. In our case, we would like to have exclusive use of it.

Now that the keyboard's cooperative level set is set, we can inform Direct Input of the type of data it will receive. For the keyboard, this is c_dfDIKeyboard. The final step in initializing our keyboard is acquiring it. This is the step that most people tend to forget. Currently, we have an object that we have told to accept keyboard data and take exclusive access of the keyboard. But we have not told it that it has permission to take control of the object. So, we make a call and that's that.

We are now ready to use the application. That means we need to have a look at the code to read the keyboard—unless, of course, you would prefer to simply make a call and never see the code in your life. Oh my! What kind of programmer are you? I can't believe you just thought that! Here's the code anyway:

```
;##############################################################################
; DI_Read_Keyboard          Procedure
;##############################################################################
DI_Read_Keyboard           PROC


               ;=====================================================
               ; This function will read the keyboard and set the input state
               ;=====================================================


               ;===========================
               ; Read if it exists
               ;===========================
               .IF lpdikey != NULL
                       ;=======================
                       ; Now read the state
                       ;=======================
                       DIDEVINVOKE GetDeviceState, lpdikey, 256, ADDR keyboard_state
                       .IF EAX != DI_OK
                               JMP     err
                       .ENDIF
               .ELSE
                       ;=========================================
                       ; keyboard isn't plugged in, zero out state
                       ;=========================================
                       DIINITSTRUCT ADDR keyboard_state, 256
                       JMP     err

               .ENDIF

done:
       ;=================
       ; We completed
       ;=================
       return TRUE

err:
       ;=================
       ; We didn't make it
       ;=================
       return FALSE
```

```
DI_Read_Keyboard          ENDP
;##############################################################################
; END DI_Read_Keyboard
;##############################################################################
```

This code first tests to see whether we have a valid object. If not, it could be for a number of reasons, such as the keyboard not being plugged in or maybe a bad port. This is unlikely to happen, but it's better to be safe than sorry.

If we are valid, the code reads the device. In the case of the keyboard, all entries are cleared and are only set if the key has been actively pressed down at the time of the read. If so, the keyboard constant associated with that key is set to TRUE; otherwise, it is left as FALSE. The key constants are defined in the DInput.inc file. Examples are DIK_J, DIK_N, and so on.

Finally, the only thing left to do is shut down the Direct Input stuff. That can be done with the following routine:

```
;##############################################################################
; DI_ShutDown Procedure
;##############################################################################
DI_ShutDown PROC


        ;================================================================
        ; This function will close down Direct Input
        ;================================================================


        ;============================================
        ; Shutdown the Mouse
        ;============================================
        DIDEVINVOKE Unacquire, lpdimouse
        DIDEVINVOKE Release, lpdimouse


        ;============================================
        ; Shutdown the Keyboard
        ;============================================
        DIDEVINVOKE Unacquire, lpdikey
        DIDEVINVOKE Release, lpdikey


        ;============================================
        ; Shutdown the Direct Input object
        ;============================================
```

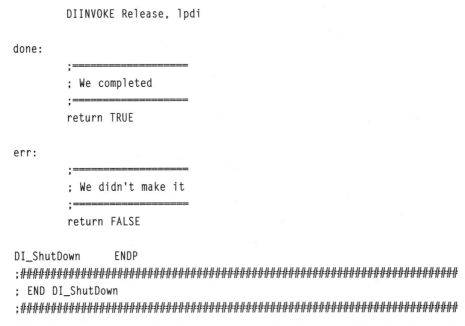

```
        DIINVOKE Release, lpdi

done:
        ;═══════════════════
        ; We completed
        ;═══════════════════
        return TRUE

err:
        ;═══════════════════
        ; We didn't make it
        ;═══════════════════
        return FALSE

DI_ShutDown     ENDP
;###############################################################
; END DI_ShutDown
;###############################################################
```

This code unacquires the devices we acquired during initialization and then releases them. It then releases the main Direct Input object that we created. That is all that needs to be done during the shutdown process.

Direct Input is one of the easiest portions of DirectX to write code in. There are very few calls you need to make, and most of them are really straightforward (with the exception of that "acquire" thing). The advantage is that we now have a high-performance input system to use and do not have to rely on Windows messages to bring us our needed information.

With Direct Input completely out of the way, we have what we need to code our menu system. Before we get to that, however, let's make a brief sojourn to the land of timing to see what kind of havoc we can INVOKE.

Timing and Windoze

Timing. Without it, your game will do some very weird things. From roller-coaster frame rates to objects that move too quickly, it all can be traced back to timing. Unfortunately, finding good documentation on timing in Windows can be a chore. Typically, you will uncover a function named GetTickCount(). Since this function deals with milliseconds, it appears to be perfect for our needs. The only problem is that it's very inaccurate and unreliable. So, we dig a little further and come up with timeGetTime() in the multimedia library of Windows. This is a much better function, it is more reliable, and it still works with milliseconds, which is what we need.

It kind of makes you wonder, though. If we are writing high-performance games, shouldn't we have a "high-performance" timer? Indeed, we do. Getting it to work nicely, however, can be a bit of a trick. But we will cover that in a moment.

First, what are our functionality needs? Obviously, we will want a function to initialize our timing system. We also will want one to return the current time and one to delay for the amount of time you pass in to it. Then we will want to add timer routines to control our frame rate. Of course, we will need one to start a timer and one to wait until the specified amount of time has elapsed. That should be it.

Here is the code for the Init_Time() function:

```
;##############################################################################
; Init_Time Procedure
;##############################################################################
Init_Time       PROC


        ;====================================================
        ; This function will find out if we can use the HP timer
        ; and will set the needed vars to use it
        ;====================================================


        ;====================================================
        ; Get the timer Frequency, at least try to.
        ;====================================================
        INVOKE QueryPerformanceFrequency, ADDR HPTimerVar

        .IF EAX == FALSE

                ;==================
                ; Set to use no HP
                ;==================
                MOV     UseHP, FALSE
                JMP     done

        .ENDIF


        ;====================================
        ; We can use it so set the Var and Freq
        ;====================================
```

```
        MOV     UseHP, TRUE
        MOV     EAX, HPTimerVar
        MOV     HPTimerFreq, EAX
        MOV     ECX, 1000
        XOR     EDX, EDX
        DIV     ECX
        MOV     HPTicksPerMS, EAX

done:

        ;===================
        ; We completed
        ;===================
        return TRUE

Init_Time       ENDP
;##############################################################################
; END Init_Time
;##############################################################################
```

This code performs the task of finding out whether we have a high-performance timer on the system to use. If not, it falls back on timeGetTime() since that is guaranteed to be there. We start out by calling the function QueryPerformaceFrequency(). If this succeeds, we have a high-performance timer on the system, and this call returns the frequency of it. If not, we set the things up to not use the HP timer.

Presuming we do have one, the code saves the timer frequency and calculates the number of ticks per millisecond. The reason for this value is that the HP timer may have a resolution far smaller than 1 millisecond. So, we need to determine how many ticks of the HP timer are equal to 1 millisecond. That is all the setup procedure needs to do to get things ready.

The next function we will cover is Start_Time(). This function is used to start a timer with the variable you pass in to it. This will be used to control our frame rate, as you will see later.

```
;##############################################################################
; Start_Time Procedure
;##############################################################################
Start_Time      PROC    ptr_time_var:DWORD

        ;=================================================
        ; This function will start our timer going and store
```

```
; the value in a variable that you pass it the ADDR of
;================================================================


;================================================
; Are we using the Highperformance timer
;================================================
.IF UseHP == TRUE
        ;================================================
        ; Yes. We are using the HP timer
        ;================================================
        INVOKE  QueryPerformanceCounter, ADDR HPTimerVar
        MOV     EAX, HPTimerVar
        MOV     EBX, ptr_time_var
        MOV     DWORD PTR [EBX], EAX

.ELSE
        ;================================================
        ; No. Use timeGetTime instead.
        ;================================================


        ;================================================
        ; Get our starting time
        ;================================================
        INVOKE  timeGetTime


        ;================================================
        ; Set our variable
        ;================================================
        MOV     EBX, ptr_time_var
        MOV     DWORD PTR [EBX], EAX

.ENDIF

done:
        ;==================
        ; We completed
        ;==================
        return TRUE

Start_Time      ENDP
```

```
;###############################################################
; END Start_Time
;###############################################################
```

The code is relatively simple. If we have access to the high-performance timer, we make a call to `QueryPerformanceCounter()`. If not, we make the call to `timeGetTime()` instead. The only thing that may be confusing is the notation used to store the value that these functions return:

```
MOV      EBX, ptr_time_var
MOV      DWORD PTR [ EBX], EAX
```

What this code does is move the value of `ptr_time_var` into the register `EBX`. In this case, `ptr_time_var` is the address of a variable that was passed in to hold the starting time. Next, the code moves the value of register `EAX` into the address that `EBX` contains. In assembly, that is what [XXX] means—"the address of". The `DWORD PTR` will let the assembler know that we will be moving a `DWORD` and that `[EBX]` is a pointer. This will effectively store the value `EAX` in the location pointed to by `ptr_time_var`.

The final timing function we will go over here is `Wait_Time()`. This is the sister function for `Start_Time()`. Together, they are used to control our game's frame rate.

```
;###############################################################
; Wait_Time Procedure
;###############################################################
Wait_Time        PROC     time_var:DWORD, time:DWORD


              ;=================================================
              ; This function will wait for the passed time in MS based
              ; on the distance from the passed start time. It returns
              ; time it took the loop to complete in MS
              ;=================================================


              ;=========================================
              ; Are we using the Highperformance timer
              ;=========================================
              .IF UseHP == TRUE

                    ;=================================
                    ; Yes. We are using the HP timer
                    ;=================================
```

```
        ;========================================
        ; Adjust time for frequency
        ;========================================
        MOV     EAX, 1000
        MOV     ECX, time
        XOR     EDX, EDX
        DIV     ECX
        MOV     ECX, EAX
        MOV     EAX, HPTimerFreq
        XOR     EDX, EDX
        DIV     ECX
        MOV     time, EAX


        ;========================================
        ; A push so we can pop evenly
        ;========================================
        PUSH    EAX

again1:
        ;========================================
        ; Pop last time or misc push off
        ;========================================
        POP     EAX


        ;========================================
        ; Get the current time
        ;========================================
        INVOKE QueryPerformanceCounter, ADDR HPTimerVar
        MOV     EAX, HPTimerVar


        ;========================================
        ; Subtract from start time
        ;========================================
        MOV     ECX, time_var
        MOV     EBX, time
        SUB     EAX, ECX


        ;========================================
        ; Save how long it took
        ;========================================
        PUSH    EAX
```

```
;==================================
; Go up and do it again if we were not
; yet to zero or less than the time
;==================================
SUB     EAX, EBX
JLE     again1


;==================================
; Pop the final time off of the stack
;==================================
POP     EAX


;==================================
; Adjust it to MS
;==================================
MOV     ECX, HPTicksPerMS
XOR     EDX, EDX
DIV     ECX
```

.ELSE

```
;==================================
; No. Use timeGetTime instead.
;==================================


;==================================
; A push so we can pop evenly
;==================================
PUSH    EAX
```

again:

```
;==================================
; Pop last time or misc push off
;==================================
POP     EAX


;==================================
; Get the current time
;==================================
INVOKE timeGetTime
```

```
;========================================
; Subtract from start time
;========================================
MOV     ECX, time_var
MOV     EBX, time
SUB     EAX, ECX


;========================================
; Save how long it took
;========================================
PUSH    EAX


;========================================
; Go up and do it again if we were not
; yet to zero or less than the time
;========================================
SUB     EAX, EBX
JLE     again


;========================================
; Pop the final time off of the stack
;========================================
POP     EAX

.ENDIF


;=====================
; return from here
;=====================
RET

Wait_Time       ENDP
;#############################################################################
; END Wait_Time
;#############################################################################
```

This routine is probably the most complex of the timing routines. What it does is
wait for the passed-in amount of time to elapse *past* the starting time that was
passed in. In other words, if your start time was 100 and you told it to wait for 50,
the function would not return until the current time was >= 150. It returns the
actual elapsed time between finish and start.

Let's view this code one section at a time.

First, if we can use the HP timer, we do. If not, we fall back to the default timer. This code first converts the passed-in time to the same frequency as the HP timer. It does this by dividing 1,000 by the passed time. This gives it a number relative to times per second. Then it divides the frequency by that number to retrieve the equivalent amount of time needed at our HP frequency level. This is done by way of setup because it determines the "finish" time for the function. It saves this value on the stack so that we can pop evenly in our loop.

Next, it enters our main compare loop. It POPs the value of elapsed time off the stack to clear it.

We then retrieve the current value of the counter. We subtract the start value from the current value to calculate the time that has elapsed so far. We then save this "time" by pushing it onto the stack.

> **NOTE**
>
> During the first iteration, this value is not the elapsed time but the finish time.

Now we can subtract the wait time from the elapsed time. If the result is less than zero, we haven't waited long enough, so we do the preceding step again. Otherwise, we continue on down to the next step.

Here we POP the elapsed time off the stack and divide that by however many ticks were in a millisecond. That allows us to return a millisecond value even if we use the high-performance timer.

The code for if we do not have a high-performance timer does the same exact thing, but it doesn't perform the conversions because the function is in milliseconds by default and can't be changed.

That's it for timing. The other two functions merely perform variations of the two routines we just covered. Therefore, I am not going to cover those. I'll leave it to you to take a look-see at them and comprehend what they do.

The Menu System

A menu can be a complex thing in a game. Lucky for us, it's not. The general idea is to provide some sort of selection process for features of your game. Most of the time, this will consist of drawing a bitmap and having another "selector" bitmap drawn on top to choose an item or feature for the game. I have chosen to do this a little bit differently. Instead of having a selector, I am simply going to have certain keys correspond to the choices in the menu, kind of like the good old days of DOS but different.

The other important consideration is how you want to set up your system. Do you want the code to go into a "menu loop" and never return until the user makes a selection? Or do you want to call the menu function over and over again? In the case of Windows, the second choice is a million times better since we need to process messages. If we had coded in the first manner, the user could hit Alt+Tab while we are in the menu code, and we would potentially crash at some point. So, we are going to set up the second type of system.

The initialization and shutdown routines are nothing you haven't seen before. All they do is load in our two menu bitmaps. One of them is for the main menu, and one is for the file menu. The shutdown code simply frees their associated memory that we allocated.

NOTE

The game does not have Alt+Tab support yet. This will come in a later version of the code in this chapter.

The interesting code is in the Process_XXXX_Menu() functions. We will look in detail at the Process_Main_Menu() function. So, as usual, here is the code for that procedure:

```
;#######################################################################
; Process_Main_Menu Procedure
;#######################################################################
Process_Main_Menu         PROC


          ;===========================================================
          ; This function will process the main menu for the game
          ;===========================================================


          ;=================================
          ; Local Variables
          ;=================================


          ;=================================
          ; Lock the DirectDraw back buffer
          ;=================================
          INVOKE DD_Lock_Surface, lpddsback, ADDR lPitch


          ;=========================
          ; Check for an error
          ;=========================
```

```
.IF EAX == FALSE

            ;==================
            ; Jump to err
            ;==================
            JMP     err

.ENDIF

;====================================
; Draw the bitmap onto the surface
;====================================
INVOKE Draw_Bitmap, EAX, ptr_MAIN_MENU, lPitch, screen_bpp

;====================================
; Unlock the back buffer
;====================================
INVOKE DD_Unlock_Surface, lpddsback

;====================================
; Check for an error
;====================================
.IF EAX == FALSE

            ;==================
            ; Jump to err
            ;==================
            JMP     err

.ENDIF

;====================================
; Everything okay so flip displayed
; surfaces and make loading visible
;====================================
INVOKE DD_Flip

;====================================
; Check for an error
;====================================
.IF EAX == FALSE
```

```
                ;===================
                ; Jump to err
                ;===================
                JMP      err

        .ENDIF


;=============================================================
; Now read the keyboard to see if they have pressed
; any keys corresponding to our menu
;=============================================================
INVOKE DI_Read_Keyboard


;=============================
; Did they press a valid key
;=============================
.IF keyboard_state[DIK_N]
                ;====================
                ; The new game key
                ;====================
                return   MENU_NEW

.ELSEIF keyboard_state[DIK_G]
                ;====================
                ; The game files key
                ;====================
                return MENU_FILES

.ELSEIF keyboard_state[DIK_R]
                ;====================
                ; Return to game key
                ;====================
                return MENU_GAME

.ELSEIF keyboard_state[DIK_E]
                ;====================
                ; The exit game key
                ;====================
                return MENU_EXIT
```

```
        .ENDIF

done:
        ;===================
        ; We completed w/o
        ; doing anything
        ;===================
        return MENU_NOTHING

err:
        ;===================
        ; We didn't make it
        ;===================
        return MENU_ERROR


Process_Main_Menu        ENDP
;###################################################################
; END Process_Main_Menu
;###################################################################
```

An interesting routine, isn't it? Okay . . . maybe not. If interesting is what you want, though, I doubt you will find it in code (unless you are really weird like I am). Anyway, what does it do?

The answer in simple terms is this: It starts out by locking the back buffer and drawing our menu bitmap onto it. Then it unlocks the back buffer and flips surfaces so that we can see it. This is boring, not to mention the fact that it is nothing new. But wait . . . there on the next line. See it? Yes! Something we haven't covered!

We get to call one of our Direct Input routines, `DI_Read_Keyboard()`. If you recall, this function gets the state of every key on the keyboard. So, when we make this call, everything is set for us to check and see which keys were pressed. We do this by just checking the key values we care about. They can be in any order you want, but be aware that, the way it is coded right now, the code will only perform the code for one value, even if two valid keys are hit. This is because the keys are in one huge `IF-ELSE` statement. So, at the first valid entry, the code falls in, executes, and leaves—forgetting all about the other keys it needed to check. Thus, if you want/need to support multiple key presses, make every "character check" a separate `IF` statement and set flags so that you can process based on the combination the user entered.

We check each key on which we want information. If the key has been pressed, we return a value that corresponds to what was pressed. For example, if the user hits the N key for a new game, we will return the value MENU_NEW to the caller. These values are known as equates and are defined at the top of the code module in the section entitled "EQUATES." They are the equivalent of #DEFINE in C. They do nothing more than let you, as a programmer, associate a value to a string of characters for readability.

Finally, if nothing was pressed that we care about, we just return a value reflecting that. The same applies if an error occurs in the code.

This same method has been used for the Process_File_Menu() function. There are many other ways to handle menus, and a little creativity will expose them to you. This setup is fairly straightforward, however, and I kind of like it. So, that is what we are using. We have now tied the Direct Input code to our menu system. All that we have left to do is tie the menu and timer code we just wrote to our main game loop somehow.

Putting the Pieces Together

We are almost finished. It's time to tie all of the little things we did together into one, nice, neat package. So, we will start off with the game initialization routine.

```
;##############################################################################
; Game_Init Procedure
;##############################################################################
Game_Init        PROC


        ;==================================================
        ; This function will set up the game
        ;==================================================


        ;==================================================
        ; Initialize Direct Draw — 640, 480, bpp
        ;==================================================
        INVOKE DD_Init, 640, 480, screen_bpp


        ;==================================================
        ; Test for an error
        ;==================================================
        .IF EAX == FALSE
```

```
            ;======================
            ; We failed so leave
            ;======================
            JMP     err

.ENDIF

;=================================
; Read in the bitmap and create buffer
;=================================
INVOKE Create_From_SFP, ADDR ptr_BMP_LOAD, ADDR szLoading, screen_bpp

;=================================
; Test for an error
;=================================
.IF EAX == FALSE
            ;======================
            ; We failed so leave
            ;======================
            JMP     err

.ENDIF

;=================================
; Lock the DirectDraw back buffer
;=================================
INVOKE DD_Lock_Surface, lpddsback, ADDR lPitch

;=================================
; Check for an error
;=================================
.IF EAX == FALSE
            ;======================
            ; Jump to err
            ;======================
            JMP     err

.ENDIF
```

```
;=====================================
; Draw the bitmap onto the surface
;=====================================
INVOKE Draw_Bitmap, EAX, ptr_BMP_LOAD, lPitch, screen_bpp


;=====================================
; Unlock the back buffer
;=====================================
INVOKE DD_Unlock_Surface, lpddsback


;=============================
; Check for an error
;=============================
.IF EAX == FALSE

        ;=================
        ; Jump to err
        ;=================
        JMP     err

.ENDIF


;=====================================
; Everything okay so flip displayed
; surfaces and make loading visible
;=====================================
INVOKE DD_Flip


;=============================
; Check for an error
;=============================
.IF EAX == FALSE

        ;=================
        ; Jump to err
        ;=================
        JMP     err

.ENDIF


;=====================================
; Initialize Direct Input
;=====================================
```

```
        INVOKE  DI_Init


        ;=================================
        ; Test for an error
        ;=================================
        .IF EAX == FALSE

                ;=========================
                ; We failed so leave
                ;=========================
                JMP     err


        .ENDIF

        ;=========================================
        ; Initialize the timing system
        ;=========================================
        INVOKE  Init_Time


        ;=========================================
        ; Initialize Our Menus
        ;=========================================
        INVOKE  Init_Menu


        ;=========================================
        ; Test for an error
        ;=========================================
        .IF EAX == FALSE

                ;=========================
                ; We failed so leave
                ;=========================
                JMP     err


        .ENDIF


        ;=====================================
        ; Set the game state to the menu
        ; state since that is our first stop
        ;=====================================
        MOV     GameState, GS_MENU
```

```
            ;========================
            ; Free the bitmap memory
            ;========================
            INVOKE GlobalFree, ptr_BMP_LOAD

done:
            ;==================
            ; We completed
            ;==================
            return TRUE

err:
            ;==================
            ; We didn't make it
            ;==================
            return FALSE


Game_Init        ENDP
;##################################################################
; END Game_Init
;##################################################################
```

This routine has had a little bit of alteration since you last saw it. First we added some calls. We added one to initialize our timing system, one for our menu system, and one for our Direct Input library. We also deleted the loading game screen at the end of the routine. This is so that we do not have memory being used by a bitmap that will never be seen again. The main thing to notice, though, is the addition of a global variable called GameState. This variable holds the current state of the game. At the end of the game initialization routine, we set this variable to the value GS_MENU. This lets our main game loop know what state to process. There are equivalents for all states in the game.

That's pretty much all that has been altered for the initialization. The shutdown code has been altered to call the shutdown routines for the Direct Input module and for the menu module. The only other changes we had to make were in the main game loop. Actually, we didn't have to change anything since the routine was empty the last time we saw it.

Here is the new main game loop:

```
;##################################################################
; Game_Main Procedure
;##################################################################
```

```
Game_Main        PROC

        ;========================================================
        ; This is the heart of the game it gets called over and over
        ; even if we process a message!
        ;========================================================


        ;============================================
        ; Local Variables
        ;============================================
        LOCAL    StartTime        :DWORD

        ;==================================
        ; Get the starting time for the loop
        ;==================================
        INVOKE Start_Time, ADDR StartTime


        ;============================================================
        ; Take the proper action(s) based on the GameState variable
        ;============================================================
        .IF GameState == GS_MENU
                ;====================================
                ; We are in the main menu state
                ;====================================
                INVOKE Process_Main_Menu

                ;====================================
                ; What did they want to do
                ;====================================
                .IF EAX == MENU_NOTHING
                        ;==============================
                        ; They didn't select anything yet
                        ; so don't do anything
                        ;==============================

                .ELSEIF EAX == MENU_ERROR
                        ;==============================
                        ; This is where error code would go
                        ;==============================

                .ELSEIF EAX == MENU_NEW
```

```
                            ;===================================
                            ; They want to start a new game
                            ;===================================

                    .ELSEIF EAX == MENU_FILES

                            ;===================================
                            ; They want the file menu
                            ;===================================
                            MOV     GameState, GS_FILE

                    .ELSEIF EAX == MENU_GAME

                            ;===================================
                            ; They want to return to the game
                            ;===================================

                    .ELSEIF EAX == MENU_EXIT

                            ;===================================
                            ; They want to exit the game
                            ;===================================
                            MOV     GameState, GS_EXIT

                    .ENDIF


            .ELSEIF GameState == GS_FILE

                    ;===================================
                    ; We are in the file menu state
                    ;===================================
                    INVOKE Process_File_Menu


                    ;===================================
                    ; What did they want to do
                    ;===================================
                    .IF EAX == MENU_NOTHING

                            ;===================================
                            ; They didn't select anything yet
                            ; so don't do anything
                            ;===================================

                    .ELSEIF EAX == MENU_ERROR
```

```
                        ;==============================
                        ; This is where error code would go
                        ;==============================

            .ELSEIF EAX == MENU_LOAD
                        ;==============================
                        ; They want to load game
                        ;==============================

            .ELSEIF EAX == MENU_SAVE
                        ;==============================
                        ; They want to save their game
                        ;==============================


            .ELSEIF EAX == MENU_MAIN
                        ;==============================
                        ; They want to return to main menu
                        ;==============================
                        MOV     GameState, GS_MENU

            .ENDIF


.ELSEIF GameState == GS_PLAY
                ;==============================
                ; We are in the gameplay mode
                ;==============================

.ELSEIF GameState == GS_DIE
                ;==============================
                ; We died so perform that code
                ;==============================

.ENDIF

;==============================
; Wait to synchronize the time
;==============================
INVOKE Wait_Time, StartTime, sync_time
```

```
done:
                ;===================
                ; We completed
                ;===================
                return TRUE

err:
                ;===================
                ; We didn't make it
                ;===================
                return FALSE


Game_Main       ENDP
;####################################################################
; END Game_Main
;####################################################################
```

The first thing you should notice about the code is that it is wrapped in calls to Start_Time() at the top and Wait_Time() at the bottom. These calls control our frame rate. I have it set to 25fps, or 40 milliseconds. Thus, 25 frames per second (or thereabouts) is the fastest our game will ever run. This is one of the most basic methods of game control, and it basically locks our game to a reasonable rate so that it will run the same on all systems that are powerful enough to reach 25fps. Weaker systems are out of luck, but those should be few and far between with this style of game.

Next, we have one large IF-ELSE statement that selects the proper game state based on our global variable that we dedicated for that purpose. So, whether we want to run a menu or perform the death code, it is all right there to manage it.

Inside our GS_MENU and GS_FILE states is their corresponding code. They make the calls to the correct menu-processing function and react based on the value returned to them. There's nothing fancy in this section, just simple IF-ELSE statements.

The new game loop is nothing more than a state manager. It simply looks at what the current state is and performs the code based on that state. All games have something very (if not exactly) similar in their core. This is the heart of the game, and without it, you would have nothing more than inactive modules, just like we had before this section.

Conclusion

Yes! We have a really nice, clean setup that is just begging for the actual game code. I, for one, am getting tired of all these setup modules.

In the next section, we will cover some more advanced material. In fact, we will hit on almost everything involved in the game play code itself, including basic animation, the loop, and structure setup.

The other thing I should mention is that this game is incomplete. I know that this is obvious, but many of you are probably wondering why there aren't any transitions, sounds, or cool FX in the game yet. The answer is because we haven't gotten to it, and we have to crawl before we can walk. Honestly, I plan to cover it all. So, for those of you who are more advanced and think I am going way too slow, just hang in there.

WIN32 ASM—PART 4

To this point, we have made some good progress. We have a nice framework for our game to sit in, and more importantly, we are all set to create the actual game. Coincidentally, that's just what we are going to do in this section. So, instead of just "good" progress, be prepared for some extraordinary progress.

Here's the current lineup:

Leading off today is Animation. He is a very important player on our team, so we want him up first. Without him, we won't be able to play at all.

Next, we have Mr. Structures. Mr. S, as he is often called, has the job of keeping everything organized. He is the guy in the dugout often stacking things or keeping track of statistics. He plays a more important role later in the season when we start playing "real games" and keeping score.

Third, we have the New Shape maker. He is responsible for setting things up for the later players. He is often overlooked since he works behind the scenes.

Batting cleanup for us is Update. Update is a big boy. He has many responsibilities but does a great job of delegating things he needs to other people. Often known as our power hitter, he is the most recognized of all members.

Batting fifth and sixth for us are twins Move Shape and Rotate Shape. They are the ones we rely on to keep things going. If they strike out, we know something has gone amiss somewhere along the line.

The seventh in our lineup is Line Test. He typically will clear the bases . . . but only if certain conditions are met.

The eighth and ninth positions are filled by another set of twins, Draw Grid and Draw Shape. They are the publicity freaks on the team, and they make sure the fans can see everything that is happening.

Our Manager is of course "the loop." He is the leader and holds everything together. It is his job to dictate what needs to be done and to make sure nobody fails. He will not hesitate to act on any error and is very demanding; he likes to make sure everything is done on his clock.

We have a good, solid team and are ready to take a look at their statistics, background, and of course, how they think. Are you ready? Play ball!

Stepping to the Plate

Animation is a very complicated player. He can play in many different ways and has numerous styles. On our team, he has adopted the style commonly referred to as "preset." This means that everything he does was determined before the game even started. This occurred in the initialization section, of course.

In our game, we have single blocks that are selected at random. These random blocks are used with random shapes. The shapes that exist are the same ones as in the original Tetris. The animation sequences needed by the shapes are relatively simple—you merely rotate the shapes. Therefore, I had the following three choices when deciding how to animate them:

- I could make bitmaps of every shape prebuilt and rotate them at runtime as needed.

- I could do the same as in the preceding except prerotate them and then save many bitmaps and cycle through them at runtime as they are needed.

- I could build every shape from a block and use some sort of table to tell me how the shape is to be built for that frame.

Because of speed and size, I decided to go with the third method. It is a little bit more complex, but I think the speed gain and size drop are worth it.

Now that we know what we want, how do we accomplish it? The first thing I did was sit down with a piece of paper to determine the

> **NOTE**
>
> As a programmer, if you have the capability to make a piece of code more robust, more user friendly, smaller, or faster, then do so.

patterns available. Then I took those patterns, encapsulated them into mini grids, and made them represent either ON or OFF states, depending on whether a block was in that position. Here is an example for a square:

```
0 0 0 0
   0 1 1 0
   0 1 1 0
   0 0 0 0
```

Notice that the grid is 4×4. This is because the largest a shape can be is four squares wide or tall. The 1s are the places where the blocks are, and the zeros are empty locations.

With that gigantic list built, I needed a way to organize them into lookup tables. The decision was to pad the left of each line with four zeros and thus get an 8×4 grid. I could then use an array of 4 bytes for each frame where a single bit represented a block. This caused a 2-byte waste for every block, yet it made the code about 100,000 times easier to understand.

The table access is really simple. We just offset into the table according to the shape we want. Then we offset into that address by the frame we want. Every shape has four frames no matter what, and all are aligned to 4 bytes. So, we can easily adjust our "frame pointer" with a few simple arithmetic operations.

This is how Animation works in our game. You simply tell him when to adjust to a new frame and he does. Need a new shape? No problem, just point him where it is, and he will know what to do.

Here is our internal lookup table:

```
;==================================================
            ; Here is our shape table it contains every possible
            ; combination of values for the different shapes.
            ; In order to give us the correct shape for every
            ; possible rotation.
            ;==================================================
ShapeTable       \                              ; Here is our square
                  \
        DB       00000000b                     ; Position 1
        DB       00000110b
        DB       00000110b
        DB       00000000b

        DB       00000000b                     ; Position 2
        DB       00000110b
        DB       00000110b
        DB       00000000b

        DB       00000000b                     ; Position 3
        DB       00000110b
        DB       00000110b
        DB       00000000b
```

```
        DB        00000000b                  ; Position 4
        DB        00000110b
        DB        00000110b
        DB        00000000b
                                  ; Here is our Line

        DB        00001000b                  ; Position 1
        DB        00001000b
        DB        00001000b
        DB        00001000b

        DB        00000000b                  ; Position 2
        DB        00000000b
        DB        00000000b
        DB        00001111b

        DB        00000001b                  ; Position 3
        DB        00000001b
        DB        00000001b
        DB        00000001b

        DB        00001111b                  ; Position 4
        DB        00000000b
        DB        00000000b
        DB        00000000b
                                  ; Here is our Pyramid

        DB        00001110b                  ; Position 1
        DB        00000100b
        DB        00000000b
        DB        00000000b

        DB        00001000b                  ; Position 2
        DB        00001100b
        DB        00001000b
        DB        00000000b

        DB        00000000b                  ; Position 3
        DB        00000100b
        DB        00001110b
```

```
        DB      00000000b


        DB      00000001b                    ; Position 4
        DB      00000011b
        DB      00000001b
        DB      00000000b

                                 ; Here is our L

        DB      00001000b                    ; Position 1
        DB      00001000b
        DB      00001100b
        DB      00000000b


        DB      00000000b                    ; Position 2
        DB      00000010b
        DB      00001110b
        DB      00000000b


        DB      00000110b                    ; Position 3
        DB      00000010b
        DB      00000010b
        DB      00000000b


        DB      00001110b                    ; Position 4
        DB      00001000b
        DB      00000000b
        DB      00000000b

                                 ; Here is our Backwards L

        DB      00001100b                    ; Position 1
        DB      00001000b
        DB      00001000b
        DB      00000000b


        DB      00000000b                    ; Position 2
        DB      00001000b
        DB      00001110b
        DB      00000000b


        DB      00000001b                    ; Position 3
        DB      00000001b
```

```
DB      00000011b
DB      00000000b

DB      00001110b                    ; Position 4
DB      00000010b
DB      00000000b
DB      00000000b
                            ; Here is our Backwards Z

DB      00000100b                    ; Position 1
DB      00000110b
DB      00000010b
DB      00000000b

DB      00000110b                    ; Position 2
DB      00001100b
DB      00000000b
DB      00000000b

DB      00000100b                    ; Position 3
DB      00000110b
DB      00000010b
DB      00000000b

DB      00000110b                    ; Position 4
DB      00001100b
DB      00000000b
DB      00000000b
                            ; Here is our Z

DB      00000010b                    ; Position 1
DB      00000110b
DB      00000100b
DB      00000000b

DB      00001100b                    ; Position 2
DB      00000110b
DB      00000000b
DB      00000000b

DB      00000010b                    ; Position 3
```

```
        DB      00000110b
        DB      00000100b
        DB      00000000b

        DB      00001100b              ; Position 4
        DB      00000110b
        DB      00000000b
        DB      00000000b
```

Mr. Structure

Oh, yes . . . Mr. Structure. He often looks like a container, but in our game he is spread out. It is his responsibility to hold the x and y coordinates, the current shape, the current shape block to use, and the current frame. He has just a few variables to keep things semi-organized.

As previously mentioned, he will have a larger job when it comes to keeping score and managing any other statistics.

He is a really open guy, global to be precise. He doesn't mind helping people and, of course, will let anybody know what he knows.

The declarations for him are in Shapes.asm and, for the time being, are relatively simple.

Because Mr. Structure is so open, bad things can *possibly* happen. It is your job, as a programmer, to make sure that those bad things can *never* happen. If you let him be corrupted in some manner, your whole game might go down the toilet.

The New Shape Maker

With the dreary setup stuff behind us, we are ready for the New Shape maker. His responsibility is fairly straightforward, so let's take a look at the code before I start explaining things.

```
;##############################################################################
; New_Shape Procedure
;##############################################################################
New_Shape       PROC
```

```
;=================================================
; This function will select a new shape at random
; for the current shape
;=================================================


;=================================================
; First make sure they haven't reached
; the top of the grid yet
;
; Begin by calculating the start of
; the very last row where the piece
; is initialized at ... aka (5,19)
;=================================================
MOV     EAX, 13
MOV     ECX, 19
MUL     ECX
ADD     EAX, 5
MOV     EBX, BlockGrid
ADD     EAX, EBX
MOV     ECX, EAX
ADD     ECX, 4


;=========================
; Loop through and test the
; next 4 positions
;=========================
.WHILE EAX <= ECX
        ;====================
        ; Is this one filled?
        ;====================
        MOV     BL, BYTE PTR [EAX]
        .IF BL != 0
                ;==================
                ; They are dead
                ;==================
                JMP     err

        .ENDIF
```

```
                    ;================
                    ; Inc the counter
                    ;================
                    INC     EAX
            .ENDW


            ;================================
            ; Use a random number to get
            ; the current shape to use
            ;
            ; For this we will just use
            ; the time returned by the
            ; Get_Time() function
            ;================================
            INVOKE Get_Time


            ;================================
            ; Mod this number with 7
            ; since there are 7 shapes
            ;================================
            MOV     ECX, 7
            XOR     EDX, EDX
            DIV     ECX
            MOV     EAX, EDX


            ;================================
            ; Multiply by 16 since there
            ; are 16 bytes per shape
            ;================================
            SHL     EAX, 4


            ;================================
            ; Use that number to select
            ; the shape from the table
            ;================================
            MOV     EBX, OFFSET ShapeTable
            ADD     EAX, EBX
            MOV     CurShape, EAX
```

```
        ;===============================
        ; Use a random number to get
        ; the block surface to use
        ;
        ; For this we will just use
        ; the time returned by the
        ; Get_Time() function
        ;===============================
        INVOKE  Get_Time


        ;===============================
        ; And this result with 7
        ; since there are 8 blocks
        ;===============================
        AND     EAX, 7


        ;===============================
        ; Use it as the block surface
        ;===============================
        MOV     CurShapeColor, EAX


        ;===============================
        ; Initialize the Starting Coords
        ;===============================
        MOV     CurShapeX, 5
        MOV     CurShapeY, 24


        ;===============================
        ; Set the Current Frame Variable
        ;===============================
        MOV     CurShapeFrame, 0

done:
        ;=========================
        ; They have a new piece
        ;=========================
        return TRUE

err:
```

```
;====================
; They died!
;====================
    return FALSE

New_Shape        ENDP
;####################################################################
; END New_Shape
;####################################################################
```

Do you see what I am doing with the code? You should start having at least a general idea when looking at the code segments. If not, start studying more. That means writing code, not staring at mine!

To start with, we check the area directly under where we want the block to start to see if there are blocks already in there. If so, they died. It is a really simple concept. No more room on grid = DEATH!

Next we grab some random numbers to use for the block texture and the shape. I chose to just use the Get_Time() function that we have. We'll write a true random-number generator later in this chapter. For now, this function call will serve our purposes.

To get a number between zero and six, we divide by seven and take the remainder. (This is placed in EDX after a DIV.) This way, the highest number we could have is six and the lowest is zero, which is perfect since we have seven shapes to choose from.

We do something a bit different for the blocks. Instead of performing a MOD operation, we AND the number with N-1, where N is the number you would normally MOD with. This only works for numbers that are powers of two, however. We are taking advantage of another bit manipulation operation to speed things up.

The next step is to merely initialize the starting X and Y coordinates along with the starting frame to use.

That is all we need to do to create a new shape during the game. Once this function is finished, everything is set up to start moving and manipulating the current shape, whatever it may be.

Update Takes a Few Practice Swings

Update is our power hitter. He has the job of handling all updates. Let's take a look at exactly what he does.

```
;###############################################################################
; Update_Shape Procedure
;###############################################################################
Update_Shape    PROC


                ;===============================================
                ; This function will update our shape ... or
                ; drop it down by a grid notch and test for
                ; a collision with the grid
                ;===============================================


                ;========================
                ; Can we move down???
                ;========================
                INVOKE Test_Collision
                .IF EAX == TRUE

                        ;========================
                        ; NO... we hit something
                        ;========================


                        ;============================
                        ; Place the piece in the grid
                        ;============================
                        INVOKE Place_In_Grid


                        ;========================
                        ; Jmp & Return with False
                        ;========================
                        JMP     err

                .ELSE

                        ;============================
                        ; yes we can drop down
                        ;============================
```

```
        ;═══════════════════════════════
        ; Drop our piece down by a notch
        ;═══════════════════════════════
        DEC     CurShapeY

    .ENDIF

done:
        ;═════════════════════
        ; We hit nothing
        ;═════════════════════
        return TRUE

err:
        ;═════════════════════
        ; We hit something
        ;═════════════════════
        return FALSE


Update_Shape    ENDP
;##########################################################################
; END Update_Shape
;##########################################################################
```

Wow! For somebody so important, he sure doesn't do very much. Almost like real life, what do you think?

To begin with, we make a call to test the collision status of the current shape. If the call returns TRUE, we cannot move the shape any more and need to place it in the grid. So, he makes a call to Place_In_Grid(). However, if the call returns FALSE, we can still move the shape. So, we drop it down a notch by decrementing the Y coordinate of the shape.

The last thing we need to do is return to our manager and tell him whether we succeeded or failed. Before we continue, though, let's take a closer look at Test_Collision() and Place_In_Grid() since they are the ones who really do the work.

```
;##########################################################################
; Place_In_Grid Procedure
;##########################################################################
Place_In_Grid   PROC
```

```
;===============================================
; This function will place the current shape
; into the grid
;===============================================


;=================================
; Local Variables
;=================================
LOCAL     DrawY:          DWORD
LOCAL     DrawX:          DWORD
LOCAL     CurRow:         DWORD
LOCAL     CurCol:         DWORD
LOCAL     CurLine:        DWORD
LOCAL     CurGrid:        DWORD


;=================================
; Get the Current Shape Pos
;=================================
MOV       EBX, CurShape
MOV       EAX, CurShapeFrame
SHL       EAX, 2
ADD       EBX, EAX
MOV       CurLine, EBX


;=================================
; Set the Starting Row and Column
; for the placement of the block
;=================================
MOV       EAX, CurShapeX
MOV       EBX, CurShapeY
MOV       DrawX, EAX
MOV       DrawY, EBX


;=================================
; Loop through all four rows
;=================================
MOV       CurRow, 0
.WHILE CurRow < 4
          ;=================================
          ; Loop through all four Columns
          ;=================================
```

```
MOV     CurCol, 4
.WHILE CurCol > 0
                ;================================
                ; Shift the CurLine Byte over
                ; by our CurCol
                ;================================
                MOV     ECX, 4
                SUB     ECX, CurCol
                MOV     EBX, CurLine
                XOR     EAX, EAX
                MOV     AL, BYTE PTR [EBX]
                SHR     EAX, CL


                ;================================
                ; Is it a valid block?
                ;================================
                .IF ( EAX & 1 )
                        ;================================
                        ; Yes it was a valid block
                        ;================================


                        ;================================
                        ; Calculate the Block in our
                        ; BlockGrid to place it in
                        ;================================
                        MOV     EAX, DrawY
                        MOV     ECX, 13
                        MUL     ECX
                        MOV     EBX, DrawX
                        ADD     EBX, CurCol
                        DEC     EBX
                        ADD     EAX, EBX
                        MOV     ECX, BlockGrid
                        ADD     EAX, ECX


                        ;================================
                        ; Store the Color in the Block
                        ; add one since we let 0 mean
                        ; the block is empty
                        ;================================
                        MOV     EBX, CurShapeColor
```

```
                    INC     EBX
                    MOV     BYTE PTR [EAX], BL


            .ENDIF


            ;====================
            ; Dec our col counter
            ;====================
            DEC     CurCol


    .ENDW


            ;====================
            ; Inc the CurLine
            ;====================
            INC     CurLine


            ;====================
            ; decrement Y coord
            ;====================
            DEC     DrawY


            ;====================
            ; Inc the row counter
            ;====================
            INC     CurRow


    .ENDW


done:
            ;====================
            ; We completed
            ;====================
            return TRUE


err:
            ;====================
            ; We didn't make it
            ;====================
            return FALSE
```

```
Place_In_Grid    ENDP
;##################################################################
; END Place_In_Grid
;##################################################################


;##################################################################
; Test_Collision Procedure
;##################################################################
Test_Collision  PROC


                ;==========================================
                ; This function will test for a collision between
                ; the grid and the current shape
                ;==========================================


                ;==========================================
                ; Local Variables
                ;==========================================
                LOCAL    Index:  DWORD
                LOCAL    Adjust: DWORD


                ;==========================================
                ; Loop through and find the first block
                ; in each of the four columns
                ;
                ; NOTE: 0 = RIGHT 3 = LEFT
                ;==========================================
                MOV      Index, 0
                .WHILE Index < 4
                        ;==================================
                        ; Start at the bottom of the Current Frame
                        ;==================================
                        MOV      EBX, CurShape
                        MOV      EAX, CurShapeFrame
                        SHL      EAX, 2
                        ADD      EBX, EAX
                        ADD      EBX, 3
```

```
;===================================
; Now loop until we have a one in the
; current column we are working on or we
; reach the top
;===================================
MOV     Adjust, 4
.WHILE  Adjust > 0
        ;===========================
        ; Get the Current Line
        ;===========================
        XOR     EAX, EAX
        MOV     AL, BYTE PTR [EBX]


        ;===========================
        ; Adjust by the Column
        ;===========================
        MOV     ECX, Index
        SHR     EAX, CL


        ;===========================
        ; Was there a block there
        ;===========================
        .IF ( EAX & 1 )
                ;===================
                ; Yes there was a block
                ;===================


                ;===========================
                ; Have we hit Bottom
                ;===========================
                MOV     EAX, CurShapeY
                SUB     EAX, Adjust
                INC     EAX                 ; Off by 1 syndrome
                .IF EAX == 0
                        ;===============
                        ; Bottom of grid
                        ;===============
                        JMP     done

        .ENDIF
```

```
                              ;============================
                              ; Calculate the Block right
                              ; under it on the grid
                              ;============================
                              DEC       EAX                    ; Move Under it
                              MOV       ECX, 13
                              MUL       ECX
                              ADD       EAX, CurShapeX
                              ADD       EAX, 3
                              SUB       EAX, Index
                              MOV       ECX, BlockGrid
                              ADD       ECX, EAX


                              ;============================
                              ; Does the Block have one
                              ; underneath it on the grid?
                              ;============================
                              MOV    AL, BYTE PTR [ECX]
                              .IF AL != 0
                                        ;============================
                                        ; We had a valid collision
                                        ;============================
                                        JMP       done

                              .ENDIF

                    .ENDIF

            ;============================
            ; No Block -- Previous Line Please
            ;============================
            DEC     EBX


            ;============================
            ; Decrement the Adjust counter
            ;============================
            DEC     Adjust

    .ENDW
```

```
                ;==================================
                ; Next Column Please!
                ;==================================
                INC      Index

        .ENDW

err:

                ;===================
                ; We didn't collide
                ;===================
                return FALSE

done:

                ;===================
                ; We collided
                ;===================
                return TRUE

Test_Collision   ENDP
;###############################################################################
; END Test_Collision
;###############################################################################
```

The `Place_In_Grid()` function is the simpler of the two, so let's cover that one first. It moves to the location in grid memory based on where our current shape is located. Once there, it simply loops through every row in the frame, and if there is a block in that bit position, it sets the block to TRUE by indicating the current block texture + 1. The reason we had to do texture + 1 is because we use zero to indicate that no blocks are there.

`Test_Collision()` is not quite so simple. It loops through all four columns and, inside that, loops through all four rows of the current frame. It then tests the bit at its own (row, col) location. If there is a bit turned ON there, it checks whether or not the grid has a block in the position directly under it. If it fails this test on *any* bit, the block cannot be moved, so we return TRUE. Otherwise, at the end there have been no collisions, and we return FALSE. At this point, we also check to see if it is at the bottom of the grid. This constitutes the same thing as having a block underneath it.

As you can see, although Update() is very important to our team, he has so much to do that you *always* want to have him to delegate his responsibilities out to others. Then just let him pretend to do what he is supposed to do.

Let's Get Moving

Now that we have a piece to play with, we need to do just that—play with it. Get your minds out of the gutter and look at the code!

```
;##############################################################################
; Rotate_Shape Procedure
;##############################################################################
Rotate_Shape    PROC


            ;============================================
            ; This function will rotate the current shape it tests
            ; to make sure there are no blocks already in the place
            ; where it would rotate.
            ;
            ; NOTE: It is missing the check for out of the grid on
            ; rotation. That is left for the time being as an
            ; exercise.
            ;
            ; My solution will be shown in the next section.
            ;============================================


            ;============================================
            ; Local Variables
            ;============================================
            LOCAL   Index:          DWORD
            LOCAL   CurBlock:       DWORD
            LOCAL   Spot:           BYTE
```

```
;====================================
; Are they at the last frame?
;====================================
.IF CurShapeFrame == 3

            ;==========================================
            ; Yep ... make sure they can rotate
            ;==========================================


            ;===============================================
            ; Adjust to the current Block they are at
            ;===============================================
            MOV     EAX, CurShapeY
            MOV     ECX, 13
            MUL     ECX
            ADD     EAX, CurShapeX
            ADD     EAX, BlockGrid
            MOV     CurBlock, EAX


            ;================================================
            ; Loop through all four rows of our Shape
            ;================================================
            MOV     Index, 0
            .WHILE Index < 4

                    ;=============================
                    ; Get the current line
                    ;=============================
                    MOV     EBX, CurShape    ; Same as Frame 0
                    ADD     EBX, Index
                    XOR     ECX, ECX
                    MOV     CL, BYTE PTR [EBX]
                    MOV     Spot, CL


                    ;===================================
                    ; Test all 4 of the valid bits
                    ;===================================


                    ;=====================
                    ; Position 4
                    ;=====================
                    .IF ( Spot & 8 )            ; 2^3
```

```
                              ;========================
                              ; Test this on the Grid
                              ;========================
                              MOV     EAX, CurBlock
                              .IF ( BYTE PTR [EAX] ) != 0
                                          ;========================
                                          ; Failed! Can't rotate
                                          ;========================
                                          JMP     err

                              .ENDIF

        .ENDIF

;==================
; Inc our CurBlock
;==================
INC     CurBlock

;========================
; Position 3
;========================
.IF ( Spot & 4 )          ; 2^2
                              ;========================
                              ; Test this on the Grid
                              ;========================
                              MOV     EAX, CurBlock
                              .IF ( BYTE PTR [EAX] ) != 0
                                          ;========================
                                          ; Failed! Can't rotate
                                          ;========================
                                          JMP     err

                              .ENDIF

        .ENDIF

;==================
; Inc our CurBlock
;==================
```

```
INC      CurBlock


;===================
; Position 2
;===================
.IF ( Spot & 2 )           ; 2^1
        ;===================
        ; Test this on the Grid
        ;===================
        MOV      EAX, CurBlock
        .IF ( BYTE PTR [EAX] ) != 0
                ;===================
                ; Failed! Can't rotate
                ;===================
                JMP      err

        .ENDIF

.ENDIF

;===================
; Inc our CurBlock
;===================
INC      CurBlock


;===================
; Position 1
;===================
.IF ( Spot & 1 )           ; 2^0
        ;===================
        ; Test this on the Grid
        ;===================
        MOV     EAX, CurBlock
        .IF ( BYTE PTR [EAX] ) != 0
                ;===================
                ; Failed! Can't rotate
                ;===================
                JMP      err

        .ENDIF
```

```
            .ENDIF

            ;========================
            ; Drop Down by a line
            ; plus the amount we
            ; Incremented over by
            ;========================
            SUB     CurBlock, 16


            ;========================
            ; Increment our Index
            ;========================
            INC     Index

    .ENDW

    ;========================
    ; Ok ... start over
    ;========================
    MOV     CurShapeFrame, 0

.ELSE
    ;=============================
    ; NO ... make sure they can rotate
    ;=============================


    ;=================================
    ; Adjust to the current Block they are at
    ;=================================
    MOV     EAX, CurShapeY
    MOV     ECX, 13
    MUL     ECX
    ADD     EAX, CurShapeX
    ADD     EAX, BlockGrid
    MOV     CurBlock, EAX


    ;=================================
    ; Loop through all four rows of our Shape
    ;=================================
    MOV     Index, 0
    .WHILE Index < 4
```

```
;=======================
; Get the current line
;=======================
MOV     EBX, CurShape
MOV     EAX, CurShapeFrame
INC     EAX        ; Get to new frame
SHL     EAX, 2
ADD     EBX, Index
ADD     EBX, EAX
MOV     CL, BYTE PTR [EBX]
MOV     Spot, CL


;============================
; Test all 4 of the valid bits
;============================


;===================
; Position 4
;===================
.IF ( Spot & 8 )            ; 2^3

            ;=======================
            ; Test this on the Grid
            ;=======================
            MOV     EAX, CurBlock
            .IF ( BYTE PTR [EAX] ) != 0

                        ;=====================
                        ; Failed! Can't rotate
                        ;=====================
                        JMP      err

            .ENDIF

.ENDIF

;===============
; Inc our CurBlock
;===============
INC     CurBlock
```

```
;=================
; Position 3
;=================
.IF ( Spot & 4 )          ; 2^2
                ;=====================
                ; Test this on the Grid
                ;=====================
                MOV     EAX, CurBlock
                .IF ( BYTE PTR [EAX] ) != 0
                        ;=====================
                        ; Failed! Can't rotate
                        ;=====================
                        JMP     err

                .ENDIF

.ENDIF

;=================
; Inc our CurBlock
;=================
INC     CurBlock

;=================
; Position 2
;=================
.IF ( Spot & 2 )        ; 2^1
                ;=====================
                ; Test this on the Grid
                ;=====================
                MOV     EAX, CurBlock
                .IF ( BYTE PTR [EAX] ) != 0
                        ;=====================
                        ; Failed! Can't rotate
                        ;=====================
                        JMP     err

                .ENDIF

.ENDIF
```

```
;=====================
; Inc our CurBlock
;=====================
INC     CurBlock


;=====================
; Position 1
;=====================
.IF ( Spot & 1 )            ; 2^0
            ;=====================
            ; Test this on the Grid
            ;=====================
            MOV     EAX, CurBlock
            .IF ( BYTE PTR [EAX] ) != 0
                        ;=====================
                        ; Failed! Can't rotate
                        ;=====================
                        JMP     err

            .ENDIF

.ENDIF

;=====================
; Drop Down by a line
; plus the amount we
; Incremented over by
;=====================
SUB     CurBlock, 16


;=====================
; Increment our Index
;=====================
INC     Index

.ENDW


;=====================
; OK ... just increment
;=====================
```

```
                INC     CurShapeFrame

        .ENDIF

done:
        ;==================
        ; Wc completed
        ;==================
        return TRUE

err:
        ;==================
        ; We didn't make it
        ;==================
        return FALSE


Rotate_Shape    ENDP
;###############################################################################
; END Rotate_Shape
;###############################################################################


;###############################################################################
; Move_Shape Procedure
;###############################################################################
Move_Shape      PROC    Direction:DWORD

        ;=======================================
        ; This function will move the shape in the
        ; desired direction
        ;=======================================


        ;=========================
        ; Local Variables
        ;=========================
        LOCAL   CurCol:         DWORD
        LOCAL   CurRow:         DWORD
        LOCAL   CanMove:        DWORD
```

```
;===================================
; Set CanMove to true; it will
; be false later if we can't move
;===================================
MOV     CanMove, TRUE


;=========================================
; Perform the Tests based on direction they want
;=========================================
.IF Direction == MOVE_LEFT

        ;=========================================
        ; They want to move to the left
        ;=========================================


        ;=========================================
        ; Find the Leftmost column with a
        ; valid block inside of it
        ;=========================================
        MOV     CurCol, 0
        .WHILE CurCol < 4
                ;===========================
                ; Calculate Our Mask
                ;===========================
                MOV     EAX, 1
                MOV     ECX, 3  ; Start from the Left
                SUB     ECX, CurCol
                SHL     EAX, CL
                MOV     EDX, EAX
                PUSH    EDX


                ;===========================
                ; Go through all 4 rows
                ;===========================
                MOV     CurRow, 0
                .WHILE CurRow < 4
                        ;===========================
                        ; Get the Current Line of Blocks
                        ;===========================
                        MOV     EBX, CurShape
                        MOV     EAX, CurShapeFrame
                        SHL     EAX, 2
```

```
ADD     EBX, EAX
ADD     EBX, CurRow
XOR     ECX, ECX
MOV     CL, BYTE PTR [EBX]


;======================
; Test the Mask and the
; current line of blocks
;======================
POP     EDX
PUSH    EDX
.IF ( EDX & ECX )
        ;==================
        ; There was a Block
        ;==================


        ;==================
        ; Calculate the
        ; block's X value
        ;==================
        MOV     EAX, CurShapeX
        ADD     EAX, CurCol


        ;==================
        ; Can we move?
        ;==================
        .IF EAX == 0
                ;============
                ; Nope
                ;============
                MOV     CanMove, FALSE

        .ELSE
                ;====================
                ; Calculate the block to
                ; the left of us
                ;====================
                MOV     EAX, CurShapeY
                SUB     EAX, CurRow
                MOV     ECX, 13
                MUL     ECX
```

```
                                        ADD     EAX, CurShapeX
                                        ADD     EAX, CurCol
                                                ; 1 to the Left
                                        DEC     EAX
                                        MOV     ECX, BlockGrid
                                        ADD     ECX, EAX
                                        MOV     AL, BYTE PTR [ECX]


                                        ;=======================
                                        ; Are we blocked?
                                        ;=======================
                                        .IF AL != 0
                                                ;=================
                                                ; We are blocked
                                                ;=================
                                                MOV     CanMove, FALSE

                                        .ENDIF

                            .ENDIF

                    .ENDIF

                    ;===========================
                    ; Inc our current row
                    ;===========================
                    INC     CurRow

            .ENDW

            ;===========================
            ; Clean Off the stack
            ;===========================
            POP     EDX


            ;===========================
            ; Inc our current column
            ;===========================
            INC     CurCol

    .ENDW
```

```
;================================
; Can we Still Move
;================================
.IF CanMove == TRUE
        ;========================
        ; yes we can
        ;========================
        DEC     CurShapeX

.ENDIF

.ELSEIF Direction == MOVE_RIGHT
        ;================================
        ; They want to move to the right
        ;================================


        ;================================
        ; Find the Rightmost column with a
        ; valid block inside of it
        ;================================
        MOV     CurCol, 4
        .WHILE CurCol > 0
                ;========================
                ; Calculate Our Mask
                ;========================
                MOV     EAX, 1
                MOV     ECX, 4   ; Start from the Right
                SUB     ECX, CurCol
                SHL     EAX, CL
                MOV     EDX, EAX
                PUSH    EDX


                ;========================
                ; Go through all 4 rows
                ;========================
                MOV     CurRow,0
                .WHILE CurRow < 4
                        ;================================
                        ; Get the Current Line of Blocks
                        ;================================
```

```
MOV     EBX, CurShape
MOV     EAX, CurShapeFrame
SHL     EAX, 2
ADD     EBX, EAX
ADD     EBX, CurRow
XOR     ECX, ECX
MOV     CL, BYTE PTR [EBX]


;========================
; Test the Mask and the
; current line of blocks
;========================
POP     EDX
PUSH    EDX
.IF ( EDX & ECX )
        ;==================
        ; There was a Block
        ;==================


        ;==================
        ; Calculate the
        ; block's X value
        ;==================
        MOV     EAX, CurShapeX
        ADD     EAX, CurCol
        DEC     EAX


        ;==================
        ; Can we move?
        ;==================
        .IF EAX == 12
                ;============
                ; Nope
                ;============
                MOV     CanMove, FALSE

        .ELSE
                ;======================
                ; Calculate the block to
                ; the right of us
                ;======================
```

```
                                    MOV      EAX, CurShapeY
                                    SUB      EAX, CurRow
                                    MOV      ECX, 13
                                    MUL      ECX
                                    ADD      EAX, CurShapeX

                                    ; Already one to the right
                                    ADD      EAX, CurCol
                                    MOV      ECX, BlockGrid
                                    ADD      ECX, EAX
                                    MOV      AL, BYTE PTR [ECX]


                                    ;====================
                                    ; Are we blocked?
                                    ;====================
                                    .IF AL != 0
                                            ;===============
                                            ; We are blocked
                                            ;===============
                                            MOV    CanMove, FALSE

                                    .ENDIF

                            .ENDIF

                    .ENDIF

                    ;=========================
                    ; Inc our current row
                    ;=========================
                    INC    CurRow

            .ENDW

            ;=========================
            ; Clean Off the stack
            ;=========================
            POP    EDX
```

```
                        ;============================
                        ; dec our current column
                        ;============================
                        DEC       CurCol

        .ENDW

        ;====================================
        ; Can we Still Move
        ;====================================
        .IF CanMove == TRUE
                        ;========================
                        ; yes we can
                        ;========================
                        INC       CurShapeX

                .ENDIF

        .ELSEIF Direction == MOVE_DOWN
                        ;==================================
                        ; They want to move the piece down
                        ;==================================


                        ;==================================
                        ; Test for a collision
                        ;==================================
                        INVOKE Test_Collision
                        .IF EAX == FALSE
                                        ;==========================
                                        ; It is safe to drop a notch
                                        ;==========================
                                        DEC       CurShapeY

                        .ENDIF

        .ELSE
                        ;==================================
                        ; They passed an invalid direction
                        ;==================================
                        JMP       err
```

```
        .ENDIF

done:

        ;==================
        ; We completed
        ;==================
        return TRUE

err:

        ;==================
        ; We didn't make it
        ;==================
        return FALSE

Move_Shape     ENDP
;#######################################################################
; END Move_Shape
;#######################################################################
```

—

These two functions, Rotate_Shape() and Move_Shape(), are pretty big, so it is good that they are twins. Despite their size, what they do is fairly cut and dried. Let's cover, just in general, what it is that they do.

The rotate function first decides whether it is at the last frame. If so, it has code to wrap it around for the entire test; otherwise, it just uses the next frame. Then it loops through all of the bits, finding the valid ones just like Test_Collision(). If there is already a bit set in the place where the shape would be, it is not allowed to move and the call fails.

Back to the code at hand: Move_Shape(). This function will move the shape to the left or to the right, depending on the value passed into it. It merely tests the bits once again, only this time we have to find the leftmost or rightmost valid bit in each row. Then we check the grid

NOTE

There is not code to check for out of bounds on the grid. So, if you rotate at a corner, you may slide out of the grid and into the background area. This has been left as an exercise for you. I wanted to see something interactive come out of this section, and I decided that this would be as good a place as any to start asking for it. I will present my solution in the next section. Compare yours to mine at that time.

block to the left or right and see if it is empty. Accordingly, either we move it or we don't, and then we return to the caller.

There isn't much else to talk about in this section. You have seen how to access everything many times now. The only thing that changes is what we need to access or the order in which we test stuff. These are the kinds of things that need to be resolved at design time.

Time to Clear the Bases

When it comes time to clear the grid, we call on Line_Test. This function will return TRUE if it clears a line. It will return FALSE if it doesn't have a valid line on the grid. Examine its contents.

```
;##############################################################
; Line_Test Procedure
;##############################################################
Line_Test        PROC


        ;=========================================
        ; This function will test to see if they earned a
        ; line ... if so it will eliminate that line
        ; and update our grid of blocks
        ;=========================================


        ;=========================
        ; Local Variables
        ;=========================
        LOCAL    CurLine:        DWORD
        LOCAL    CurBlock:       DWORD


        ;===============================
        ; Start at the Base of the Grid
        ;===============================
        MOV      CurLine, 0


        ;===============================
        ; Loop through all possible Lines
        ;===============================
        .WHILE CurLine < (GRID_HEIGHT - 4)
```

```
;====================================
; Go to the base of the current line
;====================================
MOV     EAX, CurLine
MOV     ECX, 13
MUL     ECX
ADD     EAX, BlockGrid


;====================================
; Loop through every block,
; testing to see if it is valid
;====================================
MOV     CurBlock, 0
.WHILE CurBlock < (GRID_WIDTH)
        ;============================
        ; Is this Block IN-Valid?
        ;============================
        MOV     BL, BYTE PTR [EAX]
        .IF BL == 0
                ;====================
                ; Yes, so break
                ;====================
                .BREAK

        .ENDIF

        ;========================
        ; Next Block
        ;========================
        INC     EAX


        ;========================
        ; Inc the counter
        ;========================
        INC     CurBlock

.ENDW
```

```
;================================
; Did our inner loop go all
; of the way through??
;================================
.IF CurBlock == (GRID_WIDTH)

        ;================================
        ; Yes. That means it was
        ; a valid line we just earned
        ;================================


        ;================================
        ; Calculate How much memory to move
        ; TOTAL - Amount_IN = TO_MOVE
        ;================================
        MOV     EBX, (GRID_WIDTH * (GRID_HEIGHT -5))
        MOV     EAX, CurLine
        MOV     ECX, 13
        MUL     ECX
        PUSH    EAX
        SUB     EBX, EAX


        ;================================
        ; Move the memory one line
        ; up to our current line
        ;================================
        POP     EAX
        ADD     EAX, BlockGrid
        MOV     EDX, EAX
        ADD     EDX, 13


        ;================================
        ; Move the memory down a notch
        ;================================
        INVOKE RtlMoveMemory, EAX, EDX, EBX


        ;================================
        ; Jump down and return TRUE
        ;================================
        JMP     done
```

```
                .ENDIF

                ;==============================
                ; Increment our Line counter
                ;==============================
                INC     CurLine

        .ENDW

err:
                ;==================
                ; We didn't get one
                ;==================
                return FALSE

done:
                ;==================
                ; We earned a line
                ;==================
                return TRUE


Line_Test       ENDP
;##############################################################################
; END Line_Test
;##############################################################################
```

The code loops through every line in our grid memory and tests for blocks. If it finds that a grid location is empty, it continues with the next line. If every location has a valid block inside of it, the function moves all of the memory above it to the row that had the line. It does this by calling the Win32 API function RTLMoveMemory().

We have it return after every valid line it finds and eliminates because, when we want to keep score, it will be easier to track how many lines they earn. It is always a good thing to keep future expansion in mind while programming.

The Final Batters

Our two final hitters are the publicity hounds Draw_Shape() and Draw_Grid(). The following is their code.

```
;###########################################################################
; Draw_Shape Procedure
;###########################################################################
Draw_Shape      PROC

                ;=================================================
                ; This function will draw our current shape at its
                ; proper location on the screen
                ;=================================================


                ;=================================
                ; Local Variables
                ;=================================
                LOCAL   DrawY:          DWORD
                LOCAL   DrawX:          DWORD
                LOCAL   CurRow:         DWORD
                LOCAL   CurCol:         DWORD
                LOCAL   CurLine:        DWORD
                LOCAL   XPos:           DWORD
                LOCAL   YPos:           DWORD


                ;=================================
                ; Get the Current Shape Pos
                ;=================================
                MOV     EBX, CurShape
                MOV     EAX, CurShapeFrame
                SHL     EAX, 2
                ADD     EBX, EAX
                MOV     CurLine, EBX


                ;=================================
                ; Set the Starting Row and Column
                ; for the drawing
                ;=================================
                MOV     EAX, CurShapeX
                MOV     EBX, CurShapeY
```

```
MOV      DrawX, EAX
MOV      DrawY, EBX


;=======================================
; Loop through all four rows
;=======================================
MOV      CurRow, 0
.WHILE CurRow < 4
            ;===============================
            ; Loop through all four Columns if
            ; the Y Coord is in the screen
            ;===============================
            MOV      CurCol, 4
            .WHILE CurCol > 0 && DrawY < 20
                    ;=======================
                    ; Shift the CurLine Byte over
                    ; by our CurCol
                    ;=======================
                    MOV      ECX, 4
                    SUB      ECX, CurCol
                    MOV      EBX, CurLine
                    XOR      EAX, EAX
                    MOV      AL, BYTE PTR [EBX]
                    SHR      EAX, CL


                    ;=======================
                    ; Is it a valid block?
                    ;=======================
                    .IF ( EAX & 1 )
                            ;===============
                            ; Yes, it was a valid block
                            ;===============

                            ;===============
                            ; Calculate the Y coord
                            ;===============
                            MOV      EAX, (GRID_HEIGHT - 5)
                            SUB      EAX, DrawY
                            MOV      ECX, BLOCK_HEIGHT
                            MUL      ECX
                            MOV      YPos, EAX
```

```
;==============================
; Calculate the X coord
;==============================
        MOV     EAX, DrawX
        ADD     EAX, CurCol
        DEC     EAX
        MOV     ECX, BLOCK_WIDTH
        MUL     ECX
        ADD     EAX, 251
        MOV     XPos, EAX


;==============================
; Calculate the surface to use
;==============================
        MOV     EAX, CurShapeColor
        SHL     EAX, 2
        MOV     EBX, DWORD PTR BlockSurface[EAX]


;==============================
; Blit the block
;==============================
        DDS4INVOKE BltFast, lpddsback, XPos, YPos, \
            EBX, ADDR SrcRect, \
            DDBLTFAST_NOCOLORKEY OR DDBLTFAST_WAIT


    .ENDIF


;==============================
; Dec our col counter
;==============================
    DEC     CurCol


.ENDW


;==============================
; Inc the CurLine
;==============================
INC     CurLine
```

```
            ;═══════════════════
            ; decrement Y coord
            ;═══════════════════
            DEC     DrawY


            ;═══════════════════
            ; Inc the row counter
            ;═══════════════════
            INC     CurRow

    .ENDW

done:
            ;═══════════════════
            ; We completed
            ;═══════════════════
            return TRUE

err:
            ;═══════════════════
            ; We didn't make it
            ;═══════════════════
            return FALSE


Draw_Shape      ENDP
;###############################################################################
; END Draw_Shape
;###############################################################################


;###############################################################################
; Draw_Grid Procedure
;###############################################################################
Draw_Grid       PROC

            ;═══════════════════════════════════════════════════
            ; This function will draw our grid. If the value is zero
            ; there is no block; otherwise the value is the block#
            ;═══════════════════════════════════════════════════
```

```
;===================
; Local Variables
;===================
LOCAL    CurRow:         DWORD
LOCAL    CurCol:         DWORD
LOCAL    CurBlock:       DWORD
LOCAL    YPos:           DWORD
LOCAL    XPos:           DWORD


;============================
; Start the current block at
; the beginning of our grid
;============================
MOV      EAX, BlockGrid
MOV      CurBlock, EAX


;============================
; Initialize the current row
;============================
MOV      CurRow, 0


;============================
; Loop through all of our rows
;============================
.WHILE CurRow < ( GRID_HEIGHT - 4 )


        ;===============================
        ; Initialize the current column
        ;===============================
        MOV      CurCol, 0


        ;============================
        ; Loop through all of our cols
        ;============================
        .WHILE CurCol < GRID_WIDTH
                ;======================
                ; Is there a Block here
                ;======================
                XOR      EAX, EAX
                MOV      EBX, CurBlock
                MOV      AL, BYTE PTR [EBX]
```

```
.IF AL != 0
            ;=============================
            ; Yes there was a block here
            ;=============================


            ;=============================
            ; Get the surface to use
            ;=============================
            DEC     EAX
            SHL     EAX, 2
            MOV     EBX, DWORD PTR BlockSurface[EAX]


            ;=============================
            ; Calculate the Y coord
            ;=============================
            MOV     EAX, ( GRID_HEIGHT - 5 )
            SUB     EAX, CurRow
            MOV     ECX, BLOCK_HEIGHT
            MUL     ECX
            MOV     YPos, EAX


            ;=============================
            ; Calculate the X coord
            ;=============================
            MOV     EAX, CurCol
            MOV     ECX, BLOCK_WIDTH
            MUL     ECX
            ADD     EAX, 251
            MOV     XPos, EAX


            ;=============================
            ; Blit the block
            ;=============================
            DDS4INVOKE BltFast, lpddsback, XPos, YPos, \
                EBX, ADDR SrcRect, \
                DDBLTFAST_NOCOLORKEY OR DDBLTFAST_WAIT


            ;=============================
            ; Did we succeed?
            ;=============================
            .IF EAX == DDERR_SURFACELOST
```

```
                                  ;=====================
                                  ; We lost the surface
                                  ;=====================


                       .ELSEIF EAX != DD_OK
                                  ;=====================
                                  ; We failed in some way
                                  ;=====================
                                  JMP     err

                       .ENDIF

              .ENDIF

              ;===========================
              ; Inc the Current Block
              ;===========================
              INC     CurBlock


              ;===========================
              ; Increment the Cur column
              ;===========================
              INC     CurCol

         .ENDW

         ;====================
         ; Increment the row
         ;====================
         INC     CurRow

    .ENDW

done:
    ;====================
    ; We completed
    ;====================
    return TRUE

err:
```

```
;===================
; We didn't make it
;===================
    return FALSE


Draw_Grid        ENDP
;##############################################################################
;  END Draw_Grid
;##############################################################################
```

If you have been able to keep up with this series so far, this code should be a breeze to understand. Both of them do the same basic thing. The only difference between the two is that one operates on the current shape and the other draws everything currently in the grid.

The basic idea is to loop through every bit in the frame for the shape or every byte for the grid. (You should be very used to this looping concept by now.) Then we use either the current shape color or the number stored in the grid to access the proper block texture to use. The rest involves a call to draw the surface on the back buffer.

The one thing you need to make sure you don't forget, however, is that you need to convert from grid to screen coordinates. If you do not, everything will be drawn at the left-hand side with *a lot* of overlap.

Also, keep in mind that since we use the DX blitting function, the back buffer must *not* be locked prior to the call. If you did lock it, make sure you unlock it before you make the call; otherwise, you will crash.

That is all our functions do, and more importantly, it is all we need to have on our team for the time being. Now it is the Manager's job to get the game running for us. So, let's go investigate "The Loop."

The Loop and His Team

The loop is a very complex manager. He does his best to organize things, though. He has state variables (that way, he doesn't process what he doesn't need to), and he also uses many different timers to make sure things are getting done. Here's a look at his innards.

```
;##############################################################################
; Game_Main Procedure
;##############################################################################
Game_Main        PROC

                 ;=====================================================
                 ; This is the heart of the game; it gets called over and over
                 ; and even if we process a message!
                 ;=====================================================


                 ;==========================================
                 ; Local Variables
                 ;==========================================
LOCAL    StartTime        :DWORD

                 ;==========================================
                 ; Get the starting time for the loop
                 ;==========================================
INVOKE Start_Time, ADDR StartTime


                 ;============================================
                 ; Take the proper action(s) based on the GameState variable
                 ;============================================
.IF GameState == GS_MENU
                 ;==================================
                 ; We are in the main menu state
                 ;==================================
                 INVOKE Process_Main_Menu

                 ;==================================
                 ; What did they want to do
                 ;==================================
                 .IF EAX == MENU_NOTHING
                          ;==========================
                          ; They didn't select anything yet
                          ; so don't do anything
                          ;==========================

                 .ELSEIF EAX == MENU_ERROR
```

```
        ;================================
        ; This is where error code would go
        ;================================

.ELSEIF EAX == MENU_NEW
        ;================================
        ; They want to start a new game
        ;================================


        ;==============================
        ; Re-Init the grid
        ;==============================
        INVOKE Init_Grid


        ;==============================
        ; Get a new Starting Shape
        ;==============================
        INVOKE New_Shape


        ;================================
        ; Get starting time for the input
        ;================================
        INVOKE Get_Time
        MOV     Input_Time, EAX


        ;================================
        ; Get starting time for the updates
        ;================================
        INVOKE Get_Time
        MOV     Update_Time, EAX


        ;==============================
        ; Set the Game state to playing
        ;==============================
        MOV     GameState, GS_PLAY

.ELSEIF EAX == MENU_FILES
        ;================================
        ; They want the file menu
        ;================================
        MOV     GameState, GS_FILE
```

```
                .ELSEIF EAX == MENU_GAME
                        ;=================================
                        ; They want to return to the game
                        ;=================================

                        ;=================================
                        ; Set the Game state to playing
                        ;=================================
                        MOV     GameState, GS_PLAY

                .ELSEIF EAX == MENU_EXIT
                        ;=================================
                        ; They want to exit the game
                        ;=================================
                        MOV     GameState, GS_EXIT

                .ENDIF


.ELSEIF GameState == GS_FILE
        ;=================================
        ; We are in the file menu state
        ;=================================
        INVOKE Process_File_Menu

        ;=================================
        ; What did they want to do
        ;=================================
        .IF EAX == MENU_NOTHING
                ;=================================
                ; They didn't select anything yet
                ; so don't do anything
                ;=================================

        .ELSEIF EAX == MENU_ERROR
                ;=================================
                ; This is where error code would go
                ;=================================

        .ELSEIF EAX == MENU_LOAD
```

```
                        ;===============================
                        ; They want to load game
                        ;===============================

            .ELSEIF EAX == MENU_SAVE
                        ;===============================
                        ; They want to save their game
                        ;===============================


            .ELSEIF EAX == MENU_MAIN
                        ;===============================
                        ; They want to return to main menu
                        ;===============================
                        MOV     GameState, GS_MENU

            .ENDIF


    .ELSEIF GameState == GS_PLAY
                ;==============================
                ; We are in the gameplay mode
                ;==============================


                ;==============================
                ; Load the main bitmap into the
                ; back buffer
                ;==============================
                INVOKE DD_Load_Bitmap, lpddsback, ptr_BMP_MAIN, \
                        640, 480, screen_bpp


                ;==============================
                ; Is it time to process input yet?
                ;==============================
                INVOKE Get_Time
                SUB     EAX, INPUT_DELAY
                .IF EAX  > Input_Time
                        ;=================
                        ; It is time.
                        ;=================
```

```
;===========================================
; Read the Keyboard
;===========================================
INVOKE DI_Read_Keyboard


;=======================================
; What do they want to do
;=======================================
.IF keyboard_state[DIK_ESCAPE]

        ;=============================
        ; The return to menu key
        ;=============================
        MOV     GameState, GS_MENU

.ELSEIF keyboard_state[DIK_UP]

        ;=============================
        ; Rotate the shape
        ;=============================
        INVOKE Rotate_Shape

.ELSEIF keyboard_state[DIK_DOWN]

        ;=============================
        ; Move the shape down
        ;=============================
        INVOKE Move_Shape, MOVE_DOWN

.ELSEIF keyboard_state[DIK_LEFT]

        ;=============================
        ; Move the shape left
        ;=============================
        INVOKE Move_Shape, MOVE_LEFT

.ELSEIF keyboard_state[DIK_RIGHT]

        ;=============================
        ; Move the shape Right
        ;=============================
        INVOKE Move_Shape, MOVE_RIGHT

.ENDIF
```

```
        ;=================================
        ; Get a New Input Time
        ;=================================
        INVOKE Get_Time
        MOV     Input_Time, EAX

.ENDIF


;=========================================
; Is it time to update the shape yet?
;=========================================
INVOKE Get_Time
SUB     EAX, UPDATE_DELAY
.IF EAX  > Update_Time
        ;=================
        ; It is time.
        ;=================


        ;=================================
        ; Update the current shape
        ;=================================
        INVOKE Update_Shape

        ;=================================
        ; Did we not succeed at updating
        ;=================================
        .IF EAX == FALSE
                ;=========================
                ; They had a collision
                ;=========================

                ;=========================
                ; Test for a line
                ;=========================
                INVOKE Line_Test

                ;=========================
                ; Did they earn one?
                ;=========================
                .WHILE EAX == TRUE
```

```
                        ;================
                        ; They got one
                        ;================


                        ;================
                        ; Test for another
                        ;================
                        INVOKE Line_Test

            .ENDW


            ;=========================
            ; Start a new piece
            ;=========================
            INVOKE New_Shape


            ;=========================
            ; Did we make it?
            ;=========================
            .IF EAX == FALSE
                        ;================
                        ; They died!
                        ;================
                        MOV     GameState, GS_DIE

            .ENDIF


        .ENDIF


        ;===========================
        ; Get a New Update Time
        ;===========================
        INVOKE Get_Time
        MOV     Update_Time, EAX

    .ENDIF


    ;============================
    ; Draw our current grid
    ;============================
```

```
            INVOKE Draw_Grid

            ;=====================================
            ; Draw our current shape
            ;=====================================
            INVOKE Draw_Shape

            ;=====================================
            ; Flip the buffers
            ;=====================================
            INVOKE DD_Flip

    .ELSEIF GameState == GS_DIE
            ;=====================================
            ; We died so perform that code
            ;=====================================

            ;=====================================
            ; Wait for a couple of seconds so
            ; they know that they have died
            ;=====================================
            INVOKE Sleep, 2000

            ;=====================================
            ; ReInit the Grid
            ;=====================================
            INVOKE Init_Grid

            ;=====================================
            ; Get a New shape
            ;=====================================
            INVOKE New_Shape

            ;=====================================
            ; Back to the Main Menu
            ;=====================================
            MOV     GameState, GS_MENU

    .ENDIF
```

```
        ;=======================================
        ; Wait to synchronize the time
        ;=======================================
        INVOKE Wait_Time, StartTime, sync_time

done:

        ;===================
        ; We completed
        ;===================
        return TRUE

err:

        ;===================
        ; We didn't make it
        ;===================
        return FALSE

Game_Main       ENDP
;###########################################################################
; END Game_Main
;###########################################################################
```

As you can see, if the user selects to have a new game, "loop" makes a bunch of calls. First he makes a call to initialize our grid and then one to create a new shape. Next he makes a couple of calls to get the starting time for input and the starting time for updates, and then finally he sets the game state to playing.

We have now entered the game. Every frame, he draws the bitmap onto the back buffer and decides if it is time to process some input. If so, he makes a call to process the input and then reacts based on the keys that are pressed. With that completed, he reinitializes the input time. Otherwise, if enough time hasn't passed, he skips the input phase altogether.

The same thing is done with updating. He first finds out if it is time. If enough time has not yet elapsed, he skips over the updating and makes calls to draw everything. If it has, he calls the update function and reacts to what Update has to tell him. If Update fails, that means it is time for a new shape. But first we call the test to see if there are valid lines. We keep doing this until no more valid lines exist, and then we create the new shape and reinitialize our update time.

During this time, if the call to create a new shape fails, the user has died and the game state is set to reflect that. Finally, he updates the display by flipping our primary and back buffers. Then he does it all over again, synchronizing it to the desired frame rate.

The one thing I want to comment on here is the use of time-based updates. This is a very crucial part of developing a game. If we had updated the input every frame, things would be flying everywhere, and the user would be in a state of shock. The same thing applies to updating the shapes. Also, your machine may achieve 100fps, and yet another machine might only be able to do 25fps. This means that, if you are using frame-based code, the game will look/react in different ways across the two machines.

By using time, you can come close to a guarantee that it will look the same across all capable machines. The reason for this is that time, unlike a frame rate, cannot change across machines. The rate at which a second occurs is the same no matter what you run it on.

The code we have here is a simple implementation of this premise. You can definitely get more complex. Still, this code works and works well for what it needs to do.

Conclusion

I told you we would cover a lot of material! We now have a fully working—albeit limited—game to show for all this work. It has all the rudimentary elements it needs. The only thing the game lacks is the bells and whistles that make it pretty.

The next sections are going to cover those bells and whistles. We will be covering Direct Sound implementation, adding screen transitions, and I will show you my answer for the rotation clipping code.

In the meantime, experiment with some things we haven't done yet or even just try tweaking some things that we have. Everybody has to start someplace and sometime. There is no time and place better to do so than the present. At worst, you will crash your game, and we have all done that. The important thing is to try and to learn.

WIN32 ASM—PART 5

Until the last section, SPACE-TRIS was not even a game; it was merely an exercise in coding modules. Well, now we have a game that is working, and it is just ugly. Sadly enough, though, we are back to coding modules. The good news is these modules will pretty things up by a large margin.

The modules we will be covering today are Direct Sound (yuck!) and screen transitions (yay!). The Direct Sound module isn't going to be anything too complex; it's just a simple sound effects manager that allows you to play, stop, delete, add, or set variables on the sounds themselves. The screen transitions module is going to consist of one main function that gets called, and then a transition is selected at random to perform.

The game also needed a way to check for an out-of-bounds occurrence while rotating pieces. You guys were working on it like I told you too, right? Yeah, I'm sure. Anyway, I will present my quick hack of a solution in a few moments. First, however, I want to say that I am going to be glossing over many of the things we have already covered in past sections. For instance, in the Direct Sound module, you have already seen how to check for an error, so I won't be explaining that again. If you skipped ahead, do yourself a favor and skim the beginning if you need to. This isn't your favorite TV series where you can just pop by on any old day and know exactly what is going on. We are going to be moving at warp speed through a lot of things. All I am really going to provide now is an overview of the techniques I use. It is up to you to understand them.

With that said, let's get right down to business with that solution to the rotation problem.

Rotation Solution

The solution to our rotation problem is fairly straightforward. Basically, we already have all of the routines we need. What we have to know is if, at any given frame, the current piece is out of bounds—and MoveShape() does this for us. So, the fix we have is a simple one. We can just call that routine with the frame it would be on next, right? Wrong. That's what I tried at first because it seemed to make sense. But there is a hidden problem with that method.

The problem lies in the fact that any piece could already be out of bounds when you adjust the frame. Move_Shape() only tells you if you can move the shape to the left or right and does so if it can. If we fake our next frame for that call, it may succeed because it is already out of bounds by one column if it was on the edges previously. This means we need a way to prevent it from ever being out of bounds to begin with.

The solution is to move it in toward the center by one column beforehand. Then, when we make the call, the shape is guaranteed to be on the edge or in the middle, never outside the grid. The way we decide if we can go to the next frame is by seeing if the X coordinate sent before we made the call matches the one we have after the call. If it does, that means the shape can be rotated. If they don't match, the shape cannot be rotated.

This method has the advantage of eliminating the need for any other code. The Move_Shape() function will not succeed if something else is blocking its move. Therefore, we do not need to do any other tests on the shape to see if other blocks are in the way. We just need that simple call based on the next frame. So, we not only solved the problem, we made the routine shorter in the process.

```
;###################################################################
; Rotate_Shape Procedure
;###################################################################
Rotate_Shape    PROC

                ;==========================================
                ; This function will rotate the current shape; it tests
                ; to make sure there are no blocks already in the place
                ; where it would rotate.
                ;==========================================


                ;==========================================
                ; Local Variables
                ;==========================================
                LOCAL    Index:          DWORD
                LOCAL    CurBlock:       DWORD
                LOCAL    Spot:           BYTE


                ;==========================================
                ; Make sure they are low enough
                ;==========================================
```

```
        .IF CurShapeY > 21
                JMP     err
        .ENDIF


        ;================================
        ; Are they at the last frame?
        ;================================
        .IF CurShapeFrame == 3
                ;================================
                ; Yep ... make sure they can rotate
                ;================================


                ;====================================
                ; We will start by seeing which half of
                ; the grid they are currently on; that way
                ; we know how  much to move the shape
                ;====================================
                .IF CurShapeX < 6
                        ;========================
                        ; They are on the left half
                        ; of the grid
                        ;========================


                        ;========================
                        ; So start by moving them one
                        ; coord right and saving the
                        ; old coordinate
                        ;========================
                        PUSH    CurShapeX
                        INC     CurShapeX


                        ;========================
                        ; Now adjust the frame to what
                        ; it would be
                        ;========================
                        MOV     CurShapeFrame, 0


                        ;========================
                        ; Try to move them to the left
                        ;========================
                        INVOKE Move_Shape, MOVE_LEFT
```

```
;===================
; If we succeeded then the old
; X will be equal to·the new
; X coordinate
;===================
MOV     EAX, CurShapeX
POP     CurShapeX
.IF     EAX == CurShapeX
        JMP     done
.ELSE
                ;================
                ; Can't rotate
                ;================
                MOV     CurShapeFrame, 3
                JMP     err

.ENDIF

.ELSE
                ;=========================
                ; They are on the right half
                ; of the grid
                ;=========================


                ;=========================
                ; So start by moving them one
                ; coord left and saving the
                ; old coordinate
                ;=========================
PUSH    CurShapeX
DEC     CurShapeX


                ;=========================
                ; Now adjust the frame to what
                ; it would be
                ;=========================
MOV     CurShapeFrame, 0
```

```
        ;================================
        ; Try & move them to the right
        ;================================
        INVOKE Move_Shape, MOVE_RIGHT


        ;================================
        ; If we succeeded then the old
        ; X will be equal to the new
        ; X coordinate
        ;================================
        MOV     EAX, CurShapeX
        POP     CurShapeX
        .IF     EAX == CurShapeX

                ;================
                ; Can rotate
                ;================
                JMP     done

        .ELSE

                ;================
                ; Can't rotate
                ;================
                MOV     CurShapeFrame, 3
                JMP     err

        .ENDIF

    .ENDIF

.ELSE

    ;====================================
    ; NO ... make sure they can rotate
    ;====================================


    ;======================================
    ; We will start by seeing which half of
    ; the grid they are currently on; that way
    ; we know how much to move the shape
    ;======================================
    .IF CurShapeX < 6
```

```
;===================
; They are on the left half
; of the grid
;===================


;===================
; So start by moving them one
; coord right and saving the
; old coordinate
;===================
PUSH     CurShapeX
INC      CurShapeX


;===================
; Now adjust the frame to what
; it would be
;===================
INC      CurShapeFrame


;===================
; Try to move them to the left
;===================
INVOKE Move_Shape, MOVE_LEFT


;===================
; If we succeeded then the old
; X will be equal to the new
; X coordinate
;===================
MOV      EAX, CurShapeX
POP      CurShapeX
.IF      EAX == CurShapeX
            ;==========
            ; Can rotate
            ;==========
            JMP     done

.ELSE
            ;==========
            ; Can't rotate
            ;==========
```

```
                    DEC     CurShapeFrame
                    JMP     err


        .ENDIF

    .ELSE
            ;===========================
            ; They are on the right half
            ; of the grid
            ;===========================


            ;===========================
            ; So start by moving them one
            ; coord left and saving the
            ; old coordinate
            ;===========================
            PUSH    CurShapeX
            DEC     CurShapeX


            ;===========================
            ; Now adjust the frame to what
            ; it would be
            ;===========================
            INC     CurShapeFrame


            ;===========================
            ; Try & move them to the right
            ;===========================
            INVOKE Move_Shape, MOVE_RIGHT


            ;===========================
            ; If we succeeded then the old
            ; X will be equal to the new
            ; X coordinate
            ;===========================
            MOV     EAX, CurShapeX
            POP     CurShapeX
            .IF     EAX == CurShapeX
                    ;===============
                    ; Can rotate
                    ;===============
```

```
                        JMP       done

              .ELSE

                        ;================
                        ; Can't rotate
                        ;================
                        DEC       CurShapeFrame
                        JMP       err

                  .ENDIF

              .ENDIF

          .ENDIF

done:

          ;=======================
          ; We completed
          ;=======================
          return TRUE

err:

          ;===================
          ; We didn't make it
          ;===================
          return FALSE

Rotate_Shape    ENDP
;###############################################################
; END Rotate_Shape
;###############################################################
```

The Sound Module

The sound module for this game is pretty simple. It merely presents an interface to
load WAV files, play the sounds, delete them, and edit properties about them.
However, there are a few tricky things to watch out for in the module.

The first thing I want to illustrate is how to create an array of structures. Take a
look at the following modified code snippet.

```
;###############################################################################
;###############################################################################
; STRUCTURES
;###############################################################################
;###############################################################################


        ;==================================
        ; this holds a single sound
        ;==================================
        pcm_sound       STRUCT
            dsbuffer        DD 0      ; the ds buffer for the sound
            state           DD 0      ; state of the sound
            rate            DD 0      ; playback rate
            lsize           DD 0      ; size of sound
        pcm_sound       ENDS


        ;==================================
        ; max number of sounds in
        ; the game at once
        ;==================================
        MAX_SOUNDS      EQU     16


        ;======================================
        ; Our array of sound effects
        ;======================================
        sound_fx        pcm_sound       MAX_SOUNDS dup(<0,0,0,0>)
```

You will notice that any time we declare a structure, we need to use angle brackets or curly braces (not shown) for them. The numbers inside consist of the members of your structure and nothing more. Whatever you place there is what things get initialized to. Also, pay attention to how the structure is defined. It consists of normal variable declarations in between a couple of keywords and a tag to give it a name.

Of special note is that you must use another set of braces or brackets if you want to have nested structures. The way we get an array with a structure is the same as any other variable. We use the number we want followed by the DUP pseudo command and then, in parentheses, what you want the values initialized to.

We are going to skip over the DS_Init() and DS_Shutdown() procedures since they do the same exact things as the other DX counterparts. Instead, let's take a look at Play_Sound().

```
;############################################################
; Play_Sound Procedure
;############################################################
Play_Sound PROC id:DWORD, flags:DWORD


        ;===============================================
        ; This function will play the sound contained in the
        ; id passed in along with the flags which can be either
        ; NULL or DSBPLAY_LOOPING
        ;===============================================


        ;==============================
        ; Make sure this buffer exists
        ;==============================
        MOV     EAX, sizeof(pcm_sound)
        MOV     ECX, id
        MUL     ECX
        MOV     ECX, EAX
        .IF sound_fx[ECX].dsbuffer != NULL
                ;==============================
                ; We exists so reset the position
                ; to the start of the sound
                ;==============================
                PUSH    ECX
                DSBINVOKE SetCurrentPosition, sound_fx[ECX].dsbuffer, 0
                POP     ECX


                ;=====================
                ; Did the call fail?
                ;=====================
                .IF EAX != DS_OK
                        ;=====================
                        ; Nope, didn't make it
                        ;=====================
                        JMP     err

                .ENDIF


                ;===========================
                ; Now, we can play the sound
                ;===========================
```

```
            DSBINVOKE Play, sound_fx[ECX].dsbuffer, 0, 0, flags

            ;=====================
            ; Did the call fail?
            ;=====================
            .IF EAX != DS_OK

                    ;=====================
                    ; Nope, didn't make it
                    ;=====================
                    JMP     err

            .ENDIF

        .ELSE

            ;=====================
            ; No buffer for sound
            ;=====================
            JMP     err

        .ENDIF

done:

        ;==================
        ; We completed
        ;==================
        return TRUE

err:

        ;==================
        ; We didn't make it
        ;==================
        return FALSE

Play_Sound      ENDP
;################################################################################
; END Play_Sound
;################################################################################
```

This is the routine we use to start a sound playing. You can pass it flags to alter how it sounds. As far as I know, there are only two options for the flags. If you pass in

NULL, it plays the sound once. If you pass in DSBPLAY_LOOPING, it will play the sound repeatedly.

The routine begins by checking that the sound has a valid buffer associated with it. If so, it sets the position of that sound to the beginning and then makes a call to begin playing it with whatever flags were passed in.

The only thing worth illustrating in this routine is how the structure element is referenced. To begin with, we obtain the size of the structure and multiply that by the ID of the sound to give us our position in the array. Then, to reference a member, you treat it just like you would in C/C++ . . . StructName[position].member.

> **NOTE**
>
> It is important not to forget to multiply the element you want to access by the size of the structure. Arrays are contiguous in memory.

The next three routines allow you to set the volume, frequency, and pan of a sound. There is nothing to these routines; they are just wrappers for the Direct Sound function calls. If you want to use anything but Set_Sound_Volume(), however, you need to tell Direct Sound that you want those attributes enabled when you load the sound. This is done by passing in DSBCAPS_CTRL_PAN or DSBCAPS_CTRLFREQ, respectively. If you do not specify these flags when you load your sound, you will not be able to manipulate those items.

The next two functions are for stopping sounds from playing. One will stop the specific sound you pass in, and the other will stop all of the sounds from playing. Here is the code from the module. Once again, these are merely wrapper functions to shield you from the DX headache.

```
;##################################################################
; Stop_Sound Procedure
;##################################################################
Stop_Sound PROC id:DWORD

        ;=========================================
        ; This function will stop the passed-in sound from
        ; playing and will reset its position
        ;=========================================


        ;=============================
        ; Make sure the sound exists
        ;=============================
```

```
        MOV     EAX, sizeof(pcm_sound)
        MOV     ECX, id
        MUL     ECX
        MOV     ECX, EAX
        .IF sound_fx[ECX].dsbuffer != NULL

                ;===================================
                ; We exist so stop the sound
                ;===================================
                PUSH    ECX
                DSBINVOKE Stop, sound_fx[ECX].dsbuffer
                POP     ECX


                ;===================================
                ; Now reset the sound position
                ;===================================
                DSBINVOKE SetCurrentPosition, sound_fx[ECX].dsbuffer, 0


        .ENDIF

done:

        ;==================
        ; We completed
        ;==================
        return TRUE


err:

        ;==================
        ; We didn't make it
        ;==================
        return FALSE


Stop_Sound      ENDP
;###############################################################################
; END Stop_Sound
;###############################################################################


;###############################################################################
; Stop_All_Sounds Procedure
;###############################################################################
Stop_All_Sounds PROC
```

```
;==================================================
; This function will stop all sounds from playing
;==================================================


;==================================================
; Local Variables
;==================================================
LOCAL    index    :DWORD


;==================================================
; Loop through all sounds
;==================================================
MOV      index, 0
.WHILE index < MAX_SOUNDS
         ;==========================================
         ; Stop this sound from playing
         ;==========================================
         INVOKE Stop_Sound, index

         ;==================
         ; Inc the counter
         ;==================
         INC      index

    .ENDW

done:
    ;==================
    ; We completed
    ;==================
    return TRUE

err:
    ;==================
    ; We didn't make it
    ;==================
    return FALSE

Stop_All_Sounds ENDP
```

```
;#####################################################################
; END Stop_All_Sounds
;#####################################################################
```

Notice that Stop_All_Sounds() is just a wrapper function for our Stop_Sound() routine. We simply iterate through our array, making a call to stop every sound. The routine to actually stop the sound makes a call to stop and reset the current position if the buffer is a valid one.

Delete_Sound() and Delete_All_Sounds() are remarkably similar to the sound-stopping functions. The only difference is that you make a different function call to DX. In the sound module, Delete_Sound() will call Stop_Sound() first to make sure the sound isn't trying to be played while you are trying to delete it. The interesting thing about these two functions is that you do not personally have to release any of your sounds if you don't want to. During shutdown of Direct Sound, all the sounds you loaded will be deleted. If you have reached your maximum in sounds and want to free one up, however, you will need to manually delete it.

There is also a function named Status_Sound() that is yet another wrapper routine. It is used when you need to find out if a sound is still playing or has stopped already. You will see this function put to use later on.

Now that 90 percent of that stupid module is out of the way, we need to move on to the final 10 percent of that code, the Load_WAV() procedure.

One Big Headache

Loading file formats is always a pain. Loading a WAV file proves to be no different. It is a long function that probably could have been broken up a little bit better, but for now it will have to do. It works and that is all I am concerned about. So, have a gander at it.

```
;#####################################################################
; Load_WAV Procedure
;#####################################################################
Load_WAV        PROC    fname_ptr:DWORD, flags:DWORD

        ;=================================================
        ; This function will load the passed in WAV file;
        ; it returns the id of the sound, or -1 if failed
        ;=================================================
```

```
;===============================
; Local Variables
;===============================
LOCAL    sound_id        :DWORD
LOCAL    index           :DWORD


;===============================
; Init the sound_id to -1
;===============================
MOV      sound_id, -1


;===============================
; First we need to make sure there
; is an open id for our new sound
;===============================
MOV      index, 0
.WHILE index < MAX_SOUNDS

        ;===============================
        ; Is this sound empty??
        ;===============================
        MOV     EAX, sizeof(pcm_sound)
        MOV     ECX, index
        MUL     ECX
        MOV     ECX, EAX
        .IF sound_fx[ECX].state == SOUND_NULL

                ;===============================
                ; We have found one, so set
                ; the id and leave our loop
                ;===============================
                MOV     EAX, index
                MOV     sound_id, EAX
                .BREAK


        .ENDIF

        ;===============
        ; Inc the counter
        ;===============
        INC     index
```

```
        .ENDW

        ;=================================
        ; Make sure we have a valid id now
        ;=================================
        .IF sound_id == -1

                ;=========================
                ; Give err msg
                ;=========================
                INVOKE MessageBox, hMainWnd, ADDR szNoID, NULL, MB_OK


                ;=========================
                ; Jump and return out
                ;=========================
                JMP     err

        .ENDIF


        ;=========================
        ; Set up the parent "chunk"
        ; info structure
        ;=========================
        MOV     parent.ckid, 0
        MOV     parent.ckSize, 0
        MOV     parent.fccType, 0
        MOV     parent.dwDataOffset, 0
        MOV     parent.dwFlags, 0


        ;=========================
        ; Do the same with the child
        ;=========================
        MOV     child.ckid, 0
        MOV     child.ckSize, 0
        MOV     child.fccType, 0
        MOV     child.dwDataOffset, 0
        MOV     child.dwFlags, 0


        ;=================================
        ; Now open the WAV file using the MMIO
        ; API function
        ;=================================
```

```
INVOKE mmioOpen, fname_ptr, NULL, (MMIO_READ OR MMIO_ALLOCBUF)
MOV     hwav, EAX


;===================================
; Make sure the call was successful
;===================================
.IF EAX == NULL

        ;====================
        ; Give err msg
        ;====================
        INVOKE MessageBox, hMainWnd, ADDR szNoOp, NULL, MB_OK


        ;====================
        ; Jump and return out
        ;====================
        JMP     err

.ENDIF


;===================================
; Set the type in the parent
;===================================
mmioFOURCC 'W', 'A', 'V', 'E'
MOV     parent.fccType, EAX


;===================================
; Descend into the RIFF
;===================================
INVOKE mmioDescend, hwav, ADDR parent, NULL, MMIO_FINDRIFF
.IF EAX != NULL

        ;====================
        ; Close the file
        ;====================
        INVOKE mmioClose, hwav, NULL


        ;====================
        ; Jump and return out
        ;====================
        JMP     err
```

```
        .ENDIF

        ;=============================
        ; Set the child id to format
        ;=============================
        mmioFOURCC 'f', 'm', 't', ' '
        MOV     child.ckid, EAX


        ;===================================
        ; Descend into the WAVE format
        ;===================================
        INVOKE mmioDescend, hwav, ADDR child, ADDR parent, NULL
        .IF EAX != NULL
                ;==================
                ; Close the file
                ;==================
                INVOKE mmioClose, hwav, NULL


                ;=====================
                ; Jump and return out
                ;=====================
                JMP     err

        .ENDIF

        ;================================
        ; Now read the wave format info in
        ;================================
        INVOKE mmioRead, hwav, ADDR wfmtx, sizeof(WAVEFORMATEX)
        MOV     EBX, sizeof(WAVEFORMATEX)
        .IF EAX != EBX
                ;==================
                ; Close the file
                ;==================
                INVOKE mmioClose, hwav, NULL


                ;=====================
                ; Jump and return out
                ;=====================
                JMP     err
```

```
        .ENDIF

        ;═══════════════════════════════════
        ; Make sure the data format is PCM
        ;═══════════════════════════════════
        .IF wfmtx.wFormatTag != WAVE_FORMAT_PCM
                ;═══════════════════
                ; Close the file
                ;═══════════════════
                INVOKE mmioClose, hwav, NULL

                ;═══════════════════
                ; Jump and return out
                ;═══════════════════
                JMP     err

        .ENDIF

        ;═══════════════════════════════════
        ; Ascend up one level
        ;═══════════════════════════════════
        INVOKE mmioAscend, hwav, ADDR child, NULL
        .IF EAX != NULL
                ;═══════════════════
                ; Close the file
                ;═══════════════════
                INVOKE mmioClose, hwav, NULL

                ;═══════════════════
                ; Jump and return out
                ;═══════════════════
                JMP     err

        .ENDIF

        ;═══════════════════════════════════
        ; Set the child id to data
        ;═══════════════════════════════════
        mmioFOURCC 'd', 'a', 't', 'a'
        MOV     child.ckid, EAX
```

```
;==============================
; Descend into the data chunk
;==============================
INVOKE mmioDescend, hwav, ADDR child, ADDR parent, MMIO_FINDCHUNK
.IF EAX != NULL
        ;==========================
        ; Close the file
        ;==========================
        INVOKE mmioClose, hwav, NULL

        ;==========================
        ; Jump and return out
        ;==========================
        JMP     err

.ENDIF


;==================================
; Now allocate memory for the sound
;==================================
INVOKE GlobalAlloc, GMEM_FIXED, child.ckSize
MOV     snd_buffer, EAX
.IF EAX == NULL
        ;==========================
        ; Close the file
        ;==========================
        INVOKE mmioClose, hwav, NULL

        ;==========================
        ; Jump and return out
        ;==========================
        JMP     err

.ENDIF

;====================================
; Read the WAV data and close the file
;====================================
INVOKE mmioRead, hwav, snd_buffer, child.ckSize
```

```
           INVOKE mmioClose, hwav, 0


           ;==============================
           ; Set the rate, size, & state
           ;==============================
           MOV     EAX, sizeof(pcm_sound)
           MOV     ECX, sound_id
           MUL     ECX
           MOV     ECX, EAX
           MOV     EAX, wfmtx.nSamplesPerSec
           MOV     sound_fx[ECX].rate, EAX
           MOV     EAX, child.ckSize
           MOV     sound_fx[ECX].lsize, EAX
           MOV     sound_fx[ECX].state, SOUND_LOADED


           ;========================
           ; Clear the format struc
           ;========================
           INVOKE RtlFillMemory, ADDR pcmwf, sizeof(WAVEFORMATEX), 0


           ;==============================
           ; Now fill our desired fields
           ;==============================
           MOV     pcmwf.wFormatTag, WAVE_FORMAT_PCM
           MOV     AX, wfmtx.nChannels
           MOV     pcmwf.nChannels, AX
           MOV     EAX, wfmtx.nSamplesPerSec
           MOV     pcmwf.nSamplesPerSec, EAX
           XOR     EAX, EAX
           MOV     AX, wfmtx.nBlockAlign
           MOV     pcmwf.nBlockAlign, AX
           MOV     EAX, pcmwf.nSamplesPerSec
           XOR     ECX, ECX
           MOV     CX, pcmwf.nBlockAlign
           MUL     ECX
           MOV     pcmwf.nAvgBytesPerSec, EAX
           MOV     AX, wfmtx.wBitsPerSample
           MOV     pcmwf.wBitsPerSample, AX
           MOV     pcmwf.cbSize, 0
```

```
;===============================
; Prepare to create the DS buffer
;===============================
DSINITSTRUCT ADDR dsbd, sizeof(DSBUFFERDESC)
MOV     dsbd.dwSize, sizeof(DSBUFFERDESC)
        ; Put other flags you want to play with in here such
        ; as CTRL_PAN, CTRL_FREQ, etc or pass them in
MOV     EAX, flags
MOV     dsbd.dwFlags, EAX
OR      dsbd.dwFlags, DSBCAPS_STATIC OR DSBCAPS_CTRLVOLUME \
                OR DSBCAPS_LOCSOFTWARE
MOV     EBX, child.ckSize
MOV     EAX, OFFSET pcmwf
MOV     dsbd.dwBufferBytes, EBX
MOV     dsbd.lpwfxFormat, EAX


;===============================
; Create the sound buffer
;===============================
MOV     EAX, sizeof(pcm_sound)
MOV     ECX, sound_id
MUL     ECX
LEA     ECX, sound_fx[EAX].dsbuffer
DSINVOKE CreateSoundBuffer, lpds, ADDR dsbd, ECX, NULL
.IF EAX != DS_OK
        ;=================
        ; Free the buffer
        ;=================
        INVOKE GlobalFree, snd_buffer

        ;=================
        ; Jump and return out
        ;=================
        JMP     err

.ENDIF


;===============================
; Lock the buffer so we can copy
; our sound data into it
;===============================
```

```
MOV     EAX, sizeof(pcm_sound)
MOV     ECX, sound_id
MUL     ECX
MOV     ECX, EAX
DSBINVOKE mLock, sound_fx[ECX].dsbuffer, NULL, child.ckSize,
        ADDR audio_ptr_1, ADDR audio_length_1, ADDR audio_ptr_2,\
        ADDR audio_length_2, DSBLOCK_FROMWRITECURSOR
.IF EAX != DS_OK
        ;==================
        ; Free the buffer
        ;==================
        INVOKE GlobalFree, snd_buffer


        ;==================
        ; Jump and return out
        ;==================
        JMP     err

.ENDIF

;============================
; Copy first section of buffer and
; then the second section
;============================
        ; First buffer
MOV     ESI, snd_buffer
MOV     EDI, audio_ptr_1
MOV     ECX, audio_length_1
AND     ECX, 3
REP     movsb
MOV     ECX, audio_length_1
SHR     ECX, 2
REP     movsd

        ; Second buffer
MOV     ESI, snd_buffer
ADD     ESI, audio_length_1
MOV     EDI, audio_ptr_2
MOV     ECX, audio_length_2
AND     ECX, 3
REP     movsd
```

```
MOV     ECX, audio_length_2
SHR     ECX, 2
REP     movsd


;===============================
; Unlock the buffer
;===============================
MOV     EAX, sizeof(pcm_sound)
MOV     ECX, sound_id
MUL     ECX
MOV     ECX, EAX
DSBINVOKE Unlock, sound_fx[ECX].dsbuffer, audio_ptr_1,
          audio_length_1, audio_ptr_2, audio_length_2
.IF EAX != DS_OK
        ;==================
        ; Free the buffer
        ;==================
        INVOKE GlobalFree, snd_buffer

        ;====================
        ; Jump and return out
        ;====================
        JMP     err

.ENDIF

;====================
; Free the buffer
;====================
INVOKE GlobalFree, snd_buffer
```

done:

```
;==================
; We completed
;==================
return sound_id
```

err:

```
;==================
; We didn't make it
;==================
```

```
            return -1

Load_WAV        ENDP
;###############################################################################
; END Load_WAV
;###############################################################################
```

The code is fairly simple, but it is long. I will skim over the first few parts since they are just setting things up. The code starts out by finding the first available sound in our array. If it finds none, it issues an error and then returns to the caller. Once we have a valid sound ID to hold our new sound, we can start playing with the file and setting up the structures for use.

We start by initializing the structures to 0 to make sure we don't have any leftover remnants from previous loads. When that is complete, we get to open up our WAV file using the multimedia I/O functions found in the Winmm.lib file.

Once the file is opened successfully, we descend into the internals of the file. This merely takes us to relevant sections in the header so that we can set up our structures for loading. A few sections need to be traversed, and then we are ready to get the WAV format information, which is the actual header we will need.

With our WAV header information intact, we can ascend up the file and then down into our data chunk. Once "inside," we allocate memory for our data and then grab it with the mmioRead() function. Finally, we can close the file, and the ugly part is over.

Next we do some more setting of values in structures and clearing things out. It's all stuff you have seen before, so it should look familiar by now. We are getting ready to create the sound buffer with all these assignments.

Normally, I would just say "Here is where we create the sound buffer," but there is something very weird going on here. Have you noticed that we aren't able to pass in the sound buffer parameter? The reason is that we need to pass in the address. So, the line right before the call uses the Load Effective Address (LEA) instruction to obtain the address of our variable. The reason for this is just a quirk in the INVOKE syntax, and it's something we need to work around. By

> **NOTE**
>
> Another small thing you might want to jot down is that we can't use EAX to hold that value. The reason is that the macro I defined, DSBINVOKE, uses EAX when manipulating things. This, however, is the only reason. Normally, you could use it without trouble. Never forget that macros are just direct replacements into your code, even if they don't make sense.

loading the address before the call, we can place it in the modified invoke statement without any trouble.

Once we have our buffer created, we lock it, copy the memory over to the new buffer locations, and then unlock it. One thing that might seem a little confusing is the method I have chosen to copy the sound data over. Remember how we copied using DWORDs in our Draw_Bitmap() routine? If not, go back and refresh your memory because it is very important. For those of you who do recall, that is almost exactly what we are doing here.

The only thing that is different is that we have to make sure our data is on a 4-byte boundary. We do this by ANDing the length with 3 and then moving byte by byte until we hit zero. At that point, we are on a 4-byte boundary and can move DWORDs until the end.

It is the same basic concept we have seen before, only this time we have to do the checking for alignment ourselves since the data is not guaranteed to be on even 4-byte boundaries.

> **TIP**
>
> Using the AND instruction with N-1, when N is a power of 2, is the same as using number MOD N.

Once all of that is out of the way, we can free the buffer—along with our headache—and we are finished. The sound is now loaded in the buffer, and we can return the sound's ID to the caller so that they can play the sound later on. One thing I do want to mention is that this WAV loader should be able to load WAV files of any format (8-bit, 16-bit, stereo, mono, and so on). Yet only 8-bit sounds can be utilized in the Direct Sound buffers. The reason is because we only set the cooperative level to normal instead of exclusive. So, if you want to load in and play 16-bit sounds, you will need to alter the DS_Init() procedure and put Direct Sound into exclusive mode.

With that, our sound module is complete. It is definitely not state-of-the-art, but it works fine and removes a lot of the DirectX burden that would normally be placed on us. Luckily, though, we now get to talk about something a lot more fun: screen transitions.

Screen Transitions

Screen transitions are usually fun to write. Of course, most anything would be fun after playing with Direct Sound. The screen transition is often one of the most important things in a game. If you have a lot of places where the view/screen completely changes, a transition is typically needed to smooth things out. You do not want the user to be "jarred" to the next scene. To the user, a transition is like riding in a Lexus, whereas having none is like riding an old Harley Davidson. In other words, you don't want the user to feel the road; you want him to enjoy the scenery.

I have taken an interesting approach with the screen transitions in this game. I decided there would be one main interface function. This function, intelligently called Transition(), is responsible for selecting a screen transition at random and calling it. This provides some break from the monotony of calling the same one over and over again. Of course, I have only provided one simple transition (with two options); it is your job to write more. All transitions require that the surface you want to transition from be on the primary buffer and the surface you want to transition to be on the back buffer.

Here is the code for the interface function:

```
;###############################################################
; Transition Procedure
;###############################################################
Transition      PROC

                ;============================================
                ; This function will call one of our transitions
                ; based on a random number. All transitions require
                ; the primary buffer to be the surface you want
                ; to transition from and the back buffer to be the
                ; surface you want to transition to. Both need to
                ; be unlocked.
                ;============================================


                ;============================
                ; Get a random number
                ;============================
                INVOKE Get_Time


                ;============================
                ; Mod the result with 2
                ;============================
                AND     EAX, 1
```

```
;==========================
; Select the transition based
; on our number
;==========================
.IF EAX == 0
        ;==========================
        ; Perform a Horizontal Wipe
        ;==========================
        INVOKE Wipe_Trans, 6, WIPE_HORZ


        ;==========================
        ; Universal error check
        ;==========================
        .IF EAX == FALSE
                JMP     err
        .ENDIF

.ELSEIF EAX == 1
        ;==========================
        ; Perform a Vertical Wipe
        ;==========================
        INVOKE Wipe_Trans, 4, WIPE_VERT


        ;==========================
        ; Universal error check
        ;==========================
        .IF EAX == FALSE
                JMP     err
        .ENDIF


.ENDIF

done:
;==================
; We completed
;==================
return TRUE

err:
```

```
;====================
; We didn't make it
;====================
    return FALSE

Transition    ENDP
;###############################################################
; END Transition
;###############################################################
```

The `Transition()` function grabs a random number by using the same method as our random shape generator, obtaining the time. This is not the optimum method, and we will be replacing it with a true random-number generator later on. For now, however, it will have to do. The proper transition is then made based on the time; you can play with the parameters if you want. I just selected a couple that didn't seem to take away too much of the screen each iteration.

That's all that is there for the management function. It just keeps things random. You can still call a transition directly; I just thought it was more interesting to do it like this. Besides, on a large project, after four to six months of looking at the same transitions, you would probably be insane.

Now we can look at the actual screen transition, `Wipe_Trans()`. This routine allows us to perform either a vertical (top to bottom) or horizontal (left to right) transition, taking away a width that is passed in each time. So, have a look at the following code before we continue.

```
;###############################################################
; Wipe_Trans Procedure
;###############################################################
Wipe_Trans    PROC    strip_width:DWORD, direction:DWORD

    ;=================================================
    ; This function will perform either a horizontal or
    ; a vertical wipe, depending on what you pass in for the
    ; direction parameter. The width of each step is
    ; determined by the width you pass in to it.
    ;=================================================


    ;=================================================
    ; Local Variables
    ;=================================================
```

```
LOCAL     StartTime          :DWORD


;===========================================
; Set up the source rectangle and the
; destination rectangle
;
; For the first iteration, the strip may
; not be the height passed in. This is to
; make sure we are on an even boundary
; during the loop below
;===========================================
.IF direction == WIPE_HORZ
        MOV       SrcRect.top, 0
        MOV       SrcRect.left, 0
        MOV       EAX, app_width
        MOV       ECX, strip_width
        XOR       EDX, EDX
        DIV       ECX
        .IF EDX == 0
                MOV       EDX, strip_width
        .ENDIF
        MOV       EBX, app_height
        MOV       SrcRect.bottom, EBX
        MOV       SrcRect.right, EDX
        MOV       DestRect.top, 0
        MOV       DestRect.left, 0
        MOV       DestRect.bottom, EBX
        MOV       DestRect.right, EDX


.ELSEIF direction == WIPE_VERT
        MOV       SrcRect.top, 0
        MOV       SrcRect.left, 0
        MOV       EAX, app_height
        MOV       ECX, strip_width
        XOR       EDX, EDX
        DIV       ECX
        MOV       EAX, app_width
        .IF EDX == 0
                MOV       EDX, strip_width
        .ENDIF
        MOV       SrcRect.bottom, EDX
```

```
            MOV       SrcRect.right, EAX
            MOV       DestRect.top, 0
            MOV       DestRect.left, 0
            MOV       DestRect.bottom, EDX
            MOV       DestRect.right, EAX

    .ELSE

            ;================
            ; Invalid direction
            ;================
            JMP       err

    .ENDIF

    ;========================
    ; Get the starting time
    ;========================
    INVOKE Start_Time, ADDR StartTime


    ;========================
    ; Blit the strip onto the screen
    ;========================
    DDS4INVOKE BltFast, lpddsprimary, SrcRect.left, SrcRect.top,\
            lpddsback, ADDR DestRect, DDBLTFAST_WAIT


    ;========================
    ; Make sure we succeeded
    ;========================
    .IF EAX != DD_OK
            JMP       err
    .ENDIF


    ;==============================
    ; Now adjust the distance between the left &
    ; right, or top and bottom, so that the top, or
    ; left, corner is where the right-hand side was
    ; at ... and the bottom, or right, is strip_width
    ; away from the opposite corner.
    ;==============================
    MOV    EAX, strip_width
    .IF direction == WIPE_HORZ
```

```
        MOV     EBX, SrcRect.right
        MOV     SrcRect.left, EBX
        MOV     DestRect.left, EBX
        ADD     EBX, EAX
        MOV     DestRect.right, EBX
        MOV     SrcRect.right, EBX


.ELSEIF direction == WIPE_VERT
        MOV     EBX, SrcRect.bottom
        MOV     SrcRect.top, EBX
        MOV     DestRect.top, EBX
        ADD     EBX, EAX
        MOV     DestRect.bottom, EBX
        MOV     SrcRect.bottom, EBX


.ENDIF


;================================
; Wait to synchronize the time
;================================
INVOKE Wait_Time, StartTime, TRANS_TIME


;====================================
; Drop into a while loop and blit all
; of the strips synching to our
; desired transition rate
;====================================
.WHILE TRUE

        ;============================
        ; Get the starting time
        ;============================
        INVOKE Start_Time, ADDR StartTime


        ;============================
        ; Blit the strip onto the screen
        ;============================
        DDS4INVOKE BltFast, lpddsprimary, SrcRect.left, SrcRect.top,\
                lpddsback, ADDR DestRect, DDBLTFAST_WAIT
```

```
;==============================
; Make sure we succeeded
;==============================
.IF EAX != DD_OK
        JMP      err
.ENDIF


;==================================
; Have we reached our extents yet
;==================================
MOV      EAX, SrcRect.bottom
MOV      EBX, app_height
MOV      ECX, SrcRect.right
MOV      EDX, app_width
.IF EAX == EBX && ECX == EDX

        ;=========================
        ; Trans complete
        ;=========================
        .BREAK

.ELSE

        ;=========================
        ; Adjust by the strip
        ;=========================
        MOV      EAX, strip_width
        .IF direction == WIPE_HORZ
                ADD      SrcRect.left, EAX
                ADD      SrcRect.right, EAX
                ADD      DestRect.left, EAX
                ADD      DestRect.right, EAX

        .ELSEIF direction == WIPE_VERT
                ADD      SrcRect.top, EAX
                ADD      SrcRect.bottom, EAX
                ADD      DestRect.top, EAX
                ADD      DestRect.bottom, EAX

        .ENDIF

.ENDIF
```

```
            ;=====================================
            ; Wait to synchronize the time
            ;=====================================
            INVOKE Wait_Time, StartTime, TRANS_TIME

       .ENDW

done:

            ;====================
            ; We completed
            ;====================
            return TRUE

err:

            ;====================
            ; We didn't make it
            ;====================
            return FALSE


Wipe_Trans      ENDP
;##########################################################################
; END Wipe_Trans
;##########################################################################
```

Notice that the first thing we do is set up the source and destination rectangles. We are going to be working with "strips" of the bitmap. I am going to walk you through exactly what happens when the routine is called.

Pretend the user passed in a 7 for the strip_width parameter and wants a horizontal transition. The first section finds out if the strip's width can go evenly into the screen width. If the strip can go in evenly, it sets the length to be equal to the width. If it can't, the remainder is placed in the width. The reason why we place the remainder in is because the strip is going to have that little strip left over when we finish. For example, with a 7 and a screen width of 640, you will have 91 sections of 7 and a section of 3 left over. So, for the first strip, we would store a 3 for the width.

Next we blit that small 3-pixel strip over from the back buffer onto the primary buffer. With that out of the way, we can get set up to do blits with a 7-pixel width. The way we set up is by moving

NOTE

You would do the exact same thing— except for the height/top/bottom—if you were doing a vertical wipe.

the right-hand side of the rectangle over to the left-hand side. Then we add the strip_width, in this case 7, to the left-hand side to obtain the new right-hand side. So, for our example, the left coordinate of the rectangles would now have a 3, and the right coordinate would now have a 10. We need this adjustment since our loop is only going to work with 7-pixel strips in the bitmap instead of an increasing portion of the bitmap.

We are now ready to delve into our loop. The first thing we do, aside from getting the starting time, is blit the current strip. (This is why we had to set up the rectangles out of the loop.) Then we check that the right-hand and bottom sides of our source rectangle are still inside the limits of our screen. If they have met the extents, we break from the loop because we are finished. If we haven't yet reached the edges, we adjust the rectangles. To adjust the rectangles, we add the strip_width to both the left and right of our source and destination rectangles. By adding to both sides, we are able to blit in strips of 7 pixels. If we only added to the right-hand side, we would blit in pixels of 7, 14, 21, and so on. Needless to say, that would be much, much slower than the way we are doing it. It is almost always faster to use deltas instead. Finally, we synchronize the time to our desired rate and keep doing the loop until we are finished.

There isn't very much to the routine, but it should give you a starting point in making screen transitions. Here are some suggestions in case you are lacking in creativity: Make a modified wipe that would have a bunch of strips at intervals grow to meet each other, like something you would see with a set of blinds in your house. Design a transition that zooms in to a single pixel and then zooms out to the new picture. Create a circular wipe or even a spiral one. There are many good articles out there on demo effects, and I suggest reading some of them if you find this stuff interesting. Finally, if you are really desperate for an idea, just go and play a game and see how its transitions work. Mimicry is one of the first steps in learning.

At any rate, everything in our modules is complete. We now have everything that we need to pretty up the game. In the next section, we will tie everything into a nice little bow, just as we always do.

Putting More Pieces Together

The title to this little section is really accurate. Most programming, at least in some way, is like a jigsaw puzzle. It is about combining pieces in the manner that works best. Oftentimes, you will obtain a completely different result just by reordering some of the steps. In this sense, programming is intellectually stimulating. There are many millions of ways to accomplish any given task. Keep that in mind while reviewing the code I provide. It isn't written in blood anywhere that you have to do things a certain way. At least, I don't think it is.

The module we are going to look at for the changes is the Menu module. The reason we are using this module is because it makes use of all of our new features.

You should have a glance at the code for the new module before we go any further.

```
;##########################################################################
;##########################################################################
; ABOUT Menu:
;
;        This code module contains all of the functions that relate to
; the menu that we use.
;
;        There are routines for each menu we will have. One for the main
; menu and one for the load/save menu stuff.
;
;        NOTE: We could have combined these two functions into one generic
; function that used parameters to determine the behavior. But by coding
; it explicitly, we get a better idea of what is going on in the code.
;
;##########################################################################
;##########################################################################


;##########################################################################
;##########################################################################
; THE COMPILER OPTIONS
;##########################################################################
;##########################################################################

        .386
        .MODEL flat, stdcall
        OPTION CASEMAP :none    ; case sensitive
```

```
;###############################################################################
;###############################################################################
; THE INCLUDES SECTION
;###############################################################################
;###############################################################################


        ;===============================================================
        ; These are the Include files for Window stuff
        ;===============================================================
        INCLUDE \masm32\include\windows.inc
        INCLUDE \masm32\include\comctl32.inc
        INCLUDE \masm32\include\comdlg32.inc
        INCLUDE \masm32\include\shell32.inc
        INCLUDE \masm32\include\user32.inc
        INCLUDE \masm32\include\kernel32.inc
        INCLUDE \masm32\include\gdi32.inc


        ;===============================================================
        ; The Libs for those included files
        ;===============================================================
        INCLUDELIB \masm32\lib\comctl32.lib
        INCLUDELIB \masm32\lib\comdlg32.lib
        INCLUDELIB \masm32\lib\shell32.lib
        INCLUDELIB \masm32\lib\gdi32.lib
        INCLUDELIB \masm32\lib\user32.lib
        INCLUDELIB \masm32\lib\kernel32.lib


        ;==================================
        ; The Direct Draw include file
        ;==================================
        INCLUDE Includes\DDraw.inc


        ;==================================
        ; The Direct Input include file
        ;==================================
        INCLUDE Includes\DInput.inc


        ;==================================
        ; The Direct Sound include file
        ;==================================
```

```
        INCLUDE Includes\DSound.inc


        ;================================================
        ; Include the file that has our protos
        ;================================================
        INCLUDE Protos.inc

;################################################################################
;################################################################################
; LOCAL MACROS
;################################################################################
;################################################################################


        m2m MACRO M1, M2
                PUSH              M2
                POP               M1
        ENDM

        return MACRO arg
                MOV       EAX, arg
                RET
        ENDM


;################################################################################
;################################################################################
; Variables we want to use in other modules
;################################################################################
;################################################################################



;################################################################################
;################################################################################
; External variables
;################################################################################
;################################################################################


        ;================================
        ; The DirectDraw stuff
        ;================================
        EXTERN  lpddsprimary      :LPDIRECTDRAWSURFACE4
```

```
        EXTERN  lpddsback           :LPDIRECTDRAWSURFACE4


        ;=========================================
        ; The Input Device state variables
        ;=========================================
        EXTERN keyboard_state    :BYTE


;###############################################################################
;###############################################################################
; BEGIN INITIALIZED DATA
;###############################################################################
;###############################################################################

    .DATA


        ;=================================
        ; Strings for the bitmaps
        ;=================================
        szMainMenu      DB "Art\Menu.sfp",0
        szFileMenu      DB "Art\FileMenu.sfp",0


        ;=================================
        ; Our very cool menu sound
        ;=================================
        szMenuSnd       DB "Sound\Background.wav",0


        ;=================================
        ; PTR to the BMPs
        ;=================================
        ptr_MAIN_MENU   DD 0
        ptr_FILE_MENU   DD 0


        ;=================================
        ; ID for the Menu sound
        ;=================================
        Menu_ID         DD 0


        ;=================================
        ; A value to hold lPitch when locking
        ;=================================
        lPitch          DD 0
```

```
          ;=======================================
          ; Lets us know if we need to transition
          ;=======================================
          first_time      DD 0


;############################################################################
;############################################################################
; BEGIN CONSTANTS
;############################################################################
;############################################################################



;############################################################################
;############################################################################
; BEGIN EQUATES
;############################################################################
;############################################################################


          ;===================
          ;Utility Equates
          ;===================
FALSE             EQU     0
TRUE              EQU     1


          ;===================
          ; The Screen BPP
          ;===================
screen_bpp        EQU     16


;===================
; The Menu Codes
;===================
          ; Generic
MENU_ERROR        EQU     0h
MENU_NOTHING      EQU     1h

          ; Main Menu
MENU_NEW          EQU     2h
MENU_FILES        EQU     3h
MENU_GAME         EQU     4h
```

```
MENU_EXIT          EQU      5h

              ; File Menu
MENU_LOAD          EQU      6h
MENU_SAVE          EQU      7h
MENU_MAIN          EQU      8h
```

```
;##############################################################################
;##############################################################################
; BEGIN THE CODE SECTION
;##############################################################################
;##############################################################################


   .CODE


;##############################################################################
; Init_Menu Procedure
;##############################################################################
Init_Menu         PROC


              ;=================================================
              ; This function will initialize our menu systems
              ;=================================================


              ;=================================
              ; Local Variables
              ;=================================


              ;=================================
              ; Read in the bitmap and create buffer
              ;=================================
              INVOKE Create_From_SFP, ADDR ptr_MAIN_MENU, ADDR szMainMenu,\
                      screen_bpp


              ;=================================
              ; Test for an error
              ;=================================
              .IF EAX == FALSE

                      ;=====================
                      ; We failed so leave
                      ;=====================
```

```
            JMP       err

    .ENDIF

    ;===================================
    ; Read in the bitmap and create buffer
    ;===================================
    INVOKE Create_From_SFP, ADDR ptr_FILE_MENU, ADDR szFileMenu,\
            screen_bpp

    ;===================================
    ; Test for an error
    ;===================================
    .IF EAX == FALSE
            ;=======================
            ; We failed so leave
            ;=======================
            JMP       err

    .ENDIF

    ;========================
    ; Load in the menu sound
    ;========================
    INVOKE Load_WAV, ADDR szMenuSnd, NULL
    MOV       Menu_ID, EAX

    ;==============================
    ; Set first_time to true so that we
    ; will do a trans when we first
    ; enter the menu routines
    ;==============================
    MOV       first_time, TRUE

done:
    ;==================
    ; We completed
    ;==================
    return TRUE

err:
```

```
                ;==================
                ; We didn't make it
                ;==================
                return FALSE

Init_Menu       ENDP
;############################################################################
; END Init_Menu
;############################################################################


;############################################################################
; Shutdown_Menu Procedure
;############################################################################
Shutdown_Menu   PROC

                ;========================================================
                ; This function will shut down our menu systems
                ;========================================================


                ;===============================
                ; Local Variables
                ;===============================


                ;===========================
                ; Free the bitmap memory
                ;===========================
                INVOKE GlobalFree, ptr_MAIN_MENU
                INVOKE GlobalFree, ptr_FILE_MENU

done:
                ;==================
                ; We completed
                ;==================
                return TRUE

err:
                ;==================
                ; We didn't make it
                ;==================
                return FALSE
```

```
Shutdown_Menu    ENDP
;##############################################################################
; END Shutdown_Menu
;##############################################################################


;##############################################################################
; Process_Main_Menu Procedure
;##############################################################################
Process_Main_Menu        PROC


                ;============================================================
                ; This function will process the main menu for the game
                ;============================================================


                ;===================================
                ; Local Variables
                ;===================================


                ;===================================
                ; Lock the Direct Draw back buffer
                ;===================================
                INVOKE DD_Lock_Surface, lpddsback, ADDR lPitch


                ;===========================
                ; Check for an error
                ;===========================
                .IF EAX == FALSE

                        ;===================
                        ; Jump to err
                        ;===================
                        JMP      err

                .ENDIF


                ;===================================
                ; Draw the bitmap onto the surface
                ;===================================
                INVOKE Draw_Bitmap, EAX, ptr_MAIN_MENU, lPitch, 640, 480, screen_bpp
```

```
;=================================
; Unlock the back buffer
;=================================
INVOKE DD_Unlock_Surface, lpddsback


;=================================
; Check for an error
;=================================
.IF EAX == FALSE
        ;=====================
        ; Jump to err
        ;=====================
        JMP     err

.ENDIF


;=====================================
; Make sure the Menu sound is playing
;=====================================
INVOKE Status_Sound, Menu_ID
.IF !(EAX & DSBSTATUS_PLAYING)
        ;=====================
        ; Play the sound
        ;=====================
        INVOKE Play_Sound, Menu_ID, DSBPLAY_LOOPING

.ENDIF


;=====================================
; Everything okay, so flip displayed
; surfaces and make loading visible
; or call transition if needed
;=====================================
.IF first_time == TRUE
        INVOKE Transition
        MOV     first_time, FALSE
.ELSE
        INVOKE DD_Flip
.ENDIF
```

```
;===============================
; Check for an error
;===============================
.IF EAX == FALSE
        ;=====================
        ; Jump to err
        ;=====================
        JMP     err

.ENDIF


;===========================================================
; Now read the keyboard to see if they have pressed
; any keys corresponding to our menu
;===========================================================
INVOKE DI_Read_Keyboard


;===============================
; Did they press a valid key
;===============================
.IF keyboard_state[DIK_N]
        ;=====================
        ; Stop the menu music
        ;=====================
        INVOKE Stop_Sound, Menu_ID

        ;===========================
        ; Reset the first time variable
        ;===========================
        MOV     first_time, TRUE

        ;=====================
        ; The new game key
        ;=====================
        return  MENU_NEW

.ELSEIF keyboard_state[DIK_G]
        ;===========================
        ; Reset the first time variable
        ;===========================
```

```
                MOV       first_time, TRUE


                ;======================
                ; The game files key
                ;======================
                return MENU_FILES

    .ELSEIF keyboard_state[DIK_R]

                ;================================
                ; Reset the first time variable
                ;================================
                MOV       first_time, TRUE


                ;======================
                ; Stop the menu music
                ;======================
                INVOKE Stop_Sound, Menu_ID


                ;======================
                ; Return to game key
                ;======================
                return MENU_GAME

    .ELSEIF keyboard_state[DIK_E]

                ;======================
                ; Stop the menu music
                ;======================
                INVOKE Stop_Sound, Menu_ID


                ;======================
                ; The exit game key
                ;======================
                return MENU_EXIT

    .ENDIF

done:
        ;==================
        ; We completed w/o
        ; doing anything
        ;==================
```

```
        return MENU_NOTHING

err:
        ;===================
        ; We didn't make it
        ;===================
        return MENU_ERROR

Process_Main_Menu        ENDP
;##############################################################################
; END Process_Main_Menu
;##############################################################################


;##############################################################################
; Process_File_Menu Procedure
;##############################################################################
Process_File_Menu        PROC


        ;=========================================================
        ; This function will process the file menu for the game
        ;=========================================================


        ;===================================
        ; Local Variables
        ;===================================


        ;===================================
        ; Lock the Direct Draw back buffer
        ;===================================
        INVOKE DD_Lock_Surface, lpddsback, ADDR lPitch


        ;===========================
        ; Check for an error
        ;===========================
        .IF EAX == FALSE
                ;=================
                ; Jump to err
                ;=================
                JMP     err
```

```
        .ENDIF

        ;==============================
        ; Draw the bitmap onto the surface
        ;==============================
        INVOKE Draw_Bitmap, EAX, ptr_FILE_MENU, lPitch, 640, 480, screen_bpp


        ;==============================
        ; Unlock the back buffer
        ;==============================
        INVOKE DD_Unlock_Surface, lpddsback


        ;==============================
        ; Check for an error
        ;==============================
        .IF EAX == FALSE
                ;==================
                ; Jump to err
                ;==================
                JMP      err

        .ENDIF

        ;==============================
        ; Make sure the Menu sound is playing
        ;==============================
        INVOKE Status_Sound, Menu_ID
        .IF !(EAX & DSBSTATUS_PLAYING)
                ;==================
                ; Play the sound
                ;==================
                INVOKE Play_Sound, Menu_ID, DSBPLAY_LOOPING

        .ENDIF

        ;==============================
        ; Everything okay, so flip displayed
        ; surfaces and make loading visible
        ; or call transition if needed
        ;==============================
        .IF first_time == TRUE
```

```
        INVOKE  Transition
        MOV     first_time, FALSE
.ELSE
        INVOKE  DD_Flip
.ENDIF


;============================
; Check for an error
;============================
.IF EAX == FALSE

        ;====================
        ; Jump to err
        ;====================
        JMP     err


.ENDIF



;=====================================================
; Now read the keyboard to see if they have pressed
; any keys corresponding to our menu
;=====================================================
INVOKE DI_Read_Keyboard


;============================
; Did they press a valid key
;============================
.IF keyboard_state[DIK_L]

        ;====================
        ; The load game key
        ;====================
        return  MENU_LOAD

.ELSEIF keyboard_state[DIK_S]

        ;====================
        ; The save game key
        ;====================
        return MENU_SAVE


.ELSEIF keyboard_state[DIK_B]
```

```
            ;===============================
            ; Reset the first time variable
            ;===============================
            MOV     first_time, TRUE


            ;=====================
            ; Return to main key
            ;=====================
            return MENU_MAIN


    .ENDIF

done:
            ;==================
            ; We completed w/o
            ; doing anything
            ;==================
            return MENU_NOTHING

err:
            ;==================
            ; We didn't make it
            ;==================
            return MENU_ERROR

Process_File_Menu       ENDP
;##################################################################
; END Process_File_Menu
;##################################################################

;#######################################
; THIS IS THE END OF THE PROGRAM CODE #
;#######################################
END
```

Now I will help you locate all of the new stuff. To begin with, in Init_Menu() we load in the WAV file for the menu music, and we set a new variable called first_time to TRUE. I hope the Load_WAV() call is self-explanatory. The new variable, on the other hand, is probably going to need a quick explanation. Basically, when we are drawing one of the menus, we need a way to find out whether we need to perform a transition or just draw it plain. Since we only want to transition once (upon entrance), we set up a variable to hold state information.

Looking at the Process_Main_Menu() procedure, we can see how to use the new routines. After the stuff has been drawn and is ready to be displayed, we call Status_Sound() with our menu's music ID. The function returns the status of the sound, and we AND it with DSBSTATUS_PLAYING to find out if our sound is currently playing. If it is not yet playing, we make the call to play the sound and pass in DSB-PLAY_LOOPING so that we don't have to keep calling Play_Sound(). It is important that we get the status on any sound that might be looping because, by calling Play_Sound(), we reset its position to the beginning. It ends up sounding very interesting, and you know right away that you have botched it someplace.

Once the sound is going, we are ready to display our menu screen. If our first_time variable is still TRUE, we transition in; otherwise, we just draw the screen normal. We also set the state to FALSE after we transition in so that we don't keep performing a transition. The variable also gets reset when certain menu items are selected.

That's about all for the new stuff. I have scattered things around the Menu module, and there is some sound stuff in the Shapes module. I showed you how to implement the new things, which is extremely simple. If you can think of anything else to add, feel free to do so. It is good practice.

Conclusion

Yet another part of the game is complete. I really hope that you aren't just reading these things. Programming is just that, programming. Without practice, no amount of reading is going to help you.

As always, let me remind you that this code is sample code. It is meant to illustrate beginning/intermediate techniques. It isn't fully optimized, although because it is in pure assembly, it is usually smaller and faster than any compiler could produce on its own. So, improve the code! With time and practice, you will start fully understanding these concepts, and then you will be able to produce optimum code.

Most importantly, take the time to sit back and savor what we have accomplished so far. In about a week and a half of coding time, which is what I estimate I have actually spent programming this game, we have the following: an executable that is under 30KB, a fully working game, a few bells and whistles, and we learned many new things. If you were somebody who was hesitant about assembly language before this section, these things should definitely make up your mind for you.

Assembly language is still quite useful and should still be considered a viable language for producing programs.

In the next section, we will be adding a scoring system and a preview system for the pieces. These additions will almost make a fully complete game. In the last section, I will cover some more additions that are a little bit more on the advanced side and should make the game quite a bit better. Most importantly, these last two sections will polish the game off.

Finally, take note of the totally awesome sounds that are in the game. After I threw together a few, I decided that you guys needed something much better, so I contacted Jason Pitt of EvilX Systems (**www.evilx.com**). Jason, aside from making totally unique games, has amazing musical talent. If you are a musically challenged programmer or even just want to take the music in your game to the next level, contact him. You might be surprised at what he can do—I sure was.

WIN32 ASM—PART 6

Okay, it's time to get back to work. In the last section, we added the totally awesome sound effects and made some simple screen transitions. I also showed the solution to the rotation problem we had. It may not sound like much, but trust me—those things had a significant impact on the game.

In this section, we'll start off by adding the capability to see the preview piece, which means we'll have to add a preview piece to our list of needed data (duh!). Once that is taken care of, we'll add the capability to draw text of different font sizes. The text drawing will take a few new routines and the alteration of an old one. Then we'll write the code to draw text for our level, score, and the current lines we have earned. Finally, we can add the scoring system (along with a primitive level system) to the game.

Okay, that's the plan. I suppose I should stop chattering and get to the good stuff.

Next Piece, Please

Integrating a new piece into the "pipeline" was very easy. Basically, what I wanted was a piece that would stand in line. Then, when the current piece finished dropping, the next piece in line would become current, and the new piece that was just created would take its place waiting.

I started out by copying all the variables that the current piece had. Then I just gave them new names to show that they were for the next piece and not the current one. Then I needed to alter the New_Shape() procedure. Take a look at the code I added.

```
;###############################################################################
; New_Shape Procedure
;###############################################################################
New_Shape          proc
```

```
;==========================================
; This function will select a new shape at random
; for the Next shape and will assign the old next
; shape values to the current shape
;==========================================


;==========================================
; Do the swaps if this isn't our
; very first piece of the game
;==========================================
again:
        .if NextShape != -1
                m2m     CurShape, NextShape
                m2m     CurShapeColor, NextShapeColor
                m2m     CurShapeX, NextShapeX
                m2m     CurShapeY, NextShapeY
                m2m     CurShapeFrame, NextShapeFrame
        .endif


;==========================================
; First make sure they haven't reached
; the top of the grid yet
;
; Begin by calculating the start of
; the very last row where the piece
; is initialized at ... aka (5,19)
;==========================================
mov     eax, 13
mov     ecx, 19
mul     ecx
add     eax, 5
mov     ebx, BlockGrid
add     eax, ebx
mov     ecx, eax
add     ecx, 4


;==========================
; Loop through and test the
; next 4 positions
;==========================
.while eax <= ecx
```

```
                ;===================
                ; Is this one filled?
                ;===================
                mov     bl, BYTE PTR [eax]
                .if bl != 0
                        ;=================
                        ; They are dead
                        ;=================
                        jmp     err

                .endif

                ;=================
                ; Inc the counter
                ;=================
                inc     eax
        .endw

        ;============================
        ; Use a random number to get
        ; the current shape to use
        ;
        ; For this we will just use
        ; the time returned by the
        ; Get_Time() function
        ;============================
        invoke Get_Time

        ;============================
        ; Mod this number with 7
        ; since there are 7 shapes
        ;============================
        mov     ecx, 7
        xor     edx, edx
        div     ecx
        mov     eax, edx

        ;============================
        ; Multiply by 16 since there
        ; are 16 bytes per shape
        ;============================
```

```
        shl     eax, 4


        ;===============================
        ; Use that number to select
        ; the shape from the table
        ;===============================
        mov     ebx, offset ShapeTable
        add     eax, ebx
        mov     NextShape, eax


        ;===============================
        ; Use a random number to get
        ; the block surface to use
        ;
        ; For this we will just use
        ; the time returned by the
        ; Get_Time() function
        ;===============================
        invoke Get_Time


        ;===============================
        ; And this result with 7
        ; since there are 8 blocks
        ;===============================
        and     eax, 7


        ;===============================
        ; Use it as the block surface
        ;===============================
        mov     NextShapeColor, eax


        ;===============================
        ; Initialize the Starting Coords
        ;===============================
        mov     NextShapeX, 5
        mov     NextShapeY, 24


        ;===============================
        ; Set the Current Frame Variable
        ;===============================
```

```
        mov       NextShapeFrame, 0

        ;===================================
        ; Go back to the top and load again
        ; if this was our very first piece
        ;===================================
        .if CurShape == -1
                jmp       again
        .endif

done:

        ;=======================
        ; They have a new piece
        ;=======================
        return TRUE

err:

        ;==================
        ; They died!
        ;==================
        return FALSE

New_Shape       ENDP
;###############################################################################
; END New_Shape
;###############################################################################
```

Notice that the first thing I do is test to see if NextShape is currently −1. I assign
NextShape this value during initialization to show that I need to create two new
shapes, one for the current and one for the next. After that special very first iteration, though, everything runs as normal. I place the values in the next shape into
the current shape's variables. Then I create everything just as before, except I store
the values in my next shape instead of the current one. At the bottom, I test the
current shape to see if it is −1. If so, I know I need to create another shape, so I
jump back to the top and do it all over again.

The only other modification I had to make was, as I mentioned, during initialization. At that point, both the current shape and the next shape were set equal to −1
to indicate that they needed to be created.

I Can't See It!

After getting the application to create and store the piece, I just needed a way to draw it on the screen. I decided to simply modify the existing Draw_Shape() procedure. The idea was to have it either draw the current shape or the next shape, based on a variable that was passed in. Have a look at the new version.

```
;##############################################################################
; Draw_Shape Procedure
;##############################################################################
Draw_Shape      proc    UseNext:BYTE


        ;==========================================================
        ; This function will draw our current shape at its
        ; proper location on the screen, or it will draw the next
        ; shape on the screen in the next window
        ;==========================================================


        ;==============================
        ; Local Variables
        ;==============================
        LOCAL   DrawY:          DWORD
        LOCAL   DrawX:          DWORD
        LOCAL   CurRow:         DWORD
        LOCAL   CurCol:         DWORD
        LOCAL   CurLine:        DWORD
        LOCAL   XPos:           DWORD
        LOCAL   YPos:           DWORD


        ;==================================
        ; Get the Current Shape Pos
        ;==================================
        .if UseNext == FALSE
                mov     ebx, CurShape
                mov     eax, CurShapeFrame
        .else
                mov     ebx, NextShape
                mov     eax, NextShapeFrame
        .endif
        shl     eax, 2
        add     ebx, eax
```

```
mov     CurLine, ebx


;===================================
; Set the Starting Row and Column
; for the drawing
;===================================
.if UseNext == FALSE
        mov     eax, CurShapeX
        mov     ebx, CurShapeY
.else
        mov     eax, 2          ; X Coord
        mov     ebx, 4          ; Y Coord
.endif
mov     DrawX, eax
mov     DrawY, ebx


;===================================
; Loop through all four rows
;===================================
mov     CurRow, 0
.while CurRow < 4
        ;===================================
        ; Loop through all four Columns if
        ; the Y Coord is in the screen
        ;===================================
        mov     CurCol, 4
        .while CurCol > 0 && DrawY < 20
                ;===================================
                ; Shift the CurLine Byte over
                ; by our CurCol
                ;===================================
                mov     ecx, 4
                sub     ecx, CurCol
                mov     ebx, CurLine
                xor     eax, eax
                mov     al, BYTE PTR [ebx]
                shr     eax, cl


                ;===================================
                ; Is it a valid block?
                ;===================================
```

```
.if ( eax & 1 )
            ;==============================
            ; Yes, it was a valid block
            ;==============================


            ;==============================
            ; Calculate the Y coord
            ;==============================
    mov     eax, (GRID_HEIGHT - 5)
    sub     eax, DrawY
    mov     ecx, BLOCK_HEIGHT
    mul     ecx
    mov     YPos, eax


            ;==============================
            ; Adjust the Y coord for
            ; certain shapes in the next
            ; window since they are off
            ; of the center
            ;==============================
    .if UseNext == TRUE
            mov     ecx, NextShape
            .if ecx == Offset Square || \
                ecx == Offset Line
                    sub     YPos, 7
            .elseif ecx == offset Pyramid
                    add     YPos, 15
            .else
                    add     YPos, 5
            .endif
    .endif


            ;==============================
            ; Calculate the X coord
            ;==============================
    mov     eax, DrawX
    add     eax, CurCol
    dec     eax
    mov     ecx, BLOCK_WIDTH
    mul     ecx
    .if UseNext == FALSE
```

```
                add       eax, 251
.else
                add       eax, 40
                ;==============================
                ; Now adjust the X coord on a
                ; shape-by-shape basis
                ;==============================
                mov       ecx, NextShape
                .if ecx == offset Square
                        sub       eax, 12
                .elseif ecx == offset Line
                        add       eax, 25
                .elseif ecx == offset L
                        add       eax, 15
                .elseif ecx == offset Back_L
                        add       eax, 15
                .elseif ecx == offset Z
                        sub       eax, 15
                .elseif ecx == offset Back_Z
                        sub       eax, 15
                .endif
.endif
mov     XPos, eax


;==============================
; Calculate the surface to use
;==============================
.if UseNext == FALSE
        mov       eax, CurShapeColor
.else
        mov       eax, NextShapeColor
.endif
shl     eax, 2
mov     ebx, DWORD PTR BlockSurface[eax]


;==============================
; Blit the block
;==============================
DDS4INVOKE BltFast, lpddsback, XPos, YPos, \
      ebx, ADDR SrcRect, \
      DDBLTFAST_NOCOLORKEY or DDBLTFAST_WAIT
```

```
                    .endif

                    ;════════════════════
                    ; Dec our col counter
                    ;════════════════════
                    dec     CurCol

            .endw

                    ;════════════════════
                    ; Inc the CurLine
                    ;════════════════════
                    inc     CurLine

                    ;════════════════════
                    ; decrement Y coord
                    ;════════════════════
                    dec     DrawY

                    ;════════════════════
                    ; Inc the row counter
                    ;════════════════════
                    inc     CurRow

        .endw

done:
                    ;════════════════════
                    ; We completed
                    ;════════════════════
                    return TRUE

err:
                    ;════════════════════
                    ; We didn't make it
                    ;════════════════════
                    return FALSE

Draw_Shape      ENDP
```

```
;##############################################################
; END Draw_Shape
;##############################################################
```

The start of the code is pretty self-explanatory. It simply decides which variables to use based on the piece we are drawing. Take note that the coordinates 2 and 4 are not pixel coordinates. They are the number of 32×32-pixel blocks on the X-axis and the number of blocks from the bottom on the Y-axis.

There is one major change in the code, and that is where I adjust the position of the blocks that are drawn. Because the window we are trying to draw them in is square but our shapes typically aren't, we needed a way to center them. So, I decided to hard-code the coordinate adjustments.

I used a special technique to do this, though. You'll notice that I labeled the start of each shape's declaration in the shape table. Remember when we were declaring the shapes by using bits? Well, all I did was place a label before the start of every new shape. This is very, very powerful. I am now able to address the middle of a huge table by name. Needless to say, this adds to the clarity of what would have been a very difficult thing to understand. This is the equivalent of being able to name `variable[12][12]` with an alias in C so that you can access it directly.

Finally, in the main code, we call this routine both with TRUE and with FALSE so that we can have both pieces drawn. Keep in mind that this routine could have been broken apart into two routines. We chose this route simply because the changes were easy to make and made sense. The next step is to modify the drawing routine to let us change fonts to draw our text.

> **NOTE**
>
> The only exception to this modification was the square. Because the square was the first shape, I couldn't have two names both at the same place (the first name being, of course, our variable name ShapeTable). So, at the end of ShapeTable, I put an equate that said to treat Square the same as ShapeTable. In code, I could have easily just used ShapeTable directly, but then it wouldn't have been as clear what I was doing.

The New Text

The text support didn't require too much alteration. Basically, I wanted to be able to support drawing the text with GDI in different fonts instead of the system default. This is something I should have planned from the beginning, but I didn't.

I would like to be able to say I was just saving it for later, but the truth is I plum forgot about it. Oh well, I guess you'll get to see it now.

The very first thing we have to do is add in support for selecting and deselecting certain fonts. In Windows, you specify what font you want to use by selecting it into your object after you create it. This sounds pretty crazy, but the code is fairly straightforward. Here are the routines to select and deselect the font.

```
;##############################################################################
; DD_Select_Font Procedure
;##############################################################################
DD_Select_Font PROC        handle:DWORD, lfheight:DWORD, lfweight:DWORD,\
                           ptr_szName:DWORD, ptr_old_obj:DWORD


        ;=========================================================
        ; This function will create & select the font after
        ; altering the font structure based on the params
        ;=========================================================


        ;===============================
        ; Create the FONT object
        ;===============================
        INVOKE CreateFont, lfheight, 0, 0, 0, lfweight, 0, 0, \
                0, ANSI_CHARSET, OUT_DEFAULT_PRECIS, CLIP_STROKE_PRECIS,\
                DEFAULT_QUALITY, DEFAULT_PITCH OR FF_DONTCARE, ptr_szName
        MOV     temp, EAX


        ;===============================
        ; Select the font and preserve old
        ;===============================
        INVOKE SelectObject, handle, EAX
        MOV     EBX, ptr_old_obj
        MOV     [EBX], EAX

done:
        ;=================
        ; We completed
        ;=================
        return temp

err:
```

```
        ;=====================
        ; We didn't make it
        ;=====================
        return FALSE


DD_Select_Font   ENDP
;##############################################################################
; END DD_Select_Font
;##############################################################################


;##############################################################################
; DD_UnSelect_Font Procedure
;##############################################################################
DD_UnSelect_Font PROC   handle:DWORD, font_object:DWORD, old_object:DWORD


        ;=================================================
        ; This function will delete the font object and restore
        ; the old object
        ;=================================================


        ;====================================
        ; Restore old obj and delete font
        ;====================================
        INVOKE SelectObject, handle, old_object
        INVOKE DeleteObject, font_object

done:
        ;===================
        ; We completed
        ;===================
        return TRUE

err:
        ;===================
        ; We didn't make it
        ;===================
        return FALSE


DD_UnSelect_Font          ENDP
```

```
;##################################################################
; END DD_UnSelect_Font
;##################################################################
```

This probably doesn't mean too much to you right now, but here is how the routines work. To select a font for use, two steps are required. First, we must create a font object. My select function lets you control three different things: size, weight, and font name. The size is how large you want it, the weight controls bold and normal, and the name controls the actual font you use. There are many other parameters that can be played with, and I suggest reviewing the Win32 API calls for those parameters. The second step is to "select" that font object into the current device context. The only trick here is that we preserve the old object with the pointer passed in for that old object. This is all that needs to be done to select a new font.

Our routine to deselect the font is pretty much the same process but in reverse. First we select our old object back into the device context. This step is important because we may have had something else in there that we want to restore. When programming, it is best to abide by the adage that most of our mothers taught us: "Put it back the way you found it." Then, after we select the old object, we can delete our current font object and then are finished.

That is all that there is to selecting a new font to use for drawing. It doesn't do much good, however, without some code to put it on the screen.

```
;##################################################################
; Draw_Captions Procedure
;##################################################################
Draw_Captions    proc

            ;========================================================
            ; This function will draw our captions, such as the
            ; score and the current level they are on
            ;========================================================


            ;=============================
            ; Local Variables
            ;=============================
            LOCAL    hFont           :DWORD
```

```
;========================================
; Get the DC for the back buffer
;========================================
invoke DD_GetDC, lpddsback
mov     hDC, eax


;========================================
; Set the font to "IMPACT" at the
; size that we need it
;========================================
invoke DD_Select_Font, hDC, -32, FW_BOLD, ADDR szImpact, ADDR Old_Obj
mov     hFont, eax


;==============================
; Set up rect for score text
;==============================
mov     text_rect.top, 161
mov     text_rect.left, 54
mov     text_rect.right, 197
mov     text_rect.bottom, 193


;==============================
; Draw the Score Text
;==============================
RGB 255, 255, 255
push    eax
mov     eax, Score
mov     dwArgs, eax
invoke wvsprintfA, ADDR szBuffer, ADDR szScore, Offset dwArgs
pop     ebx
invoke DD_Draw_Text, hDC, ADDR szBuffer, eax, ADDR text_rect,\
        DT_CENTER or DT_VCENTER or DT_SINGLELINE, ebx


;==============================
; Set up rect for Level text
;==============================
mov     text_rect.top, 67
mov     text_rect.left, 102
mov     text_rect.right, 151
mov     text_rect.bottom, 99
```

```
;========================
; Draw the Level Text
;========================
RGB 255, 255, 0
push    eax
mov     eax, CurLevel
mov     dwArgs, eax
invoke wvsprintfA, ADDR szBuffer, ADDR szLevel, Offset dwArgs
pop     ebx
invoke DD_Draw_Text, hDC, ADDR szBuffer, eax, ADDR text_rect,\
        DT_CENTER or DT_VCENTER or DT_SINGLELINE, ebx


;============================
; Set up rect for Lines text
;============================
mov     text_rect.top, 256
mov     text_rect.left, 90
mov     text_rect.right, 162
mov     text_rect.bottom, 288


;============================
; Draw the Lines Text
;============================
RGB 255, 255, 0
push    eax
mov     eax, NumLines
mov     dwArgs, eax
invoke wvsprintfA, ADDR szBuffer, ADDR szLines, Offset dwArgs
pop     ebx
invoke DD_Draw_Text, hDC, ADDR szBuffer, eax, ADDR text_rect,\
        DT_CENTER or DT_VCENTER or DT_SINGLELINE, ebx


;========================
; Unselect the font
;========================
invoke DD_UnSelect_Font, hDC, hFont, Old_Obj


;========================
; Release the DC
;========================
```

```
        invoke DD_ReleaseDC, lpddsback, hDC

done:

        ;====================
        ; We completed
        ;====================
        return TRUE

err:

        ;====================
        ; We didn't make it
        ;====================
        return FALSE

Draw_Captions     ENDP
;################################################################
; END Draw_Captions
;################################################################
```

I have tried to keep it in the same form as the rest of what I've shown you. The code reads from a few module variables to get the current numbers to draw. It then makes a call to set the font how we want it. This isn't anything new, I hope. We then set our rectangle for the drawing and make the call. If you don't remember, wvsprintfA() is a function that is used for formatting a string buffer (almost exactly like sprintf()).

The other thing I am doing is setting the color we will use. I don't know about you, but I prefer to make things a little bit varied so that they stand out.

In short, this routine just calls on a few library routines and pieces things together as needed. As I mentioned before, programming is like one big jigsaw puzzle. It is just a matter of finding the right pieces and putting them together correctly. There is no one right way to do it, and that is why everybody creates different pictures. Make sense? Remember this fact; it helps when designing things.

Scoring and Levels

It is truly amazing how primitive I made this scoring and level system. The thing does about as much as the old Atari games, but hey, it is a start.

Inside the Line_Test() function, the code increments a variable that tests itself for a MAX condition. This is where the number of lines is counted. Once that MAX condition is exceeded, the number of lines gets reset and the level increased. Then, in our main code, another function we call is the Is_Game_Won() function. It is called to find out if they have gone over the maximum number of levels in the game. In our case, the MAX level is 10, but you can make it whatever you would like it to be.

The other function we added was one to keep track of the score. As expected, it is called Adjust_Score(), and it performs the same type of adjustment that we did for the levels. The only difference is that if the user exceeds the maximum score, we simply reset his score to the maximum amount. It's nothing fancy, but it works as it is supposed to, which is always a nice side effect. This function is called from the main module based on how many lines the user achieved in one swoop. So, the more lines he eliminates at once, the more points he would achieve.

When the user reaches the end of the game, our main code sets the state to GS_WON and simply restarts. It is in that section that we would perform credits and special winning sequences. I was lacking in both art and creativity when I coded it, however, so it just restarts the game.

Here are the Line_Test(), Adjust_Score(), and Is_Game_Won() functions. I'll let you sort through the main code yourself and see what alterations I made.

```
;##############################################################
; Line_Test Procedure
;##############################################################
Line_Test        proc


                ;=================================
                ; This function will test to see if they earned a
                ; line ... if so, it will eliminate that line
                ; and update our grid of blocks
                ;=================================


                ;=================================
                ; Local Variables
                ;=================================
                LOCAL   CurLine:        DWORD
                LOCAL   CurBlock:       DWORD


                ;=================================
                ; Start at the Base of the Grid
                ;=================================
```

```
mov     CurLine, 0


;======================================
; Loop through all possible Lines
;======================================
.while CurLine < (GRID_HEIGHT - 4)
        ;======================================
        ; Go to the base of the current line
        ;======================================
        mov     eax, CurLine
        mov     ecx, 13
        mul     ecx
        add     eax, BlockGrid


        ;======================================
        ; Loop through every block,
        ; testing to see if it is valid
        ;======================================
        mov     CurBlock, 0
        .while CurBlock < (GRID_WIDTH)
                ;========================
                ; Is this Block IN-Valid?
                ;========================
                mov     bl, BYTE PTR [eax]
                .if bl == 0
                        ;==================
                        ; Yes, so break
                        ;==================
                        .break

                .endif

                ;====================
                ; Next Block
                ;====================
                inc     eax


                ;====================
                ; Inc the counter
                ;====================
```

```
            inc     CurBlock

.endw

;==============================
; Did our inner loop go all
; of the way through??
;==============================
.if CurBlock == (GRID_WIDTH)

        ;=============================
        ; Yes. That means it was
        ; a valid line we just earned
        ;=============================


        ;=================================
        ; Calculate how much memory to move
        ; TOTAL - Amount_IN = TO_MOVE
        ;=================================
        mov     ebx, (GRID_WIDTH * (GRID_HEIGHT -5))
        mov     eax, CurLine
        mov     ecx, 13
        mul     ecx
        push    eax
        sub     ebx, eax


        ;============================
        ; Move the memory one line
        ; up to our current line
        ;============================
        pop     eax
        add     eax, BlockGrid
        mov     edx, eax
        add     edx, 13


        ;============================
        ; Move the memory down a notch
        ;============================
        invoke RtlMoveMemory, eax, edx, ebx
```

```
                        ;=============================
                        ; Jump down and return TRUE
                        ;=============================
                        jmp     done

            .endif

                        ;=============================
                        ; Increment our Line counter
                        ;=============================
                        inc     CurLine

        .endw

err:
        ;===================
        ; We didn't get one
        ;===================
        return FALSE

done:
        ;===================
        ; Play the sound
        ;===================
        invoke Play_Sound, Thud_ID, 0

        ;=========================
        ; Adjust their line count
        ;=========================
        inc     NumLines
        .if NumLines >= MAX_LINES
                mov     NumLines, 0
                inc     CurLevel
        .endif

        ;===================
        ; We earned a line
        ;===================
        return TRUE
```

```
Line_Test        ENDP
;################################################################
; END Line_Test
;################################################################


;################################################################
; Adjust_Score Procedure
;################################################################
Adjust_Score     proc     amount:DWORD


        ;================================================
        ; This function will adjust the score by the
        ; passed-in value if possible, adjusting the
        ; level if necessary
        ;================================================
        mov     eax, amount
        add     Score, eax
        .if Score > MAX_SCORE
                mov     Score, MAX_SCORE
        .endif

done:
        ;====================
        ; We earned a line
        ;====================
        return TRUE


Adjust_Score     ENDP
;################################################################
; END Adjust_Score
;################################################################


;################################################################
; Is_Game_Won Procedure
;################################################################
Is_Game_Won      proc
```

```
;==============================================
; This function will return TRUE if we have won
; the game and false otherwise
;==============================================

        .if CurLevel > MAX_LEVEL
                return TRUE
        .else
                return FALSE
        .endif

Is_Game_Won    ENDP
;##############################################################
; END Is_Game_Won
;##############################################################
```

Conclusion

Whoopie! We are finished with yet another section. So, have you been working on your different versions like I keep hounding you to? I really hope so, especially since we are going to get into the final topics in the next section, which is a little bit more advanced.

The next section will cover saving and loading, and we will utilize a new random-number-generation scheme. With what we completed in this section, the game is almost finished. What we do need, other than what we cover in the final section, is more polished artwork and some extra music and sound effects. Those are the kinds of things that really finish off a game. The important thing, though, is to be careful with what you choose. As programmers, we sometimes have views of what looks nice or sounds good even though the mainstream public (you know, the people actually playing your game) doesn't care an iota about it.

WIN32 ASM—PART 7

We are almost finished with SPACE-TRIS. The game has evolved remarkably in the last two sections, and we are getting to the point at which we can state it is completed. In fact, that is the goal we are aiming for in this last section.

To begin with, we will cover saving and loading the game out to disk. Then we will tackle writing a new random-number-generation scheme. Using a call to grab the current time, although completely functional, is a little antiquated. The saving and loading will be in a simple format, and the random-number generator will use a relatively noncomplex algorithm. They will help tidy off what has been a wonderful game for us to develop.

Once these things are complete, we can sit back and admire our work and the final product. Until then, I must crack the whip and send us back into the line of fire.

Storing Your Life

One of the most important things in a game is being able to save and load your position. In our game, we have a menu setup for doing just that. Remember the Game Files section on the main menu? Well, the menu underneath that option is where the user will save and load his game. Thus far, we have had no code at all in the handler, but we are about to change all of that.

First we will take a look at the code that will open a file and save or load the game based on what the user has selected. This is the snippet of code from the Game_Main() function inside SPACE_TRIS.asm.

```
.elseif GameState == GS_FILE
                ;===================================
                ; We are in the file menu state
                ;===================================
                invoke Process_File_Menu
```

```
;=================================
; What did they want to do
;=================================
.if eax == MENU_NOTHING
        ;=================================
        ; They didn't select anything yet,
        ; so don't do anything
        ;=================================

.elseif eax == MENU_ERROR
        ;=================================
        ; This is where error code would go
        ;=================================

.elseif eax == MENU_LOAD
        ;=================================
        ; They want to load the saved game
        ;=================================


        ;=================================
        ; Create the file to read from
        ;=================================
        invoke CreateFile, offset szSaveFile, \
                GENERIC_READ or GENERIC_WRITE, \
                FILE_SHARE_READ, NULL, OPEN_ALWAYS, \
                FILE_ATTRIBUTE_NORMAL,NULL
        mov     hFile, eax

        ;=================================
        ; Load the game off of disk
        ;=================================
        invoke Load_State, hFile
        .if eax == FALSE
                ;=================================
                ; Failed to load
                ;=================================
        .else
                ;=================================
                ; Play sound to show we loaded okay
                ;=================================
```

```
                            invoke Play_Sound, Loaded_ID, 0

              .endif

              ;═══════════════════════════════════════
              ; Close the handle to the file
              ;═══════════════════════════════════════
              invoke CloseHandle, hFile


              ;═══════════════════════════════════════
              ; Set the Game state to playing
              ;═══════════════════════════════════════
              mov      GameState, GS_PLAY

       .elseif eax == MENU_SAVE
              ;═══════════════════════════════════════
              ; They want to save their game
              ;═══════════════════════════════════════


              ;═══════════════════════════════════════
              ; Create the file to write to
              ;═══════════════════════════════════════
              invoke CreateFile, offset szSaveFile, \
                       GENERIC_READ or GENERIC_WRITE, \
                       FILE_SHARE_READ, NULL, OPEN_ALWAYS, \
                       FILE_ATTRIBUTE_NORMAL,NULL
              mov      hFile, eax


              ;═══════════════════════════════════════
              ; Save the game off to disk
              ;═══════════════════════════════════════
              invoke Save_State, hFile
              .if eax == FALSE
                      ;═══════════════════════════
                      ; Failed to save
                      ;═══════════════════════════
              .else
                      ;═══════════════════════════════════
                      ; Play sound to show we saved okay
                      ;═══════════════════════════════════
                      invoke Play_Sound, Saved_ID, 0
```

```
        .endif

        ;═══════════════════════════════════
        ; Close the handle to the file
        ;═══════════════════════════════════
        invoke CloseHandle, hFile


    .elseif eax == MENU_MAIN
        ;═══════════════════════════════════
        ; They want to return to main menu
        ;═══════════════════════════════════
        mov      GameState, GS_MENU

    .endif


.elseif GameState == GS_PLAY
```

Notice that the first thing we do—whether we want to save or load the file—is make a call to CreateFile(). This is the Win32 routine that will do the equivalent of fopen() in C. We give it the basic parameters, telling it we want to read and write to the file (although we will only use one). Then we make a call to save or load the game file off of disk.

For the time being, there is only one game file that is used. I am leaving it as an exercise for you to add the interface and capability for a user to select the file he wants to save the game into. The method currently used only allows one person to store his game and only one game at a time. If he tries to save another game, the file will be overwritten.

We then check for an error. If there is one, a block is left so you can fill in the error code you want to use. This can range from displaying a message box to throwing the user into an entirely new screen to deal with the problem. If the user succeeds, however, we play a sound to let him know that we loaded, or saved, the game. These sounds are loaded during game initialization.

After we've handled the result of the save or load, we can close the handle that Windows gave us when we cre-

NOTE

Before anybody says, "Hey Chris, you sound like a girl!" I want to let you know that these sounds were generated in a text-to-speech synthesis engine.

ated the file. Finally, we can set the state to playing if we are loading the game; that way, the user goes directly to his loaded game.

Now that we have the framework for the game loading and saving operations, we can take a look at the code that actually does all of the work for these two tasks. These are two routines in the Shapes.asm module. We place them in this module because the variables we need to access (the ones that track the game) are contained here. Browse through these two routines.

```
;###############################################################
; Save_State Procedure
;###############################################################
Save_State        proc      hFile:DWORD

        ;========================================================
        ; This function will save the current state of the game
        ; to the passed-in file handle. It returns true if
        ; successful and false otherwise.
        ;========================================================


        ;========================================================
        ; Write the user's score, the current level,
        ; and the number of lines out to disk
        ;========================================================
                ; The Score
                invoke WriteFile, hFile, ADDR Score, 4, ADDR numRW, NULL
                .if eax == 0
                        jmp     err
                .endif

                ; The current level
                invoke WriteFile, hFile, ADDR CurLevel, 4, ADDR numRW, NULL
                .if eax == 0
                        jmp     err
                .endif

                ; The number of lines
                invoke WriteFile, hFile, ADDR NumLines, 4, ADDR numRW, NULL
                .if eax == 0
                        jmp     err
                .endif
```

```
        ;====================
        ; Save out the current block grid
        ;====================
        invoke WriteFile, hFile, BlockGrid, (GRID_WIDTH * GRID_HEIGHT), \
                            ADDR numRW, NULL

        .if eax == 0
                jmp     err
        .endif


        ;====================
        ; We finished saving
        ;====================
done:
        return TRUE


err:
        return FALSE


Save_State      ENDP
;##############################################################
; END Save_State
;##############################################################


;##############################################################
; Load_State Procedure
;##############################################################
Load_State      proc    hFile:DWORD


            ;====================
            ; This function will load the current state of the game
            ; from the passed-in file handle. It returns true if
            ; successful and false otherwise.
            ;====================


            ;====================
            ; Load the user's score, the current level,
            ; and the number of lines off of disk
            ;====================
                ; The Score
                invoke ReadFile, hFile, ADDR Score, 4, ADDR numRW, NULL
                .if eax == 0
```

```
                    jmp     err
            .endif

            ; The current level
            invoke ReadFile, hFile, ADDR CurLevel, 4, ADDR numRW, NULL
            .if eax == 0
                    jmp     err
            .endif

            ; The number of lines
            invoke ReadFile, hFile, ADDR NumLines, 4, ADDR numRW, NULL
            .if eax == 0
                    jmp     err
            .endif

    ;=========================================
    ; Load in the current block grid
    ;=========================================
    invoke ReadFile, hFile, BlockGrid, (GRID_WIDTH * GRID_HEIGHT),\
                            ADDR numRW, NULL
    .if eax == 0
            jmp     err
    .endif

    ;=====================
    ; We finished saving
    ;=====================
done:
        return TRUE

err:
        return FALSE

Load_State      ENDP
;###############################################################################
; END Load_State
;###############################################################################
```

The basic premise of saving or loading a game is really well defined. We want to save every variable that contains the user's state information. In this case, these are the variables that contain the score, the number of lines the user has earned, and the current level he is on. In addition to this basic information, we want to save the entire grid so that we can re-create the user's current level when he loads it back in. Some programmers choose not to do so. The results of not saving the grid are the equivalent to starting at the beginning of a level in Super Mario Brothers as opposed to in the middle of one. There's nothing wrong with either method; I just wanted to point out the implications of not saving the grid. Some things not saved that you might also want to save are the current and next piece variables.

The call to actually write or read this information is nothing complex. We simply tell it that we want to work with the passed-in file handle, the address of the information to read/write, the number of bytes to read/write, the address of a variable to hold the actual amount read/written, and null to specify that we don't want any overlapped I/O. Make

> **NOTE**
>
> Notice the progression from variables that allow us to re-create the level to the finer points that allow us to re-create the exact state of the game. Always get the grasp before you work on the details.

sure you specify bytes and not DWORDs. Also notice that since the BlockGrid variable contains the address of the memory we allocated, we don't give the call the address of BlockGrid. Instead, we just pass the variable like normal. If we had done it in the way the other calls to the read/write file had been done, we would have specified a point to a pointer and achieved unpredictable results since we wouldn't have known what was at the memory address where our BlockGrid DWORD variable was allocated.

This is all you need to know to save and load files containing the game state information. As I previously said, you can add more game variables to get finer game preservation or fewer game variables to get a rougher preserved state. These are the type of things your game idea will dictate. Whether or not you want the user to be able to start in the middle of a level is normally determined by where the save points in your game are located. In the case of a puzzle game, the user normally can save at any time, whereas an adventure game typically only allows a save at the end of a level. It's your game, so you decide.

Come On, Lucky Number 7

One of the things I have wanted to change since I wrote it was the way our game obtains random numbers. Currently, we are making a call to get the time and then using that as the random number. The problem with this method is that it can become very predictable as the time cycles. I have been waiting to write a random-number generator until we were a little bit more accustomed to assembly language. Looking back, I could have probably introduced this sooner, but we are going to look at it now, and that's all that counts.

There are two functions that I decided to implement: Init_Random() and Random_Number(). The first initializes the random-number generator with the passed-in seed. The second function returns a random number. It's best to keep things simple. The two routines are in a module called Random.asm. Here are the two routines in that module.

```
;###############################################################
; Init_Random Procedure
;###############################################################
Init_Random      proc      seed:DWORD


                 ;=================================================
                 ; This function will seed the random-number generator
                 ;=================================================


                 ;=================================================
                 ; Store the seed they want to use
                 ;=================================================
                 mov     eax, seed
                 mov     RandomSeed, eax

done:
                 ;=================
                 ; We completed
                 ;=================
                 return TRUE

Init_Random      ENDP
;###############################################################
; END Init_Random
;###############################################################


;###############################################################
; Random_Number Procedure
;###############################################################
Random_Number    proc
```

```
;===================================
; This retrieves a random 32-bit number
;===================================


;===================================
; Grab the seed value we last used
;===================================
mov     eax, RandomSeed


;===================================
; Multiply by a constant and then adj
; the multiplier to the high 16 bits
;===================================
mov     edx, 1103515245
mul     edx
shl     edx, 16


;===================================
; Add a constant to the random number
; that is in eax and add with carry
; to our randomizing number in edx
;===================================
add     eax, 12345
adc     edx, 0ffffH


;===================================
; Store our new random number seed
;===================================
mov     RandomSeed, eax


;===================================
; Move high 16 bits of random num to
; the low 16 bits
;===================================
shr     eax, 16


;===================================
; Clear out everything but the upper
; 16 bits in our randomizing number
;===================================
```

```
        and     edx, 0ffff0000H

        ;=====================================
        ; OR the things together and we have
        ; our new random number
        ;=====================================
        or      eax, edx


        ;=====================
        ; We completed
        ;=====================
        ret

Random_Number   ENDP
;##############################################################################
; END Random_Number
;##############################################################################
```

The first routine does nothing but store the seed that is provided to initialize the random-number generator. This routine is called from the game-initialization function in the main module. We use a call to Get_Time() as the seed for the generator. Thus, we need to make sure the time is initialized before we initialize the random-number generator. The seed can be reset at any time during the game with another call to Init_Random(). Doing so will simply provide a new number to work with during the randomizing process.

The second routine is the one we really care about. It is a basic random-number-generation function. You can find these in numerous algorithm books, so I won't spend time covering why it does what it does. This routine, however, does expose some new instructions that we haven't yet seen: the bit shifting and add with carry instructions. You can find basic descriptions of what they do in the preceding comments.

That's all we needed to do to create a new random-number-generation method. So, anywhere we are currently using a call to Get_Time() to provide a random number, we replace it with a call to the new Random_Number() routine instead. There are only a couple of spots where I had to do this in our code. The first was in the Shapes.asm module when we generated a new shape.

Conclusion

That's it for SPACE-TRIS. The game is now complete (or at least as complete as I am going to make it). There are still numerous things you can do to the game. If it were destined to be a commercial product, you would want to polish off some of the artwork and provide some more sound effects. Since it isn't, I'd just focus on extending some of the game play, perhaps making levels more difficult as they advance or adding some unusual shapes. Special effects are always fun to write. Making them happen in real time is sometimes tricky and thus a perfect next step for the budding assembly language programmer. Go find an interesting algorithm and set to work implementing it in assembly. By now, you have the tools needed to make it happen.

Once you are ready, try to undertake the project of writing your own game. Granted, developing your own game from scratch is a big step for anybody, and in assembly, it is even bigger. But you have seen firsthand that it can be done. The hardest part is usually picking a game within your ability level. Most people would love to write the next Quake-killer, but it is more realistic for indie developers (especially those working solo) to focus on games that don't require as many resources. It is much better to finish an A-quality game than to say you almost made a AAA-type game.

Throughout this chapter, I have tried to illustrate the advantages of using assembly. I do realize that assembly will never be a truly mainstream programming language. I also realize that using assembly in large development houses is a fantasy (or a nightmare, depending on your skill). For the solo game developer, however, who writes games because he cares about games and because it is fun, I think assembly is a very realistic choice. After all, the typical reason for choosing to write games in the first place is because you love them. And the assembly language programming, if nothing else, is a labor of love. You will undergo ridicule, contempt, and even envy. But in the end, you are doing it for yourself and your own reasons.

The market is open and ready for those who are willing to take a chance and develop a game from start to finish. Sadly, programmers all too often start but never finish their game ideas. Do yourself a favor and see something through to completion. It doesn't matter if it takes years; you will thank yourself in the long run.

Good luck with your coding endeavors. I wish you nothing but the best in your search for greatness.

SECTION 4

Appendices

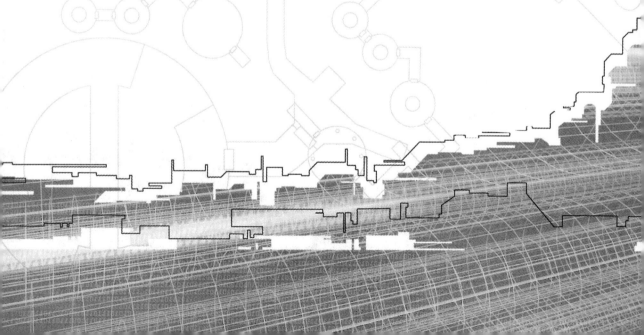

This section is filled with additional information that can also be useful! The appendices provide information using VisualStudio, C/C++ and STL primer, C++ keywords, resources on the Web, what can be found on the CD-ROM, and so on. Be sure to refer to this section to get help on the C/C++ programming and using the VisualStudio compiler. There is enough information in this section to get you out of those rough spots you may encounter from time to time. Finally, the resources listed in this section should prove very valuable as they provide you with links to information beds on the Internet that will aid you as you continue to grow and push the limits of game programming.

It has been a fun and exciting journey to this point! I hope you found the book useful and I wish you luck on all of your game programming ventures!

APPENDIX A

INTRODUCTION TO DEVSTUDIO

MASON McCUSKEY, SPIN STUDIOS,
WWW.SPIN-STUDIOS.COM

Note: This appendix originally appeared in the book Special Effects Game Programming *with DirectX 8.0 by Mason McCuskey, published by Premier Press. It's reprinted here slightly modified but in its entirety.*

"Godzilla. He is a good man . . . and he is a bad man."

—Unknown

This appendix is for all of you who haven't had that much experience using the Microsoft Development Studio (DevStudio, to its friends) to develop applications for Windows. In this appendix, you'll learn the basics of creating a project, adding source-code files, setting up library and include paths, and all the other tasks needed to create the sample programs for this book.

DevStudio is like Godzilla. It helps out with a lot of things, but in the blink of an eye, it can turn evil and cause you a lot of grief. On the good side, DevStudio comes packed with powerful features, all designed to make the life of the programmer easier. On the bad side, it also does a remarkably good job of hiding from you the details of compiling programs. If you've done C/C++ development somewhere else, you're probably familiar with make files. Make files are not at the forefront of DevStudio. They are present, but they take a back seat to DevStudio's GUI for configuring compiler and linker options. You more than likely will never edit a make file directly. Instead, you'll make changes to the way in which your source code compiles and links via myriad dialog boxes, property sheets, and drop-down lists. Like I said, it's a double-edged sword.

In this appendix, I'm going to teach you how to take the source-code files contained on the accompanying CD-ROM and create from them an executable.

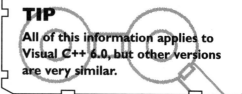

TIP

All of this information applies to Visual C++ 6.0, but other versions are very similar.

Creating a Project and Workspace

At its core, DevStudio operates on the ideas of projects and workspaces. The hierarchy looks like Figure A.1. A project contains a collection of source files and options, and a workspace contains one or more projects.

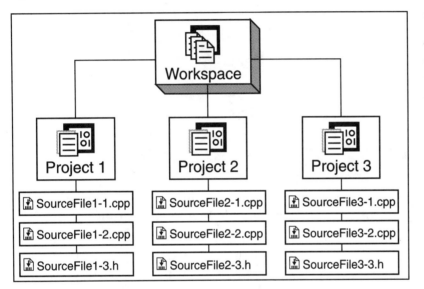

Figure A.1

A workspace is a collection of projects, and a project is a collection of source files

Most of your workspaces will contain only one project. Most programmers only put multiple projects into their workspaces if they're writing a set of DLLs or components that function together, and they need quick access to several different code collections simultaneously.

To write some new code in DevStudio, the first thing you'll want to do is create a workspace and project in which that new code will live. You do this by selecting the New command from the File drop-down menu. This presents you with a dialog box. Navigate to the Projects tab of this dialog box, and your screen will resemble Figure A.2.

To create a new project, you must first tell DevStudio what kind of application you want to create. There are many choices here, but you'll most likely want to use one of the following options:

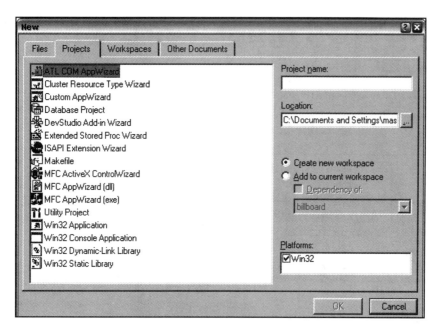

Figure A.2

The Projects tab of the New dialog box

- **Win32 Application.** This is by far the most common selection. This project type is used when you're creating a plain-old Windows application.

- **Win32 Console Application.** This project creates a console application. Console applications behave very similarly to old DOS programs. They're command-line based, they have a text window in which to do their work, and that's about it. They don't use dialog boxes, and they don't have a message pump. If you're creating a simple program that doesn't need a GUI, a console application is the way to go.

- **MFC Appwizard (exe).** This option is similar to Win32 Application, but it includes support for the Microsoft Foundation Classes (MFC). MFC is a set of classes and a framework designed to make it easy to create applications that conform to most of the user interface standards for Windows. For example, if you use MFC, you automatically gain the capability to use a multiple document interface (MDI) like Word, in which you can open multiple windows from within one "master" window. We don't use MFC in this book, but since this is a common choice for heavy-duty GUI applications (and even some games), I thought I'd mention it here.

Because Ch1p2_NormalWindow is a Windows program that doesn't use MFC, go ahead and select the Win32 Application project from the list. Also be sure to give your project a name (this is also the name of the EXE) and a location before you click OK.

When you click OK, a new dialog box comes up, asking you if you'd like to create an empty project, a simple Win32 application, or a typical "Hello World!" application (see Figure A.3).

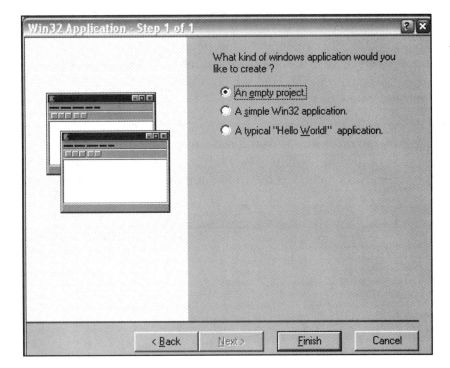

Figure A.3

After inputting a project name and clicking OK, you'll see this dialog box

These are shortcuts designed to make your life easier. For example, if you opt to create a simple Win32 application, DevStudio will give you a project and a source-code template that's already put together. If you select a "Hello World!" application, DevStudio will create a completely functional program. All you need to do is compile it; when you run the EXE you've compiled, a window containing the text "Hello World!" will appear on your screen.

That's all fine and dandy, but since we've already got source code and just need a project, go ahead and select "An empty project" and click Finish. Another dialog box will come up, summarizing the options you've selected. Click OK at this point, and DevStudio will generate your project and workspace!

Notice that out on your hard drive, you now have a DSP file and a DSW file for your project. The DSP file is the project file, and the DSW file is the workspace file. Both are human readable, so you can load them in a text editor, but you shouldn't modify them.

Adding Source-Code Files

Once you have a project and workspace created, you need to add some source code files to it. If you were creating new code from scratch, you'd again select New from the File drop-down menu, go to the Files tab, and click C++ Source File or C++ Header file to create a blank CPP or H file.

If you already have source-code files, however, you can add those directly to your project. Click the FileView tab on your left. You'll see a tree view with your workspace at the top and your project immediately beneath it. Right-click on your project, and you'll be presented with a context menu like the one shown in Figure A.4.

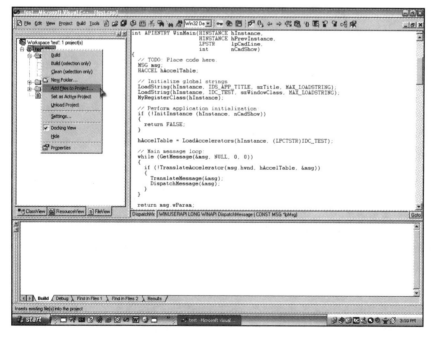

Figure A.4

Right-click on your project, and you'll be presented with this menu

Click Add Files to Project and then browse for the source-code files you want to add. (You can add multiple files at once by holding down Ctrl or Shift as you click their names).

For Ch1p2_NormalWindow, navigate to the folder containing the source code and add the one source-code file, Ch1p2_NormalWindow.cpp, to the project.

Now, if you expand the project node in your FileView tree, you'll see three folders underneath it: source-code files, header files, and resource files. Under source-code files, you should see your source file (see Figure A.5). Double-click it and you can edit it.

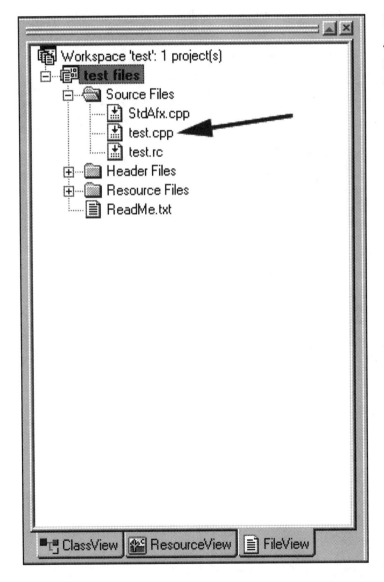

Figure A.5

After you insert a source-code file, it should appear in the FileView tree

Setting Compiler Options

Once all of your source-code files have been added, you can turn your attention to the task of setting the compiler options for your project.

There's roughly a dozen different ways to get to the Project Settings dialog box that contains all of your project options. I prefer to get there by right-clicking on the project in the FileView tree and selecting Settings from the context menu (see Figure A.6).

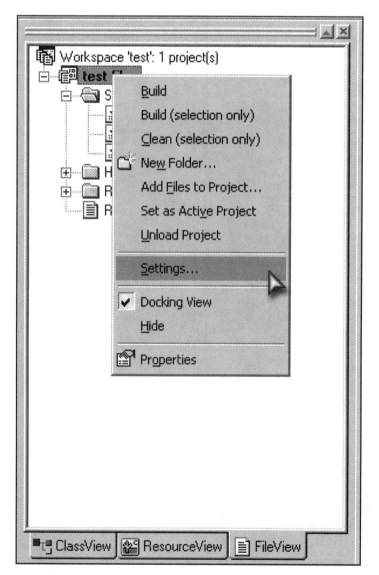

Figure A.6

To get to the project settings, right-click on the project in the FileView and select Settings

Figure A.7 shows the Project Settings dialog box.

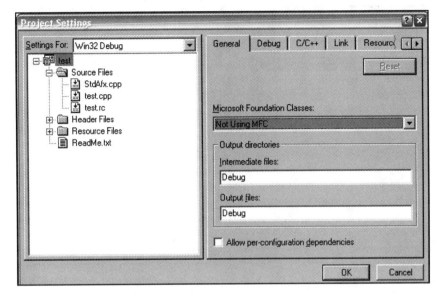

Figure A.7

The Project Settings dialog box

As you can see, on the left you have the same tree that's in your FileView. On the right are a bunch of controls to set the options. Running along the top are a whole slew of tabs for the various sections of controls.

DevStudio uses two different sets of project settings, one for debug and one for release. The idea here is that you'll probably want to compile things differently depending on whether it's just a quick build for you to test and debug things or it's a finished program that you intend to distribute to your customers (the game players!).

Most of the time, you'll be working with debug builds (that is, builds based on the debug set of project settings). Occasionally, as you're writing your program, you should create a release build to guarantee that your project settings are in sync and that certain compiler settings (optimization, lack of debug information, and so on) don't interfere with the behavior of your program. (They shouldn't, but every so often they do.)

You can change with which set of project settings you build by selecting Set Active Configuration from the Build drop-down menu. You'll be presented with the dialog box shown in Figure A.8. Select the settings you'd like to make active and then click OK. You can also do this from the toolbar.

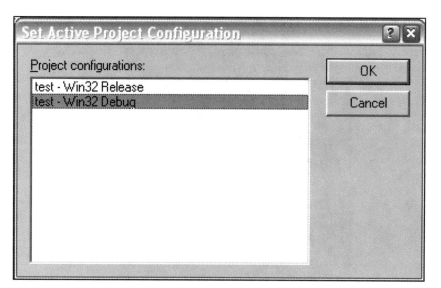

Figure A.8

This configuration dialog box appears when you select Set Active Configuration

I'm not going to cover every single option you can set. For most of the settings, the default values that DevStudio provided will work just fine. I will, however, draw your attention to the useful options or to the options you'll more than likely need to change.

TIP

You're not limited to just two sets of project settings. You can create additional sets of settings by selecting Configurations from the Build drop-down menu and then clicking the Add button. You usually won't need to do this, but I wanted to mention it in case you found yourself in a weird situation. For example, sometimes you'll want to build shareware with different options for registered and demo versions. You could set up something like that using four different sets of project settings: demo debug, demo release, registered debug, and registered release.

Setting the Warning Level

Usually the default warning level (Level 3) will work just fine, but occasionally you'll want to increase or (shame on you!) decrease the warning level of the C++ compiler so that you create the illusion that your code isn't broken. To do this, go to the C/C++ tab inside the Project Settings dialog box. Select General from the Category drop-down list, and your dialog box will change into something like Figure A.9.

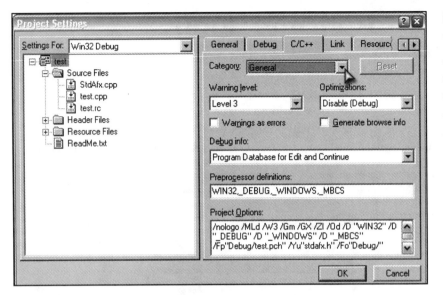

Figure A.9

*The Project
Settings dialog box
after selecting
General from the
Category drop-
down list*

Immediately below the Category drop-
down list is the drop-down for the warning level. Choose a new value (higher
numbers mean the compiler is more
strict) to set the warning level you want.

Setting the Optimization Level

> **TIP**
>
> It's usually a good idea to check the
> "Warnings as errors" check box here
> as well. Bad programmers ignore
> warnings and face the consequences of
> badly written code. Good program-
> mers solve the warnings that come up
> as if they were compiler errors.

Immediately next to the Warning level
drop-down list on the C/C++ tab of the Project Settings dialog box is another drop-
down list that controls the optimization level of the compiler. Here you can choose
to optimize for size (that is, make the EXE as small as possible even if it means the
code runs slower) or for speed (make things run fast even if it means a larger
EXE). Needless to say, most of the time you'll want to set this for speed.

You can also turn optimizations on or off individually. Select Optimizations from
the Category drop-down list, and you'll be able to enable or disable specific optimization techniques. This is extremely useful because, very rarely, a certain optimization feature might cause your program to crash or behave in strange ways.
(Visual C++ isn't perfect when it comes to this sort of thing.)

Turning on Runtime Type Identification (RTTI)

Some of the sample programs need RTTI turned on to operate correctly. (If you're not sure what RTTI is, see Appendix B.) To turn RTTI on, navigate to the C/C++ tab in the Project Settings dialog box. Select C++ Language from the Category drop-down list, and your dialog box will change into something like Figure A.10. Make sure the Enable Run-Time Type Identification (RTTI) check box is checked.

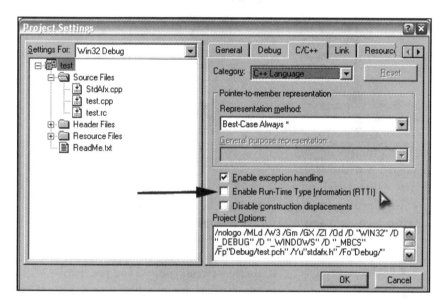

Figure A.10

Enabling RTTI is as easy as checking this check box

CAUTION

If you try to use RTTI and the active set of project settings doesn't have RTTI enabled, the compiler will warn you. If you choose to ignore its warning, your program will more than likely crash when it comes to the first chunk of code that uses RTTI.

Library and Include Search Paths

One of the most vital things to understand in DevStudio is how it handles search paths for source-code files, include files, and libraries. For each of the major categories (source-code files, include files, library files, and so on), there are actually two completely separate settings. There's a setting that's stored in the specific project you're working on and a global setting that applies to all projects.

The per-project settings take precedence over the global settings. That is, DevStudio only looks at the global settings if it can't find what it's looking for using the per-project settings.

Here's an example. Let's say we've added a #include "MyHeaderFile.h" directive to our source code. DevStudio now needs to find this include file. To do this, it first looks in the same directory as the source file it's compiling. If it can't find MyHeaderFile.h there, it looks in the folders you've specified inside the per-project include file search path (in the order you specified them). If it still can't find it, it looks in the global search path for include files (again, in the order you specified). If it can't find it even then, it gives up and the compiler spits out an error message.

Here's how to set up the two different search paths.

Per-Project Search Paths

Per-project search paths are set up through the Project Settings dialog box. You can set up per-project search paths for include files and for library files.

To set up the include file search path, go to the C/C++ tab and select Preprocessor from the Category drop-down list (see Figure A.11).

Near the bottom is an edit box labeled "Additional include directories." Insert your include directories here, separated by commas.

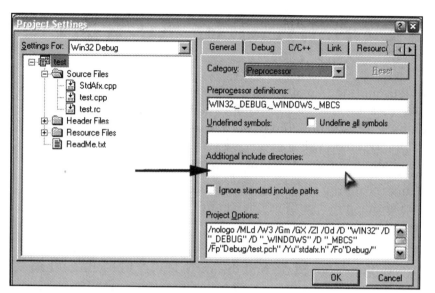

Figure A.11

Setting the per-project search paths

To set up the library search path, go to the Link tab and select Input from the Category drop-down list. At the bottom of the dialog box will be an edit box labeled "Additional library path." Enter your search paths here, separated by commas. (Again, you can use relative paths.)

TIP

You can enter relative paths in this box. That is, if you always want this particular project to search a folder one up from its current location, you can enter "..\" into the search path box.

Global Search Paths

You set up global search paths in a totally different location. Instead of going to the Project Settings dialog box, select Options from the Tools drop-down menu. Click the Directories tab, and your dialog box will look like the one in Figure A.12.

You can alter the global search path by adding or deleting entries from the list box or by clicking the up and down arrows at the top of the list, which move the current selection up or down the list. Change the search path by selecting a different entry from the combo box labeled "Show directories for."

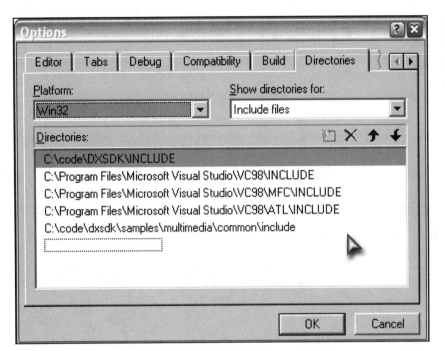

Figure A.12

The Directories tab of the Options dialog box

CAUTION

It's very important that you add the include and library paths for the DirectX API. Also, it's vital that these directories take precedence over the other include and library files. (That is, they should be at the very top of the list.) The reason is that DevStudio ships with header and library files for an older version of DirectX. If you try to compile DirectX 8 applications without adding the DirectX 8 header and library paths, everything will appear to be normal, but you'll run into all sorts of weird compiler errors that appear to be errors in the DirectX code itself. Watch out for this.

Linking in the DirectX Libraries

Now that you know all about project options and search paths, it's time to integrate DirectX into your project.

The way you do this is by adding some libraries to your linker settings. Table A.1 shows the DirectX libraries you usually need.

Table A.1 DirectX Libraries

Library Name	Description
D3D8.lib	This library contains the source code to interface with the Direct3D component of DirectX. If you're doing Direct3D programming, you need to link with this.
D3DX8.lib	This library contains the D3DX helper functions. You need to link with this if you use any D3DX items.
DDraw.lib	This library contains the DirectDraw interfaces. You won't usually need this for 3-D stuff, but if your code is written for older versions of DirectX and uses DirectDraw, you'll need to link with this.
DInput8.lib	This library contains the source code to interface with the DirectInput component of DirectX. If you're using DirectInput, you need to link with this.
Dsound.lib	This library contains the source code to interface with the DirectSound component of DirectX. If you're using DirectSound, you need to link with this.
Dxerr8.lib	This library contains source code to help you use and translate DirectX error codes (for example, the function DXGetErrorString8).
D3dxof.lib	This library contains routines used to load and save X files. If you're using anything from the dxfile.h header, you need to link with this.
Dxguid.lib	This library contains the globally unique identifiers (GUIDs) for the DirectX components. If you're using any part of DirectX, you need to link with this.

Microsoft provides other DirectX libraries, but you'll use the ones in the preceding table most often. For the sample programs in this book, you need to link with `dinput8.lib`, `d3dx8dt.lib`, `d3d8.lib`, `d3dxof.lib`, `winmm.lib`, and `dxguid.lib`.

Building and Running Programs

Finally! You've set up all your options and are now ready to build and run your programs.

The easiest way to do this is to select Build <yourproject> from the Build dropdown menu. (Don't worry, you'll learn the hotkey for Build, F7, very quickly.)

As DevStudio builds, it outputs warnings and errors to your output window at the bottom of your screen. (If this window isn't visible, select Output from the View menu to make it appear.) You can double-click on any error or warning line, and DevStudio will take you to the appropriate source-code file and line number.

Once you get your program built without any errors, you can choose to run it two different ways. First, you can launch it from DevStudio by selecting Execute <projname> from the Build drop-down menu. This is the equivalent to double-clicking the EXE from within Explorer. Your program launches as a completely separate process, and it doesn't get wired up to the DevStudio debugger.

The second way to launch the program is by selecting Go from the Start Debug submenu, which is under the Build drop-down menu. This is the most common way to run the program, so remember the hotkey (F5). If you run your program this way, you hook it up to the DevStudio debugger so that you can break into it at any time.

Debugging

When it comes to integrated debugging, DevStudio really shines. This section will explain how to accomplish the most basic debugging tasks once you've selected Go from the Start Debug menu. For a complete feature breakdown, refer to the DevStudio online help.

Breakpoints

The easiest way to set a breakpoint is to simply right-click the line of the source-code file at which you'd like to break. Select Insert/Remove breakpoint from the context menu that appears. Lines that contain a breakpoint have a little red circle out in their margin.

You can quickly delete all of your breakpoints by selecting Breakpoints from the Edit drop-down menu and clicking the Remove All button on the dialog box that appears. You can also set up conditional or data-driven breakpoints from within this dialog box.

Stepping Through Code

There are four main ways you can step through code:

- **Step over.** This is the most common way to step. Stepping over means that you execute the line you're on and then pause again. You'll quickly learn the hotkey for stepping over, F10.

- **Step into.** This is slightly different than stepping over. If the current line contains a call to a function, you can use step into to follow the code down into that function (whereas step over just completes the entire function call in one step).

- **Step out.** Use this command to get out of function calls. Step out runs until you return from the function you're in. Use it to quickly get out of function calls once you've determined that the bug you're looking for isn't in the function you stepped into.

- **Run to cursor.** Use this command to skip over large segments of code. When you select this command, the debugger will execute the code until it arrives at the line the cursor is at. It will then stop. In a way, this is like a shortcut for setting a breakpoint, running, and then removing that breakpoint immediately after you hit it.

Watches

The DevStudio integrated debugger allows you to watch the values of variables change as your program executes. There are two main windows in DevStudio that provide access to most of the watch functionality. You'll find these two windows in the bottom section of your screen when you're running a program in debug mode (see Figure A.13).

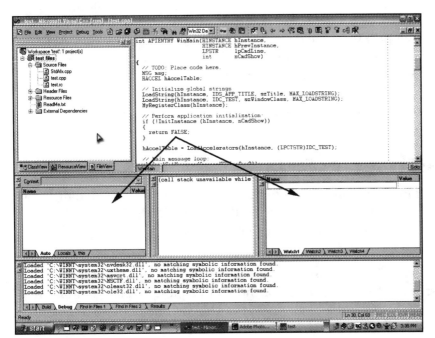

Figure A.13

The watch windows appear when running a program in the debugger

One watch window allows you to enter any variable names you like. Click on an empty list entry, type the variable name you're interested in, and DevStudio will show you its value. As you step through your program, DevStudio will update this value. It will turn red when it changes.

The second watch window automatically gives you a view of the variables you're probably most interested in. This includes variables used by the line of code that's currently executing as well as this pointers and function return values.

TIP

You can also use the memory viewer to view the contents of raw memory locations. This is most useful when you need to look at a huge chunk of data. Because DevStudio often clips huge strings in the watch window, to see the entire string, you'll need to manually copy its address into the memory viewer. You access the memory viewer by selecting **Memory** from the **Debug Windows** submenu under the **View** drop-down menu.

Debug Output

One of the most common ways to debug software is to print out diagnostic messages that let you know what your program is doing when it's impossible (or just really irritating) to break into a debugger and start stepping through the code. Microsoft provides support for these diagnostic messages through a Win32 API function called `OutputDebugString`. This function takes a single parameter—a string to send to the debugger. Any messages you push out using `OutputDebugString` end up inside your debug output, in your IDE. This allows you to keep tabs on your program without having to trace through code.

Accessing Help

I've saved the most important discussion for last! DevStudio help is something that all programmers use very frequently. This is partly because DevStudio itself is huge, and it takes a long time to get familiar with all of its features.

Thankfully, there are no office assistants in DevStudio. To get help, select Index from the Help pull-down menu. Also, DevStudio has a comprehensive context-sensitive help system, so keep an eye out for those little question mark buttons in the corners of dialog boxes and tool windows. Clicking on one of those will often-times take you exactly where you need to go.

Conclusion: DevStudio Wrap-Up

This appendix was a crash course. I didn't cover everything, but I covered the key points you need to know to get the most out of this book and DevStudio in general.

The best way to learn DevStudio is simply to use it. The IDE is the lifeblood of a programmer, and you'll quickly pick up the shortcuts and tricks by simply using it frequently. Have fun!

APPENDIX B

C/C++ PRIMER AND STL

MASON MCCUSKEY,
SPIN STUDIOS,
WWW.SPIN-STUDIOS.COM

When I was a kid, I loved flying kites. I grew up in suburban Denver, which was great, but it wasn't exactly the kite-flying utopia like Chicago or someplace that would be windier. Frequently, getting a kite off the ground required my brother's help—he'd stand a couple dozen yards away from me, holding the kite. On my signal, he would throw the kite up into the air and I would run as fast as I could away from him. In this way, we could generate just enough wind for the kite to rise and catch an actual breeze.

> **NOTE**
>
> This appendix originally appeared in the book *Special Effects Game Programming with DirectX 8.0*, by Mason McCuskey, published by Premier Press. It's reprinted here slightly modified, but in its entirety.

That's the purpose of this appendix. To continue this (cheesy?) analogy, the goal of this appendix is to give you just enough knowledge to get you off the ground and flying high enough to catch the actual breeze. This appendix isn't going to cover everything in C++ and Standard Template Library (STL); it's not really even going to scratch the surface. But, if you're not very experienced with these technologies, it's my hope that this appendix will give you what you need to know to understand the rest of the chapters in this book.

> **CAUTION**
>
> I'm going to move fast, and won't cover each topic in complete detail. If you're completely new to a topic, you should do yourself a favor and devote more time to it than I have. There are several great C++ / STL Web sites (listed on your CD-ROM) that you can cruise to and learn some of the finer points.

Selected C++ Topics

As I wrote the sample code for this book, I used what many programmers refer to as a "sane subset" of C++. C++ is a feature-rich language, and every C++ feature is useful in certain situations. However, the code for this book does not venture into all of those situations. It does hit some of them, though, so I'm going to devote a little time to each of these features now. I'll progress from what I consider the easier stuff to the more complex features.

Let's start with inline functions.

Inline Functions

Inline functions are especially valuable to game programmers, because oftentimes they can speed up the execution of a program. Carefully inlining can give you some good performance gains (at the expense of executable size, which usually isn't an issue with the size of today's drives).

When you use the C++ keyword inline on a certain function, you're telling the compiler that function doesn't necessarily have to be a function. If it saves time, the code can be embedded directly into the "caller," without the need for a function call.

So essentially, an inline function is C++'s answer to C's #define. Inline functions behave exactly like regular functions, with one key difference: When the compiler comes across an inlined function, it doesn't create a machine-language subroutine. Instead, it just places the machine language code for the function directly "inline" with the rest of the code, just as if you had used #define to make a macro.

In this way, you get the best of both worlds—you get the speed of having the function's code directly inline. No time is wasted putting variables onto the call stack before the function's called, and popping them off when the function's done.

Also, since you're not just doing string substitutions like with #define, you get the benefit of having the compiler treat your macro as an actual function. To see why this is handy, take a look at the following code (pardon me if you've seen this one):

```
#define BoundsCheck(a) if (a < -5) a = 2; if (a > 10) a = 10;
void Foo(void) {
  int a = 0;
  BoundsCheck(++a);
  printf("%d", a);
}
```

What does that function print? It looks like it should print 1, right? Bzzt, wrong! It prints at least 2, sometimes 3. The reason: The compiler is doing simple string substitution on your #define so you actually wind up with machine language code that corresponds to this:

```
void Foo(void) {
  int a = 0;
  if (++a < -5) ++a = 2;
```

```
if (++a > 10) ++a = 10;
printf("%d", a);
}
```

Now it's easy to spot the gotcha—you didn't actually mean for a to be incremented twice—you wanted it to be incremented just once, and then passed to a BoundsCheck "function." Here's equivalent C++ code that works correctly:

```
inline void BoundsCheck(int &a) {
 if (a < -2) a = 2;
 if (a > 10) a = 10;
}
void Foo(void) {
 int a = 0;
 BoundsCheck(++a);
 printf("%d", a);
}
```

That code prints 1, which, if you'll forgive the pun, is more in line with what you'd expect it to do.

Namespaces

One of the problems with traditional C is that of naming. Frequently in C, you'll run into the problem of "name clashing"—essentially, you'll run out of good unique names for global functions. Even worse, let's say you're writing a C API, in other words, you're writing some code and then handing a library (lib file) to another C developer. Let's say that C developer has written a global function called Process, and that you've also embedded a global function called Process into your API library. That's a problem—the name of your API function is clashing with the name of the other developer's function. Unfortunately, the only remedy for this is for one of you to change your function name, which is no fun.

In C++, however, you can avoid this problem by using namespaces. Essentially, a namespace is a "folder" for your function and variable names. Just as you can group files into hierarchies of folders, in C++ you can group functions and variables into hierarchies of namespaces.

For example, let's say you're writing a 3-D game, and you'd like all of the classes for your 3-D engine grouped together. You'd use a namespace, and write code something like this:

```
namespace MyCool3DEngine {
```

```
void Initialize();
void Terminate();
void Draw();
// other variables, functions and
  classes for 3D engine go here.
};
```

Now, all of the stuff associated with your 3-D engine is contained nice and neat in a namespace called MyCool3DEngine.

You have two options for accessing the stuff you've put inside a namespace. First, you can use the scope resolution operator, ::, like so:

```
void RunGame(void) {
 // initialize 3D engine
 MyCool3DEngine::Initialize();
 // etc.
}
```

> **TIP**
>
> **You may not realize it, but you've already been dealing with namespaces regularly. Classes, structures, enums, and several other things you're already familiar with exist within namespaces. For example, if you have a static method** Foo, **of class** A, **you know you can't access** Foo **from outside class** A **without specifying** A::Foo.
>
> **The keywords** class, struct, **and** enum **do things in addition to creating a namespace. The** namespace **keyword simply creates a namespace, nothing more.**

In the example above, we use the scope resolution operator to get to the Initialize function contained in the MyCool3DEngine namespace.

Alternatively, you can specify a using namespace line, like so:

```
using namespace MyCool3DEngine;
void RunGame(void) {
 // initialize 3D engine
 Initialize();
 // etc.
}
```

This works similar to how a search path works for files. The using namespace line tells the compiler that if it can't find a function, it should look for it within the specified namespace. In the previous example, if the compiler doesn't find immediately a function called Initialize, it looks in the namespace MyCool3DEngine.

The using namespace feature is handy, not only because it saves you some keystrokes, but also because if the name of the namespace changes, you only have to adjust the code in one place (that is, you only have to change the using namespace line).

You can also "alias" a namespace. Aliasing allows you to change the name of a namespace, which can be handy if you're dealing with code that you can't change (i.e., code from other developers or companies). For example, if a company's code is irritating you

because it's named its namespace something huge like Official3DGraphicsRenderingAPIVersionOne, you can switch that to something easier to type (say, GFXRenderingAPI) by writing code like this:

```
namespace GFXRenderingAPI = Official3DGraphicsRenderingAPIVersionOne;
```

You can also nest namespaces. Think of the scope resolution operator, ::, as the equivalent to the backslash in the file system (it's not quite as versatile, but it's a good analogy for right now). For example, let's say you have namespace A embedded in namespace B, like so:

```
namespace A {
 namespace B {
  void Foo(void);
 }
}
```

You could get to Foo by writing:

```
A::B::Foo();
```

So, that's a namespace—a simple C++ feature that really adds a lot to the organization of your code. Give it a try sometime—it's handy!

Dynamic Memory Allocation the C++ Way

I'm painting with broad strokes here, but essentially, programmers have two options for memory allocation: dynamic and static. A program can allocate different amounts of dynamic memory each time it runs; however, it always uses the same amount of static memory.

When you declare a variable on the stack, that's a static allocation. Here's an example:

```
char str[256];
```

Every time this piece of code runs, you get 256 chars. There's no way to change how much is allocated, short of cracking open the source code, changing that 256 number to a different value, and then recompiling.

If you don't know for sure how much memory you'll need, static allocation becomes irritating. You have two choices: brace for the worst case, and statically allocate the maximum number of objects that you'll support (knowing that you may only use 3 of those 256 chars), or allocate the memory dynamically.

A Quick Recap of How to Dynamically Allocate Memory in C

If you're an experienced C programmer, you're probably good friends with the C standard library functions malloc and free. C programmers use these two functions extensively to perform dynamic memory allocation—that is, to have their programs allocate various amounts of memory as they run. For example, you might write something like this:

```
int iNumberOfCharsNeeded = CalculateNumCharsNeeded();
char *str = (char *)malloc(iNumberOfCharsNeeded);
```

Using malloc, we can allocate just the right amount of memory that we need. That's the C way to do it—malloc and free.

How Not to Dynamically Allocate Memory in C++

However, because you're now a C++ programmer, you need to break the malloc and free habit. malloc and free are C library calls, and as such, they have no clue about

C++. So, based on that piece of information, see if you can spot the bug in the following code:

```
class MyClass
{
public:
 MyClass() { m_Number = 10; }
private:
 int m_Number;
};
void main(void)
{
 MyClass *newClass = (MyClass *)malloc(sizeof(MyClass));
 printf("%d", newClass->m_Number);
 free(newClass);
}
```

Looks pretty innocent, right? Careful—contrary to what you'd expect, this program does not print out 10. In fact, there's no telling *what* it will print. The bug is that malloc, being an old-school C function, doesn't know about constructors. Sure, it allocates enough memory to hold a MyClass object, but it doesn't actually call the MyClass constructor. So, m_Number never gets initialized to 10.

Proper Dynamic Memory Allocation in C++

So, what we need is a way to say, "Hey, Mr. Compiler, I'm not just allocating memory here, I'm actually making a new object, so you need to call its constructor." The way we do this is with the new keyword. Here's the same code, only this time the use of new has vanquished the bug:

```
void main(void)
{
 MyClass *newClass = new MyClass;
 printf("%d", newClass->m_Number);
 delete newClass;
}
```

The first thing you should notice is that we've replaced the malloc call with new. That creates the object—notice also there's no longer a need to cast the return value from new. Not only does new properly call the constructor for MyClass, it also hands you back the correct type of pointer, so there's no more messy casts.

So, that's half the mystery. But we also need to free the object properly—we must ensure that the destructor (if any) for the object is called. To do this, we use the `delete` keyword. The `delete` keyword works just like `free`, only it also makes sure the object's destructor gets called.

Dynamic Memory Allocation for Arrays in C++

Now that you've got the basics, consider this: let's say we wanted to create five `MyClass` objects. That situation is a bit trickier, so, if you'll forgive my second bad pun in this appendix, we need to learn some more "new" stuff.

This time I'll give you the code up front:

```
void main(void)
{
 MyClass *newClass = new MyClass[5];
 for (int q=0; q < 5; q++) {
  printf("%d", newClass[q].m_Number);
 }
 delete[] newClass;
}
```

I've changed a couple of things here. First, notice the [5] at the end of the `new` line. That tells the C++ compiler that we're creating five objects, and that we'd like the constructors to be called for each of those five objects. Correspondingly, the brackets at the end of the `delete` keyword tell the compiler that it needs to call the destructors for all the objects in the array (we don't have to specify the size of the array when we call `delete[]`—the compiler remembers how many we allocated in the first place).

Note also how we get to the individual objects inside that array, just as if `newClass` were an array of `chars` or `ints`. All we have to do is put the index we want (in this example, the variable q) inside brackets.

Pause for a moment here and make sure you understand all of these concepts. Dynamic versus

CAUTION

You need to be very careful and ensure that your news and deletes are in sync. That is, make sure you use `delete` to free single objects and `delete[]` to delete object arrays. Otherwise, you'll get strange memory errors and probably access violations. Forgetting to put the brackets on the end of `delete` when killing an array of objects is one of the most common mistakes I've seen beginning C++ programmers make.

static memory allocation is a vital concept that you need to know inside and out in order to follow the examples in this book.

Polymorphism and Pure Virtual Functions

When most people think of C++, this is the topic in the forefront of their minds. As you know, C++ allows you to create classes, which are like structs but with functions, and the ability to make things private. This is the first thing most C++ programmers learn.

The second thing is that these classes can be arranged in a hierarchy, and you can leverage this hierarchy inside your programs to address things in a "generic" manner. For example, say you're writing a game about animals, and you have three classes: cat, dog, and fish. Each animal needs to eat, so you write an eat method for each class. Using a feature of C++ called polymorphism, you can treat the cat, dog, and fish classes as a generic "animal." You can tell that "animal" to eat, and C++ will take care of calling the appropriate function based on the type of object.

This is called polymorphism, one of the three key principles of object-oriented programming (the other two key principles are data abstraction and inheritance). Polymorphism is a noun, meaning "the ability to change into different forms." Essentially, that's what C++ classes can do. If you set up the situation correctly, they can change into different things without you ever knowing.

Inheritance Versus Aggregation (Is-A Versus Has-A)

Every C++ class can be derived from no classes (no inheritance), one class (single inheritance) or from many classes (multiple inheritance). To make one class "inherit" another, put the inherited class on the declaration line for the new class. For example, to make class Y inherit class X, write the following:

```
class X { /* whatever */ };
class Y : public X { /* whatever */ };
```

That tells the compiler that class Y inherits class X *publicly,* which means that the public methods and members of class X are public in class Y. C++ supports other types of inheritance, but public inheritance is the most common.

In the previous example, C++ programmers say that class Y is derived from class X. In other words, class Y derives some of its functionality (methods and members) from class X.

Now, applying that to our cat, dog, and fish example: We know that cats, dogs, and fish are all animals. So, we might want to create a class hierarchy that reflects that:

```
class CAnimal { /* whatever */ };
class CFish : public CAnimal { /* whatever */ };
class CCat : public CAnimal { /* whatever */ };
class CDog : public CAnimal { /* whatever */ };
```

That establishes a class hierarchy. The compiler now knows that fish, dog, and cat classes derive from the animal class (in other words, a fish is an animal, a dog is an animal, and a cat is an animal. For this reason, object-oriented programmers also refer to inheritance as an "is-a relationship"—a fish is-a animal, a dog is-a animal, and a cat is-a animal.

So, that's an "is-a" relationship. There's also a "has-a" relationship. For example, we know that all three types of animals, be they fish, cats, or dogs, have hearts, so we can say that an animal "has-a" heart:

```
class CHeart { /* whatever */ };
class CAnimal {
protected:
 CHeart m_Heart;
};
class CFish : public CAnimal { /* whatever */ };
class CCat : public CAnimal { /* whatever */ };
class CDog : public CAnimal { /* whatever */ };
```

In this code, we've created a CHeart class and added a member to CAnimal called m_Heart. The cat, fish, and dog classes now automatically get an m_Heart object, because they derive from CAnimal. A derived class inherits the members and methods of its base (or parent) class.

TIP

Note also the protected: **keyword. That tells the compiler that** m_Heart **is in protected storage, which means it's only visible to methods of** CAnimal, **and methods of classes derived from** CAnimal. **Protected storage is somewhere between** public **(where everything can see the member) and** private **(where only that class can see the member).**

This is called a "has-a" relationship—an animal has-a heart. Some programmers also refer to "has-a" relationships as "aggregation."

> **TIP**
>
> It can sometimes be tricky to decide between inheritance and aggregation. I've found that using "is-a" and "has-a" in a sentence about the two things in question often helps me decide whether I should make a new base class and derive from it, or if I should just give a variable to an existing class. If the "is-a" sentence makes sense, that means inheritance is the way to go; if the "has-a" sentence makes more sense that means I should use aggregation.
>
> For example, "a fish is-a heart" sounds silly, but "a fish has-a heart" is reasonable, so aggregation wins. As a counterexample, we know the animal/fish relationship is inheritance, because "a fish has-a animal" sounds ridiculous, but "a fish is-a animal" makes perfect sense.
>
> Keep this in mind as you're designing your class hierarchies.

Virtual Functions

Now that we've got hearts for our fish, dog, and cat class, we might decide to give them a little more life. We know that all animals breathe, so we can easily add a Breathe function to our code:

```
class CHeart { /* whatever */ };
class CAnimal {
protected:
 void Breathe(void);
 CHeart m_Heart;
};
class CFish : public CAnimal { /* whatever */ };
class CCat : public CAnimal { /* whatever */ };
class CDog : public CAnimal { /* whatever */ };
```

This works, but the problem is that some animals breathe differently than others. Fish breathe water; cats and dogs prefer air. Having one Breathe function for all three animal types would force us to perform a switch inside the function, and do different things depending on what kind of animal we are:

```
void CAnimal::Breathe(void)
{
 if (ThisAnimalIsADog() || ThisAnimalIsACat()) { BreatheAir(); }
```

```
  if (ThisAnimalIsAFish()) { BreatheWater(); }
}
```

There are several painful points in the previous code. For starters, how do we implement the `ThisAnimalIsADog`, `ThisAnimalIsACat`, and `ThisAnimalIsAFish` functions? Additionally, if we add new animals, we have to go back to this function and add if statements. Even worse, if none of the if statements are true, the animal doesn't breathe at all!

Polymorphism was designed to solve just this type of problem. C++ contains a feature called "virtual functions." Virtual functions are functions, which are defined for both the base and derived classes. When you call a virtual function of a class, the compiler looks at the type of class, and automatically calls the correct function.

Let's see how it looks:

```
class CHeart { /* whatever */ };
class CAnimal {
protected:
 virtual void Breathe(void) { BreatheAir(); }
 CHeart m_Heart;
};
class CFish : public CAnimal
{
protected:
 void Breate(void) { BreatheWater(); }
};
class CCat : public CAnimal { /* whatever */ };
class CDog : public CAnimal { /* whatever */ };
```

Here we've introduced a couple of things. First, we've put the `virtual` keyword before the `Breathe` prototype in `CAnimal`. This tells the compiler that `Breathe` is a virtual function. Second, we've added a `Breathe` function to `CFish`.

Now let's say we have some code as follows:

```
void Foo(void)
{
 CFish fish;
 CDog dog;

 dog.Breathe(); // calls CAnimal's Breathe
 fish.Breathe(); // calls CFish's Breathe
}
```

That's polymorphism! When we say dog.Breathe, the compiler knows that dog is of type CDog. Since CDog doesn't define a Breathe function, we end up inside CAnimal's Breathe function. Conversely, when we call fish.Breathe, the compiler notices that we've created a Breathe function just for CFish, and calls that instead of CAnimal's breathe.

Pure Virtuals

At this point our code is starting to become much more object-oriented, but there's still something that should be bothering you—not all animals breathe air. For example, if we added a CEel class, we'd have to make sure to add a Breathe function for it, otherwise, we'd incorrectly be calling BreatheAir for eels!

Right now we're saying to the compiler "unless I tell you otherwise, assume that all animals breathe air." It might be better if we could say "don't make any assumptions; I will provide a Breathe function for all derived classes." That way, we could be sure that each animal is breathing correctly.

This is where the notion of a "pure virtual function" comes into play. A pure virtual function (or pure virtual, to its friends), is a function that only exists for derived classes. It has no base class implementation.

You declare one by putting " = 0" after the function declaration in your class. Here's how we'd use one in our code:

```
class CHeart { /* whatever */ };
class CAnimal {
protected:
 virtual void Breathe(void) = 0;
 CHeart m_Heart;
};
class CFish : public CAnimal
{
protected:
 void Breate(void) { BreatheWater(); }
};
class CCat : public CAnimal
{
protected:
 void Breate(void) { BreatheAir(); }
};
class CDog : public CAnimal
```

```
{
protected:
 void Breate(void) { BreatheAir(); }
};
```

Essentially, the only thing we've done here is put an "= 0" in place of CAnimal::Breathe. That tells the compiler that our Breathe function doesn't exist in our base class, but must exist in every class that derives from our base (we get compile errors if it doesn't).

One important caveat to creating pure virtual functions: Any class with a pure virtual cannot be instantiated. That is, with the pure virtual inside CAnimal, you can't ever create a variable of type CAnimal. This makes sense, because what would the compiler do if you created a variable of type CAnimal, and then called Breathe on it? It would have no idea what kind of animal it would be dealing with, so it wouldn't know what Breathe function to call.

You can still create references and pointers to that base class, however, and in reality, that's where the power of polymorphism really shines, because it allows you to do things like this:

```
CAnimal *CreateRandomAnimal(void)
{
 CAnimal *theAnimal = NULL;
 switch(rand() % 3) {
  case 0: theAnimal = new CCat(); break;
  case 1: theAnimal = new CDog(); break;
  case 2: theAnimal = new CFish(); break;
 }
 return(theAnimal);
}
void Foo(void)
{
 CAnimal *pAnimal = CreateRandomAnimal();
 pAnimal->Breathe(); // automatically calls the correct function!
 delete pAnimal;
}
```

In the code example above, we've got a function that creates a random type of animal. It returns that random type of animal in a pointer to its base class, CAnimal. (Remember, you can't create CAnimals, but you can create pointers to CAnimals).

When Foo tells the new CAnimal pointer to breathe, the compiler automatically knows which function to call.

Think about how cool that is for a moment. Foo doesn't know or even care what type of animal it's dealing with—it just says Breathe and the compiler does the rest. In fact, we could add 500 different types of animals, and rewrite CreateRandomAnimal so that it randomly picked one of those 500 animals, and so long as all 500 animals derived from CAnimal and all 500 implemented a Breathe function, Foo would work without us changing one line of its code. That's the power of polymorphism!

Virtual Destructors

I want to cover one last, very important topic on polymorphism before moving on. We need to talk about what happens when base and derived classes are destroyed.

Each C++ class has a constructor and destructor, which tell the compiler what to do when that object is created or destroyed. Normally, if the constructor allocates any memory for the class, the destructor frees that memory. For example, let's say we wanted to create a couple of animal parts dynamically:

```
class CHeart { /* whatever */ };
class CGills { /* whatever (for the fish) */ };
class CAnimal {
public:
 CAnimal() { m_pHeart = new CHeart; }
 ~CAnimal() { delete m_pHeart; }
protected:
 virtual void Breathe(void) = 0;
 CHeart *m_pHeart;
};
class CFish : public CAnimal
{
public:
 CFish() { m_pGills = new CGills; }
 ~CFish() { delete m_pGills; }
protected:
 void Breate(void) { BreatheWater(); }
 CGills *m_pGills;
};
class CCat : public CAnimal
{
protected:
```

```
 void Breate(void) { BreatheAir(); }
};
class CDog : public CAnimal
{
protected:
 void Breate(void) { BreatheAir(); }
};
```

Here you can see I've added a couple of things. First, I changed CAnimal so that it dynamically allocates a heart when it constructs, and deletes that heart when it's destroyed. I've also added a similar mechanism to Cfish—the fish object now creates some gills when it's constructed, and destroys those gills when it's destroyed.

Unfortunately, there's a bug in that code, and it's a sneaky one. Let's say I have the same Foo function:

```
void Foo(void)
{
 CAnimal *pAnimal = CreateRandomAnimal();
 pAnimal->Breathe(); // automatically calls the correct function!
 delete pAnimal;
}
```

The problem here is that Foo only knows it's dealing with a CAnimal. So, when it says delete pAnimal, the CAnimal destructor is called, but not the destructor for any derived objects. So, if CreateRandomAnimal happens to create a fish, we'll create a heart and some gills, but when we call delete, we will end up calling only the CAnimal destructor, and wind up deleting the heart but not the gills. This is bad because we leak memory, to say nothing of the spookiness in having some disembodied gills floating around somewhere.

To fix this problem, we need to make the CAnimal destructor virtual. When we add the virtual keyword to the beginning of the destructor line, we solve our problem.

The virtual keyword has a slightly different meaning when applied to destructors. Ordinarily, virtual means "Hey, Mr. Compiler, check the derived classes for this function, and if you find it down there, don't call this one, call the derived one instead." But, when applied to the destructor, the virtual keyword

CAUTION

For the reason you've just seen, you should probably play it safe and make every destructor you create virtual. You may never derive another class from a particular class, but if you do and you don't have a virtual destructor, you run the risk of creating really hard-to-spot memory leaks.

says "Hey, Mr. Compiler, you need to call the destructor for the derived classes, *as well as* the destructor for this object." C++ does things this way because if both the base class and the derived class allocate memory, they'll both need to be called.

Polymorphism Wrap-Up

So, those are the details of polymorphism that you need in order to understand the code in this book. What I've just spoken about is by no means a complete rundown on the subject. Many books have been written on how to use polymorphism to create better-designed programs, and you should definitely check them out if you want to become a better C++ programmer.

Exception Handling

The next topic I want to glance at is exception handling, and I'll start by asking a question: How would you characterize the "robustness" of the programs you've written before? In other words, do they handle errors gracefully? Do they recover from abrupt end of files or unexpected data and issue a sensible error message, or do they simply go down in flames?

Writing a robust program has traditionally been a pain, but a C++ feature called exception handling can help make it easy. To learn why, let's first start with an example.

Life Before Exception Handling

Say someone asks you to write a function that reads a file into memory. You gladly oblige them, and hammer out a first revision that looks something like this:

```
void ReadFileIntoMem(char *filename, char **pMemory)
{
 int handle = open(filename, O_RDONLY | O_BINARY);
 int len = filelength(handle);
 (*pMemory) = new char[len+1];
 read(handle, *pMemory, len);
 close(handle);
}
```

Pretty easy to write, but not exactly robust. What happens if there's not enough memory, and new returns NULL? Crash! What happens if the file name isn't found? What happens if there's a read error? I could go on, but I hope you see my point. Virtually no error checking is done on this code.

So, let's say you notice that and decide to make a robust `ReadFileIntoMem` function. You add some code to check for common errors, like so:

```
bool ReadFileIntoMem(char *filename, char **pMemory)
{
 int handle = open(filename, O_RDONLY | O_BINARY);
 if (handle == -1) return(false);
 int len = filelength(handle);
 if (len == -1) { close(handle); return(false); }
 (*pMemory) = new char[len+1];
 if (*pMemory == NULL) { close(handle); return(false); }
 if (read(handle, *pMemory, len) != len) {
  close(handle); return(false);
 }
 close(handle);
 return(true);
}
```

Now we're a little more robust. The function will detect most errors and recover gracefully by returning false, which lets the calling function know that something went horribly wrong.

The code that does this works great, but it's now a lot harder to follow than our first, non-robust version of the function. The error handling logic is essentially interwoven with the core logic, and it can be difficult to see at a glance what the function's doing. Also, we still haven't caught all of the errors. For example, if `filename` is `NULL` coming in, we'll crash.

This painful error-checking problem is a classic irritation of C programming that C++'s exception handling feature was designed to solve.

The Basics of Exception Handling

Exception handling in C++ works by using three main constructs:

- Try blocks. These are blocks of code that begin with the statement "try {" and end with "}". You put code that might bomb inside a try block, effectively saying to the compiler, "try this."

- Catch blocks. These are blocks of code that start with "catch", followed by a variable declaration, and end with "}". These come immediately after each try block, and tell the compiler what to do if something goes wrong.

- Throw statements. When something goes wrong, you "throw" the error by using the throw keyword. Program flow jumps immediately to the appropriate catch block. You can throw anything you want—strings, ints, even C++ objects.

Here's a simple example that illustrates all three constructs:

```
try {
 // do something risky
 throw("An error has occurred!");
}
catch(const char *e) {
 printf("%s", e);
}
```

First, notice the try block. We've wrapped the risky code inside a try block, and we've immediately followed that try block with a catch block (catch blocks must always come right after try blocks). Inside the try block, we're throwing a string, which is really a const char pointer.

That catch line may look sort of strange. We're actually declaring a variable e of type const char. You can think of e as similar to a parameter of a function. It exists only within the catch block, and it's passed by value, not by reference. The compiler automatically fills in e with whatever error (of type const char) the throw statement threw. So this example code simply prints out the error string using printf.

Here's the cool thing about exception handling—you can throw from within a function and catch outside of that function. For example, the following code is completely legit:

```
void Foo(void)
{
 throw("Error in function foo!");
}
void main(void)
{
 try {
  Foo();
 }
 catch(const char *e) {
  printf("%s", e);
 }
}
```

Pretty cool, isn't it? When Foo throws, program execution jumps *up the stack* to the nearest catch statement. That is the core of the power of exceptions. Frequently an error will occur in some low-level function, and you won't have enough knowledge of what's actually going on to correctly handle the error. In C, your only recourse has been to communicate that something happened, usually through a return value, and hope that whoever called you is paying attention to what you're returning.

Another thing to keep in mind: Really low-level stuff will also throw an exception. For example, if you access memory that you shouldn't, an exception will be thrown. You can catch this exception and attempt to pull up from the nosedive you're program is in. Most standard C++ APIs, including the STL, will also throw exceptions. Also, when an exception is thrown, any objects you've statically allocated are destroyed appropriately (that is, the stack is "unwound" correctly, so you don't get memory leaks).

Catching Different Types and Catching Everything

You're not limited to just catching one type of exception. Here's an example that catches both strings and integers:

```
void Foo(void)
{
 if (rand() % 2) throw("Error in function foo!");
 else throw(5);
}
void main(void)
{
 try {
  Foo();
 }
 catch(const char *strError) {
  printf("Caught string: %s", strError);
 }
 catch(int iError) {
  printf("Caught integer: %d", iError);
 }
}
```

I've modified Foo so that it randomly throws a string or an integer. To accommodate this, I've also added a new catch handler that catches integers instead of strings.

TIP

The type you are catching doesn't necessarily need to match exactly the type you're throwing. For example, if you throw an object of class Derived, and class Derived is derived from class Base, a catch(Base &e) handler will catch the Derived class you threw. Once you're inside the catch block, you can choose to use Run-Time Type Identification (RTTI, explained in a few pages) to determine what kind of thing you caught, and act appropriately.

Also, the order you specify the catch statements in matters. Say you have a catch block for both Base and Derived objects. Be careful: If the Base catch comes before the Derived catch, any Derived objects you throw will end up in the Base catch, because it came first. Example:

```
class Base { /* yada */ };
class Derived : public Base { /* yada */ };
void main(void)
{
 try {
  throw(Derived());
 }
 catch(Base &e) {
  // Derived is caught here...
 }
 catch(Derived &e) {
  // even though you probably want it caught here.
 }
}
```

For this reason, it's always a good idea make your first catch blocks very specific, and put broader catch statements (like base classes) later:

You can also add a special catch statement, which many programmers call a catch all, that will catch anything for which you haven't specifically written a catch handler. You create a catch all by putting an ellipsis (three dots) inside the parentheses of the catch statement, like so:

```
void Foo(void)
{
 switch(rand() % 3) {
```

```
  case 0: throw("Error in function foo!");
  case 1: throw(5);
  case 2: throw(5.08f);
 }
}
void main(void)
{
 try {
  Foo();
 }
 catch(const char *e) {
  printf("Caught string: %s", e);
 }
 catch(int e) {
  printf("Caught integer: %d", e);
 }
 catch(...) {
  printf("I caught something, but I have no idea what it is.");
 }
}
```

In this example, Foo now throws strings, ints, or floats. The string and int throws end up in the string and int handler, but since we haven't defined a handler for floats, the float throw ends up in the catch-all handler.

TIP

You can't declare a variable for your catch all handler. After all, what type would it be?

Nested Try Blocks and Re-Throwing Exceptions

Yep, you can nest try blocks just like you can nest any other block of code. Here's an example:

```
void main(void)
{
 try {
  Foo();
  try {
   throw("Another Error Occurred");
  }
```

```
   catch(const char *e) {
    printf("An error occurred after Foo: %s", e);
   }
  }
  catch(const char *e) {
   printf("Caught string: %s", e);
  }
  catch(int e) {
   printf("Caught integer: %d", e);
  }
  catch(...) {
   printf("I caught something, but I have no idea what it is.");
  }
 }
```

In this example, the very first catch handler catches the "Another Error Occurred" error. You can nest try/catch blocks as deep as you'd like.

You can also re-throw an exception, if you catch something and you have no idea what to do with it. Here's an example of that:

> **TIP**
>
> The typical rule is to catch an error as close as possible to where it was thrown. You should catch errors as soon as you know enough about what's going on to properly handle them.

```
void main(void)
{
 try {
  Foo();
  try {
   throw("Another Error Occurred");
  }
  catch(const char *e) {
   // our error is caught once here
   printf("An error occurred, and I have no idea what to do"
     " about it, so I'm re-throwing.");
   throw;
  }
 }
 catch(const char *e) {
  // our error is caught again here
  printf("Caught string: %s", e);
```

```
}
catch(int e) {
 printf("Caught integer: %d", e);
}
catch(...) {
 printf("I caught something, but I have no idea what it is.");
}
}
```

In that example, I changed the inner-most catch handler, and made it re-throw the error. The error is caught by the innermost handler, which prints a message saying it doesn't know what to do with it, and then re-throws. The next handler up then catches the error. This is extremely nifty, because it allows you to log errors and then hand them off without actually doing anything about them.

> **TIP**
>
> By the way, when an exception is thrown, the C++ compiler takes care of calling the destructors of any objects that need to be destructed because you're moving up in scope. For example, if you have an object inside Foo, and you throw, the compiler will call the object's destructor, ensuring that memory is cleaned up proper-ly as you exit the function.

The Do's and Don'ts of Using Exceptions

As you now know, exceptions can be a powerful tool. However, just like any tool, exceptions are not appropriate in all situations. One of the most common errors I see beginning C++ programmers make is to sprinkle exceptions everywhere in their code. They throw at the slightest hint of something gone wrong, and often don't write catch handlers as close to the error as possible. Ironically, this leads to code that's very difficult to follow and debug.

So, here are a few bullet points on the do's and don'ts of using exceptions:

- **Don't use exceptions as a replacement for errors.** An error is an alternate flow of logic; an exception is truly something out of the ordinary. For exam-ple, if you prompt users for a password to begin play at a certain level of your game, and they enter the incorrect password, that's an error. Your program takes an alternate path of execution, probably displaying an error like "hey, your password's wrong!" and allowing them to enter it again. However, if you run out of memory while trying to validate their password, that's an excep-tion, because it's something you wouldn't normally expect to happen.

- **Do use exceptions to separate error logic from core logic.** Isolate your error-handling code in a catch block (or many catch blocks), so that you end up with the exceptional cases separated from the normal cases.

- **Don't use exceptions where a normal switch statement or other program feature would suffice.** Again, you should use exceptions only to handle truly bizarre events in your code. The normal flow of logic through your program should be exception-free.

- **Don't just drop a library that uses exceptions into a program that doesn't.** If you must, surround the library interface with a set of wrapper classes that catch the exceptions and convert them into whatever non-exception error handling system you have (return values, global variables, whatever).

- **Don't convert existing, already robust code to use exceptions.** Also, as a corollary to the last item—it's very tedious and time consuming to take a robust program that doesn't use exceptions, and change it so it does. If your program's working correctly and robustly already, don't change it.

- **Do use a class hierarchy for exceptions.** By this, I mean, create a base class called CException or something, and derive from it different exception classes —COutOfMemoryException, CArrayOutOfBoundsException, etc. Use RTTI (discussed later) to figure out what you've caught, or, create a virtual function that returns the class name of the exception as a string.

- **Don't worry about using exceptions in small programs.** If you're writing a one-page command-line utility program, exceptions are probably more trouble than what they're worth. Just because you have a great tool for making code robust doesn't mean that all of your code needs to be robust—oftentimes it's better to concentrate on the game itself at the expense of the internal tools. Just make sure that what you're releasing to your end users, the players, is robust!

Exception Handling Wrap-Up

Believe it or not, there are many exception-handling topics that I didn't cover here. Before you go charging off and using exceptions in your next 3-D engine, you should spend more time learning about the fine points of their usage. For example: What happens if you throw an exception inside a constructor? What happens if you're creating an array of objects, and midway through the construction of the objects, you throw? How many array objects are valid? Can you write a handler for exceptions that no one catches?

Don't start using exceptions heavily without first being able to answer those questions. Exceptions are new, unlike anything we've seen in C, and we need to move carefully to ensure we're using them correctly.

TIP

STL has several built-in exception classes that you may find useful. Check out your STL documentation for details.

C++ Style Casting

You're probably intimately familiar with casting—you know, saying to the compiler, "Yes, I know it's an integer, but pretend it's a char, OK?" You've probably seen code like this:

```
int i = 5;
char c = (char)(i);
```

Essentially, what you're doing here is "casting" the value (i) to a char. It's supposed to be an int, but by doing a cast you're saying "stuff this into a char and don't complain!"

Also, you've probably seen pointer casts, like what you have to do when you use malloc:

```
char *str = (char *)malloc(50);
```

You need the (char *) cast in there because malloc returns a void *, and the compiler doesn't want to automatically convert void *'s into char *'s.

So, that's how you do it in C, and C++ still allows you to do this form of casting. But, there are several ugly things about this form of casting:

- **It isn't something for which you can easily search.** Say you've got a chunk of code, and you want to know every place where that code is casting. How do you do that? You can't just search for parentheses, because they're used everywhere. If your search tool doesn't support wildcards in the search statements, you're basically out of luck, and even if it does, it'll errantly find prototypes of functions that take one argument: A cast like (char *) looks the same as part of a C function prototype, void foo(char *);

- **It doesn't differentiate between dangerous casts and innocent casts.** Say you've got a pointer to class D, which derives from class B. Casting your pointer to (B *) is safe, because we know B is a base class of D. However, casting your (D *) pointer to, say, (char *), isn't nearly as safe—in that situation, you're playing directly with bytes of memory, and that's risky. In C, you accomplish both safe and risky casts the same way.

C++ style casting was designed to solve these two main problems. C++ style casts are obvious, and they differentiate between safe and unsafe casts.

There are four new cast keywords in C++. Table B.1 summarizes them.

Table B.1 New C++ Casts

Cast Keyword	Description
reinterpret_cast	Use this cast to do anything. You can use it to convert void pointers to floats, convert chars into pointers, and do all sorts of other risky stuff.
static_cast	Use this cast to do "safe" casting, for example, to convert a derived class pointer into a base class pointer (called "upcasting"). You can also use it to perform implicit type conversions (stuff the compiler would have done anyway, like converting an int to a float if you're adding it to another float). You can also use static_cast to convert a void pointer into something more useful.
	The compiler won't let you use a static_cast for anything that's really dangerous. To program the safest possible cast, always use static_cast; don't use reinterpret_cast until the compiler says that you must.
dynamic_cast	Use this to perform dynamic downcasts (converting from a base class pointer into a derived class pointer). In other words, you can use dynamic_cast to ask "Hey Mr. Compiler, does this base pointer really point to a derived object?"
	If it does, the compiler will give you back a pointer to that derived object. If it doesn't, the compiler will give you a NULL pointer back.
	This cast is a part of doing run-time type identification, which we'll talk about a little later.
const_cast	Use this to add or remove "const-ness" from something. For example, if you have a const class and need to convert it to non-const, you can use this. You can also use it to temporarily make something const.
	You can also use const_cast to add or remove volatility from something. If you've got a volatile object, and you need it not to be, use const_cast. Or, if you need something volatile, const_cast is the tool for the job.

To use the casts, you first type the keyword for the cast you want to use. Put the thing you want to cast to inside < and > symbols immediately after the cast keyword. Then, put the stuff you want to cast from inside parentheses immediately after the >. Here's an example:

```
int i = 50;
char *pMemory =
  reinterpret_cast<char *>(&i);
```

That code is functionally equivalent to the old-school:

```
int i = 50;
char *pMemory = (char *)(&i);
```

As you can see, using C++ casts, it's possible to easily search for all "dangerous" casts. Just search for reinterpret_cast, a C++ keyword.

Here's a short example showing the new C++ casts in the wild:

> ## CAUTION
>
> Be careful using dynamic_casts with references. When you dynamic_cast a pointer, and the compiler can't safely determine that your cast is legal, it returns NULL. But, if you're dynamic_casting a reference, the compiler can't simply return NULL, because references can't ever be NULL.
>
> So, it throws! Yep, you read that right—the compiler will actually throw an exception, of type bad_cast. If you don't have a catch-all handler or a handler specifically for bad_casts, you're probably going down in flames. So, be careful any time you dynamic_cast a reference, and make sure you've got a catch block in case things go wrong.

```
class CMyClass : public CMyBaseClass { /* whatever */ };
void foo(const CMyClass *myClass, CMyBaseClass *myBaseClass)
{
 // use static cast to convert myclass into my base class
 CMyBaseClass *pStaticCastedClass =
  static_cast<CMyBaseClass *>(myClass);

 // use dynamic cast to see if a base class pointer really
 // points to a derived class
 CMyClass *pDynamicCastedClass =
  dynamic_cast<CMyClass *>(myBaseClass);
 if (pDynamicCastedClass) {
  printf("hey, myBaseClass really does point to a CMyClass.");
 }
 else {
  printf("nope, myBaseClass doesn't really point to a CMyClass.");
 }
 // use const cast to add or remove constness
```

```
CMyClass *pNotConstClass = const_cast<CMyClass *>(myClass);

// use reinterpret cast to do dangerous stuff
char *pClassMemory = reinterpret_cast<char *>(myClass);
}
```

Run-Time Type Identification (RTTI)

Now that you've gotten a grip on C++ casting, we can talk about another C++ feature—run-time type identification, or RTTI.

As its name implies, RTTI is a C++ feature that allows you to determine what type an object is. We saw a little of this in the previous section, where we learned that we can use dynamic_cast to effectively ask the compiler if something is of a given type. Technically, dynamic_cast is part of RTTI.

RTTI isn't just about dynamic_cast, however. There's another equally important keyword—typeid. The typeid keyword works very similar to how sizeof works—it's not really a function, but you use it as if it were. The sizeof "function" returns the size of whatever you gave it, in bytes. The typeid "function" gives you an object called type_info that contains type information about what you gave it.

Specifically, here's what type_info contains:

```
class type_info {
public:
  virtual ~type_info();
  int operator==(const type_info& rhs)
  const;
  int operator!=(const type_info& rhs) const;
  int before(const type_info& rhs) const;
  const char* name() const;
  const char* raw_name() const;
private:
  /* you can't see this! */
};
```

> **CAUTION**
>
> The compiler throws an exception if you pass NULL into typeid. The exception is of type bad_typeid. So, make sure you've got a bad_typeid catch block anywhere you could potentially be passing NULL into typeid.

As you can see, this type_info class consists of three functions and two overloaded operators. Let's look at each in detail.

type_info::before

The before method isn't terribly useful. You use it to determine if one type ID should be sorted before another. For example, if you have classes X and Y, you could use the before function to determine if X should come before Y:

```
if (typeid(X).before(typeid(Y))) { /* X comes before Y! */ }
else { /* Y comes before X! */ }
```

Like I said, not the most useful thing in the world, but it's handy in certain situations.

type_info::name

This method is much more useful. It returns the name of the thing you pass it:

```
class MyClass { /* yada */ };
void main(void)
{
 MyClass x;
 printf("x is a %s.", typeid(x).name());
}
```

> **TIP**
>
> Don't use the name you get back from this function to control your program logic. That is, don't use it in if statements, like if (strcmp(type-id(MyClass).name(), "MyClass")). A better way to do that is to use the overloaded operators that you'll learn about momentarily.

That code will print "x is a MyClass." I'm sure you can find myriad uses for this: For example, you can save the name of the class that generates your saved game files *inside* the save file itself, so that you'll always know what class to use to load it.

type_info::raw_name

This method is very similar to the name method, with one key difference—raw_name returns the decorated name, which isn't human readable. The decorated name has at signs—@—and weird letters all over it, because it's the name the compiler refers to the type as internally. Nonetheless, this name may be useful in situations where you need to compare things.

Overloaded Operators of *type_info*

The type_info class contains overloads for the == and != operators. These overloads allow you to compare the types of two objects directly, without having to do string comparisons on their names (or raw names).

For example:

```
class MyClass { /* yada */ };
class MyOtherClass { /* yada */ };
void main(void)
{
 MyClass x;
 MyOtherClass y;

 if (typeid(y) == typeid(MyOtherClass)) {
  printf("So far, so good...");
 }
 if (typeid(x) != typeid(MyClass)) {
  printf("Something has gone horribly, horribly wrong.");
 }
 if (typeid(MyClass) == typeid(MyOtherClass)) {
  printf("Something is still horribly, horribly wrong.");
 }
 printf("x is a %s.", typeid(x).name());
}
```

> **TIP**
>
> Keep in mind that `dynamic_cast` **can tell us the same thing however,** `dynamic_cast` **can be slightly slower than** `typeid`, **so only use** `dynamic_cast` **when you want a pointer to the object, and use** `typeid` **when you want to see if an object is equal to something.**

Here you can see that we're doing some comparisons to see whether certain variables are of certain types.

RTTI Wrap-Up

Pretend this sentence contains the standard disclaimer about how you really should not use RTTI in your own projects until you know more about it. Here's some other questions you can research on your own:

- What does `typeid` give you if you pass it a template class?
- What does `typeid` give you if you pass it a `void *` that actually points to a base class?
- Does `typeid(5) == typeid(int)`? Does `typeid(5) == typeid(float)`?

Templates

C++ supports a powerful feature, called templates, which can really help you out in certain situations. So, here's how they work.

Template Functions

Let's say you're a C programmer who's just spent the last two months coming up with the perfect function to swap two integers:

```
void swap(int *a, int *b)
{
 int temp;
 temp = *a;
 *a = *b;
 *b = temp;
}
```

Now, let's say you've just recently learned about C++ references, so you've rewritten your swap function to be even more glorious:

```
void swap(int &a, int &b)
{
 int temp;
 temp = a;
 a = b;
 b = temp;
}
```

Pretty nifty. This code is easy to read, and is reasonably optimized. You've got yourself a great tool for swapping integers.

But what about swapping floats? Arrgh! Now you have to create another function, to handle floats. You know that C++ will let you overload the function name so long as the parameters are different, so you write an overload for swap that takes floats:

```
void swap(float &a, float &b)
{
 float temp;
 temp = a;
 a = b;
 b = temp;
}
```

At this point you should be concerned, because you've used copy/paste inside your IDE. Any time you copy and paste code, you should get worried, because you're creating two identical functions. If you find a bug in the int version of swap, you'll have to go and make the exact same patch to the float version, and that wastes time (to say nothing of the headaches that come if you forget to update the other function—if you've done a lot of copy paste, you can also waste a lot of time chasing your tail, solving the same bug over and over again for different data types).

This is what C++'s template feature was designed to solve. Templates allow you to write code that operates on things of any data type—ints, floats, classes, structs, whatever. You simply tell the compiler what string you'd like to substitute for the variable type, write your algorithm, and the compiler takes care of "putting in" the correct types. In other words, you create the "template" for the code, and the compiler uses this template, along with a certain data type, to create the actual code.

It's easier to see in code than explain in words, so here's a version of swap that will work for *all* objects:

```
template<class T> void swap(T &a, T &b)
{
 T temp;
 temp = a;
 a = b;
 b = temp;
}
```

We start out with the keyword `template`, which tells the compiler we're about to define a template function. Next, we put `class T` inside a tag, which tells the compiler, "Any time you see a `T`, you should replace it with whatever type is needed." Next, we write our function, using `T` in place of int or float. `T` is effectively a placeholder for a variable type.

Now, when we call this function, the compiler automatically plugs in the correct types. For example, say we call the function like this:

```
int x=5, y=10;
swap(x, y);
```

The compiler will automatically instantiate (make) a version of swap that works for ints. If we say:

```
double x=5.0, y=10.0;
swap(x, y);
```

Then it'll make a version that works for doubles. Pretty cool, isn't it? We can even have it generate a version for a class:

```
CMyClass x, y;
swap(x,y);
```

That will work, provided we've overloaded the = operator for CMyClass.

So, that's what you *can* do. Here's what doesn't work:

```
CMyClass x; int y;
swap(x,y);
```

In this situation, we're trying to use two different data types. As it's written now, the swap template won't accept two different types. However, we could rewrite it so it does:

```
template<class T1, class T2> void swap(T1 &a, T2 &b)
{
  T1 temp;
  temp = a;
  a = b;
  b = temp;
}
```

It gets a little trickier to make that version of swap work—you'd need to have operator = overloads, or you'd have to rely on implicit conversions (i.e., the compiler automatically knowing how to set an int equal to a float). I wrote that example mainly to show that you could specify as many different template parameters (type substitutions) as you want.

Template Classes

You've now learned how to create template functions. C++ also lets you create template classes. Here's what that looks like:

```
template <class T>
class MyTemplateClass
{
public:
```

TIP

The compiler only generates the code that you need. It doesn't automatically generate every possible version of swap or other template functions. When you add code that uses a float version of swap, it creates the float version.

Because of this, it's possible that a template function may compile and link without any errors at first, but if you go back and use it for a different type, you may get errors. For example, if we didn't have an operator = overload for a class we were using swap with, we'd get an error *inside* swap complaining about us trying to set one class equal to another.

The Visual C++ compiler (and most other compilers) will also give you the line of code that caused the compiler to generate the errant template function, but it still sometimes takes a bit of thinking to deduce exactly what broke and why.

```
/* use T for the types of some variables here */
T m_MyData;
};
```

You declare a template class basically the same way you declare a template function: You type the keyword template followed by the different template arguments. You then declare the template class just as you would any other class.

To instantiate a template class, you must give the compiler all the argument types the template requires. You do this as follows:

```
MyTemplateClass<int> m_IntClass;
m_IntClass.m_MyData = 5; // m_MyData is of type int
MyTemplateClass<float> m_FloatClass;
m_FloatClass.m_MyData = 5.0f; // m_MyData is of type float
```

In that example, we're instantiating a version of `MyTemplateClass` that uses ints. See how the template argument just hangs off the class name?

If our class template used more than one type of class, we'd need to separate the data types by commas:

```
template <class T1, class T2>
class MyDualTemplateClass
{
public:
 /* use T for the types of some variables here */
 T1 m_MyData;
 T2 m_MyData2;
};
void Foo(void) {
 MyTemplateClass<int, float> m_MyClass;
 m_MyClass.m_MyData1 = 5; // m_MyData1 is of type int
 m_MyClass.m_MyData1 = 5.0f; // m_MyData2 is of type float
}
```

You can also really warp your head, because you can put template classes in other template classes:

```
template <class T>
class MyTemplateClass
{
public:
 /* use T for the types of some variables here */
```

```
   T m_MyData;
};
void Foo(void) {
  // create a template class that uses a template class that uses
  // ints
  MyTemplateClass< MyTemplateClass<int> > m_MyClass;
  // m_MyClass.m_MyData is of type MyTemplateClass, so it has another
  // m_MyData of type int.
  m_MyClass.m_MyData.m_MyData = 5;
}
```

You see this more often than you might think. The STL library includes several template classes that use other template classes as template arguments. It can get downright weird trying to think about some of these, so the best advice I can give you is to simply practice!

C++ Wrap-Up

So, there it is—a quick tour through the C++ features that are used in this book.

I hope this section has given you a deeper understanding of what C++ is all about—giving the programmers more tools they can use to make their job easier. As I said before, not all of the C++ features are useful in every situation. An experienced C++ programmer knows which tools fit the job, and uses only those tools. That means you shouldn't waste time using a C++ feature just for the sake of using it—use the feature because it reduces complexity and makes your life easier.

Also, resist the temptation to add in everything under the sun. Not every function needs to be virtual, not every program needs to use exceptions, and not everything needs its own namespace. Pick and choose your weapons carefully, and you'll be fine.

The Standard Template Library (STL)

Now that I've given you a crash course in the C++ features you need to understand this book, it's time to talk about the other thing you need to know: STL.

What Is the STL and Why Should I Care?

STL is an acronym for the Standard Template Library. Let's take that apart word-by-word. First of all, the STL is standard. The powers that be incorporated it into the American National Standards Institute (ANSI) standard of C++, so any compiler that's ANSI compliant will have a STL library. This is great, because it means that if you ever need to port your program to Linux or something, you won't have to scrap all the code that relies on the STL.

Second, the library uses templates. In fact, some of the most heavy-duty take-no-prisoners template code I've seen resides in the STL. The STL programmers used templates to make the library as useful as possible. For example, they didn't just want to make one algorithm or container class work with just ints, or just floats, or just chars, so they template-ized the whole thing so that it could work with any class you can dream up.

Finally, the L in STL means library. Real libraries are huge collections of books. The STL is a huge collection of container classes and algorithms. You will probably never use all of the STL in one program, and may never use all of it anywhere. For that reason, the STL is broken down into several components. You use each component by including a specific header file, just like what you're used to with the C runtime libraries. Usually, you don't even have to worry about linking the correct STL libraries—the compiler takes care of that for you.

We're going to concentrate on the two types of STL container classes this book uses: vectors and maps. There are many other container classes (stacks, lists, etc.), and I encourage you to learn more about them, because they can be useful in many situations.

STL Strings

One of the most useful things the STL provides is a string class. C programmers spend a lot of time wrangling fixed-length character arrays—`char buf[256]` and such. This can often lead to frustrating buffer overrun—or "I tried to put a six character string into a five element array"—errors.

C++ string classes solve this problem. The STL library provides a rather lightweight string class, called `string`. So, to create a STL string, just type something like this:

```
std::string strFilename;
```

You can then assign a value to this string as follows:

```
strFilename = "C:\\test\\myfile.txt";
```

The string class takes care of the details of allocating the right amount of memory to hold the string.

You can figure out how long a string is by using the size method:

```
printf("The length of the string \"blah\" is: %d",
 std::string("blah").size());
```

Also notice in that section of code how I created a temporary string object by passing in a character array to the string constructor.

If you need to convert your string into a character array, use the c_str method:

```
void Foo(char *strFilename)
{
 /* do something with filename */
}
void main(void)
{
 std::string str = "SomeFile.txt";
 Foo(str.c_str());
}
```

That's essentially the basics of using STL strings. Consult the STL documentation to learn about the more powerful features of STL strings that this book doesn't use.

CAUTION

Whenever you want to print a string, and you use the %s tag in your `printf` statement, remember to use the c_str method, otherwise, you'll get weird `printf` results, and sometimes program crashes!

For example, don't do this:

```
printf("The string is: %s", strSomeSTLString); // kablooey!
```

Instead, do this:

```
printf("The string is: %s", strSomeSTLString.c_str());
```

STL Vectors

Think of a STL vector as a resizable array. Once you've got a STL vector created, you can add as many items to it as you want (until you run out of memory, of course), and you can delete any item inside the array without affecting the others.

Making a STL Vector

To create a new vector, all you need to do is declare a variable of that type. Remember, vector is a template class, so you need to give it the type of stuff you'll be storing. For example, to create a vector of ints, write something like this:

```
std::vector<int> m_ArrayOfInts;
```

To create a vector of chars, write:

```
std::vector<char> m_ArrayOfChars;
```

Or to create a vector of your own classes, write:

```
std::vector<CMyClass> m_ArrayOfMyClasses;
```

Adding Items

The vector class allows you to put objects into it in a few different ways. First, there's the most common: Just call the push_back method:

```
std::vector<int> m_ArrayOfInts;
m_ArrayOfInts.push_back(5); // add 5 to array (array is now 5)
m_ArrayOfInts.push_back(3); // add 3 to array (array is now 5, 3)
m_ArrayOfInts.push_back(4); // add 4 to array (array is now 5, 3, 4)
```

The push_back method puts the new item at the very end of the array. (In case you're curious, there's also pop_back, which removes the last item from the array.)

When you push an item into a STL vector, you're actually making a copy of that item. This is a moot point when dealing with ints, but becomes important if you're using a vector to store classes.

If you want to insert stuff in the middle of the array, you can use insert. The insert method takes two

CAUTION

Your class needs to implement an operator = overload in order for this to work, and if your class allocates memory or contains pointers to different things, you need to make sure that your overload copies that memory correctly.

arguments. The first one specifies where you'd like the item placed. The insert method will place the item immediately before the one specified. The second argument is a reference to the item you want to insert.

Here's an example of insert:

```
std::vector<int> m_ArrayOfInts;
m_ArrayOfInts.push_back(5); // add 5 to array (array is now 5)
m_ArrayOfInts.push_back(3); // add 3 to array (array is now 5, 3)
// add 4 to the *beginning* of the array
m_ArrayOfInts.insert(m_ArrayOfInts.begin(), 4);
// array is now 4, 5, 3
// add 7 between 5 and 3 (that is, before element 3)
m_ArrayOfInts.insert(m_ArrayOfInts.begin()+2)
// array is now 4, 5, 7, 3
```

The only thing weird in that code is probably the m_ArrayOfInts.begin()+2 stuff. Essentially, the begin method returns an iterator. An iterator is a pointer to whatever type you're storing; in this case, it's an int *. The begin method of vector returns an iterator that points to the first thing in our vector. Since we want the third object down, we simply add two to this iterator and pass that as the location before which we want the new item inserted.

STL vectors allow you to insert things in many more ways than I've just shown. For example, you can insert a whole range of blank objects, using resize or another insert overload. However, most programmers rarely use more than push_back and the simple insert overload.

> **TIP**
>
> This sounds more complex than it is. Don't worry, you'll become more familiar with iterators after you have a chance to play with them in your own programs.

Getting and Editing Items

Once you got some stuff in the vector, you probably want to get at it. You can do this in several ways. First and oftentimes easiest: STL vectors overload the brackets operator, [ ], allowing you to pretend that your vector is really just an array:

```
std::vector<int> m_ArrayOfInts;
m_ArrayOfInts.push_back(5); // add 5 to array (array is now 5)
m_ArrayOfInts.push_back(3); // add 3 to array (array is now 5, 3)
if (m_ArrayOfInts[0] != 5) {
```

```
printf("All is not right in the universe.");
}
```

You can also loop through the entire vector by doing something like this:

```
for (std::vector<int>::iterator i = ArrayOfInts.begin();
    i != ArrayOfInts.end(); ++i) {
  printf("%d ", *i);
}
```

That's a mammoth for statement, but it comes apart fairly easily. First, we declare an iterator for a vector of integers, name it i, and set it equal to the beginning of the vector. We keep looping so long as i does not equal end. The end method of vector is very similar to begin, except it gives you an iterator that's one past the end of the array.

> **TIP**
>
> Always use ++i instead of i++ when iterating through a vector. It's faster, because the compiler does not have to create a temporary object behind the scenes.

So, essentially, we're looping from the beginning of the vector to the end. Since i is an iterator, and an iterator is just a fancy pointer to our object, all we have to do inside the for loop is de-reference the pointer and use it. If you were using classes, you would probably want to create a reference to that class element, like this:

```
for (std::vector<CMyClass>::iterator i = ArrayOfClasses.begin();
    i != ArrayOfClasses.end(); ++i) {
  CMyClass &ThisClass = *i;
  /* do whatever you need to here, using ThisClass */
} // next!
```

That code makes things a little easier to read, because once you get into your for loop, you can use a reference to the class instead of constantly having to de-reference the iterator.

> **CAUTION**
>
> Be careful if you add new items, shuffle the item order, or delete items while you're using an iterator to move through the vector. The insertion and deletion functions may actually invalidate your iterator, which will cause you to go tromping off into memory somewhere, and will probably lead to an access violation.
>
> Check the STL docs for more information on how to get around this.

Deleting Items

To delete an item from a vector, use the clear and erase methods. The clear method kills everything in the array:

```
std::vector<int> m_ArrayOfInts;
m_ArrayOfInts.push_back(5); // add 5 to array (array is now 5)
m_ArrayOfInts.push_back(3); // add 3 to array (array is now 5, 3)
m_ArrayOfInts.clear(); // array is now empty
```

The erase method, on the other hand, allows you to delete a specific item or a range of items. STL vectors provide two overloaded erase methods. The first overload takes one iterator, and simply deletes that item. The second overload takes two iterators, and deletes all items between those iterators, including the first iterator but not the second:

```
std::vector<int> m_ArrayOfInts;
m_ArrayOfInts.push_back(5); // (array is now 5)
m_ArrayOfInts.push_back(3); // (array is now 5, 3)
m_ArrayOfInts.erase(m_ArrayOfInts.begin()); // (array is now 3)
m_ArrayOfInts.push_back(4); // (array is now 3, 4)
m_ArrayOfInts.push_back(6); // (array is now 3, 4, 6)
// kill everything but the first element
m_ArrayOfInts.erase(m_ArrayOfInts.begin()+1, m_ArrayOfInts.end());
// array now contains 3
```

The code above shows how to use both erase overloads. Again, note that the end method does not return an iterator pointing to the last element of the array. It returns an iterator pointing *past* the last element of the array.

A Clever Way to Delete Vectors Full of Derived Objects

Many programmers use STL vectors to store pointers to different classes. For example, say you have three classes, CCircle, CTriangle, and CRectangle, all of which derive from a common base class, CShape. Now, let's say you need to store an arbitrary number of circles, triangles, and rectangles. An elegant way to do this is to create a vector of CShape *'s, dynamically allocate memory for each object, and then add its pointer to the vector, like so:

```
class CShape { /* blah */ };
class CCircle: public CShape { /* blah */ };
class CTriangle: public CShape { /* blah */ };
class CRectangle: public CShape { /* blah */ };
void main(void)
{
  std::vector<CShape *> shapes;
```

```
shapes.push_back(new CCircle());
shapes.push_back(new CTriangle());
shapes.push_back(new CRectangle());
// now, how do you delete these shapes?
}
```

So, the question is, "how do you delete the shapes you've just created?" This is where the cleverness comes in. For years, I used to write deletion code like this:

```
for (std::vector<CShape *>::iterator I = shapes.begin();
 i != shapes.end(); ++i) {
 delete i;
}
shapes.clear();
```

As it stands, there's nothing wrong with that code. It gets the job done just great; however, it's a bit much to write just to nuke a vector.

Yordan Gruchev, a fellow game programmer, has come up with a better way. He has used template programming to create an stlwipe function that encapsulates all of that code. Here's what stlwipe looks like:

```
template<class T>
void stlwipe(T &t)
{
 //get the first iterator
 T::iterator i=t.begin();
 //iterate to the end and delete items (should be pointers)
 for(; i!=t.end();++i) delete(*i);
 //clear the collection (now full of dead pointers)
 t.clear();
}
```

See how that works? Now that we have our template function, we can just call stl-wipe(shapes) to delete everything from our vector. Pretty slick, isn't it?

Other Useful Vector Stuff

Now that you know the basics of adding, editing, and deleting elements from a vector, here are a couple of other useful things you can do:

- You can find out if a vector's empty by calling the empty method. That method returns true if the vector's empty, false otherwise.

- You can find out how many items are in the vector by calling the `size` method.

- Behind the scenes, the STL vector allocates memory for each item you pass into it. If you know you're going to be pushing a whole bunch of items in, you can tell the vector to make room in advance, so that it does one big memory allocation instead of fragmenting your memory with several smaller allocations. The vector method to call to do this is `reserve`.

STL Vector Wrap-Up

The best way to become familiar with everything a STL vector can do is to simply crack open the `vector` header file and look at the class declaration. You'll see many more methods than what I've covered here, and you'll probably want to go through the STL docs (or some STL resources I've given at the end of the chapter) to learn about the stuff not used in this book.

STL Maps

Another critical container class is the STL Map. This section explains what a map is, and shows you some basics on how to use a map.

What Is a STL Map?

A STL map lets you find a "thing" given a "key." Maps work in pairs—every item you put into a map is bound to a key. Once you put these key/item pairs into the map, you can quickly retrieve an item if you know its key.

For example, say we're writing a search program for a library. We know that all books have an ISBN number, so we decide that the ISBN number is the key by which we'll retrieve the other book information—author, title, etc. We make a structure that contains all the book information, like so:

```
class CBook
{
public:
 CBook() { }
 CBook(string strAuthor, string strTitle, string strISBNNumber) {
  m_strAuthor = strAuthor;
  m_strTitle = strTitle;
  m_strISBNNumber = strISBNNumber;
 }
```

```
string m_strAuthor;
string m_strTitle;
string m_strISBNNumber;
/* other info - etc */
};
```

Then, for each book, we insert a key/value pair into a map (see Figure B.1).

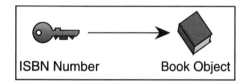

ISBN Number   Book Object

Figure B.1

Our map's key is the ISBN number; the map value is the book itself

Our key is the ISBN number; our value is the object that goes with that ISBN number.

Once we've got all our keys/values inserted into the map, we can retrieve a structure full of information about a book simply by supplying the ISBN number to the map. The map has an internal organization that lets it quickly find the book structure corresponding to the ISBN number we gave it.

Many programmers use maps to accomplish many different kinds of tasks. The example I gave above is only one way to use a map. Another way is to create something resembling a translation table, in which the key and the item the key's attached to are the same data type. For example, let's say we wanted to create a (very simply) encryption program, which would take a string and jumble the letters up (A=G, B=Y, and so on, randomly, for the rest of the alphabet). We could use a map to make the translation easier—our keys could be A-Z, and our values could be the random letter each key corresponds to. That way, when we needed to encrypt the message, we could simply ask the map, "hey, what letter is attached to key B?" The map would hand us back whatever letter we inserted attached to key B, and to encrypt our string, we'd replace all instances of B in it with that value. When we wanted to decrypt, we could make a reverse-map, where the keys are the jumbled letters and the items are the "real" letters each jumbled letter corresponds to.

If the light bulb still hasn't come on, let me try to explain maps in terms of another example, this time with some code to buttress it.

Let's say you're writing a multiplayer game. Each player is playing the game from his own computer, which has its own IP address. Let's say your networking code just received an "I quit this game!" message from a certain IP address, and now it needs to figure out the player name that IP address corresponds to, so that it can display a message saying "<player> left the game" and take the player out of the game.

That's the situation—you've got an IP address, and you need a player name. One way to solve this situation is to create a vector of objects, with each object containing an IP address and a name, like so:

```
class CPlayerInfoObject {
 public:
   CIPAddress m_IP;
   std::string m_strPlayerName;
   /* other player info */
};
std::vector<CPlayerInfoObject> g_vPlayerInfo;
```

You'd fill this vector up with all the players in the game. Then, when you needed a player name for a certain IP address, you'd loop through the elements of this vector until you found the structure you wanted, like so:

```
std::string GetPlayerNameGivenIPAddress(CIPAddress GivenIP)
{
for (std::vector<CPlayerInfoObject>::iterator i =g_vPlayerInfo.begin();
 i != g_vPlayerInfo.end(); i++) {
 if (i->m_IP == GivenIP) {
  // we've found our player! return their name!
  return(i->m_strPlayerName);
}
// we didn't find anything, so return an empty name.
return("");
}
```

This is perfectly acceptable code, but touching every single item isn't exactly the fastest way to search for something.

This kind of situation is what maps were designed to solve. The map container can essentially replace all that slow and error-prone search code:

```
std::map<CIPAddress, CPlayerInfoObject> g_mPlayerInfo;
std::string GetPlayerNameGivenIPAddress(CIPAddress GivenIP)
{
 return(g_mPlayerInfo[GivenIP].m_strPlayerName);
}
```

The bracket operator [ ] is overloaded for maps, so that you can put in your key and get back the corresponding object (or a "blank" object, made with the default constructor, if the map doesn't find a match).

So, that's essentially what a map is. Now let's look at how to create and use one in code.

Making a STL Map

To use a map, you must first include the <map> STL header:

```
#include <map>
```

Once you include the header file, creating a new map is as simple as the following:

```
std::map<CKey, CValue> myMap;
```

Here we're declaring a new map called `myMap`. The `map` template needs two template arguments. The first template argument is the data type you'd like to use as a key—in the example above, the ISBN number was the key. You can use any data type you like here, including the built-in data types.

The second template argument is the "value" data type. This is what you get back when you put in the key. Again, you can put in any type you want.

> **TIP**
>
> You'll probably want to disable warning number 4786 before you include the map header. The STL map makes heavy use of templates, and the template expansions generate gobs of a particular compiler warning—4786. The warning itself isn't terribly important, and it's next to impossible to read the output window with it present. Luckily you can easily disable the warning by typing the following:
>
> ```
> #pragma warning(disable: 4786)
> ```
>
> This will turn off the warning and allow you to make sense of your compiler output once again.

Actually, `map` has four template arguments, but most of the time you can omit the last two and let the compiler use their default value. In case you're curious, the other two arguments specify how to sort things within a map, and how to allocate memory for the elements in the map.

Adding Items

You might think that the map class would contain two different arrays of objects— one array for the keys, and another array for the values. However, it doesn't work that way. The map stores one array full of `std::pair` objects.

The `std::pair` object is a nifty little STL creation; it's a handy tool for "pairing" two objects together into one object. Essentially, `pair` simply contains two objects (of any type), called `first` and `second`. To prove that it's really that simple, here's a typical STL class definition for `pair`:

```
template<class T, class U>
 struct pair {
  typedef T first_type;
  typedef U second_type
  T first;
  U second;
  pair();
  pair(const T& x, const U& y);
  template<class V, class W>
    pair(const pair<V, W>& pr);
 };
```

See the `first` and `second` objects? This `pair` object just takes two random classes and "binds" them together into one structure.

As you've probably already surmised by now, we need to "bind" our key and our value together using `std::pair` before we can insert it into our map. Fortunately, there's a STL function called `make_pair` that does just that. Here's an example of inserting an object into a map:

```
std::map<std::string, CBook> books;
// declare a new book object
CBook SpecialEffectsBook("Mason McCuskey",
 "Special Effects Game Programming With DirectX", "0-7615-3497-0");
// add it to the map
books.insert(std::make_pair(SpecialEffectsBook.m_strISBNNumber,
 SpecialEffectsBook));
```

Notice the call to `make_pair` in the code above, to bind the ISBN number of the book with the book object itself.

Finding Items

STL maps are no fun unless you can use them to find something. Fortunately, finding something in a map is really easy. The first way is to use the `find` method of `std::map`, like so:

```
map<string, CBook>::iterator it;
```

```
it = books.find(strISBN);
if (it == books.end()) { // not found!
 cout << "I don't know about that book.";
}
else {
  CBook &theBook = it->second;
  /* etc. */
}
```

Give the `find` method a key, and it will return an iterator pointing to the object in the map with that supplied key, or pointing to `end()` if there's no match. As you can see in the previous code, the iterator doesn't point to an object of type `CBook`, it points to a `pair` object (remember, when you inserted the object you bound the key and object together in a `pair` object). The book object you're after is the `second` member of this pair object.

If you're in a hurry, you can also use the overloaded bracket operators to find something:

```
CBook &theBook = books[strISBN];
```

The only caveat to using this is that if the object doesn't exist in the map, this will actually create a blank object and associate it with that key. Note also that the brackets operator gives you back a reference to `it->second`, so there's no need for you to do anything extra. Just put in a key, get back an object—cool, isn't it?

> **TIP**
>
> Keep in mind that a map supports iterators, just as a vector does. So you can make a for loop from `map.begin()` to `map.end()` and play with each element individually, just like a vector.

Deleting Items

You can delete items you've previously added to a map by calling the `erase` method. This works the exact same way it does for a vector—simply pass in an iterator and that object is deleted.

You can also clear the entire map in one fell swoop by calling the `clear` method.

> **CAUTION**
>
> Again, just like with vectors, be careful if you add new items, shuffle the item order, or delete items while you're using an iterator to move through the `map`.

MultiMaps

Up until now, we've talked only about maps. However, even though we don't use them in this book, I feel compelled to mention the map's sibling. STL provides another class very similar to a map, called a multimap.

Essentially, the keys in a multimap can be duplicated, whereas in an ordinary map each key must be unique. For example, the whole ISBN/book database is great for an ordinary map, because we're guaranteed that two books can never have the same ISBN number. However, if you were modeling a school and wanted to key students by their last name, you would probably want to use a multimap, because there may be several students with the same last name. (I once knew three Smiths in my elementary school homeroom alone.) Alternatively, you might decide to use another piece of ID, one that more uniquely identifies a student (say, their Social Security number, for example).

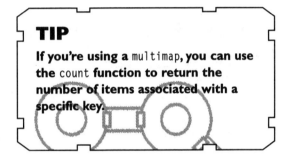

TIP

If you're using a multimap, you can use the count function to return the number of items associated with a specific key.

STL Map Wrap-Up

STL maps, like STL vectors, are a very useful tool that can save you a lot of programming time when properly used. By using a map, you're guaranteed to have a fast and very-well-tested algorithm for storing and quickly retrieving all sorts of items. Free working code! Now that's something that everyone can enjoy.

STL Summary

I realize that it's probably painful and discouraging to learn all this new STL stuff. If you're like most programmers, you've probably already got some great tools to do the STL stuff I've covered here. You may be used to a particular C++ string class or exception hierarchy.

I consider the STL valuable because it's cross platform and really is part of the C++ standard. So, no matter where you go, as long as you have C++, you have STL. That's something that can't be said for most other array toolboxes.

Also, realize that you can always wrap the STL into a form more suitable for you. For example, if you've been using a string class of your own, there's no reason why you can't re-implement that string class in terms of STL strings (that is, using a STL string behind the scenes). That's a great approach if you've already got a large code-base that's using a proprietary string class, or if you just like keeping the same names.

In general, give the STL a chance. It's a bit ugly at first, but once you spend some time working with it, the larger pattern to it clicks in, and you see the method to its madness. At that point, you start really exploiting the power of the STL. All of a sudden, complex algorithms can be written in one line, using some clever STL types and templates.

About the Example Programs

The two example programs for this appendix demonstrate STL vectors and STL maps.

ChAp1_STLVectorExample: This example program demonstrates STL vectors. I designed it so that you could step through it with the debugger and watch the vectors change as things happen.

ChAp1_STLMapExample: This example program demonstrates STL maps. Again, step through it with the debugger and watch the maps change as things happen.

Exercises

There are no exercises for this appendix. Becoming familiar with C++ and the STL is just something that takes practice.

APPENDIX C

C++ Keywords

Lorenzo D. Phillips Jr.,
www.renwareinc.com,
lorenzo.phillips@renwareinc.com

Table C.1 C++ Keywords

auto	delete	goto	register	true
bool	do	if	reinterpret_cast	try
break	double	inline	return	typedef
case	dynamic_cast	int	signed short	typeid
cast	else	long	sizeof	typename
catch	enum	mutable	static	union
char	explicit	namespace	static_cast	unsigned
class	extern	new	struct	using
const	false	operator	switch	virtual
const_cast	float	private	template	void
continue	for	protected	this	volatile
default	friend	public	throw	while

Table C.2 Visual C++ Specific Keywords

_asm	_forceinline	_single_inheritance
_assume	_finally	_virtual_inheritance
_based	_inline	naked
_cdecl	_int8	noreturn
_declspec	_int16	_stdcall
_dllexport	_int32	thread
_dllimport	_int64	_try
_except	_leave	uuid
_fastcall	_multiple_inheritance	_uuidof

APPENDIX D

RESOURCES ON THE WEB

Lorenzo D. Phillips Jr.,
www.renwareinc.com,
lorenzo.phillips@renwareinc.com

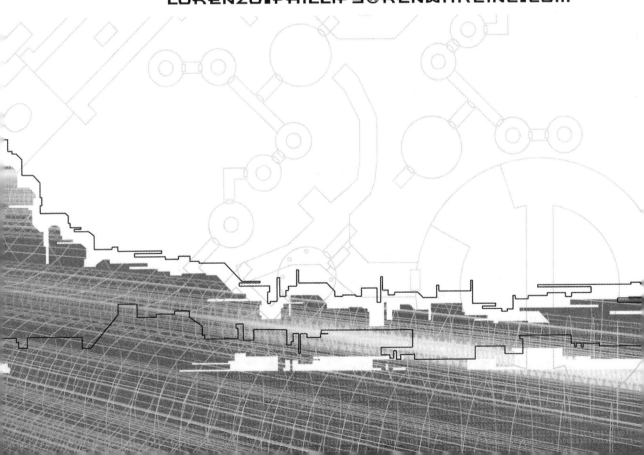

Had enough yet? Or do you crave more information? The following are lists of sites that I think will cure your appetite. If not, they are enough to get you started.

SCM Sites

Just in case you would like to search for some information on software configuration management (SCM), I have included some links to get you started. The first link is to my company. It offers SCM services on most commercial and noncommercial tools. Check out the Web site for a complete listing of services provided and keep an eye on it because we are about to release helpful scripts and white papers as well. CM Crossroads is a bulletin board system that has discussion areas for most of the tools you can think of that are available to the public. The remaining links are to some of the most notable SCM tool vendors.

RenWare, Inc.: **www.renwareinc.com**

CM Crossroads: **www.cmcrossroads.com**

Rational: **www.rational.com**

MERANT: **www.merant.com**

Serena: **www.serena.com**

Telelogic: **www.telelogic.com**

MKS: **www.mks.com**

Game Development Sites: Best of the Best

In my opinion, these are some of the best sites you can hope to find. Information is the key to success, and knowing where to find it increases your chances of being successful. These sites have all of the information a person could hope to find and then some. There are numerous tutorials, and some of them even have boards you can access to discuss game-related topics with your fellow gamers around the world or simply to chat in a lounge with other gamers while you take a break from the hours upon hours you've just spent playing the latest, hottest titles on the market.

Xtreme Games: **www.xgames3d.com**

GameDev: **www.gamedev.net**

Game Tutorials: **www.gametutorials.com**

Adrenaline Vault: **www.avault.com**

Game Institute: **www.gameinstitute.com**

Game Developer: **www.gamedeveloper.net**

Gamasutra: **www.gamasutra.com**

Game Development Search Engine: **www.gdse.com**

MSDN DirectX: **www.microsoft.com/directx**

MSDN Visual C++: **www.microsoft.com/visualc**

OpenGL: **www.opengl.org**

FlipCode: **www.flipcode.com**

IsoHex: **www.isohex.net**

CodeGuru: **www.codeguru.com**

NeHe Productions: **http://nehe.gamedev.net**

Downloads, News, and Reviews

The sites listed here are where you can go to find downloads, news, and reviews. In short, these sites can keep you up-to-date with the latest gaming news no matter where you are located in the world. Or you can simply go out and download some really cool software. It is also worth mentioning that many of the sites in the preceding section provide the latest in gaming news, but then again, that is why they are listed as the best of the best.

GamePro: **www.gamepro.com**

Games Domain: **www.gamesdomain.com**

Blue's News: **www.bluesnews.com**

Download.com: **www.download.com**

Happy Puppy: **www.happypuppy.com**

Tucows: **www.tucows.com**

Game Conferences

Finally, here are some links to some of the best places to be once a year. Although the Electronic Entertainment Expo (E3) is not technically a game-developer conference, it is the largest conference in the game community, so it deserves to get mentioned here.

Xtreme Games Developer Conference: **www.xgdc.com**

Game Developer Conference: **www.gdconf.com**

Electronic Entertainment Expo: **www.e3expo.com**

APPENDIX E

ASC11 Table

Lorenzo D. Phillips Jr.,
www.renwareinc.com,
lorenzo.phillips@renwareinc.com

Decimal	Octal	Hex	Binary	Value
000	000	000	00000000	NUL (null character)
001	001	001	00000001	SOH (start of header)
002	002	002	00000010	STX (start of text)
003	003	003	00000011	ETX (end of text)
004	004	004	00000100	EOT (end of transmission)
005	005	005	00000101	ENQ (enquiry)
006	006	006	00000110	ACK (acknowledgment)
007	007	007	00000111	BEL (bell)
008	010	008	00001000	BS (backspace)
009	011	009	00001001	HT (horizontal tab)
010	012	00A	00001010	LF (line feed)
011	013	00B	00001011	VT (vertical tab)
012	014	00C	00001100	FF (form feed)
013	015	00D	00001101	CR (carriage return)
014	016	00E	00001110	SO (shift out)
015	017	00F	00001111	SI (shift in)
016	020	010	00010000	DLE (data link escape)
017	021	011	00010001	DC1 (XON) (device control 1)
018	022	012	00010010	DC2 (device control 2)
019	023	013	00010011	DC3 (XOFF) (device control 3)
020	024	014	00010100	DC4 (device control 4)
021	025	015	00010101	NAK (negative acknowledgment)
022	026	016	00010110	SYN (synchronous idle)
023	027	017	00010111	ETB (end of transmission block)
024	030	018	00011000	CAN (cancel)
025	031	019	00011001	EM (end of medium)
026	032	01A	00011010	SUB (substitute)
027	033	01B	00011011	ESC (escape)

Decimal	Octal	Hex	Binary	Value
028	034	01C	00011100	FS (file separator)
029	035	01D	00011101	GS (group separator)
030	036	01E	00011110	RS (request to send)
031	037	01F	00011111	US (unit separator)
032	040	020	00100000	SP (space)
033	041	021	00100001	!
034	042	022	00100010	"
035	043	023	00100011	#
036	044	024	00100100	$
037	045	025	00100101	%
038	046	026	00100110	&
039	047	027	00100111	'
040	050	028	00101000	(
041	051	029	00101001	)
042	052	02A	00101010	*
043	053	02B	00101011	+
044	054	02C	00101100	,
045	055	02D	00101101	-
046	056	02E	00101110	.
047	057	02F	00101111	/
048	060	030	00110000	0
049	061	031	00110001	1
050	062	032	00110010	2
051	063	033	00110011	3
052	064	034	00110100	4
053	065	035	00110101	5
054	066	036	00110110	6
055	067	037	00110111	7

Decimal	Octal	Hex	Binary	Value
056	070	038	00111000	8
057	071	039	00111001	9
058	072	03A	00111010	:
059	073	03B	00111011	;
060	074	03C	00111100	<
061	075	03D	00111101	=
062	076	03E	00111110	>
063	077	03F	00111111	?
064	100	040	01000000	@
065	101	041	01000001	A
066	102	042	01000010	B
067	103	043	01000011	C
068	104	044	01000100	D
069	105	045	01000101	E
070	106	046	01000110	F
071	107	047	01000111	G
072	110	048	01001000	H
073	111	049	01001001	I
074	112	04A	01001010	J
075	113	04B	01001011	K
076	114	04C	01001100	L
077	115	04D	01001101	M
078	116	04E	01001110	N
079	117	04F	01001111	O
080	120	050	01010000	P
081	121	051	01010001	Q
082	122	052	01010010	R
083	123	053	01010011	S

Decimal	Octal	Hex	Binary	Value
084	124	054	01010100	T
085	125	055	01010101	U
086	126	056	01010110	V
087	127	057	01010111	W
088	130	058	01011000	X
089	131	059	01011001	Y
090	132	05A	01011010	Z
091	133	05B	01011011	[
092	134	05C	01011100	\
093	135	05D	01011101	]
094	136	05E	01011110	^
095	137	05F	01011111	_
096	140	060	01100000	`
097	141	061	01100001	a
098	142	062	01100010	b
099	143	063	01100011	c
100	144	064	01100100	d
101	145	065	01100101	e
102	146	066	01100110	f
103	147	067	01100111	g
104	150	068	01101000	h
105	151	069	01101001	i
106	152	06A	01101010	j
107	153	06B	01101011	k
108	154	06C	01101100	l
109	155	06D	01101101	m
110	156	06E	01101110	n
111	157	06F	01101111	o

Decimal	Octal	Hex	Binary	Value
112	160	070	01110000	p
113	161	071	01110001	q
114	162	072	01110010	r
115	163	073	01110011	s
116	164	074	01110100	t
117	165	075	01110101	u
118	166	076	01110110	v
119	167	077	01110111	w
120	170	078	01111000	x
121	171	079	01111001	y
122	172	07A	01111010	z
123	173	07B	01111011	{
124	174	07C	01111100	|
125	175	07D	01111101	}
126	176	07E	01111110	~
127	177	07F	01111111	DEL

APPENDIX F

WHAT'S ON THE CD-ROM

The CD-ROM included with this book contains all of the available source code from those chapters that had source code, some basic tools, and some very fun games in demo format.

The CD-ROM GUI

The Graphical User Interface (GUI) for the CD-ROM is HTML-based and has a nice menu and GUI structure to it. The GUI can be viewed in any browser, but you would be wise to stick with Netscape 4.0 or later or Internet Explorer 4.0, versions 4.0 or later.

CD-ROM File Structure

The CD-ROM contains three main folders with some goodies contained in the subdirectories beneath them.

- **Demo Games:** This folder contains several games that demonstrate the level of quality that can be achieved with the techniques discussed throughout this book.
- **Source Code:** This folder contains the source code for those tricks that used sample source code to illustrate their point. It should be noted that not all tricks required source code, and thus, some trick numbers will not be present.
- **Tools:** This folder contains the essentials to get you started on your way to making a million dollars! Well, maybe not a million dollars, but the folder contains the basic tools you will need especially when it comes time to compile your code.

System Requirements

Nowadays, the PCs contain more than enough horsepower to handle the examples in this book. However, if you're like me, you may have a couple of older machines lying around that you still use. So, the minimum requirements you need in order to work with the source code in this book are as follows:

- **CPU:** at least 350MHz; however, this would require a top-of-the-line video card to help handle the load.
- **RAM:** 32MB RAM, but I would recommend at least 64MB or better.

- **Video:** There are a number of brands still out there, so I would recommend that you have one with at least 16MB RAM, but the more video RAM your card has the better because some of the tricks are heavy on the graphics and rendering.

- **CD-ROM, DVD, CD-R, CD-RW Drive:** Since the book's content is stored on the CD-ROM medium, it only makes sense for you to have one of these drives so you can access the book's content.

- **Hard Drive:** Even if you installed everything on this CD-ROM, you don't need a huge hard drive with a ton of disk space for the contents of this book. A safe number for you is 100MB or more as some of those 3-D models can get quite hefty.

- **Browser:** As I mentioned earlier, you should be able to use any browser out there, but you would be wise to use Internet Explorer and Netscape, versions 4.0 or later.

Installation

If you are like me, then you probably skipped over the previous sections, read this section, and then went back and reviewed the previous sections while the installations were executing. Simply install the CD-ROM into your CD-ROM drive. If your operating system is Windows 95 or greater and you have the autorun feature enabled, then the menu should appear in your browser automatically. If not, then you can use *My Computer* or *Windows Explorer* to navigate to your CD-ROM drive and click (or double-click, depending on your computer and mouse settings) on the MENU.HTM file.

From that point, you should be able to use the menu navigational system to load whatever you want with ease. However, if you experience problems with the CD-ROM feel free to email me (**TricksoftheTrade@renwareinc.com**), so that I can notify the appropriate personnel at the publishing company.

Now, get on with creating those next million-dollar-best-selling games!

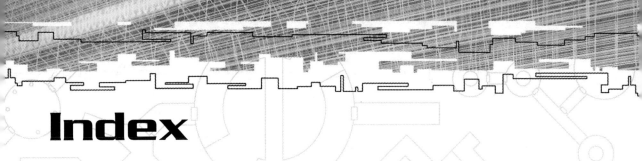

Index

N

O